PHOTOGRAPHY

Revised Fifth Edition

DIGITAL IMAGING

MARVIN J. ROSEN

CALIFORNIA STATE UNIVERSITY, FULLERTON

DAVID L. DEVRIES

KENDALL/HUNT PUBLISHING COMPANY
4050 Westmark Drive   Dubuque, Iowa 52002

Pat Gooden was born in Minneapolis, Minn. in 1954, and currently resides in Florida. She studied Painting and Printmaking at Virginia Commonwealth University in Richmond, Virginia where she received a Bachelor of Fine Arts Degree. A past recipient of the Virginia Museum Undergraduate Fellowship, she has also won numerous awards for her drawing and painting. She studied Black and White photography and darkroom technique at Polk Community College.

In 1997 she began using the computer to retouch old photographs and quickly discovered its potential as an artistic tool. Since that time, she has been creating artwork exclusively with the computer and outputting prints digitally with Epson printers. Currently all of her work is created using Photoshop 7 on a PC with dual XEON 533 processors with 2 gigs of RAM. She also uses Epson 1680 Professional scanner and prints with an Epson Stylus Photo 2000P. Her work is composed of digitally manipulated original photographs that she takes using Olympus Camedia 2100UZ and Olympus E-20 N cameras. Currently, her award winning work can be found in several private and public collections as well as a digital photography book and other print publications.

Book Team
Chairman and Chief Executive Officer Mark C. Falb
Vice President, Director of National Book Program Alfred C. Grisanti
Editorial Development Supervisor Georgia Botsford
Developmental Editor Angela Willenbring
Production Editor Angela Shaffer
Permissions Editor Renae Heacock
Project Designer Deb Howes
Senior Vice President, College Division Thomas W. Gantz
Vice President and National Field Manager Brian Johnson
Managing Editor, College Field John Coniglio
Associate Editor, College Field Janice Samuells

Brief Contents

Appendices

The following appendices are included on the CD that accompanies this book.

Contents

Preface

Our cultural history from earliest times reveals an ever-increasing use of pictorial images. Photographic images now constantly surround us in magazines, newspapers, films, television, and web pages. Photography has gained enormous social and cultural value, particularly in science, education, art, and the mass media. As a result, photography has emerged as a primary tool of communication and self-expression and is pursued by students at all levels and in all disciplines seeking to express themselves and to interact with others more effectively.

This revised fifth edition of *Photography and Digital Imaging* is a general and comprehensive guide. It includes principles and theory, general information, and step-by-step instructions for performing specific procedures and processes for making images. It is designed for those with little or no previous experience in these media as well as intermediate photographers who wish to extend their knowledge and skill.

Used as a conventional text, the book provides basic information, allowing instructors to supplement its content with their own demonstrations, lectures, and discussions. Used as a basis for independent or distance learning, the book is designed to serve as a tutor, systematically introducing each new topic, providing instruction and practice in an orderly and cumulative fashion, and building complex skills on simpler ones.

The book continues the practice of using student images extensively to illustrate various principles, because we believe that learners are motivated by peer examples. Students recognize that these images are within their grasp, that they were produced by beginners like themselves rather than by professional photographers. Works of professional photographers also appear throughout the book wherever they best serve to illustrate a point made by the text.

The technology of photography is in the midst of a great revolution. From the earliest discoveries for capturing images from nature until perhaps the 1940's, the technology of photography was based upon wet chemical processes, mostly involving metallic silver. With the development of electronic and digital imaging, capturing images from nature slowly evolved to the dry, computer-based technology that is today replacing film-based processes in the hands of professionals and amateurs alike.

The transition from film to digital technology is now in a period of rapid acceleration. Digital camera sales stood at 6.7 million units in the year 2000. A 2003 study projected that worldwide unit sales of consumer digital cameras would reach nearly 53 million in 2004, surpassing unit sales of worldwide film cameras, and are expected to experience a compound annual growth rate of 15 percent for the next four years, reaching 82 million units in 2008.

Yet today, film cameras still vastly outnumber digital cameras in common use—the majority of U.S. households possess film cameras while only a minority possess digital cameras. While most digital cameras are purchased to supplement film cameras, replacement purchases are clearly on the rise. By 2005, film camera sales are expected to be in rapid decline as new developments make digital cameras an increasingly attractive replacement: affordability, comparable images, and the availability of cost-efficient digital photo finishing. In addition, digital cameras offer other attractive benefits, such as immediate in-camera review, virtual no-cost-per-frame shooting, simple computer-based image editing, and selective printing. Moreover, the ease of sharing photos over the Internet via email and websites, has placed us on the threshold of a new era of personal visual communication.

Being in the midst of such a technological revolution poses special problems for a book such as this. The new technologies have not yet replaced the old; we find film-based photography alive and well even as digital photography becomes more ubiquitous. Many photographers use both technologies—unwilling to give up the tried and true methods they understand so well, but eager to latch onto the advantages and possibilities of the new. Most professional and amateur photographers find themselves using both the old and the new technologies. And photography education continues to require literacy in both. This book, therefore, attempts to integrate both the traditional, silver-process methodologies and the newer digital imaging technologies.

Reflecting the transition from film to digital imaging, this edition has allowed the film content of the book to give way to increased digital content. Most basic principles and methods of film-based photography continue to be covered as in previous editions, though compressed and abbreviated somewhat to make room for increased coverage of new and elaborated digital content. We hope this approach responds to the needs of instructors and students alike as they seek mastery of this changing technology.

Special Features of This Edition

New Format

The format of this revised fifth edition of *Photography & Digital Imaging* has been changed to a vertical page orientation that allows for easier handling while providing for excellent presentation of the photographs and the concepts covered. The book is printed in two colors throughout and includes 15 pages of full color plates.

As the title reflects, the technical content mirrors the rapid developments in photography, digital imaging, and teaching practices, while increasing the relative proportion of space given to digital imaging methodologies—

- A completely new chapter devoted to advanced digital photography, imaging, and print making
- New step-by-step instructions that teach digital photography, imaging, and print making techniques
- Up-to-date working practices for both chemical and digital photography
- New films, photographic materials and digital sensors
- Color processing
- Digital cameras
- Scanners, scanning and file formats
- Image editing and managing programs
- Printers
- Related materials and accessories

CD-ROM

A dual platform CD-ROM included in each book contains:

- Valuable software for image editing and managing
- Practice tests and explanatory answer keys
- Equipment and supply sources
- Workshop and program information

- Tables of current films and materials
- Model release form
- Approximate equivalent focal lengths for various film formats
- Personal film developing sheet for recording specific film developing data
- Relevant web sites
- Professional organizations and hotlines
- Publications
- Time and temperature charts
- Client licensing agreement
- Access to authors' companion web site
- Internet links to galleries, museums, and collections

Companion Web Site

A companion web site is dedicated to users of this book. http://www.introphotodigital.com

Highlights of Revised Fifth Edition

Vignettes

- Famous Photographs
- Famous Photographers
- Careers in Photography
- Special photographic techniques

Special Features

- Learning Objectives for each chapter and section
- Key Concepts
- Illustrated Instructional Concepts
- Questions to Consider
- Field and Laboratory Assignments
- Illustrated Step by Step Instructions for Photographic Techniques

- "Pix Tips" and "Helpful Hints" icon boxes contain many tricks of the trade
- Extended Glossary of Terms and Concepts
- Thorough and complete index for rapid access to specific information

Continuing Features

- No skimping on features to make a "lite" book
- Comprehensive and thorough treatment of topics
- Lavish use of quality illustrations
- Modular approach to photographic skills
- Integrated content covering both film and digital photography and image processing
- Push processing
- Assessing negatives
- Handling photochemicals
- Creative printing techniques
- Available light photography
- Processing for permanence
- Large format photography
- Law and ethics for photographers

Acknowledgments

We gratefully acknowledge the contributions of many persons to this work—Dr. J. William Maxwell and Mrs. Barbara Machado for their early encouragement and material support; Dr. Rick D. Pullen, Dr. Wendell Crow, and Mr. Rick Deitrick, California State University, Fullerton; Prof. Mac McCall, California College of Arts and Crafts; Prof. Dean Dablow, Director of the School of Art at Louisiana State Tech University; Prof. Lenma Kane, Fullerton Community College; Steve's Digicams Online, Inc.; the students and photographers whose works appear herein and in earlier editions; and our many colleagues who have provided invaluable suggestions for strengthening this book since its first publication by Kendall/Hunt Publishing Company in 1974.

And thank you, Ruth, for your patience, advice, and timely refreshments.

Historical Background

Eadweard Muybridge, "Man Running," (0.042 second) first published in 1887.
Courtesy of Kingston Museum and Heritage Service.

Unit at a Glance

The history of photography provides a background for learning about the art and craft of photography. Not only does history help us to understand how the technology has evolved, but it also helps us to understand the evolution of our visual thinking.

This unit describes how cameras and chemistry developed into a technology called photography. It also discusses how artists, journalists, and others have used photography to document the world around them and to communicate their ideas. Examples of the various styles and content that characterize photography's diverse history are presented throughout the unit.

Imaging: Expression and Representation in Pictures

Human beings expressed themselves and told their stories in pictures long before they could write. Pictures on the walls of early cave dwellings are evidence of the human compulsion to describe the world in both representational and symbolic images. Until the invention of printing in Western Europe in the fifteenth century, pictures were unique creations, each handmade, highly prized, and often thought to possess spiritual qualities.

From the beginning, these handmade images seemed to reveal dual purposes: to describe objects and events in precise objective detail, and to express feelings about them. Primitive peoples probably used these images as we use pictures today—to inform, to teach, to persuade, to inspire, and to express feelings and insights.

In Renaissance Europe, artists became preoccupied with representing the three-dimensional physical world in two dimensions. In fifteenth-century Florence, Filippo Brunelleschi and Leon Battista Alberti introduced the mathematical concept of linear perspective. This concept established a standard of realism that continues to dominate Western visual thinking and that, at the time of its invention, created a demand for mechanical aids to achieve it. From the array of visual devices that were developed during the sixteenth century, the modern camera found its beginnings.

The Tools of Photography

Interestingly, the device that gained the greatest popularity among perspective artists, the **camera obscura** (Latin for a dark room), was based on principles that had been known for centuries. As early as the fourth century B.C., Aristotle had manipulated the passage of light through a small hole in a dark room to produce images of solar eclipses and had observed that the image was sharper when the hole was smaller.

During the Dark Ages, Arab scholars preserved Aristotelean knowledge. Early in the eleventh century, Alhazan, an Arab mathematician, de-

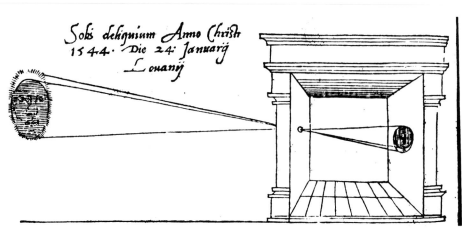

Figure 1-2. Rainer Gemma-Frisius. The first published illustration of a camera obscura showed its use to observe a solar eclipse in 1544 AD. Courtesy of Harry Ransom Humanities Research Center, The University of Texas at Austin.

scribed how to make a camera obscura in a dark tent.

In the sixteenth century, lenses and mirrors were added and various forms of the camera obscura became common artists' tools.

Until the seventeenth century, the camera obscura was an actual room, sometimes of permanent construction, sometimes portable, but large enough for persons to work within. The size of this device gradually became smaller and smaller, until finally it emerged as a small box, large enough for only the artist's hands to work in. It was often painted black inside, sometimes equipped with an opalglass focusing screen, and sometimes designed with a telescoping body to modify the image size.

One important step remained. Although images could be produced by lenses and projected onto paper or other surfaces with the camera obscura, the images were fleeting. To make the images permanent, artists had to trace them with pencil and brush. If artists could make the projected images permanent without manual tracing, they could increase the speed and the accuracy of their work.

The Chemistry of Photography
Pioneers

Early in the eighteenth century, 100 years before the first permanent photographic image was re-corded, Johann Heinrich Schulze, working in Germany, discovered that light darkened the silver salts he kept stored in bottles. Although he recognized no practical use for this phenomenon, his discovery would later become the foundation for photography.

In the mid-eighteenth century, a Swedish chemist, Carl Wilhelm Scheel, observed that although the silver salts themselves were soluble in ammonia, the metallic silver that had been freed by the action of light was not.

At the turn of the nineteenth century, several adventurous craft workers, scientists, and artists were working to capture *camera obscura* images. In Britain, Humphrey Davy and Thomas Wedgwood found that objects placed directly on materials that had been sensitized with silver chloride and exposed to sunlight would leave momentary impressions that would later fade. Wedgwood and Davy's work, however, did not progress to the point of recording an image produced by a *camera obscura*.

In the early 1800s, the French inventor Joseph Nicéphore Niépce experimented with lithography at his home near Chalon, France. Nicéphore explored light-sensitive varnishes, trying to find a coating that would record *camera obscura* drawings after exposure to light. In 1816, using a camera and paper sensitized with silver chloride, he succeeded in making a paper negative, but was

Figure 1-3. Niépce studio view, 1826. The world's second oldest known permanent camera image, bitumen on pewter, is a view taken from Niépce's second floor window. The exposure took approximately eight hours. A year earlier Niépce used light alone to make a plate from which he printed a photographic copy of a 17th century Dutch engraving of a man leading a horse.

dissatisfied because the images were reversed and could not be made permanent. He was also unable to produce a permanent positive print, although he found that nitric acid preserved the images for a while.

Failing with paper, he turned to plates of pewter coated with bitumen of Judea, a type of varnish that hardened when exposed to sunlight. After placing a drawing in contact with this plate, he exposed it to sunlight for many hours. After exposure he removed the unexposed areas with a mixture of turpentine and lavender oil to reveal a barely visible image of the original drawing. In 1822 he finally made a permanent image using a camera obscura by exposing coated pewter plates to a camera image and using the vapors from heated iodine crystals to darken the silver and heighten contrast. He named this process "heliography" or "sun writing." During the next several years he continued his attempts to produce a permanent camera image and in 1825 was finally successful.

In about 1827, Niépce met Louis Jacques Mandé Daguerre, who became interested in Niépce's work because of his uses of the camera obscura for painting and theatrical designing (see *Famous Photograph: The Daguerreotype.* Pg. 5). After working with Niépce and his son Isidore for ten years, Daguerre developed a method of producing extremely fine, luminous, and permanent images on sheets of copper plated with silver.

The Daguerreotype

Daguerre was a flamboyant theatrical entrepreneur and showman whose diorama productions had thrilled audiences in London and Paris for many years. Now, sensing a hit, he moved to promote his photographic invention. In 1839, he arranged for the French Academy of Sciences to announce the process that he named the **daguerreotype**. He cajoled the French government into buying the rights and making them public in France, and awarding him and Isidore Niépce lifetime pensions.

Figure 1-4. Gaspard-Felix Tournachon—or Nadar. "A View of Paris." 1858. First aerial photograph made from a balloon hovering at an altitude of 1600 feet. Cliché Bibliothèque nationale de France, Paris.

Figure 1-5. Honore Daumier. "Nadar Elevating Photography to a High Art," 1862. Nadar's photographic feats, including aerial shots from a balloon, inspired this lithograph. Courtesy George Eastman House.

Famous Photograph

The Daguerreotype

This daguerreotype, made in 1839 by Louis Jacques Mandé Daguerre, is generally regarded as the first photograph showing the image of a human being. Early daguerreotypes required lengthy exposures; Daguerre was fortunate that for this shot, his human subject remained in a relatively stationary position while having his boots shined, allowing his image to be captured. Meanwhile, pedestrian and carriage traffic that may have passed along the street while the image was being slowly recorded were never stationary long enough to become fixed in this memorable scene.

A showman by profession, Daguerre specialized in creating spectacular dioramas that mixed projected images, painted backdrops, and three-dimensional objects to create realistic displays of exotic subjects. He had long used the camera obscura to sketch the exacting perspectives of his elaborate illusions and quickly saw the connection between Joseph Nicéphore Niépce's work with heliography and his own. The two men entered into a partnership to perfect Niépce's process, a collaboration that continued without practical result until Niépce's death in 1831. Daguerre and Niépce's son, Isidore, continued with the experiments until, in 1837, they discovered how to make a strong, permanent image using sheets of silver-plated copper fumed with iodine vapor and processed in mercury vapor.

Early in 1839, the year of this photograph, astronomer and physicist Dominique Françoise Arago demonstrated Daguerre and Niépce's process—the daguerreotype—before the French Academy of Sciences. Later that year Arago made public the technical details and Daguerre published a detailed booklet on the process. Daguerre may not have been the "inventor" of photography, but he probably did more than any other person to make photography a matter of public interest. People from London to St. Petersburg and even in America reacted with wild enthusiasm and before long "Daguerreotypomania" had captured the public's imagination. Studios sprung up everywhere and excited amateurs clamored to buy daguerreotype apparatus.

Popular photography had been born.

Louis J.M. Daguerre. "Paris Boulevard." 1839. Daguerreotype. Bayerisches Nationalmuseum Munchen

Fascination with the daguerreotype swept Paris. Upon seeing the process for the first time, painter Paul Delaroche pronounced, "From today, painting is dead!" Daguerreotypomania, as it was dubbed in the press, seemed to take over every phase of life. Nothing like it had ever been seen before. The perfect perspective, the exquisitely etched details of cobblestone streets, carved facades, brocaded dresses, and the subtle shadings of facial features and elaborate coiffures evoked comparisons with the great artists.

The daguerreotype spread rapidly throughout Europe. Daguerreotypists appeared everywhere, offering convenient portrait services to celebrities and common folk alike. Enterprising publishers dispatched daguerreotypists to foreign lands and began illustrating their travel books with illustrations and drawings that were hand copied from daguerreotype views. Daguerreotypes also appeared as miniature works of art and as documentations of events. It seems certain that by 1843, only four years after Daguerre's announcement, every European town of consequence had at least one daguerreotype studio, and itinerant photographers served others.

Daguerre's patent restrictions made daguerreotypy costly in England, but the process spread unfettered to America. The American inventor Samuel F. B. Morse, who had also tried unsuccessfully to fix camera obscura images, learned of Daguerre's work during a visit to Paris, and by mid 1840 he and John William Draper had become partners in a portrait studio atop New York University. The craft spread rapidly in America. By 1853 New York City alone boasted an estimated 100 or more studios.

The Calotype

In the early 1830s, while Niépce and Daguerre were struggling to capture images on metal plates, others were also at work. One of these was England's Sir John Herschel, who by 1839 had succeeded in capturing images on paper that had been sensitized with carbonate of silver, and who was the first to make them permanent by fixing them in hyposulfite of soda.

The noted English scientist William Henry Fox Talbot took a direction different from Daguerre's use of metal plates. Talbot captured images on paper coated with silver chloride. By 1835 he had learned to make these images permanent by washing them in a strong salt solution. To speed up exposure, he worked with very small images, some only an inch or so square. These little negative images—curiosities at best—were of little compelling interest, even to Talbot. Between 1835 and the time of Daguerre's dramatic announcements in 1839, Talbot had all but abandoned this line of work. However, when he heard the news from France, Talbot rushed to claim prior discovery by sending letters to members of the French Academy of Science and a report of his own work with "photogenic drawings" to the Royal Society in England. Although his report was widely circulated in the press, his coarse little images could not compete for public favor with the larger, brighter, more detailed, and positive, not negative, daguerreotype images.

Embedded in Talbot's report to the Royal Society was the following observation, offered almost casually:

Figure 1-6. Henry Fox Talbot. "The Broom," 1844. Calotype from Pencil of Nature, the first book illustrated with photographs. Courtesy George Eastman House.

If the picture so obtained is first preserved so as to bear sunshine, it may be afterwards itself employed as an object to be copied, and by means of this second process the lights and shadows are brought back to their original disposition.

With this statement, Talbot advanced the negative-positive principle that was to become the basis for nearly all photography after that time.

Eclipsed by the popularity of the daguerreotype and frustrated by the lukewarm interest of the Royal Society, Talbot worked on alone, continuing his experiments with larger cameras and improved lenses. He began using hyposulfite of soda as a fixing agent, as Sir John Herschel had suggested. The following year, he discovered that latent, unseen images resided in the sensitized paper after only a brief exposure, and that they could be made visible by resensitizing the paper. Talbot was thus able to reduce exposure time from many hours to less than a minute. To produce a positive image, Talbot resurrected his negative-positive idea and invented contact printing. He waxed his paper negatives so that they would better transmit light and exposed them to sunlight in contact with photosensitive paper to produce positive prints. In 1841 he secured a patent for his process, which at first he called the **calotype**—beautiful image—but which he was later persuaded to call the **talbotype**.

Talbot set up a studio in Reading, outside of London, where he and his employees operated what was probably the world's first photo finishing company. From 1844 to 1846 he produced, probably from this studio, his landmark, six-volume work, *The Pencil of Nature,* the first photo-illustrated book, each volume containing 24 pasted-in calotypes.

Talbot's vigorous enforcement of his patent rights discouraged widespread adoption of his process in England. However, calotype studios opened elsewhere in Europe without his licensure. In 1843 David Octavius Hill, a noted landscape painter, and Robert Adamson, a calotypist, opened a studio in Edinburgh, Scotland; in their four-year association they produced more than 2,000 calotype portraits, genre and architectural views, and landscapes that remain classics of the Victorian era.

The calotype became more popular in France than elsewhere in Europe. Hippolyte Bayard, an experimenter and noted daguerreotypist, invented a method of printing in cloud formations and produced memorable calotype landscapes. Gustave Le Gray, whose seascapes were ahead of their time, developed a process for waxing the calotype paper first to reduce dramatically the paper grain and to give the sensitized paper longer storing properties. In 1851 Louis Desiré Blanquart-Evrard opened a studio in Lille primarily to produce calotype prints for book illustrations. The 125 pasted-in calotypes he produced for Maxime Du Camp's *Egypte, Nubie, Palestine et Syrie* in 1851 were a remarkable achievement for the time. He also developed a faster, sharper, glossy-surfaced printing paper using photo salts suspended in the whites of eggs, which enabled him to increase print production more than 300 percent. This **albumen paper** dominated photographic printing for more than forty years.

Figure 1-7. David Octavius Hill and Robert Adamson. "Architect George Meikle Kemp," circa 1844. This team of a Scottish painter and a chemist collaborated to explore Calotype photography and created over 1500 portraits and genre scenes. Courtesy George Eastman House.

Although the calotype never achieved the popularity of the daguerreotype, some photographers recognized the aesthetic qualities of the process. Because of its method of printing through a paper negative, the calotype was soft and lacked the fine, etched detail of the daguerreotype. Yet these same qualities produced a soft, charcoal-like impression that was better suited to the representation of shapes and masses of tone with soft edges—characteristics that appealed to the more interpretive of the early photographers. Further, unlike daguerreotypy, which produced single, unique, irreproducible images, the calotype process could be used to produce any number of identical prints.

Thus, by the mid 1840s, more than one technology of photography existed. This period of early photography, including both the popular daguerreotype and the calotype, was relatively short; it lasted only until the early 1850s. It served, however, to establish photography as an art and craft accessible to the common people.

Wet Plate Photography

Recognizing the advantages of the negative-positive process, but dissatisfied with the coarse quality of images printed through paper, numerous experimenters searched for a transparent medium. Many tried the obvious, glass, but experienced difficulty in bonding the emulsion to the surface. In 1848, however, Abel Niépce de Saint-Victor succeeded by using albumen as a coating on glass. Although his process produced a storable, dry plate, a great convenience, the required exposures were excessively long and the process never became popular.

Nevertheless, experimentation continued and, in 1851, Frederick Scott Archer succeeded in bonding a photographic emulsion to glass. The process employed **collodion**, a viscous solution of guncotton dissolved in alcohol and ether, as the transparent bonding agent. The sensitized plate had to be exposed and processed before the highly volatile collodion

could dry, for when dry it formed a shield impervious to the developing and fixing solutions. Because collodian was used in this fashion, the process became known as **collodion wet plate** photography.

The collodion wet plate process was unbelievably awkward. Imagine toting with you on even the most casual photographic outing a portable darkroom such as a light-tight tent, a supply of 8in x 10in (or larger) glass plates, photosensitive and processing chemicals in their various containers, and a bulky wooden camera and tripod. Then imagine setting up a tent, coating each glass plate with a photographic emulsion, loading the plate while still wet into a plate holder and then into the camera, immediately making an exposure, and rushing back into the tent to process the plate before it could dry; then repeating the process for each exposure.

Despite these inconveniences, the collodion wet plate rapidly superseded the daguerreotype in popularity. The materials were less costly. Exposure times were usually less than a minute, and often were as short as ten seconds. Unlike the daguerreotype, which was a single, irreproducible image, the glass collodion wet plate produced a negative from which unlimited prints could be made. The final prints, on paper, were lightweight and flexible. And, happily, the rendering of exquisitely fine detail, uncompromised by printing

Figure I-8. Artist unknown. Portable Wet Plate Darkroom Tent and equipment, circa 1877. The gear necessary for wet plate photography in the field weighed over 120 pounds. Courtesy of Harry Ransom Humanities Research Center, The University of Texas at Austin.

through paper, was comparable to that of the daguerreotype. Collodion wet plate photography began a wave of popular photography, enticed thousands of new amateurs to the craft, dominated photographic practice worldwide for nearly thirty years, and established the negative-positive process as the standard for photography thereafter.

Two variations of the collodion wet plate, which simulated the appearance of the daguerreotype, also became popular. One, the **ambrotype**, patented by James Ambrose Cutting, used underexposure or bleaching to produce a faint negative image on glass. When viewed against a deep black background, a positive image would be seen. A **union case** was used to bind the glass plate permanently with, usually, a piece of deep black velvet. Another variation was the **tintype**, introduced in 1856 by Hamilton L. Smith. In this case, the wet collodion emulsion was applied to a metal plate, usually tin, that was lacquered deep black. A faint image was produced on the surface, and when the plate was viewed against the black background, the positive image would be seen. Because ambrotypes and tintypes were inexpensive and easy to make, they became very popular in America and supported a virtual army of studio and itinerant photographers. However, these one-of-a-kind techniques would eventually go the way of the daguerreotype, superseded by the more flexible negative-positive processes.

Figure 1-9. Photographer unknown. Untitled Ambrotype, circa 1858. The black backing has been partially removed on the right to show how the backing made the negative image appear as a positive one. Courtesy of Harry Ransom Humanities Research Center, The University of Texas at Austin.

Dry Plate Photography

In 1871 Richard Leach Maddox discovered a means of bonding a dry emulsion to a glass plate using gelatin, and by 1878 a practical dry plate process was available that rapidly superseded the collodion wet plate process. Because dry plates could be mass-produced, stored, distributed through retail shops, and processed at leisure, commercial channels quickly developed.

Figure 1-10. Fred Church. "George Eastman on Board Ship," 1890. Eastman is shown here with a No. 1 Kodak identical to the one that took this picture. Courtesy George Eastman House.

9

Figure 1-11. Roger Fenton. "Bataclava Harbor during the Crimean War," 1855. Fenton was the first photographer to cover a war under fire. However, his photographs show none of the bloodshed and brutality of battle; such photographs would have offended Victorian tastes. Courtesy George Eastman House.

to say. He popularized the slogan: "You push the button and we do the rest." A year later, he replaced the paper base of his roll film with transparent nitrocellulose. By the turn of the century, Eastman was marketing his simple cameras and popular film products to ordinary people everywhere, who carried their cameras about with them on their travels, at home, at play, and in the workplace. By simply combining the hand-held camera that was easy to operate and dry roll film that was painless to process, George Eastman had made photography simple and practical for everyone.

Color Photography

The images produced by the camera obscura appeared, of course, in full color, and the artists who used the device normally produced their final works in color. When people dreamed of capturing the image of the camera obscura, they naturally dreamed in color.

The earliest photographic experimenters sought to capture not only line, shape, mass, and relative brightness, but color as well. Both Niépce and Daguerre experimented with color. The latter even expressed disappointment that his process failed to show his subjects "in the full splendor of their colors."

In 1861 the British physicist James Clerk Maxwell demonstrated the principle of color separation and linked the principle to color photography. He photographed a tartan ribbon three times, each time using a different color filter—red, green, or blue. Then, after making positive black-and-white transparencies of the three images, he projected them simultaneously on three projectors through these same filters, demonstrating the principle of **additive color mixing**. When the three images were superimposed, a kind of "photograph" of the ribbon in its original colors was produced.

In 1869 Louis Duco du Hauron and Charles Cros, working independently, simultaneously an-

However, even in the late 1880s, photography remained the domain of the very determined. Photographic plates were still heavy and fragile. Camera equipment was bulky and unwieldy. Photographers in the field were obligated to carry about the stuff of their trade by covered wagon or mule train. This was no easy craft.

One American dry plate manufacturer, George Eastman, recognized that would-be photographers represented a huge market for anyone who could simplify this process; in 1888 he did just that. He introduced a small, lightweight box camera that was easy to operate and that boasted a shutter fast enough to eliminate the need for a tripod. More important, however, was the fact that the camera came loaded with a roll of paper film. For thirty-five dollars a purchaser could shoot one hundred pictures and then return the entire camera to the Eastman Company, where the film would be removed and processed. One hundred individually mounted pictures would be returned to the purchaser together with the camera, reloaded with a fresh roll of film.

Eastman dubbed his little camera Kodak, a meaningless word that was easy to remember and easy

Figure 1-12. Roger Fenton. "Fenton's Photographic Van," 1855. Fenton carried his equipment in this horse-drawn wagon. Even though "Photographic Van" was painted boldly on its side, it was a frequent target for enemy artillery. This portable darkroom was fully equipped for making and processing wet-plate emulsions. Courtesy of the Science Museum.

nounced their discoveries of **subtractive color mixing**. They knew that passing white light through a filter caused the filter's colors to be transmitted while its complements were absorbed. Therefore, passing white light through two or more successive filters of pure secondary colors would cause the light from the filter's complementary primary to be blocked as the light passed through each filter (see Color Plate 1C). By applying this principle they were able to reproduce full-color images by passing white light through superimposed transparent cyan, magenta, and yellow images, each of varying density. A full-color image was produced as varying amounts of primary color were subtracted from the transmitted image at each filter stage.

The first commercial color film process, **Autochrome**, was an additive process introduced in 1907 in France by Auguste and Louis Lumière. They thinly coated a sensitized glass plate with grains of starch colored orange, green, and violet, and then processed it to produce a full-color transparency.

The subtractive process, however, provided the foundation for modern color photography. As early as 1912, a method for chemically forming dyes in the emulsion during development had been demonstrated. However, this process remained unreliable because the dyes tended to migrate between color layers. In 1930, Leopold Mannes and Leopold Godowsky, both musicians and amateur photo scientists who were working with the Eastman Kodak Company to develop the **Kodachrome** process for the movie industry, overcame this problem. They removed the color couplers from the emulsion and introduced them during processing instead. This process coats a single sheet of film with three layers of emulsion, each sensitive to one of the primary colors of light. A single exposure, properly processed, produces a positive transparent image. Both Kodachrome and **Agfacolor**, a similar material introduced almost simultaneously in Germany, were made available for still photography in 1935.

Many approaches to color photography have emerged subsequently. In 1950 Kodak introduced another Mannes and Godowsky invention, the color reversal film, **Ektachrome**, which provided for home processing. **Kodacolor, Ektacolor**, and other films that used nonreversal processes, by which positive color prints were produced from transparent color negatives, soon followed. Another noteworthy approach, **Cibachrome**, was based on a method of selectively removing dyes from the emulsion, a method that was described as early as 1918 by Christiansen. The modern variation produces highly stable prints of incredible sharpness. Another approach is the Polaroid line of instant color films that are based on Edwin Land's demonstration that full color may be perceived with only two superimposed images if they are illuminated by light of different colors. These films are remarkably complex layered materials that contain all photosensitive and processing chemistry in a single, integrated configuration.

Later Camera Developments

The first photographic cameras available to the public followed the announcement of the daguerreotype in 1839. These were relatively simple devices, derived directly from the camera obscura—wooden boxes with a lens mounted at one end and a ground-glass focusing screen on the other end, with some provision for altering the distance between the lens and the film plane to achieve focus. Later elaborations included aperture controls. A complete daguerreotype outfit including the camera, tripod, plate box, iodine/mercury vaporizing boxes, spirit lamp, bottles of chemicals, and the rest, weighed over 100 pounds.

Because the plates used for these early processes were very large, lenses were generally slow, requiring long exposures, often many minutes. Those long exposures generally ruled out photographs of people or other moving subjects. Several attempts were made to solve this problem. Alexander S. Wolcott patented a concave mirror camera in 1840 that was fast enough to produce 2in x 2in daguerreotype portraits. In 1841 Peter Friedrich Voigtländer marketed a barrel-shaped brass camera fitted with a relatively fast portrait lens designed by Josef Max Petzval. The lens, thirty times faster than any other lens of this period, remained the standard for portrait photography for more than fifty years.

Cameras designed for the calotype also appeared in 1839; they were similar to those designed for the daguerreotype. In 1850, Roger Fenton carried with him to Crimea a calotype camera specially designed by his assistant, Marcus Sparling, to hold ten sheets of calotype paper in special holders within the camera. In 1854, a pair of ingenious inventors designed a camera that would accept a roll of calotype paper that could be advanced to a take-up roller after exposure within the camera.

During the wet plate period, a complete wet plate outfit outweighed the comparable daguerreotype outfit by twenty pounds. It included a portable tent and water containers, in addition to everything else. Itinerant photographers often hired a porter as well as a van to carry this paraphernalia about. Roger Fenton outfitted a van to serve also as sleeping quarters during his sojourn in the Crimea, an idea quickly adopted by Civil War and expeditionary photographers later in the nineteenth century.

Unique cameras were designed for special purposes when needed. Tiny cameras seem always to have been a fascination. One pocket daguerreotype camera was designed to produce 8mm x 11mm daguerreotypes. At the other extreme, one of the largest cameras made in the nineteenth century was a horse-drawn wet plate camera designed in 1860 for John Kibble of Glasgow to accept a 44in x 36in glass plate weighing about 44 pounds. Another was the Mammoth, built in Chicago, which used a 4 1/2ft x 8ft glass plate that weighed 500 pounds and took 10 gallons of chemical solution to process.

Stereoscopic views became enormously popular after Louis Jules Dubosc commercially introduced them in 1851. Stereoscopic photography creates an illusion of 3-dimensional depth by re-creating the binocularity of human vision. Because our two eyes are separated, each eye sees the world slightly differently and these two eye-images are merged into one in the brain. The stereoscopic view was a single card on which were mounted two nearly twin photographs of the same subject taken from slightly different views—one for the left eye, one for the right—corresponding to the human binocular separation. When viewed through Sir David Brewster's lenticular stereoscope, the two images merged to present a three-dimensional view of astonishing reality.

Special cameras were designed and marketed to photograph these stereoscopic views. Some were single-lens devices providing for defined movement between successive shots. Others were

Figure 1-13. Photographer unknown. Stereograph of Photographer's Studio. Viewing stereographic photographs was an extremely popular pastime from its introduction in the 1850's until well into the 20th century. A stereopticon viewer was needed to view the twin pictures as a single, three-dimensional image. © Bettmann/Corbis

twin-lens devices designed to shoot both distinct views simultaneously. Millions of stereoscopic views were produced between the 1850s and the 1930s.

Queen Victoria and Prince Albert were presented with a stereoscopic viewer at the Crystal Palace exhibition in 1851 and the popularity of the medium soared. Oliver Wendell Holmes called for the establishment of "special stereographic collections." Entrepreneurial photographers recorded and sold stereoscopic views of local history and events, grand landscapes, quaint genre scenes, celebrity portraits, and views of architecture, war, and natural disasters. Stereo views declined in popularity in the early 1920s as movie newsreels and illustrated magazines such as *Life* replaced them.

Just as the television today appeals to the diverse needs and tastes of a complex audience, so stereoscopic views entertained and enlightened the public. Between the 1850s and the 1910s, stereoscopic views were a primary source of home entertainment and personal leisure activity.

Another popular nineteenth-century application was the **carte de visite**—the visiting card. So ubiquitous did photography become during the century that it became a social custom to exchange photographic visiting cards depicting the

parties. For this purpose, in 1854 André Adolphe Eugène Disdéri patented a camera fitted with four identical short-focus lenses corresponding to four interior compartments. Using an internal device, one could first expose one half of a plate and then the other half one lens at a time, to obtain eight separate poses on a single plate that could be made into cartes de visite.

By the end of the century, an enormous variety of cameras for use with dry plates, cut film, and roll film were produced for an enormous variety of purposes. By 1900 it was estimated that 10 percent of Britain's population—about four million people—owned cameras.

The Emergence of Motion Pictures

The ancients knew the phenomenon of the persistence of vision; the brain retains images slightly longer than the eye physically records them. During the nineteenth century, experiments with this phenomenon using still photography combined with optical projection produced a practical motion picture technology by the early 1880s.

In 1832 Joseph Plateau patented a novelty he called the **phenakistiscope**. Individual paintings on a flat, circular board were viewed in a mirror through slits in a second board while the boards

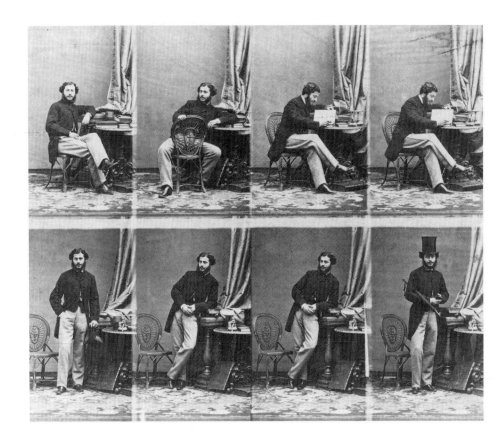

Figure 1-14. Adolphe-Eugene Disderi. Uncut print from a carte de visite negative, circa 1860. So popular was the exchange of these little images that the carte de visite album became a fashionable feature in Victorian parlors. Courtesy George Eastman House.

Figure 1-15. Phenakistiscope de Plateau. Culver Pictures. Moving demonstrations of the Phenakistiscope de Plateau can be seen on the Internet at http://allserv.rug.ac.be/~ivaeghe/mhsqent/engl-plat5.html

were rotated at high speed in opposite directions. The slits provided a kind of shutter so that the successive images would be seen one at a time rather than as a spinning blur. The result was the illusion of a single moving picture.

In *"Sur un nouveau genre d'illusions d'optique", Corresp. Math. Phys. 1832 VII p.291*, Plateau describes the construction and action of a disc with 16 slits and 16 intermediate sectors depicting a pirouetting dancer. The brilliant contribution of Plateau is that instead of putting 16 identical images in the sectors he drew 16 images each slightly different than its predecessor. The shutterlike effect and the persistence of vision gave the rapid succession of images the illusion of a single moving image. Because of this contribution, Joseph Plateau's invention is credited as the precursor of the movie or, more accurately, the animation film.

Simultaneously, Simon Ritter von Stampfer developed a similar device in Germany and dubbed it the **stroboscope**. Two years later, William George Horner created a similar device, which he named the **zoetrope**, that used a circular drum with interchangeable picture strips. That same year, Baron Franz von Uchatius experimented with similar toys combined with the **magic lantern**, a kind of candle-powered slide projector that was popular at the time. He continued these experiments for many years and by 1853 had developed the projecting phenakistiscope. All these devices relied upon hand-drawn images, similar to animated cartoons.

The first attempts at motion photography were posed still photographs that simulated movement. The stills were mounted on picture strips and displayed with the projecting phenakistiscope. The result was far from realistic, because the process was a synthesis of discrete, posed, nonmoving images. A method of breaking a single, continuous movement into discrete, sequential, photographic units was needed.

The first person to succeed in this attempt was Eadweard Muybridge, a ne'er-do-well English inventor living in California, who was hired by then governor Leland Stanford to prove that all four of a racing horse's hooves left the ground at some point in its stride. After five years without success, Muybridge devised a scheme whereby he arranged twelve cameras in a row along a racetrack, each triggered separately by a string stretched across the track. When the galloping horse tripped the wires, Muybridge had his motion picture sequence. (See Unit 4, *Famous Photograph,* p. 138.) Over the next twenty years he perfected this technique, increasing the number of cameras and the variety of subjects, and combining these photographs with his version of the projecting phenakistiscope, which he called the **zoopraxiscope**.

After seeing Muybridge's work, Etienne-Jules Marey attempted to record successive phases of movement on a single plate. He succeeded in 1882, using one camera that used a circular photographic plate that was rotated twelve times in a single second to produce twelve sequential exposures. The device looked so much like a shotgun that he referred to his activity as "shooting," and this term has been in popular use to describe making a photograph ever since. Marey's work inspired the American painter Thomas Eakins, who produced his own multiple-exposure photographs and influenced the Futurist painters and their pursuit of "simultaneity."

Figure 1-16. Thomas Eakins. "George Reynolds Pole-Vaulting," 1884. Eakins, a great American painter, made photographic studies of models in motion using multiple exposures on a single plate. The Metropolitan Museum of Art. Gift of Charles Bregler, 1941. All Rights Reserved.

All that now remained to complete the technology was a continuous photographic material capable of holding thousands of sequential images. George Eastman's celluloid roll film, developed originally for still photography in 1889, provided an answer. For nearly a decade, major experiments with motion picture photography were carried on by Thomas Edison in America and by Auguste and Louis Lumière in France, among others, using roll film. But it was the Lumières who most influenced motion picture photography, establishing sixteen frames per second and a film width of 35mm as standards that survive to this day.

Still photographers naturally conceived of the idea that cine-film might be used in a still camera. As early as 1912 George P. Smith of Missouri designed a camera that would use 35mm motion picture film, and by 1914 Oscar Barnack had developed a prototype of his Leica camera, which would later transform the industry. The Leica went into full-scale production following World War I, equipped with a fast Elmar lens and a lens-coupled rangefinder for accurate focusing. An era of true miniature cameras had begun.

The Emergence of Halftone Technology

The invention of halftone technology in the late nineteenth century not only made possible the widespread dissemination of photographic images in print, but also foreshadowed the later development of digital imaging. (See page 87.) In order to reproduce a continuous tone image with black ink on paper, Stephen T. Horgan figured out a way to simulate the gray tones in an image by printing many closely spaced tiny black dots of varying size on white paper. By varying the size of these nearly invisible dots, the image would appear as varying shades of gray, simulating a continuous tone image.

To produce the halftone plate one was required to contact print the original continuous tone image through halftone screens of the desired frequency (lines per inch). This was a very complex and costly process. However, by defining a continuous tone image as a matrix of discrete dots, or points of data, the halftone process laid the foundation for the development of digital imaging technology that would follow a century later.

Twentieth-Century Developments

Developments since that time include twin-lens and single-lens reflex designs, variable focal length and zoom lenses, automatic exposure systems, digital cameras, digitizers and scanners, electronic tools for creating, manipulating, and distributing images, and a host of special-purpose cameras, attachments, materials, and technologies far too numerous to describe. In little more than a century and a half, photography advanced from Niépce's first crude heliograph of his pigeon loft, to NASA's computer-enhanced images of Jupiter's moons, transmitted through millions of miles of space, and to the widespread dissemination of images over the Internet and the World Wide Web.

DIGITAL IMAGING

What may be considered as the most significant photographic development of the last century is the emergence of digital imaging.

Figure 1-17. Jupiter's moon Ganymede as imaged by a NASA probe. About the size of Mercury, Ganymede is 3168 miles in diameter.

What is digital imaging? Digital imaging is still too new for our culture to have produced the language needed to clearly distinguish it from its precursors. Digital imaging can encompass many processes—from capturing images in a camera, from a scanner, or from a video source, editing, enhancing, or manipulating them on a computer, and printing or distributing them via email or the World Wide Web, to name just a few. For the time being it is probably sufficient to define a digital image simply as "a two-dimensional image which originated in a lens-imaging device and was then brought to completion on a computer." (Bradley University Millennium Exhibitions) This would include images originally captured by film cameras, video cameras, still-video cameras, digital cameras, and 3D-scanners.

A digital image, therefore, might be an original image drawn manually using a computer. It might be an original image generated using a computer and image-generating software. It might be an original image produced photographically using a digital camera or by scanning traditional photographic materials. It might be an image produced using a computer to combine text, diagram, drawn images, generated images, photographic images from separate sources to create a new, seamless montage.

While defining digital imaging may be complex, evaluating the power of an image has not changed. An image touches us, demands our attention, and communicates with us if it offers us new insight. The best images, whether produced by traditional photography or by digital imaging, offer us new ways of seeing.

First introduced to the consumer market around 1994, digital cameras have experienced an explosion in popularity and have led to a revival of interest in photography. A 2003 survey reported that one in seven American households owned a digital camera. Although the boom is recent, many events contributed to the rapid technological development of digital imaging.

In 1956, the television industry put video tape recorders (VTRs) into common use that converted television images into digital data. Digital imaging technology was further developed by the government during the 1960s for use with spy satellites and space probes. In the mid-1970s, the Scitex Company found a way to use a micropro-

cessor to store the signal from a photo multiplier tube in a computer. An electromechanical scanner was introduced, similar to the halftone scanner that read a transparent or reflected image and recorded it as a digital file. Texas Instruments was the first to patent a filmless electronic camera in 1972. The George Lucas production team developed specialized imaging software for his motion picture, Star Wars, that was eventually sold, redeveloped, and repackaged as Photoshop.

At first, the makers of business computers did not embrace digital imaging technology. Although Apple built graphical display capabilities into their products and introduced desktop publishing, their market consisted mostly of families and schools. Seeing the needs of business to be significantly different, the makers of business computers initially provided only crude, monochrome graphics that were minimally suitable for graphs and charts.

However, in 1986 Kodak created a 1.4 megapixel sensor and, in 1991, introduced the first commercial digital camera. Following rapidly in the early 1990s, other companies such as Sony, Canon, and Nikon began producing digital cameras. Over the next decade, image quality improved significantly and compact, removable storage media were developed that could be read directly from the camera to a computer. Other features important to photographers, such as zoom and interchangeable lenses, were also incorporated into camera designs.

Almost from the moment that computers first appeared on desktops, however, users demanded more imaging functions, not only for entertainment, but for education, research, commerce, communication, manufacture, and design as well. Color rapidly displaced monochrome as the standard desktop computer display. Computers, digitizers, scanners, and color printers became more affordable. The Internet and World Wide Web grew at a phenomenal rate through the 1990s. By the end of the Millennium, people of all walks of life, of all ages, throughout the world were creating, manipulating storing, retrieving, disseminating, and publishing photographic images on a scale never before seen.

Two major factors help account for the accelerating commercial popularity of digital imaging. One is that images need not be chemically processed and printed before they can be seen and used. Unlike a film-based photograph, a digital image can be viewed and distributed electronically within moments of its capture. The second is that image controls such as cropping, dodging, burning-in, and contrast enhancement need not be labor-intensive activities carried out in a wet-process darkroom. Unlike a film-based photograph, a digital image can be edited and enhanced quickly and efficiently using image editing programs on a computer in a light room without chemicals.

As sales of digital cameras were poised to overtake sales of film cameras in 2004, Eastman Kodak announced that it would stop selling traditional film cameras in the United States, Canada, and Western Europe in favor of digital products. Although committed to continue the manufacture and sale of films, the move indicates that this photography pioneer is transitioning its focus toward digital imaging technology.

A Visual History of Photography

One cannot view the visual history of photography as a simple chronology. Its technical history was bound intimately to its visual history, as technology interacted with personal visions and purposes. From its earliest beginnings, photography was used to record the commonplace, to document the unusual, to comment upon social life, to express aesthetic ideas, to inform, to teach, and to influence. These many uses help to explain how photography developed simultaneously in many directions under the influence of visionary individuals, social and aesthetic movements, and technical possibilities. They help explain, too, why this brief visual history may appear episodic and discontinuous—reflecting the very nature of photography's evolutionary development.

Prior to photography, hand-painted family portraits, decorative landscapes, and pictures of exotic places were much in demand by the affluent classes for the walls and libraries of their homes. From its introduction, photography represented a less expensive alternative to painting and was rapidly adopted by the middle classes for these same purposes. However, it was also apparent that this new craft offered a means to represent the physical world with greater detail and fidelity than previously had been possible. So as demand for family and celebrity portraits, landscapes, cityscapes, and architectural views increased, a new aesthetic began also to emerge—one based primarily upon the play of light and shadow on physical objects.

This new aesthetic vision did not appear at once. To achieve critical recognition, many early photographers attempted to mimic the aesthetics of contemporary artists. Early portrait photographers, for example, posed their subjects in the fashion of contemporary portrait painters, and many photographers staged elaborate setups intended to resemble the style of fashionable paintings.

For the most part, however, the daguerreotypes that survive are portraits and depictions of simple, realistic subjects. They suggest a kind of static world, mostly unpeopled, except for those people who appear in stiff, formal, stern-looking portraits or family groups. Because exposures were long, subjects had to pose motionless. Because daguerreotypes had to be processed immediately following exposure, most were taken within studios or from studio windows. Although the constraints were extreme, a few masters emerged to point the way toward a new photographic aesthetic that eventually broke away from the traditions of painting.

As faster processes emerged and exposure times decreased, the need for posing was gradually eliminated, making it possible to photograph moving subjects. People, animals, and other subjects in natural motion appeared increasingly in calotypes. With the introduction of collodion wet plates, photographic images virtually sprang to life as photographers discovered and exploited the medium's capacity to freeze life's fleeting moments. When dry plates, and later roll film, were introduced, photographers gained greater freedom to carry their cameras to places formerly denied them, to use their cameras as unobtrusive extensions of their own eyes, to record not only moments but motions. Further advances enabled them to extend their vision into microworlds and even into outer space.

Throughout the entire development of photographic technology, photographers explored their increasing ability to freeze on film their impressions of the natural world as they found it, to transform their impressions by selecting and controlling photographic elements, to extend their vision of the physical world beyond the limits of sight, and to expand their personal visions of physical reality. However, these personal visions varied widely.

A Brief History of Styles

High Art and Pictorialism
The earliest attempts to advance photography as a fine art tended to mimic the aesthetics of painting. One early effort was that of J. E. Mayall, who in 1845 produced a series of daguerreotypes illustrating the Lord's Prayer and who later exhibited other works to "illustrate poetry and sentiment." Apart from Mayall's efforts, only simple photographs of the physical world seemed to characterize the first fifteen years of photography.

Though Mayall's pictures were criticized as "a mistake . . . imagination supplanted by the presence of fact," others were to follow his lead. The Photographic Society of London encouraged photographers to produce pictures for exhibition and critical review. But the critics did not know how to deal with this new medium. They drew invidious comparisons between photography's "mere reproduction of reality" and fine art's loftier, ennobling themes. They encouraged photographers to produce the historical, allegorical, and literary images of fine art.

This attitude encouraged many painters to approach photography as they would brush and canvas, an approach exemplified by the works of William Lake Price, Oscar G. Rejlander, and Henry Peach Robinson, which were praised as **high art photography** by critics of the time. Their method involved first sketching a detailed composition, then making numerous individual negatives of its various parts, and finally combining these negatives, with generous retouching, into a composite image. Rejlander's allegorical masterwork, *The Two Ways of Life,* a 16in x 31in composite of thirty negatives, was an instant success when exhibited in 1857. Queen Victoria's purchase of this work legitimized the high art approach and encouraged others.

Robinson followed Rejlander's lead into high art photography, producing a five-negative composite called *Fading Away* in 1858 that also was purchased by the Queen. For more than thirty years

Figure 1-18. Oscar G. Rejlander. "The Two Ways of Life," 1856. A composite photograph made from thirty separate negatives. Although initially considered risqué, this image so impressed Queen Victoria that she purchased a copy, which gave credibility to photography as an art. The creation of images bearing a strong relationship to allegorical painting became a cornerstone of art photography during the Victorian era. Courtesy George Eastman House.

Figure 1-19. Peter Henry Emerson. "Gathering Water Lilies," 1886. In a reaction against the artificial devices of pictorial photography, Emerson urged a return to nature for inspiration, setting forth his views in Naturalistic Photography (1889), and influencing generations of landscape photographers who followed. Courtesy George Eastman House.

Robinson exhibited his composite pictures at every exhibition of the Photographic Society of London, wrote prolifically on his style of **pictorial photography**, and influenced generations of photographers until well after World War I, particularly with his classic book, *Picture Making by Photography.*

Naturalism Daguerre recognized that photography's uniqueness was its superior ability to reproduce nature in fine detail. He wrote, "Nature has the artlessness which must not be destroyed." Others intuitively followed his lead, expressing discomfort with contrived picture making. Using the medium to create fictitious allegories produces "at best, only the impression of a scene on the stage," they said. Nevertheless, throughout the late nineteenth century, photographic exhibitions were dominated by the artificiality and pompous sentiment of the high art pictorialists.

One of those to take up the challenge in the mid-1880s was Dr. Peter Henry Emerson, an American living in England, who boldly urged photographers to look instead to nature for inspiration and subject matter. He spent more than a decade photographing ordinary life and landscapes around the Norfolk Broads, effectively demonstrating that the photographer can reveal a personal aesthetic vision of natural subjects. He strongly advocated soft focus to simulate human vision, and he suggested that a photograph's prin-

cipal elements be in sharp focus against soft-focus backgrounds and foregrounds. He published his theories in *Naturalistic Photography* in 1889, asserting that naturalistic photographs should be truthful in appearance, naturally sentimental, and decorative.

His example led to a revived interest in landscape photography, exemplified in the works of Benjamin Gay Wilkinson, Joseph Gale, Lyddell Sawyer, Frederick Evans, Frank Sutcliffe, and George Davison. These naturalistic photographers formed a movement in 1892 called the Linked Ring Brotherhood, which advocated more impressionistic images of natural subjects—soft focus and coarse textures. Within a short time, the Linked Ring included leading art photographers from all over Europe and America. Its annual international exhibitions became the premier events in aesthetic photography through 1914.

Straight Photography Many photographers in Europe applied photography to the realistic documentation of objects and events. As early as 1851, Richard Beard produced daguerreotypes of the London poor, and these appeared as woodcuts in Henry Mayhew's *London Labour and the London Poor.* In 1855, Roger Fenton was commissioned by Queen Victoria to photograph the Crimean War, becoming the first to carry a camera into battle. John Thomson, a Scottish explorer and photographer, published studies of the Far East in the

Figure 1-20. George Davison. "The Onion Field," 1890. By combining soft focus and rough-textured paper, Davison introduced impressionism to photography. Courtesy George Eastman House.

1860s and his classic *Street Life in London* in 1877.

In America, realistic photography that aimed at producing accurate factual records of families, celebrities, war, and topography had become a preoccupation. Mathew Brady, a staid portrait photographer to the rich and famous, was compelled by a "spirit in my feet" to carry his camera into the battles of the Civil War. Later recruiting a dozen others, such as Alexander Gardner and Timothy O'Sullivan, he amassed more than 7,000 negatives that documented that tragic American conflict. Following the war, many of these same photographers joined teams commissioned to survey the western lands of the United States. These works were never seen as photographs in the popular press of their times because no technology existed for reproducing photographs in printer's ink. However, they did appear as handmade block prints and engravings copied from the original photographs. These scenes generated in America an appreciation for truthfulness and objectivity in photographic images. This almost

tangible preference for factual, unadorned representations of reality helps to explain why America showed little interest in the aesthetic movements of Europe, which were dominated by the standards of contemporary painting.

Toward the beginning of the new century, however, the spiritual center of aesthetic photography began to tilt toward America, largely due to the influence of one American, Alfred Stieglitz. Stieglitz had gone to Europe as an engineering student in 1882 and became captivated by photography, winning a medal at the Linked Ring exhibition in 1888. Returning to New York in 1890, influenced by the aesthetic movements of Europe, he encountered the American documentarians, including Jacob Riis, a police photographer who documented the tenement life of poor immigrants. Stieglitz became a principal advocate for photography as an independent art form, rooted in objective reality but adhering to its own aesthetic principles. In 1902 he started the Photo-Secession, a group

Figure 1-21. Timothy H. O'Sullivan. "A Harvest of Death, Gettysburg," 1863. One of Mathew Brady's staff of nineteen photographers who covered the battlefields of the American Civil War. Their Civil War photographs make up one of the most remarkable and treasured collections of documentary photographs in American history although they were little appreciated in their own time.

Figure 1-22. Alfred Stieglitz. "The Steerage," 1907. Seeking to regenerate photography as art in America toward the end of the nineteenth century, Stieglitz was a purist who advocated straight, unmanipulated images of everyday subjects to reveal a romantic vision. Courtesy George Eastman House.

dedicated to photography as an art form, and the following year he brought out the first edition of *Camera Work,* a prestigious quarterly that he edited for the next fifteen years. In 1905 the Photo-Secession opened the Little Gallery at 291 Fifth Avenue in New York City. Usually referred to simply as 291, the gallery featured the most innovative works in the visual arts and introduced to America such avant-garde masters as Picasso, Cèzanne, Matisse, Braque, and Rodin.

Though his own art grew from the pictorialist tradition, Stieglitz gradually shifted his focus to straight photography—an approach that eschewed darkroom manipulations, retouching, or other artificialities in favor of straightforward, truthful photographs of natural subjects taken so as to integrate their natural elements into cohesive, romantic, idealized compositions of light, shade, tone, and texture. He considered his photograph *The Steerage* to be his finest work.

Others who emerged from Stieglitz's Photo-Secession and took up the straight photography approach were Gertrude Käsebier, Paul Strand, Imogen Cunningham, Alvin Langdon Coburn, Edward Weston, Ansel Adams, and Edward Steichen. Steichen, as director of photography for the Museum of Modern Art, organized over fifty photography exhibitions, including "The Family of Man," which is probably the most famous.

Despite its enormous influence on the direction taken by aesthetic photography, the Photo-Secession still represented a self-conscious approach that would eventually yield to more direct interactions with subjects.

Abstractionism In the last two issues of *Camera Work* in 1917, there appeared some photographs by Paul Strand that manifested a break with traditional subject matter and style. Strand observed abstract forms and patterns in ordinary subjects that did not rely upon fine detail or even subject recognition to achieve their powerful aesthetic appeal. In other works, Strand deliberately avoided traditional representations of perspective to emphasize these abstract qualities in ordinary subjects. He used this same technique effectively to startle his viewers into a confrontation with his subjects, unadorned by romantic idealism.

Although Strand's subjects did not rely upon recognition for impact, they were, in fact, recognizable objects. Other photographers, however, experimented with the purely abstract. In 1917, Coburn produced *Vortographs,* a series of photographs of bits of wood and crystal, photographed with three mirrors, that derived their power from their patterns and arrangements of light and shadow rather than from their depiction of recognizable detail. In the aftermath of World War I, artists worldwide tended to cast aside traditional principles of composition in search of new forms. This was true of many photographers as well. Some, such as Christian Schad, Tristan Tzara, and Man Ray, experimented with cameraless images, producing their abstract designs by placing objects directly on photosensitive paper in a manner reminiscent of Talbot's early work.

In the 1920s and 1930s, the Bauhaus School in Germany encouraged a group of avant-garde artists and crafts workers, including photographers, to experiment with new techniques and materials. The Bauhaus had much influence on photography as well as on furniture design, typography, and architecture. From the Bauhaus emerged

Figure 1-23. Paul Strand. "The White Fence," 1916. Strand explored the abstract forms found in everyday subjects. In this image, Strand intentionally avoids any effect of perspective to emphasize the abstract qualities of his subject. Paul Strand: The White Fence, Port Kent, New York, 1916. © 1971, Aperture Foundation Inc., Paul Strand Archive.

László Moholy-Nagy, who experimented with photomontage, photograms, X-rays, microphotography, solarization, and other manipulations to produce a fascinating array of creative works that employed photographic processes, if not photography, to achieve his purposes. These techniques were aimed at abstracting light patterns and shapes from objective detail and tonal gradations. The contribution of abstractionism to photographic style was its extension of photographic vision to include the abstract qualities of subjects, a vision that forcefully influenced both aesthetic and realistic photographers thereafter. Its influence can be seen in later works of photo illustration, fashion, and portraits, as well as documentaries, as in the works of Bert Stern, Richard Avedon, Joel Meyerowitz, and Aaron Siskind.

New Realism In contrast to these experiments with abstractionism, some photographers began expressing a renewed fascination with natural subjects. Albert Renger-Patzch, for example, trained his camera closely on everyday objects, revealing their beauty of form and texture with the utmost possible fidelity. His 1928 book, *Die Welt ist Schön* (the world is beautiful) supports his view that photographs "can stand alone on account of their photographic quality—without borrowing from art." The *Neue Sachlichkeit,* the New Realism, as Gustav Hartlaub of the Mannheim Museum of Art dubbed it, was a reaction against sentimentality, falsification, and self-conscious abstraction in art, which found expression as well in cinema and photography.

Although it was arrived at independently, Renger-Patzch's approach echoed those of Paul Strand and Edward Steichen in America a decade earlier. By 1925, Edward Weston had adopted this approach as well, exhibiting landscapes, portraits, and close-ups of ordinary objects remarkable for their form and texture. In the "International Film and Photo Exhibition" in Stuttgart in 1929, Edward Weston, his son Brett Weston, Imogen Cunningham, Beren-

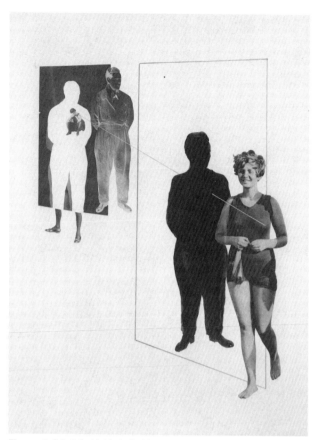

Figure 1-24. László Moholy-Nagy. "Jealously," 1927. A member of the German Bauhaus group of artists who were dedicated to rethinking art in all its forms, Moholy-Nagy experimented with photographic technique and darkroom manipulations to achieve novel designs and images. This image is a photomontage combining pieces of several photographs. Courtesy George Eastman House. © 2001 Artists Rights Society (ARS), New York/VG Bild-Kunst, Bonn.

Since World War II, other approaches have emerged, influenced largely by the small, hand-held camera. The documentary, journalistic styles of such photographers as Henri Cartier-Bresson and W. Eugene Smith, made possible by the small camera, reasserted the importance of content in photographic art. The drama of everyday life was made intimate and compelling by the proximate camera, sophisticated composition, and widespread publication in the press.

Robert Frank's post World War II book *Les Americains* revealed an outsider's view of a strange and troubled America and led the documentary style of photography into new directions. It had a great influence on photographic artists, such as Diane Arbus, Lee Friedlander, and Garry Winogrand, all of whom had backgrounds in photojournalism. Winogrand and Friedlander photographed contemporary American genre scenes in an apparently casual, but visually sophisticated, snapshot style. Arbus, who began as a fashion photographer, was later attracted to the odd and unusual, such as nudist camps, transvestites, giants, and dwarfs that she photographed in a starkly direct and involved way.

Later documentary photography explored topographics—the detailed and accurate description of particular places, cities, towns, districts, or tracts of land. The works of Robert Adams, Joe Deal, Nicholas Nixon, and Stephen Shore, for example, portray "man-altered landscapes" that include human habitations albeit without humans. While these directions were rooted in the "modernist" style of photography, they signaled a bridge to an eventual break from tradition.

From these non-traditional beginnings there emerged a new, postmodernist aesthetic, represented by such artists as Sherrie Levine, Cindy Sherman, and Richard Prince, who used words like "appropriation", "deconstruction", and "manipulation" to describe their work. They explore the roles people play, but rather than creating settings and subjects, they "appropriate" images from advertising, mass media, and other works, take them apart, put them together again, and manipulate them to make their visual points.

For some, penetrating the surface of physical reality became their preoccupation. Psychological themes are evident in the works of Minor White,

ice Abbot, and Charles Sheeler greatly influenced the direction of photographic style. In 1930, Ansel Adams, encouraged by Edward Weston, also moved in this direction before turning to the great landscapes for which he became known. In 1932, Willard Van Dyke formed the f/64 group, which included Weston, Cunningham, Adams, and Peter Stackpole, and which was dedicated to achieving honesty, directness, and naturalism by making brilliant, sharp images with the greatest possible depth of field using only unmanipulated contact prints with large, usually 8in x 10in, plates. Today, the objective, straightforward style pioneered by the New Realists remains a contemporary standard for realistic photography. The work of Stieglitz, Steichen, Weston, Strand, and Adams inspired many who followed such as Harry Callahan, Minor White, Nicholas Nixon, Arnold Newman, Wynn Bullock, Larry Fink, and Chauncey Hare.

Ralph Hattersley, Robert Frank, Diane Arbus, Gary Winogrand, and Les Krims.

Photography itself remains neutral, open to experimenters and practitioners to use for their purposes as they will.

A Brief History of Content

Portraits From the start of photography, portraits were probably the most popular form. Although daguerreotype portraits were awkward, requiring subjects to be held motionless by mechanical devices during long exposures, it is clear that many were willing to put up with the inconvenience to obtain the product. Mathew Brady, John Plumbe, and the firm of Southworth and Hawes exhibited daguerreotype portraits of high quality in America in the 1840s. In Europe, the calotype portraits produced by Hill and Adamson in Edinburgh stand today as remarkable achievements of early photography, combining the soft qualities of calotype with painterly compositions.

André Adolphe Eugène Disdéri, a Parisian photographer, realized early that there was a demand for

Figure 1-26. Julia Margaret Cameron. "Sir John Herschel," 1867. Taking up photography for pleasure at age forty-eight, Cameron deplored the shallowness of the carte de visite portraits and sought to record "the greatness of the inner as well as the features of the outer man." Courtesy George Eastman House.

cheap portraits to give away. He invented a way to produce eight inexpensive images on a single plate and introduced the **carte de visite**—a visiting card with a picture. It was not popular at first, but a carte de visite craze swept Europe after Napoleon III halted his army to visit Disdéri's studio in 1859. The popularity of the carte de visite was surpassed after 1866 by the larger cabinet portrait, which dominated portrait photography until World War I.

Gaspard Félix Tournachon, a flamboyant French balloonist and photographer who called himself Nadar, dominated French portraiture with both his skill and his personality. His red-painted studio was a meeting place for celebrities. In 1858, Nadar ascended in his balloon with a camera to become the first aerial photographer, and he later was the first to shoot underground by electric arc light. In later years, he pioneered the photo interview in a classic series of images featuring the hundredth birthday of chemist M. E. Chevreul.

Julia Margaret Cameron, a latecomer to photography in the 1860s, advocated soft-focus portraits in her work with celebrities, and pioneered the close-up portrait

Figure 1-25. Edward Weston. "Dunes, Oceano," 1936. Weston's penetrating vision enabled him to present a precise description of a subject while simultaneously revealing its abstract, rhythmic, emotional, and almost musical qualities. Dunes, Oceano, 1936. Photograph by Edward Weston. Collection Center for Creative Photography, The University of Arizona. 1981 Center for Creative Photography, Arizona Board of Regents.

Figure 1-27. Robert Demachy. "Au Bord Du Lac," circa 1905. Oil print. Influenced by Degas and the impressionists, Demachy used every sort of darkroom manipulation of his negatives and prints in order to "endow" his images with maximum interpretive effect. Courtesy of The Royal Photographic Society, Bath.

to reveal something of the inner personality of her subjects.

Modern portraiture was advanced in the early part of the twentieth century by Edward Steichen and, more recently, by Arnold Newman, Philippe Halsman, and Yousuf Karsh, whose work spans forty years.

Landscape One of the earliest landscape photographers was Henry White of London, whose close-ups of natural subjects in the 1850s were highly regarded by his contemporaries and foreshadowed the New Realist movement of the 1920s. Other noteworthy early landscapists were Gustave Le Gray, who captured clouds and moving waves in his seascapes, and Hippolyte Bayard, who invented the technique for printing-in from separate negatives.

From the 1870s until the turn of the century, landscape photography was dominated by the English tradition espoused by Henry Peach Robinson, Peter H. Emerson, George Davison, the French photographer Robert Demachy, and others of the pictorial and naturalist schools. The central aesthetic principle of this approach was to produce sentimental, pretty pictures that looked like paintings.

After 1900, the influence of the Photo-Secession appeared in landscape and other photography. Influenced by Stieglitz, Steichen, and others, landscape photographers broke away from imitating painting to search for purely photographic idioms. The forms, shapes, and textures of landscape subjects as revealed by the play of light and shadow became the basis for a new aesthetic of landscape. This aesthetic of landscape continued to evolve in later years under

Figure 1-28. Ansel Adams. "Mt. Williamson, The Sierra Nevada, From Manzanar, California," 1945. A founding member of the f/64 group, Adams was a master at revealing with impeccable clarity and precision the formal beauty of natural objects, from trees, roots, and driftwood to landscapes of the grandest scale. © Ansel Adams Publishing Rights Trust/CORBIS

Figure 1-29. Francis Frith. "Pyramids of Dahshoor, Egypt," 1858. Frith journeyed three times to Egypt, Palestine, and Syria between 1856 and 1860, enduring sand, flies, and intense heat in his portable wet-plate darktent to obtain some of the finest travel and topographical views of those regions ever seen. Courtesy George Eastman House.

the influence of Edward and Brett Weston, Ansel Adams, Wynn Bullock, Imogen Cunningham, Paul Caponigro, George Tice, and others, who advocated scrupulous honesty, ultra-sharp detail, nearly tangible textures, and unlimited depth of field, without manipulation or artifice.

Natural Documentary A distinction should be made between landscape and natural documentary photography. Landscape photography was motivated initially by the goals of fine art and originally adopted the traditions of English landscape painting. Natural documentary photography, on the other hand, was motivated primarily by a need to document the exploration of geographical and topographical subjects with great fidelity.

Thus, driven by objectives quite different from those of the landscapists, early photographers took up their cameras to record their observations of distant lands. As early as 1841, John Lloyd Stephens and Frederick Catherwood carried a daguerreotype camera with them during their archeological exploration of the Yucatan. In the 1850s, the British Army was photographing its activities in India and Roger Fenton was recording his observations of Moscow. Similarly, in 1851 Maxime du Camp published *Egypte, Nubie, Palestine et Syrie* with 125 pasted-in calotypes of these regions.

Photographs of lands and sights that previously had been known only from drawings and writings enabled viewers to gain new insights about the world. Between 1856 and 1860, Francis Frith took three journeys to Egypt, Palestine, and Syria, traveling 1,500 miles beyond the Nile Delta by horse and carriage, and producing wet plate photographs as large as 16in x 20in, copies of which appeared in many publications. Frith became Europe's largest publisher of topographical photographs.

The stereopticon viewer and its accompanying stereoscopic pictures became one of the major entertainments of the Victorian age. When viewed through the stereopticon, twin images mounted on cards produced three-dimensional images that captivated viewers for three generations, providing a form of home entertainment akin to television today. William England, chief photographer of the London Stereoscopic Company in the 1850s, took thousands of pictures of distant lands, finally specializing in Alpine views, as did Adolphe Braun and the Bisson brothers.

Photographers became standard fixtures on a wide range of expeditions and explorations during the latter half of the nineteenth century. Philip Egerton photographed the Shigri Glacier and the natives of Spiti near Tibet; Samuel Bourne photographed the Himalayas and in thousands of photographs revealed the beauties of India to the people of Europe; John Thomson of Scotland spent ten years in the Orient photographing the wonders of China, Siam, and Cambodia.

In America, San Francisco photographer Carlton E. Watkins was the first to discover the photographic potential of the Yosemite Valley, exhibiting some astonishing views in 1867 in Paris. Eadweard Muybridge, who learned photography from Watkins, worked as a photographer on an official survey of Alaska in 1868, and later made hundreds of topographical photographs for railroad and steamship companies before embarking on the animal locomotion studies for which he is primarily remembered.

Many photographers accompanied the government's numerous geologic surveys of the American West. Between 1870 and 1877, William Henry Jackson accompanied eight such surveys, and his photographs of the Yellowstone region, distributed in Congress, were said to be instrumental in the passage of legislation establishing the first national park. Timothy H. O'Sullivan accompanied surveys of the fortieth parallel, the Isthmus of Panama, and the canyons of the Colorado River and Arizona.

Herbert Ponting, who was official photographer to Robert Scott's second South Pole exploration during 1910–1912, produced outstanding expedition shots and topographical views of the Antarctic; Captain Frank Hurley held the same position on five subsequent Antarctic expeditions.

Similarly motivated were the architectural and cityscape photographers, who faithfully recorded the details of manmade structures and city scenes. During 1853–1854, Philip Henry Delamonte documented the rebuilding of the Crystal Palace at Sydenham in hundreds of photographs, starting with the leveling of the site and continuing through the opening ceremonies a year later. Other noteworthy architectural photographers were Robert MacPherson, who depicted Roman antiquities in a striking way; the Alin-

Figure 1-30. Timothy O'Sullivan. "Ruins of White House, Canyon de Chelly," 1873. After the Civil War, O'Sullivan served in several surveys of the American West conducted by the United States government. This photograph is one taken during the Wheeler Survey of what was to become the State of Arizona. Courtesy George Eastman House.

Figure 1-31. Eugene Atget. "Cour, 7 rue de Valence," 1922. For thirty years Atget photographed street scenes in Paris. Unappreciated, he died in poverty, leaving a remarkable legacy of over 10,000 photographs documenting Paris street life. Atget, Eugène. Cour, 7 rue de Valence. June 1922. AP:6379. Albumen-silver print from a glass negative, 6 3/4in x 8 3/4in (17.1cm × 22.2cm). The Museum of Modern Art, New York. Abbott-Levy Collection. Partial gift of Shirley C. Burden. Copy print © 2001 The Museum of Modern Art, New York.

ari brothers, who specialized in Italian cathedrals and works of art; and Roger Fenton, who turned out a fine series of English cathedrals after returning from the Crimea in 1856.

Another approach was that exemplified by Eugène Atget in Paris and Sir Benjamin Stone in England. Both undertook in similar ways the documenting of city life, in a nonjudgmental manner, to capture for all time the physical characteristics of their respective locales. Stone left a collection of some 22,000 photographs of English townscapes, festivals, pageants, and ceremonies, whereas Atget left nearly ten thousand prints of buildings, staircases, shop fronts, and common street life.

Social Documentary The ability of photography to record the most complete array of details with dazzling accuracy did not escape the attention of journalists and social commentators, even from the beginnings of the craft. Hermann Biow and Carl Ferdinand Stelzner had produced what was perhaps the first news photograph—a daguerreotype of the devastation following the Great Fire of Hamburg in 1842. Individual photographers also recorded scenes of the Mexican War, 1846–1848.

The first extensive war reportage was carried out in 1855 by Roger Fenton and James Robertson during the Siege of Sebastopol in the Crimea. Though somewhat romanticized, in keeping with the public tastes of the day, the 360 photographs produced by this team provided a convincing and intimate view of life at the front in a way that the public had never seen before.

Mathew Brady's organized coverage of the American Civil War is legendary. Driven by motives that he himself was unable to explain entirely in later years, Brady left his successful portrait studios in New York and Washington to direct a staff of nineteen photographers in documenting almost every scene of the war. His photographic wagons, dubbed "what's-it wagons" by the troops, were familiar features at encampments and battle sites. His staff included such luminaries as Alexander Gardner, Timothy O'Sullivan, George Barnard, James Gibson, and others known only from their credit lines in albums published after the war. The government took little interest in the project before, during, or after the war, and Brady received little compensation for producing one of the most treasured documents of American history.

A major problem facing these new photojournalists and social documentarians was the fact that no means existed to reproduce photographic images in printer's ink until very late in the century. Until then, the works of these photographers could be viewed only in the form of photographic prints, which were expensive to distribute in great numbers, or as hand-drawn woodcuts or metal plates copied from the original photographs. Nevertheless, the images produced by these early war photographers found their way into the view of most citizens, mostly through hand-cut block prints in newspapers and magazines. Even in this form,

they conveyed an authenticity more intimate, more brutal, than the artists' hand-drawn interpretations of earlier times.

As a tool of mass communication, photography's greatest impact has been felt since the introduction of the halftone process late in the nineteenth century, and with it the technology to reproduce photographs rapidly, mechanically, and faithfully in the press. Though it seems surprising, nearly forty years elapsed between Stephen Horgan's demonstration that halftone images could be printed together with type and the appearance in 1919 of the exclusively photographic *Illustrated Daily News*.

Since that time, social documentarians and photojournalists have been able to share their visions with far wider audiences, and their influence has increased accordingly. War photography has been increasingly truthful, conveying more vividly than ever before possible the senselessness, brutality, and horror of war. A much greater proportion of the population than ever saw the works of Fenton or Brady for example, saw the war photographs of Robert Capa, David Douglas Duncan, and Eliot Elisofon, firsthand.

Other social phenomena attracted photographers. The everyday life of ordinary people, for example, interested many early photographers. In the late

Figure 1-32. Jacob A. Riis. "Sabbath Eve in a Coal Cellar, Ludlow Street," circa 1890. One of the many photographs Riis made that documented life among the poor immigrants in the tenements of New York City in the 1890's. Photographs like this led eventually to his book, *How the Other Half Lives*, that inspired Theodore Roosevelt, as Governor and later President, to implement social reforms. *Ludlow Street Hebrew Making Ready for Sabbath Eve in His Coal Cellar*. Circa 1898. Museum of the City of New York, The Jacob A. Riis Collection.

Figure 1-33. Lewis Wickes Hine. "Breaker Boys," 1911. As staff photographer to the National Child Labor Committee, Hine exposed the deplorable conditions of working children in factories and mines. His work influenced passage of child labor laws.

1840s, Hill and Adamson did a series of genre photographs sentimentally depicting ordinary life around the port town of Newhaven. Ordinary life was also the subject for Frank Sutcliffe, who in the 1880s applied his naturalistic style to depict a quaint, idealized life around Whitby in England.

But extraordinary life—life among the poor, the exploited, and the ill—attracted the attention of an emerging breed of social documentarians and photojournalists. We have already noted the social concerns of Richard Beard in 1851 for London's poor and of John Thomson in the 1870s for the street folk of London. In the same spirit, Jacob Riis, a New York police reporter-photographer, consciously used his camera to arouse the public conscience over the intolerable living conditions in the city's tenements. His books, *How the Other Half Lives* (1890) and *Children of the*

Poor (1892), so influenced New Yorkers and their governor, Theodore Roosevelt, that many reforms were legislated to relieve these conditions. Riis was

Figure 1-34. Edward S. Curtis. "Kutenai, Duck Hunter," 1910. From 1896 to 1930, Curtis recorded more than 40,000 images of the disappearing Native American culture, nearly all on glass plates. Curtis' work, *The American Indian*, is among the most ambitious projects ever undertaken by one person. Each one of its twenty volumes was accompanied by a portfolio of photographs that sensitively portrayed life among many of the vanishing tribes. Edward S. Curtis, Flury & Company, Seattle.

one of the first to use flash powder to capture his devastating images in the dark back alleys, sweatshops, and tenement houses of New York City.

Lewis Wickes Hine, a sociologist, used his camera to dramatize the plight of poor European immigrants, ironworkers, miners, and mill workers between 1905 and 1909. His photographs of immigrants arriving at Ellis Island and his magazine exposés of child exploitation and working conditions in mills and factories shocked the public. Hine was engaged as staff photographer to the National Child Labor Committee, and his photographs of children working under appalling conditions were instrumental in stimulating passage of child labor legislation.

Around the turn of the century, several photographers took note of the fact that the American Indian cultures were disappearing from the American scene and undertook to document these dying cultures while they still could be found. Edward S. Curtis was one among these; from 1892 to 1927 he attempted to chronicle all the surviving Native American tribes. Similarly, Adam Clarke Vroman sought to document what remained of the original inhabitants of the Southwest.

One of the more influential documentary photojournalists, Henri Cartier-Bresson, began photographically documenting the workings of human nature in France in the 1930s. His 1952 book, *The Decisive Moment,* formalized an approach to docu-

Figure 1-35. Henri Cartier-Bresson. "Place de la Europe, Paris," 1932. Cartier-Bresson says that his intent in photography is to guess what the next moment will bring. In his best work, he believes he is working by intuition to anticipate one "decisive moment" when all elements come together. © Henri Cartier-Bresson/Magnum Photos

Figure 1-36. Arthur Rothstein. "A Farmer and His Sons Walking in a Dust Storm, Cimmarron, Oklahoma," 1936. One of many photographs made for the Farm Security Administration (FSA) to illustrate the plight of the dispossessed and the unemployed during the Great Depression. Many of the photographs made by the FSA photographers have become symbols of that era.

mentary photography that remains a cornerstone of modern photojournalism. Cartier-Bresson's approach is characterized by the merging of strong documentary content with precise aesthetic composition. Photography, he said, requires the simultaneous recognition of the significance of an event and a proper organization of form to express it. To capture this coalescence of form and content, Cartier-Bresson would become intensely involved in the continuous action of an event. He would move about within the action, his camera held closely to his eye, until that "decisive moment" when all elements would visually converge. To recognize and capture that moment, he said, required that the photographer be intellectually, emotionally, and physically ready.

During the 1930s, the Farm Security Administration (FSA) sponsored one of the more ambitious projects of social documentation. Under the direction of Roy Stryker, a Columbia University professor, a unique staff of photographers was assembled that included Dorothea Lange, Walker Evans, Ben Shahn, Arthur Rothstein, John Vachon, Carl Mydans, and Russell Lee, some of America's leading documentary photographers of the time. The FSA project was commissioned to chronicle the

economic, physical, and social disaster that was the Great Depression. For eight years, under Stryker's brilliant leadership, this group produced a body of straight, unmanipulated, unsentimental, yet insightful photographs that profoundly influenced the course of American photojournalism.

Picture magazines actually had their roots in pre-Nazi Germany, but when the new government shut these magazines down in the 1930s, many of their photographers migrated to America, where they joined in the creation of *Life* and *Look* magazines in 1936. Many of the FSA photographers also found their way to the staffs of these publications, and there began to emerge an American magazine idiom, the photo essay. Probably the leading exponent of this form was W. Eugene Smith, whose *Life* photo essay "The Spanish Village" (1950) explored life and death in a poor country village where Smith lived for a year while doing the essay.

Smith's later work, *Minimata,* published in book form after the demise of *Life,* exposed the effects of willful industrial contamination by the Chisso Company in the Japanese town of Minimata. For years, the company had been dumping its mercury-

Figure 1-37. W. Eugene Smith. One of the photographs from his photo essay, "The Spanish Village," 1950. Smith explored and developed the photo essay form as a way of more completely reporting extended stories. One strategy he developed may be termed "A Day in the Life of . . .", which has become a popular photojournalistic approach. W. Eugene Smith, © Heirs of W. Eugene Smith. Courtesy of Black Star.

laden wastes into the bay off the town, poisoning the fish and the townspeople who ate those fish. Smith's investigations apparently aroused company officials, for Smith was badly beaten by a large group of men hired by the company, and sustained injuries that cost him part of his eyesight and affected his health for the rest of his life. Notwithstanding his awful experience, Smith finally published his photo essay exposing the company's actions and their effects on the lives of the townspeople. (See Famous Photographer feature, page 479.)

Contemporary Directions

Since World War II, the uses of photography have multiplied in both style and content. The small, hand-held camera has enabled photographers to examine their subjects ever more closely, entering into areas both physical and psychological that were denied them in earlier times. Examination of the works of Robert Frank, Diane Arbus, and Gary Winogrand suggests the complex psychological themes that are often the concern of contemporary photographers. Harry Callahan, Wynn Bullock, Lee Friedlander, and Aaron Siskind provide us with fresh visions of landscapes and cityscapes. Irving Penn, Bert Stern, and Richard Avedon suggest new directions taken in fashion and product photography. Yousuf Karsh, Philippe Halsman, Arnold Newman, Judy Dater, Nicholas Nixon, Chauncey Hare, and Annie Leibovitz provide insightful portraits.

Although the variety of directions and styles that has emerged in the last quarter century is overwhelming, some threads of continuity may be discerned. Many documentary photographers seem intent on making objective, nonjudgmental, formally organized, dispassionate images. Nevertheless, many continue to pursue social themes of passionate concern in an attempt to arouse response and effect change.

Many photographers have turned to highly personal themes, involving themselves and their immediate friends and families, with little attempt to generalize. Few photographers seem intent

upon making pretty pictures or on touching up the physical, social, or cultural blemishes that the camera reveals. In the arena of persuasive photography, however—the advertisements we see daily in print, on television, and on the Internet—our skill in idealizing, romanticizing, and glorifying our subjects has never been greater.

Modern Photojournalists and the Extended Essay

Today's photojournalists often choose to document long-term projects, as exemplified by Eugene Richards's compelling study of the drama and tragedy of a late-night hospital emergency room, The *Knife and Gun Club*, and his works on cancer and poverty. Mary Ellen Mark, one of the new breed of graduate-school-trained photojournalists, has made extended photo essays exposing the problems of teenage runaways, prostitutes, and the mentally ill. Both Richards and Mark are

Figure 1-38. Yousuf Karsh. "Georgia O'Keefe," 1956. Karsh is known for his portraits of the famous and powerful. This image of painter Georgia O'Keefe shows Karsh's distinctive preference for photographing in his subject's own environment and his precise attention to light, shadow, tone, and detail. Courtesy of Woodfin Camp & Associates, Inc.

Figure 1-39. Keith Carter, "Fireflies," 1992. Carter's signature works are images that merge fact and dream. Here, for example, he uses shallow depth of field to create a magical, dreamlike vision of two young boys discovering the radiant wonder of light and nature. "Fireflies" by Keith Carter. Copyright © 1992 by Keith Carter.

drawn to examine life on the fringes of society, and both make penetrating and insightful images of the most significant social events of our time.

Fabricating the Settings and Situations

Fabrication of photographic settings and situations provided another avenue of expression. Beginning in the 1980s, some workers actually constructed stage sets and tableaux designed especially to be photographed. Sandy Skoglund fabricated complex room interiors filled with life-size and wildly colored cats, as well as goldfish and babies, that appear to overrun the room and its occupants in an urban nightmare. Laurie Simmons and Ellen Brooks both produce miniature stage sets populated with dolls that are then photographed as comments on a gender-oriented society.

Other photographers have elected to construct and control the content of their work by choreographing the actions of their subjects. Like movie directors, Joel-Peter Witkin, Nic Nicosa, Bruce Charlesworth, Cindy Sherman, and others spend weeks gathering costumes, props, and sets in which to position their models to create theatrical versions of contemporary domestic life. The photographs that result from these domestic dramas are often printed as extremely large-scale color prints that invite the viewer to enter into the human conflicts depicted. Through the literal fabrication of scenes and situations photographers have broken their dependence on a preexisting subject matter and extended the medium's creative range.

Manipulating Images

Contemporary photographers also continue to work in the realm of the manipulated image, a tradition defined as early as the 1850s by O. G. Rejlander and Henry Peach Robinson. The Starn twins, Douglas and Michael, tear up and reassemble the print itself, making a "new" photograph using the torn and crumpled pieces, tape, and other artifacts of the destruction-reconstruction process.

Rather than manipulating and collaging the print, John Pfahl chooses to make physical alterations to his landscapes by adding bits of colored yarn, aluminum foil, and wooden stakes that change the way the viewer perceives the scene. His altered

Figure 1-40. Jim Dine, Diptych (Self-Portrait), 1996. A renowned artist of the late 20th century, Jim Dine has recently adopted photography as one of his expressive media. This image is one of a series made with both conventional and digital cameras that focus on issues of mortality and the self. Here Dine pairs his own face with a leering skull to create a moody reflection on both art and the shortness of life. Copyright © 1998 by Jim Dine. Courtesy of the artist and Pace/MacGill Gallery, New York.

landscapes are rich and beautiful but also contain witty spatial and scale distortions that question the photograph's illusion of three dimensions. In a similar manner, John Divola has applied stripes and patterns of paint to abandoned beach houses to alter their presence. Divola also transforms banal landscapes into suggestive narratives by placing intruding objects and figures lit by garish colored light in the frame. Barbara Kasten also manipulates colored filters of light in her formal studies of geometric mirror-covered forms juxtaposed against contemporary urban architecture.

Appropriating Images

Interest in "appropriation" of imagery resurfaced in recent years. Pop artists of the 1960s commonly based their work on the omnipresent imagery of society, such as soup cans, cartoons, and maps; the work of some photographers reflects their fascination with this same kind of imagery. Vicky Alexander and Richard Prince clip images directly from published sources, glue them together and present the new imagery as their own. Robert Heinecken reprints unaltered images from fashion magazines but presents them along with fictional narratives he has written. In similar fashion, Barbara Kruger overprints her appropriated photographs with blocks of written text from books, newspapers, and advertising slogans to shift and skew the original meaning of the images.

These photographers and others choose to question the authorship, ownership, and manipulation of social information. Many who appropriate images attempt to investigate and demonstrate

Figure 1-41. "Drottingholm, Sweden," 1967, Kenneth Josephson. Josephson was one of the leaders in conceptual photography in the 1970s. His photographs often explore the act of picture-making and offer playful comments on the nature of photographic truth and illusion. Museum of Art, Rhode Island School of Design. Gift of Mr. and Mrs. Gilman Agier. Photography by Cathy Carver.

the pervasive cultural impact of everyday visuals. Their works are concerned more with the manipulation of signs and symbols than with the making of an art object, and the viewer is often regarded simply as the receptor of these media-produced messages.

The Impact of Color in Contemporary Photography

Color photography has clearly increased in importance in the last decade, perhaps catalyzed by the broad range of color images in the press and media that have become so much a part of contemporary culture. The expressive capabilities of color were fully recognized in the last quarter century, which has led to a furious production of large-scale color prints throughout our visual landscape. Many workers take advantage of the higher film speeds, reduced processing times, and greater image stability of the new color film and print materials. Newspapers, books, and galleries are alive with color images.

Viewers were tantalized by the sensuous colors and luminous shades of Joel Meyerowitz's quiet and compelling *Cape Light* photographs and were treated to hauntingly beautiful yet disturbing wasteland images by Richard Misrach. Color has become a staple of contemporary photojournal-ism, too, and the photo essays of Susan Meiselas and James Nachtwey led the way in demonstrating the role color could play in news coverage.

The Impact of Digital Imaging: Reality Revisited

As traditional and newer technologies began to merge toward the end of the twentieth century, the hard edges of straight, documentary, and journalistic photography began to soften. The emergence of digital imaging, telecommunications, and the Internet began a revolution in the way pictures were produced, disseminated, and ultimately in how they were used to represent reality.

Imaging Although conventional photography and digital imaging may appear as two technologies designed to produce similar products, their differences are profound. Conventional photographs are created by chemically processing film that is altered by the action of light to create a unique, immutable, original image. The successor images produced from this original can be further enhanced and manipulated during printing by a variety of exposure and chemical techniques, but all are based upon the original. By comparison, digital images are created by the action of light upon sensors that convert the image into a binary numerical code that is stored electronically. This code can be al-

HISTORY *of* PHOTOGRAPHY

A CAPSULE HISTORY OF PHOTOGRAPHY: 1826—PRESENT DAY

4th Century BC Aristotle manipulates passage of light through small hole in dark room to observe image of solar eclipse.

1521 Cesare Cesariano publishes brief account of camera obscura.

1544 Rainer Gemma-Frisius publishes illustration of camera obscura.

1550 Girolama Cardano recommends use of bi-convex lens in camera obscura to brighten image.

1558 Giovanni Battista della Porta describes camera obscura as drawing aid for artists.

17th Century Camera obscura develops from permanent roomlike device into portable and finally into tabletop model utilizing complex arrangements of convex and concave lenses, mirrors, and aperture controls to invert and sharpen the image.

1725 Johann Heinrich Schulze observes light sensitivity of silver salts.

1777 Carl Wilhelm Scheele demonstrates that sensitivity of silver salts varies with wavelength and that exposed salts are insoluble in ammonia.

1802 Thomas Wedgwood publishes results of his experiments with sun prints.

1826 Joseph Nicéphore Niépce invents heliography.

1832 Joseph Plateau patents phenkistiscope (moving image device).

1835 William Henry Fox Talbot makes first photographic negative.

1839 Louis Jacques Mandé Daguerre invents daguerreotype.

Talbot describes his "photogenic drawing."

Hippolyte Bayard makes direct positives on paper.

1840 Alexander Wolcott and John Johnson open first portrait studio in New York.

1841 Talbot patents his Calotype process.

1843 David Octavius Hill and Robert Adamson collaborate to make calotype portraits.

1844 Talbot describes calotype process in *The Pencil of Nature.*

1847 Niépce de Saint-Victor develops albumen glass plates.

1850 Louis Désiré Blanquart-Evrard develops albumen paper for positive prints.

1851 Frederick Scott Archer introduces wet collodion process.

1854–56 Ambrotypes, *cartes de visite*, and tintypes patented.

1861 Sir James Clerk Maxwell demonstrates principle of additive color mixing.

1869 Charles Cros and Louis Ducos du Hauron announce discovery of subtractive color mixing.

1871 Richard Leach Maddox introduces gelatin dry plate process.

1878 Eadweard Muybridge captures horse-in-motion sequence on film.

1880 *New York Daily Graphic* prints first halftone reproduction of a photograph on a printing press.

1882 Etienne-Jules Marey invents twelve-image multiple exposure camera.

1888 George Eastman introduces No. 1 Kodak camera.

1889	Eastman introduces celluloid roll film.
	Peter Henry Emerson publishes *Naturalistic Photography*.
1890	Jacob Riis publishes *How the Other Half Lives*.
	Ferdinand Hurter and Vero C. Driffield lay foundations for sensitometry by describing characteristic density curve.
1892	Frederick E. Ives invents Kromstop color transparency camera.
	Linked Ring Brotherhood formed.
1893	Charles Jasper (John) Joly introduces screen plate color process.
1895	Louis Lumière introduces roll film motion picture camera.
1902	Photo-Secession exhibition held.
1907	Auguste and Louis Lumière invent Autochrome color process.
1911	Lewis Hine begins photographing for National Child Labor Committee.
1912	Illustrated Newspapers appear in Europe.
	George Smith designs still camera to use 35mm motion picture film.
1919	Exclusively photographic *Illustrated Daily News* appears in New York.
1924	Oscar Barnack introduces his 35mm cine-film Leica camera.
1924	Leopold Mannes and Leopold Godowsky receive first patent on color process.
1930	Alfred Stieglitz opens *An American Place* gallery.
1935	Farm Security Administration Photography Unit formed under Roy Stryker
	Associated Press members send photographs by wire.
	Kodachrome professional color film introduced.
1936	First issue of *Life* published.
1941	Edward Farber's stroboflash introduced.
1942	University of Missouri begins photojournalism program.
	First Pulitzer Prize in photography awarded to Milton (Pete) Brooks of the *Detroit News*
	Ektachrome amateur color film introduced.
1945	National Press Photographers Association formed.
1947	Magnum Picture Agency formed.
1947	Edwin H. Land invents 60-second Polaroid instant camera.
1951	W. Eugene Smith's seminal photo essay *Spanish Village* published
1952	Henri Cartier-Bresson publishes *The Decisive Moment*.
1955	Edward Steichen's "The Family of Man" photography exhibit opens at Museum of Modern Art.
1961	Holography demonstrated.
1962	Edwin H. Land of Polaroid announces 60-second Polacolor process.
1969	Department of Defense establishes ARPANet to link widely distant computers.
1972	110-format cameras introduced by Kodak with a 13mm x 17mm frame.
1973	C-41 color negative process introduced, replacing C-22.
	Susan Sontag publishes *On Photography*.
1980–85	Scitex, Hell, and Crossfield introduce computer imaging systems.

1982   Sony demonstrates Mavica "still video" camera.

1983   Kodak introduces disk camera, using an 8mm x 11mm frame (the same as in the Minox spy camera).

1984   Sony introduces digital camera.
Canon demonstrates first electronic still camera.

1985   Pixar introduces digital imaging processor.

1986   Minolta introduces first professional auto focus camera, the Maxxum 9000.

1987   Eastman Kodak announces the 1.4 megapixel CCD for digital cameras.
Canon produces RC-760 Still Video Camera with a 600,000 Pixel CCD.

1988   Sony and Fuji announce new digital cameras.
Eastman Kodak announces a 4 megapixel CCD.
PhotoMac is the first image manipulation program available for the Macintosh computer.
Video to computer transmissions demonstrated.

1989   NPPA publishes an all-electronic newspaper
150th anniversary of photography celebrated worldwide.

1990   Kodak announces the development of its Photo CD system.
Adobe Photoshop 1.0 (TM) image manipulation program becomes available for Macintosh computers.
Dr. Tim Berners-Lee invents the hyperlink to simplify linking computers on the Internet.

1991   Kodak introduces its Professional Digital Camera System.
Sony, Rollei, and Arca Swiss announce digital studio cameras.

1992   Kodak markets PhotoCD system.

1993   Steven Spielberg's *Jurassic Park* uses computer-generated creatures.
Nikon, Canon, Leaf Systems, and others announce new digital cameras for photojournalists and studio photographers.
Adobe Photoshop becomes available for MS-DOS/Windows platforms.
Marc Andreeson invents the first browser software to simplify searching and linking on the Internet

1994   Apple Computer, Sony, and Kodak announce new digital cameras.
Associated Press announces the AP/Kodak NC2000 digital camera for photojournalists.

1995   *Toy Story* becomes the first full-length feature composed completely of computer animation.

1996   Advanced Photo System (APS) is introduced.

tered at will to fundamentally change the stored image without leaving a trace. Not only can simple details be altered, such as removing unwanted features, but entirely synthetic details and entire images can be created that never really existed at all. In a sense, each successive image variation becomes a new original.

The power to alter computer code to change the original recorded image, for whatever purpose, brought many photographers to confront what they probably knew all along—that a photograph, after all, is only a picture and not objective reality. As one historian stated, "The digital image represents the final erosion of any remaining assumptions about the 'simple' nature of representation."

That photographs never represented objective reality was obvious from the start. After all, photographs were two-dimensional; the real world, three-dimensional. Until quite recently, photographs were black and white; the real world, rich in color. Photographs were framed by the edges of the print; the real world was frameless. Photographs were smooth and flat; the real world, rich in textures and other three-dimensional tactile details. Photographs captured but a single moment in time; the real world existed in a time continuum.

ETHICAL CONSIDERATIONS

Digital imaging, however, concerns more than simply advances in technology. It raises many ethical questions that challenge the popular belief that a photograph is, or at least ought to be, a truthful document based upon a reality captured unaltered by the camera.

However, during the early days of digital photography respected publishers sometimes created abuses and outrageous fakes. This is not new in our time, of course—the first images published in newspapers and magazines were etchings that usually left truth to the imagination of an artist or engraver who did not even witness an event. The invention of photography and the halftone process did not halt these practices—cropping, stripping, airbrushing, hand re-touching, creating composites, and staging or re-creating events continued to be used to alter the representation of events.

Though generations of documentary photographers, photojournalists, and photo essayists strived to adhere to an ideal of objective truth, many of history's more memorable photographs were posed or manipulated in some way to capture truths that lay just beyond the photograph's confining limits. Even Civil War photographers Mathew Brady and Timothy O'Sullivan reportedly "moved at least one dead body to compose a photograph." The Pulitzer Prize winning photograph by AP photographer, Joe Rosenthal, was arguably a re-staged event of the flag raising on the island of Iwo Jima that had occurred days earlier.

Look again at Hine's "Little Spinner in North Carolina" (page 517), Wolcott's "Coal Miner's Child" (page 348), or Smith's "Spanish Village" photographs (page 34) and ask what is true. Each photographer posed and manipulated the physical details of the scene to frame, emphasize, and illuminate their metaphysical qualities.

The ideal of objective reality for photographers such as these transcends the straightforward recording of physical details. As they reach to represent metaphysical realities, many contemporary photographers, at least partly as a result of the digital revolution, use what they find in nature

Figure 1-42. Joe Rosenthal: Flag-Raising on Iwo Jima. Associated Press photographer, Joe Rosenthal, made this Pulitzer Prize winning photograph atop Mt. Suribachi, a Japanese observation post on the island of Iwo Jima during World War II. It became the most reproduced photograph in history. Its authenticity has been questioned resulting from a remark Rosenthal made later to a reporter. He denied the charge saying, "Had I posed the shot, I would, of course, have ruined it. I would . . . have made them turn their heads so that they could be identified for AP members throughout the country." *Flag raising on Iwo Jima. (NWDNS-80-G413988)* © Corbis.

simply as a starting point in an extended process. In this process they seem more willing to pose and stage their scenes and to manipulate their images in ways that refer back to reality to better capture spiritual and emotional values or make conceptual connections and statements.

Today, however, easily mastered image editing tools enable any digital pre-press operator to alter images at will, without the ethical constraints that photographers once imposed upon themselves. Photography can no longer be relied upon to document the truth (though perhaps it never could) since it is so easily subverted in a process now termed "image enhancement" or "digital correction." Three corporations pioneered these processes—Scitex, Hell Graphics Systems, and Crossfield—who together revolutionized the Digital Pre-Press industry. Even today, publishers use the word "scitex" as a verb to describe digital manipulation. Before these systems, pre-press was labor-intensive and required years of training and apprenticeship. Now with available digital technology, a competent technician can easily and quickly alter an image so significantly as to totally misrepresent its factual content.

To an increasing extent, the public is becoming more aware that the "factual" images they see can be so easily altered and manipulated as to raise questions about their veracity. Adding information, changing emphasis, adopting a new "slant" have always been accepted as tools journalists and artists use to communicate the truth. Now, however, digital imaging vastly expands the photographer's and the digital technician's tools not only to achieve a similar result but also to misrepresent the truth altogether.

National Geographic was embarrassed when it featured a digitally altered pyramid on its February 1982 cover to better fit the cover's format. New York Newsday showed Tonya Harding and Nancy Kerrigan apparently skating in very close proximity to each other on its February 16, 1994, front page. Actually, the image was a composite of two images shot some months before. Referring to this photograph, Leonard Downie Jr., then executive editor of the Washington Post said, "this paper had decided not to publish altered photographs showing imaginary events."

Ethical newspaper photo editors uniformly reject the use of all forms of unethical manipulation.

Nevertheless, the technology tempts photographers and technicians to abandon ethical standards to achieve a more dramatic, attention-grabbing image, even if the result is not quite true. And this applies to professionals as well as non-professionals who produce photographic images for whatever their purpose might be.

Dissemination Simultaneous with the development of digital imaging technology was the growth of the Internet and the World Wide Web. Digital technology made possible the widespread dissemination of multimedia messages, including photographs, text, sound, and films.

The Internet is a loosely defined global network of computer networks that interconnects computer users worldwide. Somewhat analogous to a telephone system, the Internet allows any computer connected to the Internet to link to any other computer connected to the Internet. Unlike

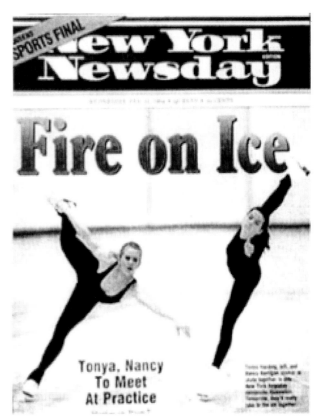

Figure 1-43. Following an attack on Nancy Kerrigan by an associate of Tonya Harding's husband, and shortly before the much-anticipated women's Olympic figure skating competition, New York NEWSDAY published this photo composite showing the ice skating rivals appearing to practice together. Although composed of two separate images taken at different times, the composite appeared to show the adversaries skating together. New York Newsday, February 16, 1994, front page. © 1994 by New York Newsday. Reprinted by permission.

the telephone, however, computers can exchange pictures, text, motion pictures, and sound recordings, as well as voice, although these technologies are merging rapidly.

The most popular way of getting around on the Internet is called **browsing**. By using a software program called a browser, one can freely connect to any of the millions of **web sites** connected to the Internet. Most of these sites contain text and pictures, much of which may be easily downloaded to the user's computer.

From its beginnings in 1969 as ARPANet under the Department of Defense (DOD), use of the Internet was largely confined to the DOD, research universities, defense contractors, and a few people with the technical expertise to use it. Internet use accelerated rapidly after Dr. Tim Berners-Lee invented the **hyperlink** in 1990 and Marc Andreeson developed the first **browser** in 1993. From then, Internet use accelerated phenomenally. Although estimating how many computers are connected to the Internet worldwide is an inexact art at best, an "educated guess" based on recent surveys is that there were nearly 606 million Internet users connected as of September, 2002.

The primary uses of the Internet are sending and receiving e-mail, browsing, research, and commerce. Every application displays a propensity to include at least text and pictures, but the use of the Internet for other multimedia purposes is expanding rapidly to include the distribution of music, motion pictures, and videos as well as interactive commercial activities.

Classic Photo Collections

The computer improves access to classic photographs, contemporary and historical, creative and documentary, famous and not-so-famous images. Thousands of photographs have been digitized and assembled into collections that are available on the Internet. With a desktop computer and a connection to the Internet, one can freely browse through some of the world's most compelling photo exhibitions, portfolios, museums, and galleries.

E-zines, E-newspapers, E-galleries and Other Web Sites

Many magazines, newspapers, and TV/radio networks maintain web sites that are updated regularly and contain many of the photographs and film clips used in their published editions. In addition, many unique magazines exist only in electronic form, called e-zines. Photographers, working singly or in groups, routinely exhibit their work to a global audience in virtual galleries. Anyone with a computer connected to the Internet can create their own web site or publish their

Figure 1-44. Lois Conner, Ngo Gach Street, Hanoi, Viet Nam, 1994. Lois Conner makes extensive use of the panoramic format to capture delicate visions of cultural landscapes. Inspired by ancient Chinese landscape painting, Conner uses an old 7in × 17in banquet camera to experiment with panoramic composites that combine as many as seven individual 7in × 17in negatives, as in this composite image of a Hanoi street. Courtesy of Lois Conner and the Laurence Miller Gallery.

Figure 1-45. Peter Campus, "decay," 1991. Peter Campus began experimenting with digital images in the late 1970s. In computer-generated images such as this, he contrasts emblems of both synthetic and natural worlds. Because digital tools allow him to "control every nook and cranny of a picture," he believes that a digital image is not a photograph. Unlike photographs, the connection between digital images and direct visual experience is severed. Peter Campus "Decay," 1991. Courtesy Paula Cooper Gallery, New York.

own e-zine. So publishing a portfolio of photographic work to share with the world is as simple as setting up a personal web site.

Summary

Many styles and visions stretched the boundaries of photography in the last quarter century; yet the medium has survived intact. Influenced by performance and conceptual art, some photographers turned away from work based on capturing actual life experiences. Instead they chose to use photography as a vehicle for ideas in a manner similar to conceptual art. Although these activities have contributed significantly to the range and scope of the medium, some critics question the staying power of the resulting images. Other photographers have continued to use the documentary power of the medium, enhanced by the tools of digital imaging, to challenge and shape our view of society and the world and to communicate their personal visions of the metaphysical content of the physical world they photograph. The beauty of life, too, often has been rediscovered. This is particularly evident in the stunning formality and color quality of the large-scale prints that became so popular. Ultimately, at the beginning of the third millennium, we see the medium of photography vibrantly alive, encompassing a greater variety of approaches to content and dissemination than ever before.

HOW TO USE THIS BOOK

From this point on, the units in this book are organized to provide systematic, practical instruction in the craft of photography.

You will learn what equipment and materials are currently available and how to use them.

You will learn how to control the photographic process to obtain the effects that you want.

And you will develop your ability to see, to visualize, and to communicate with photographs.

Unit 2 contains specific instructions on how to use the special features of this book most effectively.

Cameras, Lenses, and Accessories

"Street scene," taken with a Widelux camera with a moving lens. Michelle Warmotts

<table>
<tr><td>

**Unit
at a
Glance**

</td><td>

Cameras and accessories come in a bewildering assortment of types, sizes, and features. Choosing the right camera to solve a photographic problem can be difficult. This unit examines film and digital cameras by viewing system, film size and image format, and exposure system. The advantages and disadvantages of the various camera designs are explained to help you determine what kind of camera best suits your requirements. Special-function cameras, such as instant and underwater cameras, are described, as well as the kinds of photographic assignments for which they are likely to be used.

Characteristics of lenses, including speed, focal length, and angle of view are examined and the effects of telephoto and wide-angle lenses are explained in this unit. A discussion of common camera accessories and their use is included, followed by recommendations for proper camera care and tips for use.

</td></tr>
</table>

The Human Camera

Objective 2-A Compare the human eye and the camera in terms of their basic parts and functions.

Key Concepts lens, light sensitive, retina, film, digital imaging sensor, body, shutter, aperture, iris diaphragm

The human eye provides a good starting point for learning how a camera works. The lens of the eye is like the **lens** of the camera. In both instruments the lens focuses an image on a **light-sensitive** surface—the **retina** of the eye and the **film** or **digital imaging sensor** in the camera. In both, the light-sensitive material is protected within a light-tight container—the eyeball of the eye and the **body** of the camera. Both eye and camera have a mechanism for shutting off light passing through the lens to the light sensitive interior—the lid of the eye and the **shutter** of the camera. In the eye, the size of the lens opening, or pupil, is regulated by the iris; in the camera, the size of the lens opening, or **aperture**, is regulated by an **iris diaphragm**. Study Figure 2-2 to compare the eye and the camera.

The eye adjusts automatically to high and low light conditions. In a darkened room the iris of the eye opens wide to allow as much light as possible to enter. In bright light the iris of the eye closes down to prevent too much light from entering. Observe the iris of your own eye in a mirror as you switch a bright light on and off. You will see that it adjusts the size of your pupil for each condition.

Most modern adjustable cameras, even as the eye, adjust themselves automatically for varying light conditions. Having set the camera for the sensitivity of the film that is loaded in it, these cameras automatically adjust for the existing light conditions. Nevertheless, some adjustable cameras do *not* adjust automatically for high and low light conditions and must be adjusted manually to regulate the amount of light that enters. To help with this manual adjustment, many cameras have built-in light meters that inform you of changing light conditions.

The eye also adjusts automatically to focus on the details of interest to you. Small muscles attached to the lens of the eye alter its shape to focus on

<table>
<tr><td>

HOW TO USE THIS BOOK

Objectives and Key Concepts

Starting with Unit 2, each unit is divided into sections preceded by numbered objectives. For example, in Unit 2, the objectives are numbered 2-A, 2-B, 2-C, and so forth. The first objective, 2-A, is about the human camera. The objective describes what you will learn to do: Compare the human eye and the camera in terms of their basic parts and functions.

Following each objective is a list of key concepts—the important terms and ideas that are included in this objective. The key concepts are **boldfaced** in the text when they are defined for the first time in each unit.

</td></tr>
</table>

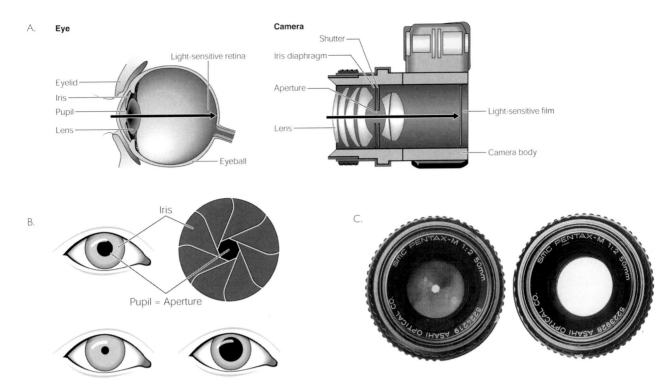

Figure 2-2. Eye and camera. A) Notice the similarity of the structures. B) The iris of the eye regulates the size of the pupil opening. The aperture setting on the camera determines how the iris diaphragm regulates the size of the lens opening (aperture). C) Actual appearance of small and large apertures.

nearby or distant objects. Many modern adjustable cameras also adjust focus automatically using a built-in computer. However, some cameras require you to manually adjust the focus on the details of interest to you. To help you with this adjustment, most cameras provide built-in features that indicate which details are in and out of focus on the film. Thus in many ways the camera functions much as the human eye.

One important difference between eye and camera is that the eye sees selectively, whereas the camera sees indiscriminately. Human beings tend to observe only those elements that are important to them, because their minds filter out the unimportant information. The camera, on the other hand, sees all the details in view and records them with equal emphasis on the film. It cannot judge which are important and which are not. That explains why sometimes a strange object may appear in the finished print that the photographer did not notice when taking the picture—the photographer focused attention only on the subject of the shot whereas the camera recorded all the details in view. Photographers must train themselves to see what the camera sees. (See Figure 2-3.)

Basic Camera Types

Objective 2-B Identify several basic camera types and describe their similarities and differences.

Key Concepts pinhole camera, box camera, disposable camera, viewfinder (VF), fixed focus or focus-free, manual focus, auto focus, auto-focus lock, rangefinder focus, single-lens reflex (SLR), follow focusing, twin-lens reflex (TLR), view camera, bellows, swings and tilts, parallax, small format, 35mm camera, APS camera, medium format, large format, sheet film, digital cameras, digicam, photosites, pixels, megapixel, compact flash, smart memory, memory stick, floppy, mini CD-R, between-the-lens (BTL) shutter, focal plane (FP) shutter, self-timer, fixed exposure, manual exposure, match-needle, automatic exposure, shutter priority, aperture priority, fully automatic, programmed automatic, exposure override, instant cameras and films, wide-format camera, underwater camera, underwater housing, stereo camera, press camera

As camera technology has developed in many directions, cameras themselves have taken many

Figure 2-3. Eye's view and camera's view. What did the camera see that the photographer failed to see?

forms. Modern cameras may be classified according to body type, film and digital sensor size, image formats, shutter system, viewing and focusing system, exposure-setting system, and special functions. Regardless of their complexity, all cameras operate on common principles and share the basic elements found in even the simplest cameras.

Simple Cameras

To gain an understanding of camera architecture, consider first some of the earlier, simpler camera types.

Pinhole Camera

The **pinhole camera**, page 51, is the simplest of all cameras. It is basically a light-tight box with a pinhole in one end and the film at the opposite end. The camera has no lens; rather, a small pinhole forms the image on the film. A flap serves as a shutter to control the light entering the pinhole. All other cameras merely add refinements to this basic design.

Three important refinements are the lens, which substitutes for the pinhole and provides a much sharper and brighter image, the iris diaphragm, which allows the photographer to vary the intensity of the light entering the camera, and the electric or mechanical shutter, a device that precisely controls exposure times and which substitutes for the flap on a pinhole camera.

Box Camera

The **box camera** (Figure 2-4) is an inexpensive refinement of the pinhole camera and is equipped with a simple lens and a shutter. The widely sold **disposable cameras** are modern examples of the box camera. Usually these cameras have a nonadjustable lens set to focus on objects about ten feet or more from the camera. The nonadjustable shutter, usually placed behind the lens, is preset for 1/60–1/125 sec., suitable only for shooting relatively stationary objects under average lighting conditions. The early box cameras and their modern counterparts can take excellent photographs under these conditions. Close-ups, action shots, and weak lighting conditions usually limit a box camera's capabilities.

Camera Types by Viewing System

One way of classifying cameras is by viewing system. In general, four types of viewing and focus-

Figure 2-4. Disposable cameras, a type of box camera, now come in many forms, including telephoto models and even simple underwater cameras. All are pre-loaded with film and are designed for one-time use.

TECHNICAL FEATURE

Pinhole Camera

WHAT IS PINHOLE PHOTOGRAPHY

Pinhole photography is a quick, direct, and entertaining way to experiment with photographic principles while creating unique and exciting images. A pinhole camera is nothing more than a light-tight box with a piece of light-sensitive film (or photographic paper) at one end, and a pinhole for a lens at the other. Working pinhole cameras can be made from any container that can be made light-proof, such as oatmeal boxes or coffee cans. Even shoes have been used as successful cameras.

WHY MAKE A PINHOLE CAMERA?

Pinhole cameras are fun to make, easy to use, and produce images that have a unique and impressionistic look. You can make long wide-format cameras, curved wide-angle cameras, long focal length "telephoto" cameras—even cameras with multiple pinhole lenses that see like an insect's eye. Pinhole optics are also unique in having infinite depth of field. In a pinhole photograph everything—regardless of distance—is equally sharp—or should we say, equally a bit unsharp.

HOW TO MAKE A PINHOLE CAMERA

First, find or make a light-tight box—one with a deep and snug-fitting lid is ideal. It can be any size, but a container large enough to use 4in x 5in film or photographic paper is especially convenient. Devise some method for holding the film in the back of the camera. You can simply tape the film in place or create a pair of cardboard rails to slip it under. Paint the inside of the camera black to minimize reflections. Cut a small hole, about 1/2in in diameter, opposite the film side of the box. This is where the pinhole will be mounted.

MAKING A PINHOLE "LENS"

The best and sharpest pictures are made from perfectly round, small pinholes with clean edges. Smaller pinholes give sharper images up to the point of diffraction. You may use the chart below to select an appropriate sewing needle to make the pinhole for your camera, but you needn't be too accurate about this.

Using an appropriate-size sewing needle, carefully drill through a small piece of aluminum foil or other thin sheet metal. Make the hole as smooth and round as possible. Now mount your "lens" on the

A pinhole camera can be made from any light-tight container. The photographer used a discarded film box and attached a 4in x 5in. Polaroid film back for instant pinhole photographs. The resulting image is characteristic of the quality a pinhole camera can produce. Pinhole images are adequately sharp and possess nearly infinite depth-of-field.

camera and design some sort of shutter. The shutter could be simply a flap of black tape that you lift to make the exposure.

TAKING PINHOLE PICTURES

Unless you devise a viewfinder you will have to estimate what will be included in the picture. Exposures, too, will need to be estimated until you gain experience with your individual camera. As a starting guide, pinhole photography exposures with ISO 400 film under bright daylight will need to be about 1–2 seconds long. If you are shooting with enlarging paper

Table FB1. Selecting Needles for Pinhole Cameras

Best Focal Length	Needle #	Size	Approximate f/stop
20"	#4	.036"	f/555
15"	#5	.031"	f/483
13"	#6	.029"	f/448
10"	#7	.026"	f/384
8"	#8	.023"	f/347
6.5"	#9	.020"	f/325
5"	#10	.018"	f/277
4"	#12	.016"	f/250
2.5"	#13	.013"	f/192

instead of film, its effective film speed of about 3 will require longer exposures—about 30–90 seconds. Develop and print the film or paper in the conventional manner.

OTHER POSSIBILITIES

If you have a 35mm camera with interchangeable lenses, you could substitute a pinhole lens and save yourself the trouble of constructing a camera box. You would then be able to make multiple pictures without reloading and it would be simple to use roll film.

The longer the camera you make, the larger the image you make can be. Make the longest camera you can for telescope-like effects or very large images. If you want to, you can even shoot on mural paper.

Pinhole photographers have created sensible cameras equipped with such features as Polaroid backs; they have also made highly fanciful and imaginative cameras in strange shapes. Have fun!

FOR MORE INFORMATION

Chernewski, A. (1999). *How to make three corrugated 8x10 pinhole cameras: Wide-angle, normal, telephoto.* Issaquah, WA: The Pinhole Format Co.

Renner, E. (1999). *Pinhole photography: Rediscovering a historic technique.* Woburn, MA: Focal Press.

Shull, J. (1974). *The hole thing: A manual of pinhole photography.* Dobbs Ferry, NY: Morgan and Morgan.

Shull, J. (1999). *The beginner's guide to pinhole photography.* Buffalo, NY: Amherst Media.

Smith, L. (1985). *The visionary pinhole.* Salt Lake City, UT: Peregrine Smith Books.

Eastman Kodak Company, *How to make and use a pinhole camera.* (Publication AA-5). Rochester, NY.

ing systems are commonly used: viewfinder (VF), single-lens reflex (SLR), twin-lens reflex (TLR), and view cameras.

Viewfinder Cameras

The **viewfinder (VF)** camera (Figure 2-5) is distinguished by a separate eye-level window through which the photographer can plan and compose the picture within illuminated frame lines. The viewfinder system is easy and fast to use, especially in low light. The advantages of this type of camera include a small compact design, lightweight, mechanical simplicity, quiet operation, and relative durability. Many photographers also feel that looking through a viewing window rather than looking at a ground-glass focusing screen allows a more direct and immediate interaction with the subject.

Viewfinder cameras have one major disadvantage—**parallax**. Because the viewing window is separate from the picture-taking lens, the two views do not completely coincide; thus, what the photographer sees through the viewer may not exactly match what is recorded onto film. (See Figure 2-11.) Another disadvantage of most VF cameras is their lack of interchangeable lenses and their inability to shoot close-ups.

VF cameras use a variety of systems to achieve sharp focus, ranging from simple fixed focus de-

A.

B.

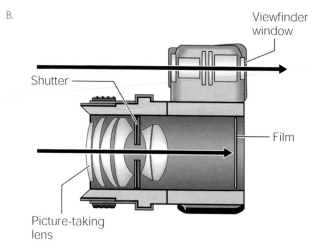

Figure 2-5. A) An example of the popular point-and-shoot 35mm cameras which feature automatic exposure, autoflash, and motorized film transport. B) Viewfinding and picture-taking systems.

signs to wondrous electronic auto-focus systems. Many digital cameras use both a viewfinder and a display screen for viewing and focusing. Note that the viewfinder camera typically uses a leaf-type shutter that is located either behind the lens or between the lens elements.

Fixed Focus or Focus-Free A **fixed focus** or **focus-free** viewfinder camera uses an eye-level window for composing the image; however, it possesses no focusing system at all. Fixed focus cameras are designed to provide acceptably sharp images of all objects that are beyond some specified minimum distance from the camera, usually 7–10 feet. Note that focus-free cameras are not the same as auto-focus cameras. Focus-free cameras have a single, fixed focus setting and provide no focus adjustments; they rely instead on depth of field to render most objects at medium distance and farther adequately sharp. Auto-focus cameras, discussed below, feature automatic, adjustable focusing.

Manual Focus A **manual focus** VF camera also uses an eye-level window for composing the image; however, it uses a separate focusing system. Typically, manual focus cameras are equipped with an adjustable lens on which is inscribed a distance scale. By turning the focusing ring according to the distance scale, the lens can be set for the estimated or measured distance between the camera and the subject. Some manual focus cameras provide only a few focusing positions—for distance, medium range, or close-up shots. Manual systems for viewing and focusing are typical of simple, inexpensive cameras that do not provide precise focusing controls. (See Figure 2-6.)

Auto-Focus Many modern cameras are equipped with focusing systems that automatically focus the lens as the shutter is released. These **auto-focus** cameras differ in design from fixed focus cameras. Some emit a signal pulse of either sound or infra-red light in the direction the lens is pointed. In the manner of sonar or radar, the camera's receiver then translates the return reflection of the pulse into a distance reading and automatically sets the camera to focus on the subject. Others use a combination of optical and electronic sensors to focus the lens.

Using this technology, the camera makes its own focusing adjustments. However, the camera does not have the benefit of the photographer's judgment as to which objects should be in focus and which should not. These cameras typically focus automatically on the nearest object encountered at the center of the image field. To provide the photographer with some control, some auto-focus systems offer an **auto-focus lock** feature, which allows the photographer to prefocus on an object of choice and then lock the system to that focus distance.

Rangefinder Focus Classic VF cameras such as the Leica have a separate rangefinding optical system built into them. This rangefinder system is coupled to the picture-taking lens in such a way that adjustments in the rangefinder automatically produce like adjustments in the picture-taking lens. In this way the photographer can be certain that objects in focus in the rangefinder will be in focus in the final picture. (See Figure 2-7.)

Figure 2-6. Close-up of a manual focus camera showing the focusing ring and distance scale.

Figure 2-7. A modern viewfinder type camera. This precision made Leica even offers interchangeable lenses.

Single-Lens Reflex Cameras (SLR)

Single-lens reflex (SLR) cameras have an optical system that allows both viewing and picture taking to be performed by the same camera lens. When using an SLR camera, the photographer views an image on a screen that is generated by the camera's taking lens, rather than by a separate viewing lens. In this way, the photographer views a scene exactly as it will be recorded.

Film and digital cameras accomplish the SLR function in different ways. Film-based SLRs transmit the image from the taking lens to a ground-glass screen by means of a mirror set at an angle between the lens and the film. A **focal-plane shutter** protects the film from exposure during viewing while allowing the image to be reflected to the viewing screen. When the shutter is released, the mirror flips up out of the way, the shutter opens, and the film is exposed to the image. When the shutter closes, the mirror returns to its viewing position. In this way the photographer sees exactly what the camera's lens sees and gains precise control over focus and composition. Figure 2-8 shows a typical film-based SLR camera with its mirror in both viewing and taking positions. Film-based SLR cameras are manufactured primarily for use with 35mm, 120, or 220 films.

Digital SLRs sometimes employ different principles for viewing and recording images through the same lens. Both viewing and recording operations are performed by the camera's sensor. Instead of a mechanical mirror, however, the image may be directed electronically to a display screen for viewing.

Typically, the display screen is integrated into the back of the camera body, although some digital cameras also provide for viewing the same image through an eye-level viewfinder. When the shutter is released, the image is simply redirected electronically to record the image and to store it in the camera's memory.

Whether film-based or digital, the SLR camera has the ability to frame precisely what will be recorded in the final image, an advantage shared only by the view camera. SLR viewing eliminates parallax at all working distances and gives the photographer an exact view through any lens or accessory mounted on the camera body.

Many SLRs are available with automatic focusing and even advanced focusing features. **Follow focusing**, for example, used for moving objects, has the ability to release the shutter when the subject enters a predetermined distance zone.

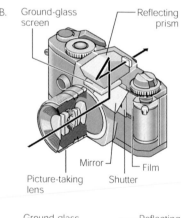

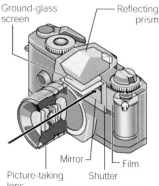

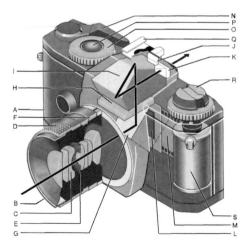

A. Body
B. Lens
C. Lens elements
D. Focusing ring
E. Iris diaphragm
F. Aperture ring
G. Mirror
H. Viewing screen
I. Pentaprism
J. Metering cell

K. Viewfinder eyepiece
L. Shutter
M. Film
N. Film advance
O. Shutter speed dial
P. Shutter release
Q. Hot shoe
R. Rewind mechanism
S. Film cassette

Figure 2-8. A) A single-lens reflex (SLR) camera. B) A cross section of an SLR camera showing focal plane shutter. Note that the mirror moves up and down. C) Detailed cutaway of SLR camera.

Another advantage of an SLR system is the wide range of interchangeable lenses that is available, such as zoom, telephoto and wide-angle lenses. Further, SLRs equipped with a normal lens usually focus much closer than VF type cameras, often to less than one foot. Their ability to do close focus work may be extended even further with the addition of bellows, extension tubes, or special macro lenses. (See Figure 2-41)

The SLR camera is not, however, without disadvantages. Compared to other camera types, the SLR is electronically and mechanically more complex, resulting in higher prices, larger bodies, greater weight, more noise, and more fragile workings.

Twin-Lens Reflex Cameras (TLR)

The **twin-lens reflex (TLR)** camera (Figure 2-9), designed primarily for film, is distinguished by two separate but quite similar lenses that are mounted on the lens board at the front of the camera—one to view the scene and the other to take the picture. By using two lenses of similar optical characteristics, the photographer can separate the viewing and picture-taking functions and at the same time couple them to act in unison. As with the SLR camera, viewing is accomplished by means of an image focused on a ground-glass screen, which is mounted on top of the TLR camera.

Typically the upper lens of the TLR camera is for viewing, whereas the lower lens is for picture taking. The focusing adjustment moves the entire frontal lens board, including both lenses, in such a way that the images produced by both lenses are in focus at the same time. In other words, when the image on the ground-glass screen is in focus, the image at the film plane is in focus also. Note that unlike SLR cameras, the TLR camera normally uses a leaf-type shutter located between or just behind the lens elements. This type of shutter and camera is very quiet in use and is often chosen when the typical "clank" of an SLR firing would be obtrusive.

Because the photographer views a subject through a lens mounted above the one used for picture taking, problems with parallax can occur, especially when focusing up close. Thus, most inexpensive TLR cameras usually focus no closer than three feet. Some TLR cameras do feature inter-

A.

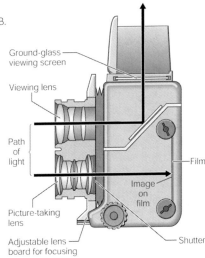

B.

Ground-glass viewing screen

Viewing lens

Path of light

Picture-taking lens

Adjustable lens board for focusing

Film

Image on film

Shutter

Figure 2-9. A) A twin-lens reflex (TLR) camera. B) A side-view cross section of a TLR camera. Note that the viewing and picture-taking lenses move together when focusing.

changeable lenses, but these are relatively expensive items, because the manufacturer must make a matched pair of lenses—one for viewing and one for picture taking. The latter must also include a shutter mechanism.

TLRs have long been favored for their durability and reasonable price, both qualities that result from the mechanical simplicity of the design. TLR cameras have been produced in many sizes and formats; the ones most commonly available today are designed for use with 120 and 220 film; photographers often select a TLR when they desire the greater image quality that such a medium-format film size provides.

Figure 2-10. The studio or view camera. Offers many adjustments for controlling perspective.

View Cameras

View cameras are the oldest type of camera, descending directly from the historic camera obscura. (See Figure 1-2) They represent the simplest camera design, consisting of little more than a flexible **bellows** with a lens and shutter mounted at one end and a ground-glass focusing screen and film plane affixed at the other. Despite their apparent simplicity, view cameras are powerful tools for work that requires precise control of perspective, depth of field, sharpness, and tone. For this reason, they are often chosen for use in portraiture, product photography, architecture, scenic photography, and technical and scientific photography. (See Figure 2-10.)

View cameras commonly use single sheets of film, usually large format and typically 4in x 5in, although they have been commercially produced for film sizes as large as 20in x 24in and as small as 35mm. Most can also be outfitted with an accessory digital back. Composing and focusing is accomplished through the picture-taking lens. The photographer, draped under a dark cloth, studies the image on a ground-glass screen at the back of the camera and makes the necessary adjustments before the film or digital sensor is put in place. The view seen by the photographer exactly matches that which will be recorded, and the large size of the ground-glass screen encourages an awareness

of the design elements of the picture and a studious fine-tuning of its composition.

The main advantage of the view camera is its many physical adjustments, which allow precise control over the shape and sharpness of an image. In addition to focus adjustments, the relationship between the lens and the film plane can be widely modified by means of movements called **swings and tilts**. This makes the camera extremely useful for correcting and controlling perspective and optical distortions. The angular relationship between the lens board and the film plane can be adjusted by these camera movements to control the shape and sharpness of objects depicted in the photograph. Lens boards are easily removed for accepting a variety of lenses, and interchangeable backs permit the use of Polaroid instant films, digital backs, roll film backs, and other sizes of sheet films.

Using a view camera is a time-consuming and deliberate process, not well suited for situations involving action or moving subjects. View cameras are also large, heavy, awkward to carry, require many adjustments, and generally must be used on a tripod or other camera support. Despite these disadvantages, however, the view camera remains the premier tool for the creation of exquisitely controlled and highly evocative images and has been the choice of many of the great photographers.

Parallax Error

The viewing system of the SLR and view type cameras provides a view of the subject that precisely matches the scene that will be recorded when the shutter is released. It does not matter if the subject is far or near, because the view presented to the photographer is formed by the picture-taking lens. Thus, what the photographer sees in the viewfinder is what will be recorded in the final image.

Other types of cameras use different optical systems for viewing and focusing, as we have seen in the cases of VF and TLR cameras. When separate optical systems are used, the viewing system is displaced slightly from the optical axis of the picture-taking system. As a result, the image seen in the viewfinder may be slightly different from the image formed at the focal plane—the two systems see the subject from slightly different angles.

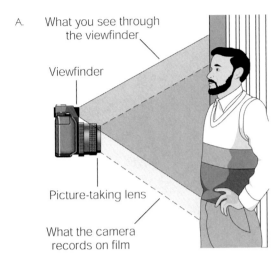

A. What you see through the viewfinder

Viewfinder

Picture-taking lens

What the camera records on film

Figure 2-12. Most viewfinder type cameras display additional parallex-correcting frame lines for close-up work.

B.

C.

Figure 2-11. Parallex effect. A) Image seen in viewfinder may differ from image seen by the picture-taking lens. B) Subject may appear perfectly centered in viewfinder while C) picture-taking lens is seeing off-center view. To remedy parallax effect, tip camera slightly in direction of viewfinder.

Separate viewfinding systems are designed so that the field of view closely matches that of the picture-taking lens at average snapshot distances. However, at close-up distances, the two images may be sufficiently different as to cause a problem. This discrepancy between the image seen through a camera's viewfinder and that which is recorded is what photographers call **parallax error**. Some cameras compensate for this discrepancy by providing a visual close-up frame within the viewfinder; others correct the view by optically displacing the viewfinder image as the picture-taking lens is focused at close-up distances. Some cameras do not correct for parallax error at all. If a camera provides no means to correct for parallax error, it can be corrected by tipping the camera slightly in the direction of the viewfinder when taking close-up pictures.

Camera Types by Film Size, Format, and Digital Resolution

Cameras are often classified by the size of the film or digital sensor they use or the format of the images they produce. The major types are small-, medium-, and large-format cameras. Digital cameras, on the other hand, are often classified by their digital resolution, as measured by the number of megapixels (millions of pixels) their sensor can record. Typical types are 2, 3, 4, 5, 6, and 8 megapixel cameras, or larger.

Because a photographic image can be magnified only to a certain degree without visibly degrading its quality and sharpness, film size, format, or digital resolution should be considered in relation to how the images will be used. The larger the recorded image or the higher the digital resolution, the larger the image can be magnified without visible degradation. For enlargement to album-size prints ("snapshots") or small-room projection, small-image formats or lower resolution may be quite suitable. For exhibit-size enlargements, auditorium projection, or print publication, larger formats or higher resolution may be required. Keep in mind that as image size and resolution increase, costs also increase. Choice of film size, format, or digital resolution should reflect, therefore, the expected uses of the recorded images.

Film Cameras

SMALL FORMAT

One type of **small-format** camera is the **35mm** camera, so called because it uses 35mm film. A camera of this type loads with a **magazine**, a light-tight container holding a strip of film sufficient for a number of images, each measuring 24mm x 36 mm. These magazines are available in many different sizes, some sufficient for twelve exposures, some for as many as seventy-two exposures. The most common sizes provide for twelve, twenty-four, or thirty-six exposures. Some 35mm films are available in 50-ft. and 100-ft. rolls so you can load them into your own magazines to the exact length you prefer.

The 35mm camera is the most popular type of film camera. It is available in many varieties, from simple, nonadjustable models suitable for a limited range of uses, to highly complex models with interchangeable and adjustable components suited for a wide range of uses. Small-format cameras are easy to carry, versatile, compact, easy to handle, and their small image format is suitable for most types of photographic assignments.

APS Format APS format is 24mm wide, smaller than 35mm, and is packaged in a smaller, "intelligent" film cartridge. Introduced in 1996, the Advanced Photo System was co-developed by Kodak, Fuji, Nikon, Canon, and Minolta, to build advanced technology into cameras that were simple to use. Hundreds of compact, APS cameras have appeared on the market since.

APS offers true, drop-in loading, that eliminates the need to thread film leader onto a take-up spool, or even to line up the leader to an index mark as required by "autoloading" cameras. Loading APS film is as simple as dropping the film cartridge into the camera's film compartment and closing the compartment door. The cartridge cannot be loaded

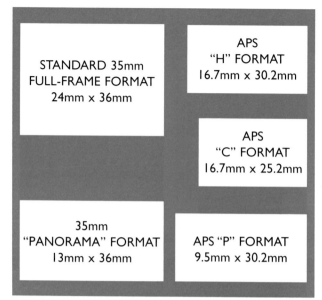

Figure 2-13. Comparison of 35mm and APS formats. APS cameras offer up to three image formats for each shot—C, H, & P.

incorrectly as it fits into the compartment only one way. The camera automatically pulls the film from the cartridge, winds it to the first frame, and sets the system to the correct film speed, film type, and length.

APS offers several automatic features to prevent common errors such as double exposures. The cartridge indicates whether it contains unexposed film, a partially exposed roll, a fully exposed roll, or a processed roll. APS cameras prevent loading exposed or processed cartridges, although some advanced APS cameras offer "MRC"—midroll change capability—whereby a partially exposed cartridge may be removed from the camera, replaced by another, and reloaded at a later time without losing a frame.

APS cameras offer choices of up to three image formats for each shot: C, H, and P. Some cameras offer all three; others, only one or two. Although all images are actually recorded in the full frame H format measuring 16.7mm x 30.2mm, the images are coded to yield prints of different aspect ratios. C format is the standard 2:3 aspect ratio that yields 4in x 6in prints; H is the 9:16 aspect ratio used by High Definition Television (HDTV) that yields 4in x 7in prints; and P is a panoramic aspect ratio of approximately 1:3 that yields 3.5in x 10in or 4in x 11.5in prints. Unlike the negatives from standard 35mm cameras, APS negatives can be printed in any of the three formats during processing.

Figure 2-14. Index print from roll of APS film.

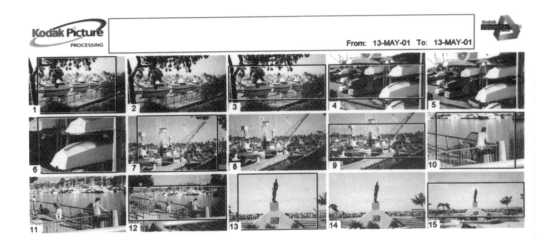

Kodak Picture PROCESSING

From: 13-MAY-01 To: 13-MAY-01

ID059-622

MEDIUM FORMAT

The most popular **medium-format** cameras are designed to use 120 or 220 film, which is supplied in rolls containing sufficient film for twelve or twenty-four images respectively, each measuring 2 1/4in square (6cm x 6cm). Some medium-format cameras using this size film are designed to produce rectangular images measuring 6cm x 7cm (2 1/4in x 2 3/4in), for example, or 4.5cm x 6cm (1 5/8in x 2 1/4in). The advantage of these formats is that they are close to the proportions of a standard 8in x 10in print. (See Figures 2-15 and 2-16.) Many medium format cameras will also accept digital backs for high quality digital imaging.

Medium-format cameras are often chosen for assignments that demand high-quality reproduction of nonstationary subjects; the film size offers greater detail and a richer tonal rendering than the smaller 35mm format. Medium-format cameras are often the tools of choice for professionals in the fields of commercial, industrial, editorial, and portrait photography.

LARGE FORMAT

Large-format cameras are designed to use **sheet film**, film supplied in individual sheets to fit standard film holders or large digital imaging sensors. Sheet films are commercially produced in many sizes and formats for both photographic and graphic arts purposes. The sizes most commonly used for photography are 2 1/4in x 3 1/4in (6cm x 8cm), 4in x 5in (10cm x 13cm), 5in x 7in (13cm x 18cm), and 8in x 10in (20cm x 25cm). Larger sizes up to 20in x 24in (52cm x 62cm) are produced for graphic arts and scientific purposes. These large-format films require little enlargement to produce relatively large prints; therefore, grain is virtually nonexistent in the final display. Large negatives and transparencies offer the ultimate in photographic reproduction, because they record even the most minute details and textures of a scene.

Figure 2-15. An example of a medium format camera that uses 120 or 220 size film.

Metrication

In the field of photography, both U.S. customary measures (inches, quarts, pounds, degrees Fahrenheit) and metric measures (centimeters, liters, grams, degrees Celsius) are commonly used. Some standard product measures may be expressed in one system and some in the other, depending on where or for what market the product is manufactured. For example, some cameras are known as 4in x 5in cameras because of their image format; other cameras are known as 6cm x 7cm cameras because of theirs.

In this book, when appropriate, we have provided metric equivalents in parentheses wherever U.S. customary measures are commonly used and U.S. customary equivalents in parentheses wherever metric measures are commonly used. For example, a statement such as the following might be found: A 2 1/4in x 2 1/4in (6cm x 6cm) camera uses the same size film as a 6cm x 7cm (2 1/4in x 2 3/4in) camera. A table of metric conversions is provided in Appendix C, found on the accompanying CD-ROM.

Figure 2-16. Comparison of small-, medium- and large-format film sizes.

Most large-format cameras can also be equipped with digital backs. Because of their large sensor size they yield very high quality and detailed digital files of up to 100MB in size.

In selecting an image format, consider the tradeoff between image size and camera size. In general, obtaining larger images requires the use of larger, bulkier, and usually more expensive camera equipment. To obtain the convenience of smaller, lighter, portable, and usually less expensive camera equipment, smaller image formats must generally be accepted. Except to solve special problems and for studio uses, today's professional photographers rely heavily on small- and medium-format cameras for most purposes, particularly those using 35mm, 120, and 220 film sizes and their digital equivalents. (See Figure 2-16.)

Digital Cameras

The architecture of digital cameras is very similar to their film counterparts. Both use a lens to form an image, have a system for focusing and viewing, control exposure with shutter speeds and apertures, and produce images. The main difference, of course, is that a **digicam** uses a digital sensor instead of film to record the image.

The sensor, a silicon chip the size of a small postage stamp, contain millions of photosensitive diodes called **photosites**. During exposure, each photosite records the intensity of light falling on it by accumulating an electrical charge—the more light, the greater the charge. The pattern of charged elements is then converted electronically to digital data (a sequence of 1s and 0s) and stored as a coded file. That file is used to set the color and brightness of dots on a computer screen or ink on a printed page. These dots of various colors and intensities are called **pixels** and form the resulting photographic image. (The word "pixel" is contracted from the words "picture elements".)

Figure 2-17. Example of digital camera. Most digital cameras have a LCD monitor screen for instantly reviewing your photos.

Pixels and Pictures The imaging chip used in digicams might be a CCD (Charge Coupled Device) or a CMOS (Complementary Metal-Oxide Semiconductor) and its size and the number of photo sites it contains determines the maximum resolution of the camera. Think of a picture created with small mosaic tiles. If the tiles are very tiny, the mosaic-tile picture can be viewed close-up and remain detailed and lifelike. If the tiles are larger, the image appears detailed and lifelike only if viewed from a greater distance.

Figure 2-18. An example of a digital single-lens reflex camera.

Similarly the number of pixels used to form the image determines the resolution of the image and the size of acceptable print it can produce. For this reason, the number of pixels in the resulting image—its resolution—is an important basis for classifying digital cameras. (See Unit 4, Films and Digital Materials.)

Despite the similarity of film and digital cameras, no common architecture has yet emerged for digital cameras. Most film cameras have acquired familiar structures that provide for film transport, the passage of light, and the placement of such artifacts as mirrors and prisms. Although manufacturers initially designed their digital cameras to look like familiar 35mm cameras, they soon realized they were free to design new forms. As a result, you'll find many new, sometimes strange camera shapes in today's market.

In general, digital cameras can be classified by their viewing systems. Two viewing systems have emerged that correspond to their film counterparts:

- Viewfinder (VF) cameras, which provide separate optical systems for viewing and picture taking.
- Single Lens Reflex (SLR) cameras, which provide for viewing and picture taking through the same lens.

Twin Lens Reflex (TLR), View, and other larger format cameras, often preferred by studio and commercial photographers, are not commonly manufactured as digital cameras. Nevertheless, some of these cameras can be converted for digital use with a **digital scanback**. This is a scanning device that fits to the back of the camera and captures the image using scanning technology rather than a CCD or CMOS sensor. They offer superior resolution

and precise image controls but often need to be tethered to a computer—making them suitable only for studio work. They are also usually quite expensive and require longer exposures.

Digital Video (DV) cameras, although designed mainly to produce movies, may also include a "still" setting. In this mode one "frame" of information is captured and can be stored as a still image. In general, digital video cameras do not produce still images with the same sharpness and resolution of a digital camera, but can be acceptable for small prints or web work.

Digital cameras may also be classified into roughly three tiers by image resolution and features.

- In the first tier are **consumer** cameras that are fully automatic, point-and-shoot cameras with resolutions of 3 to 4 megapixels. These are typically VF cameras that feature a zoom lens and internal flash only. Compact and lightweight, they are well suited to snapshots. The least expensive digital cameras, they are fully automatic and usually don't provide much in the way of adjustable controls. Still, their images can produce great prints up to 8in x 10in or so.

Figure 2-19. Typical consumer point-and-shoot camera.

Figure 2-20. Typical prosumer camera. Courtesy of Steves-Digicams.com

- In the next tier are **prosumer** cameras that provide many creative, adjustable controls with 4 to 8 megapixels. These include both VF and SLR cameras with both internal and external flash. They typically offer more advanced features such as through-the-lens (TTL) focusing and many creative controls and appeal to those who want precise control of their camera's settings. Some provide for interchangeable lenses and many attachable camera accessories. Their images can easily enlarge to 8in x 10in prints or larger.

- In the top tier are **professional** cameras that provide a wide range of creative, adjustable controls, with 6 to 14 megapixels. These are typically SLR cameras that often offer the same features, such as exposure controls, and accessories, such as lenses, that were designed for the film-based predecessors made by the same manufacturer.

Figure 2-21. Typical professional digital SLR camera. Courtesy of Steves-Digicams.com

Four Thirds System Recently, a new common standard for image sensor size and camera body lens mounts was jointly developed by Olympus and Kodak and has been adopted by Fuji and others. Known as the Four Thirds System, it departs from existing standards for 35mm film SLR camera systems and establishes a new common standard for the interchange of lenses that meet the optical requirements of digital SLRs. By creating a standard for camera body lens mounts and sensor size, the system will allow photographers to combine camera bodies and lenses from different manufacturers for a wider choice.

Advantages of Digital Cameras Digicams offer several advantages over film cameras, including:

- Instant viewing of pictures—allowing you to erase the ones you do not like and re-shoot until you're happy with the results

- Low operating costs—no film or processing to pay for

- Freedom to experiment creatively without worrying about the costs of film and processing

- Freedom to photograph under artificial light without special film or filters

- The ability to use image-editing software for retouching, control, and creative manipulation that would be difficult or impossible in a conventional darkroom

- Make and distribute copies without any loss of quality

- Send images to friends by e-mail or post them on a web site

- Use the images in multimedia presentations and even databases

Disadvantages of digital cameras Digicams are not without their disadvantages. These include:

- Digital cameras cost more than their film equivalents.

- Digital cameras have more controls and seem more complicated.

- The quality of large digital prints may not match that of film, although the quality of digital prints continues to improve rapidly.

- The lag time between shots with a digital camera is usually greater than that with a film camera. The latter requires only advancing the film. Digital cameras must process the image data recorded by the sensor and write it to the memory media. Some, more expensive, digital cameras provide an internal memory buffer to shorten this lag time.

■ Digicams consume battery power rapidly, especially when using the built-in display and flash unit.

■ Editing digital images requires sophisticated image-editing software and a moderately high level computer system.

Common Features of Digital Cameras Most digital cameras offer the following features:

■ Autofocus

■ Built-in flash

■ An LCD screen or monitor for framing, focusing, and viewing

■ An eye-level viewfinder

■ A optical zoom lens

Figure 2-22. Full-featured consumer type digital camera.

Table 2-1. Comparing 35mm vs digital cameras	
35mm	**Digital**
35mm cameras generally cost less than digital cameras with similar features.	Digital cameras cost a little more than 35mm cameras with similar features, but they are getting cheaper and better.
Every photo costs money, whether you make prints or not. You have to buy the film then pay for processing for every photo you shoot.	After you purchase a memory card, your photos are virtually free. You can erase photos or upload them to your computer, then reuse the memory card indefinitely.
You cannot see your photos until you get them back from the developer.	You can see your photos immediately on the LCD viewer on your digital camera.
You must develop photographic skills because you can't know for sure how a photo will look like until the film is processed. Even poor shots will cost for film, processing, and printing.	You can rely more upon the camera to focus and expose correctly. Since you can view the images immediately, you can shoot many times at no additional cost, delete unwanted photos, and print only those you choose.
Making additional copies of your photos costs money, time, and a trip to the film processor.	Making 100% exact duplicate copies of your digital images is free and as easy as a few clicks with your mouse.
Photos made using 35mm film are not immediately ready for e-mailing or for publishing to a web page. After paying for film and processing, you must also digitize them.	Photos made using a digital camera are stored in a digitized format and are immediately ready to be e-mailed or used on your web page.
35mm camera film is produced in rolls of 36 or fewer exposures. You must reload the camera with a new roll of film after making the maximum number of exposures.	Digital memory cards hold far more images than 35mm film rolls depending upon the card's capacity and the resolution of the images, e.g. a 128MB memory card can hold about 150 images for good quality 5in x 7in prints.
We often give away prints to friends and relatives intending to make another for ourselves later. Often we never do.	We can e-mail 100% exact copies of digital images to others without giving away the original.
When traveling you must mail photos back to others or make them wait to see them until you get home.	When traveling you can e-mail your photos to others using a laptop computer or one of the many cyber cafés in cities and towns worldwide.

TECHNICAL FEATURE

Shopping for a Digital Camera

Digital cameras are changing rapidly. New high-tech features appear every day, such as improved sensors and lens systems. Such rapid evolution prevents giving specific buying advice, but you will find it useful to consider the following factors when choosing a new digicam.

FORM FACTOR, SIZE, AND VIEWING SYSTEM

As with film cameras, viewfinder digital cameras tend to be the smallest while digital SLRs tend to be the largest.

ULTRA-SMALL CAMERAS

Many manufacturers make ultra-small, compact digital cameras that easily fit into a shirt pocket. Though convenient for quick and easy photography, these popular cameras generally scale back many features, such as zoom range, exposure modes, image enhancements, accessory flash connectors, and extended battery life.

MEDIUM-SIZE CAMERAS

Medium size viewfinder digital cameras are popular with advanced amateurs and may still fit nicely in a larger pocket or small pack. With about the same form factor as point-and-shoot 35mm film cameras, they usually offer a long zoom range, advanced exposure modes, numerous resolution and white balance settings, an accessory flash connection, and extended battery life. Cameras in this range offer a rich blend of features for their price.

LARGER SLR TYPE CAMERAS

Although single lens reflex digital cameras are larger and bulkier, they tend to be favored by advanced amateur and professional photographers. They offer the same advantages as those offered by film SLRs—precise viewfinding and image control, easy close-ups, long zoom ratios, interchangeable lenses, a large range of exposure and image settings, long battery life, accessory flash connections, and high resolution. They also tend to have larger interface controls for easier handling.

RESOLUTION

An old adage in real estate is "location, location, location." For digital photographers it is "resolution, resolution, resolution." When only one- or two-

megapixel cameras were available, resolution was the primary concern of buyers. Today, when cameras boasting 5-megapixels and beyond are common, it is less important.

Higher digital resolution generally equates to greater image quality, but only up to a point. Image quality is affected by many other factors, including optical resolution, printer and monitor resolution, the quality of the camera's electronic circuits, the size of the digital sensor, and noise reduction. Look for cameras that not only have high resolution figures but also advanced imaging processing technologies, and a variety of color management, noise reduction, ISO, file format, and white balance settings.

CAPTURE SPEED AND SHUTTER LAG

Film photographers are often disturbed to find their new digital cameras less responsive. The digital electronics take time to perform their wonders. One time lag occurs between switching the camera on and the camera's readiness to take your first shot. Another time lag occurs, called shutter lag, between depressing the shutter button and actually capturing the image. The digital sensor needs a moment to charge for each shot, the focus system needs to evaluate the image and adjust the lens, and the exposure system needs to evaluate and adjust the shutter and aperture. All of these factors affect the responsiveness of the camera. Professional and prosumer cameras tend to be more responsive than consumer grade cameras. Test cameras before purchasing to determine their capture speed and shutter lag and to test how many shots can be taken consecutively before the camera's buffer is full.

THE LENS

Before light can reach the digital sensor it passes through an image-forming lens, and this component is important in determining image quality and the versatility of the camera. Most small and medium sized digicams have non-interchangeable zoom lenses.

ZOOM LENSES

Look for a lens that offers at least a 3X optical zoom range of about 35mm–105mm (35mm equivalent). Such zoom lenses will handle most normal picture requirements from close-up portraits, to mid-range group shots, to long range scenic photographs.

Sometimes, however, you might want an extended optical zoom range, such as in sports or wildlife photography. Although you might not use this full range often, it is a nice feature. A few medium-sized digicams are available that offer up to a 10x optical zoom range. Note that the optical zoom range is a function of the lens; digital zoom range, also offered on many cameras, is an enlarging function of the camera that tends to degrade image quality.

This digital camera has a powerful zoom lens and a built-in flash.

If you expect to shoot under low-light conditions, you should also consider the lenses speed. Many compact zoom lenses are relatively slow and not well suited to low-light conditions.

ACCESSORY LENSES

If your camera can be fitted with photographic filters, you can probably obtain auxiliary lenses for it. These lenses mount in front of the existing lens to either increase its wide-angle coverage or its telephoto strength. Lenses made by the camera manufacturer usually have the best optical quality; however, after-market lenses may be less expensive.

INTERCHANGEABLE LENSES

Many digital SLRs can be fitted with a wide variety of interchangeable lenses. Choose such lenses carefully to get the best mix of image quality, zoom range, and lens speed.

Some digital SLRs will accept lenses from their 35mm film counterparts; however, sensor sizes differ on most digicams and usually are smaller than a 35mm film frame. Thus, their effective focal length may change when used with a digital SLR. What may have been a moderate wide-angle on a 35mm film camera often becomes a normal lens on a digicam. When considering a digital SLR with interchangeable lenses, look at the camera's specifications to determine the magnification ratio, if any.

THE LCD MONITOR

One big advantage of a digital camera is its ability to preview shots and to review recorded images instantly on the camera's built-in display monitor. This provides an instant check on composition, exposure, framing, lighting, and the subject's action or expres-

sion. However, not all monitor screens are created equal—some tilt out and swivel, some are larger and some smaller, and some are difficult to see in bright sunlight where you will often work.

Compare LCD screens in person; do not rely solely on specifications or on sales claims. View the screen image both in the store and outside.

SHOOTING MODES

Many digital cameras offer a variety of shooting modes beyond the usual aperture and shutter priority. Many have specialized scene modes tuned specifically for sports, portraits, and landscapes to name a few. These modes make capturing even tricky scenes easier and give less experienced users great results. These shooting modes are usually selected by setting an external dial to the icon-selected mode.

For advanced photographers full manual and priority modes are necessary. Many advanced cameras also provide options for manual focus and spot metering. To better control the camera's response to changing light sources, look for a camera with adjustable white balance settings. This provides the ability to set a custom white balance by taking a light reading from a target white card.

Many cameras also include a movie mode for capturing short bursts of multi-image recording, even accompanied by sound. Although both the resolution and length of the movie clips produced with a digicam are low, they can be fun to explore and to e-mail to family and friends for playback on a computer or television set.

MEMORY CARDS

All common memory cards are small, offer high image stability, and have fallen in price dramatically. Thus, the memory card used by a digital camera is of minor importance in a purchase decision. However, if you already own a digital camera, or other device that uses a memory card, you may find it useful to buy a digicam that uses the same system, all other factors being equal.

You will want to buy additional memory cards for your camera because most new digicams come supplied with only a small capacity card. If you expect to be recording high-resolution images with little or no compression, you'll need a lot of storage capacity. Buy large capacity memory cards and carry multiple cards with you on important shooting excursions.

At a Glance

Size:

- Ask to examine a variety of cameras in the size and price range you desire. Compare features and viewfinders.
- Handle many cameras to find one that feels comfortable and offers a friendly interface with buttons and menus that are quick and easy to use.

Resolution:

- Get enough resolution for the size of prints you expect to make.
- Resolution may not be the only important specification, but it is still a primary one. Look for at least 4–6 megapixels in smaller cameras and 8-megapixels and beyond for SLRs.

Capture Speed and Shutter Lag:

- Compare the start-up times of several models when first switched on.
- Beware of cameras that have too long a time lag between the pressing of the shutter and the exposure. Test by photographing a moving object.
- Compare how many consecutive shots can be taken in a short time.

The Lens:

- Select a camera with a sufficiently long optical zoom range for your shooting needs.

- Consider cameras that accept auxiliary lenses that can extend your range.
- Professionals and enthusiasts often use interchangeable lenses. Consider a camera that offers interchangeable lenses if your needs require them. Check to see if the camera adds a magnification factor to the lens.

The LCD Monitor:

- Bigger LCD monitors are easier to read and provide greater detail. Examine the screen image of many models both indoors and in bright sunlight.
- Consider a tilt-out monitor screen to increase your capacity to view the image in a variety of circumstances.

Shooting Modes:

- Consider cameras that have many programmed scene modes to provide a variety of automatic shooting modes.
- Consider cameras that feature multiple light-meter settings, white balance options, and manual exposure and focus controls. These will be useful as you gain experience.

Memory Cards:

- Although not an important factor for selecting a camera, purchase additional memory cards to supplement the small card supplied with the camera.

Some digicams also feature some or all of the following features:

- A digital zoom—a not very useful feature that crops and digitally enlarges a small portion of the image, lowering resolution

- Video output to view images on TV

- Spot metering

- Backlight compensation

- Several program modes such as aperture priority, shutter priority and manual exposure

- Manual distance setting for focus

- A variety of white balance settings to match lighting conditions

- A self-timer or remote control

- Extra flash settings such as red-eye reduction, rearcurtain synch, and the ability to use external flash units.

- Image stabilization to reduce camera movement for sharper results.

Some manufacturers are reflecting the convergence of visual and other information technologies in the feature sets of their digital cameras. For example, many digicams can record sounds and film clips, some can play MP3 music files, and a few can even be used to access e-mail and transmit images directly to a web site. Similarly, cell phones and personal digital assistants (PDAs) are now also featuring built-in digital cameras.

Image Modes All digicams record full-color images and many offer other imaging modes such as black-and-white, sepia tone, negative images where the tones and colors are reversed, posterization, and the ability to "stitch" together many shots into a panorama with special software.

Most digicams also provide the user with a choice of image file type, such as JPEG. TIFF or RAW (see page 157), and offer various resolution settings for various applications. Many also offer user-selected choices of electronic image sharpening including soft, normal, hard and user-defined, although most experienced digital photographers prefer to apply sharpening during the image editing process for better results.

Storage Media The capacity of the flash memory card used with a camera defines how many images can be stored before the card is full. This removable memory or "digital film" comes in a variety of sizes and shapes. The photographer can carry additional memory cards along in the field. Like additional rolls of film, extra memory modules allow for further picture-taking. Popular flash memory storage media include **Compact Flash** (CF), **Smart Memory** (SM), **Secure Digital** (SD), and **xD** memory cards. Other storage options include **Memory Sticks**, miniature writable compact disks or **Mini-CD-R**s, and miniature hard-drives. First generation digicams sometimes stored images on standard floppy disks, but these are not generally suited to the large file sizes of modern high-resolution cameras.

The choice of storage media will be dictated by the brand and model of camera selected, but all are effective. Some card types do record faster, but the difference is unlikely to be noticeable in daily picture-taking. Do, however, get a large-capacity storage card and carry plenty of extra memory with you so that you can take numerous high-resolution images in one session. Unlike film, the images stored on flash memory cards can be erased or transferred to a computer, releasing the card to be used over and over again. Photographing with a digital camera is fun and addictive! (See further discussion in Chapter 4.)

Digital Accessories Every digital camera owner should carry a spare memory card, both to extend shooting opportunities and to serve as a back up in case one card is damaged. Memory card readers attach to the computer via USB, Firewire or serial cables. Although most digicams can be cabled directly to the host computer, these card readers are a much faster and more convenient way of transferring files. Many manufacturers offer accessory lenses to extend the range of focal lengths your camera can cover. Sold in both wide-angle and telephoto models, these devices enhance your photographic vision.

In addition to a digicam you'll need a computer, a software program to organize and manage your photo files, an image-editing program like Photoshop, and access to a quality color printer. Modern ink-jet printers designed for photo-realistic prints are surprisingly inexpensive and capable of producing exceptional quality on specially coated paper. Large files can be transported on Zip disks, CD's, DVD's, or USB plug-in storage devices. Writable CD-ROM or DVD drives are fairly inexpensive and CD's and DVD's are a popular way to archive image files, exchange pictures, or submit portfolios.

Battery Power Batteries power all automatic exposure cameras. Without battery power, the automatic features will not function; sometimes even the camera will not function. A desirable feature for an automatic film camera is the ability to function in a manual mode even without battery power in case the batteries fail and cannot be quickly replaced.

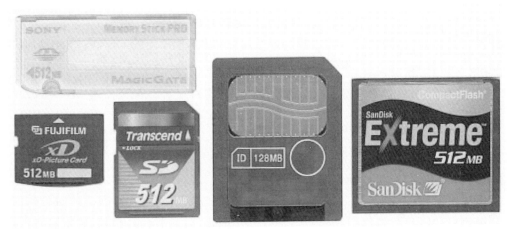

Figure 2-23. Flash Memory Cards, sometimes called storage cards or digital film, are used to record images in a digital camera. The digital camera dictates the type of flash memory card you use. The most popular types are: CompactFlash (CF), SmartMedia (SM), Memory Stick (MS), MultiMediaCard (MMC), Secure Digital (SD), and xD-Picture Card (xD), all available in different capacities. These cards are physically different and are **NOT** interchangeable. Courtesy of Steves-Digicams.com

Table 2-2. File compression, file size, and memory card capacity

Flash memory is available in several formats, including CompactFlash™, SmartMedia™, MultiMedia (MMC), Secure Digital (SD), xD-Picture Card™, and Memory Stick™. To figure out which format(s) of flash memory is compatible with your camera, consult the owner's manual. Flash memory cards are available in various capacities, up to 4GB or more. Select a card that is suitable for your storage needs.

Most digital cameras allow you to adjust your image quality, so your memory card can contain both high-resolution and low-resolution images. Use high resolution when you know you will want to make prints; use lower resolution when you want to e-mail the images to others. The table below will give you a general idea of how many images you might expect to record on memory cards of various capacities. These ranges are only approximate. This will vary depending upon resolution, compression, color format, camera model, and shooting conditions.

No. of Pixels in Image**	Card Capacity 16MB**	Card Capacity 32MB**	Card Capacity 64MB**	Card Capacity 128MB**	Card Capacity 256MB**	Card Capacity 512MB**	Card Capacity 1GB**
1 MP	20–44	40–88	80–150	160–250	320–550	640–1200	1280–2500
2 MP	16–32	32–64	64–122	128–220	256–480	512–980	1024–2000
3 MP	10–20	20–40	40–90	80–150	160–300	320–600	640–1300
4 MP	6–16	12–32	24–64	48–128	96–256	192–512	384–1024
5 MP	3–12	8–28	19–58	38–92	76–180	150–350	300–700
6 MP	2–10	6–23	15–48	31–76	63–150	125–291	250–583

Number of images of various resolutions you might expect to store on a memory card of this capacity. Size of actual image files will vary depending on resolution, compression, color format, camera model and shooting conditions.
**MB = megabytes, GB = gigabytes, MP = megapixels

Digital cameras are rapid consumers of battery power, more so than their film-based siblings. The combination of a CCD or CMOS image sensor, color LCD panel, built-in flash and zoom lens makes a digital camera a power-hungry beast. So the right choice in batteries can make the difference between looking at a great shot or looking at a "low-battery" warning. Batteries are rated in milliampere-hours (mAh), which tells you how much current a battery can supply and for how long.

Disposable batteries

Alkaline vs. Lithium. Traditional alkaline batteries often are packaged with a new digital camera. As digital cameras quickly exhaust standard alkalines, you should consider replacing them with either lithium batteries or hi-power alkaline cells, which offer the best power source from a disposable battery. Disposables can serve as an excellent backup to rechargeable cells, especially when you're in the field and unable to recharge batteries. If your camera will not be used for a long time, remove alkaline batteries—they have a tendency to leak caustic chemicals. Never mix rechargeables with alkalines, as leakage can damage electrical contacts and ruin your camera.

Among disposable batteries, lithium AA batteries are the best choice. The lithium's higher power capacity and reliable performance throughout its life make it preferable over alkaline. It also provides great performance in colder temperatures, which is something to consider if you expect to shoot under such conditions. Moreover, lithium batteries last for years and do not leak.

Rechargeable batteries

The most common rechargeable batteries are Nickel Cadmium (NiCd) and Nickel Metal Hydride (NiMH) of which the latter are more powerful. They last through hundreds of recharges, yet they will lose their charge slowly if not in use. Nickel-Metal Hydride (NiMH) batteries are the most cost-effective batteries for cameras that use AA-sized cells. Available up to 2200 mAh, these cells deliver excellent performance in both compact and SLR-type digital cameras. They also perform well under extreme temperatures. NiCd or NiMH rechargeables do not leak and can safely be left in place. They will also help preserve the small back-up battery or condenser, common in digicams, that serves to remember the internal time and date.

Many digicams consume some power even when the camera is switched off. To avoid damage from total battery discharge during long periods of non-use, recharge NiMH batteries about once a month. This will also ensure the reliability of the camera's clock. Unlike NiMH batteries, NiCds should be fully discharged before charging. NiCds suffer from "memory effect," i.e. they "remember" their last state of charge and will hold less power over time.

If your camera uses a proprietary rechargeable lithium-ion or NiMH battery, invest in batteries from the manufacturer or from a name-brand company. Purchase three separate sets—one in the camera, the second fully charged in your camera bag, and the third on the charger. With this arrangement, you'll always have two fully charged batteries available.

Two main types of chargers are available for rechargeable batteries—quick chargers and slow ones. If you use a **smart charger** designed for your type of battery, the charger will stop charging when the batteries are full. The most common cause of premature battery failure is overcharging, which can occur with chargers designed to operate for a fixed period of time. Smart chargers are designed to monitor temperature, time, and current to ensure that batteries are not overcharged. Most manufacturers do not recommend trickle charging with a continuous low charge. Instead, fully charge your batteries and then store them in a cold place such as a refrigerator. They will hold their charge for many months. However, let them adjust to room temperature before use.

Words of caution—never try to charge non-rechargeable batteries as they might overheat or even explode. Remember too that batteries often contain harmful materials, so dispose of them safely.

Shutter Systems

Two types of shutter systems are in common use: between-the-lens (BTL) shutters and focal plane (FP) shutters.

Between-the-Lens Shutters

Between-the-lens shutters are made of thin, overlapping metal leaves designed to pivot outward from the center to admit light. Installed between the lens elements close to the optical center, the BTL shutter admits light to the entire film area throughout its exposure cycle. As the shutter begins its cycle, dim image-forming light is admitted to the entire picture area. As the shutter opens more widely, the illumination brightens until the shutter reaches its maximum opening. Then, as the shutter closes, the illumination dims again until the shutter is closed. The design of the BTL shutter imposes mechanical limitations on how quickly the blades can open and close. For this reason, BTL shutters rarely have top speeds of more than 1/500 of a second. (See Figure 2-24.)

Focal Plane Shutters

Focal plane (FP) shutters may be made of metal or cloth in the form of two overlapping curtains

Figure 2-24. A) A between-the-lens (BTL) shutter in action showing the opening and B) closing of the metal blades.

Table 2-3. Selecting a type of film or digital camera

Subject or Situation	Commonly used camera type	Other choices	Notes
Fast, easy to use for casual snapshots and general family photographs	Fully automatic viewfinder type of point-and-shoot camera	SLR with autofocus and program exposure	Easy and quick to use, but gives the photographer little control over the results
Backpacking	Point-and-shoot type of camera, or viewfinder with exposure settings	Compact SLR	Look for cameras that are light-weight and ruggedly constructed
Photography student or advanced amateur	SLR with manual mode to control both shutter and lens openings	SLR with aperture and shutter priority modes	Could also use viewfinder or medium-format camera with manual control of exposure
Sports Photography	SLR with shutter priority or action program mode	SLR with manual exposure	Select fast shutter speeds when stop-action is desired
Landscape Photography	SLR with aperture priority or landscape program mode	SLR with manual exposure	Select small lens openings when great depth of field is desired. Medium- or large-format cameras are also used
Portraiture	SLR with moderate telephoto or zoom lens	Medium-format camera with moderate telephoto lens. Could also use a point-and-shoot viewfinder camera with zoom lens	Professionals usually choose medium format for its higher resolution images
General commercial work	Medium-format camera	SLR	
Architecture	Large-format, 4 × 5 view camera	SLR with perspective control lens	Large format cameras permit precise control of a building's perspective
Product advertising	Large-format, 4 × 5 view camera	SLR with medium telephoto or zoom lens	Large format cameras permit precise control of a product's perspective

or sets of blinds that open and close in rapid succession so that the opening between them admits light to the film. Installed in the rear of the camera close to the surface of the film or digital sensor—at the focal plane—the FP shutter admits light successively to portions of the film as the opening between the curtains traverses the film gate. By varying the rate of travel and the width of the shutter opening, manufacturers can achieve a wide variety of shutter speeds. Some focal plane shutters offer exposure times as short as 1/8000 of a second, a duration almost fast enough to freeze a bullet in flight. (See Figure 2-25.)

Each type of shutter has its advantages and disadvantages. The BTL shutter is more flexible for flash synchronization, allowing electronic flash units to be used at all shutter speeds. This is a great boon for "fill-in" flash work. Its location between the lens elements, however, prevents its common use in single-lens reflex camera designs. The FP shutter, on the other hand, is more suitable for single-lens reflex cameras and offers higher shutter speeds, but its method of exposure limits its usefulness with electronic flash. This subject will be treated more fully in Unit 13, *Flash Photography.*

The range of shutter speeds varies with shutter design. Most modern adjustable cameras provide a range of speeds from several seconds or more to 1/8000 of a second or less. In addition, some provide a setting for manually timing longer exposures that allows the photographer to open and close the shutter at will. A further feature available with some cameras is a **self-timer**, which provides for delaying the exposure by ten seconds or so after the shutter is released. This feature is useful for stabilizing the camera on its support before releasing the shutter for a long exposure. It can also be used for self-portraits of the photographer.

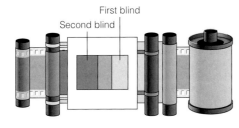

First blind
Second blind

1

2

3

Figure 2-25. The two curtains of a focal plane shutter form a narrow opening that moves across the film gate to expose successively the whole picture. Some cameras use FP shutters that transverse the film gate horizontally, as shown; some move vertically.

Digital Camera Shutters

Just as in a traditional camera, a shutter controls light entering the camera through the lens. Most compact digicams use between-the-lens (BTL) shutters, while a few professional-level cameras use focal plane (FP) shutters. A growing number use the image sensor itself to set the exposure time. A computer-controlled timing circuit tells the image chip when to start and stop recording light. This system is the functional equivalent of a shutter.

Exposure-Setting Systems

Two basic controls on an adjustable camera determine the amount of light that strikes the film—shutter speed and aperture. The length of time the shutter remains open affects the duration of the exposure; the size of the aperture affects its intensity. The simplest cameras use a **fixed exposure** system that possesses a single combination of shutter speed and aperture. Such nonadjustable cameras may be used effectively with a certain type of film under prescribed shooting conditions. Most cameras, however, are designed so that shutter speed and aperture can be adjusted to various settings, permitting use of the camera with films or digital sensors of various types and speeds and under many shooting conditions. Exposure-setting systems may be divided into two major classes: manual and automatic.

Manual Exposure

A **manual exposure** system allows you to set the aperture, shutter speed, and focus by hand separately and independently. Most veteran photographers advise beginners to use a camera that lets you choose these settings manually if you wish. Most discontinued 35mm SLR cameras, whether they are mechanical or fully electronic models, have metered manual or manual override for users who wish to have complete control over their exposure settings.

Exposure may be determined by using a published exposure guide and estimating lighting conditions or by using a built-in or hand-held exposure meter to measure the lighting conditions. Most photographers prefer the latter method because it is more precise.

Before the 1960s, most photographers used a separate, hand-held exposure meter to determine correct exposure settings. Most of today's manual exposure systems use built-in microelectronics to combine the reading and setting functions into a smooth, efficient one-step operation. (See Figure 2-26.)

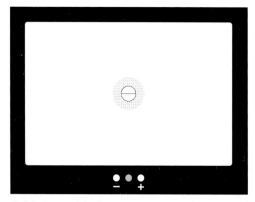

Figure 2-26. A match indicator exposure setting system. Adjust the aperture and/or shutter speed until the indicator light or needle shown in the viewfinder is properly aligned.

Automatic Exposure

An **automatic exposure** system automatically sets the shutter speed, aperture, and focus without your intervention. This allows you to concentrate on composition without having to pay attention to the exposure settings.

Many automatic exposure cameras, both film and digital, allow the photographer to select from among four general modes of operation—fully automatic, shutter priority, aperture priority, and programmed.

- The **fully automatic** exposure mode automatically sets the shutter speed, aperture, and focus without your intervention to standard exposure settings. This mode allows you to shoot without paying attention to these settings so you can concentrate on composition.

- The **shutter priority** mode lets you choose the shutter speed manually while the camera sets the aperture automatically to provide proper exposure in response to lighting conditions. Select this mode whenever you wish to freeze motion or deliberately blur movement in the image. This is useful when dealing with rapidly moving subjects, such as in sports photography. (See Exposure and Action in Chapter 3.)

- The **aperture priority** mode lets you select the aperture manually while the camera sets the shutter speed automatically to provide proper exposure in response to lighting conditions. Select this mode whenever depth of field is most important—to control the range of focus in the image. This is useful when dealing

with near-far spatial relationships, such as those found in landscape, scenic, portrait, and still life photography. (See Depth of Field in Chapter 3.)

- The **programmed exposure** mode utilizes a built-in computer program that selects an optimal combination of shutter. Cameras with advanced features often offer multiple program modes designed to give optimum results in a specific situation such as action, landscapes, close-ups, or night scenes. Some cameras even allow the photographer to design a custom-tailored program mode.

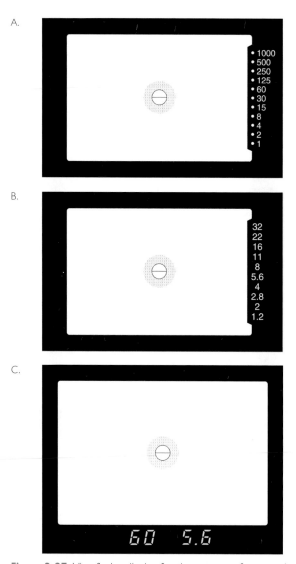

Figure 2-27. Viewfinder display for three types of automatic exposure systems. A) Aperture priority; the window displays the corresponding shutter speed automatically selected for the camera. B) Shutter priority; the window displays the corresponding automatically set lens opening. C) Programmed automatic; window displays both the shutter speed and aperture selected by the camera.

Most cameras with automatic exposure systems display a viewfinder readout of the camera's settings. This feature provides the photographer with the information needed to retain creative control. Although automatic exposure systems are accurate and normally produce properly exposed images, at times the photographer may wish to alter the automatic settings to achieve a particular result. Cameras equipped with an **exposure override** control allow the photographer to disengage the automatic functions and to revert to manual exposure control. (See Figure 2-27.)

Special-Function Cameras

Many cameras have been developed to meet particular needs or to perform special functions. A few of these are mentioned here to provide an idea of the variety of **special-function cameras** that exist today.

Instant Cameras and Film

One type of camera worth special mention is the **instant camera**. Using special instant film, this camera produces a finished print immediately after the picture is taken, without darkroom processing. The modern instant camera is designed to use a special film pack containing a complete system of chemically treated film and paper for either black-and-white or color prints. The processing chemicals are activated within the camera and, in seconds, a finished print is produced. (See Figure 2-28.)

Figure 2-28. A camera designed specifically for use with instant films.

A.

B.

Figure 2-29. A) Some professional cameras offer instant film backs as accessories B) which may be attached to the camera in place of the conventional film magazine.

The major advantage of instant photography, of course, is that a finished print is immediately available. A major disadvantage, however, is that duplicates and enlargements of the finished picture cannot be made easily. Although printable negatives can be obtained with a special type of instant film, duplicates and enlargements are usually available only by copying the original print. Some Polaroid materials produce instant positive transparencies in the same manner as the print films produce prints.

Many camera manufacturers provide interchangeable backs for their cameras suitable for the use of instant films. With such an accessory instant films can be used with most conventional medium- and large-format cameras. Working photographers commonly use such instant prints made with their normal cameras as proofs to check exposure, composition, lighting, and other critical factors before shooting their final exposure on conventional film. (See Figure 2-29.)

Special instant films are available for use in regular 35mm cameras. After exposure, the roll of special 35mm film is inserted along with a chemical pod into a small processing box. The user then turns a crank to combine the film and processing chemicals, waits a few seconds, and removes the developed film.

Various types of 35mm black-and-white instant transparency films are available, including a continuous tone material for pictorial use and a special high-contrast black-and-white positive film that is useful for producing slides of charts, graphs, and computer screens for public presentations. An instant 35mm color slide film is also available.

Panoramic or Wide-Format Cameras

There are essentially three ways to obtain photographic images that take in a wider angle of view than is normally seen by the human eye. One is to use what is called a wide-angle lens, which is discussed later in this unit. Another is to create a **montage** of several photographs, each of which has been taken from precisely the same camera position but with the camera pointed in a slightly different direction. (See Figure 2-30A.) These several photographs are then carefully trimmed,

aligned, and mounted so as to created a single, panoramic image. The third way is to use a **wide-format camera**. These cameras have either an external revolving lens and shutter or a special wide-angle optical system and produce long narrow images. They are especially useful for architectural work, panoramic landscapes, and large group photographs. (See Figures 2-1 and 2-30B.)

Underwater Cameras

Circumstances that require protecting camera equipment from water arise more often than we think. Certainly we might like to take a camera underwater on occasion to photograph the flora, fauna, and terrain. However, we may also find ourselves in the rain, in snow, on a canoe trip, or exposed to ocean spray. In all of these cases an ordinary camera may not be up to the task. The **underwater camera** is a specialized piece of equipment that is designed for use when fully submersed in water down to some specified depth. In addition, some manufacturers offer **underwater housings** designed for deep-water use of their particular models. Also, some specialty manufacturers make Plexiglas housings for general camera use. These, however, are generally not designed for

A.

B.

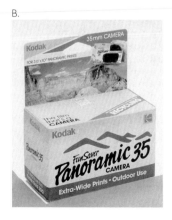

Figure 2-30. A) A montage of two or more frames may be used to create a panoramic effect. B) A special wide-format camera designed to produce panoramic views that are twice as wide as a normal postcard size print.

deep-water applications. Equipment designed for underwater use will also serve with other kinds of wet or severe shooting conditions.

Stereo Cameras

Stereo cameras are designed to take two pictures simultaneously through two separate but identical optical lenses spaced a few inches apart—like human eyes. The resulting image pair may then be mounted for use in a stereo viewer to obtain a three-dimensional view of the original scene. Some camera manufacturers make stereo attachments for use with their own models.

Press Cameras

Press cameras are often identified as special-function cameras. For many years press photographers preferred large-format cameras that could be used in a wide variety of situations—2 1/4in x 3 1/4in or 4in x 5in, for example—so that the images would not require great magnification. These old press cameras were simplified forms of view cameras fitted with optical, eye-level viewfinders and grips for hand-holding. For a long time the Speed Graphic camera was the standard of the industry. It was bulky, heavy, and hard to manage, but it was reliable and rugged. It used 4in x 5in sheet film, had an adjustable bellows, and certain versions had both focal plane and between-the-lens shutters. Figure 2-31 shows a 4in x 5in press camera.

Today's press photographer, however, often uses a variety of cameras, and any camera preferred by a press photographer may serve as a press camera. The availability of high-speed, fine-grained films, electronic flash units, and fast, high-resolution lenses makes possible the use of medium- and small-format cameras for press purposes. The press also routinely uses digital cameras, which are especially useful for working under tight deadline conditions. The press photographer often carries several lightweight cameras, supplementary lenses, and accessories for use under various conditions and for the many purposes encountered in press work.

Summary

Many types of cameras are available to suit a variety of needs, tastes, and special purposes. Cam-

Figure 2-31. A press camera is so-called because this type of camera was formerly used by photojournalists. Now they are a favorite of large-format photographers working on location.

eras are tools designed to solve specific problems; no one type of camera is ideally suited to all image-making situations. The choice of what camera to use or purchase depends on the kind of photographic subjects most often encountered. Working photographers who are called upon daily to handle a variety of subjects will probably have different and specialized camera systems for each need; their camera "tool-boxes" will likely grow as their photographic skills develop and their tastes expand.

Selecting a camera can prove a confusing and frustrating task for those with little prior experience in photography. In recent times, new camera technologies have developed so rapidly that today's newest model is likely to become obsolete within a few years. In fact, the economics of camera manufacture encourages rapid turnover of models so that owners will want to upgrade their equipment frequently and thereby create a constant market for new camera products.

No one camera or set of features will satisfy all needs and purposes. Each photographer develops unique working habits and becomes especially comfortable with some particular camera configuration. In the long run, only experience will reveal to you what features you are likely or unlikely to use. Only experience will show you what type of camera will best serve your own picture-taking style. Obviously, there is little economic advantage to paying a premium for features that you do not need and will not use. The novice photographer, therefore, is usually well advised to begin with a borrowed, hand-me-down, or inexpensive camera that provides adjustable focus, aperture, and shutter speed. A little experience will improve one's judgment about what additional features will be likely to prove useful in the longer run. A good beginning camera for the serious photographer would be a moderately priced 35mm SLR or digital camera with a manual exposure override. Such cameras are relatively easy to use, and the exposure override allows the photographer to explore the fundamentals of photography as well as maintain creative control.

Although there are many quality camera brands on the market—almost all of them capable of producing fine images—certain makes and especially certain models within brands tend to stand out and are most often chosen by professional photographers for their combination of features, quality, durability, and adaptability. If you are seriously considering a career in photography, you would be well advised to investigate which major brands and models are most used by the working professionals in your area and select your camera system accordingly. If you own the brand most popular with local professionals, you will have access to a greater range of rental and company-supplied "pool" equipment and lenses than will those who own cameras with other styles and brands of lens mounts.

Lens Characteristics

Objective 2-C Describe two major characteristics of a camera lens and their effects on picture taking.

Key Concepts focal length (F), focal point, object at infinity, normal lens, image format, angle of view, telephoto lens, wide-angle, zoom lens, perspective, telephoto effect, wide-angle effect, speed, maximum aperture, f-number, f-number = F/d, optical zoom, digital zoom, bayonet mount, threaded mount, mounting adapter

Two major characteristics of the camera lens that affect the image are its focal length and its speed.

Focal Length

The **focal length (F)** of a lens is the distance between the lens and the **focal point** at which a sharp image of an **object at infinity** is formed. Have you ever used a magnifying glass to focus an image of the sun on a piece of paper or a leaf? The focal length of the magnifying glass is the distance between the glass and the image of the sun on the paper when it is in sharp focus. The sun, of course, is very far away and we may consider it an object at infinity. Practically speaking, we may consider any object more than fifty feet away from the lens an object at infinity. Figure 2-32 shows how the focal length (F) of a lens is determined.

The manufacturer inscribes the focal length on the lens barrel. The focal length of some lenses never changes because it is a characteristic of the design to which the lens is ground. Zoom lenses, however, may be set to perform as the equivalent of many different focal lengths.

Normally a camera is fitted with a "normal" lens that has a field of view approximately the same as that seen by a human when staring straight ahead with one eye closed. Such normal lenses have a focal length roughly equal to the diagonal of the **image format** used in that camera. Thus the **normal lens** for a 35mm camera using a 24mm x 36mm format would be approximately 50mm. The normal lens for a medium-format camera producing 2 1/4in x 2 1/4in (6cm x 6 cm) images would be approximately 3in (80mm). Figure 2-33 shows how this was calculated using the formula for finding the diagonal of a square based on the length of the image format.

Lenses with longer or shorter focal lengths have differing **angles of view**. That is, they usually see less or more of the peripheral details in a scene than would a normal lens at the same distance. Figure 2-34 shows the different angles of view usually associated with lenses of differing focal lengths.

Lenses having a longer-than-normal focal length are commonly known as **telephoto lenses**; they increase the size of the image on the film. Objects are effectively brought closer to the camera; the effect is similar to looking through a telescope. For 35mm size cameras, any lens with a focal length much longer than the normal 50mm is considered to be a telephoto; for example, a 105mm lens is moderate telephoto.

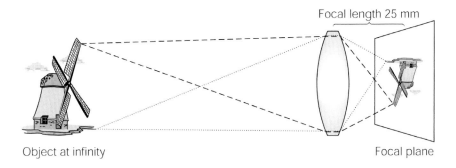

Focal length 25 mm

Object at infinity

Focal plane

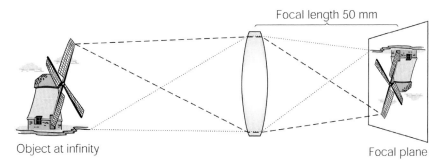

Focal length 50 mm

Object at infinity

Focal plane

Figure 2-32. Focal length (F) is the distance between the optical center of a lens and the focal point for an object at infinity. Note that increasing focal length also increases the size of the image on the focal plane.

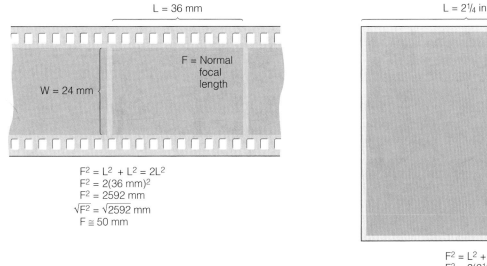

L = 36 mm

W = 24 mm

F = Normal focal length

$$F^2 = L^2 + L^2 = 2L^2$$
$$F^2 = 2(36 \text{ mm})^2$$
$$F^2 = 2592 \text{ mm}$$
$$\sqrt{F^2} = \sqrt{2592} \text{ mm}$$
$$F \cong 50 \text{ mm}$$

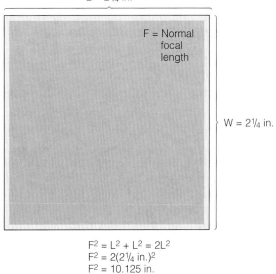

L = 2¼ in.

F = Normal focal length

W = 2¼ in.

$$F^2 = L^2 + L^2 = 2L^2$$
$$F^2 = 2(2¼ \text{ in.})^2$$
$$F^2 = 10.125 \text{ in.}$$
$$\sqrt{F^2} = \sqrt{10.125} \text{ in.}$$
$$F \cong 3 \text{ in. (or about 80 mm)}$$

Figure 2-33. The focal length (F) of a normal lens is approximately equal to the diagonal of a square based on the length of the image format. Thus, for a standard 35mm negative format normal F = 50mm. The normal F for 2 1/4in x 2 1/4in (6cm x 6cm) film is approximately 3in (80mm).

The magnifying ability of a telephoto lens, or its ability to apparently bring objects closer to the camera, can be estimated by comparing the focal length of the telephoto lens to that of a normal lens for the same camera. Thus a 200mm lens on a 35mm film size camera has a focal length that is four times as long as the 50mm normal lens; such a telephoto lens can be expected to produce an image on film that is four times as large. Similarly, a 300mm lens might be thought of as a six-power telephoto.

Lenses with shorter-than-normal focal length are known as **wide-angle lenses**; their use will increase the camera's field of view. The effect is to reduce the image size of specific objects on the film; however, more peripheral detail is included in the picture at any given distance. As focal length

Focal Lengths

For practical purposes you can think of different lenses on a 35mm camera in this way:

■ Around 50mm = a normal focal length lens

■ Greater than 50mm = telephoto lens, has the effect of bringing objects closer, for example, an 80mm lens

■ Less than 50mm = a wide-angle lens, has the effect of seeing more in the frame, for example a 28mm

As a practical guide:

■ Doubling the focal length will double the image size. An object will be twice as big in a photograph taken with a 100mm lens compared to one made with a 50mm lens at the same camera position.

■ Cutting the focal length in half will double the field of view. A 24mm lens sees an area about twice as wide as a 50mm lens.

See Figures 10-19 A, B, C, D, E on page 353 for examples.

Approximate Equivalent Focal Lengths for Various Film Formats

	Film Size				Angle of View
	35mm	2¼ × 2¼	2¼ × 2¾	4 × 5	
Wide-angle lenses	15mm	22mm	28mm	54mm	100°
	21mm	32mm	40mm	75mm	81°
	28mm	45mm	50mm	90mm	65–68°
	35mm	50mm	65mm	125mm	53–55°
Normal lenses	**50mm**	**80mm**	**90mm**	**180mm**	**39–44°**
Telephoto lenses	70mm	100mm	125mm	210mm	30–35°
	85mm	125mm	150mm	300mm	24°
	100mm	150mm	180mm	350mm	20°
	135mm	180mm	250mm	450mm	15–17°
	200mm	300mm	375mm	700mm	10°
	400mm	600mm			5°

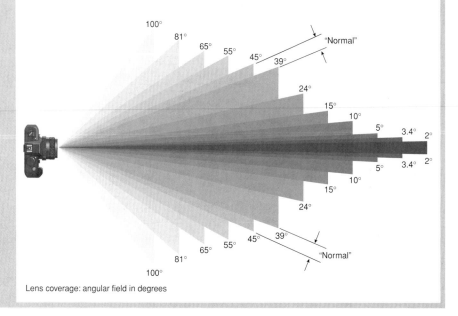

Lens coverage: angular field in degrees

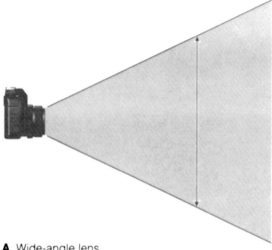

A Wide-angle lens.
The field of view is expanded, but image size of specific details is reduced.

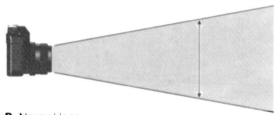

B Normal lens.
The field of view is smaller than with a wide-angle lens, but the image size is larger.

C Telephoto lens.
The size of the image is increased, but the field of view is reduced.

Figure 2-34. Angles of view with various lenses. As focal length increases, the angle of view decreases.

decreases, the image magnification likewise decreases, but the angle of view increases. For example, switching from a 50mm normal lens to a 25mm wide-angle lens would result in an angle of view that is twice as wide, and individual objects in the resulting image would be only half as large.

A **zoom lens** has a variable focal length designed to be set at any point between the limits of its range. A 28-85mm zoom lens, for example, may be set at any focal length between a 28mm wide-angle and an 85mm telephoto by adjusting a ring on its barrel. Zoom lenses permit the photographer to instantly change focal lengths and offer a

compact and affordable alternative to carrying several conventional lenses. Zoom lenses rarely match the maximum apertures and speed of fixed-focal-length lenses, however, and less expensive zooms may not be quite as sharp.

Perspective In addition to changing the angle of view, the focal length of the lens used is also related to linear **perspective**—different focal lengths affect the relative size and spacing of objects at different distances from the camera. A long lens not only photographs a smaller target area than a wide-angle; it also produces a different spatial rendering of the subject. Photographers often speak of a **telephoto effect** whereby objects in a scene seem abnormally compressed and the space appears flattened. The opposite perspective distortion occurs when wide-angle lenses are used. In a **wide-angle effect**, space appears to be stretched, and the distance between near and far objects looks exaggerated. These variations from normal perspective can be powerful tools with which the creative worker can interpret a scene, and photographers often consider these factors when selecting a lens to create a particular statement. (See Figure 2-35.)

For more information on lens use and selection, see Unit 3, *Camera Controls*.

Speed

A second major characteristic of a lens is its **speed**. The speed of a lens indicates how much light the lens will transmit when it is open to its widest aperture. Just as a large window allows much light into a room, a large lens opening allows much light into the camera. Smaller windows, like smaller apertures, allow less light to pass. The speed of a lens is expressed by the symbol f/-, such as f/1.4, or f/2.0. The more light the lens allows to pass, the "faster" the lens and the smaller the f-number.

The f-numbering system is a precise way of expressing the relationship between the diameter (d) of the lens at its **maximum aperture** and the focal length (F) of the lens. The **f-number** of a lens is calculated as follows:

f-number = focal length/lens diameter

For example, if the focal length is 50mm and the diameter of the lens at its maximum aperture is 25mm, then the speed of that lens is

A.

B.

Figure 2-35. A) Telephoto compression. Notice how the ascending rows of stadium bleachers have been compressed into a single plane in this view made with a 400mm telephoto lens. B) Wide-angle effect. Wide-angle lenses tend to open up and exaggerate near-far perspectives as in this photograph made with a 24mm wide-angle lens.

50mm/25mm = f/2.0

The manufacturer inscribes the maximum f-number on the barrel of the lens. An f/2.0 lens has a diameter that measures one-half of its focal length; an f/4.0 lens has a diameter one-fourth of its focal length, and so on. The greater the diameter of the lens, the more light can pass through it at its widest aperture. Thus for any given focal length, larger diameter lenses are faster lenses; f/2.0 is faster than f/4.0, f/4.0 is faster than f/5.6, and so on.

Any given f-number defines an exact relationship between the lens aperture and the area of the image format no matter what camera or lens is in use. Thus f/8 on a normal lens of a 35mm film-sized camera represents the same exposure setting as f/8 on a telephoto lens of a large-format view camera. The system of f-numbers provides a common standard of light measurement for all cameras under all conditions.

Lenses for Digital Cameras

Apart from the CCD in a digicam, the lens is the most important element that affects image quality. Most consumer-grade digital cameras use an imaging sensor chip that is much smaller than a frame of 35mm film, often 1/2in to 2/3in in size. Due to their small size, the "normal" digicam lenses have much smaller focal lengths than the equivalent "normal" lenses of 35mm cameras.

Unlike 35mm cameras, however, the image format of digicams varies from one camera to another. So a "normal" focal length for one digicam will not necessarily be a "normal" focal length for another. Any film-camera lens will perform as a longer focal length lens when used with most digicams. For example, a 50mm lens, considered "normal" for a 35mm camera, will perform as a telephoto lens with a digicam. To provide a standard base of comparison, most manufacturers describe digicam focal lengths with their 35mm camera equivalents. Digicam manufacturers typically provide a table of equivalent 35mm focal lengths.

While entry-level digicams usually have an optical viewfinder and a fixed lens, the more popular models come equipped with a zoom lens that may vary from wide-angle to telephoto—typically from about 5mm to 15mm. Thus, a 5–15mm digicam zoom lens might be described as the 35mm equivalent of a 28-110mm zoom lens. It should be noted, however, that zoom lenses on digicams are usually not interchangeable among cameras from different manufacturers. However, professional SLR digicams often accept the same interchangeable lenses as their film camera siblings from the same manufacturer. Every lens will have three specifications: focal length, aperture, and close (macro) focus.

Zoom lenses on digicams operate manually, allowing the photographer to zoom in, increasing the focal length and narrowing the angle of view, or to zoom out, decreasing the focal length and widening the angle of view. Most digicams offer both **optical zoom** and **digital zoom** features. Optical zoom is a true zoom, performed by the lens, which resolves an image on the entire CCD. **Digital zoom**, on the other hand, is an enlarging process, performed by the camera, which programmatically "blows up" the image and crops in on a section of it. This process results in a reduction in image quality since you are asking the camera to create pixels that don't exist as it increases the size of the image.

The total zoom capability of a camera is the product of its optical and digital zoom magnification. Thus a camera with 4X optical zoom and 3X digital zoom will have 12X total zoom capability. If you must enlarge a portion of the image, using digital zoom with the camera will usually result in a cleaner image than enlarging after the fact in an image editor. In all cases digitally enlarging an image will produce lower quality results than using optical zoom.

Some digicams can also accept add-on wide-angle and telephoto conversion lenses to extend the range of focal lengths. Those designed especially for your make and model camera will likely provide the best quality. These add-on lenses are additional pieces of gear that add to your picture-taking tasks, however, so it's better to get as much range as possible in the standard zoom that you'll use with your camera.

Mounting Systems

Cameras that allow photographers to change lenses employ lens mounting systems for attaching lenses to the camera body. Most such cameras employ a **bayonet mount** system, in which the lens is aligned and seated in the mount and rotated a quarter turn to lock it in place. Some cameras use a **threaded mount** system, in which the lens is screwed into place in the camera body. Most manufacturers use their own mounting design, so that one manufacturer's lenses generally will not fit the camera body of another brand. However, some in-

Figure 2-36. A bayonet-type lens mounting system. Notice how the flanges on the lens interconnect with the corresponding openings on the camera. Also visible are the electronic connections for auto focusing.

Table 2-4. Selecting a lens for a 35mm camera

Subject or Setting	Commonly used lens type	Other choices	Notes
Working in cramped interiors	Extreme wide-angle lens, 15mm to 20mm	Wide-angle lens, 24 to 28mm	Wide-angle zoom
Landscape or cityscape grand views	20mm to 35mm focal length lens	28–80 or similar zoom	"Stitch" together multiple shots in image editing program to form a panorama
Large groups of people	28mm or wide-angle zoom	24mm in smaller rooms	35mm wide-angle lens
Indoors without a flash	"Fast" 50mm f/1.8 or f/1.4 lens	f/2.8 lens	Use a tripod or select a faster film or digital setting
Close-up photography of stamps, flowers and the like	A true macro lens for up to life-size magnifications	Macro setting on zoom lens for lower magnifications	Extension tubes or supplemental close-up lens
Portraits of people framed head and shoulders	85mm to 135mm lens	80–200 zoom lens or similar	Teleconverter used with a shorter lens
Outdoor sports at various distances	100–300 zoom lens or similar	80–200 zoom lens or similar	Teleconverter with zoom
Distant sports events	400mm or longer telephoto	Long telephoto zoom	Teleconverter with zoom
Wildlife	300mm to 500mm telephoto lens	Very long telephoto zoom	Teleconverter with zoom

dependent lens makers manufacture **mounting adapters** that make it possible to mount their lenses to many popular camera bodies.

Common Accessories

Objective 2-D Describe several common accessories used with adjustable cameras.

Key Concepts lens hood, LCD hood, UV (ultraviolet) and skylight filter, lens cap, tripod, cable or remote release, camera case, camera or gadget bag, memory cards, batteries, exposure meter, flash meter, flash unit, filters, automatic winder, supplementary lenses, teleconverter, dioptric correction lens, printer dock, interface cables

Hundreds of accessories are commonly available for simple as well as for complex cameras. Many are frequently, even constantly, useful, while others are useful only rarely for special purposes. Some of these accessories are described briefly here in the general order of their usefulness in beginning photography.

Lens Hood A **lens hood** is a detachable device fitted to the front of the lens to shade the lens surface from extraneous light. Use of a lens hood can improve image quality by reducing internal flare.

Eliminating stray light can, at times, dramatically improve color saturation, increase contrast, and even boost apparent sharpness. A lens hood also helps protect the lens from accidental damage; many professionals use heavy-duty metal hoods to help protect their expensive lenses against damage from severe impact.

LCD Hood Similarly, an **LCD hood** is often useful to shield the LCD viewing screen found on most digital cameras. The LCD hood is a cone-like attachment that blocks stray light from striking the screen and makes it easier to view the displayed image as well as to navigate the camera's menu screens.

UV and Skylight Filter To prevent accidental bumps and scratches of the lens surface, almost all photographers semi-permanently mount a clear **UV** or **skylight filter** on each lens in their bag.

Lens Cap A **lens cap** is a detachable, opaque cover fitted to the front of the lens to protect it and to block the passage of light. The lens cap is generally used when storing the camera, but it must be removed for picture taking. Some cameras with battery-operated light meters rely on use of the lens cap between shots to reduce battery drain. (See Figure 2-37.)

A.

B.

Figure 2-37. A) Lens hood and B) Lens cap

Tripod A **tripod** is a portable, three-legged device used to support and stabilize the camera when a photographer needs precise framing control or during lengthy setups and long exposures. When slow shutter speeds are used (as they are in weak lighting situations), the slightest movement of the camera will blur the image to some degree. A tripod is useful in such situations to eliminate the unavoidable movement of the hand-held camera.

Cable or Remote Release For slow shutter speeds, the use of a **cable release**—or a remote release in the case of electronic cameras—is also recommended. Such devices enable the photographer to release the shutter without touching any part of the camera body, thereby avoiding camera movement. (See Figure 2-38.)

Camera Case A snug-fitting **camera case** designed to enclose and protect the camera is generally available for most cameras. These cases are designed so that the camera can be used quickly, without being removed from the case. Most photographers, however, prefer to remove the camera case altogether while shooting, to reduce weight and to simplify camera handling and film chang-

ing. Many manufacturers also make hard-bodied, fitted camera cases for their equipment, designed to hold the camera along with several accessories in neat compartments for storing and shipping.

Camera or Gadget Bag Probably more useful in actual shooting is the soft-bodied **camera bag**, often called a **gadget bag**, designed to be carried from the shoulder. These are made in a great variety of sizes and shapes with various, often adjustable, interior compartments and pockets, suitable for any photographer's camera equipment and shooting style. (See Figure 2-39.)

Memory Cards Carrying extra **memory cards** is a useful guarantee that your digital camera won't run out of storage space. If you fill your memory card with pictures that you want to keep and you have no immediate way to download them to your computer, you'll be ready to take more pictures with extra memory cards.

Batteries Carrying extra **batteries** also will guarantee that you won't run out of power at some critical moment. To be sure that you never

Figure 2-38. A tripod mounted camera with a cable release.

Figure 2-39. Soft-bodied camera bag.

miss a picture, keep an extra set of batteries on hand.

Exposure Meter Although many modern cameras are equipped with built-in exposure meters, a separate **meter** is an essential accessory for the precision use of an adjustable camera. It is used to measure the intensity of light in various parts of a given scene and to aid in determining exposure. Many external meters also function as **flash meters** to determine exposure with professional strobe units. Use of exposure meters is explained in Unit 3, and flash meters are covered in Unit 13. (See Figure 2-40.)

Flash Unit Although many modern cameras are equipped with built-in flash units, an external **flash unit** is essential for controlling, supplementing, and improving lighting conditions for any photography beyond simple snapshots. The electronic flash or strobe units in common use provide a measured burst of light synchronized with the camera's shutter. The use of flash units is explained in Unit 13.

Filters The way the human eye perceives colors does not always agree with the way film or digital sensors record those colors. To be sure that colors are recorded the way you wish them to appear, it is often necessary to use filters. A **filter** is a detachable device fitted to the front of the lens and designed to alter the color, intensity, or quality of the transmitted light. By this means, the recording of various colors can be controlled

to obtain the desired or special effects. Use of filters is explained in Unit 11.

Automatic Winder Although most newer cameras have built-in automatic winders, accessory **automatic winders** are generally available for those that do not. An automatic winder advances the film automatically after each exposure. Because the viewfinder need not be taken from the eye to advance the film, it is useful for photographing rapid action or fast-moving events.

Supplementary Lenses **Supplementary lenses** can help you enhance your pictures in several ways:

- A telephoto lens brings the action closer to you.
- A wide-angle lens captures a wider field of view.
- A close-up lens allows you to focus on objects only inches from your camera.

On some cameras, you may use separate, interchangeable lenses for these effects. In other cases, you may attach supplementary lenses to other lenses to change their optical performance. For example, you may use a **teleconverter** to increase the focal length of a lens. Commonly available as 2X, 3X, or 4X converters, these accesso-

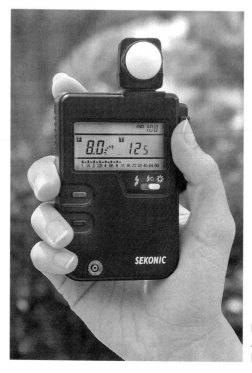

Figure 2-40. A hand-held light meter.

ries will double, triple, or quadruple, respectively, the focal length of any lens used with them. A 50mm lens used with a 3X converter, for example, becomes a 150mm lens.

In addition, lens attachments may be used to change a lens's focal length to produce telephoto, wide-angle, and close-focusing performance. Such attachments are generally available for consumer-grade digital cameras. The most common supplementary lenses are used for portraits, close-ups, and special effects. A special adapter may be required to attach supplementary lenses to your camera.

Extension Tubes and Bellows These devices are sometimes used with interchangeable lenses to make extreme close-ups. (See Figure 2-41.)

Dioptric Correction Lens Eyeglass wearers may find that their glasses interfere with eye-level viewing and focusing. To view and focus without glasses, a **dioptric correction lens** may be attached to the viewfinder. The manufacturers of

most adjustable cameras make dioptric lenses in various strengths that can be attached easily to the viewfinder to correct most common vision problems. In addition, some modern cameras provide a built-in, adjustable dioptric correction. For more severe vision problems, many manufacturers will grind special lenses to prescription.

Printer Dock Some manufacturers of digital cameras offer a **printer dock** that simplifies printing pictures directly from the camera. A printer dock is an external printing device that interfaces directly with the digital camera and produces hard copy paper prints from the recorded images.

Interface Cables Digital cameras provide built-in connectors that allow you to connect the camera directly to your computer or to an external display device, such as your television set. Completing these connections requires special **interface cables** that link the camera to the external devices so that you can copy, print, or display your pictures.

Figure 2-41. Camera accessories designed to extend the uses of lenses. A) Teleconverter (extender) B) Extension tubes C) Extension bellows D) Supplemental lenses

C.

A.

B.

D.

The accessories discussed here are those that are most commonly used in general photography, although hundreds of others are made and sold to meet a great variety of special needs and purposes.

Care of the Camera

Objective 2-E Describe some important camera "housekeeping" practices.

Key Concepts lens tissue, lens-cleaning solvent, lens cap, lens brush, spring tension, light fog, AC power adapter

Good housekeeping in photography begins with the camera. If you want to lengthen your camera's life and get the most out of it, you should take good care of it. The best resource for camera care and safety advice is the user's manual that came with your camera. Whether it is a film camera or digital camera, these guidelines will help.

1. Keep the lens clean and protect it from chips, scratches, dampness, and heat.

   The most vulnerable part of your camera is the lens. It is especially important to keep the lens clean, because dust particles can show up as dots on photos. It is a precision instrument—in most cases, a combination of several soft glass elements. Some are cemented together with a resin that is affected by heat or dampness. For safe cleaning:

   - Wipe the entire surface of the camera using a clean, dry, soft cloth.
   - Use an air blower, soft brush, a clean, soft, lint-free cloth, or special **lens tissue** on the camera lens and LCD screen to eliminate dust.

   Some caveats regarding safe lens cleaning:

   - Avoid blowing on the lens as breath contains moisture and acids that may harm the lens.
   - Avoid chemically treated tissues that may cause scratching.
   - Avoid lens tissue designed for eyeglasses.
   - Avoid soiled cloth and facial tissue that may contain dust or brittle fibers that could scratch the soft lens surface.

   - Do not touch the lens surface with your fingers—they will deposit oils and acids harmful to your lens.
   - Do not apply pressure when cleaning the surface of a photographic lens.
   - For a lens too thickly coated with dirt or fingerprints, use a drop or two of photographic **lens-cleaning solvent**. Avoid lens-cleaning solutions designed for eyeglasses. Apply lens-cleaning solvent to a lens tissue and then gently to the lens—never directly to the surface of the lens.
   - Hand-held canisters of compressed air made to photographic standards are available commercially and may be used for cleaning lenses. A rubber bulb syringe is also handy for blowing away dust particles.

   For protection: If the lens does not fold back into the camera body, where it is protected, use a **lens cap** and store the camera in a case or drawer. Many photographers prefer to use a UV or skylight filter over the lens at all times to protect it from scratches. When the camera is idle, keep it in a cool, dry, clean place.

2. Keep your camera clean and protect it from heat, shock, and dampness.

   You can purchase camera-cleaning kits that include an air blower, a soft cloth, and everything else you need to keep your camera in top condition.

   Cleaning your camera not only keeps it looking shiny and new, but it also improves the quality of your photos.

   Dust sometimes seeps into the interior of a camera. Dust on the film or image sensor shows up as black blemishes on the finished prints. Make it a habit to keep the inner face of the lens and inner surfaces of the camera dust free. Use a soft **lens brush** for cleaning the interior of the camera when changing film, but avoid touching the fragile shutter mechanism. For film cameras, clean the film pressure plate on the camera's back occasionally with a lightly moistened cloth to remove any accumulated film particles.

   Keep everything together in a padded case with a good strap for easy transport. A good camera case or bag will protect against dust

Famous Photograph

First Halftone, March 4, 1880

Although photography was widely used for personal and artistic purposes in its first sixty years, it was not used much for news reporting. There was no practical way to print a photograph with ink on paper and to preserve the gradations of tones. Pictures that did appear in magazines and newspapers were printed from wood and metal engravings that were cut by hand. Photography was used only to provide the original image from which the engravings were copied.

Almost from the beginning of photography, printers and crafts workers sought a means for printing photographs in printers ink on newsprint along with the type. Many attempts were made dating from the early 1860s, but it was not until the *New York Daily Graphic* published this photograph in its March 4, 1880, issue that a practical means for doing so was demonstrated.

The *New York Daily Graphic* was established in 1873 expressly to promote the use of photography in news reporting. Stephen J. Horgan was hired as photographer and soon became manager of the newspaper's photomechanical printing operations. Horgan built upon the earlier work of F. W. von Egglofstein, Georg Meisenbach, and Frederic E. Ives to develop the halftone process by which this photograph was printed.

Describing this picture when it appeared, the *Daily Graphic* wrote:

We have dealt heretofore with pictures made from drawing or engravings. Here we have one direct from nature. . . . We are still experimenting with it . . . and feel confident . . . that pictures will eventually be regularly printed in our pages direct from photographs without the intervention of drawing.

Stephen T. Horgan, "Shanty Town Dwellings," March 4, 1880.

Despite its early success, it took more than a generation before halftones significantly replaced hand engraving as a method of reproducing news pictures in the press.

By defining a continuous tone image as a matrix of discrete dots, or points of data, Horgan's halftone process laid the foundation for the development of digital imaging technology that would follow a century later.

and shield the camera from casual bumps and shocks. Also, most digital camera cases have built-in pockets for batteries and memory cards.

Store your camera in a cool, dry place away from dampness, heat, and direct sunlight.

Keep your camera equipment with you as carry-on when traveling. Do not check it through with suitcases—rough handling and extreme temperatures can damage it.

3. **Relax all mechanical tensions and remove batteries during inactive periods.**

Do not leave the mechanical shutter of your camera cocked when the camera is to be stored for a period of time. It is good practice with an older film camera to release all **spring tension** adjustments built into it before storing it. Springs under tension tend to lose their strength over time and shutter speeds or other fine adjustments may become unreliable.

It is good practice with battery-powered cameras and accessories to remove batteries to prevent damage from leakage if they are to be stored for any significant length of time.

4. **Load film in subdued light, store it in a cool, dry place, and avoid exposure to high-energy electromagnetic radiation, such as X-rays.**

Light fog is the unwanted exposure of the film to some ambient source of light. The packaging of modern film provides excellent protection from light, and with reasonable care all danger of light fog can be eliminated. Nevertheless, you should avoid loading film in direct sunlight. Handling film in direct, strong sunlight may expose the edges of the film and thus damage the film.

A similar fog can result from multiple passes through the X-ray detectors used by airport security. Some photographers protect their film with lead bags or request a visual baggage inspection to avoid all possibility of such a fog occurring.

Likewise, avoid storing film where it may be exposed to heat. During summer months, any place that has high temperatures from trapped heat should be avoided. A suitcase carried on top of a car and exposed to the sun may become excessively hot during a trip; it is a poor

place to store film. Buy fresh film as you need it. Many photographers refrigerate film in its unopened, original, airtight packaging for maximum freshness. Refrigerated film must be brought to normal temperature before use.

5. Handle digital "film" carefully.

The small postage-stamp-sized memory cards that are used to record digital images are thin and delicate. Handle them carefully and transport them only in special card storage boxes where they cannot be damaged. Download the images to a computer after every important photo shoot, and be sure to make a back-up zip disk or CD-ROM of the new files.

6. Have the camera inspected regularly.

Have an expert inspect the camera for light leaks and internal dirt in the lens approximately once a year. The shutter and diaphragm should be tested for accuracy. For film cameras, the mechanism for holding the film flat during exposures should be checked. Small maladjustments in your camera can lead to major disappointments in the final photographs.

7. Never attempt to repair or service the camera yourself.

Never open your camera's casing or attempt to repair the camera yourself. Touching the inside of a digital camera can result in electric shock. Cameras are precision instruments. Only a skilled, reputable technician should perform repairs and service. Resist any temptation to do this work yourself; you will avoid needless expense and regret.

8. Weatherproof your camera.

Properly care for your camera when you're on the go. Avoid extreme temperatures. Protect it from direct sunlight when it is hot; tuck it under your coat when it is cold. Carry your camera close to your body in cold climates since abrupt temperature changes can cause condensation. In wet weather, protect your camera with a plain, old plastic bag. Make a hole for the lens and secure it with a rubber band.

If moisture does seep into your camera, turn it off immediately and remove the batteries.

Remove the memory card from digital cameras. Allow the camera to air-dry for 24 hours before operating it again.

9. **Care for your batteries.**

Most modern cameras work with rechargeable nickel cadmium (NiCd), nickel metal hydride (NiMH) or lithium ion batteries. Always keep spares on hand to avoid losing battery power in the midst of a shoot.

You should care for your camera's batteries carefully. Here are some guidelines:

- Do not expose batteries to temperatures above 110° F (43° C).
- Do not overcharge batteries.
- Recharge batteries before or after longterm storage. They will discharge over time and, if not recharged, may leak and damage the camera.
- Do not mix old and new batteries or batteries of different types.
- Do not incinerate or puncture batteries or throw old batteries away. They are chemical waste. Follow the manufacturer's or other recommended guidelines for disposal and recycling batteries.

10. **Use a proper AC adapter.**

Most modern and digital cameras provide for using an **AC power adapter** to operate without batteries or to recharge the batteries. Adapters are manufactured to various power specifications and it is important to use only an AC power adapter approved by the camera's manufacturer. Failure to do so can damage the camera, cause a fire, and void the camera's warranty.

Travelers should note that the electrical systems of the United States and those of other countries are different. The U.S. system is based on 120 volts, 60Hz; overseas it is based on 220 volts, 50Hz. Wall outlets and plugs also differ. You will need an adapter kit with a universal plug and voltage adapter if you want to plug in your battery charger, AC adapter, and other equipment overseas. Consult your camera's manual.

Good Habits of Camera Use

Objective 2-F Describe some good habits of camera use.

Key Concepts expiration date, outdated film, film advance, viewfinder, range, focus setting, infinity setting (∞), camera shake

1. Label a film camera with the kind of film in it and its expiration date.

The kind of film loaded in a film camera and its **expiration date** may be forgotten over time. Different films have different photographic qualities and, as film ages, its sensitivity to light and color may become impaired. Eventually the film may become totally useless. Never shoot with **outdated film**. If your camera has one, use the film identification window to note the type of film loaded in the camera and its expiration date. Otherwise, affix a small tab of masking tape to the camera noting this information.

2. Make sure the film is loaded properly into a film camera.

Improper film loading of 35mm cameras has resulted in countless lost images for amateurs and professionals alike. If you thread the film improperly on the take-up spool, the film will not advance from shot to shot. Some cameras are designed to indicate proper film movement and some load film automatically. Check the camera's user manual for film advance indicator it provides.

3. For film cameras, advance the film after each exposure.

To be sure you do not lose picture opportunities, operate the **film advance** after each exposure. Battery operated cameras advance the film automatically; however, older cameras require you to advance the film manually. In any case, you will want the camera ready when your next shot presents itself. For manual cameras, be sure to shoot off the last picture to release the shutter spring before putting the camera away.

4. Carry extra film or flash memory cards.

Do not risk running out of your recording medium on a photographic expedition. Always carry a few extra rolls of film or an extra flash memory card. Be prepared for any extraordinary lighting conditions you may encounter.

5. Use your viewfinder.

A grand scenic view may dazzle the eye, but the camera won't take in anything outside the image frame. The camera's **viewfinder** is designed to show exactly what details will appear in the image frame. Use the viewfinder or, in the case of digital cameras, the LCD viewing screen, to carefully compose the photograph within that frame.

A camera that has automatic focusing may focus only on objects near the middle of the frame, even though you may prefer a less centered composition. Careful pre-focusing and use of the focus-lock feature will solve this problem.

6. Correct for parallax error when shooting close-ups with a viewfinder camera.

With cameras that have optical viewfinding systems that are separate from the picture-taking system, the viewfinder may not see exactly the same image as the picture-taking lens, especially when the subject is a close-up. If necessary, correct for this discrepancy by pointing the camera slightly in the direction of the viewfinder after composing your image. (See Figures 2-11 and 2-12.)

7. Know the camera's capabilities.

Do not try to take pictures beyond the camera's capabilities. If shutter speeds or lens apertures faster than those that are possible with the camera are necessary, the finished photographs will be disappointing. Know how your camera works and what it will do so that picture taking will become automatic.

8. Get the range.

The **focus setting** should be accurate for subjects at any distance, but it is especially important at shorter camera-to-subject distances. For distances less than 6 feet, focus especially carefully. For distances of 30 feet or more, focusing has wider latitude—the distance need only be approximated. With a normal focal length lens, the **infinity setting** (∞) can be used if the camera-to-subject distance exceeds 50 feet.

9. Avoid camera shake.

Camera shake, or any movement of the camera while the shutter is in motion, results in a blurred image. Learn to handle the camera so that the shutter release is operated by one finger using a gentle squeeze, while the rest of the hand holds the camera steady. Stand firmly with legs apart. Support the camera not only with your hands but also with your whole body. If you are using an eye-level viewfinder, snuggle the camera against your cheekbone. When using slow shutter speeds, hold your breath while releasing the shutter. When using very slow shutter speeds, rest the camera on a solid object, lean against a stable object, or use a tripod while shooting.

10. Wait before loading up with accessories.

Do not succumb to the temptation to buy too many accessories until you know how you will use the camera and what the camera can do without them. A good camera, used well, will probably produce results that are as good as or better than those produced by a mediocre camera that is used poorly and is cluttered with unnecessary accessories.

HOW TO USE THIS BOOK

At the end of each unit, starting with this one, you will find Questions to Consider. These questions are intended to help you check your own understanding and knowledge of the topics. Concluding each unit are Suggested Field and Laboratory Assignments. These assignments are designed to give you practical photographic experience by providing opportunities for you to assemble equipment as well as to shoot, process, print, and display pictures using the techniques and principles discussed in the unit.

You may also wish to refer to any of the many references at the back of the book for further study and clarification of the topics in each unit.

Questions to Consider

1. How do the viewing systems used by the four camera types (VF, SLR, TLR, and view camera) differ, and how are they the same? Which viewing type or types is the most accurate? Which is the fastest to use?

2. Compare a typical viewfinder type camera to a single-lens reflex camera. What are the advantages and disadvantages of each? Consider size, cost, speed, versatility, and ease of use, among other factors.

3. How does a focus-free camera differ from one with auto focus?

4. What are the advantages of a medium-format film size? How would you calculate the focal length of a normal lens for a medium-format film camera that produces negatives 6cm x 7cm (2 1/4in x 2 3/4in)? Compare film and digital cameras with respect to format and resolution.

5. What are four advantages and disadvantages of digital cameras?

6. Look at a current copy of *National Geographic*. Can you tell which photographs were made with telephoto lenses and which were made with wide-angle lenses? Were any special types of cameras or accessories used to produce the photographs in that issue?

Suggested Field and Laboratory Assignments

1. Make an appointment to meet with a local professional who works in the area of photography in which you are most interested. Ask what type of equipment he or she uses most often and what brands and models are commonly used by colleagues in the field. You may also wish to ask about rental and repair facilities in your area for the brand of camera you are considering. Working photographers can provide a wealth of information as well as become valuable career contacts. You will find that most professional photographers are very willing to meet with students who courteously book an appointment with them in advance.

2. Assemble your camera kit and supplies. Make a list of optional equipment and accessories you might consider purchasing at a later date. Suggested starter lists are provided in Appendix A.

3. Arrange for the use of a photographic darkroom and equipment. Darkrooms and equipment are often available through schools, community centers, recreation centers, photographic retailers, and photography clubs. Try looking up Darkroom Rentals in the Yellow Pages.

4. Arrange to use "digital darkroom" equipment such as a film scanner and a computer equipped with image-editing software like Photoshop. Such workstations are often available in schools or can be rented by the hour at service bureaus.

5. Explore the "photography" category on the Yahoo home page and visit several web sites devoted to photography. Then look up "digital cameras" in your search engine and visit some of those sites. You'll also find many useful web links on the CD that came with this book.

Camera Controls

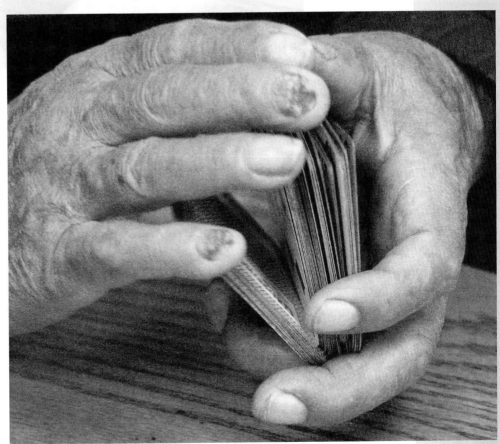

Lisa Hart,
"Hands at Senior Center."

Unit at a Glance

Modern cameras are complex devices that incorporate advanced electronic, mechanical, and optical features. Although they are designed to be easy to use, their appearance often belies their sophisticated engineering. Within most modern cameras are features that control focus, aperture, shutter speed, flash synchronization, and viewfinding—sometimes managed manually by the photographer and sometimes automatically by internal computerized devices.

The final appearance of a photograph is governed as much by the interaction of all of these variables at the time of exposure as it is by the image processing and printing controls that occur afterwards.

The amount of light that is captured by the film or digital sensor is called exposure. Recording media vary in their sensitivity to light, but to record an image of normal exposure, all need a specific amount of light at a given sensitivity. Too little light will lead to a darker than normal or underexposed image; too much will yield a lighter than normal or overexposed image. Exposure is determined by the combination of the recording medium's sensitivity or ISO speed, the lens aperture, and the shutter speed.

In general, proper exposure will produce details in both highlights and shadows. Most automatic cameras, film or digital, can calculate and set an optimal exposure for such a well-balanced image. However, to obtain particular results, the photographer will sometimes wish to override the camera's automatic setting.

This unit provides instruction on the many controls available on modern cameras and how these controls affect the recorded image.

Basic Camera Settings

Objective 3-A Name three basic settings found on adjustable cameras and describe their functions.

Key Concepts amount of light, sharpness, shutter speed, B-setting, T-setting, X-setting, aperture, f/stop, stopping down, opening up, maximum aperture, lens speed, full stop, half-stop, focus, split-image focusing, superimposed-image focusing, ground-glass focusing, automatic focusing

The three basic settings found on an adjustable camera are its shutter speed, lens opening, and focus. The shutter speed and lens opening determine the **amount of light** that strikes the film; the focus determines the **sharpness** of the image formed on the film.

Shutter Speed

Originally, a photographer would load film into the camera, remove the lens cap, time the exposure, and put the lens cap back on. With more

sensitive materials, exposures became shorter and shutters became more sophisticated. Two types of shutters emerged that are still used today.

Between the lens or leaf shutters operate like an iris with overlapping shutter blades. To make an exposure the shutter blades move apart for a brief moment and then close again. Adjusting the timing between the opening and closing of the iris controls exposure.

Focal plane shutters utilize two overlapping, opaque curtains that move either horizontally or vertically just in front of the film plane. The first curtain blocks the light path. During exposure it moves out of the way and is followed by the second curtain that covers the exposed film or CCD. Adjusting the timing between the two curtains controls exposure.

Although digicams often use mechanical shutters of similar design, some models use a CCD shutter. Adjusting the active sampling time of the sensor controls exposure. This method is completely

Figure 3-2. Shutter speed settings. A) Dial type focal plane shutter. B) Digital shutter display. C) Leaf shutter setting on lens barrel.

electronic, precise, and reliable and requires no mechanical movement. Because the exposure is completely silent, some models employ an audible "click" to indicate the exposure.

When the shutter is closed, no light can enter the camera body. When the shutter opens, light enters, striking the film until the shutter closes. The interval between the shutter's opening and closing is known as the **shutter speed**. Simple cameras may have only a single, fixed shutter speed; adjustable cameras have many.

Shutter speed settings are marked on the camera or displayed on a screen with numbers such as 30, 60, 125, 250, and 500. These numbers represent fractions of a second—1/30, 1/60, 1/125, 1/250, and 1/500 sec., respectively. A shutter speed of 30 will thus let in exactly twice as much light as a shutter speed of 60, because 1/30 sec. is twice as long as 1/60 sec. Figure 3-2 shows three types of shutter speed settings commonly found on adjustable cameras. This setting is sometimes found on the barrel of the lens, sometimes on the body of the camera, and sometimes in a digital display.

On most adjustable cameras the standard sequence of shutter settings is as follows: 1, 2, 4, 8, 15, 30, 60, 125, 250, 500, and 1,000.

Note that each shutter setting is approximately double the preceding one. Depending on the direction in which the shutter speed is adjusted, the exposure will be doubled or halved at each successive setting. Adjusting the shutter speed to double or halve the exposure is called adjusting the exposure by "one stop." Some cameras also provide shutter speeds slower than one second, often including settings up to more than a minute.

Often cameras with electronic shutters have additional speeds that are not listed above such as:

(1000) 800, 650, (500), 400, 320, (250), 200, 160, (125), 100, 80, (60), 50, 40, (30), 25, 20, (15), 13, 10, (8), 6, 5, (4), 3, 2.5, (2) 1.6, 1.3, and (1).

These additional shutter speeds represent intermediate settings. These intermediate speeds are usually spaced 1/3 of a stop apart.

Some older cameras also are equipped with a **B-setting** to allow the shutter to remain open as long as the release is depressed. When the release returns to its normal position, the shutter closes. Some cameras also are equipped with a **T-setting** to allow the shutter to open when the release is depressed and will remain open until the release is depressed a second time. Both B- and T-settings are used for time exposures longer than those provided by the shutter.

Aperture

Light passes through the lens and into the body of the camera through an opening called the **aperture**. If the aperture is large, much light will pass through; if it is small, little light will pass through. Simple cameras may have only a single fixed aperture; adjustable cameras have many aperture settings.

A number, called the **f-stop**, indicates the size of the aperture, or lens opening. F/stop settings are marked on the camera with numbers such as 22, 16, 11, 8, and 5.6. These numbers also represent fractions—1/22, 1/16, 1/11, 1/8, 1/5.6, respectively. They represent the ratio of the diameter of the aperture to the focal length of the lens. F-stops need never be computed, because they are calibrated by the manufacturer and engraved on the lens barrel or read on a camera's display screen. Both the aperture and the shutter speed must be properly set for each photograph to obtain a correct exposure for the film or sensor in use.

Figure 3-3. Aperture setting on (A) LCD panel and on (B) lens barrel.

Because these f-stops are fractions, the larger numbers represent smaller lens openings and the smaller numbers represent larger lens openings. Changing the lens opening from one f-stop to the next is called adjusting the aperture "one stop." If the stops are changed to make the aperture smaller (for example, f/16 to f/22), this is called **stopping down** one stop. If the stops are changed to make the aperture larger (for example, f/16 to f/11), this is called **opening up** one stop.

The f-stops are arranged so that as the aperture is stopped down, each subsequent stop allows half the amount of light to pass through as the previous stop. Stopping down one stop—from f/16 to f/22, for example—reduces by half the amount of light passing through the lens. Opening up one stop—from f/16 to f/11, for example—doubles the amount of light passing through. The standard sequence of f-stops is as follows: f/1.0, f/1.4, f/2, f/2.8, f/4, f/5.6, f/8, f/11, f/16, f/22, f/32, f/45.

In the above sequence f/1.0 would let in the most light and f/45 would let in the least light. Note that not all of these f-stops are found on every lens. Figures 3-3A and 3-3B show the general appearance of the aperture setting on a typical camera.

The **maximum aperture** to which a lens can be set is sometimes referred to as the **lens speed**. This f-stop is generally inscribed on the front of the lens barrel near the focal length. For example, on the front of a lens barrel might appear the numbers 50mm and 1:1.4. This means that the focal length of the lens is 50mm and its speed, or maximum aperture, is f/1.4.

Some cameras provide intermediate apertures. In other words, the aperture can be set not only at these **full stops**, but also at points in between. Normally the in-between f-stops are in values that represent 1/3 of a whole stop. For example: (1), 1.1, 1.25, (1.4), 1.6, 1.8, (2), 2.2, 2.5, (2.8), 3.2, 3.6, (4), 4.5, 5, (5.6) 6.3, 7, (8), 9, 10, (11), 13, 14, (16), 18, 20, (22).

Figure 3-5 shows the relative size of the aperture at various f-stops and its relationship to the amount of light passing through it in any fixed interval of time.

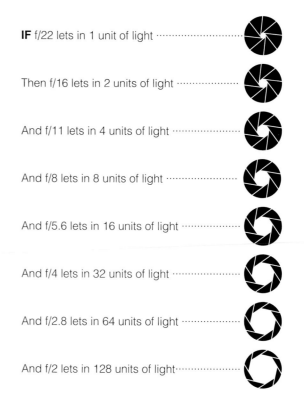

IF f/22 lets in 1 unit of light

Then f/16 lets in 2 units of light

And f/11 lets in 4 units of light

And f/8 lets in 8 units of light

And f/5.6 lets in 16 units of light

And f/4 lets in 32 units of light

And f/2.8 lets in 64 units of light

And f/2 lets in 128 units of light

Figure 3-4. Relationship of f-stops to exposure. Note that the f-numbers double every other stop, but amount of light doubles every stop.

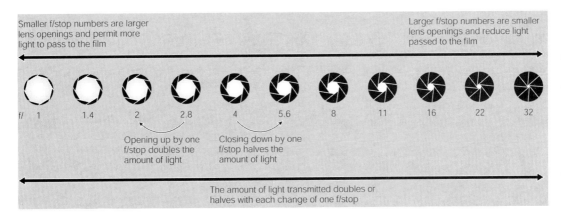

Focus

The third setting on an adjustable camera is **focus**. As the camera is moved closer to or farther away from various objects in the camera's field of view, images become more or less sharp. Simple cameras may have only one fixed-focus setting, requiring the camera to be positioned some given minimum distance from the subject. As long as the camera is positioned at or beyond this distance, the subject will be in sharp focus. Should the camera be moved closer than the minimum distance, the subject will be out of focus in the picture. Adjustable cameras provide a range of focus settings, allowing the camera to be positioned at various distances from the subject while adjusting the image's sharpness on the film.

tips *Confusing Exposure Terms*

- **Shutter speed** controls the amount of time the shutter is open and light is admitted to the film. Standard speeds are 1, 2, 4, 8, 15, 30, 60, 125, 250, 1000, and 2000 where each number represents a fraction of a second, i.e. the marking 250 represents 1/250 second.

- **Aperture** is the variable opening in the lens that admits light.

- **F-stop** is a measure of the aperture's setting. Standard f-stops are sequenced in multiples of the square root of two: 1, 1.4, 2, 2.8, 4, 5.6, 8, 11, 16, 22, 32, etc. Increasing the f-stop by one step halves the light reaching the film, decreasing a step doubles the light.

- **Stop** The term stop refers to changing either the shutter speed or the lens opening by one "standard" number, which will double or halve the light reaching the film.

- **Opening up** a stop means changing to a bigger lens opening (smaller number) or a slower shutter speed (smaller number) to double the amount of light admitted to the film.

- **Stopping down** means changing to a smaller lens opening (bigger number) or a faster shutter speed (bigger number) to reduce the exposure.

- **Exposure** is the total light reaching the film. It is a combination of the aperture setting, the shutter speed, the speed of the film in use and the amount of light reflected off the subject.

- **Lens Speed** The speed of a lens is its maximum aperture setting, i.e. its biggest lens opening (smallest number).

- **Film speed** is a measure of a film's sensitivity to light. Faster films tend to have more grain and less resolving power. Bigger ISO numbers indicate faster films, i.e. a 400-speed film is "faster" than a 100-speed film and would require less light to make a picture.

With very simple adjustable cameras the distance between the subject and the camera may need to be estimated or measured and then the lens set for that distance. Because this procedure is slow and imprecise, most popular adjustable cameras provide some type of focusing system to aid in setting the focus correctly. Some of the common types are described below.

Split-image Focusing **Split-image focusing** is found most often on professional or advanced amateur SLR cameras. As the subject is viewed through the viewfinder, part of the image is split; one-half of the image is displaced somewhat from the other half. By operating the focusing ring of the lens, the two halves of the image can be brought together. When the two halves of the image are aligned properly, the image is in focus on the film. (See Figure 3-6A.)

Superimposed-image Focusing **Superimposed-image focusing** is also found most often on professional or advanced amateur viewfinder cameras. As the subject is viewed through the viewfinder, a part of the image is doubled. Two images appear, one offset slightly from the other. By operating the focusing ring of the camera, the two images can be lined up so that they appear as one. When this has been done, the image is in focus on the film. (See Figure 3-6B.)

Ground-glass Focusing **Ground-glass focusing** is typical of medium- and large-format cameras, but is also found on small-format cameras. This system allows the image to be viewed as it appears in the film plane. If the image is out of focus, it will appear unfocused on the ground-glass viewing screen. By operating the focusing adjustments on the camera, the image can be adjusted until it appears at maximum sharpness. Whatever appears in sharp focus on the ground-glass screen will be in focus on the film. (See Figure 3-6C.)

Automatic Focusing Auto-focus (AF) could be called power-focus, as it uses a computer chip to control a miniature motor that focuses the lens for you. There are two types of auto-focus: **active** and **passive**.

Cameras with **active auto-focus** systems work in a way similar to radar or sonar devices. As the shutter is released, the camera emits a short pulse of sound or infrared light in a narrow beam along the lens's axis. When it strikes an object in its path,

HELPFUL **H**INT

Whatever the type of auto-focusing system, make sure that your main subject is within the brackets that indicate the viewfinder area used by the focusing system. On simple cameras the focus area is usually centered in the middle of the picture. If your subject is off center the camera will focus on the background, resulting in poor focus. To correct this common problem first focus by placing the auto-focus brackets on the main subject; on many cameras this can be done by pressing halfway down on the shutter button to lock the focus. Next, reframe your picture while maintaining pressure on the shutter button and completely depress the shutter to take the picture. The result will be a sharply focused main subject—even in off-center compositions.

the pulse is reflected back to a sensor on the camera. By timing the interval between the emission of the pulse and its return, the focusing system determines the distance between the object and the camera and sets the focus for that distance just as the shutter begins to open. One advantage of active automatic focusing is that it works well in the dark, making it especially suitable for flash photography. A disadvantage is that the focusing system cannot function accurately through a sheet of glass because it reflects the active focusing beams. Landscape photographs taken through a car window will be out of focus, for example.

Passive auto-focus systems are commonly found on single-lens-reflex (SLR) auto-focus cameras. This system determines the point of sharp focus through a computer analysis of the contrast of an image formed on an electronic sensor. Passive auto-focus systems are very effective but they must have light and subjects containing some detail and contrast to perform well. If you try to take a picture of a blank wall the camera can't detect any detail and so cannot focus.

Depth of Field

Objective 3-B Define depth of field and describe the major factors that affect it.

Key Concepts depth of field, out of focus, in focus, zone of focus, control, shallow depth of field, maximum depth of field, infinity (∞), hyperfocal distance, hyperfocal focusing

A.

B.

C.

D.

Figure 3-6. Different out-of-focus views. A) Out-of-focus view through split-image rangefinder. B) Out-of-focus view through superimposed-image rangefinder. C) Out-of-focus view through ground glass screen. D) In-focus view. Whatever type of focusing system is used the in-focus view is a clear and sharp image.

Various objects will appear focused or unfocused in the photograph depending on their distance from the camera. The distance range within which objects appear in acceptably sharp focus is commonly called the **depth of field**. For example, suppose all objects between 10 feet and 20 feet from the camera appeared in sharp focus, whereas objects that were closer or farther away appeared **out of focus**. The depth of field would be said to be from 10 to 20 feet, meaning that objects within that distance range appeared **in focus**. This distance range is also sometimes called the **zone of focus**.

Depth of field is an imprecise concept. The degree of sharpness apparent in an image is due only partly to the physical characteristics of the image itself; it is partly due to the subjective judgment of the viewer—what the viewer considers acceptably sharp under the circumstances.

Several factors affect the apparent sharpness of objects within an image. Physical sharpness diminishes gradually from the point of maximum focus out to the boundaries of the depth of field. It is the viewer's judgment that determines just where objects within the image are no longer acceptably sharp. Also, apparent sharpness diminishes as the image is magnified—what appears acceptably sharp in an image of one size may become unacceptable as the image is enlarged. Further, apparent sharpness diminishes more rapidly when coarse-grain films are magnified than when fine-grain films are magnified. Similarly, low resolution digital images have less apparent depth of field than their high resolution counterparts.

Because of these many factors, depth of field should be regarded as a useful concept rather than as a precise measuring tool.

Depth of field can be used as a **control** in picture taking; that is, control can be exercised over the relative physical sharpness of objects at various distances from the camera. Suppose, for example, that the photographer wishes only the subject to appear in sharp focus and everything in front of and beyond to appear out of focus. On a portrait, for example, this approach would concentrate the viewer's attention on the subject. To obtain this effect, the camera would be set to achieve a very **shallow depth of field**. In Figure 3-7A the aperture has been set to f/4 and the focus has been

A.

B.

C.

Figure 3-7. Estimating depth of field. A) With aperature set at f/4 at a distance of 12 feet, scale shows a depth of field from 10 to 14 feet. B) Depth of field scale for aperature set at f/22 at a distance of 12 feet shows a depth of field ranging from 6 feet to infinity. C) Some cameras feature a depth of field preview button that permits viewing through a stopped-down aperture. This helps estimate what depth of field will be present.

set to about 12 feet. At those settings, the depth of field scale shows that objects between 10 feet and 14 feet will be in focus; objects outside the depth of field will fall progressively out of focus.

On another occasion, the photographer might wish everything in the picture, from the nearest objects to the farthest, to appear acceptably sharp, as in a landscape. In this case, the camera should be set to achieve **maximum depth of field**. In

Figure 3-7B the aperture has been set to f/22 and the focus has been set to 12 feet. At those settings, the depth of field scale shows that objects between 6 feet and infinity will be in focus. (See the discussion of hyperfocal focusing later in this unit.)

Some SLR cameras provide a preview feature, which allows the photographer to view the scene through the lens at the selected aperture. This helps to estimate what objects lie within the depth of field. At very small apertures, however, the preview feature displays an image too dim to ascertain the relative sharpness of objects within the scene. (See Figure 3-7C.)

Some auto-focus SLR cameras offer a special focusing mode that calculates depth of field and sets the appropriate lens setting. While in this special mode the photographer first positions the viewfinder's focusing bracket on the closest object desired to be in sharp focus and slightly depresses the shutter or another control button. The photographer repositions the frame to place the farthest object desired sharp within the focus indicator and presses the control button again. The camera's microprocessor then determines and selects the proper focus point and lens opening to achieve the desired depth of field.

Aperture and Depth of Field

As the size of the aperture changes, the amount of light passing through the lens also changes. It is important to note, however, that the depth of field changes as well. At small lens apertures the depth of field is greater than at large lens apertures; objects will appear sharp over a greater range of distance at smaller apertures than at larger ones. When a large aperture is used, the depth of field is reduced; objects will appear sharp over a shorter range of distance at large apertures than at smaller ones. This principle is illustrated in Figure 3-8.

Focal Length and Depth of Field

At any given aperture, the shorter the focal length of the lens, the greater the depth of field. Conversely, the longer the focal length of the lens, the shallower the depth of field. At given apertures, therefore, wide-angle lenses will produce greater-than-normal depth of field, whereas telephoto

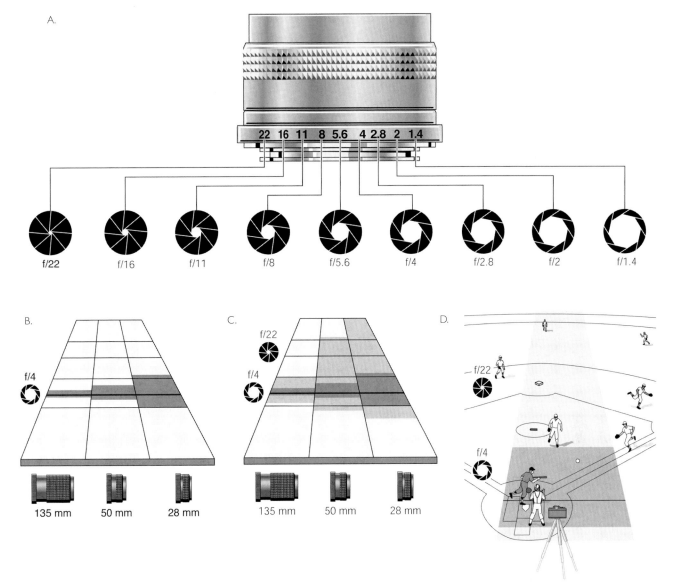

Figure 3-8. Depth of field A) f-number affects aperture size. B) The effect of focal length on depth of field. C) Depth of field at two different apertures. D) Range of subject focus at two different apertures.

lenses will produce shallower-than-normal depth of field. Figure 3-9 illustrates this principle.

Distance Setting and Depth of Field

The focus setting of an adjustable camera is marked for various distances. Focusing on an object at any given distance from the camera ensures that the object will appear in maximum sharp focus. Objects nearer or farther from the camera but within the depth of field will also appear in relatively sharp focus.

The distance at which the lens is focused, however, also affects the depth of field. When focused on objects close to the camera, the depth of field is reduced; when focused on objects farther away, it is increased.

This principle is illustrated in Figure 3-10. Note that approximately one-third of the depth of field lies between the camera and the point of sharpest focus; approximately two-thirds lies beyond it. The maximum distance shown on the focus setting is **infinity (∞)**, a theoretical distance from the camera beyond which all image-forming light rays entering the camera are parallel and all objects appear to be in focus. For practical purposes, for normal focal length lenses infinity starts at a point approximately 50 feet (15 meters) from the camera. If infinity is within the depth of field,

Figure 3-9. A) Depth of field using 35mm wide-angle lens. Note inset is equivalent to view produced by 105mm telephoto lens from same position as shown in Figure 3-9C. B) Enlarged view of inset shown in Figure 3-9A. Although the field of view is the same as that produced by a 105mm lens from the same position and at the same aperture (shown in Figure 3-9C), note difference in depth of field. C) Same view from the same position at same aperture using a 105mm lens. Even though the perspective produced by a cropped version of a wide-angle picture is the same, the depth of field differs substantially.

A.

B.

C.

Figure 3-10. Distance setting affects depth of field at any given aperture. A) Depth of field is reduced when focused at close distances. B) Depth of field is longer when focus setting is far away.

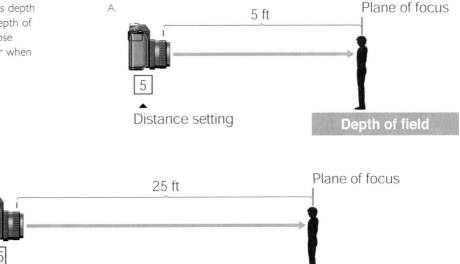

then all objects 50 feet (15 meters) from the camera and beyond will be in acceptable focus. Figures 3-10 A, B and 3-11 A, B, C illustrates the many factors that affect depth of field.

Zone Focusing

When subjects are moving or changing rapidly, many photographers avoid refocusing for every shot by setting the depth of field in advance for a wide range of distances. This is achieved by setting the focus to the *average* camera-to-subject distance that is expected, and then setting the ap-

erture to provide a **zone of focus** that includes the expected range of distances.

For example, if action is expected between 6 feet and 25 feet from the camera, you would adjust the camera's focusing ring until 6 and 25 are equally spaced on either side of the focusing index mark. You would then set the aperture to the setting closest to these numbers. Figure 3-12B shows that if the focusing index mark is set midway between 6 feet and 25 feet and the aperture is set at f/16, the zone of focus extends from 6 feet to 25 feet. For auto-focus cameras without a

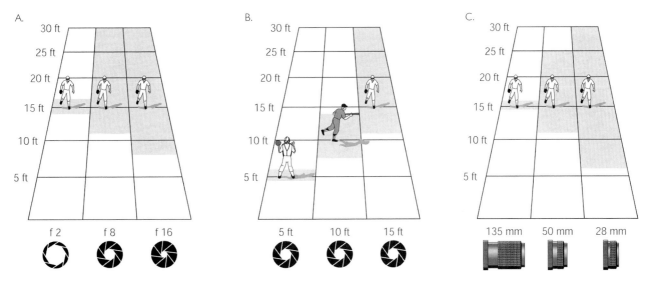

Figure 3-11. A) How aperture affects depth of field. B) How subject distance affects depth of field. C) How focal length affects depth of field.

A.

B.

Figure 3-12. Zone focusing. Set camera to an f-stop that sets the depth of field to the desired distance range. For example: A) Set depth of field index midway between 6 ft. and 25 ft. Read the aperture that will provide depth of field (f/16). B) Then set the aperture to f/16. Now any object within the range of 6 ft. to 25 ft. will fall within the range of focus. No need to continually refocus for objects within this range.

manual focus mode a similar result can be obtained by positioning the focusing indicator bracket on an object one-third into the desired range of focus and pressing the focus lock button. In the above example this would entail prefocusing on an object about 12 feet from the camera.

Hyperfocal Focusing

At any given f-stop, when the lens is focused at infinity (∞), the distance between the camera and the nearest point of acceptable focus is called the **hyperfocal distance**. Figure 3-13A illustrates that when the lens is focused on a point at infinity (∞)

only a portion of the potential depth of field is used.

To obtain maximum depth of field to infinity, the technique of **hyperfocal focusing** is used. By focusing the camera on a point at the hyperfocal distance, as in Figure 3-13B, the depth of field is extended to a point closer to the camera and still reaches to infinity.

Another way to achieve hyperfocal focusing is to align the infinity marker (∞) with the current aperture setting on the depth of field scale. For example, with the aperture set at f/16, align the in-

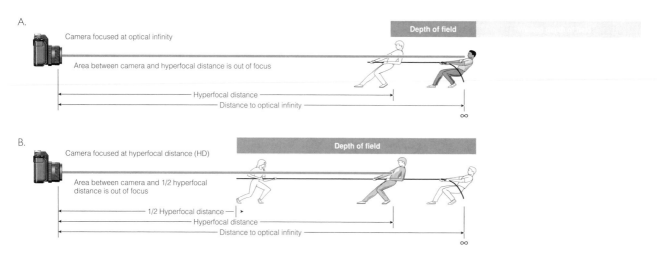

Figure 3-13. Hyperfocal focusing. A) First focus camera at infinity. Note near point of focus on the depth of field scale that corresponds to your aperture setting; this is the hyperfocal distance. B) Then set the lens focus to the hyperfocal distance. Observe that the new depth of field now extends from half the hyperfocal distance to infinity.

Famous Photograph

William Henry Jackson's "Old Faithful"

In 1871, William Henry Jackson was hired as a photographer by the U.S. Geological Survey's expedition to the Yellowstone area of Wyoming. From then until 1879, Jackson was official photographer of the United States Geological Survey Territories. Often traveling by mule with more than 200 pounds of photographic equipment, including a 20in x 24in glass plate view camera and a stereo camera, Jackson took some of the most breathtaking photographs ever recorded of the pristine western wilderness.

Jackson's employer, Dr. Ferdinand V. Hayden, was bent on a mission to preserve America's wilderness and to protect it from commercial exploitation. Hoping that the federal government would enact legislation to create a Yellowstone National Park, Hayden prepared a report on the region. Having a keen appreciation of the power of photography, he illustrated his report using Jackson's pictures and presented to every member of the House and Senate a bound volume containing nine of Jackson's most powerful and majestic images, including this dramatic photograph of Old Faithful. His actions resulted in the drafting of a bill that laid the foundation for the National Park System and was signed into law by President Ulysses S. Grant in 1872.

Jackson, called by many "the grand old man of the National Parks," died in 1942 at the age of ninety-nine. He was the last of the great frontier photographers.

William Henry Jackson, "Old Faithful." Courtesy of Denver Public Library, Western History Department.

finity marker with the f/16 mark on the depth of field scale. This technique yields the maximum depth of field possible for any given focal length and aperture setting by gaining additional foreground sharpness.

Summary

Depth of field is a concept that refers generally to the distance range within which objects will appear in acceptably sharp focus in the finished image. Five major factors operate to influence sharpness and depth of field in any given circumstance:

1. Aperture
2. Focal length of the lens
3. Focus setting (subject-to-camera distance)
4. Grain size or the resolution setting on a digital camera
5. Degree of magnification of finished image

To obtain the maximum range within which objects will appear acceptably sharp, use the smallest possible aperture, a lens with the shortest possible focal length, hyperfocal focusing, film and processing to produce the finest possible grain (or with digital cameras use the highest possible resolution setting), and the least possible image enlargement. Some adjustable cameras have a depth of field scale built into the lens that indicates the distance range of focus at various apertures and distance settings. Many cameras with ground-glass focusing allow direct observation of the depth of field before the shutter is released.

Aperture and Shutter Speed Combinations

Objective 3-C Demonstrate how to select, using an exposure guide or your camera's light meter, appropriate combinations of apertures and shutter speeds under various conditions.

Key Concepts exposure, intensity, time, E = I × T, reciprocity law, exposure guide, equivalent exposures, camera shake, stop action, blur action, control depth of field, reciprocity failure (RF) factor

Achieving the Correct Exposure

Exposure, the amount of light acting on the film or digital sensor, is the product of the **intensity** of the light and the **time** during which the light acts. This relationship may be expressed as **E = I × T** (Exposure = Intensity × Time). As long as the product of the light intensity and the time remains constant, the response of the film or digital imaging sensor also remains constant. Thus if light intensity is doubled and time is halved, their product remains the same, as does their effect upon the image. The greater the intensity, the less the necessary time, and vice versa. This relationship is known as the **reciprocity law**.

The size of the aperture controls the intensity of the light reaching the film or image sensor; the speed of the shutter controls the time. The combination of these two controls determines how much light acts on the film or image sensor when the shutter is triggered. These settings determine exposure.

How does the photographer know how to set these two controls? Films and digital sensors of

HELPFUL HINT

Basic Exposure Rule

If you do not have an exposure table or your light meter stops working, you can use the following basic exposure rule—a rule of thumb for determining shutter speed and lens opening: f/16 at a shutter speed of 1/ISO sec. for average subjects in sunlight. For example, shooting with a film or digital camera rated at ISO 125/22°, you could shoot at f/16 at 1/125 sec. for average subjects in sunlight. From these basic data you can estimate needed adjustments for different light conditions. For hazy sun, open up one stop; for very bright subjects, stop down one stop.

different speeds require different exposures. Most films used with adjustable cameras have instructions packaged with them. Table 3-1 is a daylight **exposure guide** for film or sensor rated ISO 100. This guide suggests a shutter speed of 1/250 sec. and a lens opening of f/11 to photograph an average subject on a bright, sunny day with film or sensor rated ISO 100.

Many combinations of lens opening and shutter speed will produce the same exposure. The various combinations that produce the same amount of light are called **equivalent exposures**.

For example, suppose that the exposure guide suggested a setting of f/11 at 1/250 sec. The lens could be opened one stop to f/8 (doubling the amount of light) and the next faster shutter speed, 1/500 sec. (halving the amount of light), used to obtain an equivalent exposure. Or, the lens could be stopped down one stop to f/16 and the next slower shutter speed, 1/125 sec., used. The exposure would be the same in all cases. There are four reasons to select an equivalent exposure rather than the one specified in the exposure table:

Table 3-1. Outdoor Exposure Guide for average subjects for film or digital sensor rated ISO 100			
Shutter Speed at 1/250 Sec.		Shutter Speed at 1/125 Sec.	
Bright or Hazy Sun Very Light Subjects f/16 Average Subjects f/11 [a]	Cloudy Bright f/8	Heavy Overcast f/5.6	Open Shade [b] f/5.6

[a] at 1/125 sec. for backlighted, closeup subjects
[b] Subject shaded from the sun but lighted by a large area of sky

1. To reduce the effect of camera movement

   With a hand-held camera, **camera shake** during exposure is the most common cause of blurred pictures. Using a normal lens and taking reasonable care can avoid camera shake at speeds as slow as 1/60 sec. To avoid the effect of camera shake at this or slower speeds, use a tripod or stabilizing support to hold the camera steady.

2. To stop action

   The image of a moving object moves across the film or image sensor while the shutter remains open. Thus, a moving object will produce a blurred image if the shutter remains open too long. The recommended shutter speed of 1/250 sec. helps to stop the blurring of most moving objects. However, to photograph rapidly moving objects, such as those found at sporting or racing events, a faster shutter will be needed to "freeze" or **stop the action**. In such cases the photographer would select an equivalent exposure with a faster shutter speed.

3. To blur action

   Sometimes, to enhance the impression of speed and movement, the photographer may wish the moving object to appear blurred against its stationary background or to appear fixed against a blurred background. To accomplish this, a slower shutter speed will be needed than the one recommended. Photographing a rapidly moving object with a shutter speed of 1/8 sec or slower will visibly **blur the action** of a rapidly moving object and/or its background. In this case the photographer would select an equivalent exposure with a slower shutter speed.

4. To control depth of field

   Shooting at small apertures, such as f/16, provides maximum depth of field, allowing objects both close to and far from the camera to appear acceptably sharp. A larger aperture may be used to reduce depth of field. The photographer may wish, however, to have some of the nearer or farther objects in the scene appear out of focus. Setting the camera for an equivalent exposure with a larger aperture allows **control of depth of field**. (See Figure 3-8 to review f-numbers and aperture sizes.)

Table 3-2. Exposures equivalent to f/11 at 1/250 sec.

Sec.	1/30	1/60	1/125	1/250	1/500	1/1000
f/	32	22	16	11	8	5.6

The beginner should note that the photographer cannot always select an ideal equivalent exposure. Some cameras may not provide an ideal aperture or an ideal shutter speed for a given situation because the scale of settings is not long enough. In most situations the exposure that most nearly approaches the ideal setting must be selected.

Selecting a film of appropriate speed, or choosing a higher ISO setting on a digital camera, may often improve the range of acceptable exposures in a given situation. An ISO 400/27° film is four times faster than an ISO 100/21° film. Thus, if a proper exposure using the faster film is f/5.6 at 1/250 sec., a proper exposure with the slower film under the same conditions would be f/2.8 at 1/250 sec.—a two-stop (four times) exposure increase to compensate for the slower film speed.

One can see, therefore, that the range of equivalent exposures comes under the control of the photographer largely through the selection of film or appropriate ISO setting of the image sensor for use under any given set of conditions.

Reciprocity Failure

For most practical purposes under normal conditions, the reciprocity law holds true. But it is not always so; there are times when films do not respond as the reciprocity law would lead one to expect. For example, when light intensities are reduced to a very low level, requiring extremely slow shutter speeds, increases in exposure time fail to produce proportionate responses in the film. Similarly, when light intensities require extremely short exposures, as when some kinds of electronic flash are used, changes in exposure time also fail to produce proportionate responses. This departure from the normal film response is known as **reciprocity failure. Reciprocity failure (RF) factors** are published for each black-and-white film to help one calculate a corrected exposure. To compensate for long exposures of 1–10 sec., double the normal exposure; for longer

Table 3-3. Typical RF corrections for black-and-white films

If indicated exposure time is (seconds)	either increase aperture	or increase exposure time to	and change developing time to
1/1000 sec. or less	none	none	20% more
1–10 sec.	1–1.5 stops	2–30 sec.	10–15% less
10–50 sec.	1.5–2.5 stops	30–300 sec.	15–20% less
50–100 sec.	2.5–3 stops	300–800 sec.	20–30% less

exposures, quadruple it. Table 3-3 shows typical RF corrections for black-and-white film.

With color films, reciprocity failure is more complex because it affects the three color emulsions unevenly; thus, the effect is not only underexposure, but also a shift in color balance. One way to compensate for this effect is to use special filters (discussed further in Unit 11), or to use special films designed for extremely long or short exposures. Ordinarily, however, it is most convenient to avoid excessively long exposures.

Digital imaging sensors may or may not be affected by reciprocity law failure depending on their design. For best results view your just-captured photographs on the camera's playback screen and adjust the next picture's settings accordingly. Note that almost all digital cameras suffer from "noise" and random "speckles" in the image when used for very long exposures. You will need to use a photo editing program, like Photoshop, to correct such spots.

Exposure and Action

Objective 3-D Given basic exposure data, describe techniques for photographing the action of a moving subject.

Key Concepts stop or freeze action, object speed, camera-to-subject distance, angle of movement, panning or panoramming

Freezing Action

Very fast shutter speeds are normally thought necessary to **stop or freeze the action** of a fast-moving subject. Yet a shutter speed of 1/1000 sec. is not needed to take good action photographs. Good action shots can be obtained by using a few basic principles about speed, light, film and image sensor rating, and camera technique.

Speed is relative. The actual speed of an object is less important than its apparent speed from the point of view of the camera. Sometimes fast-moving objects appear slow-moving, and vice versa. Three factors affect the apparent speed of the object: (1) the speed of the object itself, (2) the distance between the object and the camera, and (3) the angle of movement relative to the camera's axis.

1. *Object speed* Obviously a faster shutter is needed to freeze the action of a speeding car or a football player streaking for the goal line than is needed for a person walking slowly down the street. To freeze the action of a moving object, the **object speed** must be considered—the shutter must open and close again before the image of the object on the film or image sensor perceptibly changes position. Consequently, faster shutter speeds are normally required to stop the action of faster-moving objects.

2. *Camera-to-subject distance* From close to the highway, speeding cars may seem to zoom rapidly past. Farther back from the edge of the highway, the apparent speed of the cars is considerably less, due to the greater **camera-to-subject distance**. Speeding cars on the horizon may appear to be moving hardly at all. Translated into shutter settings, a general guideline for this effect might state: The closer the camera is to the moving object, the faster the shutter setting needed to stop or freeze its apparent movement.

3. *Angle of movement* A third factor that affects the choice of shutter speed is the object's **angle of movement** relative to the axis of the camera. A car moving directly toward the photographer may appear to be moving hardly at all, whereas the same car at the same distance moving across the line of vision may appear to be moving quite rapidly. If the cam-

era is positioned to photograph an object moving along the camera's axis rather than across it, the object's action can be stopped with a slower shutter speed.

Stopping fast-moving action most often requires fast shutter speeds, however. Fast shutter speeds, in turn, require larger aperture settings to maintain equivalent exposure. Because large apertures decrease depth of field, obtaining great depth of field tends to pose a problem in action photography, as in any situation requiring a fast shutter.

How can both a fast shutter and a small aperture be used? One way is to select a faster film or image-chip setting. As film speed is increased, the amount of exposure required is reduced, permitting the use of smaller apertures with a fast shutter setting. Another way is to use some form of supplementary lighting, such as flash. Additional light intensity also will permit smaller apertures with a fast shutter setting. (This topic is discussed further in Units 12 and 13.)

Blurring Action

Good action shots do not always require freezing the action of an object. Using a slow shutter and deliberately allowing moving objects to blur on the film can enhance the sense of movement. By using a very slow shutter and stationary camera, for example, a fast-moving object may be made to appear blurred against a static background. Another slow shutter technique known as **panning** or **panoramming** may also be chosen. Panning is similar to the technique used by skeet shooters to aim at clay targets in flight. They aim and pivot their bodies, keeping the gun barrel moving in the direction of the target's flight.

In panning, the camera is used in a similar manner. The photographer uses the eye-level viewfinder and spots the object as it moves into view, then pivots head and shoulders, keeping the object in the viewfinder at all times. When the object is in correct view, the shutter is released without interrupting the pivot. It is important to follow through after snapping the shutter. The trick is to have the camera moving at the same relative speed and in the same direction as the object.

The resulting photograph will show the object—car, motorcycle, runner, surfer—frozen in rela-

tively clear focus. The background and foreground, however, will be a mass of blurs and streaks caused by the camera's movement during exposure. Panning gives a visual sense of speed, and the object's movement will have stopped with a relatively slow shutter speed. Panning works best at shutter speeds under 1/30 sec, and 1/8 sec is commonly used. Figure 3-14 A, B, C, D, and E shows the effects of various techniques for shooting fast-moving objects.

Image Control with Automatic Exposure Cameras

Objective 3-E Describe some methods of working with automatic camera features to retain image control.

Key Concepts focus lock, automatic exposure modes, auto exposure disable, exposure lock, backlight compensation, exposure compensation, ISO reset, autoflash, autoflash disable, anti-red-eye, flash-fill

Many modern cameras provide features designed to make photography simpler by automatically setting focus, exposure, and flash engagement. Unfortunately, automation tends to encourage mental laziness. The photographer may be lulled into a false sense of confidence, knowing that the camera will at least provide correct focus and exposure. Creative image possibilities that might exist through the use of override and disable controls may be lost.

Some automatic cameras provide override and disable features, which allow the photographer to maintain control over the image. Fully automatic cameras without override or disable features restrict image control and limit the range of image possibilities available to the photographer. By using the override and disable features, the photographer often can exercise far greater image control than would be possible by relying on automatic features.

Auto-Focus Override Features

Auto-focus features are designed to focus automatically on a prominent detail in the image. An internal computer calculates the distance between the camera and an object near the center of the frame and focuses on it. This function works on

A.

B.

C.

D.

E.

Figure 3-14. A) Blurred action. Moving object is blurred using slow shutter. B) Stopped action with fast shutter. Moving object is not blurred if fast shutter is used. C) Panning. Moving object is stopped against blurred background by panning along with the moving object and using a slow shutter speed. D) Stopped action with slow shutter. Object moving toward camera is stopped with a slower shutter. E) Stopped action with fast shutter. Moving object is stopped using fast shutter.

the assumption that an object at the center of the frame is the object of principal interest; should your object of principal interest lie off the center of the frame, the auto-focus feature may well focus the camera on something else, leaving your principal object out of focus.

To overcome this possibility, many auto-focus cameras provide a **focus lock** feature, which allows you to point your camera at any object you choose, lock the focus in that position, and then point your

camera elsewhere for best composition. Using a focus lock feature allows you to decide for yourself what object is of principal interest in your image, rather than having the auto-focus feature decide for you. Some cameras also permit you to disable the auto-focus feature altogether and retain manual focus control.

More advanced auto-focus cameras have several focus sensors arrayed horizontally across the viewfinder to allow greater variety in subject placement. Some cameras even track the movement of your eye as you look through the viewfinder and then set the focus point accordingly. This is often referred to as eye-tracking auto-focus.

Automatic Exposure Override Features

Many advanced automatic cameras provide several different **automatic exposure modes**.

Aperture priority mode is one of the more popular exposure setting systems. Such cameras allow you to set the aperture as you wish. They then evaluate the light available in a scene and automatically set the shutter to obtain a proper exposure. This mode works especially well when the photographer wishes to control the range of sharpness in the picture.

Shutter priority mode cameras provide automatic exposure control using a shutter priority exposure setting system. Such cameras require you to set the shutter to any speed you wish. They then evaluate the light available in a scene and automatically set the aperture to obtain a proper exposure.

Using automatic exposure modes such as these allows you to select shutter speed and aperture combinations most appropriate for the image you wish to create. Keep in mind, however, that these options do not actually increase or decrease exposure; they simply provide the settings you prefer for any given exposure value. To increase or decrease exposure to compensate for unusual lighting situations, you will need to utilize **autoexposure disable** or override controls. In this way you can modify the exposure that would otherwise be set by the automatic system.

The built-in light meter that automatically sets the camera for a proper exposure by adjusting the aperture and/or shutter speed is designed to produce well-exposed negatives under average lighting conditions. However, when the subject and background are unequally illuminated, the exposure-setting system may not determine the best exposure for your purpose. A meter cannot tell the difference between the subject and its background; it reads the average intensity of light in the scene reflected from all sources. If this average is significantly more or less than the light reflected from the main subject, the system setting

may under- or overexpose your principal subject. To overcome this effect manufacturers sometimes build exposure override or disable controls into their automatic cameras.

Manual Mode Some cameras may possess a manual mode that allows you to disable the automatic exposure features and set exposure manually. Manual mode usually allows you to use the internal meter to obtain a reading of the subject and then set the aperture and shutter speed manually to the exposure of your choice. Manual mode provides maximum flexibility for setting exposure but none of the convenience of automatic exposure setting.

Exposure Lock Some automatic exposure cameras provide an **exposure lock** feature that allows you to point your camera momentarily at any object you choose for obtaining an exposure setting, lock the exposure in that position, and then point your camera elsewhere for best composition. Using an exposure lock feature allows you to decide for yourself what exposure will best represent the tonal values of a scene and avoid having the automatic exposure feature decide for you. In that way, any object you choose can be represented as a middle gray tone in your final image, regardless of its location within the frame, without sacrificing the convenience of automatic exposure setting. This control is often used in landscape photographs that feature a large expanse of bright sky. The photographer would first point the camera slightly down to exclude the sky while the light meter reading is taken. He would then lock in the exposure, and tilt the camera back up to reframe as desired.

Backlight Compensation Some automatic cameras also provide a **backlight compensation** feature. Using this feature while shooting allows you to increase exposure for that image about 1.5 stops, providing about three times the normal exposure and thereby brightening the entire image. This procedure usually serves to brighten objects that might otherwise be underexposed because of strong light in the background. (See Figure 3-15B.)

Exposure Compensation Some automatic cameras provide even more control with an **exposure compensation** feature. This feature allows exposure to be increased or decreased to compensate for any kind of out-of-the-ordinary lighting situation.

A.

B.

C.

Figure 3-15. A) Readjusting the ISO setting of an automatic camera. B) Backlight compensation. Some automatic cameras have a button that will increase exposure to compensate for backlighting situations. Pressing the backlight compensation button while shooting usually increases exposure about 1.5 stops. C) Exposure compensation. Many automatic cameras have an adjustment to manually increase or decrease exposure one or two stops. This allows the photographer to compensate for unusual lighting situations.

Figure 3-15C shows an exposure compensating dial that permits automatic settings of one-fourth and one-half of normal exposure, two and four times normal exposure, as well as normal exposure, while retaining the underlying automatic exposure setting features.

ISO Reset If your camera provides no override features and operates only in an automatic mode, you may still have an option, though a more limited one, for controlling exposure. Facing unusual lighting situations, such as strong backlight or overall darkness, you may use an **ISO reset** to alter the automatic exposure. By resetting the ISO film speed index programmed into your camera, you can fool the internal meter into increasing or decreasing its normal exposure setting. If you double the ISO setting, you will reduce normal exposure by one stop. If you halve the ISO setting, you will increase normal exposure by one stop. This technique is not applicable with most digital cameras.

Automatic Flash Features

Flash photography is the main topic of Unit 13 and is discussed in greater detail there. However, automatic cameras often possess unique automatic flash features. For example, fully automatic cameras often possess an **autoflash** mode that automatically engages the flash unit whenever there is insufficient light. Such cameras may also possess an **autoflash disable** feature that allows the photographer to turn off this automatic feature.

In addition to the autoflash feature, some cameras provide flash features designed to overcome unusual lighting situations. For example, some provide an **anti-red-eye** feature designed to offset the conditions likely to produce the red-eye phenomenon in color pictures. Usually the system fires off one or more bursts of flash before making the exposure. This has the effect of causing the subject's pupils to contract prior to the exposure, thus reducing a principal cause of red-eye.

Some automatic cameras may provide a **flash-fill** setting to engage the flash unit when the principal subject reflects substantially less light than the background areas of the image.

Fill flash is often used when taking pictures of people against a bright background or in backlight settings.

Table 3-4 provides a checklist of many features often found on automatic cameras. When evaluating an automatic camera, consider which of these features are most important to you.

Determining Exposure

Objective 3-F Describe the desirable characteristics of negatives and digital images and explain how to use an exposure meter to determine proper exposure.

Key Concepts density, characteristic curve, exposure, underexposed, range of density, overexposed, bracketing, scene modes, highlight areas, blocked up, shadow areas, latitude, exposure meter, incident-light meter, reflected-light meter, spot meter, built-in meter, averaging meter, center-weighted meter, multisegment meter, film speed setting, exposure scale, average gray, overall reading, close-up reading, highlight reading, shadow reading, range of brightness

Range of Density in Film Images

Just as the amount of light reaching the film varies, the amount of silver deposited on the film also varies. Areas of the film receiving much light will possess greater silver **density** than areas receiving little light. These variations of silver density create the image in the negative and later in the final print.

Each film responds to light in a unique and characteristic way. This response can be graphed to show how much the silver density will increase for any given increase in the amount of light. (See Figure 3-16.) This **characteristic curve** (also known as an H & D curve after its inventors, Hurter and Driffield) shows how a particular film's silver density will respond to varying amounts of exposure.

Table 3-4. Automatic camera feature checklist

Manufacturer: _____

Model: _____

Focus Controls
- Auto-focus
- Focus lock
- Manual mode
- Macro (close-up) focusing

Focal Length Control
- Normal lens
- Telephoto lens
- Wide-angle lens
- Manual zoom lens
- Power zoom lens

Exposure Controls
- Fully automatic
- Aperture priority
- Shutter priority
- Programmed exposure
- Variable shutter speeds
- Continuously variable apertures
- Exposure lock
- Backlight compensation
- Exposure compensation
- Spot metering
- Fully manual mode

Flash Controls
- Automatic flash
- Flash-fill
- Anti-red-eye feature
- Automatic flash disable
- Multiflash (strobe)
- Wide-angle flash
- Telephoto flash

Other Controls
- Automatic load
- Autoread DX codes to set ISO index
- Automatic rewind at end of film
- Remote release
- Self-timer
- Automatic advance
- Continuous shooting

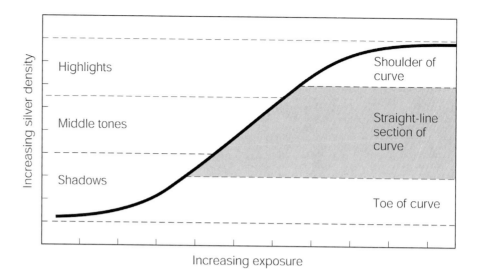

Figure 3-16. The characteristic (H & D) curve.

Examining the characteristic curve of any film reveals that silver density does not increase in proportion to increases in exposure at all levels of brightness. At both low and high levels of exposure, the so-called toe and shoulder of the curve, great increases in brightness produce only slight increases in density. Only in the middle of the curve, the straight line section, does density increase in proportion to increases in exposure. That is why it is important to make exposures near the middle part of the curve—so that areas of different brightness within the scene will be recorded with maximum differences in silver density.

Underexposed negatives are those that receive too little light. The entire brightness range of a scene is recorded near the low end of the curve. As a result, the darkest and brightest objects in the scene differ little in silver density, and, overall, the negative appears thin and exhibits a narrow **range of density**. The negative will produce a dark print that will possess little tonal separation in the middle tones and shadows. (See Figure 3-17 A, B.)

Overexposed negatives are those that receive too much light. The entire brightness range of a scene is recorded near the high end of the curve. Here, too, the darkest and brightest objects in the scene differ little in silver density; however, overall, this negative appears dense with silver and exhibits a narrow range of density. The negative will produce a light, grainy print that will possess little tonal separation in the middle tones and highlights. (See Figure 3-17 E, F.)

Range of Density in Digital Images

Like conventional film cameras, digital cameras produce images by capturing the amount of lightness and darkness in a scene. Digital imaging sensors behave in a way that is similar to film. As the amount of light striking the sensor varies so does the electrical charge produced by the imaging sensor. Areas of the sensor receiving more light produce a stronger electrical charge than areas receiving less light. These variations in electrical charges are translated into digital data by a processor inside the camera. These digital data are then used to create an image on the viewing monitor and later on the final print.

Each type of imaging sensor behaves in a unique way, but in general their response to light also follows a characteristic curve. Like its film counterpart, an image sensor's electrical output does not increase in direct proportion to increases in exposure from all levels of brightness. At both low and high levels of exposure, the toe and shoulder of the curve, great increases in brightness produce only slight changes in the cells' electrical current. Like film, it is only in the middle of the curve, the so-called straight-line section, that the imaging sensor responds proportionally to light. Unlike film, imaging sensors have a short straight-line section and very abbreviated toe and shoulder regions. This means they have very little exposure latitude. The result is that even slight exposure differences will result in considerable differences in image detail.

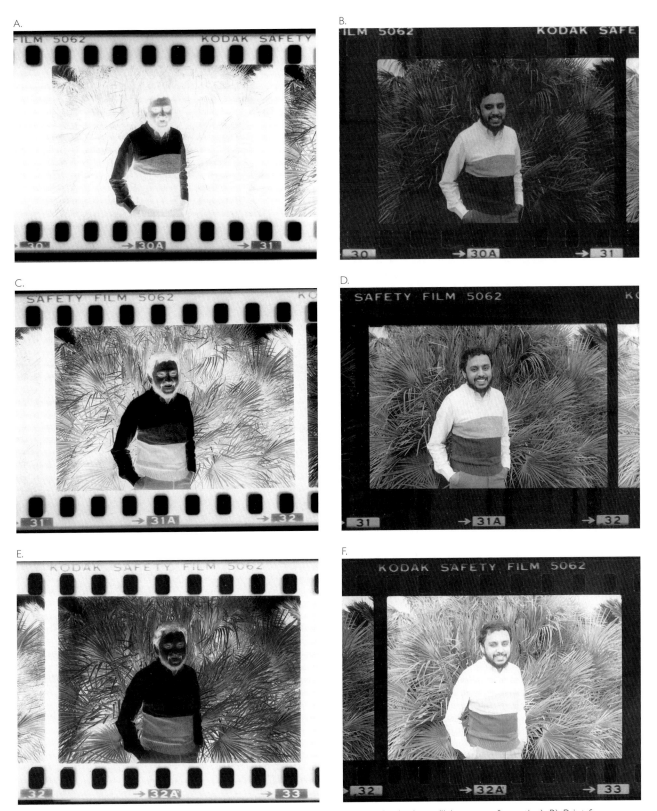

Figure 3-17. Improper exposure of negative. A) Underexposure: detail is lost in shadows (light areas of negative). B) Print from underexposed negative. Print appears muddy; details in shadow lost. C) Normal negative. Well-exposed negative records details with optimal contrast over the full brightness range of the scene. Shadow and highlight details present. D) Print from normal negative. Prints full range of details throughout the brightness range. E) Overexposed negative. Detail is lost in highlights (dark areas of negative. F) Print from overexposed negative. Print appears washed out; details in highlights obscured.

Underexposed digital images are those that receive too little light. The entire brightness range of the scene is recorded too low on the curve and some shadow details will be lost. Overall, the image appears dark with reduced separation between shadows and midtones. Subsequent processing with image-editing software can lighten the image and make a better print; however, the shadow detail can never be fully restored.

Overexposed digital images are those that have received too much light. The entire brightness range of the scene is recorded too high up on the curve and some highlight details will be lost. Overall, the image appears too light and separation between the midtones and highlights is reduced. Highlights become featureless blocks of flat white devoid of detail and tone. Image editing can be applied to darken the print; however, the highlight detail is forever gone.

Bracketing

Bracketing is an easy way to assure that you get an accurate exposure in uncertain lighting conditions. To bracket exposures manually, simply take several shots, altering the shutter speeds or aperture by 1/2 to 1 stop for each image. Usually 3–5 shots are sufficient to obtain an accurate exposure.

Many automatic cameras provide an auto-bracketing feature that allows the camera to take a sequence of 2 to 5 shots using different exposure settings. Typically, these shots will be made at, over, and under the indicated exposure.

You need not bracket every shot you take; just those for which your camera's meter might indicate a wrong exposure. This usually occurs when dark tones or light tones dominate a scene, or when the range of density is too great for the camera to record.

For example, a night shot of a building lit by floodlight might produce a contrast range between the spotlights and the dark sky that will be too high for film or sensor. This is a situation where bracketing might help. Take a few shots at, under, and over the indicated exposure, or use the auto-bracketing feature, and then review the images to see which one best records the lit buildings and the surroundings.

Scene Modes

To make setting exposure simpler, many modern cameras offer a variety of **scene modes** that correspond to your subject. One standard is usually a fully programmed mode in which the camera sets both the aperture and shutter speed automatically based on brightness, contrast, film speed, and subject distance. Other scene modes are frequently offered as well.

A few typical examples could be:

Figure 3-18. Scene Mode Icons

Landscape mode will set a small aperture to maximize depth of field. Your image will be sharp in the foreground and background.

Portrait mode will choose a large aperture to keep the background out of focus and direct attention to your subject.

Action mode will select fast shutter speeds to freeze the action.

Night scene will balance a burst of fill-in flash with a long exposure for the background.

Close-up or macro mode combines a medium aperture with a faster shutter speed to avoid camera shake. These modes allow you to focus on objects at amazingly small distances.

You may also find sunset; beach; or party modes.

Apart from these fully automatic modes some cameras also offer shutter priority and aperture priority modes that allow you to set the shutter speed or aperture manually while the camera automatically sets the other control to obtain a correct exposure.

Desirable Characteristics of Negatives and Digital Images

The preceding discussion emphasizes the importance of determining a proper exposure that will record the entire brightness range of the scene, with the middle tones being recorded near the middle part of the curve. In this way, brightness differences in the scene will produce optimum tonal separations throughout the brightness range. Under most circumstances it is advisable to strive to expose for the middle of the curve in order to record the widest range of tones and the maximum tonal separations. To accomplish this, proper exposure must be used. (See Figure 3-17 C, D.)

The well-exposed image will be rich in detail. The **highlight areas** (the densest areas of a negative) will reveal many distinct details and variations in density. For example, the image of a white shirt in sunlight should reveal the texture of the cloth, its folds and wrinkles, and the separation of the collar against the front lapel. If these areas are overexposed, such details will be **blocked up**—lost in the density of the silver deposits that record that highlight area on a negative or pushed to a pure white on a digital image. Blocked-up areas are difficult and often impossible to print well.

Similarly, the **shadow areas** (the thinnest areas of a film negative) will reveal distinct details and variations in density. The image of a black flannel suit in the shade of a tree should also reveal its texture, folds, wrinkles, and lapels. If these areas are underexposed, such details will not be recorded at all. No printing technique can replace details that are not recorded on the negative or image sensor.

Important characteristics of a well-exposed image, therefore, are its recording of detail in both highlight and shadow areas and its possession of tonal variations corresponding to brightness differences throughout the brightness range. Nevertheless, if the brightness range is very great, some of the darker tones will be recorded near the low end of the curve and some of the brighter tones near the high end. And even though tonal differences may be seen in the scene's shadows and highlights, even the most responsive film or image sensor may not record effectively all that the eye can see.

Thus, a film or image chip's **latitude** is less than that of the eye; that is, both are less sensitive to the range of brightness. In those cases in which the range of brightness in the scene exceeds a film's latitude, it is usually preferable to favor the shadow areas by exposing toward the shoulder of the curve. This tends to preserve the shadow detail while overexposing the extreme highlights, a

type of exposure that can be partially corrected when the final print is made. Figure 3-17 A–F illustrates these principles of proper exposure.

If a digital image sensor's latitude is less than the brightness range the reverse is suggested. When digital imaging under extreme brightness ranges it is preferable to favor the highlight areas of the scene while perhaps underexposing the extreme shadows. This prevents the loss of important highlight detail and the shadow areas can be partially corrected with image-editing software.

Correct exposure is best determined with an **exposure meter**. By measuring precisely the intensity of light in various parts of the scene, the meter serves as a tool for determining an exposure that will record the scene with exactly the desired tonal range.

Using Exposure Meters

There are two basic kinds of exposure meters— **incident-light meters** and **reflected-light meters**. Incident-light meters read the intensity of light reaching the scene from all sources; reflected-light meters read the intensity of light being reflected from the various objects in the scene. Incident-light meters are designed to measure the relatively brighter intensity of light sources; reflected-light meters are designed to measure the much lower intensities of reflected light. Sometimes a single meter can be adjusted for use either way. Cameras with built-in exposure meters generally measure reflected light.

Usually a light meter admits light through a small aperture or diffusion screen to a photosensitive cell. When light strikes this cell a small current of electricity is induced proportional to the intensity of the light. This current deflects the meter's indicator needle. The brighter the light that strikes the cell, the more the needle is deflected. The needle is referenced to an exposure scale that helps the photographer determine a proper exposure.

Incident-light Meters Incident-light meters are designed to measure light falling on the subject. To measure incident light, the meter is placed in the subject area, and its light-sensitive cell is pointed in the direction of the camera. The diffuser bulb or panel must be used if the meter requires it. Light falling on the subject then will fall on the photosensitive cell, and the needle will indicate its intensity. From this reading a set of equivalent exposures is easily determined.

Use of the incident-light meter assumes that the scene has an average contrast range and the suggested exposure setting will yield correct shadows, midtones and highlights. If the light falling on the subject varies in intensity, as when a pattern of shadows falls upon the scene, readings taken from both the brighter and darker light sources must be averaged to measure the average light intensity. (See Figure 3-19 A, B.)

Reflected-light Meters Reflected-light meters are designed to measure light reflected from the subject. Cameras with built-in light meters use this type of meter. To measure reflected light, the meter is placed between the camera and the subject and its light-sensitive cell is pointed in the direction of the subject. A diffuser bulb or panel must not be used when measuring reflected light. Light reflected from the subject toward the camera then will fall on the photosensitive cell and the needle will indicate its intensity.

Various objects within a scene reflect different intensities of light; white objects, for example, reflect more light than black ones. The meter may be used to measure these various intensities separately by bringing it close to the various objects in the scene. A major advantage of the reflected-light meter is that it can be used to measure the light reflected from different areas of the scene and to evaluate the different effects these areas will have upon the negative image. Exposure may then be set to obtain optimal negative density for the more important elements in a scene. (See Figure 3-20 A, B, C.)

Use of the reflected-light meter assumes that the objects in the scene have average reflectance and the suggested exposure setting will yield correct middletones. If the highlights or shadows in the scene are excessively light or dark, the indicated

A.

B.

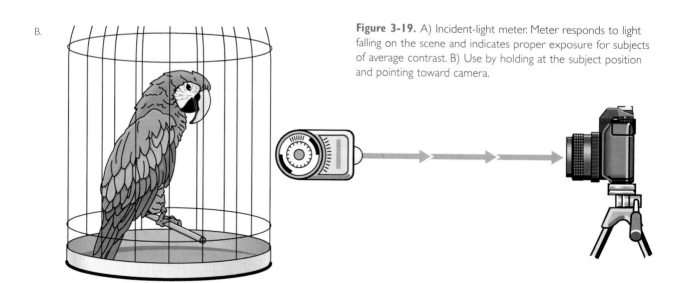

Figure 3-19. A) Incident-light meter. Meter responds to light falling on the scene and indicates proper exposure for subjects of average contrast. B) Use by holding at the subject position and pointing toward camera.

A.

B.

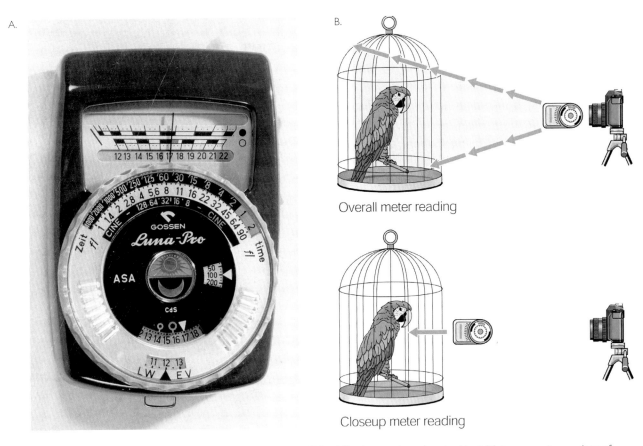

Overall meter reading

Closeup meter reading

Figure 3-20. A) Hand-held reflecting light meter. Set meter to ISO of film in use, then aim at subject. Meter suggests a variety of equivalent exposures. B) Hold near the camera for an overall reading of the scene. C) Hold near the subject for a close-up light meter reading of a detail.

exposures must be decreased or increased accordingly to retain their detail.

Spot Meters The **spot meter** is a special type of reflected-light meter that is designed to obtain reflected-light measurements from very small areas within a scene with the meter positioned at some distance from the subject. From on the shore, for example, the spot meter can be used to obtain separate readings from the sailboats on the lake, the surface of the lake, the forest areas on the far side, the snowcapped mountains in the distance, and the sky. (See Figure 3-21.)

Built-In Meters

Both amateur and professional photographers commonly use light meters built into the camera itself. There are many types of **built-in meters**. Some simply report the intensity of light in the scene toward which the camera is directed and permit the camera to be set manually to an appropriate exposure. Some automatically set the camera to an appropriate exposure based upon the

Figure 3-21. Spot meter with digital readout.

Figure 3-22. Built-in meters. A) Averaging meters combine measurements from all areas of the frame. If important details are not dominant, they may not be properly exposed. Here, bright sky in half of frame caused important details to be underexposed, producing a muddy-looking print. B) Here, a correct exposure was determined by pointing the camera downward to emphasize details in the darker half of the frame. Then the indicated exposure was used to make this shot.

A.

B.

meter's reading. Some permit a choice between manual and automatic operation.

Among built-in light meters, the three most common types are **averaging meters**, **center-weighted meters** and **multisegment meters**. The more common type is the averaging meter; it is designed to measure the average brightness reflected from all parts of the scene and to determine an appropriate setting based on this average. This works well for subjects of limited contrast and even lighting, but for scenes of high contrast, care must be taken to ensure that important objects in the scene are well exposed.

The center-weighted meter assumes that the important objects in a scene usually appear near the center of the frame. The meter is designed, therefore, to base its measurement mainly on light from this center area. This works well when the important objects are near the center of the scene, but care must be taken to ensure that important objects are well exposed when they occur elsewhere in the scene.

Some cameras use **multisegment meters**. This type of system is sometimes called matrix metering and uses a computer program to analyze individual light measurements from various parts of the scene. The software has been programmed to

C.

D.

Figure 3-22. (continued). Built-in meters. C) Center-weighted meters are more sensitive to areas near the center of the frame. Here, bright window at the center causes surrounding details to be underexposed. D) A correct exposure was determined by pointing the camera downward to exclude window. Then the indicated exposure setting was used to make this shot.

adjust for some typical exposure problems such as backlighting. (See Figure 3-22 A, B, C, D.)

Using a Hand-held Light Meter

The most common type of light meter in use today is the reflected-light meter. The meter itself measures the amount of light available in the scene. The film speed must be programmed into the meter by adjusting the **film speed setting**. Then, by matching the **exposure scale** to the meter reading, the exposure data can be read directly off the scale. Figure 3-20A shows a meter that has been set for a film speed of ISO 100, which appears in a small window. Observe also

that the indicator needle has been deflected to 17. Using this information, the photographer has adjusted the outer dial of the exposure scale to place the indicator arrow in the next lower window, also at 17. The set of equivalent exposures appropriate to the scene now may be read directly from the exposure scale at the top of the dial. In this case the set of equivalent exposures includes 1/250 sec. at f/4, 1/125 sec. at f/5.6, and so forth.

What do these indicated exposures mean? What is recorded on the film if one of these indicated exposures is used? To control the effects of exposure on the film and to select an exposure that will produce the desired results, the photographer

Table 3-5. Exposure override settings

Setting or condition	Metering and exposure problem	Common overrides	Alternate solution
Landscape or cityscape with sun in the frame	Meter is fooled by the sun resulting in considerable underexposure	Increase exposure by +2.5 stops	Take meter reading with camera pointed down to exclude the sun
Backlit person or subject against the sun or a window	Meter will underexpose and turn subject into a silhouette	Increase exposure by +2 stops	Use spot meter or take a close-up meter reading, use fill flash
Snow-covered landscape or white beach	Meter will underexpose and make the snow gray	Increase exposure +1.5 to +2 stops	Take a substitute reading from a gray card
Person on snow or white beach	Meter will underexpose and make the person too dark	Increase exposure by +1.5 stops	Use spot meter or take a close-up meter reading
Landscape or cityscape with most of the frame showing bright sky	Meter is fooled by the bright sky and will make the foreground too dark	Increase exposure by +1 stop	Take meter reading with camera pointed down to exclude the sky
Very dark subject nearly fills frame	Meter will overexpose and make the subject gray	Decrease exposure by −1 to −1.5 stops	Take a substiture reading from a gray card
Spotlight entertainer surrounded by dark region	Overexposure may occur	Decrease exposure by −1 stop. Bracket exposures.	Use spot meter

should understand what the meter is reporting. Light reflected from various areas in the scene acts on the photoelectric cell, with light areas reflecting more light and dark areas reflecting less. The meter reports the *average* of all these various light intensities in the scene. The exposure scale has been calibrated in manufacture to give an exposure setting that, using standard procedures, will produce a negative that will print objects of average brightness as an average shade of gray. Thus, if an indicated exposure is used, objects of average brightness in the scene will be rendered an **average gray**, no matter how light or dark the scene is overall.

Imagine three blank cards, one black, one gray, and one white. Using a reflected-light meter, suppose you obtain a reading from the black card and use the indicated exposure to shoot its picture. You then do the same for each of the remaining cards, obtaining two more readings and using the indicated exposures to shoot two more pictures. What do you find when the three pictures are processed and printed using standard procedures? The three cards are no longer black, gray, and white; they all appear the same average shade of gray in their respective photographs. (See Figure

3-23 A, B, C.) The meter indicates the exposure to use to make the average brightness seen by the meter appear as an average shade of gray. To obtain tones darker or lighter than this in the final print, the indicated exposure must be modified. This is especially true for scenes with an average brightness that is darker or lighter than average gray. It is also true if the photographer wishes to make a final print that is darker or lighter than the average brightness in the original scene.

Average Reading When photographing a large scene in which the light intensities are distributed fairly evenly—such as a landscape, seascape, or group photo under overcast skies—a reflected-light meter can be used from the camera position. Point the meter toward the scene to obtain an **overall** or **average reading**, and use one of the indicated exposures. Be careful not to point the meter toward the sky; tip it slightly downward. If the meter reads too much skylight, it will inflate the average reading, leading to underexposure of the shadow areas.

Close-up Reading When photographing a scene in which there are extreme highlight and shadow areas, an average reading may not be satisfactory.

A.

B.

C.

Figure 3-23. A) Exposure set at white card light reading. Note the white card appears gray. B) Exposure set at gray card light reading. Note the gray card appears gray. C) Exposure set at black card light reading. Note the black card appears gray

Suppose the subject is a sunlit girl in a white dress against a background of dark, shadowed trees. At some distance the overall reading will be influenced unduly by the darkness of the trees, leading to indicated exposures that will overexpose the subject. In such cases, take the meter closer to the subject, to a point at which subject and background are represented more equally. Such a **close-up reading** will assure you that the indicated exposure is not influenced excessively by irrelevant background details.

Whether the average or the close-up method is used, the meter should be pointed along the axis of the camera, viewing the subject from the same angle as the camera. Figure 3-20 depicts both methods.

Range of Brightness When a scene has a wide range of brightness, with extreme highlight and shadow areas, selecting a proper exposure is more difficult. If exposure is based on the brightest areas in the scene, the darkest areas may be underexposed and hence fail to record details in the shadow areas. If exposure is based on the darkest areas of the scene, the brightest areas may be overexposed, so that details in the highlight areas may be too dense and blocked up to print well. To overcome these difficulties, the photographer must find an optimal exposure between the two extremes that will record the maximum detail within the full range of brightness.

One way to determine this exposure is to take the light meter to several points in the scene for close-up readings. Find the brightest important area in the scene and take a **highlight reading**. Then find the darkest important area in the scene and take a **shadow reading**. Average the two readings and select an exposure midway between the two extremes. This exposure will record light intensities midway in the brightness

Careers in Photography

Publications and Media Photography

The field generally defined as publications photography includes photography for a wide range of visual media, including newspapers, magazines, motion pictures, and television. It may also include not only news and promotional photography, but also advertising photography and photo illustration. Many of the larger media organizations, such as daily newspapers, wire services, television networks, and major television stations, employ their own photographers who carry out specific news and promotional assignments. Assignment work, however, falls far short of satisfying the needs of most major media, which must then compete with one another for the work of freelance photographers who service this market and who are willing to sell their work to all comers.

News photography is a form of photojournalism that focuses on events of current public interest—such fast-breaking events as war, crime, catastrophe, political or sporting events, or even ordinary human activities of timely general interest. One characteristic that distinguishes news photography is its timeliness—a

A. Photo Illustration refers to making photographs that visually interpret, present, or clarify a concept or an idea.

B. The spot news photographer must be fast and resourceful to cover events, such as this fire, and get the photograph back to the home office in time to make the deadline.

news photograph must usually be published within hours of an event for it to have news value. The news photographer must find a way to get to the scene fast, even when an event occurs in an inaccessible area, to get the story, and to deliver the photographs rapidly for timely publication. To become a successful news photographer, one must possess uncommon single-mindedness about making photographs that tell the story—to a degree that obstacles, including the photographer's personal safety, are often ignored. Many find the frequent exposure to such dangers as fire, flood, crime, and conflict stimulating and develop a kind of insulation from the emotions that might impede their work. (See Careers in Photography: News and Photojournalism, in Unit 6.)

Generally, advertising photography creates pictures that are published in the print, film, television, or internet media for the primary purpose of selling products, services, or organizational images. Freelance or commercial photographers under the direction of advertising designers typically carry it out, although some larger advertising agencies employ their own photographers. Unlike photography for personal expression or photojournalism, photography for advertising requires photographers to subordinate their personal attitudes and points of view to the selling task, upon which all imagination and creativity are focused. Although most advertising photographs are made in studios, a trend toward realism in advertising has led to an increased preference for photographs made in natural locations. Advertising photographers, therefore, must be able to work under any conditions that may be required by the client or the job. Today, a good deal of the work of an advertising photographer consists of finding suitable locations, interviewing and hiring models, working with clothing stylists and makeup artists, and producing numerous proofs and test prints for approval before actually shooting an assignment.

Photo illustration refers to making photographs that visually interpret, present, or clarify a concept or an idea. Photo illustrations may be made by freelance or commercial photographers, or by in-house industrial photographers that many larger companies employ. Photographic illustrations are published most frequently in brochures, annual reports, calendars, slide shows, and multi-media presentations. Typically, a photo illustration is made from a carefully planned setup, in the studio or on location, for the specific purpose of visually communicating an abstract idea so that a lay audience may more easily understand it.

Although publications and media photography is a field that is easily entered, it is a highly competitive and speculative business in which the freelancer can expend enormous time and resources without selling very much. The business tends to favor those who possess not only photographic skills but also reportorial, writing, and communication skills. Freelance media photographers who can put a story together, write effective copy and captions, and create images that effectively communicate abstract ideas are more likely receive freelance assignments and to sell their work than their counterparts who possesses only technical photographic skills.

range as an average gray and maximize details recorded between the two extremes. This procedure is known as the **range-of-brightness** method for determining exposure. For best results with this method, obtain readings only from areas that are important. Ignore unimportant areas, even though they may be lighter or darker. If the shadow details are of special importance, using an exposure about two-thirds of the way toward the shadow exposure will improve the overall results.

Sometimes, of course, the photographer may not be interested in recording the entire range of detail and tone. Suppose, for example, that the subject is a sunlit portrait against a dark background of trees. In this case a full range of detail and tone in the face may be desired; the detail and tone in the trees is not important. One approach would be to take both highlight and shadow readings from the face of the subject, selecting an exposure between these extremes and ignoring the darker shadows of the background altogether.

Exposure for Shadows or Highlights The latitude of most black-and-white films and digital sensors approximates four stops—they will record details within a range of brightness in which highlight areas are as much as sixteen times brighter than shadow areas. If the brightness range in a scene exceeds these limits, the range of brightness method may result in loss of detail in both the highlights and the shadows. One approach to solving this problem is to obey the dictum "expose for the shadows," or, more precisely, expose for at least a minimum of shadow density. One way to use this technique is to first obtain a meter reading for the darkest important shadow area in the scene. Then reduce exposure two stops from the indicated meter reading. This renders the darkest area as thin as possible on the negative while preserving details in the shadows. Of course, highlight areas may be overexposed because the exposure is not reduced enough to unblock them; however, overexposure can be compensated for somewhat during processing and printing. Details that have not been recorded on the film in the first place can never be recovered. For this reason, many photographers give priority to shadow areas when determining exposure, even when it means that highlight areas will be overexposed.

When using digital cameras or slide films the highlight areas are generally more important than shadows. In these cases, priority may be given to the highlights, even if it means sacrificing details in the shadows. To do so, first obtain a meter reading of the brightest important highlight area in that scene. Then increase exposure two stops from the indicated meter reading. In this way the brightest areas will be rendered correctly while preserving details in the highlights. The shadow areas may be underexposed and detail lost, however, because the exposure has not been increased sufficiently to record them.

These procedures for exposing for shadows or for highlights may produce more satisfying results than the other methods discussed whenever the range of brightness exceeds the latitude of the film. They are simple adaptations of the zone system, which is discussed further in Unit 15.

The 18 Percent Gray Card Reflected-light meters are designed to indicate exposures that will record an average light reflectance as a middle tone of gray. The industry standard for this average light level is 18 percent reflectance. This means that an object that reflects 18 percent of the light falling on it would be seen as average by a reflected-light meter. The exposures indicated by the meter would record that object as a middle tone of gray.

One way to take advantage of this feature is to obtain a meter reading from an object of average reflectance and then use an exposure indicated by the meter. Because it is difficult to judge which objects in a scene are of average reflectance, an 18 percent gray card may be substituted for this purpose. A gray card will simplify many metering situations, especially those characterized by out-of-the-ordinary lighting conditions.

Use of an 18 percent gray card will not solve the problem of a scene with a range of brightness greater than the latitude of the film. It will only ensure recording the average portions of the scene as middle gray tones. If the scene has an excessively wide brightness range, both highlight and shadow details may be lost in the process. In such situations it may be better to modify the indicated exposures to expose for the shadows, as discussed earlier.

The 18 percent gray card is also useful for color printing and electronic image editing. Because the card has standard reflectance and neutral color, it may be used to serve as a reference tone to guide the image processing. Many photographers using color negative film will start each roll by shooting a frame showing an 18 percent gray card. This frame then serves as a color reference to help determine the precise color balance of the original scene.

Most commercially made gray cards have a white surface of 90-percent reflectance on the opposite side. The white side may be used in low-light levels when the gray side does not reflect enough light to obtain an accurate reading. If the white side is used, the indicated exposure must be increased by two and one-half stops to obtain the reading equivalent to 18 percent reflectance.

Simulating Close-up Readings If the scene is such that close-up readings cannot be taken (and a spot meter is not available), the lighting situation can be simulated using objects close at hand. Consider the view across the lake, for example, with sailboats on the lake, trees on the far side, and snowcapped mountains in the distance. A close-up reading from a white sheet of paper can simulate the white sails and snow, and a reading from a nearby tree can simulate a distant tree. The palm of the hand can be used to simulate similar flesh tones at a distance. Remember, however, that these substitutes will serve only if they are of similar reflectance and are viewed in the same type of illumination as the objects they simulate.

The use of the exposure meter to obtain previsualized tonal values is discussed in Unit 15.

The steps for using a hand-held reflected-light meter are reviewed in the Step-by-Step box.

Using a Hand-Held Reflected-Light Meter

1. *Set the meter for the speed of the film you are using.*

2. *Point the meter toward the subject or area of interest. Always position the meter between the camera and the subject so that the meter sees the subject as the camera sees it.*

3. *Set the adjustable ring of the exposure scale to correspond to the needle reading.*

4. *Read the exposure scale.*

5. *Take as many readings as necessary for the method you are using.*

6. *Select an exposure that will record the details and tones in the scene as you want them to appear.*

7. *Set your camera for the exposure you have selected.*

Questions to Consider

1. What types of focusing systems are most commonly used with 35mm cameras? What are the advantages and disadvantages of each? What type does your own camera use? How is the focus setting adjusted on your camera?

2. What are the various types of exposure setting systems most commonly used with 35mm cameras? How are the shutter and aperture adjusted on your own camera? What is the fastest shutter speed available? The fastest aperture?

3. Given exposure settings of 1/60 sec. at f/5.6 on your own camera, what might you do to double the exposure? To reduce it by half?

4. What steps would you take to obtain maximum depth of field using hyperfocal focusing with your own camera? How might you minimize the effect of a "busy background" by controlling depth of field?

5. You should be able to calculate equivalent exposures so that you can use an aperture and shutter speed appropriate for your subject. Suppose you determine that a correct exposure for your subject would be 1/125 sec. at f/5.6. If you wished to use an aperture of f/2 instead, what would be the correct shutter speed to obtain an equivalent exposure? If you wished to use a shutter speed of 1/30 sec., what would be the correct aperture to obtain an equivalent exposure?

6. What features of an automatic camera do you consider to be most important? Why?

7. How would you set your exposure settings to freeze the movement of a fast-moving subject? To blur the movement of a fast-moving subject? To freeze the movement of a fast-moving subject against a blurred background?

8. How would you use your reflected-light meter if you wanted the tones in your final image to correspond to the brightness tones in the entire scene? If you wanted a particular object to appear as a middle gray tone? If you wanted a particular object to appear as a near white tone? If you wanted a particular object to appear as a near black tone?

Suggested Field and Laboratory Assignments

1. Take your camera and light meter outside during daylight hours. Shoot a roll of color transparency film and a roll of black-and-white film. Shoot a variety of subjects under a variety of lighting conditions. Be sure to include close-ups and long shots, some in bright sunlight, some in shade, some moving subjects, and some stationary subjects. Shoot toward the light source and away from the light source. Use your meter to determine proper exposures: Try each method of determining exposure. Keep a shooting log (see Table 3-6). Record a log entry for each shot showing lighting condition, meter method, and exposure.

2. Have your color film commercially processed. Keep your black-and-white film for processing according to the directions given in the next unit.

3. Review your color slides with your shooting log in hand. Note those slides that appeared as you expected them to appear. Then note the slides that appeared otherwise. What went wrong? What should you do to improve results the next time you approach a similar situation?

4. Use a digital camera to shoot a variety of subjects in various lighting situations. Include shots in the bright sunlight, in open shade, a backlit subject, indoors by window light, indoors under artificial light, and an outdoor cityscape at night. Note how the sensors respond to various lighting conditions and what controls you can use to enhance the details in the highlights and shadows.

Table 3-6. Shooting log

Date: June 24   Roll: 1   Film: T-Max 100 (ISO 100/21°)

Shot	Lighting Condition	Method	Exposure
1	Bright sunlight	Average	f/11 @ 250
2	Backlight; face shaded	Close-up	f/5.6 @ 250
3	All in shade	Average	f/5.6 @ 250

UNIT
4

Film and Digital Materials

James Bunoan, untitled.

Unit at a Glance

Films for modern cameras are available in a great variety of types, sizes, and formats. Many films are designed to be used for general purposes, while others are designed for more specific needs. No one film is perfect for all occasions. Sometimes the photographer might select a film that possesses qualities especially suited to a particular subject, such as fast action photography, portraits, night action, or landscapes. At other times, when the exact conditions may be difficult to predict, a photographer might select a general purpose film that is adequate for many subjects and occasions.

The equivalent to film in digital cameras is a system composed of an optical imaging sensor and some form of electronic storage media. Light falling on an imaging sensor inside a digital camera or scanner produces an electrical charge that is proportional to its intensity. A measurement of the resulting electrical charge is converted into numerical form through an analog-to-digital converter and then written to magnetic or optical storage media. Although the sensors are not interchangeable, most cameras have various settings that change the sensitivity of the sensor and its response to light and color. In this way one sensor can be made to act like a variety of different conventional films.

This unit explores the way film works, the ways film is packaged, the various qualities that should be considered when selecting film, and how film should be handled and stored. The characteristics of black-and-white films, including their speed, color sensitivity, graininess, contrast, resolving power, acutance, and latitude are discussed. The characteristics of color reversal and color negative films are also explained, including the factors that affect color balance and the various products that can be obtained from them.

The unit also outlines the way digital sensors work and their characteristics, including resolution and color sensitivity. The various forms of storage media are described along with compression methods. Common file types are discussed and characterized.

Descriptions of commonly available film and electronic storage products are provided in Appendix G on the accompanying CD.

The Photographic Process

Objective 4-A Describe the photographic process and the composition of black-and-white film.

Key Concepts silver halides, gelatin, emulsion, latent image, silver process, top coating, subbing adhesive layer, support, antihalation backing, second adhesive layer

Although they are not perfect in this respect, most photographic films and digital sensors are designed to be sensitive to the visible light spectrum and to record their encounters with light energy much as the human eye does. However, were you to look at a roll of exposed but undeveloped film in full light, you would see no hint of the pictures stored there. The pictures stored in the film are totally invisible to the naked eye until the film has been chemically processed.

To better understand how the photographic process works, we will look first at the structure and composition of a typical photographic film. At first glance, ordinary film appears to consist of a flexible base on which there is a soft, smooth, cream-yellow or gray coating. The coating can be scratched if handled roughly, and it can be washed off with hot water. The back of the film may appear blue, green, or reddish gray.

Underlying this simple appearance is a complex structure that has developed over a period of 150 years as photography pioneers pieced together the chemistry that makes photography possible. Figure 4-2 shows a cross-section of a typical black-and-white film. Within the creamy coating are millions of microscopic crystals of **silver halides**—mainly silver bromide and silver iodide—suspended evenly in a thin layer of **gelatin**. This coating, called the **emulsion**, is the principal active component of the film. The silver halides are sensitive to light. An encounter with light changes their chemical structure—the greater the encounter, the greater the change. Yet the changes are so slight they cannot be seen even with a microscope. These minute alterations in the silver halide crystals form what is called a **latent image**—a hidden image waiting to be revealed.

The developing chemicals detect these changes and force the exposed silver halide crystals to release their metallic silver. As free silver is released, it clings to the latent image, slowly increasing in density until finally it creates a visible image. The fact that silver halides that have been exposed to light will release their metallic silver when developed is the basis of what is called **silver process** photography, the process that dominated the photography industry until the recent digital revolution.

A thin **top coat** protects the soft **emulsion** from casual abrasion as it moves through the camera. A **subbing adhesive layer** helps the emulsion bond to the **support** material. The support itself is a transparent, firm, flexible, chemically stable, plastic base, usually cellulose-acetate or Mylar.

Finally, a dark-colored **antihalation backing** is bonded to the back of the support by a **second adhesive layer**. The antihalation backing is a dyed gelatin that absorbs any intense light that penetrates both the emulsion and the support during exposure. If they are not absorbed, these light rays may reflect back from the far surface of the support into the emulsion and create halo effects around bright points of light in the image, such as around pictures of street lights at night.

Although they are similar in structure and composition, films vary enormously in other respects. Some are designed for black-and-white, others for color photography; some are faster, some slower; some have finer grain than others; some are more sensitive to certain colors than others; some produce negatives, others positive images. You should experiment with a variety of films to explore these special characteristics. Most photographers, however, usually settle on a few films that they use consistently.

Characteristics of Black-and-White Film

Objective 4-B Define some basic characteristics of black-and-white film and explain how these characteristics affect photographs made under various conditions.

Key Concepts speed, fast-speed films, slow-speed films, medium-speed films, film speed ratings, ISO ratings, pushing the film, color sensitivity, panchromatic (pan) film, orthochromatic film, blue-sensitive film, infrared film, grain size, coarse-grain negative, fine-grain negative, coarse-grain film, fine-grain film, graininess, medium-grain film, contrast, inherent contrast, high-contrast film, resolving power, resolution, acutance or sharpness, latitude

Films have many characteristics that affect their performance under different conditions. Some of the more important ones are speed, color sensitivity, grain, contrast, resolving power, acutance, and exposure latitude. All of these characteristics should be considered when choosing a film for a particular purpose.

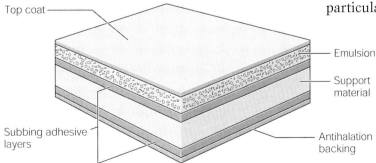

Top coat —
Emulsion
Support material
Subbing adhesive layers
Antihalation backing

Figure 4-2. Cross section of black-and-white film.

Famous Photograph

Eadweard Muybridge's Galloping Horse

Until Eadweard Muybridge's astonishing series of photographs of a galloping horse were published in *Scientific American* in 1878, people had little understanding of the actual movements of animals in motion. For example, it was commonly believed that a horse at gallop always had at least one foot on the ground at all times. Muybridge's photos proved this assumption to be false.

In 1872, Leland Stanford, former governor of California and then president of the Union Pacific Railroad, wagered $25,000 that a horse at gallop lifted all four feet off the ground at some point. He wanted a photographer to settle the bet. He brought the problem to Muybridge, who had earned a checkered reputation as a sometimes inventor, traveler, and government photographer, and who was then working in the Yosemite Valley. With limited equipment and materials, Muybridge managed to produce some "photographic impressions" of the galloping horse, but the results were apparently inconclusive, and no record of these early images remains.

Muybridge, however, was intrigued by the problem, and Stanford was determined. Six years later, in June of 1878, after further experimentation and development, they tried again, staging the event in full view of the press in San Francisco. Muybridge set up twelve cameras, each attached by a fine black thread strung across the track so that each camera would be tripped successively by the galloping horse. The resulting "automatic electric photographs" showed conclusively that all four of the horse's feet left the ground at one point.

Eadweard Muybridge. "Horse in Motion," 1878. Courtesy of Kingston Museum and Heritage Service.

Muybridge was so captivated by his experiments that he devoted the rest of his life to prolific studies of human and animal locomotion. He produced numerous books and lectured internationally on the subject. His studies influenced a generation of artists, physiologists, scientists, and engineers, who used his photographs as aids to their own work.

In 1879 Muybridge introduced the zoöpraxiscope for animating and projecting his motion photographs, producing an effect so realistic that one reporter observed, "The only thing missing was the clatter of hoofs" (sic). What had started out as a simple wager emerged as a milestone in the development of motion picture photography.

Film Speed

Films vary in their sensitivity to light. This characteristic is termed the film's **speed**. Some films are extremely sensitive to light and do not require much exposure to record a usable image. These films are called **fast-speed films**, because their emulsions are highly active and respond to low levels of illumination. Other films require much more exposure to record a usable image. They are called **slow-speed films**, because their emulsions are less active and will respond only to higher levels of illumination. **Medium-speed films**, of course, fall in between.

The **film speed rating** is a numerical index that describes a film's speed. Historically, several different film speed rating systems developed, one in North America, ASA, one in Western Europe, DIN, and one in the Soviet Union, GOST.

In an attempt to standardize film speed ratings, the International Standards Organization developed a system of **ISO ratings**, which most manufacturers now use for film distributed in Western Europe and America. Rather than create a new system, the ISO simply incorporated both ASA and DIN ratings into one rating. A film rated ASA 200 or 24° DIN would be labeled ISO 200/24°.

In general, we may refer to the relative speed of films in the following way:

Slow-speed films: Ratings up to ISO 50/18°

Medium-speed films: Ratings between ISO 64/19° and 160/23°

Fast-speed films: Ratings between ISO 200/24° and 400/27°

Ultrafast-speed films: Ratings over ISO 400/27°

One convenient feature of the ISO system is that the ASA part of the rating is directly proportional to the corresponding film speeds. The speed of an ISO 64/19° film, for example, is twice that of an ISO 32/16° film; half the amount of light will be required to obtain an equivalent exposure. The DIN system, however, works differently. As film speed doubles, the DIN rating increases by 3°. Thus the speed of 24° DIN film is twice that of a 21° DIN film and will require half the amount of light to make an equivalent exposure. Table 4-1

reports some typical film speed ratings and their equivalents in the various systems.

Bear in mind that a film's rated speed is simply a numerical index assigned by the manufacturer that indicates the standard conditions of exposure and processing under which optimal results will be obtained. This index allows the user to compare the relative speeds of films and to obtain similar results when similar standard procedures are followed.

Experienced users may alter the standard conditions, however, to obtain results that are better suited to particular conditions. When a film is processed with a more energetic developer, for example, decreased exposure and increased development time are required to obtain optimal results, and this increases the film's effective speed. Similarly, when a film is processed in a fine-grain developer, increased exposure and decreased development time are required to obtain optimal results, and this decreases the film's effective speed. This technique of varying the development is used mostly to increase the effective film speed and, for this purpose, is known as **pushing the film**.

Negatives that have been pushed may be of less than optimum quality, but the technique permits photography under extremely dim lighting conditions. For example, a photographer might choose

Table 4-1. Equivalent film speed ratings

ASA	DIN	ISO
12	12°	12/12°
20	14°	20/14°
25	15°	25/15°
32	16°	32/16°
40	17°	40/17°
50	18°	50/18°
64	19°	64/19°
80	20°	80/20°
100	21°	100/21°
125	22°	125/22°
160	23°	160/23°
200	24°	200/24°
400	27°	400/27°
800	30°	800/30°
1600	33°	1600/33°
3200	36°	3200/36°
6400	39°	6400/39°
12,500	42°	12500/42°
25,000	45°	25,000/45°

to expose film rated ISO 400/27° as though its rated speed were ISO 3200/36° and then to alter standard processing to compensate for the reduced exposure.

Color Sensitivity

Black-and-white films are sensitive to different colors in varying degrees. Colors are recorded as different shades of gray. Thus black-and-white film sees color simply as varying degrees of brightness. There are several types of film, each of which sees the brightness of various colors differently—that is, each film has a different **color sensitivity**. Four of these films are panchromatic (pan) film, orthochromatic film, blue-sensitive film, and infrared film.

Panchromatic (Pan) Film **Panchromatic (pan) films** are sensitive to all colors. They see various colors in approximately the same brightness ratio as does the human eye. Pan film thus tends to produce black-and-white prints similar in appearance to the way our vision would translate scenes into black and white.

Orthochromatic Film **Orthochromatic films** are sensitive to all colors except red. They can be developed by inspection under a red safelight. Because the film is insensitive to red, reddish objects tend to appear darker in the resulting prints than the eye would expect. This film is no longer in common use.

Blue-sensitive Film **Blue-sensitive films** see only blue. They are blind to all other colors and oversensitive to blue. The film produces high-contrast negatives and prints. Thus it is well suited for black-and-white copy work on line drawings and manuscripts, and it is used extensively in lithography.

Infrared Film **Infrared films** are sensitive primarily to the infrared and blue portions of the spectrum. They are used primarily for technical photography, such as aerial, medical, scientific, industrial, legal, documentary, and photomicrographic photography. Used with a deep orange or red filter, they may give striking and unusual effects in landscapes and similar subjects. (See Figure 11-5, page 380.)

Grain Size

Grain size refers to the grouping or clumping together of the minute silver grains that form the film's negative image. The grain pattern of the negative affects the printed image. If a negative's silver grains are clustered in relatively large clumps, we refer to it as a **coarse-grain negative**. An enlarged print produced from it may appear grainy, mottled, or sandy and may suffer a corresponding reduction in sharpness. A **fine-grain negative**, on the other hand, has the silver grains clustered in relatively small clumps. It is more likely to produce prints that appear sharp and unmottled at the same magnification.

Grain size in negatives is related to several interacting factors:

1. *Film speed.* Faster films tend to be **coarse-grain films**, as their emulsions necessarily are composed of larger, coarser, more light sensitive grains of silver halides. **Fine-grain films** are necessarily slower.
2. *Exposure and processing.* Overexposure and overdevelopment both increase the density of the silver deposits in the negative, thereby increasing negative **graininess**—the degree of coarseness in the image's grain pattern.
3. *Magnification.* Although magnification of the negative image does not alter the grain pattern of the negative, it does reveal it. Normally the graininess of a coarse-grain negative will not be apparent if the size of the final print is close to the size of the negative. But if the image is enlarged for printing, the grain pattern will also be enlarged, and thus the graininess inherent in the negative will become more apparent. Therefore, finer-grain negatives are usually used when greater magnification is required.

Graininess is not always undesirable in a print. The coarse, mottled appearance of a grainy image may serve certain aesthetic purposes. For general photographic purposes, however, many photographers prefer to work with a **medium-speed, medium-grain film** that strikes a compromise between their need for both fine grain and fast speed in a variety of circumstances.

Contrast

Contrast refers to the difference in density between light objects and dark objects in a scene. Factors that affect contrast are film choice, development time, temperature, and agitation. As these factors increase, the contrast for any particular scene's brightness will be increased in the negative. Different films may achieve the same contrast for the same scene, but may reach it in different development times. A film that reaches a given contrast more quickly is said to have higher **inherent contrast**.

The manufacturer controls a film's inherent contrast when the emulsion is prepared. In general, slower films tend to have higher inherent contrast and achieve a given contrast in shorter development times. Faster films tend to have lower inherent contrast and need a longer development time to achieve a given contrast. This built-in characteristic can be increased or decreased by varying the exposure, processing procedures, and printing procedures. For most photographic purposes, photographers prefer to work with medium-speed films that have medium inherent contrast and that achieve normal contrast in moderate development time.

A **high-contrast film** is a special type of film that records only black-and-white tones—no middle gray tones. It is used in lithography and graphic arts to reproduce line copy, to make halftone negatives, and sometimes to impart a special effect to continuous tone images.

Resolving Power

A film's ability to record distinguishable fine detail is called its **resolving power**. A film's resolving power is tested by photographing sets of parallel lines that vary in size and in distance from one another. Then the negative image is examined under a microscope to determine the number of lines per millimeter that are recognizable as separate lines—the number beyond which the lines fuse together and become indistinguishable.

The resolving power of films ranges from low, where no more than 55 lines per millimeter may be distinguished, to ultra-high, where more than 600 lines per millimeter may be distinguished.

The **resolution** evident in any given negative is very sensitive to exposure and falls off rapidly with under- or overexposure. Achieving optimal resolution with any given film depends on correct exposure, subject contrast, and other factors.

Acutance

The **acutance**, or **sharpness**, of a film is its ability to record finite edges between adjacent scenic elements. A film's acutance is tested by exposing the film to light while it is partially shaded by a sharp knife edge in contact with the emulsion. When the processed negative is viewed, the edge of the exposed portion, rather than ending abruptly at the unexposed area, can be seen to bleed into it somewhat. This bleeding is caused by the diffusion of light within the emulsion itself. Its extent is determined by the coarseness of the grain and the thickness of the emulsion, and it produces the apparent sharpness of the resulting image. To obtain the highest possible sharpness, select a film with a thin emulsion and fine grain, and avoid overexposure and overdevelopment.

Exposure Latitude

A film's **latitude** is its ability to produce a full range of tones despite variations from standard exposure and development. Films with wide latitude will produce a full range of tones even when exposure and development vary widely from the standard. Films with narrow latitude must be exposed and developed to precise standards to obtain a full range of tones. In general, the faster the film speed, the wider the exposure latitude will be; the slower the film speed, the narrower the exposure latitude will be. Thus, slow films require more accurate exposure and development to give optimal results.

Types of Black-and-White Films

Objective 4-C Name some common types of film, and describe the products and uses of each.

Key Concepts roll film, magazines, cartridges, sheet film, APS cartridge, chromogenic film

Packaging Forms

Films are packaged in forms suitable for the cameras in which they will be used. Some cameras are designed to use a long strip of film on which successive exposures are made. Films for these cameras are packaged in rolls as **roll film**, **magazines**, or **cartridges**. The entire strip of film is designed to be loaded into the camera at one time. Other cameras are designed to use rectangular **sheets** of film. Films for these cameras are packaged in boxes; the photographer preloads the sheets into special holders prior to use. (See Figure 4-3.)

Magazines and Cartridges The 35mm camera was originally designed to use standard motion-picture film. For use in this type of camera, the film is wound onto a spool and contained within a light-tight metal magazine. A short leader of film is left protruding from the magazine for loading onto a take-up spool within the camera. Once inside the camera, the film is advanced from the magazine onto the camera's take-up spool as each exposure is made. When all exposures have been made, the film must be rewound into the magazine before it is removed from the camera.

Many films display an electronic code that looks like a checkerboard pattern on the outside of the magazine or cassette. These DX codes can be read by many automatic, self-loading cameras, which will automatically set the camera's film speed setting when the film is loaded. There may be additional codings on both the film and the magazine or cartridge to identify the type and length of the film for automatic processing and printing machines.

APS film is also distributed in cartridges, but without a protruding film leader. The **APS cartridge** is designed to be inserted into an APS camera's film compartment without manual threading of any kind. The film is coded to set the camera automatically to the correct film speed, film type, and length. When it is inserted, the camera automatically advances the film to the first frame.

Roll Film For many medium format cameras, a strip of film is rolled onto a spool together with an opaque paper backing. This roll of film is inserted into the camera and threaded onto the take-up spool. The camera is sealed, and the film is advanced one exposure at a time onto the take-up spool. When exposures are completed, the take-up spool, now bearing both the film and the backing paper, is removed from the camera for processing.

Sheet Film Sheet film is packaged in boxes of 25 sheets. The boxes may be opened only in total darkness. The film, notched near the corner to aid in identification and handling, is loaded into special light-tight film holders. Each film holder holds two sheets of film. The film holder is inserted into the camera to expose one sheet of film. It is removed, inverted, and reinserted into the camera to expose the second sheet of film. After both sheets of film have been exposed, another film holder containing fresh film must be used. In the darkroom, the exposed sheets of film are removed from the holder for processing.

Figure 4-3. Film packaging: examples of bulk, roll, disc and sheet film.

Film Sizes

Films sizes are internationally standardized, assuring camera and film manufacturers a ready market for their products and assuring the user of the availability of materials throughout the world for almost all modern cameras. Some of the common film sizes are 35mm magazines; APS cartridges; 120 and 220 rolls; 2 1/4in x 3 1/4in, 3 1/4in x 4 1/4in, 4in x 5in, 5in x 7in, 8in x 10in, and 11in x 14in sheets.

Note that not all films are available in all formats. Some may be available in only one format, others in many. The characteristics of any given film may differ somewhat from format to format.

Common Black-and-White Films

Not all films will serve equally well for all purposes. Some films are especially suited for copying, providing high inherent contrast for this purpose. Others are especially suited to infrared photography, providing high sensitivity to light of this color. Some films are suited for work under low light conditions, providing the high speed needed for this work.

New films and film technologies are constantly appearing on the market. For example, in the last few years manufacturers introduced a line of **chromagenic films** that replace the metallic silver image with dyes to produce black-and-white images of extremely fine grain and exceptional detail. These films can be exposed at film speeds anywhere from ISO 100/21° to ISO 1600/33°, even within the same roll, with excellent results. In 1986 Kodak introduced its line of T-Max Professional films that utilize T-grain technology—an emulsion technology that alters the shape of the silver halide crystals to produce much finer-grain images at higher speeds. These films can be push-processed to speeds as high as ISO 6400/39° with very fine grain results.

Table 4-2, *Selecting a Black-and-White Film,* will help you select films that are especially useful for various purposes.

Color Films

Objective 4-D Describe the process of color photography and the composition of color film.

Key Concepts primary colors, integral tripack, dye image, color reversal film, positive transparencies, duplicate transparency, color print, internegative, color negative film, complementary colors, instant color print film, color balance, color temperature, Kelvin degrees (K), daylight, tungsten light, Type B films

One of the marvels of modern photography has been the development of inexpensive color materials that can be used with the same cameras and under much the same conditions as black-and-white materials. The ease with which even the beginning photographer can obtain full-color photographic images belies the long and tortuous history of color photography, which dates back well over a century.

The products of various manufacturers differ in the details of their chemical design. Nevertheless, most modern color films are similar in construction to black-and-white films in many respects, except that they consist of three emulsion layers instead of one. Each emulsion layer is designed to record the image produced by only one of the **primary colors** of light in the scene—red, green, or blue—and to produce a corresponding colored image during processing. When the film is exposed to white light in the image (a mixture of red, green, and blue), latent images are formed in all three layers. But when it is exposed to yellow light in the image (a mixture of red and green), latent images are formed in only the red- and green-sensitive layers. Because of its three emulsions, this type of film is known as an **integral tripack**.

When color negative film is processed, the images on the three emulsions are developed first as negative silver images, as with black-and-white film. At a later stage of the processing, however, each of the images is converted to a **dye image** that is the complement of the primary color of light that produced it. The red-produced image becomes cyan; the green-produced, magenta; and the blue-produced, yellow. The opaque silver and remaining silver salts are then dissolved away, leaving the three dyed image layers sandwiched close together in exact registration. When white light is transmitted through them, their images combine to produce a full range of colors that corresponds in negative form to those that were present in the original scene. When color slide

Table 4-2. Selecting a black-and-white film

Film brand and name	Sizes	Characteristics	Notes
Kodak T-MAX 100 and 400	35mm, 120 roll film, and sheets	Very fine grain, extremely sharp, good contrast with correct processing	Needs careful processing, best in T-Max chemicals
Ilford Delta 100 and 400	35mm, 120 roll film	Ultra fine grain, extremely sharp, good contrast	Some prefer to Kodak's T-Max
Kodak Plus-X and Tri-X	35mm, 120 roll film, and sheets	ISO 125 and 400, respectively	Classic films, not as fine grain as the T-Max series, but more forgiving in processing
Fuji Neopan 400	35mm, 120 roll film	Very fine grain, very sharp, good contrast	Good general purpose fast film, but may be hard to find
Kodak T-MAX P3200 Professional Film	35mm	Extremely fast film for low-light photography	Process in T-Max chemicals
Kodak Technical Pan	35mm and sheets	Kodak's slowest and finest-grained black-and-white film for pictorial photography	Film speed varies with development. Usually ISO 16-64. Best in Kodak Technidol Liquid Developer
Kodak Select Black & White/ BWC	35mm	Very wide exposure latitude, excellent image quality. Can make good prints on black and white paper.	Can be processed in color (C-41) chemicals by your local lab
Kodak Portra 400 BW	120	A roll film version of above	A roll film version of above
Ilford XP-2 Super 400	35mm, 120 roll film, and sheets	Very wide exposure latitude, excellent image quality. Can make good prints on black and white paper.	Can be processed in color (C-41) chemicals by your local lab
Agfa Scala 200X Pro	35mm, 120 roll film, and sheets	Very fine grain, very sharp, brilliant slides	Produces beautiful black and white slides but must be sent for special processing

film is processed, the negative images are converted to positive ones during processing.

Figure 4-4 shows a cross-section of a typical color film and explains the principles of its operation. Four basic types of color film are commonly available: color reversal film, color negative film, instant color print film, and instant color transparency film. Table G-2 in Appendix G on the CD describes some commonly available color films and their characteristics.

Color Reversal Film

Color reversal film is designed to produce color slides—**positive transparencies** that can be looked at through a viewer or projected onto a screen. The same film exposed in the camera is returned in the form of slides after processing.

During processing the negative images are reversed to positive ones. Then each of the three positive images is converted to a dye that is the complement of the original primary color that produced it, and the silver image is bleached away. When viewed, the three images combine by a subtractive process to form a positive color image of the scene. This reversal of the negative to a positive image gives the film its technical name, color reversal film.

The transparency also can be used to reproduce the photograph in other forms. For example, a **duplicate transparency** can be made that is virtually equivalent to the original. Among other advantages, having a duplicate protects the original from the abuses of direct handling. Also, a **color print** can be made from the original transparency. A color print is an opaque paper- or plas-

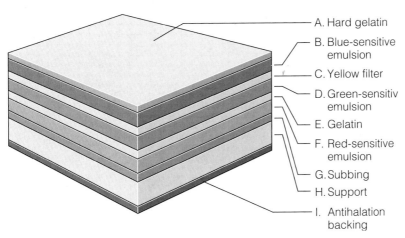

A. Hard gelatin
B. Blue-sensitive emulsion
C. Yellow filter
D. Green-sensitiv emulsion
E. Gelatin
F. Red-sensitive emulsion
G. Subbing
H. Support
I. Antihalation backing

Figure 4-4. Cross-section of modern tripack color film. A) Topcoat protects emulsion surface. B) Blue-sensitive emulsion records only the image produced by the blue light in the scene. C) Yellow filter absorbs blue light to prevent its transmission to other emulsions. D) Green-sensitive emulsion records only the image produced by the green light in the scene. (This is an orthochromatic layer. It is insensitive to red light, which passes through it to the layers beneath, and it is not exposed to blue, which has been filtered out by the layer above.) E) Gelatin layer separates green-sensitive and red-sensitive emulsions to prevent dye contamination between layers. F) Red-sensitive emulsion records only the image produced by the red light in the scene. G) Subbing aids adhesion of the emulsion to the support. H) Support, a strong, flexible, plastic base, holds all layers firmly in place. I) Antihalation backing prevents back-reflection of highlights that may penetrate through all prior layers.

tic-backed print that can be viewed without mechanical aids, mounted in an album or on a display board, and handled like any other print.

There are several methods of making color prints from transparencies; they differ in cost, complexity, and quality of the end product. Some of these methods involve direct printing on special materials using a color reversal printing process. Many of these methods are no more complex than black-and-white printing and may be performed easily in a home darkroom. Others involve making an **internegative**—copying the transparency onto **color negative film** and then using the new negative to make positive color prints. Further, an internegative can be made using black-and-white film to produce black-and-white prints from the transparency.

Color Negative Film

Color negative film is designed primarily to produce color prints. It produces a transparent negative, which is then used for making the positive prints. As with a black-and-white negative, the brightness scale is reversed—bright objects appear

dense in the negative, and dark objects appear thin. But the colors are reversed also—the original colors appear as their **complementary colors**. Thus blue objects will appear yellow in the negative, green will appear magenta, and red will appear cyan. The negative can be preserved, and reused as long as it is kept in good condition.

Color negative film is also of integral tripack construction. However, when processed, each of the three negative images is dyed the complement of its corresponding primary color. In printing, of course, both the brightness scale and the colors are reversed to correspond to the original brightness and hue in the scene.

Several end products can be made from the color negative. One of these is the color print. Positive transparencies can also be made from color negatives; in most respects these are equivalent to the transparencies obtained with color transparency film. Black-and-white prints also can be made from color negatives in a home darkroom. No internegatives, special equipment, papers, or chemicals are needed, although special printing papers are designed for this purpose to optimize results. The various products that can be made from both types of color film are summarized in Figure 4-5.

Instant Color Films

Instant color print film operates on the same general principles as conventional film and print materials. Silver halide emulsions are the basic image-forming media, and the chemical processes generally parallel those employed in color transparency films.

The primary difference between instant color print films and conventional ones is that the processing and printing materials are all sandwiched together into each sheet of film. The processing materials are held in an inactive state until they are activated following exposure. To develop the film and make the positive print, the film is squeezed between two rollers built into the camera, thus dispersing the activating chemicals throughout the emulsion.

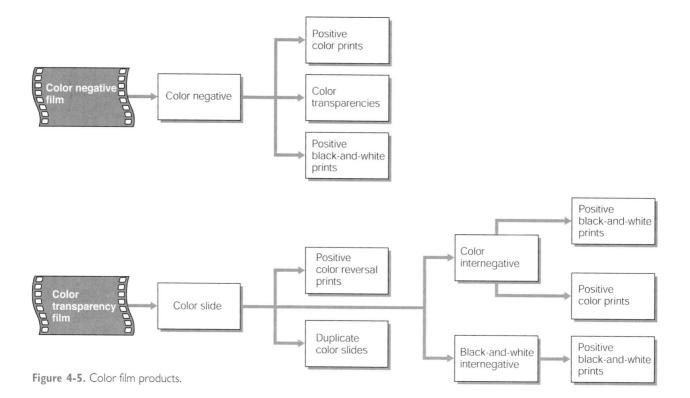

Figure 4-5. Color film products.

The action of this process is self-limiting and terminates automatically, leaving at last only the completely developed and stabilized print. As with all photochemistry, development time is related to the temperature of the materials; depending upon outside temperatures, the process will take from twenty seconds to four minutes to complete.

Color Balance

A film's ability to reproduce colors as the eye perceives them is known as its **color balance**. Just as the human eye may selectively ignore details in a scene that the camera records, the eye also may ignore shifts in the color of the dominant light source, which the film will record.

We know, for example, that sunshine in the late afternoon is redder than at noon. The color of a white car does not appear significantly different to the eye at these times, but it does to color film. Because objects reflect the characteristics of the light falling upon them, they will take on the colors of the source light. If that light is dominated by the warm, reddish hues of late afternoon sunlight or ordinary incandescent light, the film will record a reddish tinge over the entire scene. Ordinarily our minds will filter out this tinge in interpreting color, yet even a careful shopper knows

this tinge exists and often views a new tie or dress in daylight to see its "true" color. Under ideal conditions color film records colors as they are reflected from objects, not as the viewer may believe them to be.

The color of light, from the red to the blue portions of the spectrum, is described in terms of **color temperature**, which is measured in **Kelvin degrees (K)**. Figure 4-6 reports some common light sources and their approximate color temperatures in Kelvin degrees.

Color films are balanced in manufacture for the color temperatures of source lights commonly encountered in practice. One such source is **daylight** (5500 K)—the color of daylight on a sunny day between 10 a.m. and 2 p.m. is the standard. Another such source is **tungsten light**, which refers to artificial light produced by tungsten-filament lamps. Color films, known as tungsten or **Type B films**, are balanced for common indoor, incandescent lighting (3200 K). Color balance is more important for color transparency films, because no color balance adjustment can normally be made in processing; color balance can be restored when making prints from color negatives.

The most accurate color renditions are obtained when color films are used in the light for which

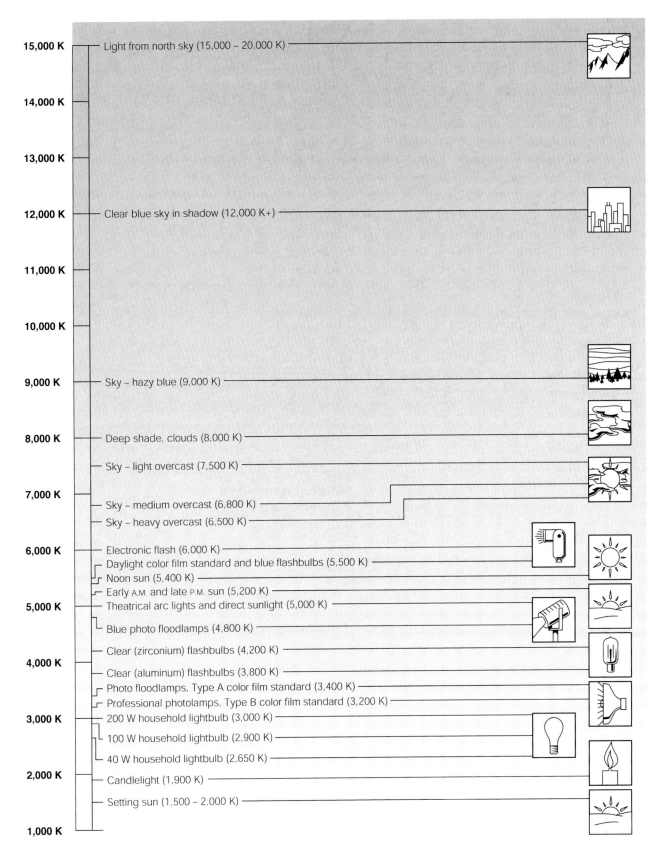

Figure 4-6. Color temperatures of various light sources.

Careers in Photography

Industrial and Commercial Photographer

The field of industrial and commercial photography defies precise definition. Generally, industrial photographers support the various activities of a business organization including administration, advertising, public and industrial relations, distribution and marketing, plant security and engineering, research and development, production and manufacturing, sales and service, purchasing, and testing. Today's industrial photographers provide service to organizations in such diverse fields as medicine, government, education, and the military, as well as the manufacturing industries. They produce a great variety of photographic works, such as portraits and product photographs for advertisements and reports, visual aids for training, technical photographs for research and development, site photographs for construction reports, product assembly photographs for time-and-motion studies, decor photographs, promotional films and videos, documentation photographs for accident and OSHA reports, and photographs for health and safety programs.

According to the 2004–2005 *Occupational Outlook Handbook*, jobs in commercial and industrial photography will be keenly competitive through 2012, growing about as fast as the average for all occupations. Photographers can expect keen competition for job openings because the work is attractive to more people than the number of available openings. Those who succeed in landing a salaried job or attracting enough work to earn a living by freelancing are likely to be the most creative, able to adapt to rapidly changing technologies, and adept at operating a business.

Job growth will likely be constrained by the widespread use of digital photography and the falling price of digital equipment. Besides increasing productivity, improvements in digital technology reduce barriers of entry into this profession and allow more individual consumers and businesses to produce, store, and access photographic images on their own.

As a specialist in visual communication, the industrial photographer may be called upon not only to perform routine photography, but also to produce highly creative solutions to visual communication problems. Engineers and scientists, for example, use photography constantly to reveal things that are otherwise invisible to the human eye—objects and events that may be too small, too fast, or too slow for normal observation. Further, the nature of many high-technology processes may be difficult to communicate visually—such as high-speed data processing or laser surgery. Therefore, the industrial photographer may be called upon to use a variety of imaginative photographic approaches and advanced techniques to solve these problems.

Many industrial photographers find their practice often extends into specialized areas such as microphotography, macrophotography, photomicrography, electron microscopy, stroboscopic photography, time-lapse photography, high speed still and motion picture photography, metallography, X-ray photography, holography,

David Coleman, "Life in Maine Industries."

infrared and ultraviolet photography, aerial photography, autoradiography, bubble chamber photography, electron and X-ray diffraction photography, nuclear photography, seismography, spectrography, stereography, oscillography, microfilming, and computer imaging. Although few industrial photographers would need to be expert in all of these specialized techniques, they would certainly need to be aware of them and be prepared to learn them as the need arose. In the final analysis, industrial photographers will succeed or fail on their ability to produce effective photographs, no matter what special technique they may need to learn in the process.

Industrial photographers generally are employed by the companies they serve; however, many small businesses must rely upon commercial photographers or freelancers to fulfill their industrial needs. Thus, independent photographers can find a lively market among smaller businesses that also need industrial and technical photographs. Freelancers should approach potential clients with a portfolio that includes photographs that show not only their versatility, variety, and technical competence, but also their ability to illustrate and communicate visual concepts.

"Rene Ego—Gagny, France," photo courtesy of Beckman Coulter, Inc.

Even in-house industrial photographers should market their services throughout their organization. Staff members and department heads may not fully comprehend how skilled industrial photography can increase productivity and internal communications. Too often photographic assignments are handed off to amateurs within a department because the availability of the in-house professional is not known. In-house industrial photographers should therefore market their services within their company much as freelancers market to their clients.

they are balanced. If daylight film is used outdoors on a sunny day at noon, for example, a white car will appear white. Early in the morning, at sunset, or under floodlights on a showroom floor, the same film will make the car appear perceptibly reddish. If Type B tungsten film is used under professional photo floodlights on the showroom floor, the white car again will appear white. However, outdoors at noon, the tungsten film will make the car appear bluish, because

the film is balanced for a lower color temperature than daylight.

It may sometimes be necessary to use a color film under conditions that vary from its rated color balance. Unit 11 discusses how to control the color shifts that might occur in such circumstances by using special filters fitted to the camera.

Control of color balance at the time of shooting is critical for color transparency films. The film in the camera ends up as the finished slide, and there is no opportunity to correct any imbalances once the picture is shot. Color negative film, however, is another story. Color imbalances in the negative may be substantially corrected during printing, with compensatory filtration. In commercial processing laboratories it is standard practice to try to balance positive prints using flesh tones or other known values as a reference. Also, many photographers will use a standard 18 percent gray card at the start of a roll, within a scene, or in the frame preceding an important shot to provide the printer with a standard reference for balancing color in the print.

Film Care and Storage

Objective 4-E Describe the conditions that may adversely affect film and describe how to store and care for films to avoid these effects.

Key Concepts humidity, heat, age, gases, X-rays and radioactive material, static electricity, professional films

Humidity, heat, age, gases, static electricity, X-rays, or radioactive materials may affect all photographic films. Some films, such as professional films, require special handling. By taking the following precautions, however, film can be protected from adverse effects.

1. Don't open a film package until you are ready to use the film.

    Most films come in vapor-tight containers or packages for protection against **humidity**. No additional protection against moisture is normally required as long as this package is intact. If the package is opened prematurely, moisture in the environment hastens the aging of the film.

2. Store unexposed film in a cool, dry place or refrigerate it in its original vapor-tight package.

    Film packages do not protect against **heat**. Do not leave undeveloped film in direct sunlight or near any heat source, such as steam pipes, heat registers, or closed compartments of a car. Special care should be taken in hot seasons or regions. Films may be refrigerated or frozen as long as they are in their original vapor-tight packages. To prevent condensation on the surface of the film, cold films should be allowed to warm to room temperature before they are removed from their vapor-tight containers.

3. Expose and process film before it spoils.

    Films are chemically active and change with **age**, even if they are not exposed to light and are stored carefully. Films are given an expiration date at the time of their manufacture and with reasonable care can be guaranteed to give good results until that date. If they are kept in a refrigerator or freezer, they will give good results long after the expiration date.

4. Expose and process film as soon as possible after opening its vapor-tight package.

    Opened, unprocessed film should be loaded into a camera and exposed in a reasonably short time. Once the vapor-tight package is opened, the film is affected by external conditions that cause aging to proceed rapidly. The loaded camera is neither vapor-tight nor heat-proof, so it should be stored in a cool, dry place. Store a loaded camera in an enclosed camera bag together with a small container of silica gel, available from most photo supply stores, to reduce relative humidity within the bag. Avoid prolonged storage of a loaded camera.

5. Avoid storing film where it may be exposed to volatile gases, X-rays, or radioactive materials.

    Certain **gases** may adversely affect the chemical composition of film. Motor exhaust, mildew preventives, camphor or formaldehyde vapors, and vapors from cleaners and solvents may seep in and damage the film. Similarly, exposure to **X-rays** and **radioactive materials** may damage the film. Special film containers should be used to ships film through customs or other X-ray security points. If no such container is available, request hand inspection.

6. Advance and rewind film slowly and handle film carefully to avoid discharges of static electricity.

    Sparks of **static electricity** at the surface of the film also can cause marks in the developed negative. Static electricity may collect at the surface of the film during dry weather when the relative humidity is very low. Just as a charge of static electricity can be built up by walking across a carpet on a dry winter day, a static charge can be built up on the film by advancing it or rewinding it too rapidly.

7. Store negatives in a clean, dry, cool place in protective envelopes or sleeves.

   The developed negatives of black-and-white film are normally very stable and require few special storage precautions. A cool, dry place will inhibit the growth of mold on the gelatin emulsion. Hydrogen sulfide and coal gas should be avoided because sulfur compounds may attack the silver in the negative image. Negatives should be kept as clean and dust-free as possible to avoid damage to the negative image.

8. Professional films require special handling.

   Most major film manufacturers produce a line of **professional films**. These films are manufactured to particularly high standards with respect to film speed and color balance. They typically have less latitude and are more sensitive to aging and temperature. Professional films are intended to be stored at 55°F (13°C) or less and to be processed immediately after use. Purchase professional films only from reputable dealers accustomed to handling these films properly.

How Digital Image Sensors Work

Objective 4-F Describe how digital sensors work including how they record color, their resolution and exposure requirements.

Key Concepts CCD, CMOS, pixel, one-shot method, filtered sensors, interpolate, three-shot method, three-chip method, megapixel, pixels-per-inch (ppi), auto-ISO, clipping, color depth, bit-depth, white balance

Light Translated into Digits

Digital image sensors, like film, capture the actions of light falling upon them. Whether in a digital camera, a flatbed scanner, or a film scanner, the mechanics of converting various intensities of light into digital bits is the same. All of these systems use an image sensor of some kind that converts light energy into electromagnetic energy and then records it in the form of digital code.

Image sensors, similar to computer chips, are solid-state devices constructed from silicon. Two technologies are currently used—charge coupled devices (**CCD**) and Complementary Metal Oxide Sensors (**CMOS.**) Both types consist of a matrix of millions of microscopic photocell sites that convert light intensity (photons) into electrical charges (electrons.) Various light intensities produce proportional electrical charges at each site.

Next, an analog-to-digital converter translates each photosite's output into a digital code that corresponds to the location, brightness, and color of the microscopic picture element that is represented by that site. Taken together, the millions of photosites form a matrix of picture elements, or **pixels**, that make up the final image.

Both CCDs and CMOSs are capable of producing high-quality images. CCDs are based on an older, more mature technology and currently produce cleaner images than some CMOSs. However, CCDs consume 100 times more power than comparable CMOSs and are more costly. Recent advances in CMOS manufacturing have produced sensors that rival the image quality of CCDs and are less costly in larger sizes. CMOS technology seems destined to replace CCDs for digital imaging.

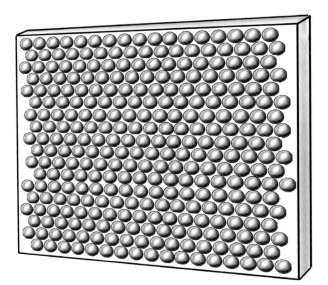

Figure 4-7. Millions of individual photosites are grouped together to form the imaging sensor in modern digital cameras.

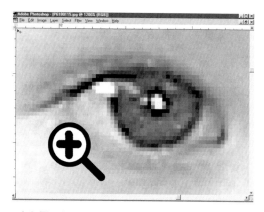

Figure 4-8. The individual pixels can be seen by enlarging the monitor's view inside most photo-editing software.

Color and Digital Sensors

Most digital image sensors like CMOSs and CCDs only measure light intensity without regard for color. In essence, they capture black-and-white images. How then do digital cameras record color images? The trick is to use red, green and blue filters to separate the red, green, and blue components of light. There are three main ways to accomplish this: a one-shot method, a three-shot method, and a three-sensor method.

The **one-shot method** uses a primary color filter applied to each individual sensor, making each photosite a **filtered sensor**, sensitive to only one particular color—red, green or blue. A computer inside the camera **interpolates** the missing colors by analyzing neighboring pixels. The interpolation process is computer intensive and often results in a slight delay while readying the camera between pictures.

This method has the advantage of capturing all three primary colors of an image simultaneously and, as the least costly to manufacture, has become the method used in most popular cameras and flatbed scanners. Unfortunately, optical resolution is reduced by about one-third because each available photosite records only one of the three colors.

The **three-shot method** is a second way of producing color images. This method requires that three separate, sequential exposures be made, each through a filter of red, green, or blue. In this way each sensor records all three primary colors one at a time. This method, while retaining full resolution by using all sensors for all colors, can-

not be used to photograph moving subjects. The three-shot method produces extraordinary high-resolution images for demanding applications and is commonly used in professional studio cameras. Some flatbed scanners also offer the user a comparable three-scan mode for the utmost in quality.

The **three-chip method**, a third method of color imaging, uses three separate image sensors, each with a different filter. Light from the camera's lens is divided into thirds by a beam splitter and redirected onto the three separate filtered sensors—red, green and blue. Each complete sensor gets an identical look at the image, but because of their respective filters, each responds only to one of the primary colors.

The advantage of this method is that the camera records each of the three color images at every pixel position simultaneously. Image processing combines data from all three chips into a very high-quality composite color image. No interpolation is necessary; images from three-chip cameras retain the full resolution of each chip. Unfortunately cameras that use this method are larger and more expensive and only available at the professional level.

Characteristics of Digital Sensors

Digital camera sensors are roughly categorized by the number of photosites they contain. Because the resulting images are made up of a correspond-

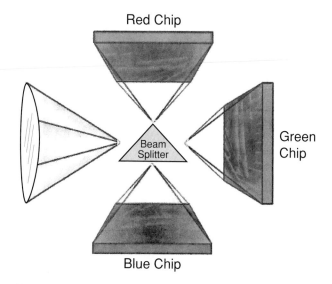

Figure 4-9. Three-chip cameras use a sensor for each primary color and record high-resolution images.

ing number of picture elements, the term pixels is commonly used to describe the sensor's size.

However, the two terms, photosites and pixels, are not exactly the same. For example, some popular cameras claim to be 4 **megapixel** cameras and can produce images that measure 2272 x 1704 pixels. But if you do the math, 2272 x 1704 = 3,871,488, or 3.87 megapixels. This is a bit less than the advertised 4 megapixel resolution. What happened to the missing pixels? The answer is that not all of the photosites are used for imaging, some are necessary to provide circuitry to other parts of the chip.

Resolution of Digital Sensors

Remember that digital images are something like mosaic tile pictures. If we make the tiles smaller and put more of them into the picture it will have greater detail and sharpness. Likewise, if we increase the number of pixels in an image, then each one will be smaller in the final output and the image will be smoother and sharper.

For practical purposes, when comparing cameras with different sensors, resolution generally equates to the number of pixels. Although many factors influence image quality, sharper and more detailed images may generally be expected from cameras with higher pixel counts.

PPI—A Measure of Output Resolution

The total pixel count also has a bearing on the ultimate print size. Output resolution is measured in **pixels-per-inch**, or **ppi**. The more pixels per inch the crisper the image that can be expected when printing larger prints. This is analogous to the relationship between grain size and image resolution in conventional film photography. Coarse-grain films equate to lower ppi; fine-grain, to higher ppi.

The ppi needed for quality reproduction depends upon the output device to be used. For display on a computer monitor, such as a web page, a resolution of 72 to 96 ppi is sufficient because most monitors cannot display anything higher. For quality hard-copy prints, 300 ppi will work well with most printers; however, as printers vary,

check the resolution guidelines that are published in the printer's manual.

To establish the maximum output size of an image at a particular resolution, divide the width or height of the picture in pixels by the desired resolution. For example, a 4 megapixel camera produces images that measure 2272 x 1704 pixels. Divide each number by 300ppi to get:

2272 / 300 = 7.572 inches in width, or

1704 / 300 = 5.56 inches in height.

Thus, at 300 ppi resolution, the largest print that could be made would be approximately 5in x 7in; at 200 dpi, approximately 8in x 10in.

For maximum print quality, print at the calculated print size **or smaller**. With the same image, smaller print sizes actually increase resolution. Larger print sizes can be expected to reduce resolution; photo-editing software cannot magically generate missing details.

Digital Film Speed

As we saw earlier in this chapter, the speed, or light sensitivity, of film is given as an ISO number indicated on the film package. Image sensors are also rated using equivalent ISO numbers. Digital cameras use sensors with ISOs ranging from 50 to 3,200 or more. The higher the number the "faster" or more sensitive the image sensor is to light.

Most digital sensors can be set to more than one ISO rating. In low-light situations, you can increase the sensor's ISO by amplifying its signal. Many cameras even increase the effective film speed automatically. This setting is often called **auto-ISO**. Amplifying ISO speeds in this way not only increases the sensor's light sensitivity, it also

Table 4-3. Pixels and print quality

Megapixels on sensor*	Good print quality	Acceptable print quality
1 megapixel	Up to 4in x 5in	Up to 5in x 7in
2 megapixel	Up to 5in x 7in	Up to 8in x 10in
3–4 megapixel	Up to 8in x 10in	Up to 11in x 14in
6–8 megapixel	Up to 11in x 14in	Up to 16in x 20in
> 12 megapixel	Up to 16in x 20in	Up to 24in x 30in

*Assumes that each sensor is set to maximum resolution.

increases noise. This is similar to tuning in a distant radio station—you can make it louder, but the static becomes louder too. Noise, in digital sensors, is analogous to grain and dust specks in traditional photography—too much can degrade an image beyond acceptability.

As with film, an image sensor with a lower ISO number needs more light for a good exposure than one with a higher ISO number. Low ISO settings produce less noisy and "cleaner" images and should be used when maximum quality is desired. Higher ISOs can be selected to enhance action stopping or permit shooting in low light without a flash.

Dynamic Range and Digital Exposure Latitude

The dynamic range of a digital sensor is determined by the depth of the wells used in the photosites. This is analogous to the depth of the bucket which would determine the number of electrons it can hold before overflowing. Professional digital SLR's and even modern consumer grade digital SLR's have considerably more dynamic range than most compact consumer digital cameras.

Digital camera sensors have less exposure latitude than negative films; therefore they require more precise control of exposure, lighting, and contrast. Digital sensors have little tolerance for even minor exposure errors, especially overexposure. Digital images quickly lose highlight detail when overexposed—light and delicately textured areas often end up as blank, white areas. In general, film photographers follow the advice "Expose for the shadows and develop for the highlights." While this advice might work well with film, it would be disastrous with digicams. Better advice for digicam photography is "Expose for the highlights, add fill light to the shadows when possible, and correct the shadows in Photoshop."

A camera's histogram display, if it has one, may be used to check the exposure and contrast range. If the tonal range spills off the histogram on either end, detail is lost in the highlights or shad-

ows, an effect known as "**clipping**." If a camera does not have a histogram display, the camera's monitor can be used to estimate proper exposure. For important pictures, make several exposures that bracket the estimated setting. Often a slight underexposure will produce the best results. Alternatively, exposures can be checked in a photo-editing program as shown in Figures 4-10 and 4-11.

Digital Color and White Balance

Color or Bit Depth   The human eye is able to differentiate millions of colors but digital images can reproduce only a limited set of colors. The number of colors an image sensor is capable of generating is referred to as **color depth**, or **bit depth**. Color depth is determined by the number of digital bits that are used to record each color. The more bits used, the richer and more varied the colors will appear.

Most consumer cameras offer 24-bit color depth —eight bits each for red, green, and blue. Professional digital cameras and many film scanners often reach 36-bit, or higher, color depth. The more bits assigned to each color, the more shades that can be stored. However, increasing the bit depth also increases the file sizes needed to store the images.

White balance is a color correction system designed to produce good color reproduction under varying lighting conditions. Our vision normally

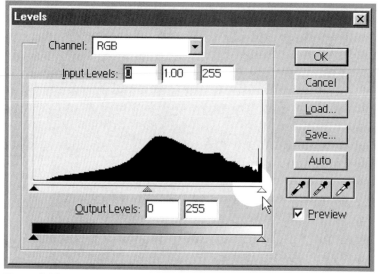

Figure 4-10. Overexposed histogram. This histogram shows the danger of overexposure with digital materials. The brightest portion of the curve spills off the chart resulting in blank highlights lacking in detail.

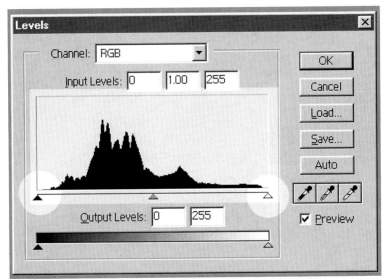

Figure 4-11. Corrrectly exposed histogram. This histogram shows an image with correct exposure and a tonal range appropriate for digital capture. Note that very few tones have been clipped at either end.

compensates for varying lighting conditions so that we perceive color accurately, whether in the warm glow of a candle or under the cool northern sky. As we have seen, film does not adapt similarly. Each film is balanced for a particular light source, such as daylight or tungsten, under which it accurately records color. To compensate for mismatches between the light source and the color balance, film photographers use color filters in front of the lens. (See Unit 11, *Filters.*)

Digital cameras, however, require no such filters. Instead, complex software programs within the camera make the needed adjustments. Most digital cameras feature automatic white balance that calculates a correct color rendering based upon the overall image color. However, because these systems may be fooled by an image dominated by one color, many digicams allow manual choice of white balance, typically from a list that includes sunlight, cloudy, fluorescent and incandescent lighting.

Some advanced digital cameras measure light reflected from a white surface to establish a white balance setting that is used until the camera is reset.

Digital Storage Media

Objective 4-G Describe the two main types of digital storage media and name common file types used for images.

Key Concepts flash memory cards, magnetic or optical disks, card reader, compression, lossless, lossy, raw, tiff, jpeg

Types of Digital Storage Media
Digital Film

Several methods for storing images in a camera and retrieving them are in common use. Very early digicams used random access memory chips (RAM) mounted permanently inside the camera. To retrieve the stored images, the camera was connected by cable to a computer. Although most of today's digital cameras can be connected directly to a computer, they also provide removable storage media—the equivalent of digital film, except that the media are reusable. When the media device becomes full, the stored images can be erased, transferred to a computer, or the device itself can be removed from the camera for later use and another media device inserted into the camera.

The alternative storage technologies fall into two broad categories—flash memory cards and magnetic or optical disks. Each camera manufacturer has chosen to use one of these technologies, but it may not be interchangeable with all other cameras.

Flash Memory Cards

Flash memory cards are small, removable, solid-state devices that have no moving parts. They are reusable, fast, and a relatively inexpensive way to store images for later transfer to a computer or printer. Five main kinds of memory cards are in use today—CompactFlash, SmartMedia, Secure Digital, XD, and Memory Sticks. Competing technologies are emerging.

Table 4-4. White balance settings	
White balance setting	*Approximate color temperature*
Sunlight	5500–6000K
Shade or Cloudy	6500K
Fluorescent	~4000–5000K
Tungsten	3000–3500K

Figure 4-12. CompactFlash memory card. Photo courtesy of Lexar Media.

Magnetic or Optical Disks

Modern high-resolution digital cameras produce large files and require correspondingly large storage spaces. Several flash memory cards might be needed to store the many images produced in an extended photo session. Flash memory in larger sizes can be very expensive; therefore, alternative technologies have produced tiny, less expensive mass storage devices for use with digital cameras.

Magnetic or optical disks use technology similar to that used for removable computer disk drives. They are placed inside the camera for recording images and are usually removed for image retrieval. Popular examples of **magnetic or optical disks** are IBM's Micro-Drive that holds image files of several gigabytes in a package no bigger than a matchbook; DataPlay's 500 MB optical disk that is the size of a postage stamp; and Sony's 156 MB 3-inch compact disk (CD-R).

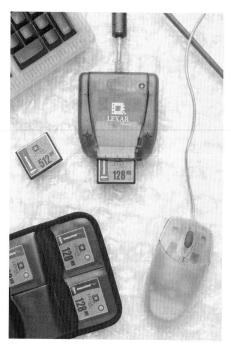

Figure 4-13. Memory card reader for transferring images to a computer. Photo courtesy of Lexar Media.

Card Readers

A **card reader** is needed to transfer files to your computer without using the camera. Just slip the digicam's memory card into a slot in these small mouselike appliances and download. The host computer treats the memory card as it would an additional hard-drive or floppy disk and can instantly copy, move, or delete image files.

File Types and Image Compression

Compression

Megapixel digital cameras generate large data files that require significant disk space to store. The process of image **compression** can considerably reduce the size of image files so that more images can be stored in less space. To compress image data, complex mathematical formulas analyze the files and remove unnecessary data. However, some image data may be lost in the process and the images may lose quality.

Two approaches to image compression are in common use—lossless and lossy. **Lossless** compression removes only redundant image data. As a result, very little image quality is lost; however, very little reduction of file size results. **Lossy** compression, on the other hand, removes more image data and results in much smaller file sizes; however, lossy compression often results in reduced image quality. In general, it may be expected that the greater the compression, the greater the loss in image quality.

Digicams typically offer a choice of file types and compression levels. Select a setting that best matches the requirements for both output quality and storage space.

File Types

Many file formats exist for recording and storing digital images. The following formats are the most

Table 4-5. File compression and file size			
File type	Approx. file size	Images per 32 MB memory	Images per 64 MB memory
TIFF uncompressed	10 MB	3	6
JPEG high quality	2.5 MB	13	27
JPEG medium quality	800K	40	80

commonly used in digital cameras: raw, TIFF and JPEG.

RAW (.RAW)

Some advanced cameras allow the unprocessed, unconverted data from the image sensor to be saved in **raw** format. Because processing and conversion is deferred to later work on a computer outside the camera, the camera's delay between shots is considerably shortened. Raw files can later be converted and saved in a variety of formats for different uses.

TIFF (.TIF)

One of the more useful formats for working with images across a variety of software programs is **TIFF** format. The term, pronounced "tiff," stands for tagged image file format. TIFF offers several compression options; selecting "none" or "LZW" results in lossless compression. One advantage of TIFF is that the format is supported by many computer systems and by most scanners, printers, and desktop publishing programs. Unfortunately, TIFF format generates relatively large file sizes.

JPEG (.JPG OR .JPEG)

Most digicam users elect to use lossy compression to save memory and storage space. Of the formats that use lossy compression, **JPEG** format, pronounced "jay-peg," is the most commonly used. Developed by the Joint Photographic Experts Group, hence the name, JPEG format offers various levels of compression to serve various output needs. Images destined for web pages, for example, do not require the same image quality as those bound for magazine publication; therefore, they can be compressed much more.

JPEG format should not be used to store images that will be modified later. When a JPEG file is opened and resaved it is re-compressed, resulting in further loss of image quality. JPEG 2000, a refinement of the original JPEG format, features near-lossless compression.

PSD, EPS, GIF, BMP, AND OTHER FILE FORMATS

Although not commonly found on cameras, many other image file formats exist. As the technology for recording and saving images continues to develop, additional formats will likely appear. PSD is Photoshop's native format and uses no compression; EPS or Encapsulated PostScript is used mainly for desktop publishing and is a file that contains both the image and instructions to a printer; GIF files use a fixed number of indexed colors and are often used on the web; BMP is a Windows bitmap format that was popular in the past but is now used primarily for desktop wallpaper.

Care and Storage of Digital Media

Objective 4-H Describe proper handling and care of digital storage materials to avoid lost data.

Key Concepts compatible, fragile, contact area, download, reformat, reconfigure, electromagnetic energy

Digital storage media are less vulnerable than film to many dangers. However, there are dangers unique to the media. Here are several precautions to be observed when using digital media to avoid damaging the materials or losing valuable images.

1. Use the proper type of storage device.

   Memory cards and devices are sold in a number of types and capacities. Not all will work in your particular camera. Check your camera's manual to determine which forms of memory are **compatible**.

2. Handle carefully.

   Digital storage media are relatively **fragile** and should be handled carefully, especially the ultrathin SmartMemory, XD, and Secure Digital cards. Do not subject the material to physical shocks or bending. Do not expose the media to excessive heat or moisture.

3. Insert media carefully.

   All memory devices need to be inserted a particular way. Check the manual for insertion instructions. Turn off the camera's power during insertion. Avoid touching the gold electrical **contact area**.

4. Don't remove the media during operation.

   Never open the card cover, eject the card, remove the batteries, or pull the plug while the camera is in record or playback mode. These actions will likely destroy the images stored on the card.

5. **Transfer files frequently.**

   Even the best memory devices sometimes fail and digicams do occasionally lock up. **Download** or transfer your files frequently to a host computer or external storage device to avoid losing valuable pictures. Make backup copies of all important picture files. Many photographers use writable CDs or DVDs for this purpose.

6. **Occasionally reformat the memory.**

   Memory cards and many memory devices will be more reliable if they are occasionally **reformatted** or **reconfigured**. Most cameras have a reformat option and it is better to reformat the media in the camera than on a computer. Note that formatting the card erases all data on it, including any write-protected images.

7. **Avoid magnetic fields**

   With the exception of optical disks, strong **electromagnetic energy** fields can damage the data on most memory devices. Don't store memory devices near televisions, computer monitors, magnets, or other sources of strong electronic or magnetic energy.

Table 4-6. Digital imaging and film speed selection guide

Setting or condition	Commonly used digital and film speeds	Options
For large enlargements	ISO 50 or 100	100 is often the slowest digital film speed on many cameras
Outdoors at a sunny beach or snow scene	ISO 50 or 100	ISO 100-200 with point-and-shoot cameras
Indoors near a window with SLR camera and accessory flash	ISO 200	ISO 400 with point-and-shoot cameras or SLR with small built-in flash
Indoors near a window, no flash	ISO 400	ISO 800
Indoors at night with bright room lighting, no flash	ISO 400	ISO 800
General family or travel photography	ISO 200	ISO 400 with point-and-shoot cameras
Sports or animals with telephoto lens	ISO 400	ISO 800

Questions to Consider

1. Describe the construction of a typical, modern black-and-white film. What are the functions of the various layers? Describe the construction of color film. What are the functions of the various layers?

2. What are the seven important characteristics of film described in this unit? What are the conditions that might lead you to select one film over another for a particular assignment?

3. Describe the several different ways that film is packaged.

4. Describe three basic types of color film and the end products obtainable from each. Describe how to obtain a positive color print from each type of color product.

5. What is meant by the color balance of a film? How is color temperature measured? For what three color balances are modern color films manufactured?

6. What steps should you take to protect your fresh film from adverse conditions?

7. What are the three main methods for capturing color images with digital sensors?

8. What are the two main types of digital storage media used in cameras?

9. Describe in general terms what is meant by lossless compared to lossy compression.

10. Calculate the output print size at 300 ppi for an image that measures 1,600 x 1,200 pixels.

Suggested Field and Laboratory Assignments

1. Obtain a roll of medium-speed black-and-white film and a roll of color transparency film to use with your camera. Study the procedures for properly loading your camera with film. Does your camera read film DX codes and automatically set itself for a correct ISO film speed index? Can you override any automatic settings and set the camera's film speed setting manually? (You will need to load your film into your camera and become familiar with your camera's features to complete the field assignments in the next unit.)

2. Experiment with various resolution settings on a digital camera. Can you tell the difference between a file saved in the TIFF format compared to one that was recorded in JPEG?

3. Use a digital camera to photograph the same scene at several different settings to bracket the exposure. Keep notes as to the amount of under- and overexposure. Open the image files in a photo-editing program that has a histogram and examine the results. Which exposures clipped the highlights? Which exposures clipped the shadows? What exposure came closest to preserving both the highlight and shadow tones?

Processing Film and Evaluating Negatives

Nicole Shibata, untitled

Unit at a Glance

This Unit describes how to process film and evaluate negatives using traditional materials, chemistry, and methods. During the transition from film to digital photography, it is not unusual to find photographers using both film and digital cameras and processing technologies for different purposes.

Processing black-and-white film is simple and requires neither a darkroom, nor much equipment. Working carefully, you can control the process to yield superior results at only a fraction of the cost of most commercial labs. Moreover, you can employ special processing techniques to match the needs of unusual shooting situations.

Processing color film employs the same general procedures and equipment as black-and-white film, except for the special chemicals used. Though requiring additional steps, the careful worker can process both color negative and color transparency films in a home darkroom.

This unit describes the theories, tools, chemicals, and step-by-step procedures used to process film. It describes how to evaluate and troubleshoot newly developed film. It also explains several special procedures including push processing and how to handle photographic chemicals safely.

Film Processing

Objective 5-A Explain and demonstrate the processing of black-and-white negative film.

Key Concepts latent image, processing, negatives, film-processing tank, developer, silver, stop bath, acetic acid, fixer, hypo, washing aid, clearing agent, wetting agent, time control, temperature control, reticulation, agitation, material safety data sheets (MSDS), ground fault interceptors (GFIs), changing bag, stock solutions, working solutions, time-and-temperature chart, one-shot developer, replenisher

Once the film has been exposed in the camera, the photographic image is recorded. Were one to look at the film at this time, however, it would appear no different from unexposed film. This recorded but invisible image on the film is called a **latent image**. To transform this latent image into a visible image, it is necessary to process the film. In **processing**, the film is passed through several chemical baths in total darkness, then washed free of all active chemicals, and finally dried. When this process is complete, the exposed film has been transformed into a set of **negatives**. In the negative image, everything on the black-and-white scale has

been reversed: objects that were white in the scene are black in the negative; objects that were black in the scene are transparent in the negative. To make a positive print from the negative, further steps must be taken; these will be discussed in the next unit. For now, let us study the processing of the film to produce negatives.

An Overview

An overview of the entire process might be helpful. First, keep in mind that most popular black-and-white films are panchromatic—that is, they are sensitive to all visible colors of light. Therefore, unprocessed panchromatic film cannot be viewed under any visible light without exposing it. All handling of panchromatic film before and during processing, then, must be accomplished in total darkness. (Certain films, such as orthochromatic film, are not sensitive to all colors of light. These films can be examined before and during processing under special lights.)

Before processing, the film is normally loaded into a lightproof **film-processing tank**. The loading must be done in total darkness to protect the film from exposure to light. However, once the film is in the tank with the tank lid properly sealed, it can be processed under normal lighting conditions. The chemical baths can be poured into and out of the tank through its light-tight openings without exposing the film to light.

How Developer Works

Once in its lightproof tank, the film is first bathed in a chemical **developer**. The developer attacks the crystals of silver bromide that have been exposed to light so that the bromine is freed, or dissociated, from the silver. The free bromine is carried off into the developer solution, while the **silver** remains in the emulsion. The greater the amount of exposure to light, the more silver remains. These silver deposits are actually tangled webs of tiny grains of silver. They appear black to the naked eye and make up the dark portions of the negative. To stop the action of a developer, the film is immersed briefly in a clear water rinse or an acid **stop bath**. The active ingredient of most stop baths is **acetic acid**.

The Purpose of Fixer

The developer attacks only the silver bromide crystals that were exposed to light; the unexposed, undeveloped crystals remain in the emulsion after development. A chemical **fixer** eliminates these still-active silver bromide crystals. Because the first chemical used as a fixing bath was hyposulfite of soda, many photographers refer to any fixer as **hypo**.

The fixing bath dissolves all the undeveloped silver bromide crystals, the antihalation backing, and all other unneeded chemicals and backings. All that remains after the fixing bath is the metallic silver image produced by the action of the developer. This image, embedded in the gelatin emulsion coated on an acetate backing, is the negative that will be used to make the finished photograph.

When all light-sensitive ingredients are removed from the film, the tank may be opened and the negatives viewed in normal light. Processing, however, is not yet complete. All traces of the processing chemicals must be washed away. Any traces of these chemicals remaining after processing will stain the negatives. Use a **washing aid**, or **clearing agent**, to reduce the amount of time and water needed to completely wash the film.

Following washing, the negatives must be dried properly. The wet gelatin emulsion is very soft and particles of dust or grit may lodge on it and become firmly embedded. These will appear as white specks on the finished photographs. Also, water droplets may dry on the surface of the emulsion and be visible in the finished photographs. Use a **wetting agent** together with correct drying procedures to assure that the processed film will dry free of dust, scratches, and water spots.

The Time/Temperature Processing Method

Chemical processes are sensitive to time and temperature. Therefore, precise **time control** and **temperature control** during processing is important—just the right amount of time at a proper temperature is needed. If you remove the film from the developer too soon, the film will be underdeveloped; if you leave it too long, the film will be overdeveloped. Underdeveloping reduces contrast and produces images that lack detail; overdeveloping increases contrast and produces dense, grainy negatives.

Precise temperature control over all solutions is equally important. Heat speeds up chemical processes, whereas lower temperatures slow them down, so precise temperature control is essential for proper timing. Furthermore, if solution temperatures vary, any sudden change in temperature may cause the gelatin emulsion to crack, producing a "craze pattern." This effect is called **reticulation**.

Proper **agitation** of the solutions is necessary throughout chemical processing. Without proper agitation, processing will be uneven. Small air bubbles will cling to the film's surface and cause tiny undeveloped spots on the negative. Further, developer will become exhausted in contact with heavily exposed areas, causing the process to slow down, while developer will remain active in contact with less exposed areas. Thus, the solution must be agitated properly to assure even development.

Agitation must be carefully controlled. If overly vigorous, agitation may cause streaks and excessive contrast.

☠ C A U T I O N ☠

Handling Photographic Chemicals Safely

Many **photochemicals** are poisonous or caustic. They should be handled carefully and kept away from children. All photochemicals pose dangers, particularly developers, sepia and selenium toners, and acetic acid. In addition, persons allergic to certain photochemicals should use plastic or rubber gloves.

IN AN EMERGENCY If you accidentally swallow or splash chemicals in your eyes, go to your doctor or local hospital. If possible, take with you the chemical container that shows the health and safety information on the label as well as the **material safety data sheet (MSDS)** usually packaged with it.

If photographic chemicals get in your eyes, immediately flush them with water for at least fifteen minutes.

Keep emergency hotline information posted clearly in your darkroom. Twenty-four hour emergency phone numbers for poison control centers for all states can be obtained from the following web site:

http://www.dorway.com/poisons.html

Dangers of Photographic Chemicals

If handled improperly, photochemicals can cause respiratory problems, allergic reactions, mental confusion, eye irritation, and other health hazards. Many skin, eye, and respiratory conditions can be cumulative, develop slowly, and may not be noticed for years.

Toxins can enter the body three ways: by ingestion, inhalation, or skin absorption. Health problems can generally be avoided by using common sense in the darkroom: Keep chemicals out of the mouth and eyes, work in a well-ventilated area, and avoid prolonged skin contact with chemicals.

Specific Guidelines for Safe Handling of Photographic Materials

KNOW WHAT YOU ARE WORKING WITH Know what chemicals you are using. Read the product label for safety information. Manufacturers are required by law to make available material safety data sheets (MSDS), which describe their products, first aid treatment, and guidelines for safe storage and disposal.

RESPECT THE MATERIALS Respect the hazardous nature of the materials. Try to avoid splashes. Pour powders slowly to avoid airborne dust. Use liquid concentrates or premixed chemicals whenever possible. When mixing water and acid, *always add the acid to the water* to prevent violent splashing. Clean spills promptly; chemicals that dry on the floor produce fine dust. Keep all equipment spotlessly clean, rinse graduates, funnels, and the like before and after each use.

USE PROPER VENTILATION Work only in well-ventilated areas—Kodak recommends ten to fifteen air changes per hour. Some processes may require local exhaust. Avoid working for long periods directly over chemicals where vapors tend to concentrate.

AVOID CHEMICAL INGESTION Never store photochemicals in food containers—they could be mistaken for the real thing. Do not eat, drink, or smoke in the darkroom, as chemical residues on the counter may contaminate these.

MINIMIZE SKIN CONTACT Protect your skin. Always use tongs to handle prints in trays. Avoid immersing your hands in chemicals. Wear form-fitting, rubber gloves with a heavy lining, and do not contaminate the cloth lining. Avoid thinner surgical gloves that may trap chemicals in the latex.

WASH YOUR HANDS AFTER HANDLING CHEMICALS Wash hands thoroughly with mild soap and dry them completely after handling photographic chemicals. Wash towels frequently.

ELIMINATE OTHER DARKROOM HAZARDS Lay out the darkroom for safe traffic flow. Round the corners of counters and tables. Attach small luminescent dots to edges and corners. Keep a fire extinguisher handy and know how to use it.

Avoid splashes—wet, slippery floors are a hazard. Avoid handling electrical equipment with wet hands. Use commonly available **ground fault interceptors (GFIs)** in place of conventional wall outlets to prevent electrical shock.

DISPOSE OF CHEMICALS PROPERLY Check and observe local regulations in your area for disposing of photo chemicals. If possible, reclaim the silver from photo processing solutions.

FOR MORE INFORMATION Consult the manufacturer's Material Safety Data Sheets (MSDS) for information on specific photo chemicals. General information on ventilation, safe handling, and potential health hazards may be found in the following publication:

Safe Handling of Photographic Processing Chemicals, Publication J-98A. Rochester, NY: Eastman Kodak Company, Revised 10/97.

This publication is available by free download from Kodak at:

http://www.kodak.com/global/en/corp/environment/kes/pubs/pdfs/J98A.pdf

This is a recommended agitation method:

> For each step in chemical processing agitate the solution gently and continuously for the first thirty seconds; after that, agitate for five full seconds every thirty seconds until the step is complete. Table J-3 in Appendix J (located on the CD Rom) describes some typical film developers.

Film-Processing Tanks

The key piece of equipment used for film processing is the **film-processing tank**. Most tanks are made of plastic or stainless steel and designed for use with either roll films or sheet film. All processing tanks are designed to hold the film so that it will not touch anything during processing. Should the emulsion touch anything—the sides of the tank, another sheet of film, or another part of the film roll—the processing chemicals will not act properly at the point of contact, and the negatives will be damaged.

Tanks for sheet films provide separate compartments or hangers for the separate sheets of film. Roll-film tanks provide a reel onto which the film can be wound. Some reels are rigid; some, flexible. Some load from the center outward; others, from the outside toward the center. (See Figure 5-2.)

The reels, cages, and hangers are designed for use with particular sizes of films. Some are adjustable, some are not. Virtually all processing tanks are designed to be loaded in complete darkness and then sealed for processing. Once sealed, processing may continue under normal lighting conditions.

Using the manufacturer's instructions and a roll of surplus film, practice loading your tank and reel in total darkness as many times as necessary to ensure proficiency. *Do not load your first tank with a valued roll of exposed film.* Until you develop the necessary skills, expect to make a few mistakes.

Now study each step in the Step-by-Step Procedure, *Black-and-White Film Processing.* Note those steps described for total darkness. If a photographic darkroom is not available, a film **changing bag** may be useful. Changing bags are light-tight, zippered fabric containers with tightly sealed sleeves through which you can insert your arms. Another alternative is to seal a bathroom with blankets over the windows and around the doors. Test the darkroom by turning off all lights and placing a white sheet of paper on the counter. If after two minutes you cannot discern the white paper, the room is dark enough for handling light-sensitive materials.

Processing Color Films

Objective 5-B Explain and demonstrate the processing of color films.

Key Concepts C-41 process, blix, stabilizer, E-6 process, reversal bath, color developer, pre-bleach, bleach

Most color film processing is carried out with the same equipment used for black-and-white film. Best results depend upon fresh chemicals, painstaking standards, and consistency, so most photographers prefer to use commercial color film processing labs for their color film. Well-run, automated, 1-hour mini-labs generally do a good job of processing popular color negative films and making prints. Custom laboratories, though more expensive, process larger negative formats and color transparency films. Unless you are processing a large volume of color film, it is usually more cost- and time-effective to use a mini lab. However, if you prefer to process your own color film, easy-to-use processing kits are commonly available.

Figure 5-2. A variety of processing tanks and reels for roll film.

Black-and-White Film Processing

Lights On

1. **Prepare the processing solutions.** *Prepare the three chemical solutions—developer, stop bath, and fixer. Some chemicals are prepared in concentrated form and diluted before use. The concentrated forms are called* **stock solutions**; *the diluted forms,* **working solutions**. *Mix powdered chemicals in advance to allow them to dissolve thoroughly.*

   Bring all processing solutions to the recommended temperature. (See Figure 5-3 A, B, C.)

   Process most black-and-white film within a range of 65°–75°F (18°–24°C). The manufacturer's **time-and-temperature chart** *will provide exact developing time and temperature combinations. (See Figure 5-4A.)*

2. **Set up the equipment and materials.** *Separate the work area into dry and wet areas. Keep wet materials out of the dry area. Before processing, handle film in the dry area using lintless cloth gloves.*

A.

B.

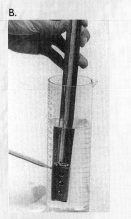

C.

Figure 5-3. Temperature control. A) Solution temperatures may be adjusted before use by placing storage bottles in tanks of water at correct temperature. Shortstop is the stop bath preparation used here. B) Solution temperature may be measured with a darkroom thermometer. C) Wash water temperature may be controlled with a photographic mixing valve.

A.

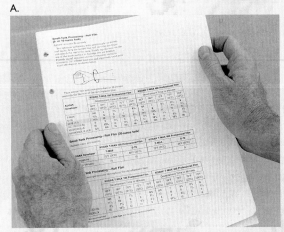

B.

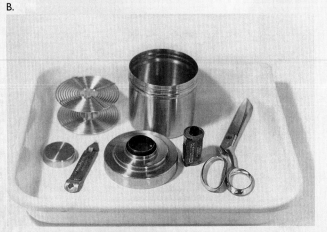

Figure 5-4. Getting ready to process film. A) Check time-and-temperature chart for normal developing time for your film and developer combination. B) Place small items in a dry tray in front of you so that you can easily locate them in the dark.

Arrange all items on the counter so you can find them easily in the dark. Use a small tray or box lid to prevent items from rolling off the counter. Place processing chemicals nearby in a sink or on the wet area counter. Arrange the following items neatly as shown:

Dry Counter	Wet Sink or Counter
Film for processing	Working-strength processing
Film-processing tank and reels or hangers	solutions
Scissors	Photo thermometer
Film cassette opener or bottle opener	Graduates
Darkroom timer	Funnel
Negative storage pages	

Check the manufacturer's time-and-temperature chart. Set the darkroom timer for the recommended developing time, but do not start the timer. Take a final look around. Turn off the lights. (See Figure 5-4.)

Figure 5-5. Electromechanical darkroom timer. May be set for intervals up to 60 minutes. Signals audibly at end of interval. Luminous face and hands can be read in total darkness. Timer is set but not switched on until processing starts.

Lights Off

3. Remove the film from its container. *For 35mm film, use the film cassette opener or a bottle opener to pry the end off of the cassette and remove the film. Unroll about 6 inches of the leader. Holding the film carefully by the edges cut off the tongue of the leader squarely. For roll films, open the seal and unwind the backing paper to uncover the film. Always handle film by the edges and do not touch the emulsion with your fingers.*

4. Load the film. *Load the film onto the processing reel or into the film hangers. Remove any tape attached to the film.*

5. Load and seal the processing tank. *Place the loaded reel or hangers into the tank. Place the lid on the tank to seal it from light. Turn on the lights. Perform the remaining steps in normal light. (See Figure 5-6.)*

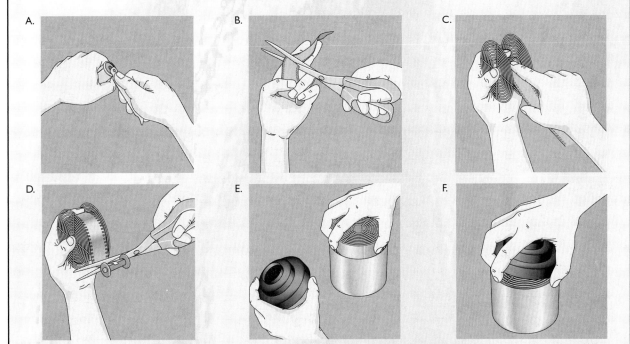

Figure 5-6. Loading film. A) In total darkness break open the film canister, magazine or roll. Remove film, handling it only by edges. B) Square off leading edge of film if necessary. C) Start to load film onto reel according to manufacturer's directions. D) Remove tape and spool at end of film. E) Place reel containing film in processing tank. F) Seal with light-tight cover. Once sealed, work lights may be turned on for processing.

Lights On

6. **Prepare for developing.** *Note the temperature of the solution. Pour the required amount of working-strength developer into a graduate. Be sure to set the darkroom timer to the time recommended on the time-and-temperature chart.*

   Optional Step: You may wish to presoak the film in plain water first to assure even processing and to dislodge air bubbles. To presoak, fill the tank with water of the same temperature as the developer, agitate for thirty seconds or so, discard the water, and continue the developing procedure.

7. **Start developing.** *Pour sufficient developer into the tank to fill it, place the cover or cap over the opening, and immediately start the timer. Always start the timer immediately after pouring each solution into the tank.*

   Optional Method: You might prefer to fill the processing tank with developer first and then, in total darkness, drop the loaded reels into the solution and place the cover on the tank. Either way, start the timer when the film is completely submerged in the solution.

8. **Begin agitation.** *Tap the tank gently a few times before starting agitation to dislodge air bubbles. Then agitate the film according to the manufacturer's instructions. Follow the same routine consistently.*

9. **Pour out the developer.** *Do not open the tank. Pour the developer from the tank when the timer cycle is complete.*

   Some developers are meant for one-time use only and are discarded after use or collected for ecological disposal. Pour these **one-shot developers** *down the drain or into a chemical refuse container. Other developers are reusable and should be poured back into their containers and retained for further use. Reusable developers often require adding a* **replenisher** *to the solution after every use or extending the developing time. There is a limit to the number of rolls that can be processed with reusable developer. (See Figures 5-7A through E.)*

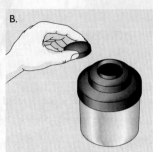
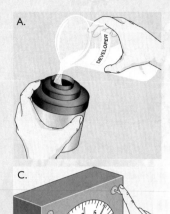
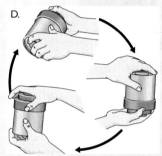
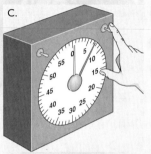

Figure 5-7. Processing film. A) Pour developer into tank through light-tight vent. (Handle later processing chemicals in same way.) B) Place vent cover over opening to prevent spillage of chemicals. C) Start timer. D) Agitate. E) Return developer to stock (or discard if one-shot developer is used). Pour all liquids from tank's light-tight vent. Never open tank during processing. F) Following development, pour water or stop bath into tank to stop developing action. G) Follow standard agitation cycle. H) Return stop bath to bottle, or discard water rinse. I) Pour fixer into tank, fix for recommended time. J) Again, follow the standard agitation cycle. K) Return used fixer to bottle.

10. Fill the tank with a clear water rinse or stop bath. *Use clear water or a chemical stop bath to stop the action of the developer quickly. Do not open the tank.*

11. Pour out the stop bath. *Discard water rinse; save stop bath for several uses. Do not open the tank.*

12. Fill the tank with fixer. *Set the timer for the recommended fixing time. Agitate during fixing. Fix film for at least the recommended time. Overfixing for a brief time will not harm the film.*

13. Pour out the fixer. *Return the fixer to its container when the timer cycle is complete. Typically, acid fixer may be reused many times. See the manufacturer's specifications to learn how long the fixer will last. Open the tank.*

14. Check the negatives. *Remove the tank cover and rinse the film briefly in water. Unroll a few frames. You should see only the black negative image against a clear background. You should see no trace of the emulsion or the colored antihalation backing; otherwise, fix longer. When clear, proceed with washing. (See Figures 5-8 A–B.)*

15. Begin the washing cycle. *Processing leaves a chemical residue in the emulsion that can damage the image. Remove chemical residues by flowing water gently around the film for twenty to thirty minutes. (See Figures 5-9 A–C.)*

    Use a high-speed washer and/or a chemical **clearing agent** *to reduce washing time and save water. High-speed washers increase the flow of water around the film; chemical clearing agents neutralize the residual chemicals.*

16. Soak the film in a wetting agent. *Water contains minerals that leave visible spots when the water dries. Use a wetting agent to avoid water spots. Immerse the washed film, still wound on the processing reel or mounted on hangers, into the wetting bath for the recommended time. Save the wetting bath for further use.*

17. Hang the film to dry. *Drain excess liquid from the film by stretching it at an angle. Hang the film by a film clip in a dry, dust-free place and attach a film clip or clothespin to weight the bottom and avoid curling. Hang film sheets by a corner.*

Figure 5-8. A) Following fixing, open tank. Give film a quick water rinse and remove it from tank. B) Inspect negatives under white light.

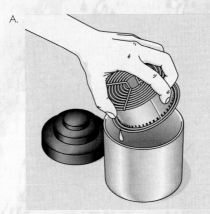

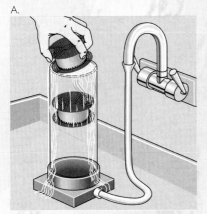
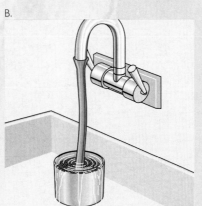
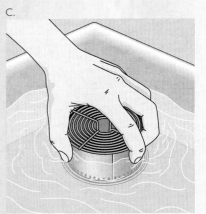

Figure 5-9. Replace film on reel for final wash. A) An efficient high speed washer will shorten wash times. B) Or, a hose can be inserted in the tank to direct a gentle stream of water through the reel. C) After a thorough wash, place film in a bath of wetting agent such as Kodak PhotoFlo.

You may gently wipe away excess liquid with a moist, clean photo chamois, squeegee tongs, viscous sponge, or absorbent cotton, or simply drip dry the wetted film. Wiping may rub floating particles into the emulsion; drip drying may form water spots. Choose a method that works well under your laboratory conditions. (See Figures 5-10 A–B.)

18. Tally and replenish the developer. *If your developer is reusable, immediately add the recommended replenisher. Tally the number of rolls developed. (See Figures 5-11 A, B.)*

19. File the negatives. *Cut and file the negatives when the film is completely dry. Cut roll-film negatives into lengths of three to six frames each, depending on the film size, and store them in plastic negative file pages or sleeves. Negatives are easily scratched without protection. (See Figures 5-12 A, B.)*

Figure 5-10. Drying processing film. A) Remove excess water or wetting agent from film with photographic sponge, squeegee tongs, or allow to drip. B) Hang film in a drying cabinet or other dustfree place until dry.

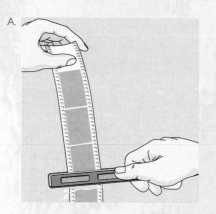
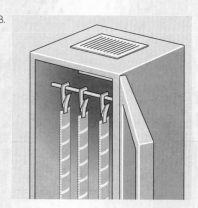

Figure 5-11. Replenishing developer (optional). A) Following use of reusable developer you may add replenisher to stock solution to revitalize developer's strength. B) Tally each roll developed on the developer container so that you'll know when stock solution is exhausted.

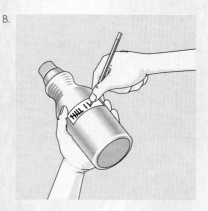

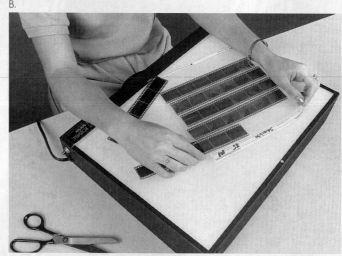

Figure 5-12. Cutting and storing negatives. A) Cut finished negatives into strips. Do not separate individual frames. B) Insert negatives into plastic negative file pages.

Color Darkroom Equipment

A darkroom set up to process black-and-white film already has most of the equipment needed for color film.

The darkroom will need the following items:

- Tanks and reels normally used for roll film.

- Deep tray and heater equipped to maintain correct temperature.

- A precise thermometer, calibrated to ± 1/4° F, to monitor solution temperatures.

- Storage containers for processing solutions. Collapsible containers keep air out and prolong solution life.

- Other typical items include a bottle opener, scissors, graduated cylinders, beakers, stirring rods, funnels, heavy-duty rubber gloves, lab apron, timer, film clips, clothespins—all things used in a black-and-white lab.

- Optionally, though expensive, a tabletop processor can make color processing easier. It holds the processing chemicals, maintains proper temperature, and provides consistent agitation.

The General Steps

Because the time, temperature, and agitation requirements for color processing are standard, films of different speeds and from different manufacturers can be processed simultaneously in the same tank, except for rolls that require push-processing. Also, note that you must process transparency and negative films separately—they use different chemistry. Follow the manufacturer's instructions.

Color Negative Processing

The industry standard for processing color negative film is the Kodak **C-41 process**. Other manufacturers offer films compatible with the C-41 process. Several manufacturers offer processing kits compatible with the C-41 process for consumer use.

Steps in Color Negative Processing

Although the chemistry differs, the general steps in processing color negatives mirrors the steps used for black-and-white film processing. (See Step-by-Step Procedure, *Film Processing* starting on page 168 for details.) The chemicals commonly used for color negative processing include the following:

- *Developer* This first, most critical step in the process establishes the density, contrast, and color balance of the image. As with black-and-white film, the **developer** first acts upon the exposed halides to produce metallic silver—only it does so *in each emulsion layer* (see Figure 4-4 on page 145). Then, by releasing dye couplers in each layer, the developer produces a primary color dye image coupled to each silver image. When development is complete, each film layer contains both a black-and-white negative and a primary color dye image.

- *Bleach/Fix or Blix* The bleach fix in this two step process, sometimes called **blix**, converts the metallic silver in each layer back to a silver halide. The fix then dissolves all the silver halides, leaving only the dye image in each layer.

HELPFUL HINT

Mixing Stop Bath

Most photochemicals are packaged with instructions for mixing and storage. Follow them carefully. Chemical stop bath, however, often is not explained. Stop bath is a 1- to 2-percent solution of acetic acid. Acetic acid can be purchased in two forms: glacial acetic acid (99 percent), which must be handled with great care, and commercial-strength acetic acid (28 percent), which is easier to store and handle. Purchase the commercial-strength if possible; if you must purchase glacial, dilute it to commercial strength for storage. Here are the dilution formulas:

3 parts glacial (99 percent) + 8 parts water = 11 parts commercial-strength acetic acid (28 percent)

1 part commercial-strength (28 percent) + 20 parts water = 21 parts working-strength stop bath

Safety Note

Proper chemical handling procedures call for mixing acid and water in a particular sequence. Always start with the required amount of water; then add the acid. Doing the reverse—that is, pouring even a small amount of water into a container of acid—could cause a dangerous reaction and/or acid splashes. Remember: acid to water, never water to acid.

- *Water Wash* Wash to remove all active chemicals.
- *Stabilizer* This last step uses formaldehyde or a derivative as a **stabilizer** to keep the color dyes from fading. A wetting agent in the stabilizer encourages uniform drying to avoid water spots.

When processing is complete, the film should be allowed to dry uniformly. Squeegee only if needed, wiping gently on both sides with a sponge soaked in stabilizer. (See Step-By-Step Procedure, *Film Processing,* Step 17, page 171.)

Processing Color Transparencies

Processing color transparencies requires more solutions and takes longer than processing color negatives. The industry standard for processing color transparency film is the Kodak **E-6 process**. Other manufacturers offer films compatible with the E-6 process. Several manufacturers offer processing kits compatible with the E-6 process for consumer use, in both six-bath and three-bath configurations.

Steps in Color Transparency Processing

The chemicals and steps commonly used for color transparency processing include the following:

- *Prewet & Prewarm Bath* Soak the film in water at the same temperature as the developer to soften the emulsion and encourage uniform development.
- *First Developer* This first critical step converts the exposed silver halides into a black-and-white negative *in each emulsion layer* and establishes the contrast and density of the image (see Figure 4-4 on page 145). The amount of silver formed affects the amount of dye formed later in the process.
- *First Wash* The first wash quickly stops development and removes developer from the film.
- *Reversal Bath* A chemical **reversal bath** prepares the unexposed, undeveloped silver halides for the chemical reversal that occurs in the color developer. Do not wash; the emulsion should enter the color developer soaked with the reversal agent.

Kodachrome Transparency Film

Kodak's Kodachrome transparency film, introduced in 1935, was originally used as a motion picture film. It was first adapted for still photography in 35mm cameras and later for larger formats. Still in use, it differs from other transparency films in that it uses no dye couplers. Instead, color is added during processing. As a result, Kodachrome processing, designated K-14 process, can only be done by specially equipped laboratories and usually takes longer than standard E-6 processing.

- *Color Developer* In this step, the reversal agent chemically "exposes" the remaining silver halides. This **color developer** then converts them to metallic silver. As the silver image is formed, the color developing agent reacts with the color couplers in each of the film's three dye layers (yellow, magenta, and cyan) to form colored dye images.
- *Pre-bleach* The **pre-bleach** prepares the metallic silver image for oxidation in the bleach step and enhances dye stability. Do not wash; the film should enter the bleach soaked with pre-bleach.
- *Bleach* The **bleach** converts the metallic silver in each layer back to a silver halide; the silver halide is later removed in the fixer.
- *Fixer* The fixer converts all the remaining silver halides into soluble compounds. Most of the silver compounds are removed in the fixer and can be recovered. Residual bleach must be neutralized by aeration or agitation to remove exhausted bleach.
- *Final Wash* Wash to remove all active chemicals remaining in the emulsion.
- *Final Rinse* The final rinse contains a wetting agent to reduce water spots and to encourage uniform drying.

When processing is complete, the film should be allowed to dry uniformly. Squeegee only if needed. (See Step-By-Step Procedure, *Film Processing,* step 17, page 171.)

Evaluating Negatives

Objective 5-C Examine and evaluate negatives for proper exposure and developing.

Key Concepts density, thin, dense, expose for the shadows and develop for the highlights, underexposure, overexposure, tonal range, contrast, overdeveloped, grainy, underdeveloped, flat

Careful visual examination of negatives can reveal much about the exposure and processing that the film received. It can also help to pinpoint problems that will need correction when the final print is made.

Evaluating Density

Lay the negatives on a light table or hold them above a brightly lit sheet of white paper. Notice that the **density**, or degree of darkness, varies within the negative corresponding to the scene's original brightness. Of course, negatives are tonally reversed: bright objects in the original scene appear darkest on the negative and dark objects in the original scene appear lightest.

In general, a technically "good" negative is one that possesses a full range of densities. The negative should be sufficiently dense to record detail in all areas, but not excessively dark. Shadows, middle tones, and highlights should all show visible separation. No large, important shadows (light areas in the negative) should be completely transparent; no important highlights (dark areas in the negative) should be completely opaque.

Examine the strip of negatives. Negatives that are very pale or mostly transparent, lacking in overall density, are often called **thin** negatives. Thin negatives will normally produce dark prints that lack detail. Negatives that are overly dark with heavy deposits of silver, or dye in the case of color negatives, are often called **dense** negatives. Dense negatives are hard to see through and will normally produce prints that are too light or too grainy. See Figure 3-17, page 117, for examples of thin, normal, and dense negatives.

Evaluate color transparencies as you would prints. Overall dark transparencies usually result from underexposure or insufficient first development. Overall light transparencies usually result from overexposure or too much first development.

Exposure and Its Relation to Shadow Density

Diagnosing negative defects can be difficult. Density defects can be caused by the amount of development, the amount of exposure, or both. Errors in both exposure and processing can create problems in tonal or color rendition, granularity, and even sharpness of the resulting images. Remember this old photographic adage when working with *negative* films: *Expose for the shadows, develop for the highlights*.

The amount of detail recorded in the shadow areas of the negative is almost entirely determined by the amount of light originally admitted into the camera. Too little light or **underexposure** produces a negative that is thin overall, but especially so in the shadows, where some details do not record at all. Underexposure results in a weak print—one that is missing texture, fullness of detail, and a sense of volume in the darker subject areas. No amount of additional development can make lost details or texture appear.

Conversely, **overexposure** results in negatives that are excessively dark overall, but especially so in the highlights, where details and textures may be lost in the dark areas of the negative. Excessive density or darkness anywhere in the negative can cause excessive grain and a loss of sharpness and detail.

A normal negative or positive transparency is neither excessively light nor excessively dark overall. It is rich in detail in all three important areas: shadows, midtones, and highlights. When negatives are viewed by reflected light, the viewer should just barely be able to see through the densest areas of the negatives.

Development and Its Relation to Highlight Density

The lighter subject tones, or highlights, are strongly affected by film development. Film developers chemically multiply the number of grains of metallic silver that form from the few atoms of silver that were originally affected by exposure. This process has a far greater effect on those areas more exposed to light than those less exposed —on the highlight areas more than the shadow areas. During development, the highlights tend to darken more than the shadows, and at a faster

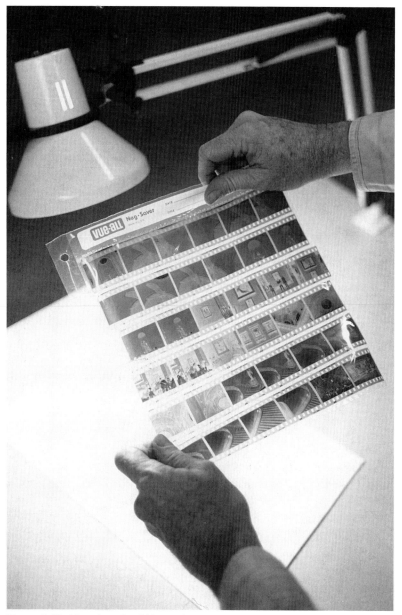

Figure 5-13. Negatives should be evaluated by an even and diffused light source. Here a desk lamp is bounced off a white card to provide proper viewing conditions.

Underdevelopment reduces highlight density, yielding a low-contrast or **flat** print. Such **underdeveloped** negatives lack the tonal separation necessary for making prints rich and bright with texture and detail. **Flat** prints are typically muddy, lacking crisp highlights, deep blacks, or both. Color images appear similarly muddy, lacking in crisp bright colors and contrasts.

Factors Affecting the Action of the Developer

The type of developer used, the temperature of the developer, the time of the development, and the amount of agitation—all of these factors affect the action of the developer on the film. If the developer is too cool, if the development time is too short, or if agitation is insufficient, an underdeveloped negative will result—one that is thin, lacking in contrast, and difficult to print well.

Conversely, if the developer is too hot, if development time is too long, or if agitation is excessive, an overdeveloped negative will result—one that is dense, grainy, contrasty, and difficult to print well.

Optimum results come only from a careful balance of development time, temperature, and agitation. Good results depend upon care and consistency. As a start, follow the manufacturers' recommendations.

rate. Thus, changing development time causes changes in the relationship between highlights and shadows, or the **tonal range**—what photographers call **contrast**.

Overdevelopment results in negatives that are excessively dark and too contrasty. Highlight areas in an **overdeveloped** negative will appear blocked or nearly solid black and will be devoid of textural information. Excess density also results in larger clumps of silver crystals on the negative, giving an enlarged print made from the negative a **grainy** or textured appearance.

Checking for Correct Film Development

Both incorrect exposure and incorrect development can cause abnormal negative density. One quick, rough way to check for correct film development is to look at the frame numbers and markings along the edge of the developed film. These letters and digits were imprinted with light at the time of manufacture and should appear crisp and dark on correctly developed film. If the numbers are excessively dark and the small spaces, or counters, within the letters appear partially filled in, the film was probably overdeveloped. Similarly, if the letters are weak and gray, the film was probably underdeveloped. For examples and descriptions of common film-developing problems, see Figure 5-14 on pages 178–179.

Summary

The ultimate test of a negative's quality is its ability to print well and easily. A good negative yields a print that is rich in detail and expresses the photographer's intent. If prints are consistently lacking in shadow detail, the film is likely being systematically underexposed. To increase detail in the darker areas, increase exposure slightly by lowering the film speed setting on the camera or meter by 25 to 50 percent. For example, for a film rated ISO 400/27°, try setting the camera's film-speed setting to ISO 320/26°, or even ISO 200/24°.

Some photographers also adjust the suggested developing times for their personal working styles and subjects. If negatives systematically lack contrast and the darkest areas of the negative are too light, increase development time to increase highlight density and contrast.

Sometimes photographers adjust developing time to compensate for an abnormal contrast range in the original scene. For example, if a roll of film were shot under low-contrast lighting, such as under heavy overcast, the resulting negatives might be too flat for normal printing. Increase contrast by slightly increasing film developing time.

Changing the film development time in this way is practical only if a whole roll of film has been exposed under the same conditions. Sheet film users can modify developing time for each negative as they wish. (See Figure 5-15.)

Adapting to Available Light

Objective 5-D Explain and demonstrate the rationale, materials, and procedures of push-processing.

Key Concepts available light, overrating, exposure index (EI), push process, high-energy developer, chromogenic films

News photographers, photojournalists, and others are often called upon to produce images by **available light** under conditions that are far from ideal. Working in low light frequently requires that the photographer use very wide aperture settings to achieve adequate exposure; however, using such large lens openings greatly reduces the range of focus and the chances for obtaining a sharply focused image. Alternatively, the photographer may select a smaller aperture to increase the range of focus and compensate for the reduced illumination by selecting a slower shutter speed; however, using a slow shutter speed increases the risk that the images will be blurred due to subject movement or camera shake.

Overrating the Film Speed

What can be done if the photographer's visual interpretation calls for higher shutter speeds or more depth of field than the lighting conditions permit? Some photographers continue to use their regular films for low light conditions, but deliberately underexpose them by **overrating** the film speed.

The ISO film speed index is an arbitrary rating set by the manufacturer and its effect may vary from camera to camera, person to person, and process to process. Variations in actual shutter speeds, personal taste in negative qualities, and individual differences in processing methods may affect the effective film speed.

The term **exposure index (EI)** is a measure of the effective film speed under given conditions. Thus, a film with a rated speed of ISO 400/27° might intentionally be shot at an exposure index of EI 1600. Overrating the film this way pretends that the film is rated ISO 1600/30° and allows you to use smaller apertures and faster shutter speeds. However, it will systematically underexpose the film by two stops.

Push-Processing

Overrating the film always results in underexposing the film. Simply switching to a faster exposure index has no effect on the actual film speed, which is determined solely by the emulsion's sensitivity. Under less than ideal lighting you may choose to overrate the film speed, despite losing shadow detail, and then **push-process** the film to

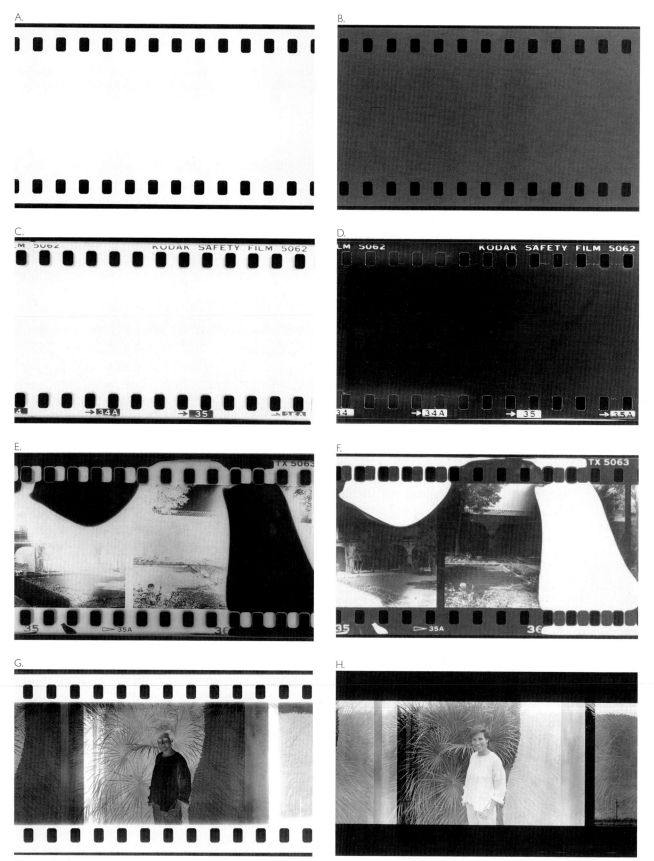

Figure 5-14. Troubleshooting film processing. A) No developer, bad developer, or fixer used first. Negative is clear with no edge markings. B) Print of A). C) No exposure. Negative is clear but edge markings are visible. Presence of edge marks assures that film was processed correctly. D) Print of C). E) Film improperly loaded onto reel. No chemicals reach areas where film touches itself, leaving gaps in image. F) Print of E). G) Film not fully advanced. One image exposed over another. H) print of G.

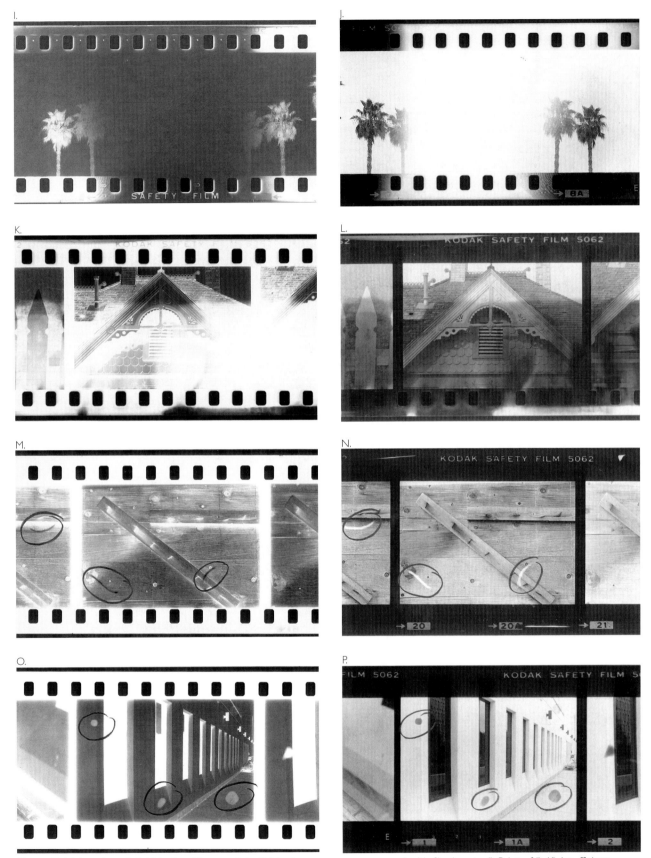

Figure 5-14 (continued). I) Light fog. Film struck by light when camera was opened with film in gate. J) Print of I). K) Insufficient developer in tank. If developer does not cover film parts of image may be underdeveloped. L) Print of K). M) Cinch marks. Film is sensitive to pressure; crimping during reel loading may cause marks such as these. N) Print of M). O) Air bells. Small bubbles formed on the surface of the film during processing prevent proper development if not dislodged by agitation. P) Print of O).

A.

B.

Figure 5-15. Contrast and processing. A) A low contrast scene given normal film development will appear flat and lifeless when printed on normal contrast paper. B) Given extended film development time the negative will gain contrast and yield a print with greater tonal separation and vitality.

compensate for the underexposure. This technique simply increases development time, increases the density of the midtones, and helps make otherwise lost images printable.

Conventional fast-speed black-and-white films can usually be overrated to double their rated index—from ISO 400/27° to EI 800/30°, for example—and still provide an acceptable print by extending development time 50 percent beyond

normal. All other processing steps remain the same.

Overrating by two stops—from ISO 400/27° to EI 1600/33°, for example, requires doubling developing time. For greater pushes, use special **high-energy developers** that allow a overrating by as much as three stops—an EI eight times the rated ISO index. (See Table J-3, Appendix J, for typical film developers.)

Famous Photograph

Imogen Cunningham

Greatly respected for her soft-form, rhythmic images, Imogen Cunningham, when ninety, said, "People often marvel at me. 'I don't know how you keep so busy,' they say. 'Keep busy!', I repeat. 'I don't keep busy. I am busy.'"

Indeed, Cunningham's career spanned more than seventy years, beginning with her study of chemistry at the University of Washington. After graduation, she took a job at the Curtis Studio, where she printed hundreds of Edward S. Curtis's photographs of North American Indians onto platinum paper. She spent a year in Dresden on a national scholarship for advanced study of photochemistry and then returned to Seattle to establish her first portrait studio.

Inspired by Gertrude Käsebier, Cunningham enjoyed her first major exhibition in 1912. She continued to exhibit throughout her life in major art museums, institutes, and universities throughout America, including the International Museum of Photography, the Art Institute of Chicago, the Library of Congress, and the Smithsonian Institution. Her work moved early toward new realism, with its emphasis on sharp focus and unmanipulated images. In 1932, she joined Willard Van Dyke, Edward Weston, Ansel Adams, and others in Group f/64. Later in her career, she taught at the San Francisco Art Institute and lectured widely in colleges and universities throughout the country.

Imogen Cunningham, "Two Callas," about 1929. Photograph by Imogen Cunningham. © 1970 The Imogen Cunningham Trust.

Although portraiture occupied a good part of Cunningham's professional activity, she is best known for her nudes, plants, and nature studies. Her images, rich with tone, palpable textures, and clean, simple form, often convey great sensuality.

You can also push-process many color films. If you push-process your own color film, increase only the developer time. Mini-labs generally won't push-process color films, but many professional labs will do so for an additional charge. You should not need to push-process color film because high-speed films are readily available and color film has a wide exposure latitude. Check the manufacturer's product sheets for push-processing instructions.

Alternatives to Conventional Films

Advances in film technology have produced black-and-white films with nearly magical film speeds and image qualities. These tabular-grain films, such as Kodak T-Max P3200 and Ilford Delta 3200, offer exceptionally high film speeds combined with reasonably fine grain.

T-Max P3200 film was designed to be shot at EI 1000/31° to EI 1600/33° without push-processing. Working photojournalists routinely process it at normal processing times to EI 3200/36° or even 6400/39° with excellent results. However, extended processing times can produce usable negatives at speeds as high as a whopping EI 25,000/45°—six stops faster than a conventional ISO 400/27° film.

Another advance in black-and-white films is a general class of **chromogenic films**, such as Kodak Portra 400BW and Ilford XP2 Super. With chromogenic film, the image is generated from dyes that are formed during development. The best balance of sharpness and grain is obtained with these films when used at EI 400/27°. However, overrated or underexposed chromogenic negatives suffer only a slight loss in quality. Chromogenic films are best processed using standard color print (C-41) processing.

These super-high-speed films present new creative opportunities for many photographers. Sports photographers can use longer, slower lenses for night football games, spot news pictures can be recorded by streetlight illumination alone, and evocative portraits can be made in the darkest environments. (See Figure 5-16.)

Figure 5-16. Sports action shots often call for extended developing times or special film developers to "push" the speed rating of the film, thus permitting action photography under available light.

Summary

Overrating and push-processing are not magic cures. Best results come from using the fastest film available and pushing as little as possible. As processing time increases, the more shadow detail decreases; moreover, extended development always results in increased contrast, bigger grain, and loss of sharpness. If light levels are too low and the picture must be captured, overrating and push-processing can help make a print that might otherwise be lost.

Questions to Consider

1. How does the developer affect the film? What is the purpose of fixer?

2. What are some of the factors that affect the action and rate of the film developer?

3. What factors can cause thin negatives? Dense negatives?

4. How does contrast relate to film developing time?

5. Explain how color processing differs from black-and-white processing. What is the function of dye couplers? How is the color image formed?

Suggested Field and Laboratory Assignments

1. Complete your acquisition of all black-and-white film processing supplies, including developer, stop bath, fixer, clearing agent, and so forth. Complete arrangements for the use of a darkroom for film processing.

2. Prepare and mix all chemical solutions following the manufacturer's instructions. Determine the working dilutions, if any, processing times and temperatures, and other pertinent data. Record this information on the film-developing summary sheet shown in Appendix K on the CD that accompanies this book for convenient reference as you develop your first rolls of film.

3. Using a processing tank, reel, and roll of dummy film, practice loading the film onto the reel under normal light. Practice until the loading becomes a reflex action. When you feel confident, practice loading the film in total darkness.

4. Develop one roll of exposed film (or more if necessary) so that you end up with a batch of usable negatives on a variety of subjects. If your first development efforts fail, shoot and process additional film until you have completed the assignment.

5. Conduct an experiment to observe the physical reaction of film to the processing chemicals. Take a strip of waste film, such as the leader tongue from an exposed roll, and process it in open containers under white light. Immerse the strip halfway into the developer tank or tray and note how the density gradually builds. Now transfer the strip through a brief rinse into a container of fixer. Immerse the entire strip in the fixing bath. Compare the action of the fixer on the developed areas to its effect on the undeveloped areas. Are frame numbers and other edge markings present? Why?

6. Shoot a roll of color negative film. Have it processed in a mini-lab. Examine the negatives. Evaluate the density, contrast, and color balance of the negatives.

Printing

Rose Tirzah, "Portrait of a Man"

Unit at a Glance

Many creative tools can be used during printing to vary the texture, color, contrast, tonality, and general appearance of a photograph. Mastering these tools allows photographers to create images that reflect their unique understanding and perception of their subjects.

During the transition from film to digital photography, many photographers continue to use traditional darkroom methods to make paper prints from negatives as well as digital image processing methods. This Unit describes how to make and evaluate prints from film negatives using traditional materials, chemistry, and darkroom methods. In general, the photographic process follows the same general chemical steps as those used film processing—exposing, developing, fixing, washing, drying. Unlike film, however, most photographic paper is processed in open trays under colored safelights, allowing you to observe a print at each step.

The unit also describes printing papers and print-processing chemistry, the control of contrast, printing controls such as burning in, dodging, split-filter printing, flashing, black-border printing, and the Sabattier effect. It discusses print-finishing techniques, including spotting, bleaching, and mounting, and provides an overview of the materials, equipment, and space necessary to create your own darkroom.

This unit describes the principles as well as step-by-step procedures used in photographic printing of both black-and-white and color images.

Tools and Materials

Objective 6-A Identify the basic printing materials and tools, including parts of a typical enlarger, and explain their functions.

Key Concepts lamp housing, condenser housing, filter drawer, color printing (CP) filters, filter pack, dichroic color head, negative carrier, condenser housing lever, bellows, enlarger lens, lensboard, elevator control crank, elevator lock knob, focusing knob, base, power plug, timer, adjustable easel, focusing magnifier, proofer, safelights, print siphon, archival washer, drying racks, heated drum dryer, voltage stabilizer, drum processor, tube, tabletop processor, color analyzer, fiber-base, resin-coated (RC), color printing paper, archival images, RA-4, R-3000

The Enlarger

At the heart of a printing darkroom is the enlarger—the principal tool for making prints from negatives and slides. Enlargers vary in complexity. Some offer adjustments for different negative sizes and formats, for modifying the optical system, for modifying perspective controls, for automatic focusing, and for adjusting color balance, to name a few possible options. Other enlargers are relatively simple mechanisms designed for a single negative format without additional features. The following discussion describes the features found on most modest enlargers, although the physical design may vary considerably among manufacturers.

The typical enlarger is designed to pass an evenly distributed beam of light through a negative and a lens so that an image of the negative is focused on a sheet of light-sensitive photographic paper. The design prevents emission of stray light from the enlarger and allows adjustments that change the size of the projected image. Some enlargers also feature a filter drawer that holds color printing (CP) filters for adjusting the color balance for color printing. Figure 6-2 A shows the functional parts of a typical enlarger.

The **lamp housing** is an enclosure for the light source—usually a photoenlarger bulb. It is designed to prevent light leaks and to dissipate heat.

The **condenser housing** usually contains one or more lenses designed to gather, concentrate, and to pass an even field of light through the negative. Some housings also contain a translucent sheet of glass to diffuse the field of light.

A **filter drawer**, often located between the lamp and the negative carrier, holds a set of **color printing (CP) filters**. This **filter pack** allows you to adjust the color balance when making color prints. Some enlargers use a complete **dichroic color head** for this purpose. See Figures 6-2 B and C.

The **negative carrier** holds the negative flat and in place during enlargement.

The **condenser housing lever** allows the entire condenser housing to be raised and lowered to allow the negative carrier to be inserted.

The **bellows** is a flexible housing that holds the lensboard and allows the distance between the lens and the negative to be adjusted for focusing.

The **enlarger lens** is mounted to a **lensboard**. The lensboard is mounted to the lower end of the bellows. Enlarger lenses of different focal lengths may be mounted to the lensboard for use with different negative formats. For any negative format, the normal enlarger lens will have the same focal length as the normal camera lens. For example, a 50mm enlarger lens is normal for 35mm negatives; a 75mm or 80mm enlarger lens is normal for 2 1/4in x 2 1/4in (6cm x 6cm) negatives; and so forth. Enlarging lenses, like camera lenses, have adjustable apertures. (See *Lens Characteristics,* page 76, for a discussion of normal focal length.)

The **elevator control crank** raises and lowers the entire enlarger head to change the size of the projected image.

The **elevator lock knob** locks the enlarger head in position.

The **focusing knob** focuses the negative image on the printing paper.

The **base** is the board or surface on which the entire enlarger assembly is mounted. A paper-holding easel is usually placed on the base.

The **power plug** provides power to the enlarger. Normally it is plugged into the timer, which in turn is plugged into the wall outlet.

Ancillary Equipment

Timer The **timer** provides for precisely timing the exposure by automatically turning off the lamp after the timed interval. It also provides for manual operation during focusing.

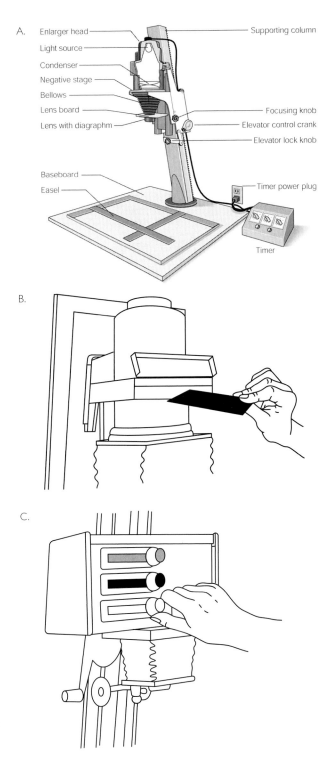

Figure 6-2. A) Anatomy of an enlarger. B) Filters can be placed in the drawer of an enlarger for color printing. C) Color heads have built-in Cyan, Magenta, and Yellow filters. Turn a dial to adjust the strength of the filters for color printing.

Easel The **adjustable easel** holds the photographic paper flat during exposure, masking the edges to create white borders.

Figure 6-3. Enlarger accessories. Electronic timer, adjustable easel, blower brush and critical focusing device.

Focusing Magnifier A **focusing magnifier** helps focus the projected image precisely. (See Figure 6-3.)

Contact Proof Frame A **proofer** consists of a sheet of plate glass mounted in a frame and hinged on a base. It provides for sandwiching negatives and photo paper under glass for contact printing. (See Figure 6-4.)

Safelights Because most black-and-white photographic paper is orthochromatic (insensitive to the red-amber portion of the spectrum), you can perform printing processes under a colored **safelight**. The most common printing safelights are light amber or yellow green. Color printing papers, however, fog easily and should be handled in total darkness until loaded into a light-tight drum or processor.

Print Washer After processing, the photographic paper must be thoroughly washed clean of chemical residues. Washing devices usually provide for removing used wash water while injecting fresh water.

A simple **print siphon** clipped to a tray makes an economical and effective print washer. Aquarium-style **ar-**

chival washers are the ultimate tool for removing all traces of chemical contaminants from fiber-based prints. (See Figure 6-5.)

Drying Racks and Lines One simple method of drying RC prints after processing is to hang them from a line by clothespins and air dry them. Alternatively, you may dry them on a fiber-glass **drying rack**. For faster drying, use an RC heat-impingement dryer that transports the prints through hot air. (See Figure 6-6.)

Fiber-based prints curl excessively if hung on a line to dry and need several hours to dry on screens. Nonetheless, racks and screens are often used to dry exhibition-quality fiber-based prints when time is not a factor.

Heated Drum Dryers To speed up the drying process with fiber-based paper, use a **heated drum dryer**. Do *not* use a heated drum dryer with RC paper; their hot surfaces will damage the RC coating. Dryers equipped with highly polished ferrotype drums impart a high gloss finish to glossy fiber-based paper.

Additional equipment that is useful for color processing includes the following:

Voltage Stabilizer A **voltage stabilizer** is useful to detect and correct variations in electric current. These variations can alter the intensity and

Figure 6-4. Proofer. Provides a convenient method for sandwiching negatives and photo paper under glass.

A.

A.

B.

B.

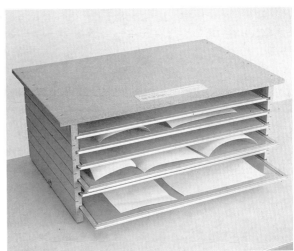

C.

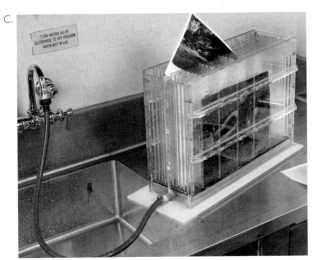

C.

Figure 6-5. Print Washers. A) Drum-type print washer. B) Tray siphon washer is convenient at work station. Especially useful for RC papers. C) Archival washer designed to remove all traces of residual chemicals and to hold individual prints separate during washing. Prints processed in archival-manner are suitable for long-term storage.

Figure 6-6. Print Dryers. A) Commercial rotary dryer with heated ferrotype drum. Not for use with RC papers. B) Fiberglass drying screens use no heat and only natural air flow, while also avoiding harsh treatment of prints, and chemical contamination. Useful for drying archival prints. May be used with fiber-based or RC papers. C) RC print dryers are designed especially for drying resin-coated papers. They squeegee the prints and quickly dry them with blasts of heated air. Not suitable for fiber-based papers.

color temperature of the enlarger light source and may affect paper exposure and print color.

Drum Processor Color prints must be processed in total darkness and should not be processed in open trays. A **drum processor**, sometimes called a **tube**, is a light tight cylinder, similar to a film processing tank, that serves for prints. The exposed color print paper is loaded into the drum in total darkness, then processed under normal room lighting. (See Figure 6-7 A)

Tabletop Processor A **tabletop processor** is a self-contained device that automates time, temperature, and agitation processes for color print processing. Some models also provide for automatically replenishing chemicals and delivering completely washed and dried color prints. (See Figures 6-7 B.)

Color Analyzer Usually found in professional color labs, a **color analyzer** uses a digital sensor to read the density and color of a color negative or transparency and to display a recommended exposure and filter array. Individual photographers usually prefer using test strips, which are less costly.

Kinds of Photographic Paper

Photographic printing papers are of two general types: **fiber-based** and **resin-coated (RC)**. The emulsion of fiber-based paper is applied directly onto the surface of porous paper. As photographic chemicals soak through the emulsion during processing they are absorbed into the paper base. Resin-coated (RC) papers differ in that the paper

base is first coated with resin, a hard, plastic-like substance that produces a good gripping surface and is impervious to water. Photographic chemicals enter the emulsion, but they do not penetrate the paper base. As a result, the paper base remains free of photographic chemicals.

Relative Advantages and Disadvantages of Photographic Papers Resin-coated (RC) papers greatly speed up darkroom work by reducing the time required to process and wash prints. Furthermore, RC prints dry faster and lay flatter than fiber-based prints. Almost all **color printing papers** are resin-coated (RC) papers.

On the other hand, fiber-based papers come in a greater variety of surface textures, base tints, and image colors than RC papers, and give photographers a wider range of expressive choices. Correctly processed, fiber-based prints are more stable and last longer than RC prints. **Archival images**, suitable for long-term storage, are best made on fiber-based paper. For these reasons, exhibition photographers and others seeking maximum print quality generally choose to print on fiber-based papers.

Print-Processing Chemicals

Black-and-white prints are generally processed in open trays of developer, stop bath, and fixer under safelight.

Color prints are processed in total darkness, generally in enclosed drums or tubes. Color printing papers must be matched to the proper processing

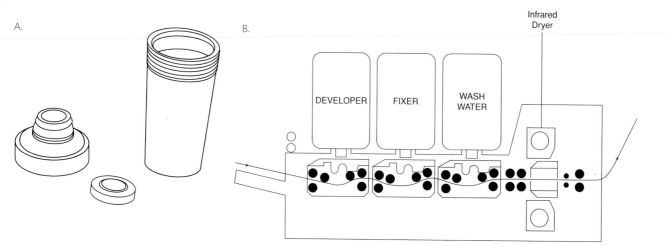

Figure 6-7. Color processing devices. A) Once loaded into drums or tubes like this, color paper can be processed in white light by pouring solutions in and out through the light tight lid. B) Tabletop processors automate color processing.

Famous Photograph

The Execution of Ruth Snyder

Convicted with her lover of murdering her wealthy husband, Ruth Snyder was sentenced to die in Sing Sing Prison's electric chair on January 12, 1928, following lurid and sensational coverage of the trial in the tabloid press. Although reporters were permitted to witness the execution, Sing Sing officials banned photographers.

In this era of "front page journalism," when every newspaper strove, by fair means or foul, to outdo and outwit the competition, the *New York Daily News* plotted a scheme to sneak a photographer into the death chamber to get the picture. City editor, Harvey Duell and picture editor Ted Dalton enlisted the aid of *Chicago Tribune* photographer Tom Howard who, they reasoned, because he was not known locally, could pass as a reporter. Duell and Dalton devised a way to strap a miniature camera to Howard's ankle and to run a cable release up his pant leg into his pocket.

With the aid of secretly obtained blueprints of the execution chamber, the men determined a shooting position and a range of focus. Howard proceeded to practice using his apparatus for a month before the execution date—they all knew that he would get only one chance at the shot.

RUTH SNYDER'S DEATH PICTURED'—This is perhaps the most remarkable exclusive picture in the history of criminology. It shows the actual scene in the Sing Sing death house as the lethal current surged through Ruth Snyder's body at 11:06 last night. Her helmeted head is stiffened in death, her face masked and an electrode strapped to her bare right leg. The autopsy table on which her body was removed is beside her. Judd Gray, mumbling a prayer, followed her down the narrow corridor at 11:11. "Father, forgive them, for they don't know what they are doing?" were Ruth's last words. The picture is the first Sing Sing execution picture and the first of a woman's electrocution.

On the night of the execution, Howard was admitted as a reporter without incident. He took up his position as planned. At the critical moment, he pointed his shoe in the direction of the condemned prisoner, hiked his trouser leg, and made one shot for each death-dealing jolt.

A few hours later, in the early morning of Friday the thirteenth, Howard's picture ran full front page in an extra edition of the *Daily News* with a one word headline: "DEAD!"

Although many consider making the illegal picture to be a breach of journalistic principles and ethics, the memorable image captures the eerie drama of the historic first execution of a woman by electrocution.

Tom Howard, "The execution of Ruth Snyder," January 12, 1928. © New York Daily News.

chemicals. **RA-4** is the Kodak designation for its system for printing from color negatives; **R-3000**, for its system of printing from color transparencies. Both RA-4 and R-3000 designations have been adopted as industry standards.

Photographic chemicals can pose health hazards if used improperly. Follow the manufacturer's recommendations for safe handling and work in a well-ventilated area. Use rubber gloves where recommended and avoid prolonged skin contact. Thoroughly wash and dry your hands after any chemical exposure. See *Handling Photographic Chemicals Safely* on page 166.

The Filter Pack

A filter pack, put together from a combination of CP filters or dialed into a dichroic color head, is a set of filter colors needed to produce a proper color balance for color printing from either negatives or transparencies. The three filter colors used most are yellow, magenta, and cyan. Other colors are available but rarely used. Filters are available in various densities: .025, .05, .10, .20, etc., the larger numbers representing greater densities. In practice, usually only two colors of filters are used. For efficient color printing, establish a standard filter pack and adjust the pack as needed for individual prints.

Making Contact Prints

Objective 6-B Explain and demonstrate the procedures used to make a contact proof sheet.

Key Concepts contact print, contact proof sheet, enlarger method, contact proofer

Contact Prints and Contact Proof Sheets

To make a **contact print** place the negative in direct contact with printing paper, the emulsions in contact with each other, and expose them to light. Because the negatives directly contact the paper, contact prints are the same size as the negatives. Thus, contact printing is generally suitable only for larger negatives.

A **contact proof sheet** is a single sheet that contains contact prints made from an entire roll of film. This provides positive views of the negative images that you can inspect with a magnifier to

evaluate composition, expression, and tonal and color balance. Many photographers bind contact sheets with their corresponding negatives in their filing system.

You can make a contact proof sheet by contact printing a whole roll of negatives at one time. Cut the roll into strips and place them on a sheet of enlarging paper, emulsion to emulsion, then expose and process them. Figure 6-8 shows the steps for making a contact proof sheet.

Light Sources, Test Prints, and General Procedures

Any accessible light source can be used for exposing contact prints, such as a table light or even an

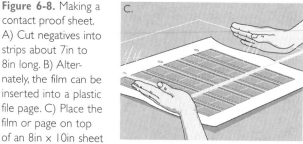

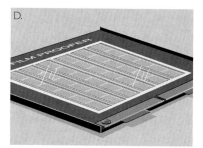

Figure 6-8. Making a contact proof sheet. A) Cut negatives into strips about 7in to 8in long. B) Alternately, the film can be inserted into a plastic file page. C) Place the film or page on top of an 8in × 10in sheet of enlarging paper, emulsion to emulsion. Cover with a clean sheet of glass and expose. (Tape edges of glass to prevent cuts.) D) A special film proofer may be used in place of a simple sheet of glass.

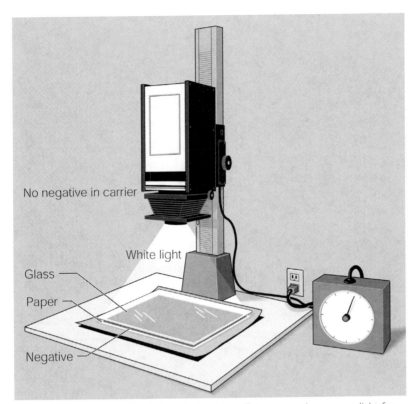

Figure 6-9. Enlarger method of contact printing. Enlarger used as source light for negatives in contact with enlarging paper on the enlarger base. Enlarging timer can be used to control exposure.

open bulb. However, enlargers are commonly used for contact printing.

The enlarger method is illustrated in Figure 6-9. The negative and enlarging paper, sandwiched together, are placed on the base of the enlarger. The enlarger timer is switched on to make the exposure. The enlarger, with no negative in the carrier, provides the light source. A **contact proofer**, **with a hinged glass lid**, can be used to hold the negative and paper. (See Figure 6-4.)

Here are some general rules to remember about contact printing:

1. For black-and-white printing, prepare all the materials and set up everything under safelight. For color printing, set up everything except the printing paper under safelight. Open the box or safe containing color printing paper in total darkness. Do not expose any unexposed printing paper to white light except during the controlled exposure.

2. Sandwich the negative and the paper so that their emulsions face each other. Then place the negative-paper sandwich on the enlarger

with the paper emulsion facing the source light. (See Fig. 6-10.)

3. Determine the amount of exposure by testing. A testing procedure is described on page 203. Do not be concerned if some frames of a contact proof sheet appear too dark and others too light; you can correct individual negatives at the time of enlarging.

4. Consider making the contact sheet with the negatives still in their clear plastic storage pages to minimize scratching or smudging the negatives during handling.

Print Processing

Objective 6-C Describe the procedures used to process prints.

Key Concepts C-prints, chromogenic prints, R-prints, reversal prints, developing, stopping, fixing, bleach/fix, clearing, washing, drying, positive print, dry area, contamination, wet area, ferrotype

Black-and-white print processing reverses the negative's densities to produce a positive print image—the dark areas of the negative appear light in the print; the light areas, dark.

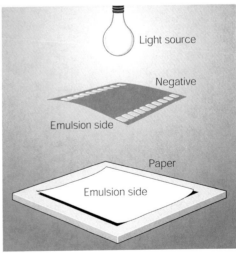

Figure 6-10. Emulsion side of negative normally faces emulsion side of paper. Occasionally the negative may be flipped to reverse the direction of the image.

Careers in Photography

News and Photojournalism

Many photographers seek to enter a career in news photography or photojournalism, which includes reporting timely news events as well as more general stories and features dealing with more complex ideas and social issues by means of photographs published in newspapers, magazines, television, and film.

The use of photography to chronicle important events began almost with the beginning of photography itself and continued a long tradition of visual journalism evident in the wood cuts and engravings made by artist-reporters found in newspapers and magazines throughout the seventeenth and eighteenth centuries. Within a decade of Daguerre's public announcement of a practical method of photography, early photographers were at work recording events such as floods, fires, earthquakes, and war, as well as noteworthy advances in science and technology. For example, in 1842 a daguerreotype was made of the Great Fire of Hamburg and in 1846 a daguerreotype was made documenting a reenactment of the first surgery using ether. The earliest examples of war photography occurred during the Mexican War, 1846–48.

Not only events but social issues also attracted these early photojournalists. In 1851, John Beard documented street life among London's poor, beginning a documentary tradition that was later pursued by John Thomson in England and Jacob Riis in America.

News photography and photojournalism are highly regarded segments of the profession and many young photographers aspire to a career in the field. Today, however, the field is crowded and few full-time positions for photographers exist on large daily newspapers, news magazines, news services, news broadcasting organizations, or magazines that feature photography. Some photographers are able to make a living by working freelance for many publications and services at the same time, usually with the help of an agent, photo agency, or other agency service. Agencies, such as Black Star, Globe Photos, and Magnum Photos, have some staff photographers who work and bill exclusively through their agency, and numerous stringers from diversified geographical areas who accept occasional assignments to supplement their local incomes.

To enter the profession, a young photographer is probably best advised to start with assignments for small–or medium-size daily or weekly newspapers. Although the assignments are not likely to be of fast-breaking events or even of regional or national interest, the experience is invaluable for preparing the photographer for the major assignments that may follow.

It is important for the news photographer and photojournalist to realize that the photographer is usually required to write captions and is often expected to write blocks of copy and design and lay out photo pages. Sometimes, the photographer may be expected to write the entire accompanying story. Smaller publications can rarely afford to have a full staff of photographers and writers to perform these specialized tasks.

Until the middle of the twentieth century, photojournalism as well as most other photographic careers were usually entered by way of apprenticeship and job ad-

A) Photojournalists must be prepared to capture fast-moving action with split-second timing.

B) Photojournalists must be ready to work in remote situations or cover events where their personal safety may be at risk.

vancement. As might be expected, progressing from washing prints and mixing chemicals to darkroom printing and original photography provided a relatively narrow, technical background, usually lacking in the aesthetic, ethical, legal, philosophical, social, cultural, and economic concerns that are central to modern photojournalism.

Today most photojournalism jobs with major news organizations require at least an undergraduate college degree. Many colleges and universities offer major degree programs in communications, journalism, and photography, which often include an internship with a professional news organization either before or after graduation. A major in another discipline, however, may also provide an appropriate education. If the photojournalist's work is to transcend the mere recording of events and to explore complex ideas and social issues, it is important to have studied the workings of society, the human condition, visual and verbal expression, as well as the techniques of photography and journalism.

Another important source of continuing education and training is the short-term workshop, which brings students into contact with working professional photojournalists and news photographers. One very successful and highly regarded short-term workshop is the Flying Short Course sponsored by the National Press Photographers Association (NPPA), which annually gathers a team of accomplished press photographers from around the country and flies them to ten regional sites. At each site the team meets with a group of working press photographers and students to deliver a dawn-to-dusk workshop during which the team makes presentations, engages participants in active question-and-answer sessions, and evaluates portfolios. Other short-term workshops are available through many colleges and associations. In addition to providing opportunities for professional evaluation and guidance, these workshops also give participants a chance to meet others in their field and to establish helpful networking relationships. (See Appendix E on the CD that accompanies this book.)

Successful news photographers and photojournalists possess a knack for recognizing events and issues that will interest and engage the public, the technical and expressive skills to tell the story effectively in photographs, as well as the determination to get the story despite the potential dangers in situations involving such calamitous events as fire, flood, crime, riot, and war.

Most color prints also are made from negatives. Processing them not only reverses the negative's densities, but also reverses the negative's colors to their positive complements. Color prints made directly from negatives are called **C-prints**, or **chromogenic** prints.

Color prints may also be made directly from positive color transparencies. The process, by reversing the transparency's positive densities and col-

ors, first produces a negative print image. This requires that the printed image be reversed in processing from negative back to positive. These are called **R-prints**, or **reversal prints**. (Ilfochrome, formerly Cibachrome, is a similar though proprietary process.)

Printing paper, like film, is coated on one side with a light-sensitive emulsion. An image is recorded on printing paper when it is exposed to

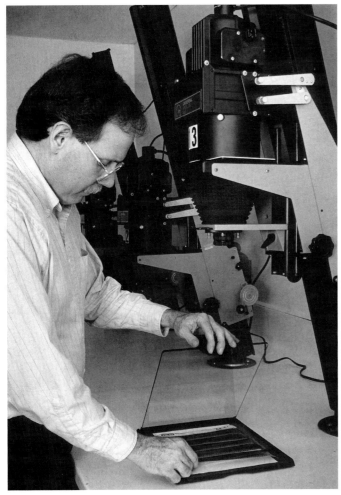

Figure 6-11. The contact proofer is positioned to receive the beam of illumination from the enlarger. The negatives are placed over the photo paper and the glass is then closed.

image-bearing light focused on its surface. Black-and-white prints may be processed in trays under darkroom safelight; color prints must be processed in total darkness, under special color printing safelights, or in a light-tight drum or tabletop processor. Once exposed, the paper is ready for processing following the same general steps as for film processing.

1. *Developing.* The latent image is transformed into patterns of metallic silver. For color prints, dye-couplers are released and dye images are formed as well. For R-prints, made from transparencies, a second color developer is used to reverse the negative image and form a positive one.
2. *Stopping.* The action of the developer is stopped.
3. *Fixing.* All remaining silver halide crystals and other light-sensitive materials are dissolved. For color prints, a **bleach/fix** process is used that also removes all metallic silver, leaving only the dye image.
4. *Clearing and washing.* All traces of processing chemicals are removed.
5. *Drying.* The wet print is dried.

The resulting print is, of course, a reverse image of the negative—a **positive print**. Den-

Making a Contact Proof Sheet Using the Enlarger Method

To make a contact proof sheet, follow these steps:

1. *Place an empty negative carrier in the enlarger and put an empty proofer on the base of the enlarger.*

2. *Turn on the enlarger. Adjust the head so that the rectangle of white light it produces is slightly larger than the proofer. Place the proofer in the center of the rectangle. Set the enlarger lens to f/8. Turn off the enlarger, leaving the proofer in place. Use safelight for black-and-white; total darkness for color.*

3. *Place an 8in x 10in (20cm x 25cm) sheet of photographic paper in the proofer, emulsion side up. Arrange your negatives on the enlarging paper, emulsion side down. Close the proofer without moving it.*

4. *Determine the exposure time through testing. As a good starting point, set the timer for fifteen seconds. Trigger the timer to start the exposure. (To determine exposure time accurately, make a test strip or test print as described in Objective 6-E on page 201.)*

5. *Process the exposed paper.*

6. *Examine the proof sheet after processing. If it is too dark overall, make another proof sheet, reducing exposure. If it is too light overall, make another proof sheet, increasing exposure. Repeat until the average prints are rendered with normal density.*

sities are reversed; and in color prints, colors also are reversed.

The printing darkroom should be organized into two areas—a **dry area** where dry materials can be handled without chemical **contamination** and a **wet area** where the processing chemicals, water taps, and sink are located. For black-and-white processing, three trays are usually set up in the wet area that contain the developer, stop bath, and fixer. (See Figure 6-12.)

Making Enlargements

Objective 6-D Describe and demonstrate how to make an enlargement.

Key Concepts framing easel, image size, image focus, aperture, timer

Figure 6-12. Three-tray setup for print processing. The first three processing steps are developer, stop bath, and fixer.

Basic Black-and-White Print Processing

1. Developing. *Immerse the exposed printing paper in the developer. Use tongs to hold the print by the edge and agitate gently throughout development. Time development to the manufacturer's recommendations, usually one to two minutes. Then remove the print from the developer, allow it to drain, and slip it edge first into the stop bath. Do not contaminate developer tongs with stop bath. (See Figure 6-13 A, B, C.)*

Figure 6-13. Print Processing. A) Immerse exposed paper evenly in the developer. B) Handle wet prints with tongs to avoid chemical contact and contamination carried on hands. C) Drain print of excess solution between trays.

(continued)

2. Stopping. *The stop bath consists of a 1 to 2 percent solution of acetic acid. (See the Helpful Hint on page 173.) Use a separate set of tongs for the stop bath. Agitate. Time to the manufacturer's recommendations, usually fifteen to thirty seconds. Then remove the print from the stop bath, allow it to drain, and slip it edge first into the fixer. Do not contaminate stop tongs with fixer.*

3. Fixing. *Use a third set of tongs to handle prints in fixer. Leave prints immersed in the fixer with occasional agitation according to the manufacturer's recommendations. Fix RC for two to three minutes; fix fiber-based prints for seven to ten minutes, depending on the type of fixer used. Slight overfixing will not harm prints.*

4. Clearing and washing. *After a few minutes, you can examine prints in the fixer under normal white light. Put unexposed printing paper away before turning on work lights.*

   After fixing, wash the print. As with film, remove all traces of processing chemicals before drying. Any remaining chemical residues may discolor the print later. Follow manufacturer's recommended wash times. RC prints can usually be washed in a few minutes; fiber-based prints usually take longer. Many photographers use a clearing agent before the final wash to remove chemicals completely in a shorter time. Avoid flowing tap water directly on the print. (See Figure 6-5.)

5. Drying. *After washing, place the prints on a smooth, clean surface and use a squeegee or a sponge to remove excess moisture. RC prints can be hung on a line by a clothespin or placed on a rack of fiberglass screens to air dry in a few minutes. (See Figure 6-14.) Fiber-based prints will take longer and may need to be flattened under weight later.*

   Fiber-based prints may also be dried using a hot drum dryer. Such dryers have a mirrorlike, heated ferrotype plate or drum. Glossy paper, if dried with the emulsion squeegeed to the drum, will obtain a high-gloss finish; if dried with the emulsion facing away from the drum, they will obtain a soft, non-glossy finish. Do not use driers designed for fiber-based papers with RC papers as that may damage the resin coating. (See Figure 6-6A.)

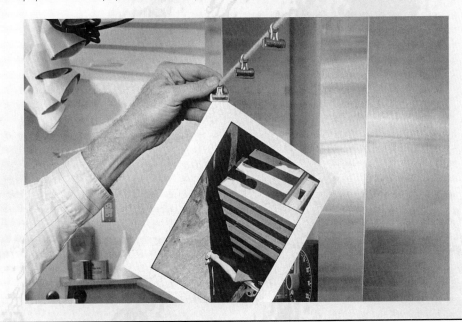

Figure 6-14. RC prints may be hung up to dry on a simple clothesline.

To make an enlargement, first place the negative in the carrier. Then place a **framing easel** on the base to hold the paper flat and to mask the borders. Place a dummy sheet of blank paper in the easel, turn the work lights off, turn the enlarger on, and project the negative image onto the paper. Raise or lower the enlarger head to change the **image size**. Rotate the focusing knob to change the **image focus** to achieve maximum sharpness. For color enlargements, adjust the filter pack to alter the color balance. When the image is framed to the desired size and focus, lock the head, turn off the enlarger, replace the dummy paper with enlarging paper, set the **aperture**, set the **timer**, and make the exposure. Then process the exposed paper as described in Objective 6-C. A typical setup for enlarging is shown in Figure 6-15.

The aperture of the enlarging lens can be set larger or smaller. As the aperture is opened wider,

Basic Color Print Processing

1. Mix processing solutions in separate beakers on the wet side of the darkroom, including one beaker of water. Keep all beakers in a deep tray of running water to control temperature. Prewarm and dry the processing drum.

2. In total darkness, roll the exposed print paper lightly, emulsion toward the center, and load it into the drum. Close the drum. Turn on the work lights.

3. Follow the manufacturer's instructions for time and temperature for each solution. Most RA-4 process (C-print) kits use the following general steps:

   A. Pour water into the drum to prewet the print. Pour water out.

   B. Pour developer into the drum. Agitate. Pour developer out.

   C. Pour stop bath into the drum. Agitate. Pour stop bath out.

   For R-3000 reversal process (R-print) kits, substitute a wash and a second, color developer for this step.

4. Wash the print with running water in the drum, or pour clean water into and out of the drum several times with agitation.

5. Pour bleach/fix into the drum. Agitate. Pour bleach/fix out.

6. Open the drum and wash the print.

7. Dry the print.

the image appears brighter; as it is stopped down, the image appears dimmer. Aperture size also affects image sharpness. Extremely large or small apertures may produce images that are less sharp overall than those produced using midsize apertures. During framing and focusing, however, use a wide open aperture to maximize brightness; then, just before exposing, stop down to a smaller aperture.

Determining Print Exposure

Objective 6-E Describe and demonstrate how to determine print exposure using the test strip method.

Key Concept test strip

Any photographer, regardless of experience, must estimate exposure for printing. With experience, most are able to make reasonable esti-

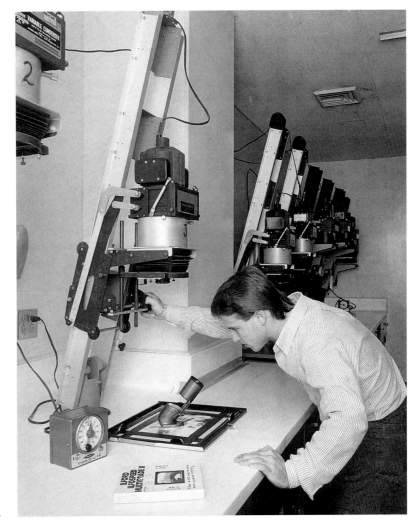

Figure 6-15. Enlarging setup. Using a critical focusing device to assure maximum sharpness.

Making an Enlargement

Follow these general steps in making a projection print or enlargement.

Enlarger is Off

1. Raise the lamp and condenser housing assembly. Remove the negative carrier and insert the negative strip into it. Adjust the strip to center the desired negative in the carrier, emulsion side toward the lens. Carefully clean all dust from the negative with a soft brush, bulb blower, or can of compressed air. Use a film cleaner to remove stains or fingerprints. Replace the carrier and negative in the enlarger. Lower the housing assembly into place.

2. If making a color print, set up the standard filter pack as recommended by the paper manufacturer.

3. Place a sheet of plain white paper in the easel. Use paper of the same weight as the paper to be used for printing. Place the easel on the enlarger base.

4. Open the enlarger lens to its widest aperture for ease of focusing and cropping.

Turn Enlarger On

5. Raise or lower the enlarger head to obtain the desired image size.

6. Adjust the focusing knob for the sharpest focus. Use a focusing magnifier, if necessary, to achieve maximum focus. Lock the elevator knob in place.

7. Position the easel and adjust for the desired framing of the image.

8. Stop down the enlarger lens to the enlarging aperture—approximately f/5.6 or f/8 for negatives of normal density.

Turn Enlarger Off

9. Do not move the easel. Make and process a test strip to determine proper exposure as described in Objective 6-E, page 201.

10. Select the proper exposure and set the timer. Without moving the easel, replace the blank paper with a sheet of enlarging paper, emulsion side up, toward the lens.

11. Trigger the timer to make the exposure.

12. Process the paper. If the overall effect is too light, make another print, increasing exposure. If it is too dark, make another print, decreasing exposure. Evaluate the color balance. If necessary, adjust the filter pack and make another print. See Table 6-1 for color balance corrections.

Table 6-1. Filter pack adjustments to correct color balance*			
	DEGREE OF CORRECTION NEEDED		
Overall Color	Small	Medium	Large
Too Blue	−5Y	−10Y	−20Y
Too Red	+5Y/+5M	+10Y/+10M	+20Y/+20M
Too Green	−5M	−10M	−20M
Too Yellow	+5Y	+10Y	+20Y
Too Cyan	−5Y/−5M	−10Y/−10M	−20Y/−20M
Too Magenta	+5M	+10M	+20M

*Assumes your standard filter pack uses only yellow and magenta filters. These adjustments are approximate and vary with the paper in use. For best results, use a **ringaround** or other reference tool that indicates the effects of various filtration adjustments.

Important: Do not try to control the darkness of the image by under- or overdeveloping. Consistently develop prints for the amount of time recommended by the manufacturer.

mates based on visual inspection of negatives. To determine optimal exposure precisely, however, they rely on experimental tests. **Test strips** are widely used for this purpose. Using this test procedure saves time, energy, and money; it reduces waste; and takes much of the guesswork out of determining exposure.

Making a Test Strip

To make a test strip, follow this step-by-step procedure.

1. With the enlarger on, the aperture wide open, and dummy sheet of blank paper in the easel, size, focus, and frame the image. Stop down to f/5.6 or f/8.

2. With the enlarger off, cut a sheet of 8in x 10in (20cm x 25cm) enlarging paper into five strips, approximately 2in x 8in (5cm x 20cm). Replace all but one of the strips into a paper safe or lightproof container. Visualize the image, place the other strip in the easel across a representative segment of the picture.

3. Use an opaque sheet of stiff, dark paper as a mask to cover the test strip, holding it over the strip as shown in Figure 6-16. Turn on the enlarger and expose successive segments of the strip for a fixed number of seconds—for example, expose a 1in (2.5cm) segment for six seconds, the next 1in (2.5cm) segment for an additional six seconds, and so forth. When you have exposed five segments, each for an additional increment of six seconds, you will have a strip with successive segments exposed for thirty, twenty-four, eighteen, twelve, and six seconds respectively as shown in Figure 6-17 A.

4. Process the test strip in the normal way.

5. Select the exposure that produced the best range of tones. If none of the segments produced an acceptable range of tones, make another test strip, increasing or decreasing the lens opening or the exposure increments.

Fixed versus Proportional Increments

The above procedure describes a sequence of fixed exposure increments: each segment was exposed for an additional six seconds. Note in Figure 6-17 A that the exposure in the 12-second seg-

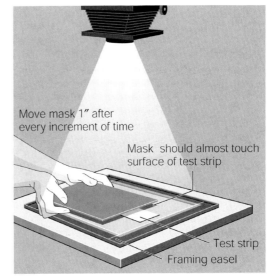

Figure 6-16. Making a test strip. Procedure for exposing successive segments for additional increments of time.

ment is 100 percent more than in the 6-second segment, but exposure in the 30-second segment is only 25 percent more than in the 24-second segment—the exposure increments in each segment represent decreasing proportions.

Another approach to incremental exposure is to increase or decrease exposure in each segment by a constant proportion, such as to halve the exposure time in each successive segment. For example, expose the first segment for 24 seconds, the next for an 12 seconds, the next for 6 seconds, the next for 3 seconds, and the last segment also for 3 seconds. The result will be a test strip such as that shown in Figure 6-17 B, with a much wider range of exposures: The successive exposures on the sheet are now 48, 24, 12, 6, and 3 seconds, with each successive increment representing a one-stop difference.

Print Materials

Objective 6-F Describe the materials used in making prints from black-and-white negatives, color negatives, and color transparencies.

Key Concepts printing paper, print-processing chemicals, contact printing paper, chloride paper, enlarging paper, bromide paper, chlorobromide paper, image tone, surface texture, weight, tint, contrast grades, low-contrast paper, normal-contrast paper, variable-contrast paper, variable-contrast filters, fiber-based papers, resin-coated (RC)

A. **Total Exposure**

30

24

18

12

6

B. **Total Exposure**

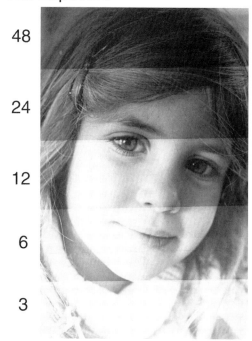

48

24

12

6

3

Figure 6-17. A) Each segment of this test strip has been exposed in fixed increments of 6 seconds. B) In each segment of this test strip exposure is doubled. To achieve this first segment was exposed for 24 sec., followed by segments of 12, 6, 3, and 3 sec. Result is a test strip where each step differs by one stop in exposure.

HELPFUL HINT

Using a Multistation Darkroom

Cooperation is essential in any multistation darkroom—one in which more than one operator can expose and process prints simultaneously.

Remember, use the dry counters for dry materials exclusively. Keep dry papers and negatives in the dry area. Only the sink should be used for chemical operations. Keep bottles and trays of chemicals in the wet area or under the sink. Wash hands thoroughly and frequently when printing and processing. If your hands become contaminated with processing chemicals, clean them promptly to avoid damaging prints. Hands contaminated with fixer, for example, may produce white smudges and fingerprints in the final print; hands contaminated with developer produce dark smudges and fingerprints. Use print tongs to handle prints, and drain them between solutions. Carry wet prints in trays to avoid dripping onto the floor and counters. Allow sufficient time following processing to wash and dry prints.

Be sure the enlarger source light is switched off before raising the condenser and lamp housing to insert or remove the negative carrier. Stray light from one enlarger may strike and ruin a neighbor's work and supplies.

paper, paper developer, stop bath, indicator stop bath, fixer, hardening fixer, clearing agent, print conditioner

Selecting the Proper Materials

In general, two types of materials are needed to make prints: **printing paper** and **print-processing chemicals**. Many varieties of these materials are available to meet individual needs. For example, consider factors such as color, image tone, texture, thickness, tint, and contrast grade when selecting a photographic paper. Consider also whether to use a quick-processing resin-coated (RC) paper or a fiber-based paper that is more durable and available in a wider range of surfaces and tones. Even the chemicals used to develop the print can be selected according to the desired image tone and amount of contrast. Creative photographers carefully select the exact printing materials necessary to meet the expressive needs of each individual photograph.

Printing Papers

Emulsions Papers are manufactured for contact printing and projection printing (enlarging). The active ingredients in these papers, as in films, are primarily silver halide salts—silver chloride and silver bromide. **Contact printing paper**, or **chloride paper**, uses primarily silver chloride in its emulsion, is relatively slow, and is rarely used today.

Enlarging papers generally use an emulsion that contains a combination of both silver chloride and **silver bromide**. The mixture of the two silver salts can be varied in manufacture to obtain a desired emulsion speed, image tone, and contrast. These **chlorobromide papers** are much faster than chloride papers. Although they are intended primarily for making enlargements, they can also be used for making contact prints and proof sheets if the enlarger is used as a light source. (See discussion on page 198.) In addition to the silver halides, color printing papers also contain the dye couplers and dyes that are used to form the color image.

Image Tone Black-and-white enlarging papers are manufactured in a wide range of tones, textures, weights, tints, and contrast grades. **Image tone** refers to the color of the actual silver image. The tone is determined by the type of emulsion and its development and may range from cold, blue-black tones through neutral-black to warm and brown-black tones. The neutral tones are most suitable for halftone reproduction processes. For exhibition, select the image tone that best suits the subject and idea of the photograph.

Surface Texture The **surface texture** of the paper refers to the glossiness or roughness of the print surface. Many types of surface textures are available, ranging from the high-gloss surface that is used most commonly for halftone reproduction to highly textured surfaces that are used more commonly for display prints. Many specialty textures are also available, such as those designed to look like rough canvas, silk, linen, or tapestry. The most commonly used textures are the glossy papers, which produce a hard, mirrorlike surface, and the semimatte papers, which produce a dull, nonreflective surface more like ordinary paper.

Thickness or Weight The paper stock is also available in several thicknesses, or **weights**, from lightweight or document stock—which is approximately the weight of ordinary typing paper—to double-weight stocks, which are about the thickness of light cardboard. The most commonly used fiber-based paper weights are single weight (.18mm) and double weight (.38mm). Resin-coated (RC) paper is available only in medium or portfolio weight.

Tint The paper base **tint** refers to the color of the paper stock itself. Papers come in a variety of tints, from brilliant snow white to natural white, cream, ivory, and buff. Specialty papers also may be obtained in pastel tints such as blue, red, and green. In general the warm-toned emulsions are matched with the warm-tinted stocks such as cream and ivory, while the cold-toned emulsions are more commonly teamed with the colder-tinted stocks.

Contrast Grade Printing papers also are manufactured in several **contrast grades**, numbered from 0 to 6, corresponding to the inherent contrast characteristics of the emulsion. The lower-grade papers, grades 0 and 1, refer to the **low-contrast papers**, which will produce prints with less contrast than the negatives from which they are made. Grade 2 paper is considered **normal-contrast paper** because it will reproduce approximately the same contrast range as the negative. The higher-grade papers, grades 3, 4 and above, refer to the **high-contrast papers**, which will produce prints with more contrast than the negatives from which they are made. Although most manufacturers market a grade 2 as a normal paper, many photographers find that they use a number 2–1/2 or number 3 grade more often to enhance the contrast characteristics of their prints.

By selecting the appropriate contrast grade, the tonal range of a negative that is too contrasty can be reduced by printing it on a low-contrast paper. This will have the effect of enhancing the gray, middle tones. Conversely, the contrast of a negative that is too flat can be increased by printing it on a high-contrast paper. This will have the effect of extending the range of tones to include deeper blacks and purer whites.

Variable-contrast Paper Another method for achieving contrast control in black-and-white printing is by using a **variable-contrast paper**, such as Kodak Polycontrast, Polymax or Ilford Multigrade, in conjunction with **variable contrast filters**. Variable-contrast papers combine all

Figure 6-18. Variable contrast filter sheets are available in two forms: as sheets for use within the lamp housing and as mounted filters for use below the enlarger lens.

However, some black-and-white printing papers are manufactured with panchromatic emulsions—they are sensitive to all colors of light. Such papers are often used for making black-and-white prints from color negatives. Panchromatic printing paper is designed to translate the different colors in the color negative into a grayscale black-and-white image. Because these papers are sensitive to all colors, you must work with these papers in complete darkness or under special safelight as recommended by the manufacturer.

Fiber-Based Papers

Fiber-based papers come in a greater variety of surface tints, image colors, surface textures, and thicknesses than RC papers. Many creative photographers use the range of options available in fiber-based paper to gain additional expressive control. Fiber-based paper is almost always chosen for exhibition work and other applications that demand the vibrant tonal rendering of a fine black-and-white print. Although fiber-based paper takes longer to process, it is inherently much more stable than RC paper and has a much longer potential lifespan. Fiber-based paper should be strongly considered for any work that is likely to have historical interest. (See Figure 6-19 A.)

Resin-Coated (RC) Papers

Resin-coated (RC) papers are sealed with a plasticlike resin before the emulsion is applied. This seal prevents processing chemicals from being absorbed into the paper base during processing. Because photochemicals are not absorbed into the paper base itself, RC papers fix, wash, and air dry very rapidly without curling. Further, glossy RC paper, unlike fiber-based paper, air dries to a hard, glossy finish without ferrotyping.

the contrast grades into a single paper product. As their name implies, these papers offer varying grades of contrast by the use of filters during exposure. (See Figure 6-18.)

The papers combine two separate emulsion layers: One emulsion has very low inherent contrast and is usually made sensitive to yellow light; the other has very high inherent contrast and is made sensitive to magenta light. A set of variable-contrast filters typically is numbered to correspond in a general way to graded paper. Variable-contrast papers offer the photographer extensive control over the range of contrast grades by allowing the selection of contrast filters in half-grade steps.

Color Sensitivity and Safelights Because the negative image from which black-and-white prints are made consists simply of patterns of light and shadow—no colors—the printing paper needs to be sensitive only to the relative presence or absence of light; it need not be sensitive to a full range of colors. Therefore, printing papers intended for normal use are basically orthochromatic—sensitive mainly to the blue portion of visible light and insensitive to the red-amber-green portions. This permits the printing darkroom to be well illuminated with amber or yellow-green safelights and allows the photographer to work conveniently in a well-lit space without exposing the light-sensitive printing papers.

Although RC papers offer many advantages to both amateur and commercial photographers, they are not without faults. First, they scratch easily while wet and must be handled carefully with print tongs. Further, if overwashed beyond the recommended time, the emulsion may separate from the paper. Special low-heat materials and procedures must be used for dry mounting RC prints in order to prevent the emulsion from

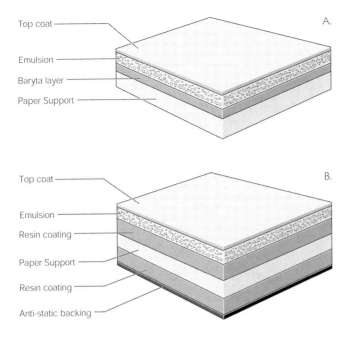

Top coat
Emulsion
Baryta layer
Paper Support

A.

Top coat
Emulsion
Resin coating
Paper Support
Resin coating
Anti-static backing

B.

Figure 6-19. A) Cross-section of fiber-base printing paper. B) Cross-section of resin-coated paper.

separating from the paper. Finally, the resins and the emulsion tend to expand and contract differently, causing the emulsion to separate from the paper as temperatures vary under normal display conditions. For this reason, RC materials are not considered suitable for archival purposes. Nevertheless, where convenience and speed of processing are more important than permanence, these materials are the contemporary standard. (See Figure 6-19 B.)

Color Printing Papers

Color printing papers come in several types. Some are intended for making color prints from negatives; others, from positive transparencies. Most negative-to-print papers can be identified by their *–color* suffix, such as Kodak's Ektacolor paper, while the *–chrome* suffix identifies the positive transparency-to-print papers, such as Kodak's Ektachrome paper. Fewer varieties of color printing papers are manufactured—most are medium weight, resin-coated, and offer few surfaces or contrast grades. Note that color balance and sensitivity may vary from one product to another, or even within the same product line from batch to batch. For this reason, note the batch number on each box of paper and make a test print every time a new box with a different batch number is opened.

Selecting the Best Paper

Various combinations of emulsions, surface textures, and developers can produce different tones, tints, and effects in black-and-white prints. Which of these possible effects is most appropriate for any particular print? The answer to that question is largely a matter of personal taste and judgment. No generalization can cover all situations.

In general, a combination of tone, tint, contrast, and surface texture should be selected that will enhance the characteristics of the image. For example, cold-tone, glossy papers are often chosen to represent industrial subjects, such as architecture and machinery, while the warm-tone matte papers are often chosen to represent the flesh tones of portraits or other human interest subjects.

Special surface textures such as canvas, silk, linen, or parchment may be used to call attention to the print as an object. Smooth-surface papers with a neutral black tone and white tint are preferred for copying or halftone reproduction. Smooth, glossy papers are preferred when every last bit of detail needs to be captured in the image.

Selecting papers for color printing offers fewer options. Because most are resin coated, the range of choices usually available with fiber-based papers is not available. Still, the choice of surface, contrast, and overall color can significantly alter the appearance of the final color print.

Surfaces available with color papers include matte, semimatte, and glossy—the high-gloss papers giving the greatest appearance of contrast, sharpness, and color saturation. Contrast grades available are generally limited to a normal and a lower-contrast grade, although some brands offer more. Nothing equivalent to variable-contrast papers is available with color paper.

The greatest control offered for color printing is control of color and overall color balance.

Paper Storage

Unless photographic printing papers are stored properly, both their physical and photographic properties may be affected adversely. Keep only the paper needed for immediate use in the darkroom. The balance of the stock should be stored in a cool, dry place. Refrigeration will help preserve freshness for long term storage. Observe the following recommendations for storing paper properly.

1. Handle all printing paper carefully, as much as possible by the edges. Avoid fingerprints, creasing, and crimping.

2. Avoid excessive heat.

3. Avoid both very dry and very damp places.

4. Avoid exposure to chemical fumes and gases such as formaldehyde, coal gas, sulfur, engine exhaust, paints, and solvents.

5. Avoid radiation. Do not store paper near X-ray or fluoroscopic devices.

6. Avoid excessive weight. Do not store paper under weight; that may cause the emulsion to fuse to the adjacent sheets.

7. Use the paper before its expiration date. Rotate the stock to use older papers first.

Table G-4 in Appendix G, on the CD that accompanies this book, lists some of the commonly available contact and enlarging papers.

Print-Processing Chemicals

Black-and-white and color processing systems employ different chemistry and somewhat different sequences of chemical processes. In general, all processing systems involve developing, fixing, and washing; however, many processes, especially color processes, include other steps along the way. Make certain the process you choose is matched to the type of print you are making.

Paper Developers The **paper developers** can affect the tone of the silver image in a black-and-white print. Depending on its chemical composition, a developer may produce warm-, neutral-, or cold-toned images. Table G-5 in Appendix G, on the CD that accompanies this book, describes several commonly used black-and-white paper developers and the tones they tend to produce.

Color printing papers must be carefully matched to a particular paper process. Color negatives are usually printed using paper and chemicals designated as Kodak RA-4 (formerly designated Kodak EP-2). Color positive transparencies are usually printed using reversal paper and chemicals designated as Kodak R-3000. These reversal color processes use two developers during processing.

Ilfochrome (formerly Cibachrome), marketed by Ilford, employs a silver dye-bleach process that differs from other reversal processes and is noted for its sharpness and color saturation. Designated as P-30P, the paper uses an emulsion with three basic dye layers already built in. During processing, the dyes are linked to the silver image and the unneeded dyes are bleached away along with the intermediate silver image. The Ilfochrome process requires only developer, bleach, and fixer.

Stop Bath The use of a **stop bath** following development is often recommended. It stops the action of the developer, helps to preserve the life of the fixer, and removes calcium scum from the print surface. For black-and-white processing, a 1- to 2-percent solution of acetic acid can be used for this purpose, as can any of several products that are available in photo stores. An **indicator stop bath** is particularly useful because it will turn dark when it is exhausted, signaling when replacement of the stop bath is needed. (See Helpful Hint on page 173.)

Color processing may or may not require a stop bath, depending upon the process and the manufacturer. Some processing systems omit the stop bath; others require it under specified conditions. Follow the manufacturer's instructions.

Fixer To make the print permanent, all the light-sensitive salts remaining in the emulsion after developing must be dissolved and removed. The **fixer** dissolves these salts. A **hardening fixer** also will toughen the soft surface of the gelatin emulsion and render it less susceptible to damage. The useful life of the fixer is limited. Do not use exhausted fixer.

In color processing, the fixer is combined with a bleaching agent designed to remove the silver image from the print after the metallic silver has been coupled to the color dyes to form a dye image.

Clearing Agent **Clearing agents** aid washing, because they neutralize all residual chemicals. A clearing agent, or washing aid, is recommended for fiber-based paper before washing to assure freedom from residual chemicals and to reduce water consumption in the washing cycle. RC papers do not require a clearing agent because they wash clean unaided in a few minutes.

Maximizing Tonal Quality

Objective 6-G Describe and demonstrate how print contrast and color balance can be controlled and how to produce relatively normal prints with flat, contrasty, and normal negatives.

Key Concepts density, contrast, high contrast, contrasty print, low contrast, flat print, normal print, contrasty negative, flat negative, normal negative, normal paper, flat paper, contrasty paper, variable-contrast paper, contrast filter, color balance, Color Print Viewing Filter Kit

Tonal Qualities of Finished Prints

We have already noted that the eye is more sensitive to minute tonal differences than film and that film does not record all the tones that the eye perceives. Therefore, one of the challenges of photography is to record on the film as much of the important visible tonal range as materials and procedures permit.

Printing paper is even less sensitive than film. Just as film loses many tones from the scene it is recording, printing paper loses many tones that may be present in the negative. To preserve richness of detail and tonal range, printing materials and techniques must be manipulated so as to maximize control of density and contrast in the final print. (See Figure 6-20.)

Density refers to the overall lightness or darkness of the print—the amount of image-forming silver or dye that it possesses. To control density, manipulate the exposure of the print. The greater the exposure, the darker the print; the less the exposure, the lighter the print.

Contrast, whether in black-and-white or color prints, refers to the range of tones and the distribution of those tones within the print. Think of the brightest values in the image, and the darkest ones. As contrast increases, the difference between the lightest and

darkest values increases and the middle values decrease; conversely, as contrast decreases, the difference between the lightest and darkest values decreases, and the middle values increase. The optimal contrast for any given print is one that best represents your personal vision of the subject.

In more technical terms, we can say that contrast refers to the range of densities present in the print between deep black (maximum density) and base white (minimum density). **High contrast** refers to the presence of maximum and minimum densities within the same print and relatively little presence of intermediate densities. A high-contrast, or **contrasty** print tends to possess deep, dark tones and base whites, with few intermediate shades. **Low contrast** refers to the presence of only a narrow range of densities. A low-

Figure 6-20. Contrast and density. Tone and mood can be varied by altering print contrast and density. A) Low contrast and high density create a darker brooding atmosphere. B) Higher contrast and reduced density considerably brightens the mood.

contrast, or **flat print** tends to possess only a few middle tones—the darkest and lightest tones in the print tend to be close in value.

A **normal print** has both a wide density range and a complete scale of middle tones. Details that stand out distinctly from their surroundings can be seen in both the high density and low density areas of the image. To achieve acceptable density and contrast in a print, select an appropriate contrast grade and exposure to yield a full tonal range—from deep, dark values to base white and a wide range of intermediate values. Examples of contrasty, normal, and flat images are illustrated in Figure 6-21.

Faithful reproduction of the original scene with clarity, definition, and sharpness is, however, only one criterion for evaluating prints. Also important is the photographer's use of these controls to express impressions of the scene, or to communicate feelings or ideas. Thus density and contrast may also be manipulated to set a mood for the scene, to emphasize important details, and to express important relationships. The use of these controls and others for effective composition will be discussed more fully in Units 10 and 14.

Negative Contrast

Not every negative has an ideal or normal contrast density range—some negatives, like prints, are flat or contrasty too. **Contrasty negatives** have a wide tonal range but weak and undefined middle tone. Pictures taken outside on a bright, sunny day at noon may tend to produce contrasty negatives because the light falling on the subject will consist of bright highlights and deep shadows. Some negatives are flat; that is, they have a relatively narrow tonal range—the difference between the lightest and darkest portions of the negative is slight. Pictures taken outside on an overcast or misty day tend to produce **flat negatives** because the light falling on the subject is even—there are no extreme highlights or deep shadows. **Normal negatives** have well-separated highlights, shadows, and middle tones. Details are clearly visible in the clearest and darkest portions of the negative.

Controlling Print Contrast

Regardless of the negative's contrast, the final print contrast can be controlled to a great degree by the photographer in the darkroom. By using contrast controls in printing, relatively normal prints can be obtained from a wide range of contrasty, flat, and normal negatives. Or, contrast can be manipulated to emphasize print details and tonal qualities. To control contrast, select printing papers that are appropriately graded for the contrast properties you desire, or use an appropriately graded **contrast filter** with a **variable-contrast paper**. Choose a higher grade paper to

A.

B.

C.

Figure 6-21. Contrast A) Low contrast. Picture is flat with little contrast between darkest and lightest tones. B) Normal contrast. Picture shows full range or dark, middle, and light tones. C) High contrast. Picture shows only darkest and lightest tones, middle tones are lacking.

increase the overall print contrast, a lower grade paper to reduce it. A photograph may need more contrast if the darkest tones are not as deep and pure as desired in an otherwise well-exposed print. Lower contrast may be indicated if details in the highlights and in the shadows are not visible in the print.

To produce a black-and-white print of normal contrast from a negative of normal contrast, use a normal contrast grade paper, such as grade 2, 2 1/2, or 3. To produce a print of normal contrast from a contrasty negative, use a lower contrast grade paper (grade 0 or 1) to flatten out the negative's contrast. To produce a print of normal contrast from a flat negative, use a higher contrast grade paper (grade 4, 5, or higher) to increase the contrast from the negative. If variable-contrast paper is used, select an appropriate grade filter to achieve the same result. (See Figure 6-22.) Table 6-2 can help you select the appropriate grade of paper or filter. (*See Objective 6-F, Print Materials*, page 203.)

Most color printing papers offer only a limited range of contrast grades. The best time to obtain a desired contrast is during original photography—by carefully positioning the camera and the subject, changing the lighting, waiting for better natural lighting to occur, or selecting a film that has better contrast properties for the subject of the photograph.

Color Balance

In addition to density and contrast, a color print's **color balance** must be evaluated. Use your standard filter pack to make the first print. Then examine areas of the print that have known color values, such as skin tones, known pastel colors, or neutral gray tones. Ignore deep colors or areas that may be affected by blue shadows or strong color reflections. To obtain a known color value, some photographers photograph a neutral gray card as the first frame of a sequence of shots using the same film under similar lighting.

Make changes to the filter pack as needed to obtain a correct color balance. When printing from color negatives, reduce a color from the print by adding that color to the filter pack; increase a color in the print by subtracting its complement from the filter pack. (See Table 6-1 on page 202.)

Table 6-2. Selecting a contrast grade or filter

With a	Use a
very low-contrast negative	very high-contrast grade or filter. (Grade 4 to 6)*
low-contrast negative	high-contrast grade or filter. (Grade 3 to 4)
normal negative	normal contrast grade or filter. (Grade 2 to 3)
high-contrast negative	low-contrast grade or filter. (Grade 1 to 2)
very high-contrast negative	very low-contrast grade or filter. (Grade 0 to 1)

*A graded paper of contrast grade 5 or 6 will generally produce a higher contrast result than the highest grade filter with variable-contrast paper.

A.

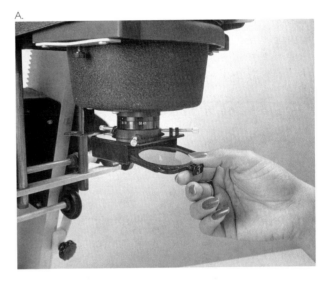

B.

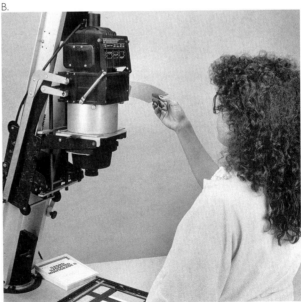

Figure 6-22. Using variable contrast filters. A) Optically correct mounted filters may be used below the enlarger lens. B) Large sheet filters should be placed in the lamp housing.

When making prints from positive transparencies, reverse this rule: reduce a color in the print by subtracting it from the filter pack; add a color to the print by adding it to the filter pack.

A useful aid for judging color balance in prints is the Kodak **Color Print Viewing Filter Kit**. The kit contains six cards with color filters mounted in them—magenta, red, yellow, green, cyan, and blue. Each card has three densities of a filter color. You can view a finished test print through the filters to find one that best corrects its color balance. Suggested changes to the filter pack are printed below each filter.

Printing Controls

Objective 6-H Describe and demonstrate cropping, burning-in and dodging, waving filters, vignetting, texture screening, convergence control, diffusion, flashing, and combination printing.

Key Concepts cropping, croppers, burning in, dodging, vignetting, texture screening, convergence control, diffusion, flashing, combination printing

In addition to normal printing techniques, there are several more specialized controls that can enhance the effectiveness of the final print. Described below are some of the commonly used controls.

Cropping

Often the negatives will contain more ambient detail than is desired in the final print. By **cropping** the print during enlargement, only that portion of the negative image that makes the best picture will be printed.

Some planning should be done before the enlargement process begins. Examine the image on the proof sheet to consider possible cropping formats. Using a felt-tipped pen or grease pencil, mark the desired cropping directly on the proof sheet. Then, during enlargement, the proof sheet will serve as a cropping guide for each print to be made. Darkroom time will be saved by not having to puzzle out each print in the darkroom. (See Figure 6-23.)

Prepare for enlarging by placing the negative in its carrier. Then place the printing easel on the base, and insert a dummy sheet of blank paper into the print frame of the easel. Turn on the enlarger and examine the image projected into the easel's picture frame. Refer to the crop marks on the proof sheet and adjust the enlarger and easel until the desired image is in focus in the print frame. Then turn off the enlarger.

Contrast Grade Selection for Black-and-White Prints

A basic guideline to remember is that highlight density is controlled by exposure, and shadow density is controlled by the contrast grade. Appropriate contrast can be achieved by using a graded paper or by using a graded filter with variable-contrast paper.

Printing Instructions

1. *Every negative has different contrast characteristics. Try starting with a normal contrast grade 2, 2 1/2, or 3.*

2. *Adjust the exposure time to make the density of the highlights look right. Make several test prints. If the highlights are too light, increase the exposure; if they are too dark, decrease the exposure.*

3. *Process the test print and evaluate the contrast. If the shadow areas are too light, increase the contrast grade. If the shadow areas are too dark and lack detail, decrease the contrast grade.*

4. *In general, to change contrast significantly, change the contrast grade by two or more grades. To fine tune contrast, change contrast by half a grade.*

5. *With variable-contrast paper, filters of contrast grade 4 and higher need twice the exposure required by filters grade 3 1/2 and lower. To double exposure, double exposure time or open the enlarger lens aperture one stop.*

Figure 6-23. Marking proof sheet with felt-tip pen or grease pencil for cropping. Planning cropping for enlargements saves much darkroom time and wasted prints.

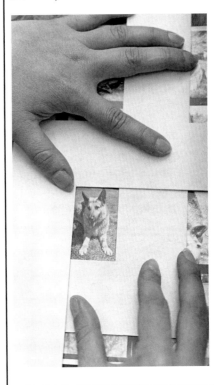
Do not rely on cropping to create effective prints from poorly planned negatives. Remember, the more any portion of a negative is enlarged, the more the print quality is diminished by increased graininess and loss of definition. Cropping may be helpful for making minor corrections in composition, but it will not usually serve for performing major surgery. Composition must begin in the viewfinder of the camera, not at the printing easel.

Burning-in and Dodging

Often the range of brightness in a negative may exceed the range of tones that the printing paper can reproduce effectively. The result can be seen in the brightest and darkest areas of the print. In the bright areas (dark on the negative), details are lost and may appear simply as blank white areas on the print. In the dark areas (light on the negative), shadow details are similarly lost. These dark areas may appear as almost solid masses in which details cannot be easily distinguished. Two techniques can be used to partially overcome this difficulty: (1) **burning-in**, which gives additional exposure only to those areas of the print that would otherwise appear too light; and (2) **dodging**, which reduces or holds back exposure in those areas that would otherwise print too dark. (See Figure 6-25.)

The typical tool for burning in small areas of the print is an opaque sheet of light cardboard or plastic with a small hole in it that serves as a mask. To burn in, first give the print its normal expo-

sure. Then insert the mask by hand under the enlarger lens about midway between the lens and the printing paper. Manipulate the mask so that only those portions of the image that need additional exposure pass through the hole. Keep the mask moving in a continuous circular motion while burning in to mask the burned-in area.

The typical tool for dodging is a sheet of opaque cardboard or plastic, or a small piece of opaque material attached to the end of a thin wire handle that looks something like a lollypop. Dodging is performed during the basic exposure so that the printing paper receives less than the normal exposure in the areas that might appear too dark in the normal print. Move the dodging tool over the area to be dodged during exposure. Keep it moving to mask its edges in the final print.

It's a good idea to make test prints to determine the amount of time needed to burn in and dodge

Figure 6-25. Burning-in and dodging. Keep tools moving during exposure to soften edges of burned-in or dodged areas. A) Technique for burning-in. B) Technique for dodging.

A.

B.

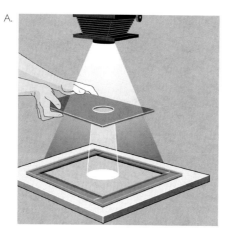
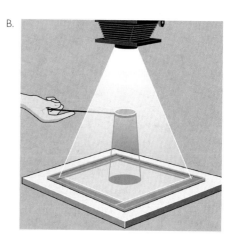

selected areas of the image. To simplify the timing of these burning-in and dodging cycles, some enlarger timers have audible clicks, much like a metronome. Without an audible timer, it is helpful to count the seconds aloud during exposure.

Burning-in and dodging can be used also to correct or alter color balance to selected areas of a color print. Color balance can be shifted by the presence of multiple light sources in the original photograph. For example, if the subject includes window light, tungsten light, and fluorescent light, the color balance will vary in different areas of the image. Burning-in and dodging techniques can be used to improve overall color balance in the print by exposing selected areas of the print with different film packs, or by waving filters over selected areas of the image during exposure. For example, waving a blue filter in a shadow area will reduce its blue cast; waving a yellow filter over the sky area will intensify the blue.

Vignetting

Vignetting can be used as a control to eliminate unwanted backgrounds and to isolate a subject against a white space. Often vignetting is used in portraits; it works best when the portrait is composed mostly of light tones. (See Figure 6-26.)

The vignetting tool is an opaque piece of cardboard or plastic with a hole cut in it in the shape of the area to be printed. The edges of the hole are feathered so that the image will fade gradually into the white paper border without its edges being clearly visible. An effective vignetting tool can be made by using pinking shears to cut an oval hole in a sheet of black cardboard. This produces

a jagged, feathered edge that helps to make a print with an image that gradually fades out to white.

Use the vignetter during the basic exposure. Insert it by hand below the lens about midway between the lens and the printing paper. Manipulate it so that only the portion of the image to be

Figure 6-26. Vignette. Technique works best with subjects set against light backgrounds.

printed is projected onto the paper below, and the unwanted portions are masked off. As with dodging and burning-in, keep the vignetter in continuous motion during use so that its edges do not appear in the final print.

Texture Screening

A textured appearance can be added to a print by printing through a **texture screen**. The texture screen itself may be made of cloth, wire, glass, or plastic. Some texture screens are sandwiched together with the negative for printing. In this case, the texture pattern varies in size with the degree of enlargement. Other texture screens are placed in contact with the printing paper. In this case, the texture pattern remains the same no matter what the degree of enlargement. Stretching a sheer cloth, or any other type of thin material that has an interesting structural pattern, over the printing paper, can make a texture screen of this type. (See Figure 6-27.)

Photographing surfaces that have interesting surface characteristics, such as grain, nap, or weave can also make texture screens. Light the textured surface with a strong side light to emphasize the texture of the material; then take a closeup pho-

HELPFUL HINT
Lost Details

Burning-in and dodging can help to control the exposure at selected local areas within the print and improve tonal quality only if the detail already exists in the negative. No amount of dodging can restore details that were never recorded on the negative in the first place. No amount of burning-in can restore details that have been lost in the dense highlights of the negative.

tograph of it and underexpose by 3 to 4 stops. The resulting semitransparent negative can then be sandwiched together with another negative during printing. Printing both negatives at the same time will impart the texture to the printed image.

Convergence Control

When a camera is pointed upward or downward, the vertical lines in the resulting picture will appear to converge toward each other. This is evident in pictures of tall buildings taken from ground level with the camera pointed upward. Although the converging verticals often may add to the feeling of height in the picture, they may

A.

B.

Figure 6-27. Texture screening. Screens are available in a wide variety of textures. Two examples are shown here. A) Canvas. B) Linen.

sometimes be distracting. The preferred method of correcting convergence is to use a camera, such as a view camera, that possesses perspective control features. However, converging verticals can be corrected to some extent during enlargement by exercising **convergence control**.

With the negative image projected on a dummy sheet of blank paper in the easel, tilt the easel by lifting up the edge closest to the point at which the converging verticals are at their widest. This tends to straighten out the convergence. Lift until the verticals appear to be parallel; then place an object under the easel to hold it in this position. Then, with the focusing knob, focus the image at a point about one-third of the way down from the high edge of the easel. If the needed correction is only slight, the image may be kept in focus over the entire picture area by stopping down the enlarging lens to f/11 or f/16 to increase the depth of field.

If the needed correction is great, however, tilt the easel to a considerable incline, then also tilt the negative carrier in the enlarger. To control for differences in exposure from one side of the easel to the other, you may need to use a cardboard mask to provide a sliding exposure from one edge of the print to the other. Note that simpler enlargers may not provide for tilting the negative carrier. (See Figure 6-28 and Figure 6-29.)

Diffusion

By using the **diffusion** technique, a hazy or soft-focus effect can be obtained during printing. This effect may be used to subdue blemishes and wrinkles in portraiture, or to create a hazy, misty effect.

This effect is obtained by introducing a diffusing medium between the enlarger lens and the printing paper during exposure. This medium may be a diffusion screen, a transparent acetate sheet such as a negative sleeve, or a thin piece of dark nylon or similar fabric stretched across the path of the light. Any transparent material that will pass the image projected from the enlarger and scatter the light rays only slightly can be used. The amount of diffusion increases as the diffusing medium is placed nearer the enlarger lens; thus the amount of diffusion that will appear in the final print can be controlled.

Usually best results are obtained if paper with slightly higher than normal contrast is used and if the diffusion technique is applied for only part of the print exposure, with the balance of the exposure made without diffusion. Figure 6-30 shows the effect of diffusion.

A.

B.

Figure 6-28. Convergence control. Parallel vertical lines that tend to converge in A) have been corrected in B) by the technique shown in the following figure.

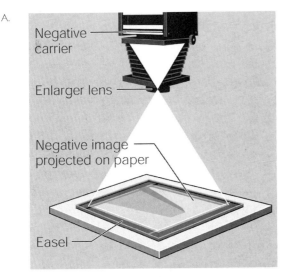

A.

Negative carrier

Enlarger lens

Negative image projected on paper

Easel

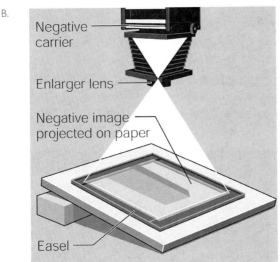

B.

Negative carrier

Enlarger lens

Negative image projected on paper

Easel

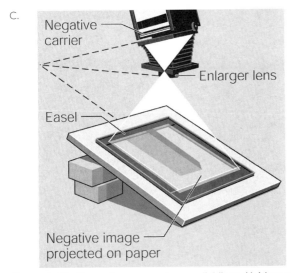

C.

Negative carrier

Enlarger lens

Easel

Negative image projected on paper

Figure 6-29. Correcting converging parallel lines. A) Normal enlargement shows converging verticals in the subject. B) Slight correction can be made by tipping the easel slightly and stopping down enlarger lens to increase depth of field. C) Extreme correction may require additional tilting of the negative carrier.

Flashing

To subdue distracting highlights in a print, the **flashing** technique is often useful. Flashing is simply a method of locally fogging small areas within a print to add density to—or darken—unwanted highlights.

Typically a small penlight is used. Roll the penlight in heavy paper to form a long, thin tube, 6 inches or so long, through which a small circle of raw, white light can be projected onto the print. For best results, the intensity of this light should be quite dim, producing a middle tone from a working distance after 6 to 8 seconds of continuous exposure.

For black-and-white prints, after exposing the print normally, place a red filter over the enlarging lens and turn on the enlarger. You will be able to see the image without exposing the print further. Then, using the modified penlight, expose the offensive highlights by "painting in" these areas with raw, white light, taking care to feather out the edges of the flashed areas. Keep the tool moving. Avoid flashing in any of the desired highlights to avoid degrading the contrast of these areas. Figure 6-31 shows the results of the flashing technique.

With color prints, flashing must be done after basic exposure with the enlarger turned off, or during basic exposure to add image-free density to selected areas. Just as the enlarger light is color balanced with a filter pack, the light used for flashing must also be color balanced. Further, without the negative's orange mask, the color equivalent of the mask must be added to the filter pack used for flashing. About 60Y + 40M may be used for this purpose. (See Table 6-1, page 202.)

The filtration used for flashing may be altered also to obtain color effects. For example, adding less yellow and/or magenta will warm the colors in the highlights while adding more yellow and/or magenta will cool them.

Combination Printing

Using more than one negative to make a single print is called **combination printing**. One common use of this technique is to add clouds to a clear sky. Basically the technique consists of expos-

A.

B.

Figure 6-30. Diffusion. Harsh complexion details in A) are softened in B) by using diffusion techniques.

A.

B.

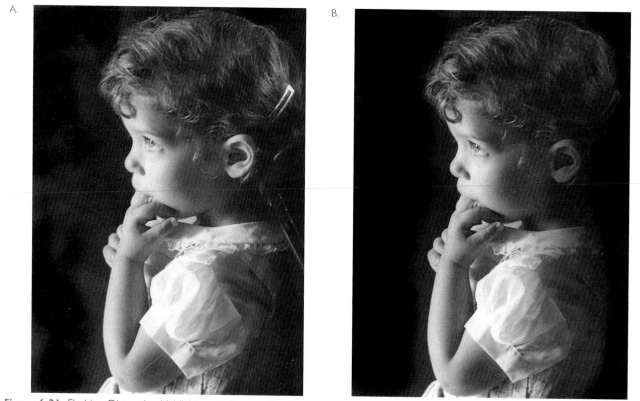

Figure 6-31. Flashing. Distracting highlights on left ear and on back of head in A) are muted in B) by flashing during exposure.

Combination Printing

The steps involved in combination printing a background, such as clouds, are as follows:

1. *Determine the correct exposure for each negative independently to ensure that the print densities of the two images are consistent.*

2. *Expose the foreground subject, masking off the original sky image to within an inch of the subject. If necessary, cut a mask to conform to the general contour of the subject. Move the mask slightly during exposure to build a slight margin of density around the subject image. This margin will help you join the two images without revealing the joint between them.*

3. *For black-and-white prints, insert a red filter below the enlarger lens. Place tape markers on the easel to indicate the position of the margin adjoining the subject image. Then replace the subject negative in the enlarger with the cloud negative. With the red filter still in place, and without moving the easel, arrange the cloud image to a suitable location and size. (The markers must be used at this point because the subject image is no longer visible.) Turn off the enlarger, remove the red filter, and proceed to expose the cloud image.*

   For color prints, these steps must be performed in total darkness. So marking the boundaries of the first image and placing the second image must be planned in advance and carried out in darkness.

4. *Mask off the previously exposed subject area, and expose the clouds. Cut the mask to conform to the subject's contour if necessary. Keep the mask moving within the marginal area to blend the second image into the first.*

Figure 6-32 provides an example of combination printing using two negatives. Combination prints may be made using many negatives if desired. The basic principles are the same.

ing a portion of the image, such as the clouds, with one negative and the remaining portion, such as a building or landscape, with a second negative. Both the subjects and the relative densities of the two portions should appear logically consistent when the print is processed, and the joining of the two images should be artfully concealed.

In selecting two negatives for combination printing, be sure that the two subjects have been shot from the same point of view. When adding clouds, for example, be sure that the clouds and the subject are seen from the same camera angle. Similarly, the lighting of the two subjects should appear to derive from the same source; if the subject is lit from the right side, the clouds also should be lit from the right. The relative size of the two images should be consistent with experience. Clouds that are supposed to be a great distance away should appear relatively small in the scale of the photograph. Violations of these logical concerns are likely to produce photographs that appear strange, artificial, and unreal. (See Figure 6-32.)

Special Black-and-White Printing Techniques

Objective 6-I Describe and demonstrate the techniques of split-filter printing, chemical control of contrast, black line border, and Sabbatier effect.

Key Concepts split-filter printing, color heads, color correction units, CC, hydroquinone, water bath development, black line border, Sabattier effect, Mackie lines, solarization

Split-Filter Printing

Split-filter printing is a process that allows precise tonal control over different areas of a black-and-white print. This technique can be used only

Figure 6-32. Combination printing. Clouds added to self-portrait by double printing—using more than one negative to make a single print. This technique may be used to add realistic features or, as in this case, to heighten psychological effect.

Careers in Photography

Portrait and Wedding Photographer

One of the more traditional careers in photography is that of portrait photographer. Portrait photography as a profession is nearly as old as photography itself, for the early Daguerreotypists and tintype photographers of the nineteenth century often supported themselves by shooting portraits for a fee. From these early times, portrait photographers have been oriented toward serving local consumer markets; even the early itinerant photographers tended to serve a few, small, relatively stable communities. Today, portrait photography generally includes wedding and school group photography that caters to the needs and wants of a local community.

Photographers who specialize in portrait photography must have a knack for dealing with people in an understanding and friendly manner. Unlike commercial photographers who generally must please third-party clients through a professional intermediary, such as an art director or an account executive, portrait photographers must learn to please the subjects themselves. These subjects, though less likely to be literate in photography, may be just as demanding and require that the photographer patiently explain photographic requirements in non-technical terms.

Carlene Duke. An example of a studio portrait.

The great majority of portrait establishments are individual proprietorships. Therefore, the field is inviting to individuals who wish to go into the photography business for themselves. Generally, a photographer may start a business in the portrait field with a minimum of equipment and capital investment. To keep overhead costs low, it is not unusual for beginning portrait photographers to work out of their own home offices and laboratories, without a studio of their own—photography may often take place outdoors or at the subject's location, such as at the subject's home, office, school, or wedding site. Because the portrait business is so easily entered, however, it is also fiercely competitive and often unprofitable for the newcomer.

If the business succeeds and develops, however, the need for a studio setting is likely to grow. The special requirements for portraits of children and groups will lead the photographer to seek greater control over backgrounds and lighting. A studio allows the photographer to control the amount of natural light, to add artificial light and flash as needed, and to provide both neutral and elaborate backgrounds as the subject may require.

Portrait photography is an art unto itself, demanding that the photographer capture the essence of the subject's personality, create an image that is itself sufficiently arresting to draw the viewer into a study of the subject, and simultaneously please the subject-client. Photographers have approached this challenge in a variety of ways, sometimes developing such a unique style and approach to their subjects that their work has achieved international and artistic recognition, such as the portraiture of Yousuf Karsh, Philippe Halsman, Arnold Newman, Richard Avedon, and Herb Ritts.

Most local portrait photographers also undertake wedding photography because it is akin to portraiture and can be a profitable, though hectic, activity. A wedding photographer needs to develop, through experience, knowledge of the significant events that make up a wedding. Because the bride and groom, and their families, usually have less wedding experience than the photographer, and are usually preoccupied with other matters during the event, the photographer must usually take the lead in planning and carrying out a plan for the photographs. The major events of a wedding include the bridal and wedding party preparations, the arrival of guests, the bridal procession, the wedding ceremony, the recession following the ceremony, the reception and party, the toasts, the cutting of the cake, the departure of the happy couple—and all significant guests must be photographed at some time or another during the event.

The self-employed portrait photographer must also possess, in addition to camera and darkroom skills, some business skills. It is important for the independent photographer to write and speak effectively, in order to prepare persuasive proposals and correspondence, and to present selling ideas to potential clients. It is important also for the independent photographer to possess some basic bookkeeping skills—to maintain records of income and expense, and payables and receivables. It is also important to maintain historical records of jobs, clients, fees, original images, rights, and permissions necessary for reproducing images on the demand of clients.

Carlene Duke.
Wedding portraits are typically made on location.

Operating a portrait business is much like operating any small service enterprise. Success or failure often rests not only on skillful performance of the service offered, but also on the communication and business skills of the proprietor.

with variable-contrast black-and-white photographic papers that use printing filters for contrast selection and control. The different contrast filters can be used to expose different areas in the print.

Variable-contrast paper is constructed of two separate emulsion layers. One layer has very low inherent contrast and is sensitive primarily to yellow-orange light; the other layer has very high inherent contrast and is sensitive to magenta or purple light.

Contrast is usually controlled by selecting a single printing filter that will pass the desired color mixture of image-forming light. However, the effective color of image-forming light also may be controlled by separate and additive exposures through two or more different contrast filters. For example, a print given half of its exposure through a number 5 high-contrast filter and half through a number 0 low-contrast filter would have an effective cumulative contrast near normal. Some photographers expose to produce good shadows with a number 5 high-contrast filter. Then, without disturbing the enlarger head, they change to a low-contrast printing filter, such as a number 0, for an overall exposure that will add density to the highlights. By varying these proportions, many different contrast renderings can be achieved.

Achieving Variable-Contrast Control With the use of separate filters, dodging and burning-in can be used together to gain precise control over different tonal areas. For example, a print could be given an overall exposure with one contrast filter, followed by a separate burning-in exposure through a different contrast filter. In this way individual areas of even the most complex negatives can be printed with appropriate contrast. (See Figure 6-33.)

Bumping Up the Blacks Split-filter printing can also be used for "bumping up the blacks." Often when an image is printed for low contrast, no rich blacks are produced, even though the exposure and contrast grade may be ideal for that image. In such cases, some photographers give a brief secondary printing exposure through a high-contrast filter. The exposure time can be short enough so as to have little effect on the overall density of the print, yet still increase the depth and richness of the deep shadow areas. Bumping up the shadows with such a second exposure often adds visual vitality and spark to an otherwise lackluster image.

Variable-Contrast Printing with Color Heads

As we have seen, some enlargers are equipped with **color heads** designed primarily for making prints from color negatives and slides. These enlargers use built-in, fade-resistant cyan, magenta, and yellow filters. The filters, and the resulting color strength, are usually adjustable from 0 to nearly 200 **color correction units**, called **CCs**. The intensity of the color is increased as the number of CCs is increased.

A color head can also be used to make black-and-white prints and is especially versatile when used with variable-contrast enlarging papers. Two of the filters found in color enlarging heads are magenta and yellow—precisely the two colors to which variable-contrast papers are sensitive. Thus, by adjusting the amounts of these two colors, the color enlarging head can be used to produce any contrast grade of image-forming light. Table 6-3 shows approximate color head equivalents for common variable-contrast filter numbers. Exact equivalents will vary with the brand of photo paper and enlarger used.

Contrast Control During Development

The print contrast of some black-and-white photographic papers can be fine-tuned by chemical

Figure 6-33. An example of split-filter printing. The main print exposure was made through a high contrast No. 5 filter to heighten the graphic shadow cast by the stairway. A low contrast No. 0 filter was then used to burn-in the bright area around the light fixture to add tone and detail.

Table 6-3. Variable-contrast printing with a color head	
Contrast Filter	Color Head Setting Y—Yellow M—Magenta
0	110Y
1/2	90Y
1	70Y
1 1/2	30Y
2	0 (white light)
2 1/2	30M
3	45M
3 1/2	55M
4	95M
4 1/2	130M
5	170M

means during paper development. This technique works best with photographic papers that have no developer incorporated into their emulsion. Fiber-based papers, especially the warm-toned chlorobromide papers, offer the most contrast control through chemical means.

Changing Development Time Minor changes in print contrast can be made simply by altering the print development time. Slightly longer developing times may be used to increase contrast a bit—but overextending the development time can have the opposite effect by fogging the whites and light grays. Experiment by developing three identically exposed prints for different times—two minutes, four minutes, and eight minutes, for example. Then carefully compare the density of the shadows and highlights to determine the effect of altering development time.

Changing Developer Chemistry Changes in print contrast can also be made by changing the developer chemistry. One method is to use more diluted developer to reduce contrast or to use more concentrated developer to increase contrast. Alternatively, selected chemicals can be added to the developer. Some photographers add a tablespoon or so of the high-contrast developing agent **hydroquinone** to a tray of conventional print developer to increase print contrast. Many manufacturers market special print developers for particular contrast effects. (See Appendix G-5 on the CD that accompanies this book.)

Water Bath Development One additional technique can be used to lower contrast when printing on fiber-based papers—the **water bath development** method. This technique works especially well with excessively harsh negatives. Expose the print normally and develop it in a conventional print developer until the image first starts to appear, usually about twenty to thirty seconds. Then transfer the print into a tray of slightly warm water and let it remain face down without agitation for one to two minutes.

Here's what happens in the water bath. The fibrous paper has absorbed enough developer to continue acting upon the image. This limited amount of developer is soon exhausted in the dark shadow areas, where there is much silver to act upon. It remains relatively fresh and strong, however, and continues to develop the less concentrated silver in the highlights. The effect is as though increased development time were given to just the highlights alone—and this reduces the overall contrast.

It is often necessary to repeat the cycle at least once more to build sufficient print density. Return the print to the developer tray and agitate for 20 seconds or so; this again saturates the paper base with developer. Then return it to the water bath for another 1 to 2 minutes.

Black Border Line Printing

You can create a print where the image is surrounded and contained by a **black line border**. The line comes from printing both the image on the negative and the clear edges of the film that surround it. Because the film border is clear, it will print as pure black. Use of the black line became popular with photographers in the 1960s. Certain street photographers and others have used the black line almost as an aesthetic statement—as proof that the picture was made using the full frame of the negative, and that the integrity and reality of the original image was not tampered with by cropping. The black line also serves to help contain and frame the photographic image and has become a commonly used stylistic and graphic device for some contemporary photographers. (See Figure 6-34.)

The simplest way to print the black line is to use an oversize negative carrier, such as one designed for the next larger film size, and then carefully adjust the easel blades. However, this technique often does not hold the negative flat enough to

Figure 6-34. An example of a black-line border print.

avoid curled negatives and problems with sharpness. A more effective technique is to file out the opening in a normal negative carrier until it is about 1/16in larger on all sides of the negative. Alternatively, a copy of the negative carrier can be traced onto heavy, black mat board and carefully cut to the same shape, slightly enlarging the film opening. Smooth all edges and darken them with a black marker.

To use the oversize negative carrier, adjust the enlarger until the blades leave an opening about 1/8in larger than the enlarged image. The easel blade will provide the sharp outer edge of the black line and control its thickness. As printing takes place, white light will pass through the clear film edge, creating a black line around the image.

The Sabattier Effect

The **Sabattier effect**, named for Armand Sabattier who first described it in 1862, is achieved by reexposing a photographic print to white light during print development. The result is a partial tonal reversal—the print is not quite a negative and not quite a positive, and the borders between tones are defined by white lines called **Mackie lines**, named after Alexander Mackie. The process is sometimes incorrectly called **solarization**. (True solarization is a reversal of tones that is caused when film is grossly overexposed.) See Figure 6-36.

The strange tonal appearance of a Sabattier print is due to the decreased sensitivity of an exposed and partially developed print to light. When such a print is re-exposed, those areas that have already partially appeared on the print act as a mask, protecting the emulsion from further exposure. The print highlights, however, have no such protection and contain many sensitive silver crystals that can still be exposed and developed. This accounts for the tonal reversal. The first development inhibits further action by the developer, thereby causing the white Mackie lines.

Sabattier printing is highly variable, and exact effects are hard to predict. In general, printing from a negative and giving only a slight second exposure will yield a print that is mainly positive but has some tonally reversed areas. Printing from a color slide or positive transparency produces the opposite effect.

The Sabattier effect works best with very high-contrast paper. Paper graded number 5 or 6 works well for this technique. With variable-contrast paper, it works best to use the highest contrast filter available for both the initial and secondary white light exposures. Experimenters have found that near-exhausted paper developer works much better than fresh. At least one manufacturer markets a developer made especially for making Sabattier prints.

Making a Sabattier Print

1. *Set up and focus the enlarger in the conventional way. Use a negative of normal to high contrast, and print with the highest contrast grade of paper or contrast filter available.*

2. *Stop down the lens to f/8 and make a stepped test print to determine the first exposure. The example in Figure 6-36 was given exposures of 5, 10, 15, and 20 seconds (top to bottom) at f/8 using a cardboard mask.*

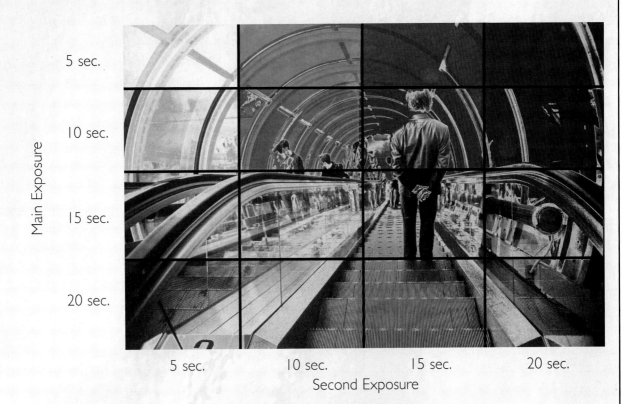

Figure 6-35. A Sabattier test print. The first or main exposure runs from top to bottom while the second, re-exposure is varied from side to side. In this manner, numerous combinations may be generated quickly and studied.

3. *Develop the print in normal or used paper developer for about half of the standard time. The example in Figure 6-36 was given a 30-sec. first development.*

4. *Move the print to a tray of running water for a 30- to 45-second rinse. Do not use acid stop bath. Remove the surface moisture from the print with a squeegee or towels. Place the damp print on a flat tray.*

5. *Place the tray with the damp print in place of the enlarging easel. Remove the negative from the enlarger but leave any contrast filters in place. Stop down the lens two stops. Make a stepped test print for the second exposure along the axis opposite that used for the first exposure. The example in Figure 6-35 was given a left-to-right stepped exposure of 5, 10, 15, and 20 seconds using a cardboard mask.*

6. *Return the print to the developer tray for the remainder of the normal developing time or until the desired effect is achieved.*

7. *Stop, fix, wash, and dry as usual.*

8. *Examine the checkerboard test print (Figure 6-35). Select one square that has the desired combination of first and second exposure times. Make a full print with these settings. For example, Figure 6-36 A was given a 10-second first exposure and a 15-second second exposure.*

A.

B.

Figure 6-36. A) A Sabattier print. Note the white lines that surround objects and the negative/positive effect. B) The same image printed in a conventional manner.

The Sabattier technique encourages experimentation. Try varying the first and second development times as well as the first and second exposures. Try burning-in and dodging during the second exposure. Exercise local control over the image by using a penlight or other small light source to reexpose and tonally reverse selected portions of the image. These and other variations of exposure and development can produce interesting variations in the resulting Sabattier effect.

Finishing Controls and Print Storage

Objective 6-J Describe and demonstrate the processes of toning, mounting, spotting, and bleaching, and describe some guidelines for the care and storage of photographs.

Key Concepts toning, dry mounting, cold mounting, wet-mounting, spray-mounting, spotting, bleaching, archival processing

Even after an enlargement has been printed and processed, certain operations can still be done to enhance its appearance. If a few small dust specks escaped attention during print exposure, they will require touching up on the print. Bathing a black-and-white print in one of many commercially available colored toning solutions can also alter the color of the image. Further, every fine print looks even more striking if it is given proper presentation by careful matting or mounting. Because all of these operations are done after the print has been made, they are called finishing

controls. Once the finishing process is complete, the photographs are in their final form. If the prints are to last for a long period of time, they must be properly stored and cared for.

Toning to Enhance a Black-and-White Image

Toning is one of several optional techniques that can be used to add a final touch to finished black-and-white prints. The toning process alters the image tone to add a color dimension to the picture. The most popular toning shades are the sepia tones, which range from light reddish brown to brown. These tones are especially effective for portraits because they convey the warmth and red-brown tones associated with the human skin. The same tones are also effective for wood subjects, trees, and landscapes, especially in the fall.

Blue is another popular toning shade. Blue tones are especially effective in communicating a sense of cold and are often used for wintry scenes of snow and ice. A blue toner may also enhance the cold, hard quality of steel.

Toner is most effectively used when it enhances the subject matter of a photograph without calling attention to itself. The use of a warm-tone toner with a cold subject or vice versa, or the use of odd or extreme colors, often will distract the viewer from the subject of the photograph. When this occurs, the viewer's concentration shifts from the subject to the technique, and the photograph may fail altogether to communicate the intended idea.

To use a typical toner, a previously processed black-and-white print is first bathed in a special toning bleach and then put through the actual toning bath. When the desired color is reached, the print is washed and dried in the conventional manner.

The actual shade obtained when any toning product is used will vary with the type of developer used, the amount of development, and the type of paper emulsion. In addition, altering dilution and immersion times may vary the intensity and shade produced by commercial toning products. Color Plate 8 is an example of toning.

Toning for Preservation

In addition to altering the image tone of black-and-white prints, toners are also used to preserve the life of photographic prints. Gold toner, for example, is designed to give any properly processed black-and-white print archival permanence. The gold in the toner combines with the silver in the image to create a print that is virtually impervious to chemical deterioration. The image tone changes very slightly toward a cooler, black-blue tone.

Selenium toner may be used for a similar purpose. In stronger concentrations, selenium toner changes the image tone toward the warmer, red-brown tones. However, in weak concentration, the selenium will combine with the silver in the image to create a chemically resistant print without noticeably changing the image tone.

Mounting

When display prints are properly mounted, they are set off from their potentially confusing surroundings by a neutral frame. This aids viewing by creating an aesthetic distance between the image and the background environment that enables the viewer to concentrate more fully on the subject. As with other finishing techniques, a mounting should enhance the subject of the picture without calling attention to itself.

Dry Mounting **Dry mounting** is the preferred mounting process because it uses no liquid adhesives and provides a relatively stable and chemically neutral bond. To dry mount a print, the following materials and equipment are needed:

- Dry-mounting tissue.
- A mounting board. Ordinary mat board will suffice for most work, but special acid-free or rag board should be used for especially valuable prints.
- An electric tacking or household iron.
- An electric dry-mounting press or household iron.

The steps in dry mounting a photo to the mounting board are listed below and shown in Figure 6-37. If a dry-mounting press is not available, a household iron may be used.

1. Lay the print face down on a counter. Lay a sheet of dry-mounting tissue over the back of the print so that the print is completely covered by tissue. Use a tacking iron or a household iron to tack the tissue to the back of the print at the center. (Set the household iron between the silk and wool temperature settings for fiber-base prints. Be sure the steam setting is off.)

2. Trim the print and tissue simultaneously in a paper cutter so that the edges of the print and the tissue are exactly even at all points.

3. Position the print on the mounting board. Hold the print in place, lift one corner of it, and tack the mounting tissue to the mount. Repeat until three corners of the mounting tissue have been tacked to the mount.

4. With a dry-mounting press: Place the mounting board, with the print and mounting tissue tacked in position, into the press with the print facing up toward the iron surface. Place a double thickness of craft paper or a special dry-mounting cover sheet over the entire mounting board surface to protect the face of the print from the heated surface. If fiber-base photo paper and standard mounting tissue are used, set the temperature of the press between 250 and 275°F (120 to 135°C). Close the press for approximately one minute, or until automatically signaled. Then remove the print from the heat, place a flat weight on its surface, and allow it to cool.

With a household iron: If a dry-mounting press is not available, a dry, electric, household iron can be used to tack and mount the print. Again, set the temperature gauge at "silk" or

SPECIAL TECHNIQUES

Photograms

A photogram is basically a contact print. Instead of using a negative, however, opaque or translucent objects are placed on light-sensitive material. This blocks out or modulates part of the light and produces a pattern or picture on the light-sensitive material when it is exposed to light and processed. The photogram has been around as long as photography itself. Many of the first images were made by laying an object on top of a light-sensitized plate of glass and setting it out in the sun to be exposed. Some eighty years later, in the 1920s, painter-photographers such as Man Ray and Lázló Moholy-Nagy, experimented with the technique to explore the "pure" actions of light in space.

Making photograms can be creative and challenging. You can use various materials and objects arranged on printing paper or film to create an infinite array of engaging images that express your own artistic vision. With opaque objects, you can produce a certain degree of realism in the image by using recognizable subjects such as leaves, keys, or lace fabrics. By shifting or moving objects during exposure, suspending them on glass, or using variations of color filters, you can alter the tones or color values in the photogram.

Although any light source can be used to produce photograms, an enlarger is generally used. Because exposure variations can profoundly alter the image produced, it is wise to make a series of test exposures first.

Any light sensitive material may be used, including black and white or color, direct or reversal photographic paper or film, or commercial blueprint paper. Even outdated or partly fogged photographic paper or film may be used.

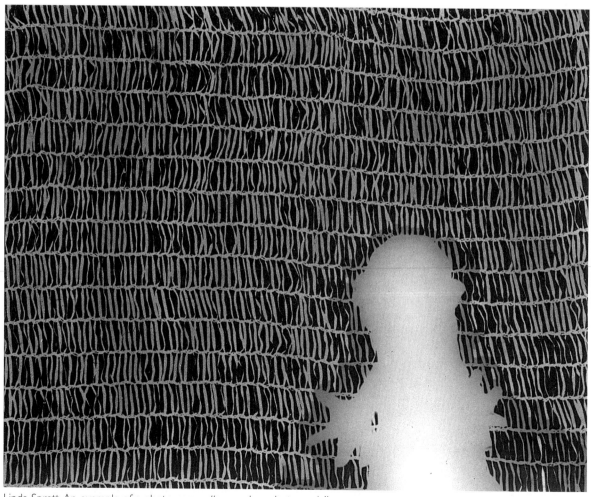

Linda Spratt. An example of a photogram or "cameraless photograph."

You can be as creative as you like when selecting the objects and materials to be used in your photogram. Some examples are these:

- flowers, leaves, or branches
- small objects such as toothpicks or pins
- seeds, marbles, or beads
- kitchen or household tools
- glassware
- plastic objects or sheets
- granular materials such as sand or salt
- fibers such as string, hair, thread, or wire
- crumpled tissue paper
- paper cutouts
- lace
- drawings on plastic or glass
- your hands
- opaque or translucent liquids poured over glass
- thinly sliced fruit
- small animals or insects

Try multiple exposures; rearranging things between exposures; multiple exposures with different colored light; different colors of paper; moving translucent colored objects between exposures; or coloring or drawing on finished prints.

In addition, you can "paint" additional exposure onto the surface by using a penlight, or you can hold back light in other areas by "dodging." You can experiment by manually moving the objects, suspending them on glass above the surface, or blowing smoke across the surface during exposure.

The key to good photograms is to experiment. Photograms offer an opportunity for the creative use of photographic materials distinct from photography itself. Used with imagination, photogram manipulations can be educational, fun, and sometimes produce worthy works of art.

A.
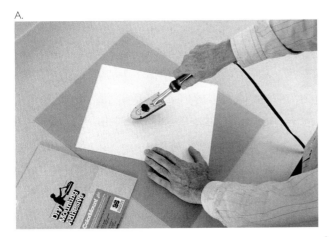

B.

C.

D.
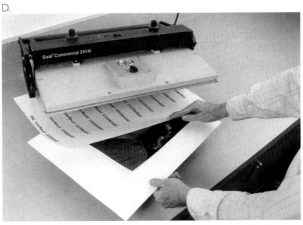

Figure 6-37. Dry mounting. A) Tack mounting tissue to back of print covering entire surface. B) Trim both print and tissue simultaneously so that all edges are even. C) Tack tissue, with print attached, to mounting board to hold it in place. D) Place print, tissue, and board in dry mounting press with protective covering sheet.

"wool." Cover the entire board and print with a double thickness of wrapping paper. Run the iron back and forth over the print area, keeping the iron moving at all times, and working from the center toward the edges of the print. Do not apply too much pressure. Continue the procedure until the mounting is firm. Place a flat weight on the print and allow it to cool. Properly mounted prints will not detach from the mounting board when the board is flexed slightly.

If RC paper is used, and this applies to most color printing paper, special low-temperature mounting tissue, designed for use at approximately 180 to 190° F (82 to 88° C), must also be used; temperatures above this level will melt the resin coating and destroy the print. Be sure to follow the paper manufacturer's recommendations for mounting.

Cold Mounting Pressure-sensitive **cold-mounting** adhesive sheets are also available for mounting prints. Cold-mounting materials need no special presses and work well with RC prints. The material is essentially a sheet of adhesive with a removable protective backing on both sides. It is applied first to the back of the print and trimmed; then the second cover sheet is peeled off and the print is adhered to the mount. Some brands are positionable; that is, the print can be moved around on the mat until it is correctly positioned. The adhesive does not chemically affect photographic materials, and the bond strengthens as it ages. (See Figure 6-38.)

Prints can also be **wet mounted** or **spray mounted**. Mounting adhesives that are specially designed for photographic purposes should be used. Do not use rubber cement or other nonphotographic adhesives, because they may contain solvents that could ruin the prints. Follow the manufacturer's instructions for wet mounting or spray mounting photographs.

Spotting and Bleaching

Despite careful printing, some prints may end up with a few tiny white spots caused by dust or lint. These may be retouched by **spotting**, using spotting dyes and brushes. Spotting dyes are available in both dry and liquid forms—the common colors are black, white, and sepia for black-and-white

A.
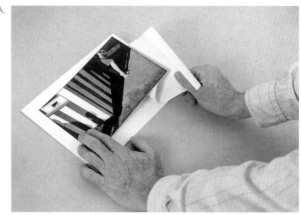

B.

Figure 6-38. Adhesive mounting. Two-sided self-sticking adhesive cards make picture mounting easy. A) Peel off backing and apply photo to adhesive surface. B) Peel backing off reverse side and apply photo to the mounting surface with even pressure.

prints. Color spotting dyes generally come in sets that contain at least red, yellow, and blue, which can be mixed to create almost any other color.

Several tools are used for spotting. To work with dyes, use very fine art brushes, usually #0 to #000. For wiping dust off the surface of a print, use a two-inch wide camel hair brush or an antistatic cloth. Wear white, lint-free cotton gloves when handling prints during spotting to prevent oils from your skin from staining the print. A small, white, ceramic dish is useful for mixing dyes to the desired color.

To spot a print, dampen the brush slightly and pick up a little of the spotting dye that appears lighter than the area around the spot. Dab lightly at the spot to overlay the dye until it matches the surrounding area. Using a fine point, apply the dye to the spot using a dotting or stippling motion. Continue until the spot disappears into the surrounding area. (See Figure 6-39.)

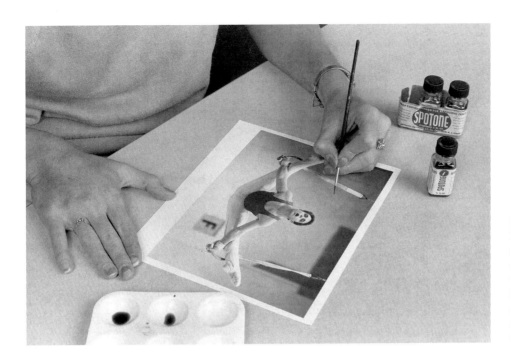

Figure 6-39. Spotting. Spotting the finished print to conceal blemishes. Spotting dyes may be diluted to match virtually any tone on the print. Liquid spotting dyes may be used with RC papers, matte or glossy fiber-based papers, warm or cold tone papers.

Occasionally a print may acquire black spots as a result of pinholes or other negative blemishes that pass light. Eliminating these spots from the print is a somewhat more complex operation that, if not meticulously executed, can easily ruin the print. The process involves **bleaching** the black spot from the print with either a weak solution of potassium ferrocyanide or ordinary laundry bleach.

Use a small, tightly twisted cotton swab to apply the bleaching agent delicately and gently to the precise area of the black spot. Try to avoid bleaching any of the surrounding area—the larger the bleached area, the more visible it will be in the final print. An alternative is to use white or opaque spotting dye to cover the spot. Then, when the black spot has been bleached or spotted away, the whitened area that remains can be spotted, as just described, to restore its tone to that of the surrounding area. Practice the technique on scrap materials before trying it with good prints.

Both spotting and bleaching are difficult, time-consuming tasks that should not be relied on to rescue carelessly made prints. Proper care in printing can save hours of laborious and often unsatisfactory retouching. See Figure 6-40 showing common print problems marked on a proof print.

Care and Storage of Photographs

The first step in caring for a photograph is to be sure that it has been properly processed. Any image that needs to last longer than fifteen to twenty years should be printed on fiber-based paper and given careful **archival processing**. See Objective 15-C for methods to use when processing for permanence.

Some of the methods available for archival processing of black-and-white prints, such as toning, are not available for color prints. Color images are especially vulnerable to fading and staining. Fortunately, the dyes in modern color materials are much more stable and long-lasting than those used only a few years ago. Nevertheless, the long-term survival of color images depends on many other factors as well. Not only is the inherent stability of the material important, but also the processing methods used and the conditions of storage and display.

In general, observing the following guidelines will extend the longevity of all photographic materials:

- Check the inherent stability of color materials as currently published.
- Store prints in light or dark conditions as recommended by the manufacturer.

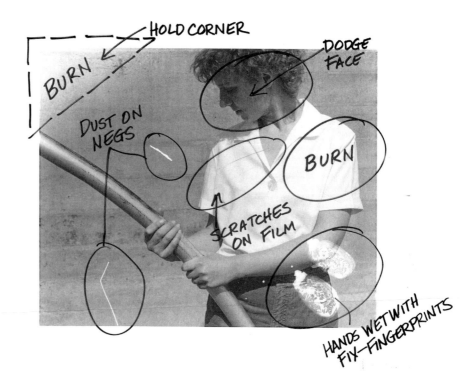

Figure 6-40. Common print problems. Note problems identified in the print. Some would be corrected by burning-in and dodging, some by spotting, and others are beyond repair. Use proper procedure to avoid them.

- If possible, process in fresh chemicals, using clean equipment, and wash thoroughly afterwards.

- Store processed films and prints at constant temperatures that do not exceed 60–70° F (16–21° C).

- Store films and prints in constant conditions that do not exceed 25–50 percent relative humidity. Avoid damp, humid conditions, such as in basements or bathrooms.

- Avoid exposing finished films and prints to excessive light, especially ultraviolet light present in sunlight and fluorescent lighting. Use duplicate slides for projection; use print materials designed with built-in UV protection; and display color prints under UV-filtered lighting. Store original materials safely and make copies or prints for display.

- Store processed film and prints in containers made of chemically inert materials that will not interact with the photographs. Use special polyethylene print storage bags or archival storage or portfolio boxes. (See Figure 6-41.) When storing several mounted prints together, place a clean layer of acid-free tissue or interleaving paper between them. (See Appendix B on the CD that accompanies this book.)

- Store photographic materials away from paints, gases, or other volatile substances, as well as airborne grit, smoke, mold, and insects.

- Avoid attaching anything to a fine print, such as paper clips or adhesive tape. If you must, use only a soft lead pencil to write on a print—never a ball point pen, marker, or anything with ink.

- For framed prints use a window or overmat to provide an air space that separates the emulsion from the glass. Without an air space, the emulsion will eventually adhere to the glass and be damaged.

Figure 6-41. Archival storage boxes. Special boxes free of contaminants are used for safe storage of valuable photographs.

Darkroom Design and Equipment

Objective 6-K Describe basic darkroom facilities and the equipment used in making prints.

Key Concepts darkroom, fogged, safelights, enlarger, color printing (CP) filters, color head, enlarging lens, enlarger optical system, contact printer, enlarger timer, printing easel, print drying racks

The basic equipment and facilities used in printing consist of the darkroom itself, safelights, white work lights, an enlarger, sometimes a contact printer, and print drying equipment.

The Physical Facility

Photographic printing procedures normally take place in a **darkroom** within which light is totally controlled. Ambient light that might affect light-sensitive materials is excluded; image-forming light is tightly controlled to prevent unwanted light leaks and reflections; and, for black-and-white printing, safelights provide overall illumination without affecting light-sensitive materials.

The size of the darkroom is determined by the type of work to be done and the number of persons to be working in it at the same time. Film processing and printmaking can be performed in the same space, but not always conveniently at the same time. If more than one person will be using the darkroom, it is useful to provide separate loading rooms where total darkness can be obtained without stopping printing operations under safelight.

The minimum requirements for a one-person printing darkroom are: (1) at least 40 square feet of space, (2) a fully grounded electrical system equipped with ground fault interceptors, (3) adequate ventilation, (4) a seal against the penetration of outside light, and (5) access to water and drainage. Highly desirable features include a minimum of 80 square feet of space and an integrated water system. (See Figure 6-42.) In planning a printing darkroom, keep in mind the Helpful Hint, *Darkroom Planning* below.

Figure 6-43 shows movable darkroom equipment adapted for use in a relatively small space. Many amateur darkrooms have been designed around a small portable cart, which can be wheeled into a bathroom and set up for operation within a few minutes. With a little imagination, any similar small space can be converted into a functioning darkroom on either a permanent or portable basis.

The Safelights

The darkroom should, of course, seal out all sources of ambient light that might fall upon the light-sensitive papers. Papers exposed unintentionally to such light may become **fogged**—that is, they may acquire an overall gray veil when developed.

Safelights should be positioned to produce the highest level of illumination possible that is con-

---

HELPFUL **H**INT *Darkroom Planning*

1. The enlarger and other printing equipment and materials should be no more than four feet from the developing position at the sink.
2. Electrical switches should be easy to reach.
3. The entire electrical system should be grounded and equipped with ground fault interceptors.
4. Electrical receptacles should be plentiful and easy to reach.
5. The countertops and the sink should be approximately 36 inches from the floor.
6. The floor should be dark, resilient underfoot, chemical- and water-resistant, and easily cleaned.
7. A light-trapped entry is desirable to provide free access and ventilation without opening doors or curtains.
8. Dust-collecting surfaces, such as pipes and open shelves, should be avoided. Provide plentiful shelf space in enclosed cabinets.
9. The walls and ceiling should be light in color—ideally white or beige—and painted with a water- and chemical-resistant paint. (Don't paint the walls and ceiling black!)
10. Provide dust-free, filtered ventilation sufficient to give at least 10 to 15 complete air exchanges per hour.
11. Provide a counter for handling dry materials—papers, negatives, and so forth—that is separate from the wet sink area, where liquid chemicals are used and processing occurs.
12. Running water and drainage are highly desirable in the darkroom. Water taps should be within easy reach.

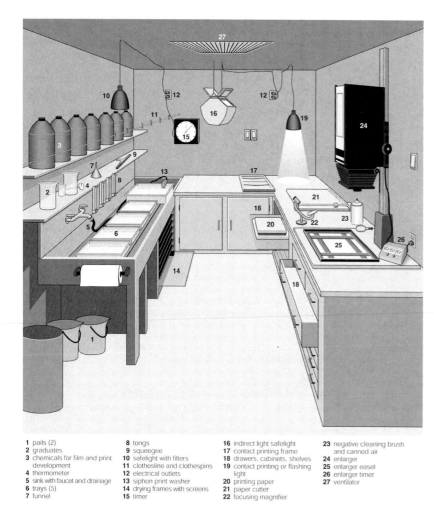

1 pails (2)
2 graduates
3 chemicals for film and print development
4 thermometer
5 sink with faucet and drainage
6 trays (5)
7 funnel
8 tongs
9 squeegee
10 safelight with filters
11 clothesline and clothespins
12 electrical outlets
13 siphon print washer
14 drying frames with screens
15 timer
16 indirect light safelight
17 contact printing frame
18 drawers, cabinets, shelves
19 contact printing or flashing light
20 printing paper
21 paper cutter
22 focusing magnifier
23 negative cleaning brush and canned air
24 enlarger
25 enlarger easel
26 enlarger timer
27 ventilator

Figure 6-42. An ideal darkroom layout. Notice that the room has been divided into a wet-side for chemical processing and a dry-side for handling film and paper.

The White Work Lights

Abundant white work light should also be available in the darkroom to aid in toning and finishing procedures as well as for general use. The color qualities of the white light are important for proper print inspection. Most workers prefer to combine ordinary household light bulbs with one or two large fluorescent fixtures for overall illumination. Several individual tungsten lights can be positioned directly over the work areas to provide increased illumination for delicate work such as print spotting. The switch for the white work lights should be placed out of normal reach so that it will not be turned on accidentally while the darkroom is in use.

For color printing, it is useful to have work light balanced for daylight (5500K) for viewing color prints. An alternative is to provide nearby a viewing booth balanced for daylight for this purpose.

sistent with the safety of the light-sensitive materials in use. Place safelights in several locations, reflecting their light off the walls and ceiling to provide an even field of safelight throughout the darkroom area. Additional safelights can be positioned directly over the work areas to provide a concentration of safelight for detailed work.

The level of safelight illumination should be tested for safety. To test safelights, expose a sheet of photo paper to a negative image. Before developing it, partially cover the exposed paper with another sheet of paper or cardboard. Then leave the partially covered photo paper exposed under the safelights for several minutes before processing it. If the safelights are affecting the paper, the covered and uncovered portions of the photo paper will have different appearances after processing. Exposed paper is used for this test because safelight fog may occur only in previously exposed portions of the print.

The Enlarger

Enlargers are designed in many varieties for many purposes. The major distinguishing features are their size, the type of light source used, and the method of distributing the light to obtain an even field of illumination during exposure. Some focus manually; others focus automatically as the head is raised and lowered.

Enlargers are designed for use with specific negative formats, from 8mm to 8 x 10 in. Most are designed to use tungsten photo-enlarger lamps, which are manufactured in various wattages. Other enlargers use other light sources such as fluorescent, quartz-halogen, and xenon arc lights. Different light sources tend to produce slightly different print characteristics.

To obtain an evenly exposed print, the light that passes through the negative should be evenly distributed—it should be free of "hot spots" and "cold spots." There should be no difference in intensity between the center and the edges of the focal plane. Two methods are used to obtain even illumination: (1) diffusing the light emanating from the light source, and (2) optically condensing the source light. Those equipped with condenser lenses tend to be heavier and sturdier, and produce prints with greater contrast and definition.

Most black-and-white enlarger heads are fitted with a filter slot or drawer, a highly desirable feature. Such a device allows individual variable-contrast filter sheets to be placed in the light path. Locating the filters between the negative and the light source eliminates any optical problems that might result from dusty or slightly scratched filters. The filter drawer can also be used to hold stacks of individual **color printing (CP) filters**, to be used when printing color photographs. Color printing with individual cut filters is possible, but not nearly as convenient as using a color head.

Color Heads Many modern enlargers are equipped with a **color head** in place of a condenser system. These heads contain three adjustable filters—cyan, yellow and magenta—and are designed especially for making prints from color negatives and slides. The filters are mounted on adjustable arms that can be extended or retracted in front of the light bulb to color the light. The user simply dials the desired filtration with calibrated knobs. After filtration, the light passes into a mixing chamber where it is further diffused and exits the head through a sheet of opal glass. Almost all color heads are of the diffusion design.

When purchasing a new enlarger, consider one equipped with a color head, or one that allows adding a color head later. Color heads can be used quite successfully for black-and-white work and even have some advantages when working with variable-contrast enlarging papers. (See Variable-Contrast Printing with Color Heads, page 222.) Color printing from slides and negatives is relatively easy when a color head enlarger is used, and many darkroom workers enjoy the added dimension that color photography offers. (See Figure 6-44.)

Enlarging Lenses The **enlarging lens** is the heart of the enlarger system. Select a lens of the highest available quality; a low-quality lens will produce photographs that noticeably lack sharpness and contrast. Enlarging lenses cost about the same as camera lenses of comparable quality.

Enlarging lenses, unlike camera lenses, are designed for flat field work. Because both the negative and the printing paper are two-dimensional, it is important that the lens possess an extremely flat field—it

Figure 6-43. Portable darkroom setup. With ingenuity, a portable or semipermanent darkroom setup can be designed for use in small home bathroom or laundry room.

HELPFUL HINT

A Basic Darkroom Kit

The basic equipment for a functioning darkroom should include the following:

- *enlarger equipped with one or more lenses of the proper focal length and negative carriers for each size of film. A built-in filter drawer is desirable; a built-in color head is preferable.*
- *variable-contrast printing filters*
- *enlarger timer*
- *brush for cleaning negatives*
- *blower or canned air*
- *safelights*
- *framing easel*
- *photographic paper*
- *paper safe*

- *paper cutter or scissors*
- *contact proofer*
- *various dodging and burning-in tools, usually homemade*
- *at least four trays: three for chemistry and one for wash*
- *darkroom tongs*
- *film-processing tank, drum or tabletop processor for color prints, graduates, funnels, and so forth*
- *darkroom chemistry*
- *chemical storage bottles*
- *thermometer*
- *print washer or siphon*
- *print drying rack or clothesline*

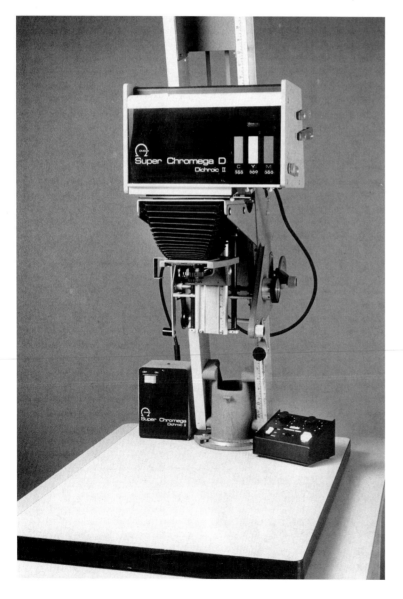

should produce sharp detail all the way from the center to the edge of the print. Enlarging lenses come in a variety of focal lengths designed to match various negative formats. Generally an enlarging lens will have the same focal length as the camera's normal lens. For example, the normal lens of a 35mm camera has a focal length of 50mm; the enlarging lens that is normally used for negatives produced by 35mm cameras also has a focal length of 50mm. Most enlargers provide a means for changing the lenses for greater flexibility.

The entire system of condenser and optical lenses, including adjustment mechanisms, is known as the **enlarger optical system**. The enlarger is used commonly with adjunct equipment, including an **enlarger timer** and a **printing easel**. The timer precisely times exposures to the nearest second, automatically turning off the source light after the selected interval. The easel holds the printing paper flat and in proper position during exposure.

Figure 6-44. An enlarger equipped with a color head. Varying strengths of cyan, yellow, and magenta filters can be dialed in or out easily.

The Contact Printer and Contact Proofer

A **contact printer** is a simple piece of equipment, usually a light-tight box containing a light source, built with one or more glass walls. A clamp tightly sandwiches the negative between the contact paper and the glass wall. A built-in timer controls the contact exposures. Like enlargers, contact printers should provide even illumination, with no "hot spots" or "cold spots." Because today some enlargement is required even to produce album-size prints from small-format negatives, contact printers have fallen out of common use. Contact proof sheets and contact prints are now generally made using the enlarger as a source light. Contact proofers, or contact printing frames, allow the negatives from an entire roll of film and a sheet of photo paper to be pressed together against a sheet of glass. (See Objective 6-B page 194.)

Print Drying Equipment

A rubber squeegee or a clean photographic sponge will remove most of the surface moisture from a well-washed print. Resin-coated prints can then be dried on a simple clothesline hung along one darkroom wall. Fiber-based prints are best air dried on **print drying racks**. Such racks can be economically built by stretching fiberglass window screening over a wooden frame. Several frames of the same size should be built at one time; they will later be stacked for use. If greater drying speed is required, a heated dryer may be used. Hot air dryers are available that quickly and automatically dry RC prints. Heated drum-type models are available for fiber-based photo paper.

Questions to Consider

1. Compare the methods used for controlling exposure in the camera to those used in photographic printing. How are they similar?

2. What is the main physical difference between RC and fiber-based photo paper? How do the processing procedures differ?

3. What are the differences in both exposure and processing between making black-and-white vs. color prints?

4. Why are contact sheets made?

5. If raising the enlarger head reduces the intensity of illumination received by the photographic paper, how would the exposure of a large print differ from that of a small one? What controls could be changed to provide the proper exposure?

6. What factors should be considered when selecting a black-and-white enlarging paper? A color printing paper?

7. Describe several methods for controlling print contrast. Describe how and why to determine a standard filter pack for making color prints.

8. How are burning-in and dodging accomplished? Which one is done during the main exposure? In what ways do dodging and burning-in differ between black-and-white vs. color printing?

9. How could split-filter printing be used with a typical landscape photograph?

10. If you were given the opportunity to design a darkroom, what size and layout would you select? How would it be equipped?

Suggested Field and Laboratory Assignments

For each of the following assignments, include either black-and-white or color printing, or both, for practice.

1. Complete your acquisition and preparation of all print-processing supplies, including developer, stop bath, fixer, clearing agent, paper, and so forth. Complete arrangements for the use of a darkroom for printing, including processing trays or tube, enlarger, safelights, and facilities for processing, washing, drying, and finishing.

2. Using the negatives and/or transparencies you produced in Unit 5, make a contact proof sheet that shows the detail in most images on the roll.

3. Carefully examine your contact sheet using a magnifying glass or loupe. Study the sheet for images that have good composition and expression. Mark frames you would like to print with a grease pencil on the proof sheet. Make additional marks or other notes on the sheet to indicate cropping or other printing manipulations.

4. Select an image from your first roll for enlargement. Set up for enlarging. Determine exposure using the test strip method. Use both the fixed and proportional increment methods.

5. Using resin-coated paper, make an 8in x 10in (20cm x 25cm) enlargement of the negative selected. Make additional prints to achieve optimal density and contrast.

6. Make at least one print on glossy paper. Make at least one other print using matte or other non-glossy paper. Compare the tonal range, sharpness, rendering of fine detail, and handling characteristics of the two prints.

7. Print the same image with at least three different contrast renditions. Change contrast grades or contrast filters to make one print with high contrast, one with low contrast, and one with moderate contrast. Experiment with various exposure times until you have a set of prints with matching highlight densities. Compare the prints. Is there a difference in the quality and interpretation of the information in the photograph? Does the viewer's emotional response to the image change?

8. Use at least one of the common printing controls—cropping, burning-in, and dodging— to refine an enlargement.

9. Experiment with one of the special printing processes such as split-filter printing, black line border, or the Sabattier effect.

10. Make two prints of the same negative, one on resin-coated (RC) photo paper and the second on fiber-based paper. Work carefully and experiment until you have two prints that match in densities and contrast. Compare the two images for tonal beauty, richness, and feeling of spatial depth.

11. Try an experiment in toning prints. Purchase a small package of sepia toner and follow the directions on the package for mixing and use. Work only in a well-ventilated area. Compare several toned prints to untoned prints.

12. Make a color print from a color negative. Experiment with dodging and burning-in to modify the color balance and densities in several areas of the print.

Basic Digital
Image Processing

Digital image processing can replace many traditional darkroom functions and offers exciting new options for creativity. The modern computers, software, and color printers found in many households are capable of quickly and easily producing prints of amazing quality. Image processing software, like Adobe's powerful Photoshop, lets users correct and modify photographs on a computer monitor and provides precise control over the final output to a computer monitor or to a printer.

This unit is organized around a typical workflow for digital photographers: image acquisition, basic corrections and manipulations, and final output. The theories and processes for working with digital images are described. Step-by-step instructions are also presented to guide you through the basic use of photo-editing software.

The objectives are illustrated with step-by-step procedures and screenshots taken from Adobe® Photoshop®. This photo-editing computer program is used by most schools and has become a professional standard. Most other photo-editing software packages on the market use similar tools and procedures.

This unit assumes at least entry-level computer skills. The user should be able to turn the computer on and off, install application software, save, delete, find, copy, and move files, use a keyboard, mouse, and printer, and perform other related tasks.

Digital Images

Objective 7-A Describe a digital image, how it differs from a continuous tone photograph, and how it is stored in an electronic file.

Key Concepts bit-mapped graphics, raster graphics, vector graphics, picture elements, pixels, binary digits, bits, file format, secondary memory

The differences between a continuous tone photographic image and a digital image are profound. Even though the results may appear alike to the naked eye, the way the images are formed, processed, and stored are very different. You may recall that after photography was invented nearly 50 years passed before photographs could be printed with ink on paper. That was because, until the invention of the halftone process, it was not possible to print the full range of gray tones that lay between the paper base color and the color of the ink.

First Steps

The invention of the halftone set forth a principle that not only made possible the printing of photographs, but also provided a theoretical basis for digital imaging technology that was to follow a century later. The halftone process provided a means for breaking down a continuous tone image into a pattern of small dots of varying sizes on a printing plate, each dot sized in such a way as to carry more or less ink during printing. Thus, each dot in the halftone plate carried the information needed to print a darkness value of a single point in the image. Taken together, all the dots, with their various darkness values, created an overall pattern that represented the original, continuous tone image.

The Digital Image

Thinking of that halftone plate as a file of data is a starting point for understanding a digital image. One important difference, of course, is that the dots are stored in a computer instead of in a metal printing plate. Two basic technologies are used to store, process, display, and print graphic images electronically—**bit-mapped** or **raster graphics** and **vector graphics**. In bit-mapped graphics, the image is composed of patterns of dots called **picture elements** or **pixels** that are conceptually similar to halftone dots. Bit-mapped graphics are most useful for representing photographic images. In vector graphics, the image is composed of lines, points, and geometric shapes that are most useful for drawing and painting tasks.

The dots, or pixels, are typically arranged on the computer screen in 1,024 rows and 1,280 columns—about 1.3 million of them. Many monitors are capable of even more. Each color pixel on the monitor is assigned an address that denotes the exact row and column of its position on the screen grid.

Bit-mapped graphic images, displayed as dot patterns, are created by digital cameras, fax machines, scanners, graphics software, and screen capture programs. The term bit-mapped refers to the fact that the image is projected, or mapped, onto the screen based on numerical codes made up solely of the digits 1 and 0, or **binary digits**, called **bits** for short. These binary coded data determine which color pixels are activated and their brightness values. Taken together, all the activated pixels, with their different colors and brightness values, create an overall pattern that represents the original, continuous tone, color image.

File Formats

As described in Objective 4-G, pages 156–157, a **file format** is a set of rules that specify how the data in a file are organized. Because many bits are needed to activate each pixel correctly and there are so many pixels to activate, bit-mapped graphic image files contain enormous amounts of data and tend to be quite large. As a consequence, in order to reduce the size of the files, many compression techniques have been developed, resulting in numerous file formats, each with different characteristics. The format of a file is noted by its filename extension—the characters after the dot that follows the filename—mydog.*tif* or mydog.*jpg*, for example. Some of the more common file formats are described in the Pix Tips *File Formats in Photoshop* on page 253.

Digital image files are stored in the **secondary memory** of a computer or digital camera. Secondary memory refers to the storage media used by the device, such as the floppy disks, hard disks, and CD avd DVD disks used by computers, or the memory cards, memory sticks, and miniature CDs, CD-Rs, and hard-drives found in digital cameras. When processed, these image files can be translated by computer programs into images that can be output to a printer to produce hard copy, to a computer monitor for viewing, or to a file that can be distributed on the Internet by e-mail or on the World Wide Web.

Image Acquisition

Objective 7-B Explain and demonstrate the process of scanning an image to a digital file. Describe other methods of digital image acquisition.

Key Concepts digitizing, USB, Firewire, SCSI, protocol, TWAIN, dots-per-inch (dpi), flatbed scanner, scanogram, transparency adapter, film scanner, drum scanner, photo multiplier tubes (PMT), pixels per inch (ppi), TIFF, PSD, JPEG, PhotoCD, frame grabber, still mode, service bureau

A computer is a machine capable only of storing, retrieving, and processing binary coded data. That means that information, including all text, images, and sound, must be coded as binary data before a computer can do anything with it. Simply stated, binary coded data is made up solely of binary digits, or bits, each either a 1 or a 0, and all computer data and the instructions for processing those data are coded in this form. The process of digitizing refers to a process whereby text, images, and sounds are coded into binary form. A digital image is a binary coded image that the computer can store, retrieve, and process.

Various methods are available to acquire images and input them into a computer. Digital still cameras, of course, produce files that are already in digital form and simply need to be transferred to the computer. Scanners can be used to copy conventional prints, negatives, or slides in digital form and transfer them to the computer. Service bureaus and many camera stores can also scan images and most labs now offer digital files along with a developed roll of film.

Scanning

The primary method of **digitizing** and loading conventional photographs into the computer is by using a scanner. Three main types of scanners are in common use: flatbed, film, and drum scanners. These devices differ in their capabilities, resolution and price. All need to be connected to the computer in some way, usually by a cable connected to a **USB**, **Firewire**, or **SCSI** port—a type of connection to the computer system. Most scanners use a special language, called a **protocol**, to communicate with the host computer. The protocol that most scanners use for this purpose is called **TWAIN**. The resolution of a scanned image is measured in **dots-per-inch**, or **dpi**.

Desktop Flatbed Scanners

The least expensive and most widely available form of scanning technology is the **flatbed** scanner. This device looks and acts much like a small photocopying machine and many can be purchased for under $100. Flatbed scanners consist of a flat piece of glass onto which a photograph, drawing, or other original image is placed. Typically, a linear digital sensor and light source are mounted on a moveable track under the glass. During scanning, the digital sensor slowly sweeps across the image and the pixel information is captured row-by-row.

The number of pixel sensors in the moving element and how fast it moves across the page determines the resolution of the scanner. For best results, a scanner should be capable of at least 600 dpi optical resolution.

The scanned image can be no better than the original print that is scanned. If the original image is too light or off-color, the scanned image will also possess these characteristics. Because enlarged 35mm color photo prints contain only a limited amount of data, they rarely yield a better image when scanned at more than 300 dpi. For this reason flatbed scanners are useful for digitizing images that will not be greatly enlarged beyond their original size.

Flatbed Scanner as a Camera

A flatbed scanner can also be used much like a camera to create original images. Various objects may be placed on the glass plate and scanned directly, a process that is akin to making a photogram with an enlarger. (See Special Techniques, Photograms, page 228.) This similarity has led to describing the process as making a **scanogram**. As with photograms, experiment—use various backgrounds such as light and dark cloth, crumpled paper, or aluminum foil. Try placing the three-dimensional objects at various angles and on their different sides to yield distinctive shadows and patterns. Try positioning a very bright desk lamp at the side of the scanner to supplement the scanner's own bulb.

Transparency Adapters

Some flatbed scanners have an accessory called a **transparency adapter** for scanning slides and other transparent materials. Light from a source in the lid passes through the transparent image to the digital sensor. This method of scanning is best used with larger format images that will not be greatly enlarged for printing. Although some flatbed scanners lack the resolution required to enlarge 35mm images for printing, these images may be satisfactory for display on the World Wide Web.

Film Scanners

A **film scanner** provides a better method of digitizing existing photographs. About the size of a shoebox, a film scanner connects to the computer and uses high-resolution digital sensors to capture the pixel information as the film is inserted into it. Film scanners are more expensive than flatbed scanners and range in price from about $200 to several thousand dollars.

These devices, sometimes called slide scanners, can be used with any kind of photographic film—color negatives, color transparencies, or black-and-white negatives. Working directly from film has two advantages over scanning prints. First, film is the original image source rather than a second-generation copy, as is a print. Also, film has greater tonal range than a print and thus it contains more detail and tonal information. Moreover, film scanners have much higher resolution than flatbeds, some more than 4,000 dpi. Higher resolution is needed because the original images are relatively small and will be substantially enlarged. For example, a scan from a 35mm negative will be enlarged about 8 times to make an 8in x 10in print.

Film scans are usually made at the highest resolution the scanner permits. This creates high-resolution files that can be resized for output without resampling and loss of quality. However, such high resolution scans result in large file sizes that place greater demand upon the computer's storage space and memory. It's not unusual to work with 20–40 MB files and some scanners produce files of up to 130 MB in size—much too large to fit on a floppy disk.

Drum Scanners

Professional trade shops and service bureaus employ sophisticated **drum scanners** to produce color separations for high-end printing. Drum scanners use large, rotating glass cylinders to carry sheets of film or prints past high quality image sensors. Instead of using CCD (Charge Coupled Devices) or CMOS (Complementary Metal Oxide Sensors) technology, drum scanners use three **photo multiplier tubes (PMT)** for greater dynamic range and color accuracy. These scanners cost tens of thousands of dollars and require highly skilled operators. However, they have powerful features not found in desktop scanners and they produce files of extraordinary size and resolution.

Scanner Resolution and Output

To make an effective scan, you must consider the final print size and the requirements of the output device. The scan should generate enough **pixels per inch (ppi)** to produce a quality image at the largest expected print size. The scan may be used to make smaller prints or images later by deleting some pixel data; but once a scan is complete, additional pixel data cannot be added.

Think of scanned images in terms of their pixel dimensions, not in terms of their final print dimensions. Scanned images don't possess dimensions other than their pixel dimensions—making a larger or a smaller print means simply that the pixels are spaced farther apart or closer together. The point is that both a larger print and a smaller one made from the same scan would contain the same total number of pixels and have the same pixel dimensions.

Let's see how this plays out in practice. Scanning a 35mm slide or negative, a typical film scanner set to 2,700 dpi will yield an image measuring 3,888 pixels long × 2,965 pixels wide. To make a print 10 inches long, those 3,888 pixels would be spread over 10 inches. Thus the print would have a resolution of 3,888/10, or about 388 ppi. Here's the formula:

$$\frac{\text{Scan size in pixels on one dimension}}{\text{Output in inches on same dimension}} = \text{output ppi}$$

The resolution from this example, 388 ppi, is more than enough to make a good inkjet or dye sublimation print. However, if only a 5-inch-long print were made, the same number of pixels would be compressed into 5 inches. Thus the resolution would be 3,888/5 = 777 ppi, which is more than most printers can use and might result in longer printing time.

Resolution problems occur when pictures are enlarged too much from their scanned resolution. To illustrate, suppose we took our example and made a print enlarged to 20 inches long. The resolution in this case would be 3,888/20 = 194 ppi, not enough to take advantage of the highest resolution possible with most printers. If printing at this lower resolution does not produce a satisfactory image, it is best to rescan the image at a higher resolution. If this is not possible, however, your photo-editing software might be able to resample the image and interpolate pixel data to simulate a higher resolution. While this may smooth the general appearance of the print, remember that such resampling will not yield additional detail; it merely adds matching pixels in the open spaces between pixels.

We can reverse the above formula to determine the ideal scanning resolution:

$$\frac{\text{Desired output length in inches}}{\text{Length of original in inches}} \times \text{desired output ppi}$$

$$= \text{needed scanner resolution}$$

For example, to scan a 6-inch-long photo that we wish to enlarge to 10 inches long and output to the printer at 300 dpi the formula would be:

$$\frac{10 \text{ inches}}{6 \text{ inches}} \times 300 \text{ ppi printer output} = \text{a scanner resolution of 500 ppi.}$$

Table 7-1 shows the recommended output resolution for various purposes:

Table 7-1. Recommended output resolutions		
Purpose	*Best resolution (ppi)*	*Acceptable resolution (ppi)*
Fujix or similar true photographic printers	400	200
Color reproduction in magazine or book	300	225
Color inkjet printers	300	180
Color laser prints	180	120
Newspapers, newsletters, flyers	180	120
Black-and-white laser printer	120	90
Web and multimedia images	72	72

File Formats for Scanning

As we saw in Unit 4, two approaches to image compression are in common use—lossless and lossy. Lossless compression removes only redundant image data and loses very little image quality; but it produces large files. Lossy compression, on the other hand, removes more image data and often results in reduced image quality; but it produces smaller files.

Scans should be saved in a file format that retains all the captured data. Thus, a lossy file format, such as **JPEG** (Joint Photographic Experts Group) **should not** be used to save an original scan since most scans will undergo further image processing. The two most common lossless file formats used for scanning are **TIFF** (Tagged Image File Format) and **PSD** (Photoshop Default). (See the Pix Tips *File Formats in Photoshop* on page 253.)

As we have noted, lossless compression formats are preferred for scans that will be edited later. Every time a lossy file is opened and resaved, a little more quality is lost. However, storage requirements may mandate smaller files to fit more images in a smaller space. In such cases, a lossy format, such as JPEG, may be the only solution. When using JPEG format, select a compression setting that will yield the highest print quality.

Alternatives to Scanning

Here are some alternatives to scanning to acquire images.

Photo CD Kodak's **Photo CD** process is one useful way to get your photographic images digitized for use with your computer without scanning.

When your film is processed by an authorized Kodak Photo CD lab you'll receive your developed film along with a CD-ROM containing a complete set of high quality digitized images. Each image is stored in six levels of resolution ranging from 128 x 192 pixels to 4,096 x 6,144 pixels. Note that Kodak also offers an alternative, lower resolution product called Picture CD and Picture Disk. The latter is delivered on a standard floppy disk.

Video Frames Video cameras are another source for digital images without scanning. Shots can be extracted directly from videotape using a **frame grabber** installed in your computer. In addition, many digital video cameras provide a **still mode** for taking single frame images. Most digital video cameras also provide for connecting the camera directly to the computer for downloading images. Although video cameras provide an inexpensive way to acquire digital images, their resolution,

Figure 7-2. Kodak Photo CDs are a high quality alternative to film scanners for acquiring digital files. Courtesy © Eastman Kodak Company.

tonal range, and color accuracy do not yet match the quality of a dedicated still digital camera.

Service Bureaus and Other Sources If you don't have access to a scanner you can take your film or prints to a **service bureau** to have scans made. Many camera stores and photocopy houses also offer scanning services at a cost of about $10 per image.

Lastly, it is possible to download digital images from the World Wide Web directly to your computer. These images might be useful for learning your photo-editing program and practicing your editing skills. However, most photos available on the Web, though acceptable for personal use, lack the quality necessary for professional publications. Note also that any public or commercial use of a downloaded image may infringe on the owner's rights and violate copyright laws. Be sure you obtain the owner's permission to use downloaded images in this way.

An Introduction to Photoshop

Objective 7-C Describe the basic tools and functions of image editing, including the steps involved in opening and saving a file, cropping, adjusting brightness, contrast and color, and sharpening a picture.

Key Concepts histogram, input levels, output levels, levels, gamma, color balance/variations, ringaround, saturation, sharpening filter, unsharp mask

Image editing programs are powerful tools for the creative photographer and offer a computerized replacement for nearly all traditional darkroom procedures. Workers can crop, adjust contrast and brightness, retouch flaws, and enlarge their images to any desired size. This section introduces the basic operations of image editing.

There are many fine image-editing software programs on the market. We have chosen to illustrate photo-editing techniques using examples from Adobe's Photoshop program because it is widely used by schools and digital photographers and has become a de facto professional standard. However, if you have another image-editing software package, you will find the basic operations and procedures to be similar.

Although not intended as an exhaustive Photoshop manual, this section will introduce you to the basic operations of the program. You will find that Photoshop is a very powerful program and you may wish to refer to a specialty book for more in-depth coverage, such as McClelland, Deke, *The Photoshop Bible*. Hoboken, NJ. John Wiley & Sons, available for both Windows and Macintosh platforms.

How to Open and Save Image Files

You'll need to open your newly acquired digital image files in the editing program to work on them. Launch Photoshop and perform one of the following:

- Choose the Open command from the File menu. A dialog box will appear that presents a list of files and folders. Point to the selected image file and double click on it.

- For faster file access try the command keyboard shortcut for open. Press Ctrl + O on a PC or ⌘ + O on a Macintosh.

Saving Files

You should develop the habit of saving image files frequently. Until you save a file, all your work since the last save could be lost in the event of a power outage or a computer crash. To protect your work, you should save it frequently. Saving your files to the hard drive during image processing will speed up your work; you can transfer the completed files to a CD, DVD, USB drive, or floppy later.

tips Navigating on the Computer

To navigate between and within programs and to issue commands on a computer requires you to press combinations of keys on the keyboard, and to manipulate a mouse or similar device. Typically you view on the screen a work area, various menus, and a mouse pointer. As you move and manipulate the mouse over a flat surface, the mouse pointer responds with corresponding movement on the screen. As you move the pointer to objects on the screen, you are able to select and execute commands. Here are some of the mouse operations:

- **Point** Move the mouse pointer to point to an object on the screen
- **Click** Tap the left mouse button once lightly
- **Double-click** Tap the left mouse button twice in rapid succession
- **Right-click** Tap the right-hand mouse button once lightly
- **Drag** Press and hold a mouse button down while moving the mouse pointer to another location
- **Drop** After completing a drag operation, release the mouse button.

Famous Photograph

Duane Michals

Duane Michals enjoys the interplay between the surrealistic and the ordinary, and the body of his work elaborates on this theme. His pictures demand involvement by the viewer to understand and experience their meaning. "Nice pictures are not enough," he says, and he studiously creates images that evoke wonder, apprehension, and sometimes fear about the mysteries of life and death.

Michals took up photography more or less by accident. While touring the Soviet Union, he borrowed a camera from a friend to record his journey. He became so captivated by the medium that he soon quit his job as a layout designer and traveled to Paris to study portraiture.

Influenced by the surrealist paintings of Balthus and Magritte, Michals is more concerned with symbolizing the personalities of his subjects and the "drama of the interior world" than with pictures of recognizable objects in recognizable surroundings. He often places his subjects in settings full of odd angles, symbolic objects, strange shafts of light, reflections, and shadows that darkly obscure details. The results are most often surrealistic expressions intended to arouse both awe and anxiety. Michals plans his photographs meticulously in advance and strives to realize a photograph that already exists in his mind. He considers the photographer's work to be 90 percent thought and only 10 percent action and technique.

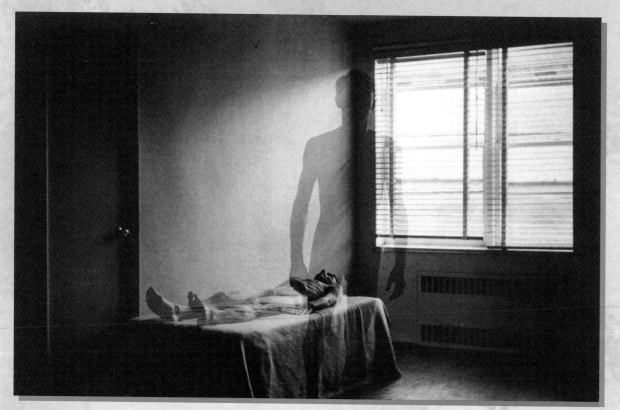

Duane Michals, "The Spirit Leaves the Body," 1969 © Duane Michals.

Always striving for something different, Michals once experimented with sequences of photographs in which each image varied only slightly from its predecessor in order to portray an event more fully. His "sequences" explore the realms of fantasy and the supernatural, often depicting the comings and goings of ghostly figures in very ordinary and realistic settings. Death is one of the recurring themes in his work, represented sometimes as spectral shadows, and sometimes as a simple, ordinary ambience as seen by a phantom spirit.

Cropping Pictures

Many photographs can benefit from judiciously cropping or trimming away unnecessary parts of the image. Cropping can be used to strengthen the composition and simplify the visual statement to add impact.

Basic Adjustments to Brightness and Contrast

Most photo-editing programs, including Photoshop, offer several ways to adjust the brightness and contrast of digital images. Some of these are reminiscent of darkroom adjustments; others offer more sophisticated control over nearly every part of the tonal range.

Auto Contrast Command One of the easiest ways to adjust the tones of your photograph is to use the Auto Contrast **COMMAND–IMAGE — > ADJUST — > AUTO CONTRAST**. As its name implies, this tool will automatically search your image and change the darkest pixel to black, the lightest pixel to white, and expand the mid-tones to fill the tonal range.

Brightness/Contrast Command A second way to adjust the tones of the image is to use the **IMAGE — > ADJUST — > BRIGHTNESS/CONTRAST** command. This command displays a dialog box with two sliders, one for brightness and one for contrast. Using this command is similar to using conventional darkroom technique. Changing the brightness slider is similar to changing the enlarger's exposure; changing the contrast slider is similar to changing paper grades or variable contrast filters. Be sure to check the **PREVIEW** box to see the effect of your adjustments before saving.

The Shadow/Highlight Command Another great tool for making global adjustments to the tonality of images is the Shadow/Highlight command. Go to **IMAGE — > ADJUSTMENTS — > SHADOW/HIGHLIGHTS** to open the dialog box. The box contains two sliders, one for the highlights and one for the shadows. Moving the Shadow slider to the right lightens the darker parts of the image, while moving the bottom slider darkens the highlights. In essence the tool allows the user to automatically burn-in the highlights and dodge the shadows by any selected amounts. This adjustment tool is especially useful to cor-

Figure 7-3. The Auto Contrast dialog box.

Saving Files

1. To save an image for the first time select FILE on the menu bar and select SAVE AS in the dropdown menu. A dialog box will appear. In the FILE NAME box, enter the file name you wish to use. Try to assign a new name to each scan to preserve the original scan as a back up. For example, if you opened a scan file named "Portrait" you might resave it as "Portrait2."

2. In the FORMAT box, select a file format. Point and click on the triangle in the format window and select the desired file format. Photoshop .PSD is the recommended format during editing—it retains all the features of the program.

3. In the SAVE IN box, enter the full path of the disk and folder in which you want to save the file.

4. Now, mouse-click on the SAVE button and you're done.

5. After this initial save, you can resave your work whenever you choose by simply using the SAVE command under the **FILE** menu. Or use just press CTRL + S on a PC or Z + S on a Mac.

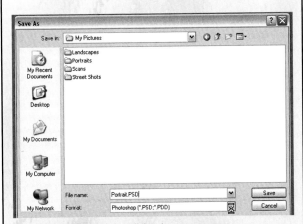

Figure 7-4. The Save-as dialog box.

Cropping

1. *The Photoshop toolbar contains an easy to use cropping tool; it's the third icon down on the left side. (Note: If the toolbar is not visible, click on the Tab button and it will appear.)*

2. *Point and click on the crop tool to engage it. Then move the mouse pointer, now a small cross-hair, to the image you wish to crop. Click and drag the pointer to draw a rectangle around the area of the image you wish to preserve. A dark marquis, or border, should appear around that part of the image that will be cut. When you drop, or release the mouse button, the crop lines remain and are adjustable. To adjust the crop, click, drag and drop one of the small handles that border the crop. If you move the mouse pointer slightly to the outside of a crop line, a double-sided arrow appears. Moving this double-arrow icon tilts the crop lines.*

3. *When the marquis precisely matches the crop you wish to make, point and double-click inside the crop to apply it, or press the keyboard **ENTER** key.*

Figure 7-5.
A) The Crop Tool.
B) The tool in use.

Oops!—Correcting a Mistake

You're bound to make a mistake or two as you work with Photoshop, and one of the first commands you should learn is the **UNDO** command. Select **EDIT** on the menu bar and click **UNDO** at the top of the drop down menu. Or you can use the keyboard command **CTRL + Z** on a PC or z + z on a Mac. The **UNDO** command deletes the previous change.

To eliminate several successive mistakes you can travel back in time with the **HISTORY** palette. Click on **WINDOWS —> SHOW HISTORY** and click on any of the History steps to return to a previous stage.

Figure 7-6. The History window lets you undo mistakes made in the past.

File Formats in Photoshop

Confused by the many file formats you can use to save an image? This Pix Tip shows you the commonly used graphic file formats available in Photoshop.

- **.BMP** (Bitmap) is the most common format used in the Microsoft Windows environment, mostly for wallpaper.
- **.GIF** (Graphics Interchange Format) is a patented format that uses a fixed number of indexed colors. Used in web pages and for downloadable online images.
- **.TIFF** or **.TIF** (Tagged Image File Format) is the industry standard for high-resolution bit-mapped images used for print publishing supported by most scanners, printers, and programs for drawing, image-editing and desktop publishing. Because it supports many color and toning protocols, TIFF is a good choice for saving scans bound for a publishing application.
- **.PCX** was originally introduced for PC Paintbrush on the IBM PC, and is now widely supported by many graphics programs, scanners, and faxes.
- **.PNG** (Portable Network Graphics) is a patent-free replacement for .GIF format.
- **.JPEG** or **.JPG** (Joint Photographic Experts Group) format is highly compressed and widely used for web pages and digital photography.
- **.RAW** is a flexible file format for transferring unprocessed, unconverted image data between applications and computer platforms for later processing and conversion.
- **.PSD** (Photoshop Default) is Photoshop's native format and uses no compression. It is the only format that supports all available image modes—Bitmap, Grayscale, Duotone, Indexed Color, RGB, CMYK, Lab, and Multichannel—and is especially useful for scans that will be edited many times.
- **.EPS** (Encapsulated PostScript) is used mainly for desktop publishing and is a file that contains both the image and instructions to a printer.
- **.PXR** (PIXAR) is designed specifically for use on high-end PIXAR image computers.
- **.SCT** (Scitex Continuous Tone) designed specifically for use on high-end Scitex image computers.
- **.TGA** (Targa) format is designed for systems using the Truevision video board.
- **.PDF** (Portable Document Format) is a cross-platform, cross-application file format based on the PostScript imaging model that accurately displays and preserves fonts, page layouts, and both vector and bitmap graphics.
- **.PCT** or **.PIC** (PICT) is widely used among Mac OS graphics and page-layout applications as an intermediary file format for transferring images between applications.

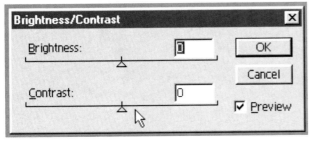

Figure 7-7. Individual sliders control brightness and contrast.

rect underexposed images. As with other tonal adjustment tools the Shadow/Highlight command can be combined with a selection for localized tonal adjustments. When used this way, this tool is especially useful to darken skies in landscape images.

Using Levels The brightness/contrast sliders affect the whole image. If you increase brightness, the entire image is brightened; if you increase contrast, the entire image gets greater contrast.

For more precise tonal control, most photographers use the **Levels** command, which allows individual adjustment of the highlights, midtones, and shadows.

When you open the **IMAGE — > ADJUST — > LEVELS** dialog box, a graph, or **histogram**, of all the image tones appears. From left to right, the histogram's width corresponds to 255 possible brightness levels from black to white. The peaks and valleys of the histogram represent the number of pixels containing those tones. An image with full tonal range will have some tones in every part of the histogram. Controls in the histogram allow you to adjust the distribution of tones in the image to modify the tonal range in the image.

The levels are adjusted either by dragging the **Input Levels** sliders to a desired level or by entering a numeral in the corresponding boxes.

- Adjusting the triangular sliders of the input levels will add contrast to the picture and adjust its brightness.

- Below the histogram is a horizontal bar of various tones called the **Output Levels**. Output levels are used to reduce image contrast by darkening lighter tones and lightening darker ones—bringing the extreme tonal values closer to the middle of the range.

Basic Levels Theory

Input levels are used to darken the darkest colors, lighten the lightest colors and adjust the middle point of an image. The numerical input boxes correspond to slider bars immediately below the histogram. When the left slider is moved, or a number from 0 to 255 is entered in the first option box, the black point is set. For example, if you raise the black value to 65, all colors with a brightness value of 65 or less in the original image will become black.

Similarly, you can map the pixels at the bright end of the scale by dragging the white slider triangle, or by entering a number from 0 to 255 in the far right option box. For example, if the white value were lowered to 220, all colors with brightness of 220 or less would become white.

The middle triangle slider and the middle numerical box adjust **gamma**, or the relative brightness of a middle value in an image. Adjustments to gamma lighten or darken the middle tones of the image without changing the shadows and highlights. The gamma value can range from 0.10 to 9.99 (1.00 is the midpoint.) If you drag the middle slider to the left, or increase the gamma number, you will lighten middle tones; if you move the slider to the right, you will darken them. Usually, you will need to brighten up the midtones of most images.

tips *Keyboard Adjustment of Levels*

When adjusting levels, the position of the triangular sliders can be precisely changed with the up and down arrow keys. Simply point and click on a slider; then each press of an arrow key will change the value by 1. Using SHIFT + an arrow key changes the value in increments of 10.

Figure 7-8. The input-levels command contains three sliding triangles that can be moved to adjust the shadows, midtones and highlights.

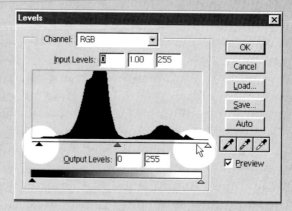

Color Balance Correction

The **color balance** of images from scanners and digital cameras often needs to be adjusted. The image might look too red overall, or perhaps too blue. Of the many techniques that Photoshop offers to adjust color balance, the three used most often are **AUTO COLOR**, **VARIATIONS**, the **COLOR BALANCE** dialog box, and **LEVELS**.

Auto Color The concept of the Auto Color command is similar to that of Photoshop's Auto Contrast command. You invoke this command under the **IMAGE — > ADJUST — > AUTO COLOR** menus. The Auto Color command analyzes the image to identify shadows, midtones, and highlights and adjusts the color balance to achieve neutral midtones, setting the dark and white points ac-cordingly. You must evaluate the results care-fully—you'll find that it works exceedingly well on some images, but that it may introduce unwanted color casts on other images, such as portraits. The command is often worth trying because it is so easy to invoke and so easy to undo if you don't like the results.

Variations The **VARIATIONS** command provides a **ringaround**—a set of images that show the effects of various color adjustments on the image you are adjusting. This tool is similar to the ringaround used in traditional color printing and has the same function. To open the **VARIATIONS** dialog box click to **IMAGE — > ADJUST — > VARIATIONS**. Thumbnail images with various color settings appear as a **ringaround**. Click on

---

Basic Level Adjustments

1. Open the Levels dialog box by IMAGE —> ADJUST —> LEVELS or CONTROL + L on a PC or z + L on a Mac.

2. The standard way to adjust the input histogram is to move the black and white sliders to a position where they begin to intersect a data point above the histogram's baseline. For example, in the histogram in Figure 7-10, you can see that the white slider (the one on the right) is positioned too far to the right to intersect any of the histogram tones. This means that nothing in this image will print as pure white. Normally you want some small part of the picture to be pure white, so move the slider to the left until it intersects the point where the histogram begins (indicated by the arrow in Figure 7-10).

3. Likewise, the black slider should be moved to the right until it just contacts a rise in the histogram.

4. What if the histogram already extends fully into the black or white areas? That means that the image already contains some pure white and pure black. If the histogram in the far left (or far right) is much above the baseline you may not want to move the sliders at all or you'll produce hot spots of dead tone in the image.

5. Set the gamma. Imagine that the middle slider, the gamma, is the fulcrum of a teeter-totter. You want to roughly set it to a point that is the gravitational center of the histogram so that about half of the tonal mass is on either side of the gamma triangle. Fine-tune the gamma adjustment until the midtones of the picture look good to you.

There is an alternate method that can be used to set the white and black points—the eyedropper icons. Select one of three eyedroppers—black, gamma, or white—and click on a pixel in the image window to automatically adjust the brightness of that pixel and all related tones. Note that the eyedropper sample also adjusts color balance in a way that is not suitable for all images.

Hints for Levels

You can apply LEVELS to a selection. Instead of burning or dodging a large area, you can select it and then use LEVELS to make the correction. (You'll learn how to make a selection in Unit 8.)

Output levels are rarely used. Adjusting the output levels reduces the contrast of an image; blacks become dark gray and the whites turn light gray.

Save Levels

The LEVELS dialog box has a SAVE button. If you save a **LEVELS** setting, you can apply it quickly to a new image or selection. This feature is useful if you have many similar images to adjust.

Figure 7-9. The Variations dialog box gives you a visual way to adjust the color balance of an image. (See Color Plate 7 for the original version.)

ADJUST — > COLOR BALANCE, or by pressing **CONTROL + B** on a PC or ⌘ + **B** on a Mac. Three sliders appear that can be set to adjust an image toward any of the three primary colors or their complements. For example, to add red to the image, click and drag the top slider toward Red; to reduce red, toward Cyan. Check the preview box to observe the effect of your adjustments on the image. Check any of the three radio buttons to adjust the shadows, midtones, and highlights separately.

Using Levels to Correct Color
You may use the **LEVELS** command to simultaneously correct an image's color and to adjust its tonal range. Previously, we corrected brightness and contrast by adjusting the red, green and blue (RGB) color channels all at once. However, the **LEVELS** command allows you to adjust each color separately. In the **LEVELS** dialog box is a window labeled **CHANNEL**. You may click the spinner to select the red, green or blue channel separately, or you may navigate with keyboard shortcuts. Check the **PREVIEW** button to see your changes. (See Figure 7-9.)

To select the red channel, press **CONTROL + 1** on a PC or ⌘ + **1** on a Mac. Then click and drag the sliders below the histogram to adjust the color. Repeat these steps for the green channel (**CONTROL + 2** on a PC or ⌘ + **2** on a Mac) and the

any thumbnail image to select a preferred color adjustment. For example, click on the **MORE RED** thumbnail to add red to the image. Click on it again for even more red. To reduce a color, click on the thumbnail of its complementary color. To reduce red, for example, click on the **MORE CYAN** thumbnail. (See Figure 7-9.)

Even more adjustments are available in **VARIATIONS**. For example, you can choose to adjust only the color in the shadows by clicking on the **SHADOWS** radio button. You can adjust only the color in the midtones or the highlights. And you can also set the relative strength of the color variations from fine to coarse.

You may try various color adjustments to see their effects on your image. You can freely experiment because you can return to the original color balance at any time by clicking the thumbnail labeled **ORIGINAL**. When the final color setting is set, click on the OK button to apply the color balance to your image.

The Color Balance Dialog Box Open the **COLOR BALANCE** dialog box by clicking to **IMAGE — >**

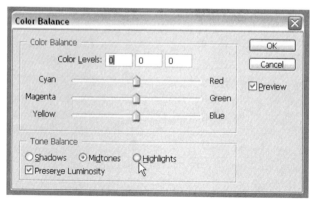

Figure 7-10. The Color Balance dialog box features three sliders that can be set to adjust the color of the shadows, midtones and highlights.

blue channel (**CONTROL + 3** on a PC or ⌘ **+ 3** on a Mac.) When the adjustments are complete, press **OK** to apply the changes.

Photoshop also provides an Auto Levels command that automatically adjusts Levels and simultaneously applies color corrections. Click to **IMAGE — > ADJUST — > AUTO LEVELS** to use this command. Be cautious, however, as this process can introduce too much contrast and unwanted color shifts in some images.

Enhancing Colors with Saturation If the colors in an image are weak, they may be intensified by applying color **saturation**. Click to **IMAGE — > ADJUST — > HUE/SATURATION (CONTROL + U** on a PC or ⌘ **+ U** on a Mac) and adjust the middle saturation slider. You can also adjust the saturation of individual colors by clicking on the **EDIT** window in the dialog box and scrolling to the color you wish to intensify. In this way you could, for example, boost the saturation of the yellows in an image without affecting any other colors.

Avoid oversaturating the colors in an image. This may create artificial colors that can destroy image detail and sharpness. Single digit saturation values are typically the most successful.

Sharpening

Almost all images lose some sharpness when digitized and can benefit from applying a **sharpening filter**. Sharpening creates the appearance of

sharper focus by increasing the contrast between the light and dark edges in an image. The dark side of an edge is made darker; the light side, lighter.

Sharpening should be applied only after all other image adjustments are complete; otherwise, it may introduce unwanted artifacts that are exaggerated with further editing. The degree of sharpening used depends upon the planned output. In general, images that will be displayed on computer monitors can use more sharpening than those that will be printed.

The Sharpen Filters Photoshop provides four sharpen filters—Sharpen, Sharpen Edges, Sharpen More and the Unsharp Mask. These are accessed from the **FILTERS** menu. Click to **FILTERS — > SHARPEN — >** .

- **Sharpen** Click to **FILTERS — > SHARPEN — > SHARPEN** for this filter. The **SHARPEN** filter slightly enhances the overall sharpness of an image. If the image already appears sharp, it may only require this minor adjustment.
- **Sharpen More** Click to **FILTERS — > SHARPEN — > SHARPEN MORE** for this filter. The **SHARPEN MORE** filter enhances the overall sharpness of an image more strongly than the **SHARPEN** filter, but often produces unwanted artifacts. For this reason, it is rarely used.

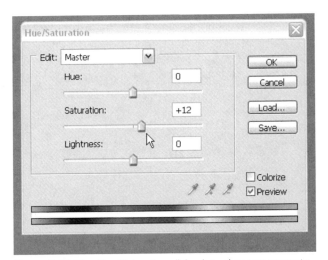

Figure 7-11. The Hue/Saturation dialog box gives you a way to adjust the saturation of all colors when set to "Master" as shown here, or to selectively enhance an individual hue such as all Reds.

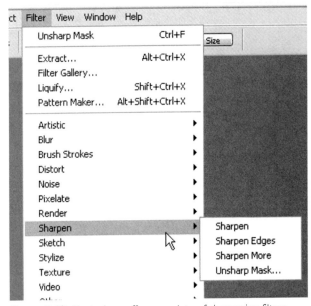

Figure 7-12. Photoshop offers a variety of sharpening filters, each creates a slightly different effect and has different applications.

Setting the Unsharp Mask

1. *Open the Unsharp Mask filter by selecting FILTERS —> SHARPEN —> UNSHARP MASK. The UNSHARP MASK dialog box contains adjustment sliders for three controls: Amount, Radius, and Threshold.*

   ■ ***Amount:*** *Change the Amount slider from 1 to 500% to control the degree of sharpening. Try an initial setting of 80%; values between 25–150% will provide moderate sharpening.*

   ■ ***Radius:*** *Change the radius slider to control the width of an edge rim between two tones. Higher values produce thicker, more contrasty edges that may appear as faint halos. A good starting point for determining the radius setting is to divide the ppi resolution of the image file by 150. Table 7-2 is derived from this formula.*

Table 7-2. Setting the radius in the unsharp mask	
Image resolution in ppi	Recommended Radius Setting
100	0.66
200	1.3
300	2
400	2.6

You can quickly check your resolution setting by clicking to IMAGE —> IMAGE SIZE

   ■ ***Threshold:*** *Change the Threshold slider to control how much two pixels must differ before they trigger sharpening action. The usual range for this setting is 0–10. Try starting with a Threshold setting of 1. Very low numbers tend to sharpen all parts of the image, but may induce unwanted sharpening of soft edges; higher settings limit sharpening to the more pronounced, higher contrast edges. For example, somewhat higher Threshold settings reduce the skin imperfections and graininess that may appear when skin texture is sharpened too much.*

2. *Start your Unsharp Mask experiments with settings derived from the above steps or copied from Figure 7-13.*

3. *Note the preview window inside the dialog box. From the image inside this window, click and drag a detail into view, such as a face. Click the + and − buttons to set the magnification to 100%. As you adjust the Amount and Threshold sliders, you will see the image appear more grainy and mottled. Reverse the adjustment slightly to just below the first appearance of graininess.*

4. *By clicking within the preview window, you can revert the image to its previous state to compare it with the effects of the filter. Try to obtain a slight increase in sharpness without graininess.*

5. *Click on **OK** to apply the setting to the image. To obtain more sharpening, apply the filter a second time by pressing **CONTROL + F** on a PC or **Z + F** on a Mac. Applying slight sharpening several times is often preferable to trying to achieve optimal sharpening in one pass.*

Note: Amount, Radius, and Threshold can be balanced in many different ways to obtain similar results. You may try the settings described in Figure 7-13 as a starting point. Try to develop an approach to these settings that produces consistently satisfying results.

■ **Sharpen Edges** Click to **FILTERS —> SHARPEN —> SHARPEN EDGES** for this filter. The **SHARPEN EDGES** filter sharpens only the outline edges of adjacent areas where appreciably different colors or tones meet. This filter is mainly used to sharpen drawings and illustration graphics.

■ **Unsharp Mask** Click to Filters **SHARPEN —> UNSHARP MASK** for this filter. The **UNSHARP MASK** filter replicates a darkroom technique by which an unsharp film negative is printed in registration with a color slide to enhance edges in the image. This gives an impression of greater focus. Not only does the **UNSHARP MASK** filter provide you control over the degree of sharpening but also allows you to choose whether to sharpen all details in an image or just the edges.

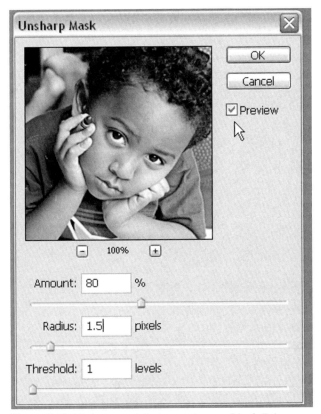

Figure 7-13. Unsharp mask is the most powerful of all the sharpening tools. Use the settings shown as a starting point.

Printing Digital Images

Objective 7-D Describe and demonstrate the process of printing a hard copy of a digital image file.

Key Concepts inkjet, dithering, CMYK, dye-sublimation, laser, photographic, dot-gain, dots per inch (dpi), resampling, downsampling

Consumer-grade computer printers have become capable of printing images that rival conventional photographs. Some advanced printers using six or more ink colors have closely matched the detail and color of traditional photographic prints. This objective describes the characteristics of various printers, criteria for selecting paper, and printing techniques.

Types of Printers

Four types of printers are in common use: inkjet, dye-sublimation, laser, and photographic. The printers vary in the quality of their output, their operating costs, and their initial purchase prices.

Inkjet **Inkjet** printers are the most popular method for reproducing color images because they offer a blend of high quality and low price. An inkjet printer works by spraying tiny drops of colored ink or pigment onto paper. The resulting image gives the illusion of continuous tones by using ink drops of many sizes to create tiny dots of various colors. Large dots of color produce darker colors; smaller dots—up to 120 dots per millimeter—produce lighter ones.

This process, called **dithering**, is similar to the halftone process. Both processes provide a means for breaking down a continuous tone image into a pattern of small dots of varying sizes, each dot sized so as to carry more or less ink during printing. Taken together, all the dots, with their various darkness and color values, create an overall pattern that represents the original, continuous-tone image.

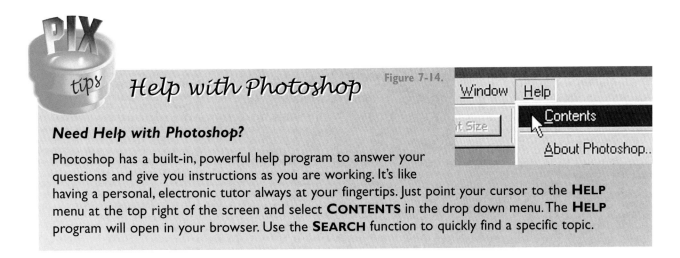

PIX tips *Help with Photoshop* Figure 7-14.

Need Help with Photoshop?

Photoshop has a built-in, powerful help program to answer your questions and give you instructions as you are working. It's like having a personal, electronic tutor always at your fingertips. Just point your cursor to the **HELP** menu at the top right of the screen and select **CONTENTS** in the drop down menu. The **HELP** program will open in your browser. Use the **SEARCH** function to quickly find a specific topic.

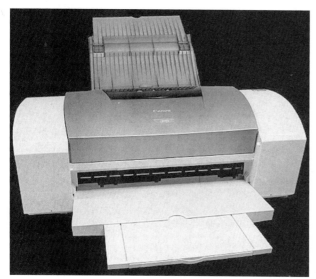

Figure 7-15. Some inkjet printers are designed specially to reproduce photos and can output images indistinguishable from conventional photographs.

Inkjet printers reproduce color images by using four different print heads, one each firing cyan, magenta, yellow, and black ink—designated as a **CMYK** process. When mixed in various proportions, these four colors produce a full-color scene. Some newer inkjets use up to seven ink colors to create smoother tones that reduce dot visibility. Even when viewed close up, the images produced by these photo-quality inkjets are nearly indistinguishable from conventional photographs.

To use an inkjet printer effectively, carefully match it to an appropriate paper. (See Paper Selection on page 261.) Note that ink jet printers, while enjoying an advantage of low purchase price and high-quality output, suffer from high operating costs. The cost of ink, for example, can run to $1 per page when the printer is set to its highest quality.

Dye-sublimation printers, dye-sub for short, produce continuous-tone images by applying heat to transfer colors from a film ribbon onto special coated paper. Each image has to pass through the printer four times, one pass for each primary color—cyan, magenta, and yellow, plus a clear coat. Unlike inkjets, dye-sublimation printers produce continuous-tone images with no visible dots. This makes dye-subs especially suitable for producing high-quality photographic prints with fine gradations of tones. Good dye-sublimation printers are generally

about double the price of inkjet printers. Their operating costs are high—a letter-size print can cost over $4.

Laser or electrophotographic printers operate on the same basic principles as xerographic photocopy machines. The action of light falling on a photosensitive drum removes a portion of the drum's negative charge in a pattern of the image. Extremely fine toner particles adhere to the remaining negatively charged areas as the drum rotates and are then fused by heat onto a sheet of paper. This creates the image. Color laser printers work by the same principle, except that they use four separate color toners—cyan, magenta, yellow, and black—during four separate rotations of the drum or, sometimes by using four different drums.

Color laser printers are expensive but feature relatively low operating costs and faster printing than inkjets. They are most suitable for reproducing lines and large areas of pure tone. Thus, they are quite suitable for large volume use in businesses and schools for printing charts, graphs, and line drawings. However, for photographic applications, color laser printers lack the clarity and contrast produced by inkjet printers on photo quality paper.

Photographic printers actually expose photographic paper to image bearing light produced by a computer and chemically process the exposed paper inside the printer. They use a near-dry process that requires only about 1 ml of distilled water per print and produce exceptional prints that look exactly like conventional color photographs. They are high-end, very expensive printers used primarily by service bureaus and photo labs.

The Fujix Pictography printers are the best known of this type. They offer the ultimate in quality, but have purchase prices in the range of $7,000 to $20,000. Their operating costs are similarly high at around $10 per print. Many photographers have Fujix prints made from their digital files for their portfolio images.

Paper Selection

To produce high-quality, near-photographic prints from an inkjet printer, it is important to select the

TECHNICAL FEATURE
Digital Imaging in News Reporting

Equipped with a digital camera that resembles a 35mm camera of the late 1990s, a photojournalist is covering the aftermath of an earthquake seventy-five miles away from his paper's San Francisco newsroom. Rescue workers search carefully for survivors amid the crumpled ruins while nearby firefighters attempt to control a burning home. The photographer captures these and other dramatic scenes on a miniature computer hard-drive inside the camera.

After making several images, the photographer pauses to review the pictures on a small display monitor and finds several newsworthy shots. One shows the daring rescue of a small boy by an exhausted fireman. The deadline for the next edition is only minutes away, but the picture can make the deadline easily—the photographer need not drive back to the office nor develop and print the film. Instead, he returns to the car where the pictures are transmitted in electronic form over a cellular telephone directly to the newsroom.

When the pictures are received, the photo editor displays the transmitted pictures on a desktop computer screen. With only a few clicks of the mouse button, she makes corrections in the densities and colors. After a quick phone conversation with the photographer in the field, the editor selects the final images and transmits digital copies to the Associated Press by fiber-optic lines. The news agency then distributes the pictures via their digital PhotoStream transmission service to newspapers around the world.

Once the computer file containing the earthquake coverage is selected for publication, it is transferred electronically to the editor who lays out the front page on a pagination terminal. Here, the color pictures are cropped, sized, and positioned on the page along with the story, which has also been transmitted electronically from a reporter at the scene. Within moments of the original event, the images and the story are on presses around the world.

right paper. Plain bond paper may be suitable for printing text documents, drawings, charts, and graphs, and for printing rough drafts, but it is not suitable for producing high quality photographic prints. The fibers in ordinary bond paper allow the individual ink drops to spread within the paper. This phenomenon, called **dot-gain**, slightly blurs the image and reduces detail. Regular bond papers typically produce prints with flat highlights, muddy blacks, uneven skin tones and dull colors.

For maximum resolution and color purity, glossy or matte photo papers especially designed for pho-

Making the Final Print

1. *Be sure that you save the image file before printing.*

2. *Click to IMAGE —> MODE —> RGB COLOR to select RGB Color. Most inkjet and other printers are designed to print red, green, and blue (RGB) file colors although they actually apply cyan, magenta, yellow and black inks to the page. Even black and white or grayscale images print best in RGB Color mode.*

3. *Click to FILE —> PRINT OPTIONS or press ALT + CTRL + P on a PC or ⌘ + OPTION + P on a Mac to preview the print. To print the image in the middle of the page, check the SHOW BOUNDING box and check the CENTER IMAGE box. If the CENTER IMAGE box is unchecked, the thumbnail image can be dragged to a new position on the page. Note: If you change the values in the SCALED PRINT SIZE box, the print will be produced from a resampled image. (See Figure 7-16.)*

4. *Click PAGE SETUP as needed to change paper type, page orientation, and output resolution of the printer.*

5. *Click PRINT to immediately make the print or select OK to save the setup and print later. To make subsequent prints, click to FILE —> PRINT or press CTRL + P on a PC or ⌘ + P on a Mac and click OK.*

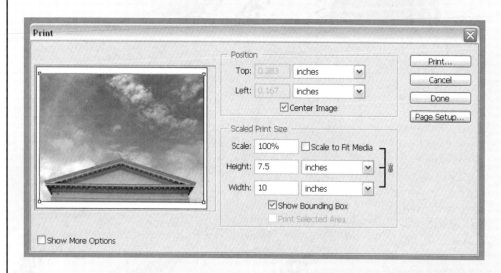

Figure 7-16. The new print Options dialog box shows a preview of the final page.

tographic prints work much better. A side-by-side comparison of a print made on plain office bond paper with one made on the highest quality photo paper will make the difference obvious. One simple way to upgrade print quality significantly is to feed the printer high quality paper.

Each printer manufacturer uses different dyes or pigments in their inks. Thus, the best results are usually produced using a paper stock sold by the printer's manufacturer. Most manufacturers offer three grades of paper for different applications:

- Inkjet paper—a high quality bond paper with a smooth coating that reduces dot-gain and increases contrast. This is the entry-level paper for photo printing and the least costly.

- Photo paper—a heavier weight, glossy-finish paper designed for photographic reproduc-

tion. Although more expensive, when used with modern printers it produces prints that look and feel like conventional photographs.

- Premium glossy photo paper—slightly heavier weight and brighter white than photo paper, its main advantage is a print with better archival qualities that will last longer and resist color shifts and fading. These are the most expensive papers.

Paper choices are not limited to only a few, however. Use your imagination and experiment with other paper stocks as many digital photographers do. Interesting results may be obtained with inkjet printers by trying papers such as *Arches, Rives BFK,* watercolor papers, handmade Japanese rice papers, or brown craft paper. Because they can be adjusted to different paper thickness, Epson inkjet printers are especially adaptable to paper experiments. Epson printers also provide for precise control of the amount and color of ink.

Inkjet printers can also be used to produce output for window decals, bumper stickers, adhesive sheets, back-light film, and canvas cloth. There is even an iron-off paper for transferring inkjet prints to fabric, such as a T-shirt.

Ink Types and Image Longevity

Typical inkjet prints have a life expectancy much shorter than that of conventional photographic prints. In general, inkjet manufacturers use one of two different ink technologies—dyes and pigments.

Most general use inkjet printers use dyes to generate their images. Dyes are capable of producing highly saturated colors and a wide range of tones. Unfortunately, dyes are not very stable and may fade when exposed to light. Indeed, prints from some dye-based printers may exhibit noticeable fading after only a few days exposed to bright sunlight.

Some manufacturers offer special photographic inkjet printers that use inks containing pigments to improve longevity. Pigments are much more resistant to fading than dyes; they can produce prints that last as long as conventional photographs when used with the proper papers.

Some printers can be fitted with after-market inks or volume ink supply systems that allow the use of either dye or pigment inks.

Adjusting Image Size and Resolution for Printing

Image size and resolution strongly affect print quality and must be carefully set for optimal results. Here are some points to consider.

- Within image editing programs such as Photoshop, image resolution is measured in ppi or pixels per inch. Image resolution of 200 ppi is sufficient for most inkjet and laser printers. However, 300 to 400 ppi files will produce somewhat better impressions with photo-quality inkjet and other printers.

- Printer resolutions, on the other hand, are often measured in **dpi** or **dots per inch**. Dpi is unrelated to ppi because inkjet printers lay down 1 to 10 ink dots for each pixel. Moreover, the printer's dpi is not set within the image-editing software and has no effect on file size or pixel resolution. Dots per inch is strictly a measure of the printer's output quality. It is set within the printer's driver program—usually to the printer's maximum dpi for the type of paper being used.

- Image size, expressed in terms of the number of pixels that make up the image, and print size, expressed in terms of the dimensions of the printed image, are interrelated. Making a larger print produces one of two results:

  1) The same number of pixels is spread over a larger print area resulting in reduced resolution.

  2) New pixels are created by the image-editing software to fill the gaps between pixels. This also results in reduced resolution although the image appears smoother. The process is called **resampling**.

Making a smaller print also produces one of two results:

1) The same number of pixels are forced to occupy a smaller print area resulting in increased resolution.

2) Some pixels are eliminated by the image-editing software, opening up the spaces between pixels. This retains the original ppi resolution. This process is called **downsampling**. In general downsampling is unnecessary; extra pixels in the image do not harm the printed output and improves the resolution of larger prints that you may wish to make later.

To calculate the largest print size at a desired ppi resolution, divide the image's pixel count along one dimension by the desired print ppi on the same dimension. The result will be the print's length or width in inches.

Here's an example. A typical film scanner might produce an image from a 35mm slide that measures 3,000 pixels long x 2,100 pixels wide. To make a print that with a resolution of 300 ppi, divide the length of 3,000 pixels by 300. The result shows that a print 10 inches long can be made at that resolution. Here's the formula:

Adjusting Image Size

Keep the points discussed in Adjusting Image Size and Resolution for Printing, page 263, in mind as you proceed.

Select IMAGE —> IMAGE SIZE and the dialog box shown in Figure 7-17 will appear.

1. *Make sure that there is **NO** check in the box labeled **RESAMPLE IMAGE**, and that the **CONSTRAIN PROPORTIONS** box is checked.*

2. *Enter the desired width or height in the appropriate box; the other dimension will appear automatically.*

3. *Note the new resolution expressed in pixels/inch. If it is appropriate to your output device, click **OK** and you are done. If the resolution in pixels/inch is less than desired, make a trial print to see if it is acceptable or resample as described in Step 4. If the resolution in pixels/inch is higher than desired, either leave it alone, or downsample as described in Step 4 to create a smaller file.*

4. *To raise or lower the resolution in pixels/inch, the software must resample the file to adjust to the new setting. Check the **RESAMPLE IMAGE** box and select **BICUBIC** from the scroll-down window. Enter the desired figure in the **RESOLUTION** box, and click **OK**. Photoshop will calculate and adjust the file to the new setting.*

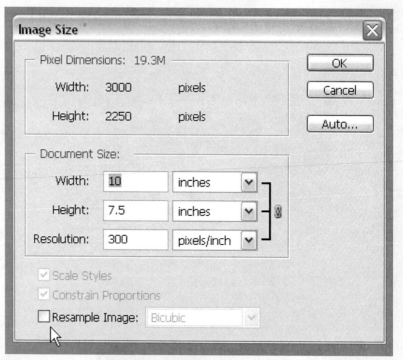

Figure 7-17. The Image Size dialog box provides control over the image dimensions, resolution and file size.

*Note: You will not see any apparent change to the monitor's image if you successfully adjusted the image size and didn't need to resample. This is normal, for you still have the same number of pixels in the display. Selecting **VIEW —> SHOW RULERS** will show that the new dimensions have been applied.*

$$\frac{\text{image size in pixels on one dimension}}{\text{desired output ppi}}$$

$$= \text{maximum output in inches on same dimension}$$

What can you do if you don't have enough pixels to yield both the desired resolution and the desired image size? Usually, it is best to choose between a smaller, higher quality print, and lowering the print ppi to see if it produces an acceptable print. A third option, less desirable but sometimes necessary, is to resample, allowing the image-editing software to interpolate the missing pixels.

Page Setup and Printing

Printer Resolution Many inkjet and other printers have controls to adjust the output resolution as measured in dpi. Higher dpi settings produce better prints but consume more ink, take longer to print, and normally require special papers. In general, photographers prefer to print at the highest dpi setting available for a particular paper stock. For example, many Epson printers can be set to 2,880 dpi with premium glossy photo paper, but can only be set to 720 dpi with regular inkjet paper. For best results use the printer's special photo papers and set the printer to the maximum dpi setting for that paper.

Step by Step — Preparing Images for Screen Viewing

1. *Open the image you want to email or use on a web site.*

2. *Select **IMAGE ––> IMAGE SIZE** and the Image Size dialog box will appear. See Figure 7-18.*

3. *Make sure there is a check mark in all three boxes at the bottom of the interface; Scale Styles, Constrain Proportions and Resample Image.*

4. *Enter the desired **HEIGHT** and **WIDTH** in the **DOCUMENT SIZE** area of the dialog box. (For example, to email a photo to a friend you might select a width of 5 inches. Since **CONSTRAINED PROPORTIONS** is checked, the new height will automatically appear once the width value is entered.)*

5. *Adjust the resolution to a setting of 72 ppi. Then click on the **OK** button.*

6. *Now go to **FILE ––> SAVE AS** and select an appropriate location and filename for saving the image. Also from the **SAVE AS** dialog box select the **JPEG** file format.*

7. *You will now be presented with the JPEG Options dialog box. See Figure 7-19.*

8. *Adjust the **QUALITY** slider to the left or right to set the desired compression. Lower quality setting numbers will make smaller files. Setting the quality to **3** or **4** is usually sufficient for web and e-mail use. Note that as you adjust the quality level the expected new file size and download time will be estimated at the bottom of the dialog box.*

9. *Under **FORMAT OPTIONS** some workers like to select **PROGRESSIVE**, which will download the image in waves of increasing resolution and appease impatient recipients.*

10. *The image is now ready to email or insert into a web page.*

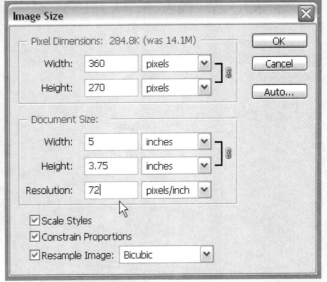

Figure 7-18. Image Size Dialog Box for Web.

Figure 7-19. JPEG Options Dialog Box for Web.

Adjusting Image Size and Resolution for Email and Web Use

If you attach a high-resolution image directly from a scanner or digital camera to an email, its large file size may require a long download time and may overload your receiver's email box. If you intend an image to be viewed on a computer monitor, you do not need high resolutions. No matter how high the resolution of the recorded image, most monitors will limit the display reso-

lution to 72 ppi. Thus, the smaller file size of low-resolution images will transmit and download faster and will display just as well.

You may record low-resolution images in most digital cameras and scan low-resolution images with most scanners, then save them in a highly compressed jpeg format. The step-by-step box above will walk you through the process of preparing images for email transmission or web use.

Questions to Consider

1.   What are the three main types of scanners? How can digital image files be acquired without a scanner?

2.   What are the advantages and disadvantages of the different file types? Which would be most suitable to use if disk space is limited? Which would be best for an image you plan to work on again?

3.   What is the method that provides the most precise way to adjust brightness and contrast?

4.   What methods can be used to sharpen an image?

5.   How do you determine the largest print size that you can make from a file at a given resolution?

Suggested Field and Laboratory Assignments

1.   Make a scanogram. Use a flatbed scanner and a variety of two- and three-dimensional objects that will form interesting patterns and shapes. Use a clear acetate sheet to protect the scanner's glass from scratches.

2.   Experiment with several methods for adjusting brightness, contrast, and color balance. Which one do you prefer? Which one allows separate control of highlights and shadows?

3.   What are the advantages and disadvantages of the four main printer types?

4.   Print the same image file on three different paper stocks—plain office bond, photo paper, and premium glossy photo paper. Compare the results.

5.   Make one print from an image file that has not been sharpened and another print with unsharp mask applied. What differences can you see?

Color Plates

1A.

Courtesy © Eastman Kodak Company.

1B.

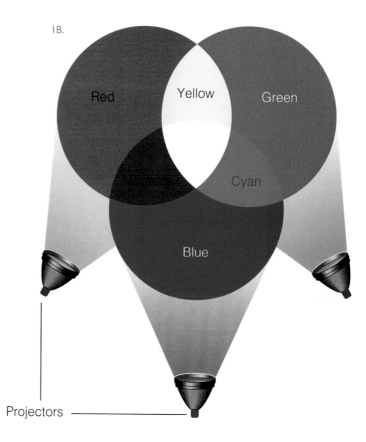

Projectors

1C.

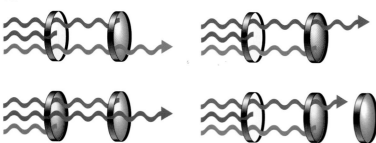

Filters

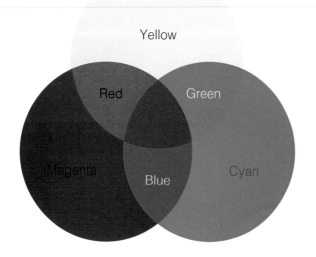

Figure 1. Color theory. A) Color wheel. Twelve arbitrary hues from visible light spectrum, including primary colors—red, blue, green—and their complements—cyan, yellow, magenta—respectively. Complements appear opposite primaries. Courtesy © Eastman Kodak Company. B) Additive color mixing. When pure monochromatic, primary colors of light are projected onto a white screen from two or more projectors, the overlapping areas produce the secondary colors. Where all three overlap, white is produced. C) Subtractive color mixing. When white light is passed through successive filters of pure secondary colors, the light from the filter's complementary primary is blocked as the light passes through each filter. Any combination of two secondary filters will block two of the primary light colors and pass only one; all three secondary filters will pass no light at all.

2A.

2B.

Figure 2. Simple composition. A) A simple composition with a major and minor element and good use of low camera angle. B) Good composition. Note lines and curves of the fabric lead your eye through the composition.

3A.

3B.

Figure 3. Color composition.
A) Monochromatic composition.
Overlapping elements and
repetition of forms and textures
combine with the overall color
scheme to generate a sense of
tranquil lushness. B) Spot color.
The bright yellow color of the
wall stands out in contrast to the
otherwise monochromatic scene
to pull your eye into the
composition.

3C.

Figure 3 *continued*. C) Contrasting colors and tones emphasize the intersecting lines and planes of this architectural composition.

3D.

Figure 3 *continued*. D) Strong contrasts of complementary colors, here yellow and blue, create dynamic separation between the figure and the background. The photographer continued this graphic treatment by likewise contrasting two opposing diagonal lines of composition.

4A.

Figure 4. Available light. A) Light coming in from an open door provided all the illumination necessary for this intimate close-up portrait.

4B.

4C.

Figure 4 *continued*. B) Available light photography often requires longer exposures. Strong side light from the doorway provided all the light needed for this image. Had flash been used from the camera position, the separation of the arches and the texture of the cobblestones would have been lost. C) Night photography. A time exposure created dynamic swirls and turned the colored lights of a Ferris wheel into a delicate tracery.

5A.

5B.

Figure 5. Color strategies. A) Spot color. A single contrasting color element attracts the eye and creates a focal point. B) Dominant color. A vividly colored wall dominates and integrates this image of two street vendors in Mexico.

5C.

Figure 5 *continued*. Color strategies. C) False or applied color. Colored gels were placed over a flashlight, then used to "paint" isolated patches of colored light onto the scene.

Figure 6. White balance or color correction. A) Use of tungsten-balanced film or tungsten white balance in daylight conditions. Uncorrected it yields a blue shift. B) Corrected by use of a conversion filter or proper white balance setting. C) Use of daylight-balanced film or daylight white balance setting in tungsten light. Uncorrected it produces an amber shift. D) Corrected by use of a conversion filter or proper white balance setting.

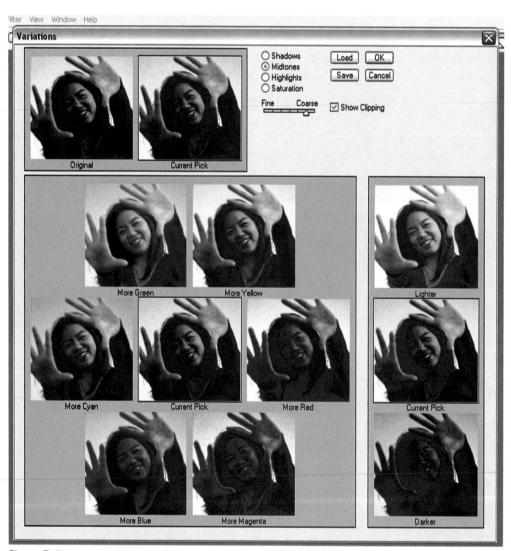

Figure 7. Photoshop's "Variations" command displays a ring-a-round of color choices to make color balancing an image easier.

Figure 8. Toning. Use of sepia tone on this black-and-white print enhances feeling of warmth and supports natural coloring of wood, earth, skin tones.

9A.

Figure 9. A) Digital artist Michael Johnson created this composite image, "Flying Circles," using six different layers in Photoshop.

9B.

Layer 1

Layer 2

Layer 3

Layer 4

Layer 5

Layer 6

Figure 9 *continued*. B) Michael Johnson used these six layers to assemble the composite shown in Figure 9 A. The opacities of each layer were adjusted to achieve the desired blend of elements.

Figure 9 *continued*. C) Student photographer built the collage "Dream Kiss" with image elements on 22 layers.

Intermediate Digital Image Processing

Digital artist Michael Johnson created this composite image, "Flying in Circles," using six different layers in Photoshop

Unit at a Glance

The digital darkroom contains many tools for modifying images to create evocative photographs. Modern image-editing programs like Adobe® Photoshop®, though complex, permit fine control over nearly every aspect of a picture's appearance. Offering many tools that are analogous to those used in a darkroom, digital image-editors additionally offer a variety of other tools as well. In addition to dodging and burning-in, for example, an image-editor allows you to make spot adjustments to color, hide or blur distracting details, restore washed-out colors, combine parts of several images, and produce many special effects. By mastering these controls, digital photographers can create images that reflect their own unique perceptions and visions.

This unit explains such image-editing features as filters, layers, and text options, and the tools used for local image control, painting and drawing, and selection. Each section contains step-by-step procedures to guide you through the processes and demonstrates the techniques.

Tools for Local Image Control

Objective 8-A Explain and demonstrate proper use of editing tools for local image control and defect correction.

Key Concepts dodging, burn, brush size, range, exposure, sponge, blur, sharpen, smudge, rubber stamp or clone, aligned, opacity, pattern stamp tool

In Unit 7 you learned several ways to change the overall appearance of an image, such as lightening, darkening, and adjusting contrast and color balance. After applying these global controls you may find that some parts of the image are still too light or too dark. In the traditional darkroom, you would correct these small, local areas within a print by using dodging and burning techniques. The digital darkroom offers similar tools—plus additional new tools—for changing small areas within an image.

Dodging

Dodging is a traditional darkroom technique used to lighten small parts of a picture. During the print's exposure, you use a small disk or paddle to block some of the enlarger's image-forming light. Photoshop features a similar tool— but one that can be set to lighten only the highlights, midtones, or shadows at the operator's discretion. The tool is used to effectively reduce the exposure of small areas of an image in order to lighten them.

The Burn Tool and Related Controls

Note that the **DODGE TOOL** button on the toolbar has a small arrow at the bottom. This indicates that a fly-out menu is available. If you click and hold on the tool button, the fly-out menu will open, offering the **BURN** and **SPONGE TOOLS**. Note the **BLUR TOOL**, represented by the raindrop icon, next to the **DODGE TOOL**. The **BLUR TOOL** also has a fly-out menu offering the **SHARPEN** and **SMUDGE TOOLS**. (See Figure 8-5.) All of these tools work much like the **DODGE TOOL** to make spot changes to an image.

Digital photographers use these tools creatively to modify an image's clarity and impact. The tools can be used also to control and direct the viewer's eye across the image, to emphasize or subordinate selected details within an image, to direct attention to the main statement, or even to alter the apparent spatial depth of the image.

The Burn Tool The **BURN TOOL** icon looks like the cupped hand used in traditional printing to give extra exposure to part of an image. Photoshop features a similar tool that is used to increase the density of small details within an image that would otherwise appear too light. When the **BURN TOOL** is selected the Options bar displays options for **BRUSH SIZE**, **RANGE**, and **EXPOSURE**. To apply these tools, hold the mouse button down while the tool is waved over the image with constant motion until the correct tone is achieved.

Using the Dodge Tool

1. Open the image file you wish to work on.

2. Click on the **DODGE TOOL** icon on the toolbar to activate the tool. It looks like a black paddle.

3. Note that the Options Bar at the top of the screen now reflects the controls available for the **DODGE TOOL**. The **DODGE TOOL** has three option settings—**BRUSH SIZE**, **RANGE** and **EXPOSURE**.

4. The **BRUSH** setting controls how large an area the tool affects. Large brushes are used to lighten large areas, such as an entire face. Small brushes are used to lighten small areas, such as an eye or a skin blemish. Click the spinner next to the **BRUSH** window to drop down a scroll box showing various brushes. Click on any brush to select it.

5. The **RANGE** setting determines which tones the tool will affect. Click the spinner next to the **RANGE** window to drop down a scroll box showing options for **HIGHLIGHTS**, **MIDTONES**, or **SHADOWS**. Choose a range setting for the image tones you wish to lighten. In the illustration, the tool is set to lighten a midtone.

6. The **EXPOSURE** window determines how much the tool will lighten an area with each pass of the Dodge icon. Work with small numbers—normally 10 to 30 percent. Click the spinner next to the **EXPOSURE** window to open a slider for adjusting the exposure setting, or type in a percentage. Try 30 percent to start. Observe the effect. If the effect is too strong, reduce the number. You can apply the tool many times for additional lightening.

7. To use the **DODGE TOOL**, simply position the Dodge cursor over the part of the image you wish to lighten. Then click and drag, waving the tool cursor around until the area is lightened to your satisfaction.

8. **HELPFUL HINT**. Figure 8-2 shows the **DODGE TOOL** in use with the default cursor setting. Note that the icon does not reflect the brush size, so the photographer cannot know exactly how the brush will affect the image. For a better way to use this and other tools, click to **EDIT —> PREFERENCES —> DISPLAY AND CURSORS**. Choose **BRUSH SIZE** in the **PAINTING CURSOR** area. The next time you use an editing tool, the cursor will reflect the actual brush size. (See Figure 8-3.)

Figure 8-2. The dodge tool in use. Adobe and Photoshop are either registered trademarks of Adobe Systems Incorporated in the United States and/or other countries.

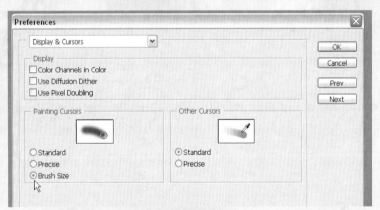

Figure 8-3. The cursor can be set to reflect the actual brush size for more accurate tool control. Adobe and Photoshop are either registered trademarks of Adobe Systems Incorporated in the United States and/or other countries.

The Sponge Tool The **SPONGE TOOL** has no equivalent in the traditional darkroom. It is a kind of dodging tool that reduces color saturation and contrast. Think of the tool as a sponge that soaks up color. When used on a color image, the sponge lowers the saturation or vividness of colors; on a grayscale image, it reduces contrast.

The **SPONGE TOOL's** option bar offers a **MODE** option that can be set to reverse its effects—to

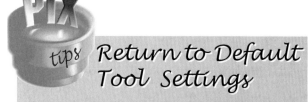

tips Return to Default Tool Settings

Have you ever changed a tool's setting on the Options Bar and then couldn't remember how to get back to normal? Just click on the tool's icon on the Options Bar. A drop down menu offers a choice of resetting the tool, or resetting all tools to their default values. Click your choice to restore the default values.

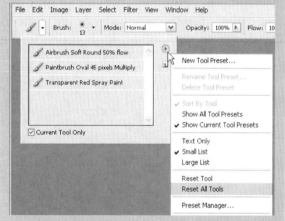

Figure 8-4. Adobe and Photoshop are either registered trademarks of Adobe Systems Incorporated in the United States and/or other countries.

increase color saturation or contrast. You can add emphasis to selected details in an image by applying the **SPONGE TOOL**. Adding saturation or contrast will make parts of the picture stand out or appear sharper and more prominent.

The Blur Tool You can find the **BLUR TOOL's** raindrop icon on the left side of the tool bar opposite the **DODGE/BURN/SPONGE TOOLS**. The **BLUR TOOL** blurs parts of an image by reducing the contrast between adjacent pixels.

For the **BLUR TOOL**, the **MODE** window includes options for selecting a type of blur—**NORMAL**, **DARKEN**, **LIGHTEN**, **HUE**, **SATURATION**, **COLOR**, and **LUMINOSITY**. For example, in the **LIGHTEN** mode, the tool blurs the lighter pixels in the image. The **HUE**, **SATURATION**, **COLOR**, and **LUMINOSITY** modes cause the tool to blur pixels based on those characteristics.

The Sharpen Tool The **SHARPEN TOOL's** icon is a steep triangle located on the **BLUR TOOL's** fly out menu. The **SHARPEN TOOL** has an effect opposite to that of the **BLUR TOOL**—rather than softening image definition, it sharpens it by increasing the contrast between adjacent pixels. The selected mode causes the tool to sharpen pixels based on the characteristic selected. Note that overuse of the **SHARPEN TOOL** can make the picture look grainy.

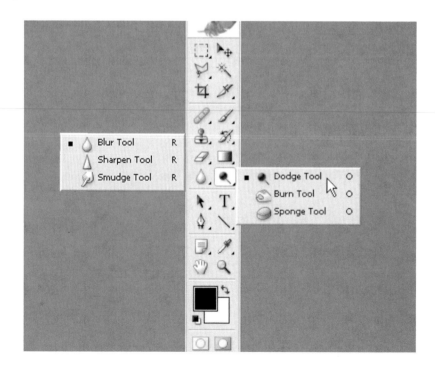

Figure 8-5. Menu flyouts reveal the six edit tools. Adobe and Photoshop are either registered trademarks of Adobe Systems Incorporated in the United States and/or other countries.

Undoing Image Changes

While using various image-editing tools, you might make a change that you now regret. After much hard work to improve the image, suddenly you make a change that ruins the whole effect. Do you have to scrap the image and start over? Certainly in a traditional darkroom that's exactly what you would have to do. Scrap the bad print and make another.

Fortunately, in Photoshop, you are able to reverse the effect of your most recent changes. If you made several changes in sequence, and you have not yet saved the image, you can step back through your changes, one at a time, and reverse or *undo* them. While you are editing an image, each change that you make is recorded in the computer's memory, allowing you to undo many successive changes, *so long as you have not yet exited the edited image.*

Here's how to undo changes: On the toolbar, click to **EDIT —> STEP BACKWARD**. As long as there are edit changes in memory, the **STEP BACKWARD** option will be displayed. Each time you click it, the next most recent edit change is reversed. Note that **EDIT —> STEP FORWARD** has the opposite effect by reinstating changes that have been reversed.

The Smudge Tool The icon of the **SMUDGE TOOL** is a pointing finger. When dragged across an image this tool smears colors and tones, making details look stretched and elastic. The result is similar to dragging your finger across a wet painting. This tool blends the edges of image elements into the background.

The Rubber Stamp or Clone Tool

Photoshop contains an editing tool, the **RUBBER STAMP TOOL**, which allows colors, textures, or parts of an image to be **cloned**—to be captured from one part of an image and imprinted into another part of the image. By using the **RUBBER STAMP TOOL**, a dust spot or image detail can be removed by cloning the texture and color of its background, then rubber stamping it over the offending object to cover it. The **RUBBER STAMP** is the preferred tool for removing dust, scratches, blemishes, or unwanted image details from a picture. In the extreme, entire persons, or other objects, can be removed from one image and imprinted into another. This tool has no equivalent in the chemical darkroom.

Additional Rubber Stamp Settings
Aligned Box Unchecked The **RUBBER STAMP TOOL** acts differently if the **ALIGNED** box on the

Options Bar is unchecked. When it is unchecked, the **RUBBER STAMP TOOL** cursor will continue to paint from the same cloned area even if it has been moved and clicked onto a new part of the target. Each new drag of the stamp will start from the same original source point. This enables you to duplicate objects several times in an image.

Opacity The Options Bar has an **OPACITY** slider that can be set to any level. Sometimes it is better to make repeated passes with less opacity than to increase opacity. By making very slight changes with each pass, you can blend parts of the image together with smoother transitions.

Pattern Stamp Tool The **RUBBER STAMP TOOL** button has a fly-out menu offering a related tool—the **PATTERN STAMP TOOL**, which is used to paint a repeating pattern. To define a pattern, draw a rectangular frame around the desired pattern using the rectangular **MARQUEE TOOL**—the dotted frame icon in the upper left corner of the toolbar. Then click to **EDIT —> DEFINE PATTERN**. The new pattern will appear in the **PATTERN** window on the **OPTIONS BAR**. Select the pattern and a brush from the Options Bar, then click and drag the tool to paint the pattern into the image. For example, you could remove a window from a wall by painting over it with a brick pattern.

Using the Rubber Stamp Tool

In Figure 8-6, note several dust spots, scratches, and an unwanted drinking fountain to be removed. Parts of the background wall were cloned and stamped to cover the scratches and the fountain. The result is shown in Figure 8-7.

1. *Open an image and select the **RUBBER STAMP TOOL**—the rubber stamp icon is fifth down on the left side of the toolbar. The button has a fly-out menu with two options—**CLONE STAMP TOOL** and **PATTERN STAMP TOOL**. Select **CLONE STAMP TOOL**.*

2. *On the Options Bar, set **MODE** to **NORMAL**, **OPACITY** to **100%** and check the **ALIGNED** box.*

3. *Use the **MAGNIFY TOOL**, the magnifying glass icon in the lower right corner of the toolbar, to enlarge the blemishes or objects you wish to correct. These are the target objects. Keyboard shortcut: **CTRL + PLUS KEY** on a PC or **Z + PLUS KEY** on a Mac.*

4. *On the Options bar, select a **BRUSH SIZE** close to the width of the object you wish to remove.*

5. *Point the **RUBBER STAMP TOOL** cursor to the area you want to copy or clone—an area that matches the background of the target object. Hold down the **ALT** key on a PC or the **OPTION** key on a Mac and mouse-click. This loads the tool with virtual ink matching the background color and texture. In Figure 8-6 the area just to the left of the top dust mark was cloned.*

6. *Next point the **RUBBER STAMP TOOL** cursor directly over all or part of the target object. Then click or click-and-drag to imprint or draw the cloned background over the target object. The **RUBBER STAMP TOOL** will apply a mark or line of the cloned color. If the result is not correct, click to **EDIT —> STEP BACKWARD**, or use **CTRL + Z** on a PC or **Z + Z** on the Mac to undo it and try again.*

7. *The **RUBBER STAMP TOOL** cursor, shaped as a cross, identifies the area that is being cloned or rubber stamped. Sometimes it is necessary to reset the cloning source or sample point. Use the **ALT** key on a PC or the **OPTION** key on a Mac and mouse-click to reload the **RUBBER STAMP TOOL** with the correct virtual ink color.*

8. *Finish removing the offending objects. Figure 8-7 shows all dust spots removed and the distracting drinking fountain eliminated.*

Figure 8-6. Dust, scratches, and undesired image elements can be removed with the rubber stamp tool.

Figure 8-7. The corrected image is blemish-free.

Photoshop comes with a few built-in patterns; however, you can add custom patterns from other images. Once added to the palette by clicking to **EDIT — > DEFINE PATTERN**, the new pattern will be available for use in any image.

Rubber Stamp Refinements The **RUBBER STAMP TOOL** is one of the most powerful and flexible tools available in Photoshop. Additional refinements are available, including:

■ The **MODE** window is usually set to **NORMAL**, but other options are available. Experiment with other modes to obtain unusual effects.

■ Try different brush sizes and shapes from the Brush palette to alter the size of the area being cloned. Change brushes frequently.

■ To retouch a straight line or scratch, mouse-click with the tool at one end of the line and then **SHIFT + CLICK** at the other. The tool will automatically fill in the middle.

■ Each mouse-click on the **RUBBER STAMP TOOL** paints with a clone of the image as it was *before* the tool was used. Occasionally this may reintroduce part of the same flaw back into the picture. If that happens, select **UNDO** and start cloning again. Be sure to end painting before the defect reappears. The resulting new image state will be used as the source next time the mouse is clicked, and you can continue painting.

The **RUBBER STAMP TOOL** can be used to clone from one image and stamp the result onto another. Just click **OPTION** (PC) or **ALT** (Mac) in the **SOURCE IMAGE's** window to load the stamp, and then drag to paint with the stamp in the second images' window.

Working with the Paint and Draw Tools

Objective 8-B Explain and demonstrate techniques of applying the painting and drawing tools.

Key Concepts foreground color, background color, color picker, hue, saturation, brightness, mode, opacity, pressure, wet edges, auto erase

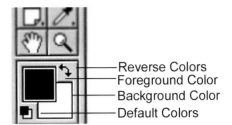

Figure 8-8. Colors are selected with these icons from the bottom of the toolbar. Adobe and Photoshop are either registered trademarks of Adobe Systems Incorporated in the United States and/or other countries.

Selecting Paint Colors

By default, Photoshop uses black as the **foreground color**—the color applied by the Pencil, Brush, and other painting tools. White is the default **background color**—the color used by the **ERASER TOOL** and for the endpoint of gradient fills. Some special effects filters also use the foreground and background colors. Eliminating a selection with the Delete key also fills it with the current background color.

You can reverse the foreground and background colors by clicking on the double-sided arrow above the square color icons at the bottom of the toolbar. You may return to the default colors at any time by clicking on the miniature icon of the color squares. (See Figure 8-8.)

Color Picker Click on the foreground or background color icon on the toolbar to open the **COLOR PICKER** dialog box. Here you will find a large color panel and a spectrum of colors arrayed along a vertical bar. Use the sliders on the vertical bar to change the colors in the panel. Then move the cursor within the panel and click on the color you wish to select. (See Figure 8-9.)

■ **Spectrum Options** Radio buttons control the color spectrum displayed in the panel. The default **H** setting displays the full range of **hues**. The **S** setting displays the **saturation** options available for the selected color. The **B** setting displays the range of **brightness** available.

■ **Chosen Color** A small panel near the top of the color slider bar displays the chosen color. When you are satisfied with the chosen color, click **OK**.

■ **Previous Color** Below the chosen color, a small panel displays the color previously set for the foreground or background.

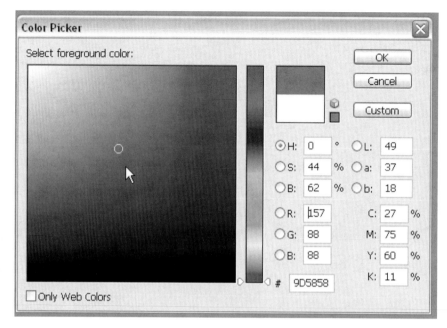

Figure 8-9. Use the color picker to select from a spectrum of possible colors. Adobe and Photoshop are either registered trademarks of Adobe Systems Incorporated in the United States and/or other countries.

- **Custom** By clicking the **CUSTOM** button inside the dialog box, many other color families are made available.

- **Other Methods** You can also select a new foreground or background color by using the **EYEDROPPER TOOL** from the toolbar, the **COLOR PALETTE** by clicking to **WINDOW — > SHOW COLOR**, or the **SWATCHES PALETTE** by clicking to **WINDOW — > SHOW SWATCHES**.

Using the Pencil, Brush, and Airbrush Tools

Painting and drawing tools extend the expressive capabilities of a digital artist in many ways. You can change the color of a specific image detail, hide minor flaws, and blend photographs with drawings to create fantasy scenes. These freehand tools work much like conventional pencils, brushes, and airbrushes.

The three main painting tools in most image-editing programs are the **PENCIL**, **PAINTBRUSH** and **AIRBRUSH TOOLS**. (See Figure 8-10.)

- **Pencil** Draws hard-edged lines of any width.

- **Paintbrush** Draws softer lines with a fuzzy edge. Different brush shapes and textures can be selected to simulate a variety of natural brushes or patterns.

- **Airbrush** Ejects a continuous stream of color that keeps coming even when the mouse is not moving. As long as the mouse button is held, paint is applied. A stationary mouse makes a rounded drop of color where the spray has built up.

Brush Options The **PAINTBRUSH**, **PENCIL**, and **AIRBRUSH TOOLS** produce lines and marks of the selected foreground color. The selected brush

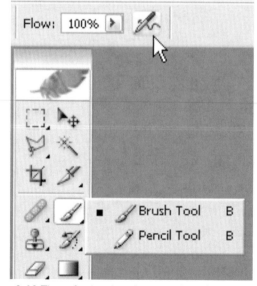

Figure 8-10. These freehand tools are used much like their real-world counterparts. Adobe and Photoshop are either registered trademarks of Adobe Systems Incorporated in the United States and/or other countries.

determines the width of the line and its sharpness. The **POP-UP BRUSH PALETTE** contains various brushes. To select a brush, first right-click on the **PAINTBRUSH/PENCIL TOOL** icon in the toolbar to select one of these tools. Then click on the spinner to the right of the **BRUSH** window on the Options Bar to display the **POP-UP BRUSH PALETTE**. Finally, click on the desired brush in the **POP-UP BRUSH PALETTE**.

You can also create a new, custom brush by clicking on the right-facing arrow in the upper right corner of the **POP-UP BRUSH PALETTE**. A pop-up menu offers a **NEW BRUSH** option for creating your own brush, a **LOAD BRUSHES** option for loading other brush assortments from Photoshop's files, and many other options. (See Figure 8-11.) To create a new brush, choose **NEW BRUSH** from the pop-up palette menu. The Preview Box in the lower right corner of the Dialog Box shows the current brush tip. The box in the lower left corner shows the current brush angle and roundness. Set the brush options you prefer. As you enter new options, the brushes in these boxes update. Then click **OK**.

Tool options provide settings for **MODE**, **OPACITY**, **FLOW**, **WET EDGES**, and **AUTO ERASE**. These options provide precise control over how any painted or drawn marks will appear.

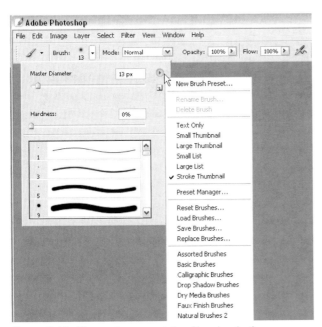

Figure 8-11. Choose from a variety of brushes in the pop-up window or make a new one. Adobe and Photoshop are either registered trademarks of Adobe Systems Incorporated in the United States and/or other countries.

■ **Mode** The **MODE** selection determines how colors are applied as the tool is used.

—**NORMAL** Selected for most painting and drawing. In this mode the tool applies the foreground color to the image.

—**DISSOLVE** Splatters colors along the edge of a brush stroke.

—**BEHIND** Applies color to any layer behind the active one.

—**MULTIPLY** Paints a darkened mix of the foreground color and the image color.

—**SCREEN** Applies a lightened mix of the foreground color and the image color.

—**OVERLAY** Applies more contrast and saturation in the drawn area.

—**SOFT LIGHT** Adds a veil of color to the image without obscuring detail.

—**HARD LIGHT** Applies a thicker wash of color that retains some of the underlying image.

—**COLOR DODGE OR BURN** Lightens or darkens the painted pixels if they are respectively lighter or darker than the foreground color.

—**DARKEN OR LIGHTEN** Applies color only if the image pixels are darker or lighter than the foreground color.

—**DIFFERENCE AND EXCLUSION** Alters expected colors and effects according to how image pixels relate to foreground color. Colors are often reversed somewhat like a negative image.

—**HUE, SATURATION, VALUE AND LUMINOSITY** Applies these color properties to the painted area.

■ **Opacity** **OPACITY** is a measure of the relative translucency of a painted color. At 100 percent, colors are totally opaque and no background shows through. At lower opacity, colors become more transparent, allowing the background image to show through. Clicking the spinner to the right of the **OPACITY** option displays a slider for setting this property.

■ **Flow** When the **AIRBRUSH TOOL** is chosen the **OPACITY** slider becomes a **PRESSURE** setting that applies less paint at lower settings.

■ **Wet Edges** Available only from the separate brush palette. **WET EDGES** makes painted lines translucent with darker edges. The re-

Famous Photographer

Alfred Stieglitz

More than any other person, Alfred Stieglitz influenced the course of photography as an art form in America. As photographer, critic, editor, publisher, curator, and forceful gadfly for the arts, he promoted influential and *avant-garde* work, not only of photographers, but also for other artists for more than 60 years.

Stieglitz's perceptions as art connoisseur and critic were far ahead of his time. His galleries, often kept afloat financially by the force of his will and personality—291, the Intimate Gallery, and An American Place—exhibited the works of many contemporary artists and photographers. With Edward Steichen, he introduced to America the works of such modern artists as Cézanne, Matisse, and Picasso. From 1903 to 1917 he edited *Camera Work,* the most influential of all photographic magazines, in which he published a wide range of photographic criticism and works that he considered to be artistically worthy, often exhibiting a surprising tolerance toward those styles he opposed. Through his influence, major museum curators and art critics eventually accepted photography as a legitimate art form.

Stieglitz twice influenced the style of photography in America: first toward the pictorial impressionistic ideal and later toward sharply realistic, "straight" photography. An early advocate of "pure," unmanipulated photography, he made his early reputation, starting in 1892, with a series of "pictorial" photographs of New York street scenes. These photographs showed convincingly that it was not necessary to manipulate images to reveal the

Alfred Stieglitz, "The Terminal," New York, 1892. © Bettmann/Corbis

pictorial qualities in everyday scenes. At first he photographed "in small," producing prints that were smaller than a playing card, mounted on a large sheet of wrinkled buff or brown paper, and would not allow his pictures to be enlarged, even in magazine reproduction.

By photographing the natural elements—clouds, rain, snowstorms—Stieglitz found a way of expressing what was in himself. "When I see something that serves as an 'equivalent' for me, of what I am experiencing myself," he said, "then I feel compelled to set down a picture of it as an honest statement . . . to represent my feelings about life." It was his opinion—quite revolutionary for his time—that any work, whether the work of a painter, pastry cook, or photographer, should be judged on its own merit and only in terms of itself.

sult appears somewhat three dimensional and tubelike. When the **PENCIL TOOL** is used this option becomes **AUTO ERASE**.

■ **Auto Erase** Available only with the **PENCIL TOOL. AUTO ERASE** turns the **PENCIL TOOL** into a self-erasing device—it draws with the foreground color, but if reapplied to a drawn line it erases the background color.

Painting and Drawing Tips Here are some tips to help you get started using the painting and drawing tools.

■ **Make Quick Color Changes** Press **ALT + CLICK** on a PC or **OPTION + CLICK** on a Mac to instantly change the drawing tool to an eyedropper. Use the eyedropper to grab a spot of color from the image with which to paint or draw.

■ **Paint or Draw Straight Lines** To paint or draw a straight line, point-and-click once at the starting point, release, then point-and-shift-click at the end point. Photoshop will connect the two points with a straight line.

■ **Draw Triangles and Rectangles** You can make straight-sided shapes such as triangles, rectangles, and polygons quickly as described above. Just continue to point-and-shift-click around the shape.

■ **Draw Horizontal or Vertical Lines** To make a straight line precisely vertical or horizontal, press the shift key immediately as you begin to drag the tool.

Selections and Their Uses

Objective 8-C Explain and demonstrate how to make, modify, and use selections.

Key Concepts selection, lasso, feather, marquee, magic wand

Making a **selection** is the act of defining a boundary around part of an image that you wish to edit in some way. You can alter a selected part of an image many ways, including modifying its brightness, contrast, color, sharpness, or by applying special-effects filters.

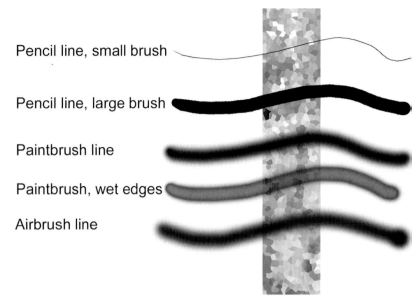

Pencil line, small brush

Pencil line, large brush

Paintbrush line

Paintbrush, wet edges

Airbrush line

Figure 8-12. Most traditional drawings and painting effects can be duplicated with the appropriate tool settings.

Any changes that you make are confined to the selected part. The boundaries of the selected part are displayed as a marquee of moving dashes, often called "marching ants." By creating selections, you can edit and fine-tune local parts of an image. You can also duplicate, move, cut, and paste selections from one image to another to form collages.

Selection Tools

Most image-editing programs provide tools for selecting parts of an image to edit. Photoshop offers three main tools to create a selection and to control its size and shape—**LASSO, MARQUEE,** and **MAGIC WAND TOOLS**. The **LASSO** and **MARQUEE TOOLS** provide fly-out menus that feature additional variations. All are shown in Figure 8-13.

Lasso Tools The **LASSO TOOL** gets its name from the rope used by cowboys to encircle a steer. Digital photographers use this freehand tool to encircle pixels.

Lasso The basic **LASSO TOOL** is simplicity itself. Click on the **LASSO** icon in the toolbar, then click-and-drag the cursor inside the image to draw your selection. Keep dragging until the cursor returns to a point near its starting point, then release it. Photoshop connects the ending and starting points with a straight line and displays the encircled selection as a line of marching ants.

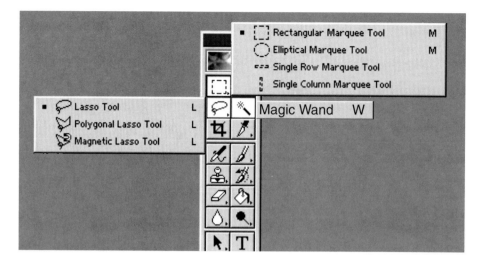

Figure 8-13. Use these tools to define the boundary of a selection you wish to edit. Adobe and Photoshop are either registered trademarks of Adobe Systems Incorporated in the United States and/or other countries.

Polygonal Lasso The **POLYGONAL LASSO** variation is often faster and easier to use than the original Lasso. This tool uses a series of connected straight lines to create a selection. To use it, click on the **POLYGONAL LASSO** icon in the fly-out menu, then click once to set a starting point for your selection. Move the cursor to a second point and click again. Photoshop connects the two points with a straight line. Continue clicking to create additional straight-line segments, varying their length and direction to shape your selection. Finally, double-click at the last point. Photoshop connects the last point with the first to complete the polygon and displays the selection as a line of marching ants.

Magnetic Lasso The **MAGNETIC LASSO** is a semiautomatic variation of the **LASSO TOOL**. The tool draws a selection outline around the edge of an object based on the color differences between the object and its background. Therefore, it works best when the object and its background are separated by fairly high contrast.

To use it, click on the **MAGNETIC LASSO** icon in the fly-out menu, then point-and-click once on the edge of the object you want to select. Follow its outline with the cursor, but do not click-and-drag; just move the cursor along the edge of the object and Photoshop will place a line of anchor points along the edge. To correct errors, you can delete to the previous anchor point by pressing **BACKSPACE** on a PC or **DELETE** on a Mac. You can add a new anchor point with a mouse-click. Continue to encircle the selection in this way. Finally, click on the beginning point to complete the

selection. Photoshop displays the selection as a line of marching ants.

The Options Bar offers several settings with the **MAGNETIC LASSO**.

- **Feather** Controls the sharpness of the selection's outline—larger numbers soften it.
- **Anti-Aliasing** Normally checked, this setting removes the jagged edges of the selection's outline.
- **Width** Sets a zone within which the cursor will trace an edge. Smaller values require more precise cursor movements.
- **Edge Contrast** Sets the contrast required for Photoshop to detect an edge. Use higher values when an object contrasts well from its background. Use lower values when the contrast is weak.
- **Frequency** Controls the number of anchor points Photoshop inserts for tracing an outline. Higher values are best for irregular shapes.

Marquee Tools The **MARQUEE TOOLS** create selections that are rectangular, oval, or round that you can use around doorways, pictures, or similar objects. You can also use them to start a complex selection that you can refine later with the **LASSO TOOL**.

The **MARQUEE TOOLS** are defined by their shapes—**RECTANGULAR MARQUEE**, **ELLIPTICAL MARQUEE**, **SINGLE ROW MARQUEE**, and **SINGLE COLUMN MARQUEE**. All operate similarly. After clicking on the tool from the fly-out

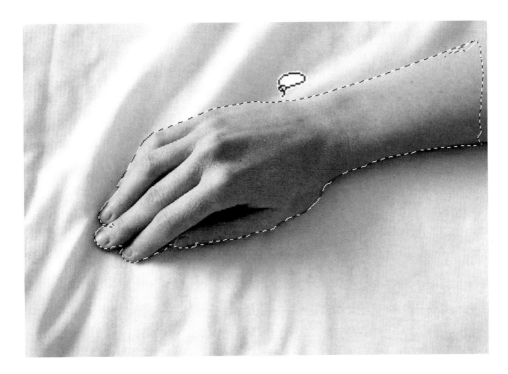

Figure 8-14. Drag the lasso tool around the perimeter of the object to be selected.

menu, click-and-drag the cursor from one corner of the area to be selected to the opposite corner. A dotted outline follows the cursor's movements and then displays the selection as a marquee of marching ants.

- **Rectangular Marquee** Use this tool to select rectangular or square parts of an image.

- **Elliptical Marquee** This tool quickly defines ovals and circles of any size.

- **Single Row Marquee** and **Single Column Marquee** These tools define a row or a column that is one pixel high or one pixel wide across the entire image. They are useful for trimming away the side of an image or inserting lines.

- **Marquee Options and Hints**

  - **Perfect Circles and Squares** To draw a perfect circle or square, press and hold **SHIFT** while dragging the **ELLIPTICAL** or **RECTANGULAR MARQUEE TOOL**.

  - **Draw Selection from Center** To enlarge the marquee from the center out, press and hold **ALT** on a PC or **OPTION** on a Mac while dragging the **ELLIPTICAL** or **RECTANGULAR MARQUEE TOOL**.

  - **Move and Draw** To move the marquee to a new location while drawing it, press and hold the **SPACE BAR** down while dragging

the cursor. Release the **SPACE BAR** to continue drawing.

- **Specific Aspect Ratio** To select an area with specific proportions, such as 4 x 5 or 5 x 7, click to **STYLE — > CONSTRAINED ASPECT RATIO** on the Options Bar and enter those values. Use the **RECTANGULAR MARQUEE TOOL** to define the selection, then click to **IMAGE — > CROP**.

- **Fixed Size** To select an area with a fixed size, such as 640 x 480 pixels used for web pages, click to **STYLE — > FIXED SIZE** on the Options Bar and enter those values. Use the **RECTANGULAR MARQUEE TOOL** to define the selection, then click to **IMAGE — > CROP**.

Magic Wand The **MAGIC WAND** is a tool that selects an area that matches the color or tonal value of the pixel where the mouse was clicked. Although easy to use, it can also be frustrating. A few hints follow:

- Tolerance The **TOLERANCE** setting determines a range of tones that the **MAGIC WAND TOOL** will select. Low **TOLERANCE** values cause the **MAGIC WAND TOOL** to select tones within a narrow range. Higher values cause the **MAGIC WAND TOOL** to select

Figure 8-15. The magic wand selects areas of matching color and tonal value. Experiment with the "tolerance" setting for best results. Adobe and Photoshop are either registered trademarks of Adobe Systems Incorporated in the United States and/or other countries.

tones within a broader range. In Figure 8-15, for example, a higher setting would include the flower's center in the selection. This may be the most important setting for successful use of the **MAGIC WAND TOOL**. Experiment with different tolerance settings for each new application.

- **Contiguous** The **CONTIGUOUS** setting, normally checked, selects only those tonal or color areas that are contiguous, or touching. If the wand were set for a flesh tone, for example, clicking on the face of one person would not select the face of a second unless they were touching.

- **All Layers** The **ALL LAYERS** setting, when checked, includes all visible layers when defining a selection.

Adding or Subtracting from a Selection

Editing an image often requires making more than one selection. To lighten two faces, for example, make two separate selections. Once the first face is selected, the second can be added and **LEVELS** applied to lighten both faces at the same

time. In other situations, you might wish to subtract from a selection. For example, you might wish to deselect a window in a wall.

It is often easier to make complex selections by combining several simpler ones. With Photoshop you can add to or subtract from a selection as often as necessary to define a selection precisely.

When a selection tool is in use the Options Bar will display a series of selection state buttons near the bar's left side. These four buttons provide for adding to, subtracting from, or intersecting a previously defined selection. To add to an existing selection, for example, choose the second button from the left and define a new selection area. The new area will be combined with the previous as one selection. (See Figure 8-16.)

Modifying and Saving Selections

Photoshop provides many tools for modifying a selection. Here are a few:

- **Feathering** Can be applied to an existing selection to blur and soften its edges. Feathered selections are used to blend image elements seamlessly. Click to **SELECT — > FEATHER** or **ALT + CTRL + D** on a PC or **OPTION + ⌘ + D** on a Mac and enter a value for the **RADIUS**. Larger values entered in the **RADIUS** window create softer edges.

- **Transform** Allows you to adjust the selection marquee to better fit an area. Click to **SELECT — > TRANSFORM** to scale, rotate, resize, or move the selection marquee to a new location.

Figure 8-16. In addition to the keyboard shortcuts Photoshop provides selection state buttons on the options bar. Adobe and Photoshop are either registered trademarks of Adobe Systems Incorporated in the United States and/or other countries.

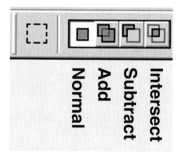

■ **Grow** Is similar to the **MAGIC WAND TOOL**. It expands a selection to include nearby colors and tones that are similar. It also uses the **TOLERANCE** setting that accompanies the **MAGIC WAND TOOL** options. After creating a selection with the **MAGIC WAND TOOL**, click to **SELECT — > GROW** to grow the selection.

■ **Similar** Works like **GROW** but includes pixels throughout the image, not just adjacent ones. After creating a selection with the **MAGIC WAND TOOL**, click to **SELECT — > SIMILAR** to expand the selection throughout the image.

■ **Color Range** A quick way to select a colored background by identifying all pixels of a matching color. After creating a selection with the **MAGIC WAND TOOL**, click to **SELECT — > COLOR RANGE**. You can also define the colors with an **EYEDROPPER TOOL** and define multiple colors by repeating the selection process.

■ **Save a Selection** Complex selections can be saved for future use. To retain a selection click to **SELECT — > SAVE SELECTION**, enter a name for the selection and press **OK**. Choose **LOAD SELECTION** from the **SELECT** menu to recall the saved selection.

■ **Invert a Selection** A selection can be inverted to select *all but* the selected area. Click to **SELECT — > INVERSE**, or **CTRL + SHIFT + I** on a PC or ⌘ **+ SHIFT + I** on a Mac. Inverting a selection is often the most efficient way to select a complicated area. In Figure 8-15, for example, the entire background could be selected with the **MAGIC WAND TOOL**, then inverted to quickly select *all but* the entire background—that is, to select the *whole* flower.

■ **Deselect** A selection can be deselected by clicking to **SELECT — > DESELECT**, or **CTRL + D** on a PC or ⌘ **+ D** on a Mac.

■ **Reselect** If you accidentally deselect a selection, you can reselect it. Click to **SELECT — > RESELECT** or **CTRL + SHIFT + D** on a PC or ⌘ **+ SHIFT + D** on a Mac to restore the most recent selection.

■ **Select All** To select the entire image **SELECT — > ALL** or **CTRL + A** on a PC or ⌘ **+ A** on a Mac.

■ **Modify** The **MODIFY** option provides four choices on its pop-up menu: **BORDER, SMOOTH, EXPAND**, and **CONTRACT**.

Figure 8-17. Selections can be refined and edited with the many tools available from the Selection menu. Adobe and Photoshop are either registered trademarks of Adobe Systems Incorporated in the United States and/or other countries.

—**BORDER** Makes a new selection that outlines the original.

—**SMOOTH** Is used to soften ragged selection edges.

—**EXPAND** Enlarges the selection marquee.

—**CONTRACT** Shrinks the selection marquee.

Working with Selections

Once a selection is defined, any effects are applied solely to that selected part of the image. You can use selections for spot control of color and contrast without changing the overall tones of the picture. First, select an area. Then perform **COLOR BALANCE** or **LEVELS** adjustments.

A digital form of burning and dodging, this technique allows the selected area to be adjusted for both density and contrast. You can brighten or subdue individual spots of color by increasing or decreasing the saturation within a selection. In this way you can fine-tune the digital image for maximum aesthetic effect.

Fill or Delete You can also fill a selection with a single color. Click to **EDIT — > FILL** to change the color of a selected object or background or to simulate hand coloring. Adjust the **OPACITY** of the fill color to retain or obscure underlying details. Entirely delete a selection by pressing **DELETE** or **BACKSPACE**. This is a useful way to quickly delete unwanted background elements.

Selection Outlines

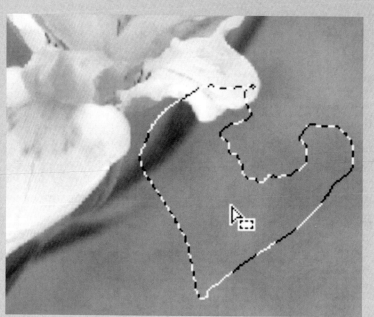

Figure 8-18. Selection outlines can be moved by dragging with a selection tool.

Moving a Selection Selection marquees can be moved without affecting their contents by dragging them with any selection tool—**LASSO TOOL, MARQUEE TOOL,** or **MAGIC WAND TOOL.** Click-and-drag the marquee to a new location. Marquees can be nudged to a new position or even moved to another image window by using the keyboard arrow keys.

Hiding a Selection The selection marquee, or marching ants, can distract you when you are previewing your changes. You can hide the selection marquee by pressing **CTRL + H** on a PC or ⌘ **+ H** on a Mac. Press the same keystrokes to unhide the selection marquee.

Collage, Copy, Move, Paste and Resize Selections You can create a collage of several elements by copying selections and pasting them as many times as needed into a new original or into another image. The Copy command is **CTRL + C** on a PC or ⌘ **+ C** on a Mac; the Paste command is **CTRL + V** on a PC or ⌘ **+ V** on a Mac. To adjust a pasted selection so that its proportions and position match its destination, click to **EDIT —> FREE TRANSFORM** to resize, stretch, or rotate it.

Use Selections to Limit Drawing and Painting Tools or Filters Because effects are limited to the selected area, selections are often used to restrict the effects of painting and drawing to a limited area. This also provides an effective way to apply filters.

Filters, Layers, and Text

Objective 8-D Explain and demonstrate how to use filters, layers, and text to modify an image.

Key Concepts filters, layers, text, layers palette, active layer, linked, adjustment layers, merging, flattening, tracking, kerning, leading, type attributes, warped text

Most of the image-editing tools and procedures discussed above have counterparts in a chemical darkroom. However, **FILTERS, LAYERS,** and **TEXT** provide tools that have no such counterparts and offer effects that were previously unavailable.

Filters are designed to digitally alter an image at the pixel level. Some, such as the **UNSHARP MASK** filter, are routinely used to enhance focus—to make the image sharper. Others, such as the **DUST AND SCRATCHES** filter, are used to automate routine retouching. Most filters, however, are designed as still-image versions of Hollywood special effects and are used to produce more spectacular results.

Layers are like sheets of glass that can be positioned over an image so that you can add additional image elements or settings. Each sheet, or layer, can be completely or partially filled; each can be adjusted to varying degrees of opacity. By using layers, you can combine a stack of image elements to produce a seamless, translucent collage. Moreover, you can edit each layer as a separate work, allowing you unlimited flexibility in composing and revising the final image.

Text is sometimes used as an image element and often as a labeling device. Photoshop offers a variety of type tools and fonts that make it easy to combine words and images and provides many choices of type font, size, color, position, **attributes**, and special effects, including boldface, outline, italics, and warping. However, Photoshop is neither a word processor nor a desktop publisher and should not be used for text editing, typesetting, or page layout.

Filters

Photoshop offers a variety of filters. Some produce effects like brush strokes, neon glows, and chroming impressions. Others can produce clouds or lens flare. A third group can be used to modify the digital composition of images, such as the **UN-SHARP MASK** filter described in Unit 7 and the **DUST AND SCRATCHES** filter.

The effect of many of the artistic-type filters can be previewed in the Filter Gallery, simply mouse to **FILTER — > FILTER GALLERY** to open. The filter gallery dialog box contains a preview window on the left and a variety of filter folders on the right. Open any folder and select a filter to see its effect previewed on the image. Note that dialog box also contains a **"New Effect Layer"** icon that looks like a pad of post-it notes near the bottom right hand corner. By adding an Effect Layer multiple filters can be stacked to make even greater modifications to the image. (See Layers on pages 287–292.)

Digital filters can create an incredible array of special effects. Although fun to play with, they often produce results whose appeal is short-lived. In general, as with all creative tools, filters will serve you best if you use them to achieve a previsualized goal. They are not magical devices that will transform any image into a masterpiece.

To apply a filter, open an image in Photoshop and select a filter from the **FILTERS** menu. If a dialog

box appears, enter any required settings, then click **OK**. A few filters require additional settings, but most that do display a preview so you can experiment with different settings. Most filters work in a similar way. See the Step-By-Step Procedure, *Applying a Motion Filter,* page 288, for an example.

Layers

LAYERS is one of the more magical tools in the digital darkroom. Working with layers is like placing parts of an artwork on many sheets of glass and then rearranging them at will—editing, repositioning, deleting them—without affecting any other sheets of glass. When you view the sheets as a stack, you can see the entire composite artwork at once. You can apply image-editing commands, such as **LEVELS** or **COLOR BALANCE**, to adjust individual layers without permanently changing the underlying image.

Every Photoshop file contains at least one layer—a background layer—that can be copied or collaged together with additional layers. All new layers are transparent until image pixels or artwork are added. You can create as many layers as you need —hundreds if you wish. Note, however, that most file formats, such as .JPG and .GIF, contain only

Figure 8-19. This pen and ink effect was produced with **FILTERS —> STYLIZE —> FIND EDGES.**

Applying a Motion Filter

1. Open an image you wish to modify. A picture of children playing was used for this example.

2. Select the area that you wish to be affected by the filter. In this example, the background was selected with the **MAGIC WAND TOOL** and refined with the **LASSO TOOL**. Using this selection prevents the children from being blurred when the filter is applied.

3. Feather the selected area to soften its edges. Click to **SELECT —> FEATHER**. A radius of 15 pixels was used in this example to soften the edges of the selected area.

4. **TO APPLY THE MOTION BLUR** filter, click to **FILTER —> BLUR —> MOTION BLUR** from the drop-down menus.

5. Photoshop displays a dialog box that requests settings for **ANGLE** and **DISTANCE**. You can experiment with various values to create the desired amount of blur. When you obtain the effect you want, click **OK** to apply the filter. This example used an **ANGLE** of 23 degrees and a **DISTANCE** of 25.

6. Apply the **LEVELS** control as necessary to heighten the blur effect.

7. Save the image file with a new name. **CLICK TO FILE —> SAVE AS** . . . and enter a new name in the dialog box for your edited image file. If you save the file with its original name, you will overwrite, or lose, your original image file.

Figure 8-20. This photograph could be enhanced to simulate panning with a careful application of the "Blur" filter.

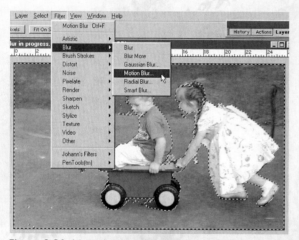

Figure 8-21. Note the "marching ants" that define the background as a selection. The motion blur will be limited to this area.

Figure 8-22. The final result is a pair of turbo-charged kids!

the final composite image and do not retain Photoshop's layers. So to preserve your layers for later editing, always save your files in Photoshop's native, .PSD format.

Using the Layers Palette Layers are controlled and applied through the **Layers Palette**. If the Layers Palette is not already present on the desktop, click to **WINDOW — > SHOW LAYERS** from the menu bar. The palette contains a thumbnail image of each layer and offers several controls for modifying the stacked image elements:

- **Active layer** Only one layer at a time can be an **active layer**—the one that will be affected by painting or editing. To make a layer active click on its name.

- **Layer order** The order of layers in the palette reflects their order in the image. Image elements high in the stack will obscure lower layers. (See *Reposition Layers* below.)

- **Eye icon** Visible layers are indicated with an icon of an eye. You can toggle visibility on and off by clicking on the eye column.

TECHNICAL FEATURE
Digital Imaging in Creative Photography

A photographic artist is hard at work refining images for two upcoming gallery exhibitions. The photographer, together with a colleague on the opposite coast, is working on a collaborative project that will combine parts of both of their photographs into several new creations. As the work continues, files containing the images in various stages of progress are quickly exchanged via the Internet from one photographer's electronic darkroom to the other.

One of the photographers has been working seriously with a new digital still camera for a few months and has found that it functions in a surprisingly comfortable and familiar way. The other photographer, working with conventional materials, later scans her original images into digital form. Personal computers in both studios are equipped with communications and image processing software capable of working with any form of digitized information.

Both photographers' transmitted images are displayed on the computer's monitor with a software package that appears much like a conventional proof sheet. Individual images or parts of images are easily selected with the click of a mouse, manipulated, and placed in a new image format. The photographers deftly assemble portions of four, separate, original images into a single new composition. Notes and preview versions of the work are exchanged instantly by email.

Even though some of the individual elements were originally shot in black-and-white, they now are colored manually in the digital darkroom to blend in with the other picture elements. The photographic artist selects from a palette of colors that appears at the edge of the computer screen and "paints" the images with a brush-like cursor. Other picture elements are then adjusted for size and rotated as needed before they are used in the new composition. Once all the picture parts have been cloned, copied, color corrected, and moved into place, the photographer uses the software's "layers" feature to blend and smooth them into a harmonious whole.

After a few more keystrokes, a full-color paper print emerges from a desktop printer. This print, along with prints of other images, will hang in a gallery on the West Coast. And what about exhibiting the prints on the East Coast? No problem—a professional photo lab in New York accepts the image files electronically. With only an Internet connection, the file is transmitted to the lab, where the images are made into large color prints ready for pick-up tomorrow morning.

Mark Yamamoto, "At Joshua Tree, California."

- **Palette pop-up** To create, duplicate, delete, merge or flatten layers, open a pop-up menu by clicking on the triangle in the upper right corner of the palette.

- **New layer** To create a new layer, click on the **NEW LAYER** icon, displayed as a stack of post-it notes, at the bottom of the palette.

- **Rename** To rename a layer or assign it a colored label, point to the layer and open the **LAYER PROPERTIES** box by pressing **ALT + DOUBLE-CLICK** on a PC or **OPTION + DOUBLE-CLICK** on a Mac.

- **Delete** To delete a layer, click on the layer and drag it to the **TRASHCAN** icon in the lower right corner of the palette.

Figure 8-23. This collage interpretation of roller-blading was built using layers and filters applied to various parts of the image.

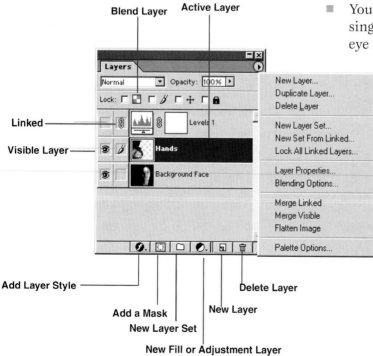

Figure 8-24. The layers palette holds the tools for creating and organizing complex image composition. Adobe and Photoshop are either registered trademarks of Adobe Systems Incorporated in the United States and/or other countries.

- **Reposition layers** To reposition a layer, click on the layer, then drag-and-drop it in its desired location in the stack.
- **Reposition image** To reposition an image within its layer, use the **MOVE TOOL** located in the upper right corner of the toolbar.
- **Links** Two or more layers can be **linked** together to move, scale, or rotate both layers together. Click on the column to the left of the thumbnail image to link that layer to the active layer. A chain icon will appear to indicate that the layers are linked. The layers can be unlinked by clicking again in the same place.
- **Opacity** The opacity of an individual layer is controlled by the value entered in the **OPACITY** window at the top of the palette. This is useful for fading in image elements.

Drag between Images You can automatically duplicate any active layer by dragging it to another image window. This is useful for building composites from several image files.

Adjustment Layers Adjustment and fill layers permit editing an image many times without permanently changing the original pixel data. Some advantages of **adjustment layers** include:

- You can compare changes that you make to a single layer by toggling it on and off with the eye icon.
  - Adjustment layers apply their changes to all layers beneath them and can be reordered at will.
  - You can create multiple adjustment layers and create a mask in each one to limit its effect to a specific part of the picture.
  - Adjustment layers can be moved and applied to other similar images or discarded as needed.
  - Adjustment and fill layers can be blended with other layers by changing the **OPACITY** value or the **BLEND** modes in the Layers palette.

Composing an Image with Layers You can assemble complex images from many composite parts with layers. Photographers use this process to create elaborate collages. You can select and copy elements from many source images and then paste them into one or more layers, gradually splicing them together into a composite. You can then rearrange individual elements within layers as well as the order of the layers themselves to achieve a desired effect. Each new layer's Opacity window can be adjusted to create the desired degree of transparency and adjustment layers can be added to control color and tonal effects.

Canvas Size When creating a layer collage you may need a larger canvas to contain all the element of the composite. You could simply create a large-sized new file (**FILE —> NEW**) with the necessary dimensions and desired resolution to hold the new collage and then add the elements in layers. However, a slightly faster approach is to expand the canvas size of the first collage image to make the necessary room to add the additional el-

ements. Go to **IMAGE —> CANVAS SIZE** and you'll see a dialog box where the expanded canvas dimensions can be set and the current image repositioned on the field. This technique is also useful for printing several smaller images on the same piece of paper.

Merging and Flattening Layers Layers are powerful tools for digital photographers, but they do come at a price. With every layer, file size grows, the demand for RAM memory increases, and computer performance may slow down. Moreover, larger files require more storage space and more time to copy or to transmit to others. Further, layered files cannot be stored in all file formats.

Photoshop offers two ways to trim the size of layered files—**MERGING** and **FLATTENING**. You should use these commands only when the af-

Making an Adjustment Layer

*Adjustment layers are the ideal tool for applying **LEVELS** or **COLOR BALANCE** effects. They can be modified to match any output device without permanently changing the image file.*

1. *Open a picture file. Then activate the **LAYERS PALETTE** by clicking to **WINDOW —> SHOW LAYERS** from the Menu Bar.*

2. *Click on the half-black circle at the bottom of the **LAYERS** window and select the type of layer desired. Options include **LEVELS**, **COLOR BALANCE**, **HUE/SATURATION**, and others. The **LEVELS** option was used for this example. See Figure 8-25.*

3. *The appropriate dialog box will now open. The Levels command displays the histogram described in Unit 7, page 256. Adjust and click OK to apply.*

4. *You can modify the adjustment layer at any time by clicking on the icon in the layer to reopen the controls. See Figure 8-26.*

5. *Save the file with a new name in Photoshop's native, .PSD format. This will retain all the layer data in your most recent edition as well as the original file before editing.*

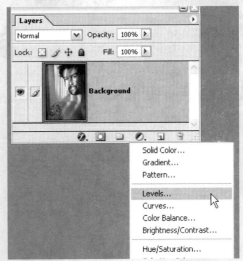

Figure 8-25. Adobe and Photoshop are either registered trademarks of Adobe Systems Incorporated in the United States and/or other countries.

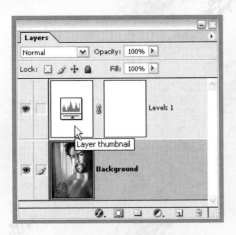

Figure 8-26. Adobe and Photoshop are either registered trademarks of Adobe Systems Incorporated in the United States and/or other countries.

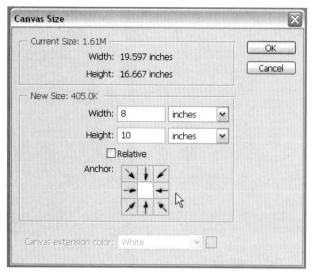

Figure 8-27. A screen shot of the Canvas Size dialog box.

fected layers are completely finished and will not need further editing.

Merging combines two or more layers into a single new layer. To merge a layer with the layer immediately below it, click to **LAYER → MERGE DOWN**. If they are visible, non-adjacent layers can also be merged—turn on the eye icon for all layers you wish to merge and click to **LAYER → MERGE VISIBLE**.

Flattening combines the data from all visible layers into a single new background layer. Flattening is required before files can be saved in many file formats, including the popular .JPEG format.

Type Tool Basics

Working with type involves more than spelling words correctly and selecting a typeface. Design-

Building a Composite with Layers

1. *Open an image that will be used as a background or start a new file. This will become the target file. In this example, the face in Figure 8-28 was used.*

2. *Open the remaining images that contain the parts you wish to combine with the background. In this example, a second photograph of hands holding teabags was used as a second source image.*

3. *To keep the same relative scale, resize each image to match the resolution of the target file. In this example, the target image is set at 300 ppi. To adjust the second source image to this resolution, click to **IMAGE → IMAGE SIZE** and set the Resolution to 300. Place a check in the **RESAMPLE** box.*

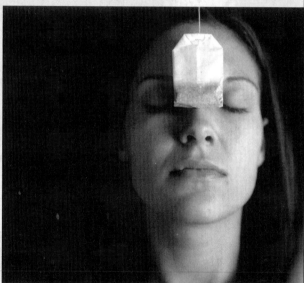

Figure 8-28. This image will be used as a target background for the composite.

4. *Draw a selection around the portion of the second source image that you wish to use in the composite. In this example, the two hands holding tea bags were selected with the **LASSO TOOL**. See Figure 8-29.*

Figure 8-29. Hands from another image were outlined with the lasso tool to make a selection.

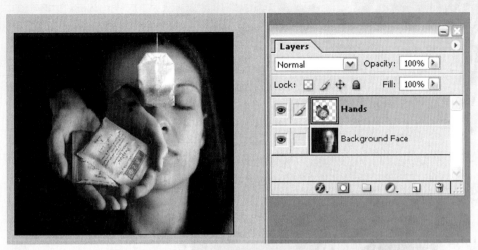

Figure 8-30. The hand selection was copied and pasted into the target window.

5. *If you wish, you can feather the selection to make a more seamless blend. In this example, the hands were feathered by clicking to* **SELECT** *—> **FEATHER** and then set to 5 pixels.*

6. *Copy the selected area from the second source image by clicking to* **EDIT** *—> **COPY**.*

7. *Next, make the target image active by clicking on its window. Then paste in the selected element by clicking to* **EDIT** *—> **PASTE**. Photoshop will automatically place the item on a new layer. See Figure 8-30.*

8. *To move the image part into place on its own layer, use the* **MOVE TOOL** *located in the upper right corner of the toolbar. Adjust the* **OPACITY** *and* **BLENDING** *options as you wish.*

9. *You can rotate, scale or transform the image on the new layer to fit the composition by clicking to* **EDIT** *—> **TRANSFORM** *—> **SCALE**.*

10. *You can create additional layers the same way, to achieve the composite that you wish.*

11. *You can also add adjustment layers. This example used an adjustment layer for Levels.*

12. *You can edit images on any selected layer to blend it with others. In this example, the* **BLUR** *and* **AIRBRUSH TOOLS** *were used to soften and blend the top edge of the two hands.*

13. *You can study your progress by turning layer visibility on and off with their eye icons. The results of editing are easier to see if the visibility of all other layers is clicked off.*

14. *Experiment with rearranging the order of the layers to create the best composite.*

15. *When finished, save the file with a new name in Photoshop's native, .PSD format. This will retain all the layer data in your most recent edition as well as the original file before editing.*

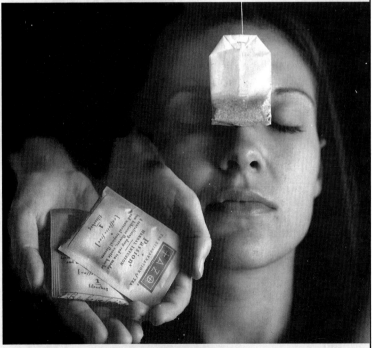

Figure 8-31. The finished composite could be used as an advertisement for herbal tea.

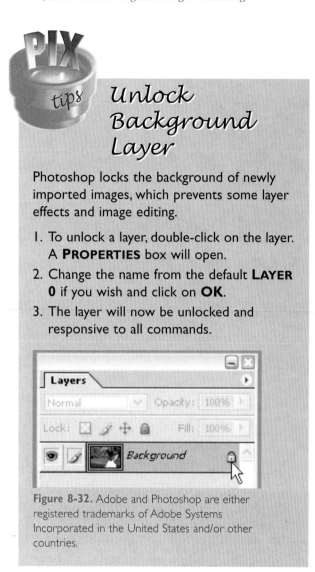

PIX tips

Unlock Background Layer

Photoshop locks the background of newly imported images, which prevents some layer effects and image editing.

1. To unlock a layer, double-click on the layer. A **PROPERTIES** box will open.

2. Change the name from the default **LAYER 0** if you wish and click on **OK**.

3. The layer will now be unlocked and responsive to all commands.

Figure 8-32. Adobe and Photoshop are either registered trademarks of Adobe Systems Incorporated in the United States and/or other countries.

ing with type fonts can add style as well as a message to an image.

Before placing any type in an image, consider where you will place it. What may look good when viewed as plain text on a blank background may get lost or confusing when placed in a colored image. The type should not only be legible, but it should make both a visual and a verbal point. Check the background to find the best place to insert the type. Consider the typeface and color contrast. Your use of type will be effective if it contributes to an overall cohesive composition.

The look and feel of a type font is determined not only by the letters themselves but by the spaces around them. Photoshop provides tools to control many of these spaces, including these:

- **Tracking** the overall spacing between letters that is characteristic of the font
- **Kerning** the spacing introduced between individual pairs of letters to fit the text in a given horizontal space
- **Leading** the spacing introduced between lines of type both for appearance and to fit the text in a given vertical space

You can access these controls and more from the **PARAGRAPH** palette and the **CHARACTER** palette. Click to **WINDOW — > SHOW PARAGRAPH** and **WINDOW — > SHOW CHARACTER**.

Warped Text

Photoshop provides a **TEXT WARP** feature for creating text effects, such as bending, bulging, glowing edges and others. No matter what complex text effects you choose to apply, the underlying text remains fully editable. For greater variety, you can apply different text effects on separate layers. Follow these steps to render **warped text** in an image:

1. Select the text layer in the **LAYERS** palette by highlighting it with the mouse.

2. Click on the **TYPE TOOL** in the toolbar and then click on the **CREATE WARPED TEXT** button on the right side of the Options Bar.

3. The **WARP TEXT** dialog box will appear. Select a warp style from the scroll box.

4. Experiment with **HORIZONTAL** and **VERTICAL DISTORTION** and **BLEND** settings until you achieve the desired effect. Preview changes in the image window.

5. Click on **OK** to render the warp effect.

6. Add additional type layers with other effects as needed to complete the composition.

7. Always click on the check mark on the far right of the Options Bar to commit your changes. (See Figure 8-33.)

Figure 8-33. The appearance of the type can be set from the options bar. Adobe and Photoshop are either registered trademarks of Adobe Systems Incorporated in the United States and/or other countries.

Figure 8-34. Photoshop offers a variety of styles for twisting and warping text.

Using Type

Use the following steps to place type in an image:

1. *Open an image to which you wish to add type.*

2. *Choose the **TYPE TOOL** by clicking on the **T** icon on the toolbar.*

3. *Select the desired **TYPE ATTRIBUTES** from the Options Bar as shown in Figure 8-35. Choices include **TYPEFACES** such as Arial and Times New Roman, **ATTRIBUTES** such as Boldface and Italics, **TYPE SIZE** in points, and **ANTI-ALIASING** method such as Crisp and Strong (normally set to Crisp).*

4. *Select a **JUSTIFICATION STYLE**, such as Left, Center, or Right.*

5. *Select a color for the type. Color defaults to the foreground color. To change color, click on the colored box in the Options Bar and select a new color.*

6. *To create a text box, click-and-drag the **TYPE** cursor within the image where you want the type to appear. A text box will appear as a dotted line. Release the mouse. Enter the message and the type will appear in the text box with the attributes you have selected.*

7. *When all of the text has been entered, click on the check mark on the far right of the Type Options Bar to commit the type. The type will appear on a new and separate layer in the image. (See Figure 8-33.)*

8. *Once the type is placed it can be repositioned with the **MOVE TOOL**.*

9. *The type is fully editable—you can correct spelling, change font size, color, and other attributes as you wish. To edit the text, point-and-click on the text to activate the **TYPE TOOL** and display the text box. Click-and-drag to highlight text you wish to edit. Click within the text to place the insertion point and then insert or delete as usual. To commit your changes, click again on the check mark on the far right of the Options Bar. (See Figure 8-33.)*

10. *Once a type layer is created, you can apply layer commands to it. You can move, reorder the stack, copy, and change the layer options of a type layer as you would do for any other layer.*

Figure 8-35. Use the character palette to set tracking, kerning and leading. Adobe and Photoshop are either registered trademarks of Adobe Systems Incorporated in the United States and/or other countries.

Questions to Consider

1. How can defects be removed from an image?

2. Describe some of the ways that selections can be used. How do you create a selection?

3. How are layers used to build composite images?

4. What factors should be considered when using type within an image?

Suggested Field and Laboratory Assignments

1. Use one of the common local image controls—Burning, Dodging, Sponge, and Sharpen—to refine a picture.

2. Enhance the color and saturation of a small part of a picture by applying image corrections to a selection.

3. Use the **RUBBER STAMP TOOL** to remove distracting elements, such as power lines, from an image. Experiment with duplicating an image element, such as a tree, and adding the duplicate to the original photograph.

4. Create an imaginary scene. Combine separate landscape photographs and various landscape elements into one new composite image made with layers.

5. Create a fantasy portrait. Use image-editing software to select and copy the image of a person from one photograph and paste it into a second background photograph. In Figure 8-36, student photographer Richard Sakall used 22 layers to assemble his complex fantasy collage, "Dream Kiss."

Figure 8-36. A fantasy portrait.

Advanced Digital Image Processing

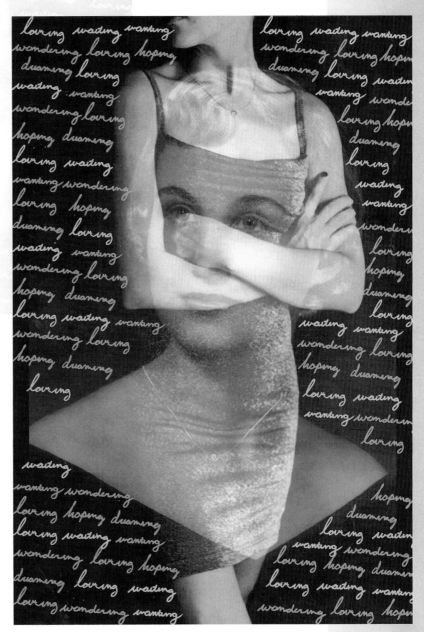

Stacia Suchon, "Writing."

Unit at a Glance

Perfecting an image in the digital darkroom can be as time-consuming as work in a conventional darkroom. Electronic imaging brought unparalleled image control to photography, but at the price of long hours of computer work. Fortunately, the digital darkroom, like its wet counterpart, can be organized and streamlined for efficient workflow.

This unit describes how to set up efficient procedures to perform the routine tasks of digital image processing so as to maximize workflow. The unit will also demonstrate ways to personalize Photoshop to work with your preferences and establish sound color management settings and policies.

Maximizing the Digital Workflow

Objective 9-A Describe and demonstrate tools and procedures in Photoshop that can be used to establish efficient and effective digital workflow.

Key Concepts file browser, RAW, flag, Metadata, EXIF, Keywords, file info, batch process, Photomerge

Use the Power of the File Browser

The **file browser** found in current versions of Photoshop is an effective control and command center for managing digital image files. The file browser operates much like a light box, displaying an array of thumbnail images, and allowing you to preview and select images for processing. You can easily scan through a day's worth of images, click on any desired thumbnail to preview an enlarged image, and select the best ones.

The real power of the file browser, however, goes beyond these ordinary tasks. In fact, the file browser is really a small image-editing program in itself. The file browser can be used to flag the best images, sort them by keywords, read the EXIF metadata embedded in the image by digital cameras, and batch process many common imaging tasks. The file browser can also import and display **RAW** files—an unmodified file format of-

Figure 9-2. The file browser window.

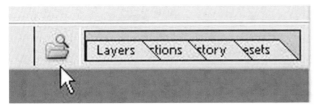

Figure 9-3. The file browser icon.

fered by many higher-level digital cameras—allowing you to adjust white balance, exposure, and other image variables in the image editor rather than in the camera at the time of exposure. This usually results in higher quality image processing.

Displaying the File Browser

You can access the file browser quickly in one of several ways:

- Click on the folder icon in the top right hand corner of the screen, just to the side of the palette dock.
- Go to the File Menu — > Browse
- Or use the keyboard Ctrl + Shift + O (PC) or Cmd + Shift + O (Mac)

Editing with the File Browser

You can open the File Browser as a window by any of these options, then resize it and drag it to a new position in the workspace. You can quickly rotate images counterclockwise or clockwise to their correct orientation by clicking on the picture and then clicking on one of the two rotate icons. You can change the size of the thumbnail images by selecting an appropriate size option under the browser's "View" command. You can also resize both the preview and directory windows by clicking and dragging the window borders. Further, you can arrange the thumbnail images in any order by clicking and dragging them around the virtual "light table."

You can quickly edit a group of images by clicking on the thumbnails of the selected images and then clicking on the "**Flag**" icon at the top of the browser's window. You can select and flag many images at once by depressing the "Apple" key on a MAC or the "Control" key on a PC as you mouse click on all the desired thumbnails. Once the selected images have been flagged, you can hide the others to complete your final editing choices. In the File Browser dialog box go to

View — > scroll down to **Flagged Files** and release the mouse. You can also sort the images by an assigned rank order. To assign a rank, select the desired thumbnail and Control/Click on a Mac or Right Mouse Click on a PC and scroll down to "Rank" where you can enter a numerical ranking value. You can display the thumbnails by rank by clicking on "**Sort**" in the browser window, scrolling down to "**Rank**," and releasing the mouse. In a like manner you can sort the images by date created, date modified, size, resolution, and other factors.

Displaying and Using Data about the Image File

METADATA

Two palette tabs become visible when you select an image in the file browser—the **Metadata** and **Keywords** tabs. As with other Photoshop tabs, you can mouse-drag these sections to other locations within the browser. For example, you might wish to move them to the "Folder" section of the browser to free up space and allow a larger preview window.

If the image was acquired with a digital camera, the Metadata window will likely contain useful **EXIF** (Exchangeable Image File Format) information—a standard format for storing information about the image, such as its creation date, camera settings used, image format, and size. The digital camera embeds this information in the image file when it captures the image. This Metadata or EXIF information is viewable but not editable within Photoshop.

USING KEYWORDS

By clicking on the "**Keywords**" tab, you open another window where you can assign labels to help you organize and sort the images. Some keyword categories and keyword folders are supplied by Photoshop, but you can easily add other suitable terms. To add a new keyword click on the New Keyword icon at the bottom of the palette that looks like a pad of sticky notes. Then type in the desired term. To create a new group of related keywords, click on the icon that looks like a file folder. In Figure 9-4 a new group called Assignments has been created with subcategories of Composition and Light.

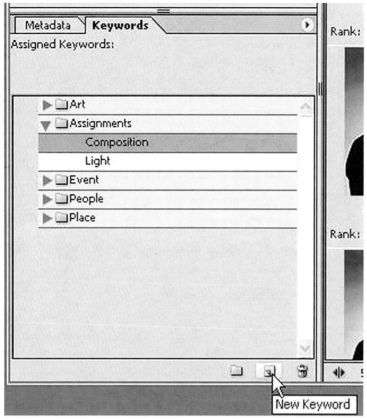

Figure 9-4. New keyword group and keyword terms.

ADDING KEYWORDS TO FILES

To assign a keyword, select the file's thumbnail in the file browser, click on the box to the left of the desired keyword or double-click on the name of the keyword. A check mark appears next to the keyword when it is assigned. One or more keywords can be added to a file.

SORTING BY KEYWORDS

Keywords are powerful tools for managing images. Instead of tediously searching through hundreds of photographs for one desired image, you can use Photoshop to quickly search by keyword. To sort by keywords, Right mouse click (PC) or Control/Click (MAC) on the desired search term. This will open a dialog box where you can specify the search criteria.

Using the File Info Window

Photoshop's **File Info** window offers another way to embed and view useful information in a file. You can access this window from the File Browser by clicking **FILE — > FILE INFO** after selecting or opening a thumbnail image.

Inside the File Info window you can assign the image a document title, keywords, an author, and copyright status. Photoshop embeds this information permanently in the file and makes it available to other users who may need it. See Figure 9-5.

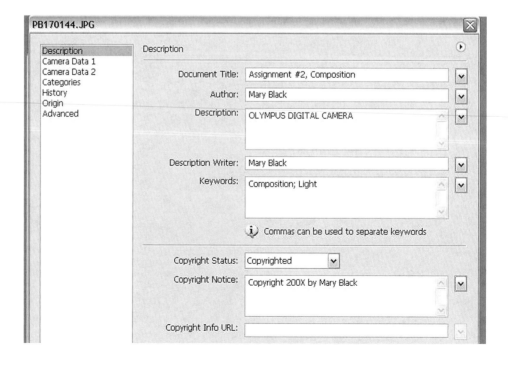

Figure 9-5. The file info window.

Using the Automate —> Photomerge Command to Create a Panorama

The photomerge function will seamlessly knit together multiple photographs taken from the same vantage point into a panoramic photograph.

Taking Photos for Merging

Select a suitable scene for a panoramic-style photograph, such as a broad sweeping landscape. Hold the camera as level as possible, preferably using a tripod, and take a series of photographs that sweeps across the scene. For best results, overlap the component images by 15–40% of their area when you take the photographs. If the overlap is less, Photoshop won't be able to generate the panorama automatically, although you can still stitch them together manually. Shoot all the images from the same location, using the same focal length, without tilting the camera between shots. For best results, shoot in a "Manual" rather than "Programmed" or "Automatic" exposure mode to maintain the same exposure throughout the series.

Merging Images with Photoshop

1. *Click on the file folder icon at the top right of the screen or **FILE —> BROWSE** to open the File Browser window.*

2. *Select the files you wish to merge into a panoramic image by holding down the Apple key (MAC) or the Ctrl key (PC) and mouse-clicking on the desired thumbnails.*

3. *Choose **AUTOMATE —> PHOTOMERGE** from the browser window. (See Figure 9-6.)*

4. *Photoshop will automatically open each image in turn, adjust the color and exposure settings, and display the combined results in a new Photomerge dialog box. (A message will appear if the image overlap is insufficient to assemble automatically; however, you can then assemble the composition manually. Photoshop will automatically lock overlapping images in place when it detects common image elements if you check "Snap to Image.")*

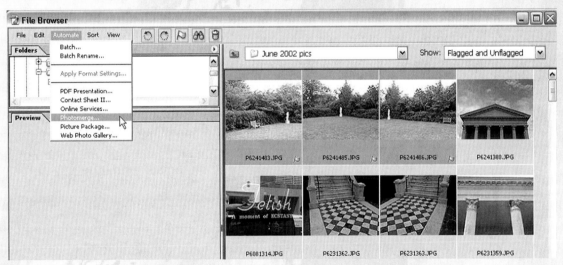

Figure 9-6. Files selected for Photomerge.

5. *Once Photomerge displays the combined panorama, you can rearrange and adjust the order of the images as you wish.*

6. *The Perspective and Composition radio dial boxes allow you to experiment with those options.*

7. *Check "Keep as Layers" and click "OK" when you complete your manual adjustments to open the image in Photoshop. (See Figure 9-7.)*

8. *Adjust the tonality and position of each layer as needed. Crop and resize the image as you wish. Then use the **FILE —> SAVE AS** command to save the file with a new name.*

9. *Your merged panorama is now complete. (See Figure 9-8.)*

(continued)

Figure 9-7. Photomerge dialog box.

Figure 9-8. Completed panorama.

The Power of Automation within the File Browser

The "Automate" menu of the File Browser is loaded with useful and timesaving features. With Automate you can rename and **batch process** a group of selected files without opening them first. This command can also be used to run a recorded "Action" on a selected group of files. For example, you can run a recorded "Action" to resize all of them for postcard-sized prints.

The Automate menu can make quick work of many repetitive tasks in digital imaging. The standard commands include:

- PDF Presentation—generates a PDF slide show of selected images
- Contact Sheet II—prepares a reference page of image thumbnails with or without file names
- Online Services—connects you directly to online photo printing services, such as Shutterfly
- **Photomerge**—automatically and seamlessly combines several images into a panorama
- Web Photo Gallery—creates hyperlinked Web pages ready to upload to a server.

Photoshop Actions

Objective 9-B Explain and demonstrate how to use and record actions to perform repetitive imaging tasks efficiently.

Key Concepts Actions, macro, Actions Palette, Actions Menu, Load Actions

Actions are miniature computer programs that can record and play back a series of steps. An action allows you to perform a long series of pre-recorded steps automatically upon one or more images at the press of a single button. Actions can save the drudgery of entering the same series of steps, one at a time, repeatedly on a folder full of images. Some actions are already built into Photoshop and many more can be downloaded from the Web. However, you can create your own Photoshop actions quickly and easily as needed. In this objective you will learn how to use and construct actions.

Photoshop Actions

A Photoshop action is a computer **macro**—a short command that executes a longer sequence of commands. For example, an action might execute a sequence of steps that automatically resizes an image for display on the Web, sharpens it, and saves it in a new folder. By using this action, you can then perform these steps on one or more images with one simple click of a button.

You can record most Photoshop commands and tools into an action, including pauses that allow the user to enter custom data. Actions created by users to meet their own imaging needs are especially powerful tools.

Photoshop provides a folder that contains some basic actions and is accessible from the "**Actions Palette**." If the "Actions Palette" is not visible you can navigate to "**WINDOW — > ACTIONS**" to bring it to the desktop. To experiment with the default actions, open an image, click on the Default Actions folder inside the Actions Palette, and select an action to play. The example below shows "Sepia Toning" as the target action to play. The selected action can now be invoked by clicking on the "Play" arrow button at the bottom of the Actions Palette. (See Figure 9-9.)

Figure 9-9. Actions palette and play button.

Loading and Using Actions Recorded by Others

You can use a recorded action on any image and share it with other Photoshop users. Thousands of Photoshop actions are available free on the Web—just search for "Photoshop actions." Once you download an action file to your computer you can load it into Photoshop and use it. Click the small arrow in the upper right corner of the Actions Palette to open the "**Actions Menu**" and scroll down to "**Load Actions**." Locate the action file you want, select it, then click on "Load." Action files for Windows computers usually end with the filename extension .atn. The new action will appear on the Actions palette; click on the "**Play**" button to use it.

Recording Your Own Custom Actions

Actions are plain text files created by Photoshop that it can read as instructions and apply to later images. The process requires you to perform all the key presses and mouse clicks one by one, in order, just once, to produce the result that you want. Photoshop records these keyboard and mouse acts as a sequence of text instructions that it can then play back on demand at another time. Simply put, Photoshop records your key presses and mouse clicks and plays them back on command. As an example, this exercise will show you how to construct an action for one common imaging task—resizing a digital image to make a

Recording an Action

1. *Create a new folder called "Postcard Prints" on the desktop or hard drive. This will be the destination folder for your adjusted images.*

2. *Open a file.*

3. *From the Actions Palette, click on the triangular button at the top right.*

4. *Be sure that "Button Mode" is not checked. Otherwise, Photoshop may assign a color or function key to the action that will be visible. You may toggle Button Mode on and off later by using the triangle at the top of the palette. Leave it off for now.)*

5. *Scroll down to "New Set." Name the set "**My Actions**." This will create a folder within the actions palette to hold the custom actions you create.*

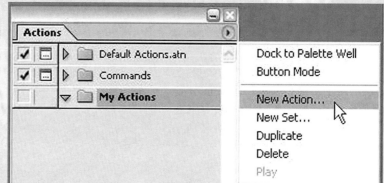

Figure 9-10. Make new action dialog box.

6. *Click once on the newly created "**My Actions**" folder to select it.*

7. *Now, either click on the triangular button and scroll down to "**New Action**" or click on the New Action icon at the bottom of the palette to create a new action—the icon looks like a pad of sticky notes. Name this new action "Postcard Prints" and click Record. (See Figure 9-10.)*

8. *Photoshop is now recording. Every key press and mouse click will be recorded and added to the action unless the recording is manually stopped. You may stop and resume recording at any time by clicking on the Stop or Record icons at the bottom of the Actions dialog box.*

9. *While recording, perform the sequence of key presses and mouse clicks needed for your tasks. They will be included in the action. In the following example the action will set the image size, set the resolution, boost the image saturation, sharpen, and finally save the file in a new folder called "postcard prints."*

10. *While recording, go to **IMAGE** —> **IMAGE SIZE**, check "Constrain Proportions" and "Resample Image." Now type in a Width of 6 inches for a standard "postcard" sized print, and set the resolution to 240 ppi for most printers. (This assumes a horizontal image proportioned to fit this print size; if not, choose a size that is appropriate for your most common images.) (See Figure 9-11.)*

11. *Photoshop recorded all the steps and entries needed to make the adjustments to the image size and resolution. The action palette should now look like this: (See Figure 9-12.)*

12. *Note that recording continues, so avoid stray key presses and mouse clicks. Go to **IMAGE** —> **ADJUSTMENTS** —> **HUE/SATURATION** to slightly boost the image color. Click and drag the Saturation slider to the right to a +5 setting. This small change will create slightly more vivid and colorful prints.*

13. *While still recording, apply the Unsharp Mask setting you prefer to sharpen the photograph by going to **FILTER** —> **SHARPEN** —> **UNSHARP MASK**. (A suggested setting for an*

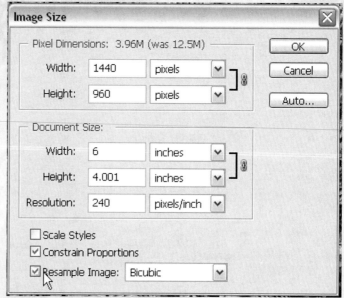

Figure 9-11. Recording size and resolution.

image file with this resolution is Amount = 80, Radius = 1.3, and Threshold = 1. If you wish to experiment, stop recording. Resume when you are ready to continue.)

14. *While still recording, go to* **FILE —>** **SAVE AS** *and select the newly created folder called "Postcard Prints" as the final destination for the file. Choose the desired file format and click on "Save." (If you select JPEG format, Photoshop will open a second dialog box for choosing a JPEG quality level. Select the quality level you wish and click "OK." You are still recording.)*

15. *While recording, go to* **FILE —>** **CLOSE** *to close the image window.*

16. *Finally, "Stop Recording" the action by clicking on the square "Stop" button at the bottom left of the Action palette. The completed action should look like Figure 9-13.*

17. *To use the action, open the image you wish to process, click once on the newly created Postcard Print action to select it, then click the play button. Your action will automatically adjust the image and save it in the new directory folder.*

18. *You can also use the action to batch process many images at one time. Open the File Browser. Select "* **AUTOMATE —>** **BATCH.**" *Select "My Actions" from the "Set" window and "Postcard Prints" from the "Action" window. Select "Folder" in the "* **Source**" *window. Click "Choose" to input the location of the folder that contains the images you wish to process. Click "OK" to apply the action automatically to all the files in the folder.*

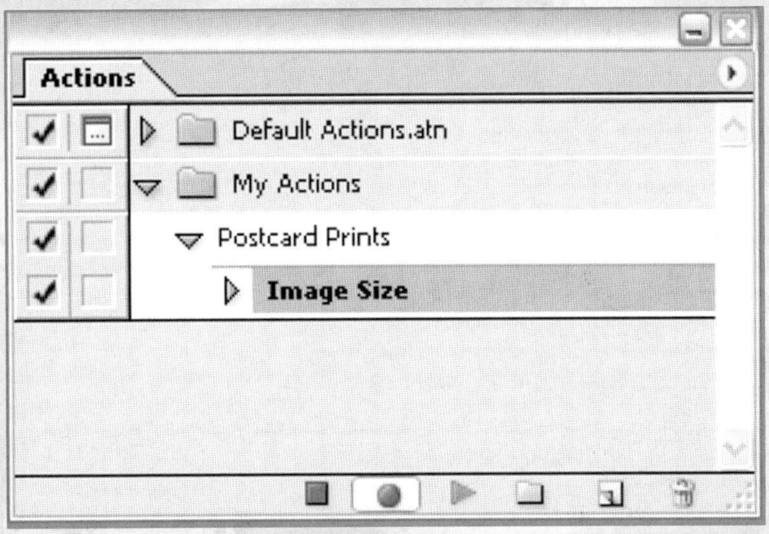

Figure 9-12. Action being recorded, part 1.

Figure 9-13. Stop recording action and finished action.

postcard sized print. To record an action, you must open the Actions Palette. If it is not visible, go to "**WINDOW — > ACTIONS**."

Fine Tuning Actions

You can edit actions to refine them. For example, you can move any step in the action to a different place in the sequence by dragging it to a new location. Similarly, you can delete steps by dragging them to the trash icon at the bottom of the Actions Palette. To add new steps in the action, select the insertion point, press the record button,

perform the new command steps, and stop recording when done.

When played, an action executes the original sequence of recorded steps. However, you may occasionally wish to omit steps to achieve a particular result. You can omit a step in the action by removing the check in the command's check box. Selecting or deselecting the checkbox toggles the command on or off. Individual action steps or groups of steps can also be selected for play by using Command-Click (MAC OS) or Control-Click (PC.) See Figure 9-14.

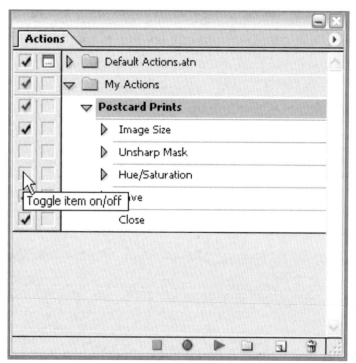

Figure 9-14. Note that removing their checkmark in this action has toggled off Unsharp Mask and Hue/Saturation.

Introduction to Color Management

Objective 9-C Explain the theory of color management and demonstrate knowledge of its use and terminology.

Key Concepts color management, color spaces, input, RGB, CMYK, central color model, CIE, color gamut, dynamic range, Color Management System (CMS), profiles, ICC, source profile, monitor profile, output profile, Color Management Module (CMM), Rendering Intent

Overview

Color management. That seemingly simple expression often strikes chords of both fear and promise in the hearts of digital photographers. What is color management? The idea is simple—providing the means to capture, view, and print your digital images with colors that match. Without effective color management, these colors can shift significantly when images are captured, viewed, or printed

and you may be disappointed with what you see. Why is color management so complicated? Different technologies are employed for capturing images (input), viewing them on a monitor (display), and printing them (output). Because of these technological differences, no perfect system of color matching is possible. Nevertheless, with correct techniques and tools, it is possible to create a workable color management system.

This section introduces theories of color management and the industry-wide terminology that is used to describe color control from Input to Output. What you learn, though not intended to make you a color management expert, will help you begin to manage color to obtain predictable results rather than trusting to chance and trial-and-error methods.

Color Management Defined

A **Color Management** system is an integrated set of software, hardware, and procedures designed to compensate for the different ways that digital imaging devices—such as digital cameras, scanners, monitors, and printers—display and produce colors. The goal of color management is to make colors look the same regardless of the hardware or platform used to capture, view, and print them. With an ideal color management

Figure 9-15. Color management assures consistent color throughout the imaging chain.

system, the colors on all monitors and all printed output should match. Color management enables you to control input, display, and output color to obtain consistently predictable results rather than having to rely on trial-and-error methods.

Color Is Not Absolute

In a large electronics store you might see a wall filled with television sets tuned to the same channel. It is apparent that they do not all look the same. And, although many of the sets may display pleasing colors, because human vision and electronic displays differ, none can truly match the original scene. Computer monitors suffer from the same problem.

To further complicate matters, colors appear differently in different viewing environments. A printed image viewed under warm tungsten lights will appear differently when viewed under fluorescent lights, or outside in sunlight, or under clouds or overcast. But which view of these colors is "true" or "correct"?

Clearly, color is perceptual and not absolute. The colors we see depend on the viewing environment. Additionally, every mechanical or electronic device in the imaging chain displays, alters, or prints colors differently. Color management provides a way to contain all these variables and attempt to display and print the same color on all devices.

Digital Color Capture

Computers cannot "understand" color. A digital camera or scanner captures color information as bits of data represented by millions of ones (1) and zeroes (0) that make up the digital code for color. The code can be sent from one device to another, but the devices cannot translate the code on their own—they need a digital definition or map to enable them to translate the code into instructions for displaying or printing colors. For example, a beautiful sunset is captured in the form of a digital code that is conveyed to a display or output device. For the device to produce an accurate and consistent color image of the sunset, it needs some form of model or map to translate the code. Computers rely on these mathematical models or color maps—referred to as **color spaces**— to represent the colors in an image.

Digital Devices & Color Models

Input devices such as digital cameras, scanners, and display devices use the Red, Green, and Blue (**RGB**) color model to reproduce color. Most printers use the Cyan, Magenta, Yellow, and Black (**CMYK**) color model to reproduce color. These two different color models reproduce colors in different ways and need a translation device to accurately convert the colors from one form of describing color to another, such as from a computer monitor to a print.

RGB or Additive Color

When red, green, and blue (RGB) colored lights are mixed in various proportions and intensities most of the visible spectrum can be represented. If red, green and blue are combined equally all visible wavelengths are transmitted back to your eye to create white. This is why these three colors are referred to as additive primary colors. RGB devices, including most digital cameras, scanners and monitors, use red (R), green (G) and blue (B) light, or channels, to reproduce color. A computer monitor, for example, creates a color image by emitting light from thousands of red, green, and blue glowing phosphors to produce the effects of many different colors. (See Color Plate 1.)

CMYK or Subtractive Color

In most, but not all, photo printing devices the red, green, and blue color is produced by using cyan (C), magenta (M) and yellow (Y) inks or dyes. The inks are laid down in layers of dots, each dot subtracting its RGB wavelength from the white background of the print to produce the colors of the spectrum. In theory, pure cyan, magenta, and yellow pigments should combine to subtract all wavelengths of light to produce black. For this reason these colors are called subtractive primary colors. (See Color Plate 1.) In practice however, because most dyes and inks contain some impurities, the three colors combined in equal quantities usually produce a muddy gray-brown. For this reason they must be combined with a fourth black (K) ink to produce a true black. (K is short for KEY, a printer term for black.) Thus, ink-jet printers and the large printing presses used by magazines and newspapers use at least four colors of ink and are sometimes called CMYK printers.

Devices Translate Color in Specific Ways

All computer devices produce color using either the RGB or CMYK color model. Further, the colors produced are dependent on the specific device and vary from one device to another. Digital cameras, scanners, and monitors typically work with color in RGB space; most printers output CMYK. Just as individual TV sets produce different colors from the same color data, different image capture, display, and output devices also produce different colors. The same type of file, such as RGB, sent from one device to another may appear differently on each device as each device uses a different map of RGB to produce color. Because of this, color descriptions such as RGB and CMYK are considered to be device-specific color descriptions, or color spaces. The most important task of a color management system, therefore, is to ensure that the destination devices, no matter what those devices may be, translate color data in an image file correctly.

Defining Color Independent of the Device

A color management system provides a means to describe color that is **not** device specific. Rather than translating the color language of one device to that of the next device in the imaging chain, color managed systems use a **central color model** or **CIE** (from *Commission Internationale De L'eclairage*, the developer of the concept). Think of CIE as an alternate, but common color

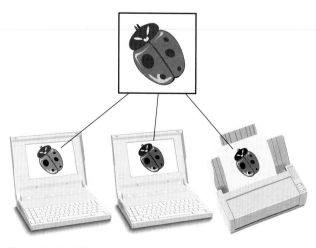

Figure 9-16. Without a color management system each device will interpret and display color in a different way.

language for each component in the imaging chain—a standard for translating color codes that is shared by all devices in the imaging chain.

Color Gamut, Dynamic Range and Device Limitations

Color Gamut All devices in the imaging chain are capable of producing a limited range of colors, referred to as their **color gamut**. As an analogy, a box of 50 different colored pencils would have a greater color gamut than the economy box of 25. Similarly, a color monitor can't produce a more saturated red, green, or blue than its design and phosphors allow. Generally speaking color gamut decreases as one moves downward through the devices in the imaging chain. Digital cameras and monitors typically have greater color gamut than printers.

Dynamic Range The range of brightness that can be recorded by a capture device, produced by a display device, or output to a printer, is called its **dynamic range**. Dynamic range is measured on a logarithmic scale. Brightness values double with each increase of 0.3. High-end digital cameras and scanners have a dynamic range of at least 3.6. Compared to film and wet-lab materials, these devices can accurately record brightness values that are as much as 12 stops apart, exceeding that of chemistry-based materials.

Generally speaking, the dynamic range of the image recorded by a digital camera or scanner is greater than that of a computer monitor, which in turn is greater than that of a color print. Thus, as you move an image downward through the imaging chain from one device to the next, you risk loosing color and brightness information unless you re-map the image for each device to approximate the dynamic range of the original.

The Goal of Standard Color and Device Compatibility

A **Color Management System** (**CMS**) allows one to utilize device-independent color spaces, such as CIE, to manage the device-dependent RGB and CMYK color values and interpret the color data in the image. A CMS compares the color space of a capture device to the color space of a display or output device, and makes the necessary adjustments to represent the color as con-

Fact Box

DEVICE INDEPENDENT COLOR

Digital imaging devices capture, display, and output RGB or CMYK color values according to their own unique physical characteristics.

The *Commission International de l'Eclairage* (International Commission on Illumination), or CIE, recognizing the need for a standard, device-independent color model, created a color space called CIE XYZ. It is based on the way humans see solid colors rather than on the characteristics of any single device. No device is expected to produce colors independently in this color space; rather, the space provides a means for converting a device-specific color space to a common standard.

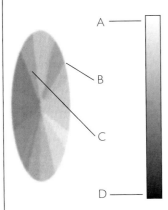

Figure 9-17. L*a*b* (Lab) model. A. Luminance = 100 (white). B. Green to red component. C. Blue to yellow component. D. Luminance = 0 (black).

Three-dimensional charts of this color model represent red, green, blue along each of the three axes of the chart. The most applicable CIE model for digital photographers is the CIE **L*a*b*** model. Developed in 1976 for managing color across digital devices, the CIE L*a*b* color space gives a good approximation of the colors visible to the eye. The acronym L*a*b* (pronounced, "L star, A star, B star") derives from its three-way description of color—L* represents the lightness, a* represents the red/blue properties, and b* represents the yellow/blue properties.

Photoshop uses L*a*b* as its device-independent color space. This intermediate color space is used by Photoshop's color management engine to convert colors from one device-specific color space to another. Generally this space remains hidden from view and needs no settings.

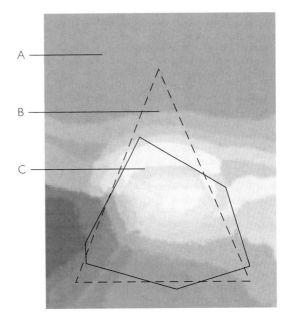

Figure 9-18. The gamuts of different color spaces. A. L*a*b* color space encompasses all visible colors. B. RGB color space. C. CMYK color space.

of computer instructions that re-maps, or converts, data from one color model to another. When an RGB image is converted to CMYK for printing, or when a CMYK image is converted to RGB for monitor display, the transform engine makes the conversion. Some examples of color transform engines are KCMS (Kodak's old color matching system,) KICC (Kodak's new version,) Apple's ColorSync and Window's ICM.

Profiles Define Color

To verify that the color information in digital images is translated consistently across all devices, a color management system (CMS) uses device and document **profiles**. Profiling refers to the process of applying a color reference to the components of the digital workflow process. A device's profile maps the color space of that device based on its capabilities to reproduce color. Profiles are CMS readable text files that define a device's color characteristics and behavior. They are generally written in the **ICC** (International Color Consortium) format and are thus sometimes called ICC profiles.

Profiles can be either custom written or generic. Custom profiles are generated using special instruments to read the color produced by the various devices—from cameras and scanners to monitors and printers. Generic profiles are written by

sistently as possible among different devices. The CMS acts as a decoder to interpret the data coming from one color space, allowing it to display or output accurately on the next device.

A transform engine, sometimes called a color management module or CMM, handles this task within the computer. The transform engine is a sequence

Fact Box

ICC PROFILES

Eight leading industry manufacturers met in 1993 and established the International Color Consortium for the purpose of creating, promoting and encouraging the standardization and evolution of an open, vendor-neutral, cross-platform color management system architecture and components.

ICC profiles are files that contain device-specific information (a map) that describes how the device works with color density and color gamut. Since various devices speak in different color terms, profiles allow the CMS (color management system) to translate device-dependent colors into or out of each specific color space based on the profile of every component in the workflow. ICC profiles use a device independent color space to act as a translator between two or more different devices.

Custom ICC profiles can be generated for each device in the imaging chain using special hardware and software. Monitors, for example, can be roughly profiled with the software known as Adobe Gamma, or they can be more accurately profiled with a special hardware device that reads the colors produced by the screen.

Generic profiles are available from the manufacturer for some devices. ICC profiles for many Epson printers, for example, are available on the Web.

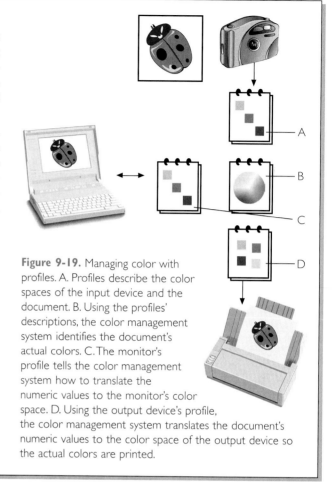

Figure 9-19. Managing color with profiles. A. Profiles describe the color spaces of the input device and the document. B. Using the profiles' descriptions, the color management system identifies the document's actual colors. C. The monitor's profile tells the color management system how to translate the numeric values to the monitor's color space. D. Using the output device's profile, the color management system translates the document's numeric values to the color space of the output device so the actual colors are printed.

the device's manufacturer and represent the average output of a particular model, such as a certain model of printer. ICC profiles contain information about how a device captures, displays, or prints color.

ICC profiles are used by the color management system to understand how a device is behaving and how to compensate for that behavior. If the display and output devices are both profiled, the CMS can change the color data it sends to them to get accurate screen or print images.

The Composition of a Color Management System

A working color management system (CMS) has the following components:

- Source Profile
- Monitor Profile
- Output Profile
- Transform Engine or Color Management Module (CMM)
- Appropriate Rendering Intent

A Color Management System is a sequence of color descriptions and software to re-map and control the color data from each device in the imaging chain. Profiles are one important component in an overall CMS. A **Source Profile** is a description of the color behavior of an imaging input device such as a scanner or a digital camera. Some digital camera and scanner manufacturers provide ICC profiles for their products or they can be created with various profiling tools. (Note that many experts question the usefulness of camera profiles because the images are captured under so many different lighting conditions.)

A **Monitor Profile** describes the color behavior of an image display device such as an LCD or CRT monitor and corrects the device's output so that it displays color accurately. Profiling a monitor is the first and most important step in building a color management system. A profile adjusts the monitor to perform to a known specification and enables one to closely predict what the image will look like on another profiled monitor. Monitors can be roughly calibrated visually with software such as Adobe Gamma for Windows or Monitor Calibrator for Mac OS, or more precisely with an external measuring device such as a spectrophotometer. The color displayed on a monitor changes with age, so monitors require frequent profiling to assure accurate results.

An **Output Profile** is a device profile for a printer or other output device. The manufacturer for each printer model often provides generic printer profiles, or you can make or purchase custom profiles. Building a custom output profile usually requires special hardware that can read the color gamut and the accuracy of a printed target. As with any profile, the more accurately the destination profile portrays the behavior of an output device, the more accurately a color management system can translate a document's numerical data into the actual colors sent to the color space of the output device.

A **Color Management Module (CMM)** performs all of the mathematical computations to transform image data from one color space to another. Using profiles for each device, the CMM calculates the color data necessary to convert colors from device to device. Current versions of Adobe Photoshop allow users to choose their desired CMM. Adobe (ACE) is the default CMM in Photoshop and is the engine used by most photographers. Other common CMM engines are Microsoft ICM, Apple ColorSync, and Apple CMM.

Rendering Intent Some colors will unfortunately fall outside the gamut of one device and/or can't be reproduced on another. Photoshop offers a way to deal with such colors through its "**rendering intent**" setting. A "Perceptual" rendering intent is designed to preserve the visual relationship between various colors and is the intent most widely chosen by photographers. Other rendering intents can be selected such as "Relative Colorimetric" which compares the extreme highlights of the source color space to that of the destination space and shifts all colors accordingly.

The CMS in Action— A Series of Color Conversions

From input to display to output, the colors in an image are portrayed based on the following key factors:

- Color space
- Monitor Profile
- Output Profile

To gain an understanding of how these factors work together, consider the path an image takes as it moves from capture to display to a printer. Starting with the color space, usually either sRGB or Adobe RGB, the image data are registered and used in image-editing software such as Photoshop.

Next, an accurate monitor profile is used by the computer's operating system and image editing software, such as Photoshop, to accurately re-map the colors on the monitor display. Finally, Photoshop or similar image editing software is supplied with an output profile for the output device, such as an inkjet printer, using appropriate photo ink and photo paper.

Because the printer's color gamut is less than that of the recorded image data, it is necessary to select an appropriate rendering intent within the image-editing software, such as "Perceptual" or "Relative Colorimetric." This enables the software to convert the image file's color data so that the printer will output the most accurate or pleasing colors.

Conclusion

Color management is a controlled system for managing digital image information so that recorded digital images may be seen and printed with colors that perceptually match. Color management is achieved by precisely calibrating and profiling each device in the imaging chain and correctly setting the color options in the preferred image editing software. Most photographers can implement a color management system with a modest investment in time and resources. A quick Web search on the phrase "Photoshop color management" will unearth much additional information and discussion. The next section of this chapter is a step-by-step guide to setting up and using a color management system using Photoshop.

A Practical Guide to Building a Color Management System

Objective 9-D Explain how to achieve a color-managed workflow and demonstrate the processes of calibrating a monitor and establishing Photoshop's color management settings.

Key Concepts Adobe Gamma, Apple Monitor Calibrator, colorimeter, spectrophotometer, generic output profiles, custom profiles, soft proof

As previously discussed, the goal of color management is to ensure that color data is processed in a consistent and predictable way throughout the entire imaging workflow.

The following diagram demonstrates a typical "color-managed workflow" and shows the image being passed along the chain—capture device → computer → monitor → printer—with ICC profiles ensuring that color data for each device is correctly described.

Creating a Monitor Profile

A computer's display monitor is one of the most important parts of a digital darkroom and requires careful calibration to yield accurate colors and tonalities. Calibration is necessary because the color and brightness of monitors vary widely, even among identical brands and models. Additionally, monitor performance changes over time requiring them to be profiled and calibrated regularly. Many professionals calibrate their monitors weekly. Old monitors may fade to a point where calibration is difficult or impossible. Note also that some inexpensive LCD or plasma screens, especially laptop screens, may not be capable of producing accurate color.

Calibrating and profiling monitors ensures that images are displayed accurately and consistently. Although color management requires more than merely standardizing the monitor, these simple procedures provide a good starting place and will greatly improve your results. Although monitors can be adequately calibrated and profiled with readily available software, instruments such as a

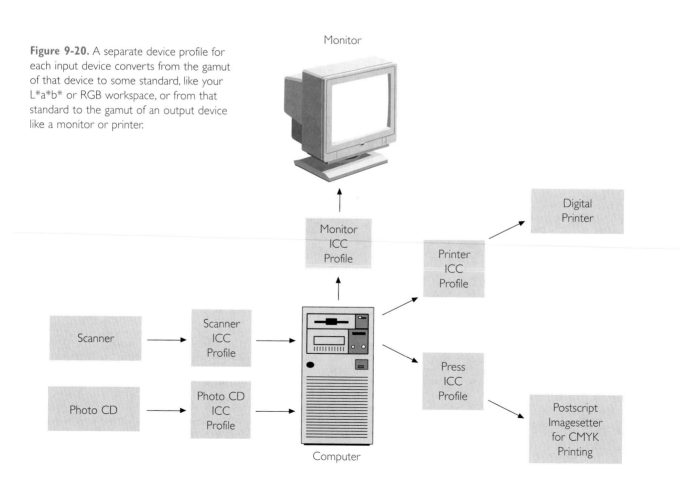

Figure 9-20. A separate device profile for each input device converts from the gamut of that device to some standard, like your L*a*b* or RGB workspace, or from that standard to the gamut of an output device like a monitor or printer.

colorimeter or spectrophotometer produce much more accurate results.

Setting Up a Monitor

Monitors used for image editing should be viewed in subdued light. Total darkness is unnecessary, but a "hood" that shields the monitor from overhead light is helpful and can be cheaply made from black foam-core or black cardboard. No strong direct light should fall upon the screen's surface. Dark areas should appear dark without distracting reflections.

You should complete several steps before attempting to calibrate the monitor. Refer to the user references of the monitor and operating system to configure these settings.

■ Remove colorful background patterns from the monitor desktop. They can interfere with accurate color perception. Use a gray colored desktop on the monitor, preferably one that uses a neutral gray setting of 128 for each of the RGB values.

■ Set the monitor's color display setting to at least 16-bits, which displays thousands of colors. Use 24-bit or 32-bit settings if the hardware allows.

■ If the monitor's white point can be adjusted, set it to 6500K (D65)—the most frequently used color temperature for image-editing.

■ Stabilize the monitor by allowing it to warm up for half an hour before calibration.

■ Set the monitor's contrast to maximum.

■ Set the monitor's brightness control (black level) so that black areas are illuminated ever so slightly.

■ If controlled through hardware, set the monitor's gamma to 2.2. The recommended gamma for the Windows operating system and the Internet sRGB color space is 2.2. The standard gamma usually quoted for Macintosh and prepress file interchange is 1.8. However, some professional image editors use a gamma of 2.2 even with Macintosh computers in the belief that this setting tends to more accurately portray the printed results.

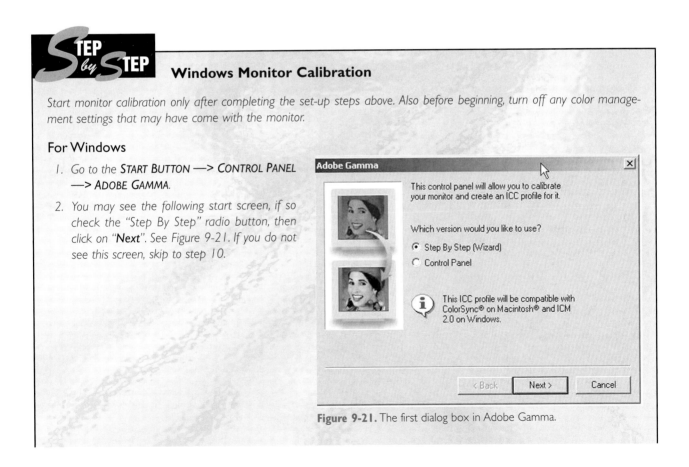

Windows Monitor Calibration

Start monitor calibration only after completing the set-up steps above. Also before beginning, turn off any color management settings that may have come with the monitor.

For Windows

1. Go to the START BUTTON —> CONTROL PANEL —> ADOBE GAMMA.

2. You may see the following start screen, if so check the "Step By Step" radio button, then click on "*Next*". See Figure 9-21. If you do not see this screen, skip to step 10.

Figure 9-21. The first dialog box in Adobe Gamma.

3. A new dialog box will open. Type in a name for your profile here, such as today's date. Click "**Next**" again. See Figure 9-22.

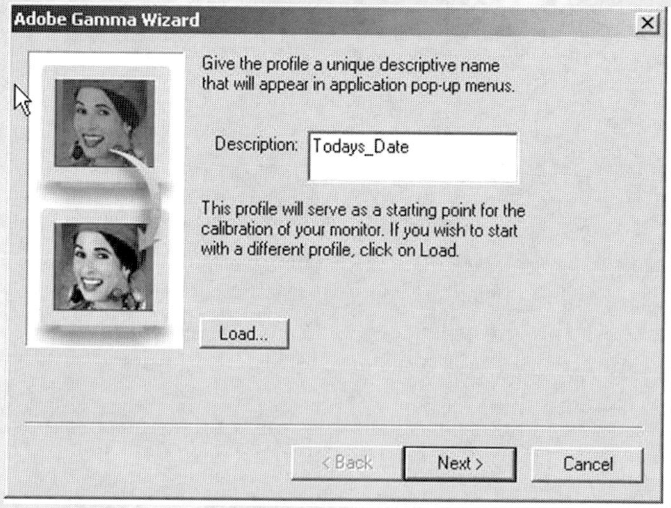

Figure 9-22. The second dialog box in Adobe Gamma, naming the profile.

4. Follow the dialog box instructions to set the monitor's contrast and brightness. When done, click "**Next**" again. See Figure 9-23.

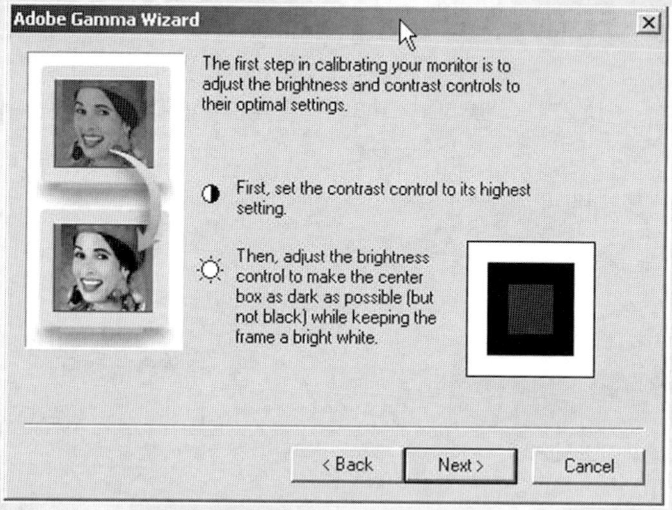

Figure 9-23. Setting contrast and brightness.

5. If you know what kind of phosphors the monitor uses enter it here; if not, accept the default setting. Then click "**Next**". See Figure 9-24.

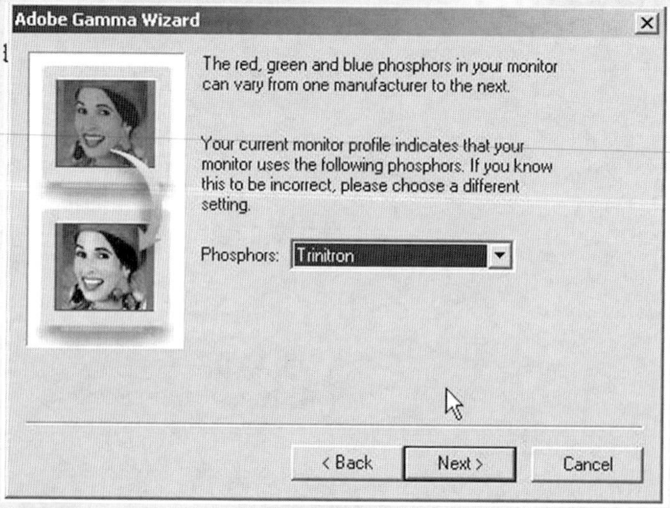

Figure 9-24. Adobe Gamma, input monitor phosphors.

(continued)

6. This next dialog box is the heart of Adobe Gamma. Select the Windows default gamma of 2.2, uncheck the "View Single Gamma Only" box, and adjust each of the three sliders until the inner boxes appear to have the density as their surrounding frames. Click "**Next**" when the adjustments are complete. See Figure 9-25.

    Although you can measure the white point of the monitor in the next box, it is better to set it manually to 6500K using the monitor's hardware controls. In the dialog box, enter 6500K (Daylight) as the white point. If the monitor in use doesn't have a white point setting, click "**Measure**". When done, click "**Next**" to continue. See Figure 9-26.

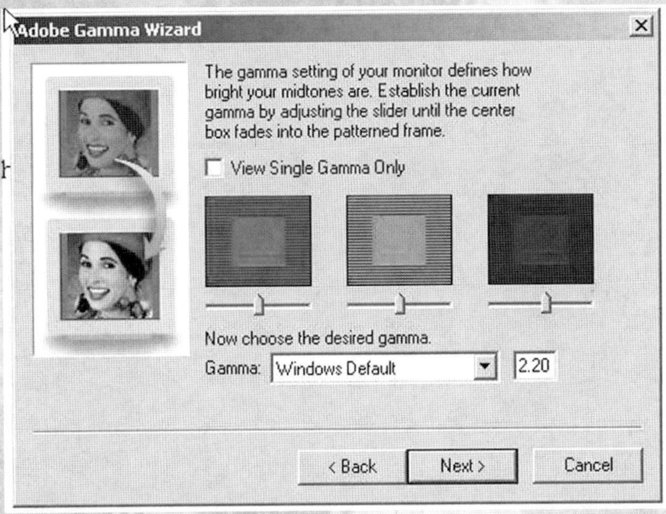

Figure 9-25. Setting the tri-color gamma visually.

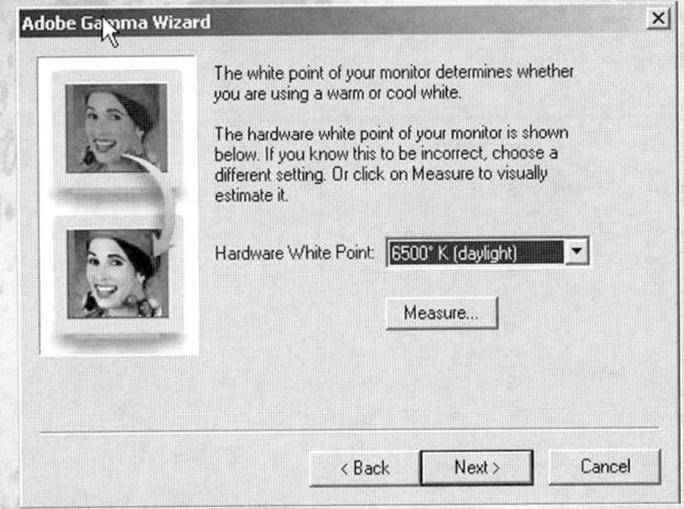

Figure 9-26. Adobe Gamma, input white point.

7. Set this next box also to 6500K. Make the selection and click "**Next**" to continue. See Figure 9-27.

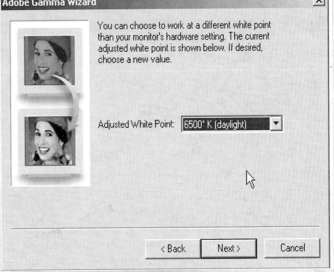

Figure 9-27. Adobe Gamma white point at 6500K.

8. *The monitor calibration is now complete. You can now make before and after comparisons with the radio buttons. To save the settings click on "Finish". See Figure 9-28.*

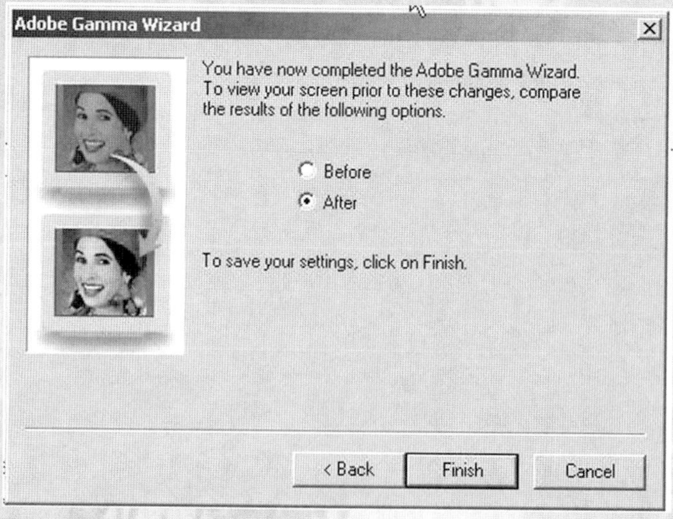

Figure 9-28. Adobe Gamma, finish button.

9. *The monitor profile will be automatically saved in the correct computer location so that ICC-compliant applications, such as Photoshop, can find it. Inasmuch as monitor output changes over time, it is useful to include a date in the profile's descriptive name. See Figure 9-29.*

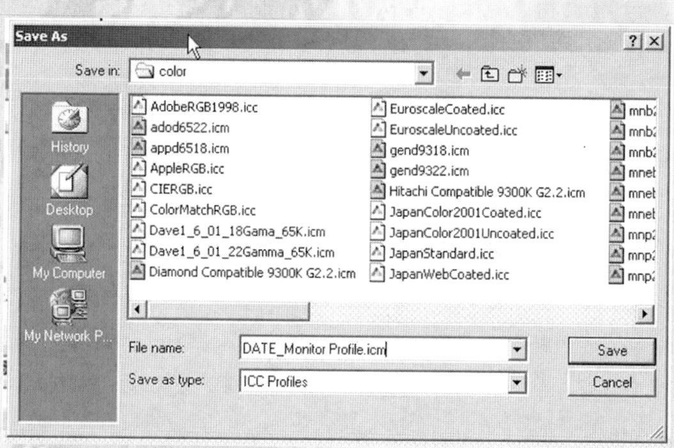

Figure 9-29. Adobe Gamma, save ICC dialog box.

10. *Your version of Adobe Gamma might open in the control panel mode where you are presented with a single dialog box rather than a sequence of steps. If so, uncheck "**View Single Gamma Only**," click on "**Wizard**," and use the settings and procedure recommended above. See Figure 9-30.*

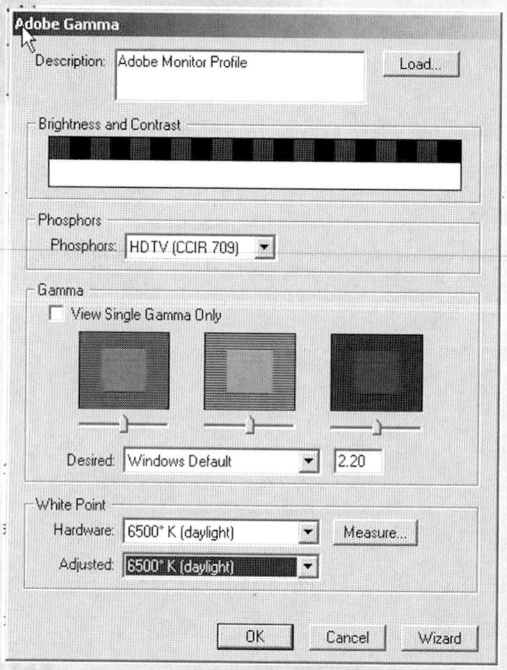

Figure 9-30. Adobe Gamma opened with a single dialog box.

Macintosh Monitor Calibration

The procedure to calibrate a Macintosh monitor is similar to the Windows instructions, but the software is slightly different.

1. Go to the "SYSTEM PREFERENCES —> DISPLAY —> COLOR" and an interface similar to the one below will appear. See Figure 9-31.

2. In the "Display Profile" dialog box select the name that matches your monitor. If that is not possible, choose the color profile of your choice, usually Adobe RGB.

3. Click on "Calibrate" and proceed.

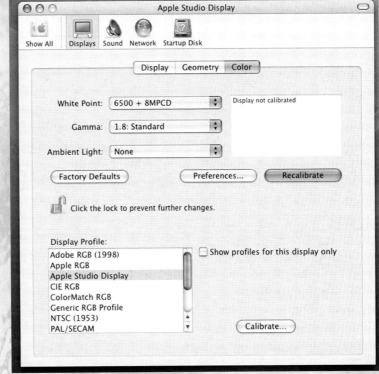

Figure 9-31. SYSTEM PREFERENCES —> DISPLAY —> COLOR.

4. The following dialog box will appear. Check the "Expert Mode" box. Click on "Continue." Proceed to the next step. See Figure 9-32.

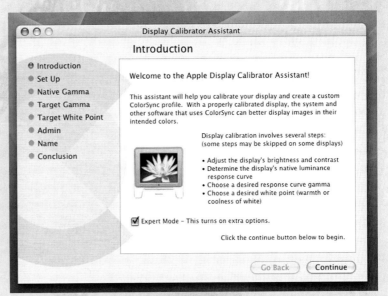

Figure 9-32. DB with expert mode checked.

5. In the next dialog box adjust both sliders until the inner boxes have the same density and color as their surrounding frames. Click on "Continue." Repeat this step in the next four similar screens. Click on "Continue" when you complete the adjustments in all five steps. See Figure 9-33.

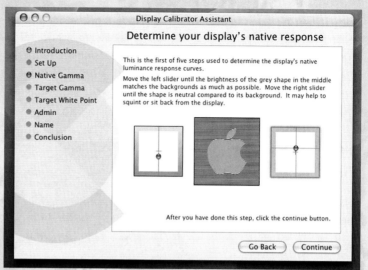

Figure 9-33. Adjust both sliders.

6. Next select a target gamma. The Macintosh default gamma is 1.8, but some users prefer to use 2.2. Make your selection. Click "Continue." Advance to the next step. See Figure 9-34.

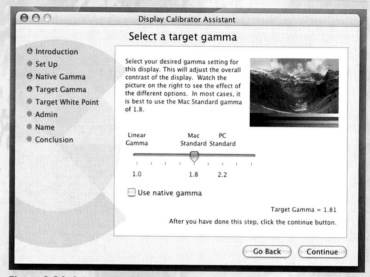

Figure 9-34. Select a target gamma.

7. Next, select a target White Point. Most digital photographers use D65 as a close approximation of daylight. Click on "Continue." Proceed to the next step. See Figure 9-35.

8. Name the profile and save it for use by the operating system.

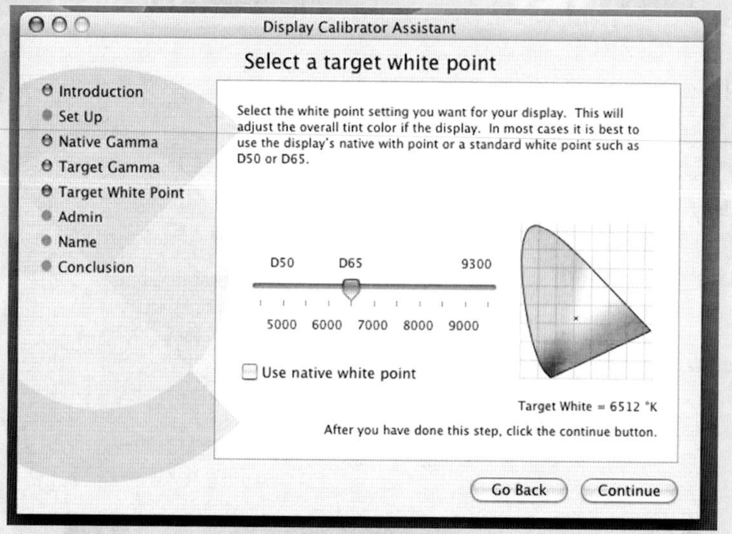

Figure 9-35. Select a white point.

Tools for Monitor Calibration

Once these basic settings are made, you can begin the monitor calibration and profiling process. You can roughly calibrate a monitor using software that leads you through several settings visually, such as **Adobe Gamma** (Windows) or the **Apple Monitor Calibrator** (Mac OS). Adobe Gamma usually ships with Windows versions of Photoshop and other Adobe products. The Apple Monitor Calibrator is part of the Macintosh operating system. These and other software products can perform a rough monitor calibration and create a profile for controlling the display. Although these software tools provide better calibration than no calibration at all, you can only achieve precise results and accurate profiles with external hardware devices, known as **colorimeters** or **spectrophotometers**.

To calibrate a monitor using external instruments, known colors and densities are sent to the screen. The device then reads the colors produced by the monitor and compares them to the colors that should have been produced. Software then adjusts the monitor based on a known set of values. Depending on their level of sophistication, colorimeters or spectrophotometers usually sell for approximately $150–$1000. Leading suppliers of such equipment include GretagMacbeth and ColorVision, both of whom have descriptive Web sites. For further information search the Web for "monitor calibration tool."

See the Step-by-Step box on Monitor Calibration.

Configuring Photoshop's Color Settings

Photoshop has a complex color engine that must be configured within the "Color Settings" dialog box. Hundreds of configurations are possible. Your particular imaging needs and output requirements will determine your best choice for each variable. Although this text cannot discuss every possible setting, it can provide general recommendations. For more information, see one of the many books devoted to color management for photographers.

Windows users will find the color setting under Photoshop's "**Edit**" menu. Macintosh users will find the settings under the "**Photoshop**" menu. See Figure 9-36.

Follow these typical settings for general photo imaging unless your requirements suggest otherwise.

Figure 9-36. Accessing Photoshop's color settings.

1. Select "**U.S. Prepress Defaults**" or "**North American General Purpose Defaults**" from the drop down menu near the top of the dialog box. This is a good starting choice for most users. You may wish to modify it to better fit your needs.

2. Make sure there is a check box in the "**Advanced Mode**" area. This expands the dialog box to look like Figure 9-37. If you hover the mouse over a selection, a brief explanation of the action appears in the "Description" area.

3. Change the "**Working Spaces**" RGB Setting from sRGB to AdobeRGB using the toggle. Change the "**Gray**" setting in "**Working Spaces**" within "**U.S. Prepress Defaults**" from "**Dot Gain 20%**" to "**Gray Gamma 2.2**" using the toggle. (Macintosh users may prefer to change the gamma to 1.8.)

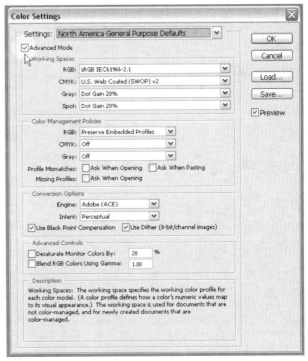

Figure 9-37. U.S. prepress defaults.

323

4. In some cases you may wish to convert a document's colors to a different color profile as it enters the Photoshop workspace. For example, many digital cameras create images using the sRGB color space. However, image-editing software commonly operates in Adobe RGB color space. So the next recommended change is in the "**Color Management Policies**" area—change the RGB policy to "**Convert to Working RGB**" and turn the "**Gray**" policy "**Off**."

5. Next, change the "**Intent**" from "**Relative Colorimetric**" to "**Perceptual**" in the "**Conversion Options.**" This recommended change re-maps colors to preserve their relative appearance rather than their numerical values.

6. Finally, press the "**Save**" button and give your custom settings a name. The finished settings should look much like Figure 9-38.

Input Profiles—Not Absolutely Necessary

An input profile, often called a source profile, describes the range of colors an input device is able to capture. For example, the profile might tell the color management system that a particular camera renders the colors in a scene with a slightly green cast. The color management system, rather than correcting the color cast, faithfully represents it in the monitor display for later image editing.

A digital camera profile describes a camera's performance with a specific light source and in a specific environment. Thus, different profiles are needed for each light source you might encounter. For example, you would need different profiles for sunny, overcast, shade, early morning, and sunset lighting. A scanner profile describes a scanner's performance with specific source material, such as a print or transparency. For critical color work, some photographers create different profiles for different types or brands of film. Some manufacturers provide generic profiles for a particular camera or scanner. You can also create a custom profile by photographing or scanning a special target with known color values. To create the custom profile, special software and hardware is used to read the RGB color codes that the input device records from the target and then to compare these RGB codes with the target's known color values.

Opinions differ about the necessity for an input device profile for producing consistent color. Some users feel that achieving consistent color is difficult without such a source profile. Others feel that input profiles are superfluous if the shooting or scanning conditions continually vary. Regardless of an input device's behavior, a well-calibrated and profiled monitor will accurately display an image's colors and contribute later to successful color correction.

Output Profiles

Profiles of your output devices, sometimes called destination profiles, describe the color space of such devices as printers and printing presses. A color management system can use output profiles in two ways. First, they can be used to re-map an image's colors to match the colors available from the output device. Second, they can be used to preview an image's colors as they will appear when printed by the output device.

To create an output profile, the output device first prints a target image of various known color patches. A spectrophotometer profiling device reads the output, then calculates and measures the known color values. The profiling software next compares the color differences between the original file and the printed patches and stores

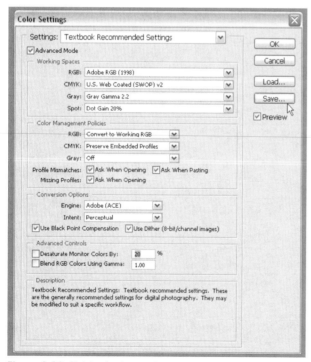

Figure 9-38. Finished color settings.

this information in the form of an output profile. The profile can then be applied during printing to ensure that images are printed correctly.

Printer manufacturers sometimes include **generic output profiles** on the disk containing the printer's drivers. Generic output profiles are also available to download from the Internet. If the manufacturer provides a profile, you can use it to help calibrate the workflow. Note that different profiles are required for different types of media— glossy photo paper, for example, displays a different range of colors than matte paper. Many ink and paper vendors also provide output profiles for their products.

Custom profiles require instruments to read the colors and values contained in the printer's output of a known target. Although some profiling products use a flatbed scanner to measure the printed target, a spectrophotometer produces a more accurate profile. These instruments vary in price and features, but entry-level models are available. You can also purchase custom profiles from third-party vendors. See the manufacturers recommended in the section on monitor calibration.

You should copy your output profiles to one of the following recommended locations in your computer system:

(Windows) Program Files/Common Files/ Adobe/Color/Profiles

(Mac OS X) Library/Application Support/ Adobe/Color/Profiles

Photoshop can then use the output profile to create a **"soft proof"** on the calibrated display that shows how a document will appear when printed to a specific device. If reliable, a soft proof can save both time and aggravation. The reliability of a soft proof depends upon the monitor's quality and accuracy, the printer profile's accuracy, and the ambient lighting conditions.

Printing with Color Management

When configured properly and used with accurate output profiles combined with soft proofing, Photoshop can color manage the printing process. Photoshop offers color managed printing through the command **FILE — > PRINT WITH PREVIEW**. However, bear in mind these points:

- Most current printers are designed for plug-and-play operation. However, the computer's plug-and-play feature might install a generic printer driver supplied by the operating system rather than the driver provided by the printer manufacturer. As a result, many of the printer's controls and features may not be fully utilized. Be sure to install the most recent driver for your printer, usually available from the printer manufacturer's Web site.

- With popular inkjet printers, use files in RGB, rather than CMYK image mode. Although these printers produce images with CMYK inks, they use drivers that work best in RGB image mode.

- The color gamut of a typical computer monitor exceeds the capability of any printer so hard copy output will never exactly match the screen image. Soft proofing offers an excellent preview, but don't expect a perfect match.

Within Photoshop select **FILE — > PRINT WITH PREVIEW** to open the dialog box shown in Figure 9-41.

Make sure the "**Show More Options**" box is checked, as shown. Then

Make the following selections:

- Under "**Source Space**" check "**Document**," which contains the image's color mode. Note that checking "**Proof**" converts to the proof profile.

- Under "**Print Space**," choose the printer profile associated with your media. Figure 9-41 shows the profile for printing an image on an

Fact Box

SOFT PROOF

In a traditional publishing workflow, a hard proof of a document is printed on paper to preview how a document's colors will look when printed. In a color-managed workflow, a soft proof of a document is displayed on a monitor, using an output profile, to preview how a document's colors will look when printed on paper by a specified device. You can then make color and density adjustments to this "proof" image to optimize the final print. Usually, you make these final, device-specific adjustments using an adjustment layer.

How to Configure Photoshop to Display a Soft Proof

With an output (printer) profile in hand, follow these steps to create a custom soft proof setup:

1. **Open Photoshop**. *If you normally use the same printer and the same paper stock for most images, then close all document windows before proceeding. This will force Photoshop to accept the newly created proof setup as the default setting.*

2. *From the View menu choose* **VIEW —> PROOF SETUP —> CUSTOM.** *See Figure 9-39.*

3. *To use an output profile as the basis for soft proofing, choose the profile from the drop down list in the "Profile" window. If the desired profile does not appear in the list, you may have saved it to the wrong location. In this case, you can access it by clicking "**Load**" and selecting the file's current location.*

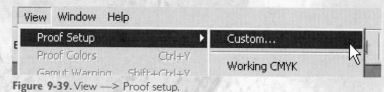

Figure 9-39. View —> Proof setup.

4. *If you are working with RGB files and outputting to an ink-jet printer, the following suggested settings in the "Proof Setup" dialog box will likely fit your needs. However, you can experiment with other settings. For more information, see Photoshop's extensive "Help" file.*

   ■ *The "Setup" and "Profile" window will display the printer defined by the selected profile.*

   ■ *Uncheck "**Preserve Color Numbers**"*

   ■ *Check "**Use Black Point Compensation**"*

   ■ *Check "**Paper White**." "Simulate Paper White" previews the base color of the print paper described in the profile. Note that not all profiles offer this option. When available, it can only be used for soft-proofing, not printing. See Figure 9-40.*

5. *Click "**Save**," and assign a new name to the newly created custom proof that indicates the printer and paper stock. To ensure that the new preset appears in the* **VIEW —> PROOF SETUP** *menu, save the preset in one of the following folders:*

   ■ *Program Files/Common Files/Adobe/Color/Proofing (Windows)*

   ■ *System Folder/Application Support/Adobe/Color/Proofing (Mac OS 9.x)*

   ■ *Library/Application Support/Adobe/Color/Proofing (Mac OS X)*

6. *You can now use this custom soft proof to preview images and to make any color and density adjustments needed to optimize the final print.*

7. *You can also toggle the soft proof view on and off by using the **Cmd/Y** (Mac) or **Crtl/Y** (Windows) keystroke command.*

You may find the resulting soft proof to be disappointing. It will probably show a reduction in the image's tonal range and perhaps a color shift as well. However, if the output profile and the color management settings were accurate and correct, the soft proof will closely match what the printer will actually produce. Better to soft proof it on a monitor and correct it before printing than to hard proof it on paper many times before achieving an optimal print.

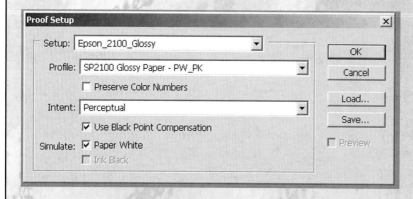

Figure 9-40. Proof setup dialog box.

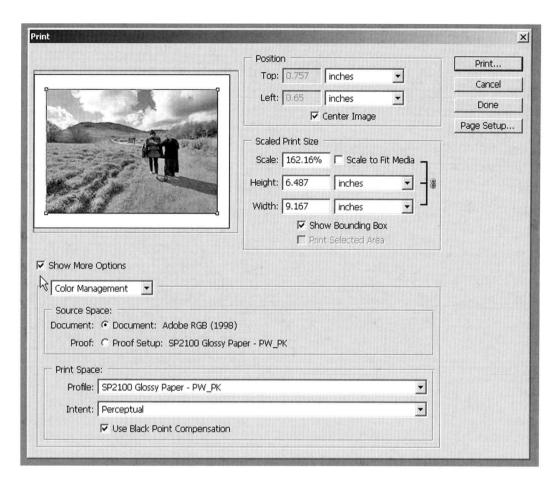

Figure 9-41. Print preview.

Epson 2100 Printer with glossy paper. If you don't have a profile for your specific printer and media choose "**Printer Color Management**."

- Under "**Intent**" most printers work best choosing "**Perceptual**." However, some newer color printers may work best choosing "**Relative Colorimetric**." Experiment to find your optimal setting.

- Finally, click on "**Print**" and go to the printer properties. Each printer brand has its own interface. The following examples show typical interface settings for popular Epson printers when used with both Macintosh and Windows operating systems. Your printer brand have different interface controls.

Typical Color Managed Printer Settings for Macintosh

Press "**Print**" from the "**Print with Preview**" box shown in Figure 9-41. Depending on the printer in use, a dialog box will open similar to the following. See Figure 9-42.

- Click "**Copies & Pages**" and select "**Print Settings**."

- Enter the type of media in use and select "**Advanced**."

- Choose the highest setting available from the "**Print Quality**" toggle. See Figure 9-43.

- Next return to the toggle near the top left and change "**Print Settings**" to "**Color Management**." If the preview box displays a printer and media profile as shown in Figure 9-41,

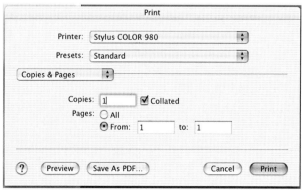

Figure 9-42. Mac print DB #1.

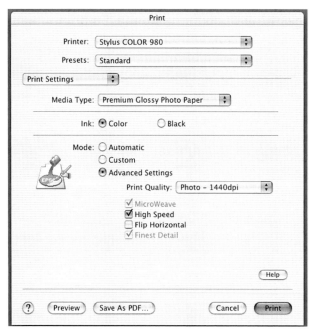

Figure 9-43. MAC print DB select paper.

Typical Color Managed Printer Settings for Windows

■ Press "**Print**" from the "**Print With Preview**" box shown in Figure 9-41. A print dialog box similar to the one in Figure 9-45 will open.

■ Select the desired printer.

■ Click on the "**Properties**" button and proceed to the next step.

■ From the "**Main**" tab, select the type of media in use.

■ Check the radio button marked "**Custom**."

■ Click "**Advanced**." See Figure 9-46.

■ If the Print Preview box displays a printer and media profile as shown in Figure 9-41, check either "**ICM**" or "**No Color Adjustment**" as shown in Figure 9-47.

■ Again, experiment to determine the optimal setting for your workflow. If you lack a specific media profile, try selecting either "**Color Control**" or "**Photo Enhance**." See Figure 9-47.

check either "**ColorSync**" or "**No Color Adjustment**." Experiment to determine the optimal setting. If you lack a specific media profile, try checking "**Color Controls**" instead.) See Figure 9-44.

With proper color management settings, your print should closely match the monitor's display of the proof view.

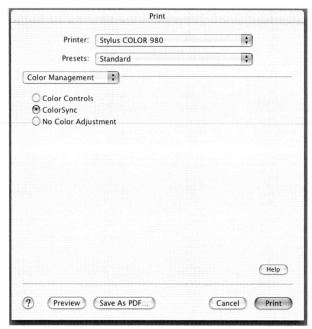

Figure 9-44. Mac print DB color synch.

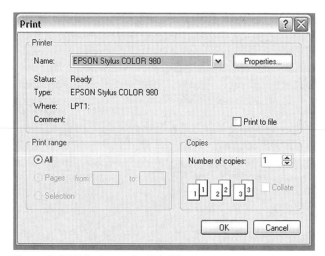

Figure 9-45. Windows print DB #1.

Figure 9-46. Windows print media selection.

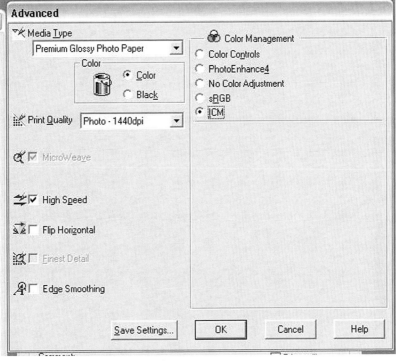

Figure 9-47. Windows print DB ICM.

Questions to Consider

1. In broad terms, describe the process color management system. Why is color management needed? What is the goal of color management?

2. What are the main components of a color managed system?

3. What is a color space? Name one common color space.

4. Explain the purpose of profiles.

5. Describe ways that a monitor can be profiled.

6. Name four factors from the recommendations made to create a good viewing environment for computer monitors.

7. What is a colorimeter? What is it used for?

8. What is the purpose of a "soft-proof?"

9. What is meant by the term "color gamut?"

10. What is meant by the term "dynamic range?" Which is better, a dynamic range of 3.3 or 3.6?

Suggested Field and Laboratory Exercises

1. Search the Web for the term "monitor calibration." Briefly describe your results.

2. Search the Web for the phrase "monitor calibration device." In general, what is the price range of software-based monitor calibrators? What are the price ranges of both colorimeter or spectrophotometer calibrators?

3. Calibrate your computer monitor using one of the methods described in the text.

4. Open Photoshop's "Color Settings" and input the values provided in the text or suggested by your instructor.

5. Search the Web for ICC profiles for your specific printer. Include in the search your printer brand, model, and the term "ICC profile." For example, search for "Epson 2400 ICC profile."

6. If you found printer profiles in this exercise, download and install them into Photoshop as described in the text.

7. Search the Web for the expression "color management" followed by your brand of printer. For example, search for "color management Canon." Briefly describe your results.

8. Search the Web for "custom printer profiles." Briefly describe your results.

Introduction to Composition

Andrea Williamson,
"Portrait of a Dancer"

Unless the visual elements in a photograph are organized and presented in a meaningful way, the image is likely to become only a shallow account of subjects and events that would have seemed far more intriguing had some planning taken place before the shutter was released. Organizing the visual elements and presenting them in such a way so as to convey meaning, mood, emotion, or insight is the function of composition.

This unit describes the elements of composition as well as the techniques photographers use to make photographs that better communicate their ideas and feelings. As photographers gain control of their medium, they increase their ability to emphasize important details and relationships, to subordinate others, to guide the attention of viewers, and to affect them intellectually and emotionally. The objectives of this unit are to provide some principles and guidelines that will help the beginning photographer to develop composition skills and judgment.

Composing Photographs

Objective 10-A Define composition and describe its elements and purposes.

Key Concepts composition, line, tone, mass, contrast, color, selection, emphasis, subordination, central or dominant idea, center of interest

Without the mind's organizing power, the visual world would be completely chaotic. There are so many details that we cannot take them all in; we cannot comprehend the visual world in its entirety. The mind helps us to pick and choose what we see—to view first this detail, then that, until a pattern of meaning emerges.

From a hillside, viewing a valley below, the naturalist may see an ecologically balanced pattern of life; the geologist, a pattern of earth formation that suggests a future earthquake; the industrialist, a pattern of valuable raw materials and energy sources; the developer, a site for a future community. Each may view the same scene, yet each sees a different pattern and derives different meaning from it.

The mind, not the camera, selects and organizes visual detail so that meaning emerges. If a photographer is to convey meaning to others, therefore, the photograph must be organized around an idea to be shared. Without an idea—without the mind of the photographer to organize the visual elements—a photograph is little more than a chaotic record of what stood before the camera when the shutter was released.

Composition, then, refers to the way in which visual details are selected and organized within a photograph to convey meaning. The organization will alter the content of the visual image and the relationships among the visual elements. The approach taken depends upon the photographer's interpretation of the details in the scene.

The Elements of Composition

Music is composed, as is a poem or a novel. We may even speak of "composing" ourselves or of retaining our "composure." The common thread in all these expressions suggests organizing diverse, confusing elements into a meaningful whole. That is what we do when we compose a photograph—we organize diverse visual elements into a meaningful pattern.

Musicians create their works and melodies from the musical elements that are the characteristics of sound, such as pitch, timbre, volume, harmony, and rhythm. Photographers create their works from the pictorial elements that are the characteristics of image, such as **line, tone, mass, contrast, and color**. Line refers to the arrangement, real or imagined, of outlines, contours, and other connecting elements within the image; mass, to areas of density within the image that cohere together; tone, to the color quality or brightness value in a portion of the image; contrast, to the magnitude or brightness differences between adjacent masses; and color, to the visual sensations produced by different wavelengths of light. Just as a musician composes sound elements to communicate ideas and feelings, so the photographer composes these image elements. In all cases composition refers to the art of organizing these diverse elements into effective communication—transmitting the composer's meaning with a minimum of distortion and ambiguity.

Compositions involving the visual elements of even a single scene may take many forms. Sometimes effective photographic compositions are simple, straightforward expositions of a single subject. Beginners often enjoy early success by concentrating on such simple compositions. However, other effective compositions may be probing explorations of complex visual patterns, communicating often subtle moods and feelings through richly varied patterns of detail and texture. A photographer's effectiveness in dealing with complex subjects tends to increase with command of the medium. (See Figure 10-2.)

Until they develop some command of the medium, beginning photographers are generally well advised to concentrate on images that tell one simple story with a single idea or dominant cen-

ter of interest. Any attempt to crowd too much within a picture's borders tends to scatter the viewer's interest and confuse understanding. When this occurs, the image fails to communicate the photographer's intent, mood, or feeling. By keeping the central idea in mind while visualizing the final print before shooting, the photographer is more likely to achieve the intended effect.

The Functions of Composition

One function of composition is to achieve emphasis within the image. Many composition guidelines primarily suggest ways to accomplish this. In an effective composition, pictorial elements within the scene are **selected** and **emphasized** so as to communicate the photographer's ideas. Other elements within the scene are **subordinated** or excluded altogether. Thus, a major function of photographic composition is to focus the viewer's attention upon certain details in the scene to the exclusion of others.

To accomplish this, a photographer selects various details to include in the photograph and others to

A.

B.

Figure 10-2. Organization of pictorial elements. A) Simple composition. B) More complex composition, probing subtle moods and feelings.

eliminate. Then, from among the included details, the photographer selects some to emphasize and others to subordinate—that is, some of the details are made to appear more prominent and others less so. This is accomplished primarily by choosing a viewpoint, selecting a camera angle, and framing the image. By selecting, emphasizing, and subordinating details in this way, the photographer seeks to communicate a **central** or **dominant idea**.

To achieve effective composition, therefore, the photographer must have clearly in mind the message, idea, feeling, or mood that the photograph is to convey; otherwise, it will be difficult to select the details of special importance. This usually means that the photograph will be about something—that some single object or group of objects will stand out unmistakably as the reason for the picture. Within the picture, one feature will usually dominate and appear especially important, significant, or interesting. Such a feature or element in a photograph is called the dominant **center of interest**. (See Figure 10-3.)

A picture without a center of interest risks being like a sentence without a subject—the audience will not understand what it is about. Nevertheless, communication is still possible. Just as musical

compositions sometimes succeed without a dominant theme on their tonal and rhythmic values alone, photographs too may succeed without a center of interest, on their tonal or rhythmic values alone. When a photograph succeeds through its use of textures, or through rhythmic repetition of pictorial elements, usually these become the central or dominant idea. The picture is then "about" these textures or rhythms. (See Figure 10-4.)

As photographers' experiences and purposes vary, so do their viewpoints. No two photographers will see the same subject in precisely the same way. Their compositions will differ as they try to communicate their own unique ideas. Their centers of interest may vary; certain details may be included by some, eliminated by others; certain details may be emphasized by some, subordinated by others. Through their compositions they direct viewers' attention to the details and relationships they think are important.

Several general principles of composition may help in composing pictures that communicate effectively. However, no rules or principles of photography will apply in all cases. Sometimes departing from these guidelines may lead to more effective communication. Ultimately photographers must

A.

B.

Figure 10-3. Center of interest. A) Single idea with careful selection of a few details. B) A single feature dominates picture, appearing especially important.

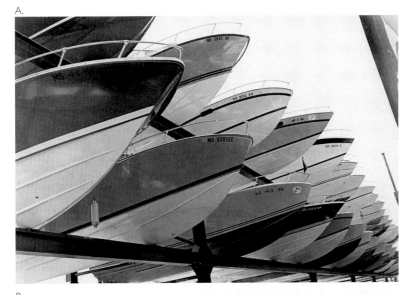

A.

B.

Figure 10-4. Central idea without center of interest. A) Repeated features establish rhythm that becomes central idea. B) The complex architectural pattern, rather than the structure itself, becomes the central idea of this image.

cumstances. The guidelines discussed below will help to make a beginning.

Control of Detail

Objective 10-B Explain and demonstrate how to achieve emphasis by controlling detail.

Key Concepts selecting details, busy background, sprout, relative sharpness, relative size, contrast, chiaroscuro, hue, primary hue, secondary hue, complement, saturation or chroma, value or brightness

Control of detail is one of the principal techniques of composition. By selecting the details to include and exclude, and by emphasizing or subordinating those that are included, the central idea of a photograph is expressed. The following discussion tells how to control details by selection, sharpness, size, and contrast.

Selection of Detail

The first major decision in composing a picture is **selecting the details** that are to be included and excluded from the photograph. One common error beginners make is to include too much detail. Decide which details are essential and which are nonessential. Then try to eliminate nonessential details that may distract the viewer from the picture's central idea by a careful choice of viewpoint and framing.

Nonessential details may be eliminated from the picture by several means. One common example of including too much detail is the **busy background**. When we view a subject against a busy background, we may have difficulty separating the subject from the other details in the scene. Such a background may so overwhelm the viewer that the subject's importance is diminished or even lost altogether. One way to avoid this problem is to select a neutral background for your subject, such as the sky or a hedgerow, thus eliminating these distracting elements and details. (See Figure 10-6.)

rely on their own senses and instincts, learn to see in their own way, and express themselves photographically in their own style. (See Figure 10-5.)

Developing an instinctive judgment about composition becomes especially important when there is little time to plan a photograph carefully. Photographers often must take their shots as they find them—in the midst of rapidly moving events and under awkward physical conditions. Only through experience and practice can photographers develop their aesthetic and learn to compose photographs quickly and effectively, even under difficult cir-

A.

B.

Figure 10-5. Composition principles. A) Composition of richly varied tones and simple line creates mood of timelessness. B) Careful timing captures spontaneous moment.

Another example of including too much detail is the **sprout**—a prominent background element directly behind the subject, such as a tree or pole, which may appear in the final print to be "sprout-

ing" from the subject. To avoid this problem, select a neutral background for your subject, eliminating such distracting background elements whenever possible.

A final example of including too much detail is the picture with no center of interest or no central idea. In this case the photograph displays many details but fails to communicate the important relationships among them. None is emphasized, none subordinated. All compete equally for the viewer's attention. The viewer cannot tell what is supposed to be important and what unimportant. By moving the camera closer to the essential details, nonessentials will be pushed out of the frame. (See Figure 10-7.)

Control of Sharpness

Another way to emphasize or subordinate details in a photograph is to control their **relative sharpness**. Once selected, details in the picture may be shown with clarity and sharpness, or they may be shown as blurred, fuzzy impressions. By using a lens's depth-of-field characteristics, background and foreground details can be shown out

A.

B.

C.

Figure 10-6. Control of background. A) Busy background. It is difficult to perceive subjects against a background of similar tonal values. B) Sprout. Metal bar appears to protrude from child's head. C) Neutral background. By selecting an appropriate angle, subject may be set against neutral background, such as sky.

Figure 10-7. Vague center of interest. What is the central idea or subject?

A.

B.

of focus while the subject is shown in sharp focus. This technique can be used, for example, when the subject cannot be framed against a neutral background. By presenting the subject in sharp focus against a background of out-of-focus details, the subject can be emphasized and the background subordinated. (See Figure 10-8.)

Control of Size

Controlling **relative size** is another way to emphasize and subordinate detail. The viewer will give greater attention to larger objects in a photograph than to smaller ones. A good guideline, then, is to move the camera as close as possible to the subject so that the subject will appear larger than other details in the picture. The presence of smaller details in a photograph tends to emphasize the larger ones. One tool photographers use to control relative size is known as a near/far approach. By this method an important part of the subject placed very close to the camera is contrasted with other elements far away. (See Figure 10-9.)

Control of Contrast

A fourth way to emphasize or subordinate detail is to use **contrast**. A bright object stands out against a dark background; a

C.

Figure 10-8. Control of sharpness. Sharpness of background detail is controlled in each picture to enhance subject.

A.

B.

Figure 10-9. Control of size. Subjects emphasized by being largest details in the scene.

dark object against a light one. The subject can be emphasized by maximizing the contrast between it and its background.

A subject presented against a noncontrasting background may lack emphasis because it does not stand out readily. The subject and the background appear to be of equal value or importance. To emphasize the subject and subordinate its background, the "light against dark; dark against light" guideline is often a good one for the beginner. This technique called **chiaroscuro**, a word borrowed from Italian "light and dark", refers to the modeling of volume by depicting light and shade by contrasting them boldly. This is one means of strengthening an illusion of depth on a two-dimensional surface and was an important technique among artists of the Renaissance. (See Figure 10-10.)

Control of Color

In color photography the additional element of color must also be controlled. By itself, color does not necessarily add impact or meaning to a photograph. In fact, improperly handled color may confuse and distract the viewer. Properly handled, however, color may help to emphasize and subordinate details and may enhance the mood, feeling, and central idea of a photograph.

Color has three major attributes:

1. **Hue**, which is the combination of wavelengths in the visible light spectrum that produces a specific color sensation. The **primary hues** are red, blue, and green; the **secondary hues**, cyan, yellow, and magenta. A primary and secondary hue are said to be **complements** when together they include all wavelengths present in light that is perceived as white.

2. **Saturation**, or **chroma**, which is the intensity or concentration of hue. When a color of a given hue is mixed with white, its saturation is reduced. The absence of saturation is no hue at all, or white.

3. **Value**, or **brightness**, which is lightness or darkness—the relative presence or absence of light rays. When a color of a given hue and saturation is mixed with black, its value is reduced. The absence of value is no light rays at all, or black.

A.

B.

Figure 10-10. Control of contrast. A) Strong contrast isolates subject. B) Silhouette isolates subject and creates atmosphere.

Although hue, saturation, and value may be separately identified, they are not independent. When one is changed, the other two are often affected as well. Nevertheless, some independent control over each attribute can be exercised. The primary control over color detail is by selection. By placing the camera and the subject in carefully chosen positions, existing color details can be included or excluded from the photograph. In addition, some opportunity may be afforded to select details,

such as clothing and backgrounds, that have desired color qualities.

As with black-and-white photography, the subject can be emphasized by presenting it against a neutral background of a simple, contrasting color. Greater emphasis can be achieved with a background of complementary color that is weaker in saturation and value.

Take care not to include too much color. A profusion of bright and varied background colors may emphasize the background at the expense of the subject. In an otherwise effective composition, even one bright-colored object in the background may draw the viewer's attention.

As with black-and-white compositions, earlier success may be enjoyed by keeping color compositions simple—by limiting the number of hues in the photographs, by keeping backgrounds uncluttered, and by subduing the saturation and value of background colors while strengthening those of the subjects.

See Color Plates 2–3 for illustrations of these principles of color composition.

Placement

Objective 10-C Explain and demonstrate how details can be emphasized or subordinated through placement.

Key Concepts rule of thirds, splitting the frame, movement into frame, camera angle, eye level, low angle, high angle

The placement of details within the frame of a photograph is a principal technique of composition. By placing details in different areas of the frame, by facing them in different directions, and by placing them against different backgrounds, the photograph's mood, feeling, and central idea can be affected.

The Rule of Thirds

One useful placement guideline for emphasizing a center of interest is the so-called **rule of thirds**. Mentally divide the picture area into thirds, both vertically and horizontally. Any of the four points at which the imaginary lines intersect within the picture space has been suggested to be a "natural"

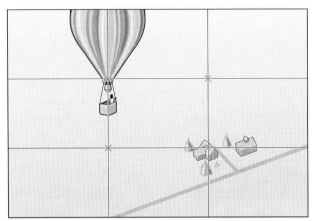

Figure 10-11. Any place marked X is a "natural" for the dominant subject. Dead center should be avoided.

for emphasizing the dominant subject. (See Figure 10-11.) It has been suggested also that secondary points of interest located at any of the other points of intersection also tend to be emphasized. According to this guideline, details elsewhere in the photograph tend to be subordinated.

The rule of thirds also cautions against certain placements within the picture frame. For example, it cautions against **splitting the frame** in equal halves with a strong horizontal element, such as the horizon. It suggests using one-third of the area for the foreground and two-thirds for the sky, or vice versa, to achieve emphasis.

Similarly, the rule cautions against splitting the frame exactly in half with a strong vertical element, such as a tree or telephone pole; it again suggests a one-third placement for emphasis.

Finally, it cautions against placing the center of interest in the exact, dead center of your picture. Such placement, being equidistant from all other points in the frame, tends to be static and uninteresting. Moving the center of interest even slightly toward the "thirds" lines may do much to add emphasis. (See Figure 10-12.)

Movement into the Frame

The direction in which a subject faces or moves creates a space expectation on the part of the viewer, whose eye is drawn in that direction. Unless space to satisfy this expectation is provided in the frame, the viewer's eye tends to move outside the frame, creating a "dead" space in the picture behind the subject. To give the subject proper emphasis, therefore, it is suggested that a space within the frame be provided for the subject to look into, face into, or move into.

For example, a leaping horse whose landing place lies outside the picture will appear to be leaping out of the picture. This draws the viewer's attention out of the picture in the direction of the leap and generally creates an uninteresting, useless area behind the subject.

Similarly, in portraiture, a face too close to the frame toward which it faces will draw the viewer's attention into the small space between the face and the frame. This will appear to crowd the subject while creating a "dead" space behind the subject. Portraits are usually more satisfying if space is provided for the subject to look into.

Figure 10-12. Placement by the rule of thirds.

In general, if there is action in a picture, it should lead into the picture, not out of it. Placement that allows **movement into the frame** generally satisfies the space expectations of the viewers of the photograph. (See Figure 10-13.)

Camera Angle

The **camera angle** from which a picture is made affects the idea that is communicated. A picture shot from a normal eye position with the axis of the camera parallel to the ground is called an **eye-level** shot. Pictures made using eye-level positions tend to present the world as we normally view it. For this reason, eye-level shots appear most natural or normal to the viewer. In a more general sense, however, any shot made with the camera axis parallel to the ground may be considered an eye-level shot, since the camera views the subject from the same level as the subject. (See Figure 10-14 C.)

A.

B.

C.

D.

Figure 10-13. Movement into frame. A) Subject too close to right-hand edge of frame, appearing confined and about to collide with frame. B) Improved placement, shifting subject to left and providing space for moving into frame. C) Portrait too close to edge, appearing to look out of frame. D) Improved placement, allowing subject to look into frame.

A.

B.

C.

The photographer can also look upward or downward toward the subject. A picture shot from a position lower than the subject is called a **low-angle** shot. Low-angle shots tend to emphasize the height, dominance, or impressiveness of objects. If the subject is a basketball player under the backboard, and the camera is pointed upward to view the subject, the player's height and elevated position will tend to be emphasized. (See Figure 10-14 B.)

A picture shot from a position higher than the subject is called a high-angle shot. **High-angle** shots tend to emphasize the smallness, dependence, or insignificance of objects. If the subject is a child playing with blocks, and the camera is pointed downward to view the subject, the child's small size and lower position will tend to be emphasized. (See Figure 10-14 A.)

Perspective Controls

Objective 10-D Describe and demonstrate how perspective controls can be used to modify apparent depth and distance in a photograph.

Key Concepts format, perspective, linear perspective, aerial perspective, selective focus, scale

The photograph's borders determine its spatial elements—its **format**. All details contained within the picture exist in relation to these borders. Each line is vertical, diagonal, or horizontal in relation to the borders; each mass is great or small in relation to the space contained by the borders.

Within this two-dimensional space, photographic elements are arranged to create an illusion of a third dimension. On the flat surface of the photograph, an illusion is created of a world that has depth. This illusion of depth is called **perspective**—the depiction of three-dimensional space on a flat surface by means of line, tonality, focus, and image size. Perspective can be controlled by several means.

Figure 10-14. Camera angle. A) High-angle shot, taken from above subject. B) Low angle shot, taken from below subject. C) Eye-level shot, taken at level of subject.

347

Famous Photographer

Roy Stryker and the FSA

In the mid-1930s, America's farmers suffered the debilitating effects of the Great Depression, mechanization, and the worst drought in history. Farm prices plummeted, a series of dust storms laid waste to the Great Plains, and thousands of small farmers were dispossessed or driven into tenancy.

To divert this tragedy, President Franklin D. Roosevelt created an agency, later the Farm Security Administration (FSA), to help relocate dispossessed farmers and appointed Columbia University economist Rexford Tugwell to head it. Tugwell planned a massive, controversial, and expensive program of subsidies, which he knew a conservative Congress would oppose. To help persuade the public of the urgent need for his program, Tugwell sent for Columbia colleague Roy Stryker.

Stryker seemed an unlikely choice—he was an engineer and an economist, not a publicist. But Tugwell knew Stryker as a fervent teacher who had animated and humanized dry statistics in his undergraduate classes by using moving and informative photographs. Stryker took the same approach to his tasks at the FSA. Of a photograph, Stryker said ". . . that little rectangle, that's one of the damndest educational devices that was ever made."

Though not a photographer himself, Stryker managed to assemble a remarkable team of photographers that included Walker Evans, Dorothea Lange, Carl Mydans, Arthur Rothstein, Russell Lee, and painter Ben Shahn, many of whom became distinguished magazine and press photographers. Using his considerable gift for teaching and persuading, Stryker taught them to be photographic anthropologists, economists, and historians as they set out across America's highways, towns, and rural pockets of poverty to document the plight of the dispossessed, the poor sharecroppers, and the tenant farmers.

With unrelenting, uncompromising honesty and the fine, sharp detail that characterized new realism, this group produced what Edward Steichen later called "the most remarkable human documents ever rendered in pictures." They brought back on film not only the bitter truth about the farmers' plight, but also a sense of their indomitable spirit, their pride, and their strength. Their pictures were widely published and succeeded in gaining both public and congressional support for the program. Just as important, however, their work inspired a generation of American photographers to seek and tell the truth.

Marion Post Wolcott. Coal miner's child taking home a can of kerosene; Pursglove, Scott's Run, West Virginia, 1938.

Linear Perspective

Linear perspective is the illusion of distance created by the relative size and location of objects. We observe linear perspective when we see the edges of a highway apparently converge to a vanishing point on the horizon. We observe it when we see roadside telephone poles apparently diminish in size as they recede into the distance. We also observe it when we look downward to view things close to our feet and farther upward to view more distant objects.

If lines we know to be parallel appear to converge in a photograph, we interpret this as depth—the lines appear to be receding into the distance. If objects we know to be the same size appear to diminish in size within a photograph, we interpret this also as depth—the smaller objects appear to be at greater distances. Similarly, objects located high in the frame usually appear more distant, whereas those near the bottom of the frame usually appear closer. Finally, objects that overlap others appear closer than those overlapped. Figure 10-15 illustrates these principles.

Control over linear perspective can be gained in several ways. For example, the camera position can be moved, increasing or decreasing its distance from the subject and thereby altering the relative size of the subject and background details. The camera can be located in a position where nearby objects will overlap more distant ones, or a frame of large foreground details can be established.

Aerial Perspective

Aerial perspective is an illusion of distance created by relative tones and contrast in a scene. Haze, dust, or smoke in the atmosphere tend to make more distant objects appear lighter and less distinct than closer objects. The effect of great distance can be created when light, hazy objects at a distance are viewed with darker, more distinct objects in the foreground.

These gradations of tone can be controlled to a degree. To darken nearby objects, a filter of a complementary color might be used in black and white photography. (See Unit 11 for discussion of filters.) For example, suppose the scene consists of a foreground of green shrubbery stretching out to a distant meadow of golden wheat under an azure blue sky. A red filter would darken the nearby green shrubbery, lighten the distant wheat, and darken the sky. Should the scene reach into the distance, the atmospheric haze might be exaggerated by using a blue filter.

A.

B.

Figure 10-15. Linear perspective. A) Converging lines and diminishing size of objects convey illusion of depth. B) Vertical location and overlapping of more distant objects convey illusion of depth.

Figure 10-16. Aerial perspective. A) Changes in tone enhance illusion of depth. B) Foreground detail and arch used as a frame enhance illusion of depth. C) Haze conveys impression of great distance.

In printing, too, aerial perspective can be controlled to a degree. For example, a foreground might be burned in to make it darker while more distant details might be dodged to make them lighter.

Including a natural frame in the photograph also can enhance the effect of aerial perspective. A foreground element, such as an overhanging branch, the trunk of a tree, or a bridge, can be used to establish a frame for a more distant subject. These frame details not only aid linear perspective but also enhance aerial perspective by tending to appear in darker tones. This combination of linear and aerial perspective increases the apparent depth of the image. Figure 10-16 illustrates aerial perspective.

Selective Focus

Perspective can also be controlled by means of **selective focus**, with objects at one distance in sharp focus, and objects at other distances out of focus. Selective focus of nearby and distant details may also be observed in the physical world. Because the human eye can focus at only one distance at a time, objects at greater and lesser distances will appear to be increasingly out of focus. The depth-of-field characteristics of the lens can be used to enhance the illusion of three dimensions by controlling which objects are in focus and which are not. The greater the difference in sharpness between objects, the greater the distance between them will appear.

This type of perspective control often is used in portraiture. The difference in degree of sharpness between the features of the face and those of the background is exaggerated to create an illusion of depth. In many portraits sharpness begins to fall

off at the subject's ears, closely approximating how a person is seen close up.

Focusing the lens and adjusting the aperture will modify depth of field. These adjustments can be used to hold certain details in sharp focus and record others out of focus. Long lenses, for example, offer greater control over selective focus, whereas short lenses afford greater depth of field. Precise control over depth of field is enhanced by using through-the-lens viewing and digital preview screens—advantages afforded by reflex and digital cameras. Figure 10-17 illustrates the effect of selective focus on perspective.

Focal Length as a Perspective Tool

Interchangeable or zoom lenses may also be used as valuable tools for controlling perspective. Lenses of various focal lengths can alter the apparent relative size of objects and thereby alter their apparent relative distances in the photograph. A lens of normal focal length approximates perspective as the human eye sees it—objects in the photograph appear to be of the same relative size and at the same relative distance as they appeared to the photographer.

Lenses of different focal lengths, however, tend to expand or compress normal perspective. For example, a shorter-than-normal focal length lens increases the size of nearby objects relative to those farther away. A short focal length lens tends to emphasize nearby objects and subordinate more distant ones by increasing the apparent distance between them. Extremely short focal length lenses distort objects close to the lens more than those farther away. Such distortion, while not normally desired, may sometimes communicate an intended idea or emphasize a particular part of the subject. (See Figure 10-18.) Telephoto or longer-than-normal focal length lenses, on the other hand, increase the size of distant objects relative to closer ones. Thus, a telephoto or telephoto-zoom lens tends to emphasize more distant objects and subordinate closer ones by decreasing the apparent distance between them.

The degree to which perspective is altered varies with the focal length of the lens—the greater the departure from normal, the more exaggerated the effect on perspective. The creative use of these

A.

B.

Figure 10-17. Selective focus. In close-ups, shallow depth of field and selective focus create illusion of depth.

Figure 10-18. Wide-angle distortion. Subjects near the camera appear distorted and display foreshortened perspective.

small hill in a photo, or a tiny insect may appear gigantic when the image is enlarged. When these objects are viewed in person, their sizes can be evaluated in relation to other familiar objects. The mountain is massive relative to the smaller size of the viewer; the insect is tiny relative to the leaf on which it sits. In a photograph, size and scale are judged by context.

Keep in mind that sizes and distances in photographs are relative. The apparent length, width, shape, volume, and distance of objects gain **scale** by their perceived relationship with other objects. If some perceived objects are of known scale, then the scale of unknown objects can become known also. Including objects of familiar size, such as trees, automobiles, houses, people, and animals, helps communicate the scale of a photograph and aids the viewer's perception of depth. Figure 10-21 illustrates this principle.

Lines of Composition

Objective 10-E Describe and demonstrate how lines of composition can be used to emphasize the center of interest and generate dynamism in a photograph.

Key Concepts lines of composition, real, implied, dynamism, horizontal, diagonal, zigzag, curved, vertical, opposing, converging

techniques to control perspective is one of the more powerful tools photographers use to express their unique perceptions of the world. Figure 10-19 illustrates the effects upon perspective of lenses of various focal lengths used at a fixed camera-to-subject distance. Figure 10-20 illustrates the effect achieved when lenses of various focal lengths are used to hold the field of view constant.

Scale

The size of unfamiliar objects is often difficult to convey. A massive mountain may appear but a

Within a photograph, various **lines of composition**, sometimes called "leading lines," tend to command attention. These lines may be **real** (visible) or merely **implied**. The edge of a building, the horizon, the edge of a road, or the top line of a fence—all are real lines in a photograph. The viewer's eye tends to travel along them.

Often these lines of composition are not visible, but they command attention just the same. A gesture, an extended arm, or the attention of many

Figure 10-19. Controlling image size with various focal length lenses. A) 28mm wide-angle lens. B) 35mm wide-angle lens. C) 50mm normal focal length lens. D) 90mm telephoto lens. E) 135mm telephoto lens. Pictures taken from the same camera position but with different focal length lenses vary the angle of view and image size. Focal length changes also alter depth of field and can be used to control selective focus.

faces directed in a single direction can create implied lines of composition. The viewer's eye tends to follow the direction of the pointed finger, the focused gaze, or the moving object. (See Figure 10-22.)

When opposing lines of composition intersect at a sharp angle, attention is drawn to the point of intersection. The viewer is held in suspense at this point, expecting something to occur there.

The intersection of composition lines acts as a powerful magnet, drawing the viewer's attention. By arranging lines of composition, the photographer can emphasize the center of interest by leading the viewer's attention directly to it.

The shapes and relationships of composition lines can also communicate **dynamism** within a photograph—a sense of force, energy, or movement. When composition lines are gently curved, they

A.

B.

C.

D.

E.

Figure 10-20. Controlling perspective with various focal length lenses. In this series, the camera distance was varied to maintain similar image size of the main subject. Note how the illusion of depth diminishes as the near-far perspective compresses. A) 28mm wide-angle lens. B) 35mm wide-angle lens. C) 50mm normal focal length lens. D) 90mm telephoto lens. E) 135mm telephoto lens.

convey a sense of flowing, graceful movement; when they abruptly change direction or intersect, they convey a sense of vigorous, even violent movement; when they are parallel, they convey a sense of simultaneous, parallel movement.

The function of composition is to organize pictorial elements to communicate the photographer's central ideas. Arranging composition lines to support a central idea is one of the photographer's es-

sential tools. Gently curving lines of composition may communicate the graceful form and movement of a ballet dancer better than can opposing lines that are full of abrupt, angular changes of direction. On the other hand, the latter may more effectively communicate the violent movements of a boxing match.

The effects of different arrangements of composition lines may vary with subject matter and treat-

A.

B.

Figure 10-21. Scale. Objects of known size establish measure for judging depth, distance, and size of unknown objects.

Diagonal lines of composition tend to convey a sense of rapid movement—the more nearly they approach the diagonal, the more rapid the movement sensed. (See Figure 10-24.)

Zigzag lines of composition—lines that abruptly change direction—tend to convey a sense of vigorous, even violent action. We often symbolize lightning with a zigzag line. (See Figure 10-25.)

Curved lines of composition, such as the S-shaped curve, tend to convey a sense of graceful, flowing movement. (See Figure 10-26.)

Vertical lines of composition tend to convey a sense of immobility, stability, and strength. (See Figure 10-27.)

Opposing lines of composition tend to convey a sense of conflict, resistance, and potential energy. (See Figure 10-28A.)

Converging lines of composition tend to convey a sense of converging, simultaneous movement and lead the eye to the point of anticipated intersection. (See Figure 10-28B.)

Because composition lines exert a powerful effect on the viewer's perception, their accidental occurrence in the middle of a picture should usually be avoided. A horizon or tree exactly splitting the image in two tends to create an image that lacks energy and resists advancing a center of interest. Usually such strong horizontal or vertical lines are best placed off-center, perhaps a third of the distance toward the picture's edge. Of course, if a sense of perfect symmetry and inactivity is to be conveyed, the exact center may be just the place for such a feature.

Use of Tone and Contrast

Objective 10-F Describe and demonstrate how tone and contrast can be used to reveal essential details, emphasize the central idea, and contribute to the mood of a photograph.

Key Concepts figure-ground contrast, silhouette, low-key photo, high-key photo, chiaroscuro

ment, and so the following suggestions should be applied with discretion. As always, select a composition that best communicates a central idea.

Horizontal lines of composition tend to convey a sense of slow movement, inactivity, restfulness, tranquility, peacefulness, and inaction. (See Figure 10-23.)

A.

B.

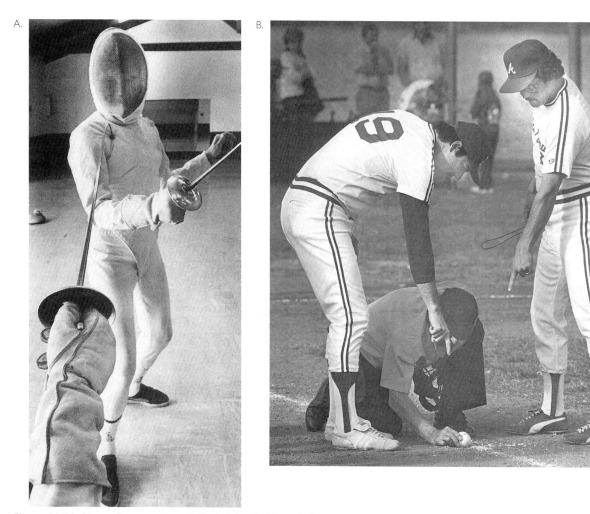

Figure 10-22. Lines of composition. A) Real. B) Implied by pointing.

Figure 10-23. Horizontal composition. Restful.

Figure 10-24. Diagonal composition. Active.

Figure 10-25. Zigzag composition. Vigorous.

Emphasis

In addition to revealing details clearly, contrast can be used for emphasis. The arrangement of black, white, and gray tones in a print should create **figure-ground contrast**, with objects standing out clearly from their backgrounds. Light objects seen against light backgrounds afford little contrast, but against dark backgrounds they stand out. The eye follows light, moving from shadows to highlights and from highlights to shadows. The greater the contrast, the greater the attraction to the eye. (See Figure 10-29.)

Figure 10-26. Curved line composition. Flowing.

Figure 10-27. Vertical composition. Strong.

357

A.

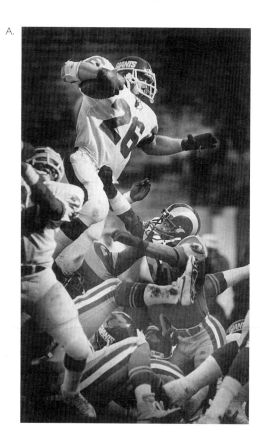

B.

Figure 10-28. Compositional arrangements. A) Opposing lines of composition convey a sense of resistance and conflict. B) Converging lines of composition lead the eye toward a point of convergence.

One central object of interest against a plain background poses no problem of emphasis. But when there are two or more objects in the same photograph and one is to be emphasized, remember that the eye is guided by the arrangement of tones. If one object is placed against a contrasting background and the other against a noncontrasting background, the eye will be drawn to the object of greater contrast first. (See Figure 10-30.)

An extreme example of figure-ground contrast may be found in the **silhouette**. Silhouette tech-nique works well when details are easily recognized by their shapes. Unless objects can be recognized by their shapes, however, the silhouette may obscure the subject, essential details, and thus the entire idea of the photograph. (See Figure 10-31.)

Mood

Contrast can also contribute to the mood of a photograph. A **low-key** photo, for example, one in which the majority of tones fall in the darkest

A.

B.

Figure 10-29. Figure-ground contrast. A) Light objects stand out against contrasting darker background. B) Dark objects stand out against contrasting lighter background.

Figure 10-30. Emphasizing objects. Eye tends to move from darker toward lighter tones.

areas of the tonal range, tends to support a somber, serious mood, or one of mystery. A **high-key** photo, on the other hand, one in which the majority of tones fall in the lightest areas of the tonal range, tends to support a light, bright mood, or one of gaiety and happiness. Photos that have little contrast tend to convey a mood of stillness, peace, and quiet. Those with a wide range of contrasts, convey a mood of activity, vitality, and energy. (See Figures 10-32 and 10-33.)

Tonal Composition

Tonal composition refers to the arrangement of light and shade in a picture—the placement of the brightest highlights and deepest shadows to bring about a harmonious and logical tonal arrangement. Scattered highlights and disjointed shadow masses can destroy a harmonious effect, despite an otherwise pleasing arrangement of details. But by juxtaposing a bright subject against a dark background, or vise versa, the tonal separation can achieve emphasis. This application of **chiaroscuro** in photog-

Figure 10-31. Silhouette. Subjects are easily interpreted by their shapes.

A.

B.

Figure 10-32. Tonality. A) High-key photograph. Majority of tones are light. B) Low-key photograph. Majority of tones are dark.

raphy leads to a conscious arrangement of light and shadow masses to reveal the subject and to direct the viewer's attention.

Color Composition

Objective 10-G Describe and demonstrate principles of color composition related to color har-

mony, psychological effects of color, effects of reflected light, and unnatural colors.

Key Concepts color harmony, contrasting colors, complementarity, monochromatic, cast

Color provides the photographer with additional controls in organizing pictorial elements to com-

A.

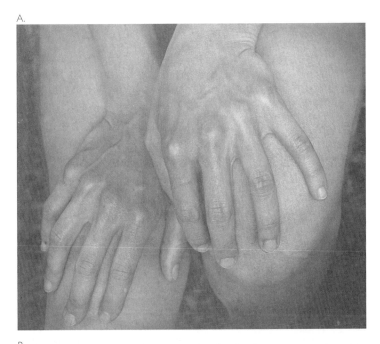

B.

Figure 10-33. Tonal contrast. A) Flat contrast conveys feeling of repose. B) High contrast conveys feeling of activity, even with stationary subjects.

municate an idea, mood, or feeling. In color photography, emphasis and subordination can be controlled not only by perspective, lines of composition, tone, and contrast, but also by the arrangement and manipulation of color details.

Color Harmony

Color harmony refers to the relationship among various color details within a photograph. Just as setting them against a background of **contrasting**

tone may emphasize black-and-white details, setting them against a background of **contrasting colors** may emphasize color details. Similarly, certain hues and values tend to appear brighter than others and thereby attract attention to themselves, providing emphasis. A harmonious organization of color elements will support the central idea of a photograph and avoid distracting color elements.

Achieving a harmonious arrangement requires an understanding of the principle of **complementarity** of colors. Because white light is made up of all wavelengths in the visible light spectrum, any given hue is made up of only some of these wavelengths. The combination of wavelengths omitted from this hue makes up its complementary hue—the color of light that, when combined with the given hue, would produce white light. The color wheel shown in Color Plate 1A shows a sample of twelve colors from the visible light spectrum. The primary colors—red, blue, and green—are connected in the figure by the solid triangle. Their complements—cyan, yellow, and magenta—are connected in the figure by the dotted triangle. The complements appear opposite their primaries. Each complementary color is a combination of two primary colors.

When any color appears against a complementary background color of lower saturation and value, its own hue is enhanced. It appears more brilliant and therefore is emphasized. Against a background of equal saturation and value, however, complementary colors compete for attention, often appearing to clash and vibrate in disharmony.

Color contrasts can be developed in other ways besides using color complements. Even objects of the same hue may contrast if one is more highly saturated than the other. A scarlet rose may be set

Famous Photographer

Margaret Bourke-White

A former student of photography at Columbia University and graduate in biology from Cornell University, Margaret Bourke-White became a commercial photographer in Cleveland, Ohio, in 1927. Her architectural and industrial photographs gained her an associate editorship at *Fortune Magazine* in 1929. Her interests soon turned toward photojournalism, however. Traveling to Russia, she began to develop her own dynamic approach to photo reportage, weaving an assortment of related images into a cohesive, thematic whole. Her first book, *Eyes on Russia,* was published in 1931.

Picture magazine publishing was at that time in ferment. New, convenient, candid cameras had led European picture magazines to experiment with picture groups, sometimes organized around a single, psychological theme that conveyed a new sense of action and immediacy. In the early 1930s, many European photographers and editors emigrated to America and brought these ideas with them.

Inspired by the success of the European magazines, Bourke-White's publisher, Henry Luce of *Time* and *Fortune,* was prompted to create a new American, large-format picture magazine—*Life.* He tapped Bourke-White, Alfred Eisenstaedt, Thomas McAvoy, and Peter Stackpole for the original photographic staff. Bourke-White was dispatched to Montana to photograph the construction of the Works Project Administration (WPA) Fort Peck Dam for *Life's* first issue, November 23, 1936.

Margaret Bourke-White,"The Living Dead of Buchenwald," 1945. © Margaret Bourke-White/TimePix

Bourke-White shot the dam; however, before leaving Fort Peck, following her own photojournalist instincts, she also shot hundreds of pictures about life among the migrant workers in the shantytowns that had sprung up around the project. Her work captured the fake-front apartments, bars, and stores, the night revelries—everything about the boomtown atmosphere, with its usual problems of prostitution, sewage, and gambling. When *Life* editor John Shaw Billings received the pictures, he quickly saw their dramatic potential and assembled them into a carefully crafted, coherent picture story—a photoessay of the form that was to characterize *Life* throughout its history. *Life's* first issue carried Bourke-White's bold, structural photograph of the dam on its cover, and inside, a nine-page photoessay about living in the shadow of the dam.

Bourke-White's photo essays are legendary. She later became an official Air Force photographer during World War II and a UN war correspondent for *Life* in Korea. Torpedoed once and awaiting rescue on a life raft, she documented the harrowing experience on film. She was on hand when the Army liberated the Nazi concentration camp at Buchenwald; she documented the surviving victims staring through barbed wire. Collections of her work are retained in the Library of Congress, Brooklyn Museum, Museum of Modern Art, Cleveland Museum of Art, and the Royal Photographic Society, London.

off nicely against a background of its pink cousin —a pink that may be identical in hue but of less saturation than the scarlet. Similarly, the dull blue of a predawn sky may provide a fitting contrast to a bright blue electric sign—a color of the same hue, perhaps, but differing in value. Thus appropriate contrast can be developed even in **monochromatic** compositions—those based on one hue or several closely related ones—by controlling their relative saturations and values. The greatest contrasts can be developed, however, between complementary colors or between colors farther apart in the visible light spectrum. (See Color Plate 3.)

Psychological Effects of Color

It is difficult to generalize about the psychological effects of color. Under one set of circumstances, green and yellow hues may convey the general idea of new life, sunshine, and springtime; under another, the feeling of jealousy, sickness, or death. Red, the traditional color of hate and anger, may suggest the feeling of love and contentment in a cozy, firelight scene. Although blue is usually the color of cold, ice, and darkness, a photograph of an azure sky over a sandy shore may give a sense of warmth and summertime. In these matters there are far more exceptions than rules, and photographers should rely on their own taste and judgment in communicating their personal vision of a scene.

Were we to generalize about color, we would advance only the following few principles:

1. The red-orange-yellow hues tend to appear brighter to the eye than the blue-green-violet hues of similar value. These red-orange-yellow hues are popularly called warm tones, in contrast to cold tones. (These popular descriptions should not be confused with the Kelvin scale, in which reds represent the cooler and blues the warmer color temperatures.) The apparent brightness of the red-orange-yellow wavelengths may draw attention to objects of those hues in a color photograph. Similarly, these red-orange-yellow hues tend to convey a greater sense of activity than the blue-green-violet hues.

2. The greater the profusion of color and contrast within a photograph, the more the photograph will tend to convey a sense of activity, dynamism, and energy.

3. Monochromatic compositions—compositions developed around a few closely related hues— will tend to convey a sense of unity, tranquility, and stillness.

The Effects of Reflected Light

We noted earlier that the color temperature of the source light can affect the color rendering of objects in a color photograph. As long as the light reaching the camera is matched to the color temperature for which the film is balanced or the appropriate white balance on a digital camera, the image will be rendered in hues that appear as they were perceived in the original scene. When the light source and receptor are not matched, the image will be rendered with an overall **cast** reflecting this mismatch. These effects and the use of filters to correct the effects are shown in Color Plate 6. (See Unit 11 for a discussion of color correction filters.)

More than the source lighting determines the light hues that illuminate objects in a scene, however. Within the scene, color is reflected from object to object. Light rays reflected from an object tend to assume the hues of the object and to lend those hues to other objects upon which they fall.

Light reflected from the green leaves of a tree, for example, would consist primarily of the green-blue wavelengths (the red wavelengths having been absorbed by the leaves). A nearby white object would reflect these predominantly green wavelengths as well as those of the source light. This phenomenon may not be apparent when the object is viewed; the mind interprets it as white. However, color photography is more faithful; the influence of this green, reflected light is recorded as a greenish cast on the white object.

Any object of strong color value can be expected to influence the cast of other, nearby objects. This effect may be useful if the cast is desirable in the color composition, or it may be a distraction. To eliminate the effect, separate strongly colored objects from other objects in the scene.

Color Manipulation

In the hands of a creative photographer, color can become a powerful tool of visual communication. Color need not be thought of as an inherent characteristic of a scene needing only to be recorded accurately on film; color should be thought of as a controllable compositional element to be managed purposefully in an image so as to convey the photographer's unique idea. An object's color may be emphasized or subdued, of course, but it can also be exaggerated, altered, or even grossly distorted for special effect. Whether the photographer chooses to be faithful to a scene or to introduce creative color manipulations is largely a matter of choice driven by a personal vision.

Special Lighting Some materials fluoresce blue-white, magenta, or other bright colors when lit by ultraviolet light, sometimes called black-light. These materials include manmade fabrics and dyes, plastics, display boards, and chalk solutions. Experiment by illuminating materials in a darkened room with a UV lamp. The eye can detect those that fluoresce immediately. To make photographs of these effects, use a clear ultraviolet lens filter and a color film balanced for daylight. If shooting digitally, experiment first with a "daylight" white balance setting, then try others.

Special Films Objects that reflect infrared light, such as vegetation, living organisms, heat-generating and heat-reflecting objects, and the like, will record false colors when viewed by infrared light. Vegetation appears to glow, sky takes on an ominous tone and flesh appears translucent. Black and white infrared film and some digital camera sensors can record infrared light. Used with deep red filters or special IR filters, these effects are further exaggerated and often produce unexpected and unpredictable results.

Misprocessing Normally exposed color slide film may be subjected to color negative processing. The resulting images show all colors reversed to their complements—blue and yellow are reversed, as are cyan and red, magenta and green. Further, the relative brightness values are reversed—the densities of the highlights and shadows. The result appears similar to a color negative, except that the image has greater density, colors are more saturated, and the overall orange-pink filter of color negatives is omitted. (Color prints made with these slides are generally unsatisfactory.) Digital manipulation in photo editing software can often achieve a similar effect; moreover, some digital cameras have a "reversal" mode designed to produce the same kind of color manipulation.

Filters A variety of filters for both black-and-white and color photography may be used effectively to manipulate the color image. These are discussed at length in Unit 11. (See Color Plates 5A, B, C.)

Printing and Display Manipulations Further color manipulation can be achieved during printing and display. Digital image processing or color printing (CP) filters can be used to alter or grossly distort color balances during printing and, combined with dodging and burning-in techniques, can be applied to selective portions of the image. Combinations of color negatives can be sandwiched together to create fantastic images; similarly, several digital image files or color transparencies can be layered together to create combined images during projection.

A creative color dimension can be added to black-and-white prints by the use of toners. Toners, normally used to tint the overall black-and-white image, may be applied to selected portions of the image. More than one toner may be used to introduce a variety of colors to selected portions of the image. Color, too, can be added to a black and white digital image in a manner akin to toning or hand coloring.

Photographic Guidelines

Objective 10-H Describe and demonstrate five photographic guidelines based upon principles of composition.

Key Concepts previsualize, move in close, select or create a neutral background, emphasize lighting contrast

Beginning photographers may apply the general principles of composition by observing a few guidelines. These guidelines are intended only as aids, not as firm rules. In many cases, these guidelines may be helpful as a start to composing photographs. However, moving beyond these starting points may prove a better way to express some intended visual ideas. When that is the case, do not hesitate to do so—experiment with a variety of ways to express ideas in photographs.

1. *Previsualize the intended image.* Compose the image around a single center of interest or

central idea and sweep it clean of anything that does not support, explain, or in some way add to that idea. Keep this central idea in mind as you **previsualize** the final print. Are the important details included? Are distracting details excluded? Are the more significant details emphasized; the less significant, subordinated? Are the important visual relationships revealed? To gain control over the final image, photographers must manipulate many variables, including camera angle, lens type and focal length, distance, aperture, exposure, contrast, and processing. Photographers can improve their compositions by selecting and arranging the visual elements so they "pull together" to support the basic idea. When the elements combine to support a basic visual statement, the shot is said to have unity.

2. *Move the camera in as close as possible to the subject without distortion.* Doing so will increase the size of the subject in relation to other objects in the picture, and will tend to force unnecessary details out of the picture. If the camera cannot physically be moved in close, use a telephoto or zoom lens to achieve a similar effect. Moving too close, however, may produce distortion. **Move in close** to exclude unwanted details, and to include only wanted details, and positioning the camera to frame the subject in the desired way are the most important ways to achieve emphasis, size, and location of the subject within the frame.

3. *Whenever possible, select or create a neutral background for the subject.* Try to move the camera into a position from which the subject can be viewed against a neutral background. If the background contains too many unnecessary or confusing elements, try a low-angle shot against the sky. If a neutral background cannot be selected, **create a neutral background** by using a shallow depth of field to throw the background details out of focus. With color photographs, select backgrounds of solid colors or colors of relatively low saturation and value. Avoid bright-colored background objects and profusions of colorful objects. Out-of-focus backgrounds tend to be neutral; the colors tend to merge as focus is diminished. To reduce confusion, avoid using too many colors in any single photograph.

Limit the colors to a few carefully chosen ones that express the visual idea.

4. *Whenever possible, emphasize the contrast between the subject and the background.* If the subject is brightly lit, try to shoot it against a dark or shadowed background. If the subject is dark, try to shoot it against a light background, such as a solid bright area or the sky. Position yourself to **emphasize lighting contrast**. With color photographs, emphasize the color of the subject by shooting against a background of contrasting or complementary hue, weaker in saturation and value. Select and organize colors within the photograph to lead the viewer's attention to the important details and relationships in the scene. Colors perceived as brighter tend to attract attention first.

5. *Use contrast to control visual energy.* Use a wide range of tones and high contrast to heighten the sense of energy and activity in a scene. Alternatively, use a narrow range of tones and low contrast to convey a sense of tranquility and repose. With color, use contrasting or complementary hues and a variety of saturations and values to heighten the sense of energy and activity. Alternatively, use similar hues, saturations, and values to reduce the visual energy conveyed in the scene.

6. *Place the subject effectively.* Except possibly for close-ups, it's often best to place the center of interest near one of the points indicated by the rule of thirds. Although the rule of thirds is a good starting point, do not hesitate to move beyond it or any other arbitrary rules if an idea is better expressed in other ways. The final test of a composition is how well it communicates the photographer's idea, mood, and feeling. As far as possible, rely upon the viewfinder to compose pictures, not on subsequent darkroom or digital processing controls.

Reading Photographs

Objective 10-I Describe and apply the process and criteria for evaluating and criticizing photographs.

Key Concepts active viewing, active questioning, photographer's intent, informed evaluation

A viewer cannot read, understand, and evaluate a photograph at a glance. Whether it is one of the viewer's own photographs, or one by a master photographer, a full understanding of the work often requires the viewer to engage in a process of **active viewing** and questioning.

The Importance of Active Viewing

Many people view photographs in the same passive way that they view a television movie. Passive viewing of this sort is unlikely to generate any enlightening information about a particular image. A more productive approach to understanding a photograph is to actively study the image, mentally describing it, and perhaps even asking questions about its origin, nature, intent, and value.

Describing the Picture One way to start an **active viewing** process is to simply describe the picture, either mentally or in discussion with another person. To describe the picture, the viewer might engage in **active questioning** about the subject, the visual elements, the technical qualities, the context, and the intended viewing medium. For example:

- *Question the subject of the picture.* What is it? What details were selectively included and what supporting elements are provided? How are they shown?

- *Question the visual elements of the picture.* What choices were made regarding the relative size and location of various objects in the picture? What are the largest and most dominant picture elements? What choices were made regarding the placement and use of mass and line in the visual design? What visual elements did the photographer choose to represent and delineate space and time?

- *Question the technical qualities of the picture.* What techniques and processes were used in making the image? Does the craftsmanship fulfill the viewer's expectations regarding the techniques and processes used?

- *Question the context in which the photograph was made.* Was the photographer working in a particular social environment? Is the location or time period relevant to understanding the photograph?

- *Question the medium in which the photograph will be presented to an audience.* Is the picture intended to be seen in a newspaper? Magazine advertisement? On a website? Gallery wall? Where?

Although the answers may initially seem obvious, the questioning process may reveal some surprising insights. At the very least, the viewer will gain a richer understanding of the photograph.

Understanding the Photographer's Intent and Interpreting the Image

The process of describing the photograph provides a basis for understanding the **photographer's intent** and interpreting the picture. The viewer might ask additional questions regarding the photographer's approach, the relative importance of detail, the manner of presentation, the photograph's formal qualities, and the use of symbols. For example:

- Certain traditional approaches may dictate the subject matter and content of a picture. Is the photographer working in an established traditional genre or style that defines the meaning and content of the photograph? These might include landscape, portraiture, street photography, still life, fashion, advertising, or photojournalism. Alternatively, does the photographer seem to be intentionally breaking away from traditional approaches?

- The importance of the details in a picture may reveal what the photographer intended to communicate. Is "what" the photographer chose to photograph important? The photographer's intent generally determines what details are selected and the relative importance given to them. Is the subject of special importance due to its rare or exotic nature? Is the subject a glimpse of the past that might otherwise be lost?

- In some photographs, "how" the subject details are presented may transcend "what" information about the subject was presented. Are the details shown in a particularly unusual or striking way?

- Certain formal qualities of a picture can reveal its purpose. Is the picture a rich visual experience?

- Many photographs have as their subject simply the interplay of light and form, volume and space, and are intended mainly to delight the eye. How significant are these formal qualities of the picture?

- How the photographer uses symbols to convey meaning can reveal intent. Has the photographer used any symbols in the photograph? Do any picture elements suggest or resemble something else? Does the photograph use metaphor, for example, to suggest a comparison between elements in the picture, and elements found in another context?

- Given the answers to these questions, can the photographer's intent be stated?

Asking these questions can help to discern the photographer's intent. Before the effectiveness of a photograph can be evaluated, the photographer's intent must be understood.

Making an Informed Evaluation

When evaluating a photograph, viewers are often tempted to immediately express approval or disapproval. Such judgments should be restrained until the image has been actively questioned and understood. Hastily expressing like or dislike for a picture suggests a less than rigorous evaluation and rarely leads to a defensible critical position.

One way to make an **informed evaluation** of a photograph's effectiveness is to compare and contrast it with similar works. The viewer might ask additional questions regarding craftsmanship, visual qualities, effectiveness, imaginativeness, salience, insightfulness, technical prowess, sufficiency, and impact. For example:

- Is the craftsmanship and method of execution appropriate to the task?

- Have such visual qualities as design, use of light, color, and form been used well?

- Is the photograph appropriate to its intended use and audience?

- Does the photograph present information in a new and imaginative way?

- Does the image present its theme in a forceful manner and compel the viewer's attention?

- Does the work stimulate new insights?

- Does the image expand the expressive or technical boundaries of the discipline?

- What, if anything, could be changed to make the photograph more effective?

- Does the viewer experience an intellectual or emotional impact?

No single set of rules can be used to read and evaluate all photographs. What viewers see in a photograph is shaped by their individual experiences, interactions with the world, fluency in photography, knowledge of art, and feelings at the time the work is viewed. Perceiving the meaning of a photograph is an intensely personal process; each viewer will find unique meanings to share with others. However, each viewer should also be able to discern some threads of meaning common to others. Ultimately, the meaning and value of an image relative to the body of valued works will be determined by social consensus.

The effective evaluation of photographs is enhanced by an understanding and appreciation of all images. Photographers who actively involve themselves in the process of reading and evaluating their own works and the works of others will increase their fluency in visual communication—and enhance their efforts toward mature and sophisticated photographic expression.

Questions to Consider

1. What is meant by the term composition? What are its purposes?

2. What are the major elements of composition?

3. Explain what controls can be used to emphasize or subordinate details in a photograph.

4. Explain the rule of thirds.

5. What is meant by the phrase "movement into frame"?

6. Describe low-angle, eye-level, and high-angle shots and what each tends to emphasize.

7. How can the illusion of depth be controlled through linear and aerial perspective?

8. How can scale be established in a photograph?

9. Describe how the mood or feeling of a photograph can be conveyed through the use of composition lines.

10. Describe how tone and contrast can be used to emphasize a center of interest and convey a mood in a photograph.

11. Describe how color can be used to emphasize a center of interest and convey a mood in a photograph.

12. What is "active viewing" of a photograph? Describe the processes suggested for describing, understanding, and evaluating photographs.

Suggested Field and Laboratory Assignments

Roll #1 (black-and-white)

1. Shoot a roll of film or a series of black-and-white digital images under daylight conditions. For one series of shots, select a scene involving at least three interacting objects, such as adult, child, and football; photographer, camera, and subject; angler, worm, and fishhook; and so forth. Shoot several shots of the scene, each time emphasizing a different object in the scene using the controls described in this unit. Note how in each shot a different interpretation of the relationship among the objects in the scene can be communicated.

2. Keep a log of every shot, recording f-stop, shutter speed, and technique(s) used to select and emphasize various details in each shot.

3. Be sure to provide at least one example of each of the following:

   ▪ a shot using tone and contrast to emphasize the center of interest

   ▪ a low-key photograph, dominated by dark tones to create a somber mood

   ▪ a high-key photograph, dominated by light tones to create a bright mood

4. Develop and proof.

5. Make enlargements of the better negatives. Crop them for best composition.

6. Record on the back of the finished prints the details taken from the log.

Roll #2 (color or digital)

Shoot several color photographs using each of the following techniques. You may include more than one technique in each picture. Keep a shooting log identifying the techniques used.

1. A long shot, including the horizon, using one or more linear perspective controls to enhance the illusion of depth.

2. A long shot, including the horizon, using one or more aerial perspective controls to enhance the illusion of depth.

3. A shot using a natural frame to enhance the illusion of depth.

4. A shot using vertical composition lines to increase the feeling of strength or dignity.

5. A shot using horizontal composition lines to increase the feeling of rest, repose, or peacefulness.

6. A shot using diagonal composition lines to increase the feeling of violence or action.

7. A shot using curved composition lines to increase the feeling of graceful movement.

8. A shot using color to emphasize the center of interest.

9. A shot using converging lines of composition to emphasize the subject or opposing lines to create a sense of conflict.

10. A low-key photograph, dominated by dark colors, to create a somber mood.

11. A high-key photograph, dominated by light colors, to create a bright mood.

12. A photograph using a color manipulation.

Filters

Mark Yamamoto, "Tree and Halfdome."

<table>
<tr><td>

**Unit
at a
Glance**

</td><td>

Filters are transparent, tinted attachments made of plastic, gelatin, optical resin, or glass. They are designed to remove certain colors from the image-forming light or to manipulate the image in other ways. Filters provide a quick and simple way to dramatically alter the appearance of a picture. Their many uses include simply reducing the amount of image-forming light, altering tones and colors, and creating a variety of special effects.

Most filters are relatively inexpensive and very useful aids. This unit explains many of the principles on which filters are based, the types and purposes of filters commonly used for black-and-white and color photography, how filters are made and how they are attached to the camera, and how exposure is adjusted to compensate for the use of filters.

</td></tr>
</table>

Principles of Filters

Objective 11-A State the principles on which filters are based and describe the general effect produced by using a filter when photographing a subject in black and white.

Key Concepts filter, primary colors, relative brightness, gray-tone rendering, correction filter, contrast filter, tone separation, law of transmission and absorption

In general, any **filter** is a device for removing unwanted portions of anything passed through it. We filter our morning breakfast coffee to remove unwanted coffee grounds, or we filter the air in a furnace to remove dust and make the air cleaner. A photographic filter removes unwanted portions of the light that reaches the camera before transmitting the desired portions through the lens to the film.

Why would a photographer wish to alter the light transmitted to the film? Remember that white light actually is made up of many colors—all colors of the rainbow, in fact—ranging from the deep violets at one end of the spectrum to the deep reds at the other. However, all these colors are made up of only the three **primary colors** of light—red, green, and blue. All the visible colors of light, including white, are composed of these three primary colors.

Black-and-white images, as their name implies, do not reproduce these colors. The film or monochrome digital file and the final black-and-white print record the **relative brightness** of objects, translating their colors into corresponding shades of gray. Thus yellow may appear in the final print as a lighter shade of gray than does red. This **gray tone rendering** is psychologically acceptable because we perceive yellow as a lighter color than red.

A photographic filter removes certain portions of the light reaching the film or digital sensor. One use of this effect is to alter the relative brightness of various objects in a scene so that they conform more closely to the way we see them and achieve the proper **gray-tone rendering** with a **correction filter**. Another use is to increase the contrast between objects and their backgrounds; a **contrast filter** to aid **tone separation**. Another use is to reduce aerial haze at high altitudes or at long distances, and another is to reduce the overall intensity of light reaching the camera so that we can shoot at slower speeds and larger apertures.

Physically, a photographic filter is a thin sheet of colored plastic, optical resin, gelatin, or glass, usually attached to the camera immediately in front of the picture-taking lens. The rays of light of various colors, reflected from the subject, strike the filter and are either absorbed or transmitted, depending on the color of the light and the color of the filter. Thus a red filter will transmit red light to the film, but will absorb blue and green light, preventing it from reaching the film. A green filter will transmit green light, but absorb red and blue light.

Law of Transmission and Absorption

A general **law of transmission and absorption** that applies to any filter may be stated thus: *A filter transmits light of its own color and absorbs light of its complementary color.*

The colors of light that a filter transmits are reproduced lighter on the final print than are those that the filter absorbs. The colors of light that the filter absorbs are reproduced darker on the final print than are those that the filter transmits. Figure 11-2 illustrates the principle of transmission and absorption using a red filter.

A red filter transmits red light, making all red objects lighter on the final print; it absorbs blue and green light, making all blue and green objects darker on the final print. Similarly, a blue filter makes blue objects lighter and red and green objects darker in the final print. A green filter makes green objects lighter and red and blue objects darker. Yellow light is a combination of red and green, so a yellow filter makes red and green objects lighter and blue objects darker. Figure 11-3 illustrates these principles. Table 11-1 shows the effects on the primary colors that result from the use of various common filters with panchromatic film or digital cameras set to image in black and white.

Forms of Filter Construction

Objective 11-B Describe two forms of filter construction and state how each is attached to the camera.

Key Concepts glass disk filters, square filters, filter holder, adapter and retaining rings, flash head filter

Red Filter
Nearly all blue and green light is absorbed by a red filter, so that blue is enhanced while red is rendered nearly white.

Green Filter
With a green filter, red light is blocked but green light admitted; reds then become darker than greens. It is useful for leaves and grass, which can often appear too dark.

Blue Filter
A blue filter absorbs red and green, making them appear the same tone. Blue objects come out as white and thus disappear against a white background.

Figure 11-2. Law of transmission and absorption.

Two common forms of filter construction are (1) glass disks bound with metal rims, and (2) squares of sheet gelatin, plastic, optical resin, or glass.

For general use the **glass disk filters** usually are easier to handle and less subject to damage. They are made of optical glass, however, and tend to be

Table 11-1. Effects of common filters with panchromatic film and digital cameras in black-and-white mode		
Filter Color	*Colors Lightened in Final Print*	*Colors Darkened in Final Print*
Red	Red	Blue, green (cyan)
Green	Green	Red, blue (magenta)
Blue	Blue	Red, green (yellow)
Yellow (red, green)	Red, green (yellow)	Blue
Light pink or skylight	None	Ultraviolet, some blue

A.

Figure 11-3. Effects of yellow and red filters. Yellow sunflowers were photographed against a blue sky. A) No filter. B) Yellow filter. C) Red filter. Figure-ground contrast is increased using filters, red filter producing most extreme contrast in this case.

more expensive than the other forms. Most modern glass disk filters are designed with threaded metal rims so that the filter can be screwed directly to the front of the lens housing. They are manufac-

tured in many millimeter sizes to fit exactly the diameters of standard lens housings. Some digital cameras require a filter adapter that slips over the lens and allows the use of standard threaded filters. (See Figure 11-4 A.) Some digital cameras require a filter adapter that slips over the lens and allows the use of standard filters.

The **square filters** are made of gelatin, plastic, optical resin, or glass. The gelatin square filters are the least expensive and are available in a wider variety of colors and special effects than glass. However, they are soft and easily damaged. They must be handled carefully by the edges, which are often taped or framed in metal, to preserve their usefulness. Plastic and optical resin filters are often made of the same high-grade polymers that are used in eyeglasses and are both more expensive and more durable than their gelatin counterparts. Glass filters tend to be more expensive and are available in fewer colors and effects. However, they are the most durable and easily handled.

To use square filters, a **filter holder** is a necessary piece of supplementary equipment. The filter holder is mounted to the lens by means of threaded **adapter** and **retaining rings** that screw into the front of the lens housing and hold the filter holder securely in place. Then the square filters can easily be inserted or removed from the filter holder as needed. One set of square filters can be used with many different sizes of adapter rings to fit a variety of lenses. This is especially handy for the photographer with many lenses. Figure 11-4 B shows a typical square-filter mounting system.

Another type of filter holder is the **flash head filter**, designed to be used with an electronic flash unit. These square plastic filters are mounted in front of the flash light source and have the same effect as a lens filter if the source light comes solely from the flash. The effect of a flash head filter is reduced if other light sources are present. (See Figure 11-4 C.)

Exposure with Filters

Objective 11-C Explain the exposure adjustments required by filters including the use of filter factors.

Key Concept filter factor

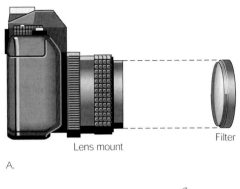

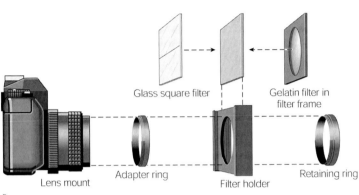

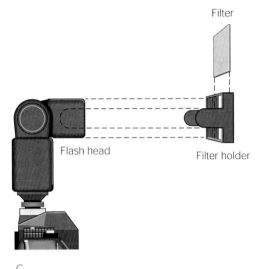

Figure 11-4. Filter mounting systems. A) Screw-in filter may be used only with lens mount of same diameter. B) Square filter mounting system. Adapter ring screws into or slips onto lens mount. Filter frame holder is inserted into adapter ring. Retaining ring screws into adapter ring to hold assembly in place. Filter squares are slipped into filter holder as needed. C) Flash head filter mounts to holder on front of flash unit to filter light emitted by the flash.

Filter

Lens mount

Filter

A.

Glass square filter

Gelatin filter in filter frame

Flash head

Filter holder

Lens mount

Adapter ring

Filter holder

Retaining ring

B.

C.

A filter absorbs part of the light passing through it, causing less light to reach the film. Therefore, to compensate for the reduction of light caused by the filter, exposure must be increased to avoid underexposure. External and through-the-lens metering systems require different procedures for increasing exposure by an appropriate amount.

Through-the-Lens Metering

Modern through-the-lens metering systems read the image-forming light through the lens and, hence, through any filter attached to the lens. With the filter mounted before the lens, the light meter reads the light intensity through the filter and thus takes into account the reduced light level. The meter will thus automatically display or set the correct exposure for the intensity of light passing through the filter. No special action by the photographer is required.

External Metering

If the camera does not have a through-the-lens metering system, the photographer must use special procedures to adjust exposure for the filter.

One approach is to read the external meter while holding the filter in place over the meter's light-sensitive cell. The meter's reading will be based upon the filtered light and take into account the reduced light level passed by the filter. The filter may then be attached to the lens and the exposure set for the reading thus obtained.

Other approaches require the use of **filter factors**. As an aid to determining the correct exposure required by a filter, the filter has a numerical value inscribed on it that corresponds to the needed increase. This number describes the factor by which the unfiltered exposure must be increased to compensate for the filter. The filter factor will vary, depending on the type of light source and type of film used. For example, a yellow filter used with panchromatic film usually has a factor of 2 in daylight and a factor of 1.5 in tungsten light. A filter factor of 2 implies that exposure must be doubled.

With an external meter, exposure must be increased manually. If an unfiltered exposure were to be f/16 at 1/125 sec., for an exposure with a yellow filter (filter factor 2) you would need to double the exposure to f/11 at 1/125 sec. or equivalent. A filter factor of 1.5 requires that exposure increase by 50 percent—to a point between f/11 and f/16 at 1/125 sec. or equivalent.

When using an external meter, many photographers find it more convenient to reset their

Famous Photographer

Jacob Riis

Sometimes credited with being America's first reporter-photographer, Jacob Riis left his native Denmark in 1870 and spent his first three years in New York often jobless, homeless, and destitute. He finally found employment with a news association and, with first hand knowledge of the plight of the poor, devoted much of his attention toward photographing and criticizing social conditions.

Often photographing in the dark interiors of tenements, in back alleys, and in bars, Riis was one of the first to use flash, which then consisted of powdered magnesium and potassium chlorate packaged in a cartridge and detonated by a device that looked like a pistol. Many of his suspicious and sometimes terrified subjects responded by brandishing weapons of their own. Riis substituted an open frying pan to hold his powder, igniting it by hand while releasing the shutter. In the blinding explosion, Riis would make his shot and then, in the resulting dense smoke, grab his camera and tripod and run off. More than once he set fire to himself and to the places he visited, once nearly blinding himself.

As a police reporter for the *New York Tribune* and the Associated Press Bureau, Riis's daily stories criticizing the poverty and squalor of immigrant life in New York tenements aroused the public conscience and led to the appointment of a Tenement House Commission in 1884. He began working for the *Evening Sun* in 1888.

He published his classic, *How the Other Half Lives,* in 1890. Heavy with moral indignation, weighted with irrefutable facts, and illustrated with thirty-eight engravings taken from his photographs, the book shocked the public. Theodore Roosevelt, then a young politician, sent Riis a note saying, "I have read your book and I have come to help." Later, as New York Police Commissioner, then Governor, and later President, Roosevelt remained true to that commitment, cracking down on the worst abuses, and joining in the reform movements that cleaned up many of the slums.

Jacob A. Riis, "Room in a Tenement," 1910. Jessie Tarbox Beals, Room in a Tenement Flat, 1910. Museum of the City of New York, The Jacob A. Riis Collection.

Riis continued his muckraking throughout his life, publishing nine photo-illustrated books that documented life among the poor immigrants of New York, and demonstrating the power of photojournalism to arouse public opinion and inspire reform.

meters to the film's ISO speed divided by the filter factor. Using an ISO 200/24° film with a yellow filter (filter factor 2), for example, they would reset the meter to read ISO 100/21° when shooting with that filter.

Digital cameras that lack through-the-lens light meters will also need exposure compensation when used with filters. With the camera set to the manual exposure mode adjust the settings to compensate for the filter factor as described above. Optionally, some digital cameras have exposure compensation settings that can be made in automatic or program exposure modes.

Two or more filters may also be used together, such as a yellow filter (factor of 2) and a polarizer (factor of 2.5). The resulting filter factor is the product of the two separate filter factors—in this case $2 \times 2.5 = 5$. Exposure in this case would need to be increased five times (approximately 2.3 stops).

In general, when the meter is read through the filter, the filter factor need not be used and the ISO setting need not be changed on either film or digital cameras. If the meter is read without the filter, then action must be taken to increase exposure by the filter factor.

Filters for Black-and-White Photography

Objective 11-D Name and describe the purposes of six types of filters commonly used in black-and-white photography, and give examples.

Key Concepts correction filters, contrast filters, ultraviolet and haze filters, polarizing filters, neutral density filters, special effects filters, tungsten light, polarized light, soft-focus filter, fog filter, cross-screen or star filter, spot filter, multiple-image filter

The filters used in black-and-white photography can be divided into six main types according to their uses and characteristics:

1. **Correction filters,** used to render the colors in a scene as shades of gray that correspond to their perceived relative brightness

2. **Contrast filters,** used to increase the tone separation between two colors that otherwise might appear as nearly the same shade of gray

3. **Ultraviolet and haze filters,** used to reduce aerial haze, particularly in distance and aerial shots

4. **Polarizing filters,** used to darken blue skies, control reflections, and penetrate aerial haze

5. **Neutral density filters,** used to reduce the amount of light passing through the lens without altering relative brightness relationships within the scene

6. **Special effect filters,** used to produce special optical effects in the recorded image

Correction Filters

Film and digital sensors differ from the human eye in the way they see the relative brightness of various colors. Thus film and many digital cameras cannot translate all colors into fully satisfying gray tones. All films are especially sensitive to violet and blue, for example, and these colors tend to appear too light in the final black-and-white print. The eye, however, tends to perceive them as relatively dark. Because of this, the white clouds we see against the darker blue sky may not appear at all in an unfiltered photograph using panchromatic film. The film sees the blue sky and the white clouds as the same light tonal value and does not record a tone separation between them.

Moreover, films are sensitive to ultraviolet light, which the eye cannot see at all, and which appears light in the final print. Conversely, panchromatic film is relatively insensitive to green. Thus, while the eye perceives green as relatively light, it appears dark in the final print.

When filters are used to correct these traits of a film—to reproduce colors with the relative brightness that most people see—they are called correction filters. For example, a yellow filter is often used with panchromatic film in daylight to reduce the amount of blue and violet light passing through the lens. The darkening of these colors in the final print serves to correct the gray tone rendering of sky and clouds and makes it appear more natural.

Similarly, **tungsten light,** such as that produced by ordinary household light bulbs, contains more red than does daylight. Because panchromatic film and digital sensors are sensitive to red, objects that reflect this additional red light may tend to appear too light in the final print. This is especially true of flesh tones. To filter out some of this red light as well as the blue and violet, a yellow-green filter is often used on the camera to obtain the most natural-looking gray tones under tungsten light.

Contrast Filters

Sometimes the perceived relative brightness of objects needs to be altered to improve contrasts and add emphasis. For example, when an object will photograph as nearly the same shade of gray as its background, the tone separation, or contrast, between the two should be increased. When filters are used for this purpose, they are called contrast filters.

For example, red and green objects tend to appear as the same shade of gray when they are photographed in black-and-white with daylight lighting. A red apple, therefore, might not stand out very well against its background of green leaves in a black-and-white photograph. A red filter, however, will transmit the red light reflected from the apple to the film or digital sensor, causing the apple to appear light in the final print. The filter will absorb the green light from the leaves, however, causing

them to appear darker in the final print. The tone separation between the two will be increased, and the apple will appear as a light object against a dark background. A green filter would produce the reverse effect. The green light from the leaves would be transmitted, whereas the red light from the apple would be absorbed. In this case the apple would appear as a dark object against a background of lighter leaves in the image.

Sometimes ordinary contrast filters can be used with special films to produce unusual effects. For example, a deep orange filter used with infrared film often produces unusual tonal renderings of landscapes. Figure 11-5 is an example of such an effect.

Both correction and contrast filters work on the same principles. The only difference between them is the use to which they are put in any given case. By mastering the use of filters, control over the relative brightness of objects in prints can be controlled. In this way contrast can be manipulated to emphasize certain objects and to subordinate others. Remember the law of transmission and absorption: *A filter transmits its own color and absorbs its complementary color. A filter's own color appears lighter in the final print; its complement darker.* Figure 11-6 illustrates some of the effects that can be achieved by using contrast filters.

Figure 11-5. This photograph was made with black-and-white infrared film and an orange filter. The trees and bushes appear white because they reflect large amounts of infrared light.

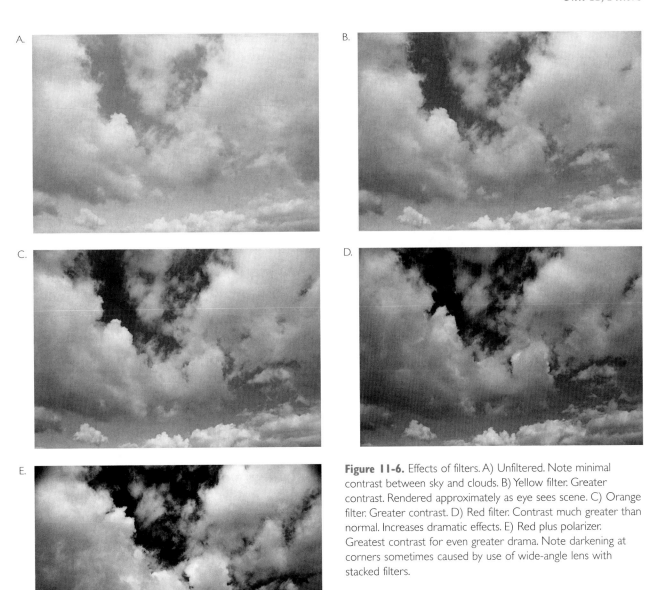

Figure 11-6. Effects of filters. A) Unfiltered. Note minimal contrast between sky and clouds. B) Yellow filter. Greater contrast. Rendered approximately as eye sees scene. C) Orange filter. Greater contrast. D) Red filter. Contrast much greater than normal. Increases dramatic effects. E) Red plus polarizer. Greatest contrast for even greater drama. Note darkening at corners sometimes caused by use of wide-angle lens with stacked filters.

Ultraviolet and Haze Filters

Atmospheric haze is often invisible to the naked eye but may appear in photographs as a light veil that masks some of the detail. In reality a bluish haze results from the scattering of light by tiny particles of dust and water vapor in the atmosphere. Because much of this haze is ultraviolet (to which the eye is insensitive), its presence may go unnoticed. Film, however, is very sensitive to ultraviolet, and hence records its presence. Most digital cameras are not very sensitive to ultraviolet light and will not record its presence.

To control haze with film cameras, use a filter that will absorb the blue and ultraviolet light that produces it. The most common filter for this purpose is the ultraviolet (UV) or haze filter. Almost clear in appearance, or very pale yellow, this filter has almost no effect on light visible to the naked eye, but gives a more precise gray-scale rendering of colors in open shade or on overcast days and reduces the effect of aerial haze in distance shots.

Many photographers keep this filter constantly attached to their lens and use it to protect the soft surface of the lens from nicks and abrasions. UV filters are commonly used for this purpose on both film and digital cameras.

For greater haze control, other filters may be used. A yellow filter will reduce haze, a deep yellow filter will reduce it more, and a red filter will almost eliminate it altogether, while simultaneously exaggerating the darkness of the sky.

A.

B.

Figure 11-7. Haze filters. A) Photo taken with red filter to eliminate haze. The darkness of the sky is exaggerated. B) Exaggerating haze can heighten sense of distance and provide contrasting background for foreground subjects.

Conversely, haze may be exaggerated in a print to create a greater feeling of distance by masking distant details in a veil of haze. To accomplish this effect, use a filter that transmits the blue and ultraviolet light and absorbs other colors. Thus a blue filter can be used to emphasize the effects of aerial haze. (See Figure 11-7.)

Polarizing Filters

A polarizing filter operates in an entirely different way. It appears grayish and does not filter out light of particular colors. All colors are transmitted equally, and no colors are absorbed. The relative brightness of various colors is unaffected by the polarizing filter. Instead, the filter acts upon light that has been polarized by reflection off nonmetallic surfaces. Such light, which vibrates at only one angle, is called **polarized light**.

Light is made up of rays that travel in straight lines and vibrate in all angles. When a light ray strikes a nonmetallic surface and is reflected from it, most of the reflected light tends to vibrate in one plane only, as shown in Figure 11-8 A. Depending on the angle of reflection, more or less of the reflected light is polarized. A polarizing filter can also polarize light, and if set at the correct angle, it will block light that has already been polarized, reducing or eliminating the reflections.

Most polarizing filters have an indicator mark or handle that designates the axis of the filter. Only light rays vibrating in a plane parallel to the filter axis will be transmitted; light rays vibrating in other planes will be absorbed.

Although direct sunlight is unpolarized, the light from a blue sky is polarized because it is made up of light reflected off particles of dust and water vapor in the atmosphere. If unpolarized light strikes the polarizing filter, only polarized light vibrating in a plane *parallel to the filter axis* will be transmitted, as shown in Figure 11-8 B. If polarized light, such as light reflected off a windowpane, strikes a polarizing filter, it will be transmitted only if the filter axis is parallel to the plane of the light's vibration, as shown in Figure 11-8 C. If the axis of the polarizing filter is rotated until its axis is *perpendicular* to the

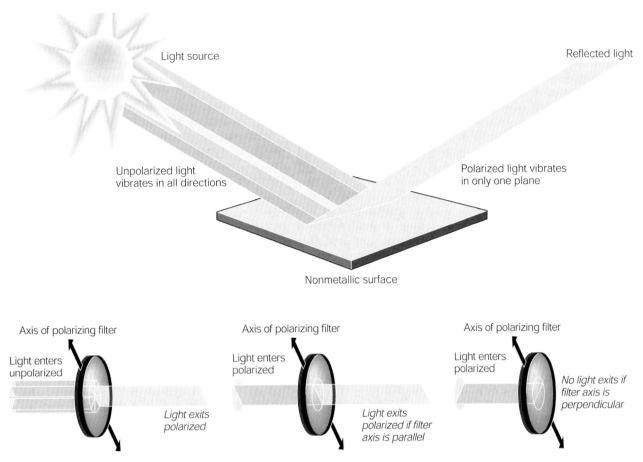

Light source

Reflected light

Unpolarized light
vibrates in all directions

Polarized light vibrates
in only one plane

Nonmetallic surface

Axis of polarizing filter

Light enters
unpolarized

*Light exits
polarized*

Axis of polarizing filter

Light enters
polarized

*Light exits
polarized if filter
axis is parallel*

Axis of polarizing filter

Light enters
polarized

*No light exits if
filter axis is
perpendicular*

Figure 11-8. Polarization of light and relation of polarized light to polarizing filter axis. A) Reflection from non-metallic surface polarizes light. B) When polarized light strikes polarizing filter, only polarized light is transmitted. C) Polarized light vibrating parallel to filter axis is transmitted. D) Polarized light vibrating perpendicular to filter axis is absorbed.

plane of the light's vibration, the polarized light will be absorbed. (See Figure 11-8 D.)

These features make the polarizing filter useful for several purposes in black-and-white photography with both film and digital cameras. Its most common uses are for darkening blue skies, for controlling reflections and glare from nonmetallic reflective surfaces, and for reducing haze without altering the relative brightness of other colors in the scene. (See Figure 11-9.)

With a rangefinder camera, look through the polarizing filter and rotate it slightly in one direction and then the other, until exactly the desired effect is obtained. Then attach the filter to the camera in this same position. With a single-lens reflex camera, of course, the filter can be attached first and then adjusted. With a twin-lens reflex camera, place the filter first on the viewing lens, adjust it to the desired position, and then relocate it on the picture-taking lens in the same position.

The polarizing filter reduces the total amount of light reaching the film. Its filter factor is 2.5 (about 1 1/3 stops) regardless of how much the filter is rotated. But in addition to the 1 1/3 stop increase needed to compensate for the filtering action, an additional 1/2 stop is usually needed because of the nature of the lighting conditions in which the filter is normally effective. The filter is most useful when the lighting is oblique—when the light strikes the subject from an extreme angle. So ordinarily slightly more exposure is needed to compensate for the deep shadows produced by such lighting. Thus, when using a polarizing filter, a two-stop increase in exposure over that indicated by the meter is typical. If the meter is read through the filter, however, exposures should be increased only 1/2 stop and the filter factor not used at all.

Figure 11-9. Controlling reflections from non-metallic surfaces. A) Reflections on windows obscure interior of building. B) Polarizer reduces reflections, revealing interior of building.

Neutral Density (ND) Filters

Neutral density filters are used to reduce the amount of light reaching the film or digital sensor without changing the relative brightness of various colors in the scene. Although you can reduce the amount of image-forming light by stopping down the aperture or by increasing the shutter speed, making these adjustments will also change the depth of field or the camera's ability to blur rapid movement. Using an ND filter for this purpose avoids changing the aperture or shutter speed.

Neutral density filters are most useful when fast film or a digital sensor with a high ISO rating is used on a bright day, conditions that often call for both smaller apertures and faster shutter speeds. Sometimes it may not be possible to open the aperture to reduce depth of field because the shutter speed is already at its fastest setting and cannot be increased. At other times it may not be possible to slow the shutter to pan with a moving object, or to synchronize the flash to fill in shadows because the aperture is already at its smallest opening. In such cases the ND filter may be useful, enabling the aperture to be opened or the shutter to be slowed without overexposing the film.

Neutral density filters are gray in color and are manufactured in various densities, which typically range from 0.10 (ND-1), requiring a 1/3 stop exposure increase, to 1.00 (ND-10), requiring a 3 1/3 stop exposure increase. Two filters may be used together to add up to a desired density. Perhaps the most useful densities are 0.30 (ND-3), 0.60 (ND-6), and 0.90 (ND-9), because they reduce exposure by 1, 2, and 3 stops, respectively.

Special Effect Filters

Many other filters are available that do not alter the color of light but produce different light patterns and effects instead. These filters may be used creatively to produce optical effects that enhance the photographic image.

One popular type of special effect filter simply diffuses the overall image. One of these is the **soft-focus filter**, which produces a soft-edged image that is often used to produce delicate, dreamlike impressions of portraits and landscapes. A more extreme version is the **fog filter**, which gives a natural misty look to scenic photographs.

Another popular type is the **cross-screen** or **star filter**, which produces star-shaped flares from any bright spots of light that appear in the image. This can be used to produce dramatic effects in night scenes or other scenes that feature bright spots of light.

Careers in Photography

Careers in Creative Photography

What Is Creative Photography?

Unlike photojournalism and commercial photography, creative or fine art photography is not a client-based career; creative photographers are not employed by a publisher or business to execute and solve visual problems. Creative photographers are motivated to produce works solely to satisfy their own need for self-discovery and self-expression. As a result, creative photographers exercise complete control over their subject matter, techniques, and aesthetics. It is this freedom of expression that attracts many to the field.

Fine arts photography lacks a specific occupational niche. Most people who engage in creative photography do so out of a passionate desire to use the medium as a way to learn more about themselves and the world around them, and, ultimately, to share and communicate these discoveries with others through their photographs. They are not primarily motivated by compensation and usually cannot depend on their photographs to support themselves financially; they usually need other sources of income. Some take on commercial photography assignments or work in another field while devoting their spare time to their personal photographic projects. Others prefer to pursue related careers, such as teaching photography or working as a staff photographer in a gallery or museum.

How to Become a Creative Photographer

Prior to the 1960s, most respected fine art photographers were self-taught or learned their craft from friends, books, or through an apprenticeship with a master photographer. Today, most photographers take formal studies in university art departments or at specialized schools of art. On the undergraduate level, many schools offer a BFA (Bachelor of Fine Arts) degree in photography.

Art school training steeps the student in the ideas and challenges of the visual arts. Student photographers learn to "see photographically" and to develop sensitivity to the interplay of light and form. They are immersed in the history and language of art and learn to critically examine and thoughtfully discuss their own work and the work of others. Guided critiques help students to advance their photographic techniques and to discover their own photographic personalities and styles.

Students interested in continuing their study of photography beyond the baccalaureate may enroll in an MFA (Master of Fine Arts) program. Graduate school perfects the student's visual, conceptual and creative senses. Most programs are designed to develop skills in critical theory and analysis in addition to the production of photographic works of art. The faculty will often include established photographic artists who can provide important links to the art world and gallery community. Graduate school is essential for those who are interested in a teaching career in photography. The MFA degree is generally required to teach art and photography on the college or university level. Choosing the right graduate school to match personal interests and goals is important.

How to Build an Exhibition Record

Many students with a passion for creative photography dream of having a major gallery exhibition of their work or perhaps publishing a book of photographs. A record of successful smaller exhibitions must be built, however, before the attention of a large gallery or book publisher can be attracted. One way for the student photographer to begin is to participate in group exhibitions on a local and national level.

Many local organizations hold annual art and photography contests that are an excellent way for beginners to gain experience in entering group competitions. Area newspapers generally carry announcements of these shows, and the contests often feature substantial prizes as an added incentive. Local contests generally require that all photographs submitted must be matted, framed, and ready to hang.

On a national level, many university galleries host juried photographic exhibitions. Group exhibitions often revolve around a theme, such as life in suburbia or the environment. The judge is usually a prominent photographer or photo critic, so receiving an award from this kind of competition is an honor that enhances a photographer's résumé.

One good source of information on upcoming exhibitions is the periodical *ARTWEEK*. Each issue contains a full page of listings for competitions and group exhibitions, including any special requirements and entry fees.

(continued)

Some national exhibitions prefer to jury and select works from 35mm slides, so most creative photographers make slide copies of their best prints. Once an image is accepted, the gallery will expect to be supplied with a finished mounted print. Frames are not normally shipped to distant shows because of their fragile nature; instead, the gallery usually takes responsibility for exhibiting works under protective sheets of glass.

One-Person Gallery Exhibitions

After compiling a record of several group shows, the aspiring fine arts photographer may wish to seek a solo exhibition in a commercial gallery. Because commercial galleries are swamped by requests from aspiring photographers, contacts and references in the art world can help to gain attention and consideration. A personal recommendation from a professor at graduate school or an established photographer can open the door.

To seriously seek a one-person show in a gallery, the photographer must

Many galleries now display fine art photographs and provide opportunities to see original prints by established masters as well as exciting experiments by new photographers.

put together a portfolio of his or her finest photographs to present to the gallery director. Most galleries prefer to see at least twenty to forty recent prints from a single project or body of work. Because galleries often receive between ten and fifty portfolios for review each week, the competition can be intense. Therefore, the photographer must make critical selections and edit the pieces carefully to ensure the best possible presentation.

A commercial gallery's financial existence depends on its ability to attract buyers and collectors; thus, gallery directors look for photographers whose works promise to contribute significantly to the field and appreciate in value. To attract the attention of a gallery director, the portfolio should demonstrate a consistency of vision and a unique perception. The director will also want to see a résumé and exhibition record to help gauge the photographer's progress and involvement with art. If the work interests the gallery and an opening is available in the exhibition schedule, the photographer will be invited to discuss details of having a one-person show. This will usually involve an agreement or contract of some kind that stipulates the date of the show, number of pieces, and the gallery's commission. Typically, the gallery will take a commission of 50 percent of the selling price and in some cases the gallery's commission can be as high as 60 percent. The photographer is responsible for delivering mounted prints to the gallery in advance of the show. The gallery will usually arrange for framing and hanging the works, printing the show announcements, and publicizing the show.

Having a show brings social and artistic recognition to the photographer as well as a chance to realize some financial reward through the sale of prints. In practice, however, works by new photographers are rarely sold. Institutional buyers and collectors usually prefer the works of established, well-known artists.

Establishing an exhibition record is a long and continuing process. With each show the photographer gains the experience and exposure necessary to advance to more sophisticated and larger galleries. Well-developed exhibition records also help creative photographers receive grant money to support their work. Grants in fine art photography are available from such groups as the National Endowment for the Arts (NEA), the Guggenheim Foundation, and various state art councils.

Summary

Although producing self-expressive photographs may be personally satisfying, only a handful of creative photographers are ever able to support themselves solely from sales of their prints. Even Ansel Adams, perhaps the most financially successful creative photographer, found it necessary to accept commercial assignments and other odd jobs for most of his career in order to support his family.

Nevertheless, fine art photographic education is excellent preparation for many professional careers in photography. The experience helps to develop good visual and creative senses, a diversity of approaches, the ability to communicate visually, and solid technical skills. These attributes are essential for professional careers in commercial and advertising photography, photographic illustration, photography education, documentary photography, and museum or gallery curatorial positions. In addition, tremendous personal satisfaction may be gained by developing one's creative talents to a high level and producing evocative works of self-expression.

A **spot filter** is designed to produce an image that is sharp at the center but whose sharpness gradually falls off toward the edges of the image.

Another type is the **multiple-image filter**, which reproduces the subject in a pattern of identical images. Variations of this filter produce three, five, or six images in several different patterns, such as parallel, circular, or pyramid-shaped arrays.

Although not all special effect devices are technically considered filters, they have been included here because of their similarity of construction and handling. Figure 11-10 shows examples of some special effect filters used with black-and-white films and digital cameras set to black-and-white mode.

Summary

Table 11-2 suggests which filters are most useful for various purposes with black-and-white panchromatic film or digital cameras used in black-and-white mode.

Filters for Color Photography

Objective 11-E Name and describe the purposes of six types of filters commonly used in color photography, and give examples.

Key Concepts conversion filters, Mired system, color-compensating (CC) filters, skylight or ultraviolet filters, polarizing filters, neutral density filters, special effect filters

Color slide films are balanced in manufacture for particular kinds of light sources—daylight

A.

B.

C.

Figure 11-10. Special effects filters. A) Fog filter. B) Star filter. C) Multi-image filter.

Table 11-2. Filters for black-and-white photographs

Subject	Desired Effect	Suggested Filter
Portraits: Outdoors	Natural skin; slightly darkened sky	Light green
Portraits: tungsten	Darker skin tones	Light green
	Lighter skin tones	Medium yellow
Blossoms and foliage	Natural	Yellow or yellow-green
	Lighter blossoms	Same color as blossom
Landscapes	Haze reduction	Medium yellow or polarizing filter
	Haze increase	Blue
Seascapes (when sky is blue)	Natural	Yellow
	Darker water	Deep yellow
Sky and clouds	Darker sky; lighter clouds	Medium yellow
	Dark sky; white clouds	Orange, red*, polarizer
	Black sky; chalky clouds	Dark red*
Architecture (sunlit)	Natural	Yellow
	Exaggerated texture	Deep yellow or red*
Sand or snow (sunlit and blue sky)	Natural	Medium yellow
	Exaggerated contrasts	Orange
Glass, polished surfaces	Reflections eliminated	Polarizer
Sunsets	Natural	Yellow
	Exaggerated brilliance	Deep yellow or red*
Natural wood furniture	Exaggerated grain pattern	Red*, orange, yellow
Aged documents and old photographs	Reduced stains	Match color of stain

*Note: Focus shifts slightly when using a red filter. This phenomenon is not usually a problem with subjects six feet or farther from the camera. For close-up work, reflex focusing and small apertures are recommended to ensure accurate focusing.

(5500K), photolamp (3400K), and tungsten (3200K). However, the lighting conditions under which a film is used often do not match the rated color balance of the film. Sometimes we may find our cameras loaded with a daylight film when we want to go indoors to shoot by artificial light, or vice versa. In other situations, we may find that the available light source is of another type altogether, such as fluorescent, arc, stage, low voltage, halogen, sodium vapor, mercury vapor, any of which may produce light of a color temperature that does not match the rated color balance of any commercial film.

At other times the available light, although of the correct type for the film, simply may not match precisely the color temperature for which the film is balanced. For example, daylight on an overcast day or in the open shade is considerably bluer than the light for which daylight film is balanced; daylight before 10 A.M. or after 3 P.M. is considerably redder. Used under any of these conditions, color reversal film will produce slides that have an overall cast that reflects the difference between the rated color temperature and the color temperature of the available light. If an appropriate filter is used, the light that reaches the film can be altered to match the color temperature for which the film is balanced. Digital cameras achieve similar results without filters by setting the white balance point.

Filters can also be used with color film and digital sensors, as with black-and-white media, to give expression to the photographer's individual perception and interpretation of a scene. To achieve the desired emphasis and subordination of detail, filters can be used to lighten or darken the color rendition of various details and thus emphasize or subdue selected colors within the scene. Filters can be used to enhance the mood of a photograph by imbuing it with an overall cast of a desired color. Filters can be used not only to obtain a natural color balance within a scene, but also to distort deliberately the color balance to conform to a particular perception or to communicate a color idea.

The use of filters is particularly important with color reversal film, because control cannot be exercised over individual images during commercial processing. Filters may be less important with color negative film because the color balance and special color effects of individual images can be manipulated significantly during the printing process. Nevertheless, it is generally good practice to provide planned filtration during shooting with color negative film as well as with reversal film. The resulting negatives will tend toward a standardized color balance, which should reduce the guesswork and labor during printing.

In general, the filters used in color photography can be divided into six main types according to their uses and characteristics:

1. **Conversion filters**, which convert the color temperature of available light to that for which a film is balanced; e.g., used to correct daylight to the color temperature of tungsten-balanced film; tungsten light to that of daylight-balanced film

2. **Color compensating (CC) filters**, which filter primary and secondary colors of light by precise amounts to provide exact control of color reproduction during photographing and printing

3. **Sky light and ultraviolet (UV) filters**, used to reduce the overall bluish cast caused by ultraviolet light, particularly in open shade, under an overcast sky, and at high altitudes; often used constantly to protect lens

4. **Polarizing filters**, used to filter out polarized light to darken blue sky, saturate colors, control reflections and glare, and penetrate haze

5. **Neutral density (ND) filters**, used to reduce the amount of light admitted to the camera without altering color rendition

6. **Special effects filters**, used to produce special optical effects in the recorded image

Conversion Filters

Slightly blue and amber in cast, **conversion filters** are designed to convert the color temperature of a given lighting source to that for which a given film is balanced. For example, a conversion filter can be used to obtain normal color rendering using a tungsten film (3200K) in daylight (5500K). Because conversion filters reduce the amount of light that reaches the film, it is necessary to increase exposure by an appropriate amount. Table 11-3 describes conversion filters that can be used with common film/light source combinations, and gives their associated filter factors. Note that film manufacturers usually provide a film-speed index to be used with a conversion filter in order to simplify exposure calculations.

Conversion filters are not generally used with digital cameras. Instead the camera's white balance is adjusted to match the source lighting and render color accurately.

A special type of conversion filter is designed to eliminate the blue-green tint that results from photographing under fluorescent lights. Fluorescent lighting poses an unusual problem because, despite its white appearance, it is made up of only a few wavelengths of light, mostly from the blue-green portion of the visible light spectrum. Converting this discontinuous spectrum of light to a color temperature that matches a film's color balance is difficult at best.

Photography under fluorescent lighting is further complicated because tubes of different types and made by different manufacturers differ. Precise conversion, therefore, requires testing under the actual fluorescent lighting conditions encountered. For general photography, filters are manufactured that represent a compromise among the various

Table 11-3. Conversion filters

| Film Balanced for | Available Light Source | | | |
	3200 K	3400 K	5500 K	Fluorescent
3200 K tungsten	None	No. 81A (1.25)	No. 85B (1.5)	FLB (2)
3400 K photolamp	No. 82A (1.25)	None	No. 85 (1.5)	FLB + 82A (2.5)
5500 K daylight	No. 80A (4)	No. 80B (3)	None	FLD (2)

Note: Filters are identified by Kodak Wratten filter numbers. Filter factors for each filter appear in parentheses. In place of filter factor, film manufacturers provide a new film-speed index for use when their film is used with a conversion filter. No exposure adjustment is needed when using automatic, through-the-lens (TTL) exposure setting.

commonly found fluorescent lighting conditions. Even though the correction is less than perfect, the results are more satisfying than they would be otherwise. The FLB filter is designed to convert fluorescent light to the approximate color temperature of tungsten-balanced film; the FLD filter is designed to convert fluorescent light to the approximate color temperature of daylight-balanced film.

Clearly there is an infinitely greater number of lighting situations in the real world than the three for which film is balanced. There is no end to the variety of filters that could be produced to convert every possible lighting situation to match the color balances of available films. One attempt to simplify this problem was the development of the **Mired system** (pronounced my-red), which stands for *micro-reciprocal degrees*. Simply described, a Mired is a standard conversion of Kelvin temperature. By using combinations of filters based on Mired units, any amount of color temperature shift can be obtained.

Typically a Mired filter system consists of two sets of filters, one composed of several bluish filters, the other composed of several reddish ones. To use the system, the Mired value of the light source and the Mired value for which the film is balanced must be determined. The difference between these values determines the amount and direction of color temperature shift needed to match the film's color balance. Then a combination of filters is selected that, used together, will closely approximate this value. Thus with six or eight filters a wide range of color shifts can be effected that are suitable for numerous film/light source combinations.

Color Plates 6 A, B, C, D illustrate the use of conversion filters.

Color-Compensating (CC) Filters

Another approach to color control is the use of **color-compensating (CC) filters**. These are used most commonly in color printing to obtain control over color during the printing stages. However, they also can be used during shooting for color conversion or to achieve special color effects.

CC filters are manufactured in six colors—red, green, blue, cyan, magenta, and yellow—the primary and secondary colors in the visible light spectrum. Each color is manufactured in six or seven densities ranging from very light tints to very strong saturations. Each filter is numbered to identify both its color and its density (measured in relation to its complement). For example, a CC20M filter is a color-compensating magenta filter of 0.20 density to green light. Color-compensating filters give the color photographer extremely precise control over color production.

When used for color conversion, CC filters provide greater precision than the more common conversion filters. They can be used, for example, to obtain a relatively normal color balance under fluorescent lighting or similar conditions where available light represents a discontinuous spectrum. Their other uses, however, are many. Color can be added to a sunset by photographing it through a yellow or red filter. Moonlight can be simulated in sunlight by using a blue filter and underexposing two or three stops. Multiple exposures can be made on the same frame, changing filters between exposures, to obtain striking and unusual effects. Or, filters can be used in combination with special purpose films to produce images never seen in nature. Color Plates 5 A, B, C illustrate some of these applications.

Skylight and Ultraviolet Filters

Daylight on overcast days, in open shade, at high altitudes or great distances, or in the snow has a higher proportion of ultraviolet and blue light than the daylight for which daylight film is balanced. Under these conditions, unfiltered daylight film will produce slides with an overall bluish cast. The **sky light filter** is a special kind of **ultraviolet filter** for color film. By filtering out ultraviolet light, the sky light filter tends to eliminate this excess bluishness and restore the reddish warmth that otherwise would be lost. Slightly pink in appearance, this filter requires no exposure increase and often is left on the camera all the time, both for its warming effect on the color balance and for the protection it provides to the camera lens. The ultraviolet (UV) filter also may be used with color film for the same purposes, but because of its slightly yellow appearance, its warming effect is somewhat less.

Polarizing Filters

The **polarizing filter** performs the same functions in color film and digital photography as it does in black-and-white photography—controlling reflections and glare, reducing haze, and darkening blue skies—without altering color balance, color rendering, or brightness ratios within the scene. In addition, when it is used with color film or color digital cameras, the polarizing filter also tends to increase color saturation of objects within the scene. Hence it is often used to obtain a deeper, richer blue sky. By filtering out polarized light reflecting from objects in the scene, however, the polarizing filter also tends to render all the colors in the scene with greater color saturation.

Neutral Density Filters

The **neutral density** filters perform the same function in color photography as they do in black-and-white photography—reducing the amount of light passing through the lens without altering the relative brightness or color balance within the scene. Suppose that, under given circumstances, a normal exposure should be f/5.6 at 1/250 sec. However, suppose also that you wish to shoot at f/2 without increasing the shutter speed. A neutral density filter would make this possible. In this case using an ND-9 filter would reduce exposure three stops, requiring a three-stop increase in the camera setting. The ND filter reduces light intensity without altering color balance, color renderings, or brightness ratios within the scene.

Special Effect Filters

The filters used for special effects in color photography are much the same as those used for black-and-white. Soft-focus, fog, cross-screen or star, spot, and multiple-image filters are equally useful in color.

One special effect filter that is uniquely useful in color photography is the **transmission diffraction grating**. Ridges etched into the surface of this filter act as prisms and reveal the color spectrum of bright spots of white light in the image. This filter produces color-enhanced flares where the specular light strikes it and can be used to create unusual spectral color effects.

Another is the **multicolored** filter, which combines several colors in different areas of the filter. For example, one multicolored filter can be used to simultaneously increase the blue in the sky and the yellow in the foreground.

Many special effect filters can be used together to obtain their combined effects. The use of filters in color photography, as in black-and-white photography, is limited only by the photographer's imagination and willingness to experiment.

Table 11-4. Uses of filters with color films

Subject	Desired Effect	Suggested Filter
All subjects	Reduce haze; protect lens; natural color	Skylight 1A or UV
Open shade; cool bluish lighting	Natural colors; reduce blue	81B Light amber
Rainy day; heavy overcast	Natural colors; reduce haze; reduce blue cast	81C Dark amber
Midday sun	Warmer colors; healthy skin tones	81A Pale amber
Glass, polished surfaces	Reduce glare	PL Polarizing filter
Landscapes, colorful foliage	Enriched, saturated colors; reduce glare	PL Polarizing filter
Sky and clouds	Enrich blue sky; increase sky/cloud contrast	PL Polarizing filter
Landscapes	Natural colors; darken bright sky	NDGrad, Graduated ND filter
Fluorescent lighting	Natural colors; remove green tint	FLD Magenta filter
Household tungsten lighting	Natural colors; remove yellow-orange tint	82A Light blue or 82C Dark blue filter*

*Use special bulbs for exact color correction

Questions to Consider

1. When using a filter with black-and-white film, which colors are lightened in the final print and which are darkened?

2. Explain why photographers and their panchromatic film do not see colors with the same relative brightness. How can using filters correct this?

3. Describe the methods by which photographic filters are attached to the camera.

4. What are filter factors, and how are they used to determine exposure? If a light meter reading is made through a filter, is it necessary to use the filter factor? Explain.

5. Given an unfiltered basic exposure of 1/125 sec. at f/16, what correction should be made for a filter factor of 2? 4? 8?

6. Describe the main types of filters used in black-and-white photography and their primary uses.

7. Describe the main types of filters used in color photography and their primary uses.

Suggested Field and Laboratory Assignments

Use a digital camera in the grayscale mode or shoot a roll of panchromatic film using filters to solve the following problems. For each shot, make one filtered and one unfiltered exposure. Keep a shooting log showing the filter used, the reason for the use of that filter, and the exposure data for each shot.

1. Use a filter to increase sky/cloud contrast.

2. Use a filter to increase subject/ground contrast between an orange or red object against green foliage.

3. Use a filter to reduce aerial haze.

4. Use a filter to exaggerate natural wood grain in furniture.

5. Use a filter to eliminate reflected glare from water, glass, or other nonmetallic surfaces.

6. Use a filter to enhance flesh tones.

Basic Lighting

Kelly Moore, "Portrait of a Man"

Unit at a Glance

The very term *photography*—which means "light writing"—tells us that light can do much more than merely illuminate a subject. Were exposure our sole concern, we would be satisfied with any light sufficient simply for recording an image. Yet many well-exposed images fail to move us or to excite our senses. Beyond illumination, light plays a central role in creating a dramatic image of a photographer's vision of a subject.

This unit introduces the principles and techniques of lighting subjects to reveal their unique visual properties—their colors, forms, textures, and fine gradations of tone. It describes approaches for using the light available at the scene to capture these qualities, as well as for arranging and manipulating supplementary lighting.

Basic Lighting Principles

Objective 12-A State and explain the basic principles of natural and arranged lighting.

Key Concepts available light, arranged light, natural light, artificial light, angle of incidence, relative intensity, inverse square law, color of light, specularity, diffused light, specular light, single dominant light source, modeling, texturing, coloring, brightness ratio, dynamic range, reflectors, tonal composition, chiaroscuro

It is the play of light over the surfaces and edges of a subject that reveals the subject's form, its textures, and its shadings and colors, and that finally determines the sensory effect of the image upon the viewer. Photographers generally refer to the lighting that occurs naturally at a scene as **available light**. By this they mean lighting conditions that have not been arranged specifically for the photographer's purposes. Lighting that has been altered or modified is referred to as **arranged light**.

Available light may consist of natural light, artificial light, or a combination of these. **Natural light** may consist of the highly specular light of the sun, the diffused light of an overcast day, moonlight, or even the subdued light found in the shade of a tree, in the interior of a room, or in the gloomy depths of a cavern. **Artificial light** refers to manmade light sources such as electronic flash, household lamps, spotlights, and fluorescent lights.

Characteristics of Light

Several characteristics of light affect the way we see a subject: angle of incidence, relative intensity, color, and specularity.

Angle of incidence refers to the angle at which light strikes the subject. From the camera's viewpoint, light can strike a subject from above, from below, or from the subject's own level. Similarly, light can strike the subject from the side, from the rear, or from the front. Because natural daylight falls on most subjects most of the time from an angle 40° to 60° above and to the side of the subject, this angle tends to produce a normal-appearing pattern of highlights and shadows.

We are most accustomed to viewing objects that are illuminated by natural light that comes from overhead. Except when a special effect of some kind is desired, therefore, subjects will tend to appear most natural when the angle of incidence emanates from a position above the camera's level. An angle of incidence from below the subject tends to produce unnatural highlights and shadows, because light from this angle is relatively rare in nature. Except in unusual settings, therefore, such as a fireplace scene, subjects tend to appear most natural when illuminated by skylight, sunlight, or artificial lights placed in overhead positions.

An angle of incidence from the front, close to the camera axis, tends to flatten out highlights and shadows, subduing the subject's contours and surface textures. An angle of incidence from the side tends to reveal textures and contours. The degree to which the subject's contours and textures are revealed can be controlled by positioning the camera and subject in such a way that the subject is illuminated from the side when viewed from the camera position.

The **relative intensity** of light reflected from the surface of an object reveals its form. It is the pattern of bright highlights, middle tones, and deep shadows that provide the information the viewer needs to interpret depth, shape, and texture. As the angle from which light falls upon the object changes, the pattern of highlights and shadows changes as well, revealing different aspects of form and texture. As we view the subject from different points of view, we see light falling upon the subject from different angles and producing different patterns of light and shadow—different representations of the object's physical form.

The distance between a light source and a subject affects the intensity of the light falling on the subject. As the distance between the source and the subject increases, the intensity of the light falling on the subject decreases. As the distance between the source and the subject decreases, the intensity of the light increases. This relationship can be expressed with mathematical precision because the intensity of light falling upon the subject is related inversely to the square of the distance between the source and the subject. Thus, if the distance between the two is doubled, the intensity of the light falling on the subject is reduced by a factor of four—a two-stop decrease. If this distance is decreased by half, the intensity of the light is increased by a factor of four. This relationship is known as the **inverse square law**.

The **color** of light has greater impact in color than in black-and-white photography. However, color affects black-and-white photographs to some degree as well. Black-and-white films have different sensitivities to different colors of light. The colors to which the film is sensitive appear lighter in the final image; the colors to which it is insensitive appear darker. By altering the color of the light transmitted to the film, we also alter the light's effect upon the film and the appearance of the subject in the final image.

The **specularity** of light refers to its direction and hardness. On an overcast day, objects and persons can be seen clearly, but no hard and distinct highlights or shadows can be seen. However, there is plenty of strong light. Light such as this, emanating from a broad light source—in this case the entire sky—is called **diffused light**. Light rays of approximately equal strength strike the object from many directions, eliminating deep shadows. (See Figures 12-2 A and B.) When the clouds clear to reveal the sun—a single, concentrated light source—immediately strong high-lights and shadows appear. This concentrated type of light, produced by intense light rays emanating from a relatively small light source or reflecting from a mirrorlike surface, is called **specular light**. Figures 12-2 C and D show how specular light striking an object from one direction produces clear highlights and shadows.

Under natural lighting conditions, such as daylight, both specular and diffused light are present. It is the presence of diffused light all around the subject that allows details in the shadows to be photographed. Were the diffused light not present, the details in the shadows would not be illuminated. The diffused light that is present in daylight is produced by sunlight reflecting off particles of dust and droplets of water vapor in the atmosphere as the light makes its way to the earth's surface. This diffusion of part of the sunlight lights up the entire sky, making it blue, and provides a broad source of diffused sky light in addition to the direct, specular rays of sunlight that also reach the earth. Additional diffusion occurs as the sunlight strikes the earth and other hard surfaces—the rays are reflected in all directions, producing additional diffused light. Thus, under natural daylight conditions, both specular and diffused light are present. When the sky is overcast, blocking out the direct light of the sun, only diffused light is present, producing a soft, even, relatively shadowless field of illumination.

Functions of Light

In addition to capturing the physical characteristics of the subject, the photographer usually wants to portray the subject in the context of an overall composition, one in which an environment of light and shadow emphasizes the relationships and contrasts that are of the most interest.

Single dominant light source refers to perhaps the most important principle governing the lighting of subjects. In nature, subjects are usually seen illuminated by a single source of light that produces a single set of dominant highlights and shadows. This source may be sunlight or sky light if the

A.

Daylight sky overcast

C.

Direct sunlight

B.

D.

Figure 12-2. Lighting. A) Diffuse light rays strike object from all directions, eliminating deep shadows. B) effects of diffused light. C) Specular light rays strike object from single direction, producing deep shadows. D) Effect of specular lighting.

subject is outdoors, or it may be ceiling light, window light, or a lamp if the subject is indoors. For the subject to appear most natural, there should be, or appear to be, a single dominant light source.

Modeling refers to revealing the three-dimensional quality of the subject. The highlights, the shadows, and the gradations of tones between them reveal the shape and contour of the subject.

Texturing refers to revealing the surface textures of the subject—the hard, crystal surface of a goblet; the soft skin texture of a young girl; the rough, weathered texture of an ancient tree.

Coloring refers to revealing the color details of the subject in color photographs or to the relative brightness of colors in black-and-white photographs.

Brightness ratio refers to the difference in the relative brightness of the highlights and the shadows at the subject position. If the difference in brightness between the highlight areas and that of the shadow areas is too great, the film or the digital sensor may not have the latitude, or **dynamic range**, to record all the details at both extremes. If the difference is too great, an exposure that is suitable for the highlights may be too little to record fully all the details in the shadows, resulting in underexposure in these areas; an exposure that is suitable for the shadow areas, on the other hand, may be too much for the highlights, resulting in overexposure in these areas.

Generally, for normal contrast, the brightness ratio between the highlights and shadows should be between 3 to 1 and 4 to 1—well within the dynamic range of most films and digital sensors. In other words, highlights that are between three and four times brighter than the shadows produce a normal contrast ratio. Translated to light meter readings, this difference between the highlight areas and shadow areas is between 1 1/2 and 2 stops.

In some circumstances, however, greater ratios occur naturally within the scene or are needed by the photographer to achieve a desired effect. Traditionally, for example, light ratios for portraiture have ranged anywhere from 2 to 1 through 8 to 1; the most popular being 3 to 1, with 8 to 1 reserved for dark, dramatic shadows. It is with these greater contrast ratios that film exhibits greater dynamic range than many digital sensors.

Film's greater latitude results from the design of the emulsion. Silver halide film is coated with crystals of various shapes and sizes that include both highly sensitive grains that respond to small amounts of light, and low sensitivity grains that respond to large amounts of light. Not all digital sensors are designed with a comparable mix of both low- and high-sensitivity pixels.

Thus, traditional digital cameras have difficulty reproducing high-contrast images containing both dark and bright areas—the dark areas tending to lose detail and whites washing out. Only more recent CCD's are designed for enhanced sensitivity and expanded dynamic range to produce a smooth and wide tonal range without losing detail in dark areas or washing out in bright areas.

Most digital cameras allow you to preview your picture on the LCD monitor and review your results immediately. This makes studio photography with a digital camera very interactive. You can explore and experiment until you are satisfied. The camera's white balance setting lets you shoot under almost any light. You can use simple, inexpensive tungsten, quartz, or fluorescent bulbs with reflectors to get good results. With the lights on during your setup, you can immediately see the effect of your arrangement.

With film negatives, overexposure could compensate for a bad lighting ratio by allowing you to capture details in the thinner shadow areas and, during printing, to burn in the denser highlight areas. With a digital camera, however, overexposure can be disastrous—it completely destroys details in the highlights that cannot be restored by any process. So, the rule of thumb with digital cameras is to underexpose if necessary. You can usually restore underexposed shadow details in the editing process, whereas overexposed areas may be lost forever.

In available light situations, the brightness ratio can be controlled by the use of **reflectors**, light-colored or polished surfaces that reflect light. When reflectors alone are not sufficient, flash may be used to fill the shadows. To reproduce a natural lighting environment artificially, one or more specular light sources can be used to produce highlight illumination. Diffused light sources can be added to illuminate the shadows.

As we discussed earlier, **tonal composition**, or **chiaroscuro** (see pages 343–344), refers to the arrangement of light and shade in a picture—the placement of the brightest highlights and deepest shadows to bring about a harmonious and logical tonal arrangement. Whether using available or arranged lighting, the photographer should seek to arrange highlights and shadow masses to reveal the subject and direct the viewer's attention in a harmonious, cohesive design.

Applying Lighting Principles

Whether the photographer is working indoors or outdoors, with natural or artificial light, available or arranged light, the most realistic lighting will usually resemble natural light, because that is what we see most often. These are some of the characteristics of natural lighting:

Main light. There will appear to be a single main source of light that creates the dominant set of highlights and shadows.

Fill light. There will be sufficient ambient lighting that the shadows are illuminated and shadow details can be discerned.

Accent light. Edges, surface, and prominent features are highlighted so as to reveal their shapes and surface textures and to set them apart from their backgrounds.

Background light. Details that lie beyond the subject are illuminated sufficiently to be discerned.

Even though the photographer may wish to alter or depart from the natural-light standard, appropriate lighting should not be left to chance or accident. Photographers need to develop an eye for the lighting of their subjects and the craft to control it. They should develop an awareness of how the highlights and shadows, shapes and textures will be recorded on the film and then act to mold them to their purpose.

Although greater control over lighting may be gained with a studio-like arrangement, control may also be exercised in available-light situations. By moving the camera or subject one way or another, or by shooting from a somewhat different angle, the way the subject is lit from the camera's point of view may be altered. Moreover, by using lighting accessories, a good deal of control over lighting may be gained, even in natural settings.

Purposes of Arranged Lighting

Even if it were possible to use natural outdoor illumination for every picture, it would not always be desirable. Outdoor lighting must be used largely as it occurs in nature. We cannot move the sun around in the sky to provide a perfect lighting angle. We can supplement daylight with reflectors, flash units, and the like, and we can move our subjects about on occasion, but we really cannot alter the quality or the source of the daylight very much.

One reason for moving indoors is to gain control over lighting and backgrounds that might be impossible to achieve outdoors. Another, of course, is to photograph subjects in their natural indoor habitats—the company executive in her office, a parent and child in the nursery, a man in his workshop, for example. When indoors, the photographer must either work under available light or create an arranged lighting setup around the subject. Except for the few photographs that may be taken using only light from a window or skylight, it will usually be necessary to arrange artificial lighting to obtain the desired image of the subject.

One principal purpose in the arranged lighting of a subject is to allow the subject's essential traits to reveal themselves. That is, the lighting is arranged partly so that the subject can be recognized for what it is—a person, a ball, a table, a bottle of wine. In most cases, however, the photographer will want to go a bit further—to emphasize certain traits and subordinate others in order to communicate a particular interpretation of the subject. The photographer may seek to *idealize the subject* by exaggerating or even distorting certain characteristics while subduing others.

Leonardo Da Vinci once said of portrait painting, "You do not paint features; you paint what is in the mind." The same may be said of photography, whatever the subject. A proper lighting arrangement is a powerful tool for expressing what the photographer thinks and feels about the subject —not just "here is a person," for example, but "here is a strong, rugged, weathered, determined farmer."

The following objectives address how these principles may be applied in available or arranged lighting, with natural or artificial sources, and by using lighting accessories.

Photographing in Available Light

Objective 12-B Describe and demonstrate techniques of available-light photography.

Key Concepts bad weather, time of day, relative position, angle of incidence

The term *available light* refers to both natural and artificial lighting that occurs naturally at a scene. Sometimes the available light may be bright and pose no special problems; often, however, a photographer is faced with uneven light situations, indoors or out, that require some combination of fast ISO speeds, slow shutter speeds, and/or large apertures to get a usable image.

Outdoors, **bad weather** and **time of day** may produce very dim natural light and unusual color shifts. Shooting in rain or mist, or shooting in very early morning, evening, or at night poses special challenges for photography. Indoors, window light may be very dim. Firelight from candles or a fireplace will flicker and produce multiple shadows from unusual directions. Indoors or outdoors, artificial light may come from several directions; its intensity may be very low and its color may be of limited range. The light may even be intermittent or blinking, such as from flashing signs or marquees.

Needless to say, such conditions often produce the barest minimum of light, often uneven, producing multiple, poorly lit shadows, high contrast, and unusual color shifts. Nevertheless, it may be necessary to shoot under available light when time or physical constraints prevent modifying, adjusting, or controlling the light at the scene. On other occasions it may even be desirable to shoot under available light to preserve the natural lighting quality or to capture a particular mood or feeling.

Dim Lighting Conditions

Just because the weather is bad, daylight has waned, or interior lighting is very dim is no reason to stop shooting. Although photography under dim available light may require special tools and techniques, the resulting photographs often convey a greater sense of atmosphere or mood than those shot in a studio or in the bright light of day. The major problem faced by the photographer is how to capture what little light exists in the scene.

Photography under dim light will generally require a fast film or high ISO speed digital sensor, a slow shutter speed, and/or a wide aperture. Photographs produced under these conditions often are relatively grainy and have shallow depth of field. Blurred images are also common—the camera as well as the subject can move during a long exposure. To make matters worse, light meters are least accurate when light is dim, and they generally underestimate the required exposure.

To answer these challenges, fast films and digital materials are essential, as are slow shutter speeds and wide apertures. When using film, exposure should be set fully for the shadow details. Slight underdevelopment of the film is also advisable to

prevent highlights and visible light sources from blocking up. You can usually compensate for overexposed highlights later during printing. When using a digital camera, exposure should be set for the highlights to avoid blocking up. You can usually tease out underexposed shadow details later in the editing process. Whenever you use a slow shutter, the camera should be stabilized to avoid camera movement during exposure.

Selected Lighting

Without modifying the available light at the scene, the photographer may often position the camera and the subject so as to gain advantageous lighting angles and qualities. The subject might be placed near a window or a lamp; the camera might be placed to achieve a maximum of illumination, modeling, and texture. Light reflected from nearby surfaces can be used to illuminate the natural shadows in the scene. When working with window light, for example, light from the window may illuminate a nearby wall or a piece of furniture. By changing the **relative position** of the camera and subject appropriately, the light reflected from these surfaces can provide fill light on the shadowed side of the subject. Thus, without modifying existing light, the photographer can select a point of view and **angle of incidence** that optimizes the lighting of the subject.

Bad Weather

Bad weather lighting is usually flat and dull. Nevertheless, in color photographs, bad weather usually produces soft, pastel shades and an overall cold, blue cast. Overall low contrast and a narrow range of tones characterize black-and-white images. These characteristics are not inherently faulty—many photographers prefer them as a true reflection of natural conditions. Alternatively, with film, the colors may be "corrected" by the use of an 81A filter or, for black and white, by the use of a yellow or orange filter. With a digital camera, equivalent effects can be achieved by adjusting the camera's white balance setting.

Falling rain itself is usually difficult to capture on film. Unless the rain is backlit and shot against a dark background, it moves too fast to be stopped by the usually slow shutter speeds required in dark, rainy weather. The effects of rain, however, are easier to capture—the glistening surfaces, puddles, flowing water, droplets on eaves and windowpanes, umbrellas, sopping hair, drenched clothing—all of these can convey the sensations of rain effectively.

Storms often provide exciting and dramatic lighting conditions. In daylight, storm clouds can become luminous as light penetrates the clouds in a rich variety of intensities. The cloud effects can be exaggerated in color by slight underexposure or by the use of a polarizing filter; in black and white by the use of a yellow, orange, or red filter; with a digital camera, by adjusting the white balance setting. (See Color Plate 000.)

When photographing lightning, it is best to use a tripod, stop down, and use an open shutter until the burst of lightning occurs. Sometimes, more than one burst recorded on the same frame provides a more dramatic image; however, if the shutter remains open too long, the sky will eventually record on the film and reduce the dramatic impact. If possible, try to cover the lens between bursts with a black card, uncovering just before the next burst is expected. This same technique can be used for photographing fireworks against the night sky.

To accomplish the same thing with a digital camera, you will need a camera that possesses a long-exposure capability, often not found on the cheaper models. Digital cameras do not have the T and B settings of film cameras that allow you to hold the shutter open as long as you wish. When long exposures are provided, they are usually limited to 15 seconds or less.

Nevertheless, it is possible to capture lightning with a digital camera by taking repeated, successive shots at the longest possible exposure. There are no film costs and you'll have the ability to preview immediately if your shots were successful.

Check your camera's manual to determine what your camera can do. You will have to compensate for shutter lag—the delay between releasing the shutter and the moment the image is actually taken. Also, some cameras won't take long exposures, limiting the longest exposure to only a few seconds.

To capture lightning, fireworks, or similar night subjects with a digital camera, use a tripod and preprogram the following settings:

- Lock the focus to infinity.
- Avoid overexposure. Cut exposure back one or two stops.
- Set the *f* stop in the middle range—about f/8.
- Keep spare batteries. Leaving the camera on depletes batteries rapidly.
- Once set up, turn off the view screen to save power. Indicator lights or audible alarms can tell you what the camera is doing.
- Capture images at the highest practical resolution. Saving the files may take longer, but you'll have a better chance of making a good print.
- If available for your camera, use an electronic remote release.

Morning and Evening Light

An exceptional sunset is irresistible as a subject for color photography. As important as the sky and cloud colors themselves are the foreground details that characterize the place from which the sunset is viewed. Against the sunset as a background, most foreground details appear in silhouette with bright edge highlights.

Sunsets are not constant; they continuously develop and change. A sunset's entire cycle lasts but a few minutes, during which the setting sun brilliantly illuminates the atmosphere and clouds and backlights foreground objects. The photographer needs to be ready as the sunset commences and must complete shooting within a few minutes. A meter reading should be taken of the sky itself, not directly from the sun. It is advisable to bracket exposures.

Light of the early morning and late afternoon is tinged with reddish hues, which many photographers prefer. For color photography, these colors may be "corrected" by the use of an 82A filter; with a digital camera, by adjusting the white balance setting.

Night Photography

Aside from the moon, stars, and lightning, few natural light sources occur to illuminate the night. Therefore, most night photography captures artificial light sources or scenes that are lit by artificial light sources. These sources include streetlights, illuminated buildings, automobile lights, fireworks, and firelight.

For many types of night photographs it is advisable to shoot in early evening, after the artificial lights have been turned on but before all sky light has disappeared. Photographs shot at this time give the impression of night photography while still preserving enough ambient light to record sky values and to fill the shadows.

At night, the light that is recorded in the picture is often the light source itself. The light coming directly from light bulbs, fluorescent and neon tubes, streetlights, and car lights is the primary image-forming light, rather than the objects illuminated by these sources. To set proper exposure for night photography, the brightness of these light sources must be accounted for, and these bright points of light must be regarded as the image highlights.

For moonlit landscapes, it is advisable to shoot at late dusk at a time when the moon rises early. The image will benefit if the sky illuminates the landscape features with dim residual daylight. Moonlight alone provides insufficient illumination for a short exposure, so if the moon appears in the picture, its movement during exposure will create a trace on the film. Often moonlit landscapes or cityscapes benefit by having some artificial light sources, such as interior building lights or signs visible in the picture.

Modifying Available Light

As noted, placing a subject near a reflecting surface may take advantage of the available light by reflecting fill light into the shadow areas. If reflecting surfaces do not exist naturally at the scene, light-colored reflectors may be placed in appropriate positions. Reflectors may be made of almost any available light-colored material—a white sheet, for example, or a large, light piece of plastic or paper. The reflector is positioned to bounce the available light into shadowed areas so that details in the shadows can be recorded. (See Figure 12-3.)

With a little imagination, the existing light can be directed and controlled to improve the image. By combining the direct main light source with reflected fill light, the photographer can control available light to produce a primary set of highlights and shadows while illuminating the shadow details.

Figure 12-3. Use of reflector to fill shadows. A) Sunlight or spotlight may produce strong highlights and shadows. Matte white reflector provides a diffused fill light. B) Effect of reflector.

Famous Photographer

Harry Callahan

Harry Callahan, a former engineering student, started work as a photoprocessor in the General Motors photo laboratories. Initially influenced by the work of Alfred Stieglitz and the approaches of Minor White and Ansel Adams, his early work was characterized by faithfully reproducing natural subjects and emphasizing the rich detail, tone, and texture that was the hallmark of new realism in the 1930s.

As his style developed, however, he experimented with complex multiple exposures and collages sometimes incorporating snippets of hundreds of photographs to produce a single image. Often favoring building façades and architectural features, he repeated the patterns of various tones and overlaid lines and masses to reveal their abstract, graphic content. Ultimately he developed a style uniquely his own that isolated the abstract qualities of his subjects by emphasizing the stark contrasts of deep black and clear white line and mass with an absolute minimum of shading and texture.

Photography in the 1950s was often described in terms of unique regional styles, and it is worth noting that the photographic style associated with Chicago at that time was generally identified with the often abstract work of Harry Callahan and Aaron Siskind. Callahan started teaching at the Illinois Institute of Design in Chicago in 1946 and later, with Siskind, presided over the photography department there for twelve years. In 1961 he accepted appointment as head of the photography department at the Rhode Island School of Design. His work has been exhibited at the Kansas City Art Institute, the International Museum of Photography in Rochester, N.Y., the Museum of Modern Art in New York City, and the Worcester Art Museum, Massachusetts.

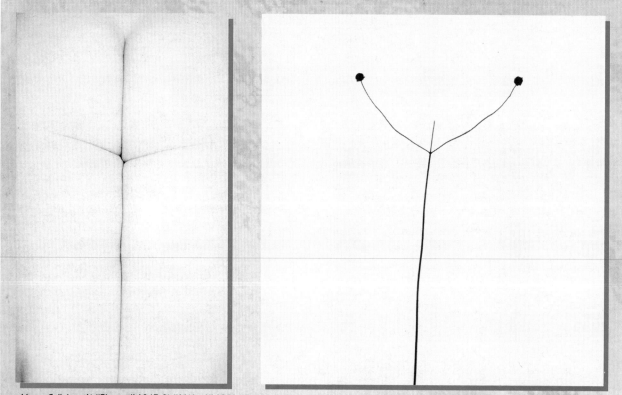

Harry Callahan. A) "Eleanor," 1947. B) "A Weed." 1951. "Eleanor," Copyright the Estate of Harry Callahan, courtesy Pace/MacGill Gallery, New York. "Weed Against Sky, Detroit," 1948, Copyright the Estate of Harry Callahan, courtesy Pace/MacGill Gallery, New York. Harry Callahan, American, 1912–1999, Weed Against the Sky, n.d., gelatin silver print, 5.7 x 5.7 cm, Peabody Photography Purchase Fund, 1952.445. The Art Institute of Chicago. All Rights Reserved.

Available-light photography under difficult conditions poses a challenge to many photographers who take special pleasure in capturing their images unaided by artificial devices. Of course, sometimes the only way to capture an image is by making do with available lighting conditions. It is advisable, therefore, to practice under a variety of available lighting conditions before adding and arranging such artificial light sources as flash and studio lighting.

A photographer can learn to appreciate the qualities and behavior of light and increase visual sensitivity by working with unmodified available light rather than trying to change it.

Artificial Lighting Tools and Their Functions

Objective 12-C Name and describe the functions of six basic lighting tools used in artificial lighting.

Key Concepts hot lights, electronic flash, strobe, tungsten-filament, tungsten-halogen, quartz lights, reflector lamp, pan-reflector light, umbrella, bounce light, softbox, spotlight, reflector cards, matte white reflectors, baffle, barn-door baffle, head screen, flag, snoot, diffusion screen, pattern screen, gels, standard, boom

When available light is insufficient or inadequate, modifying and supplementing the existing lighting can enhance the image. Preserving the original mood and quality of lighting is the real challenge. A wide variety of artificial lighting tools and auxiliary equipment is available for photographic use, but all forms of artificial lighting can be divided into two basic categories: hot lights and electronic flash. **Hot lights**, also called incandescent lights, are similar in construction to common light bulbs. They produce continuous illumination, whereas the light from an **electronic flash**, often called a **strobe** unit, produces instantaneous bursts of light.

Hot Lights

Hot lights are convenient and relatively inexpensive. Their name derives from the considerable heat that is produced by the lamps when they are in use. Hot lights may be of the tungsten-filament variety, which often resemble overgrown house-

hold light bulbs, or the more compact tungsten-halogen type favored by location photographers. **Tungsten-filament** photo lamps are available in many wattages—250 W and 500 W are the most common. **Tungsten-halogen** photo lamps, sometimes called **quartz lights**, also are available in many wattages. Although quartz lights require careful handling and their replacement is more expensive, they are efficient, lightweight, and have a high, stable light output over a long, useful life.

Photo lamps are designed to more rigorous specifications than ordinary household light bulbs. They produce a more even field of light and, more important, their color temperature is controlled carefully. Photo lamps are manufactured in both 3400 K and 3200 K ratings for Type A and Type B color film, respectively. Either may be used with black-and-white film or with digital cameras set to the appropriate white balance.

Pear-shaped photo lamps (similar in shape to household light bulbs) normally need to be inserted into a metal reflector for use, and these lamps usually are frosted to diffuse the light they produce.

The **reflector lamp** differs in shape because it has a built-in reflector coated on the inside surface of the glass bulb. Lamps with built-in reflectors are available for either flood or spot service. These self-contained units produce a broad field of relatively diffuse light for flood service or a narrow beam of specular light for spot service. Although typically a more expensive type of lamp, the reflector lamp eliminates the need for a separate metallic reflector.

Figure 12-4 A shows various forms of inexpensive hot lights. The spring-clip mounted reflector is only one of several types commonly available; it is one of the more popular types because it is convenient and easy to use.

Electronic Flash Units

In addition to hot or incandescent lights, electronic flash units also can be used in an indoor lighting setup. In commercial studios, large electronic flash units, or strobes, powered by alternating current (AC) are commonly used. Two or more flash heads may be linked to the same power pack for synchronization. Many studio

A.

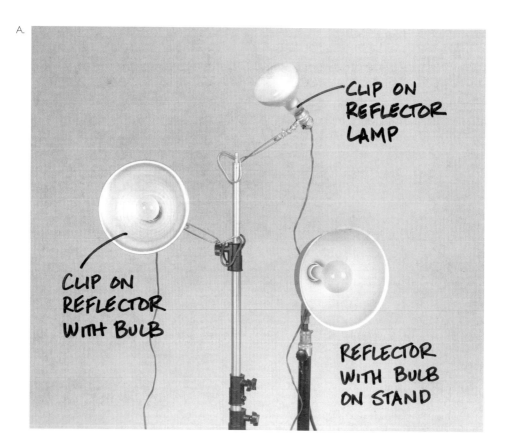

B.

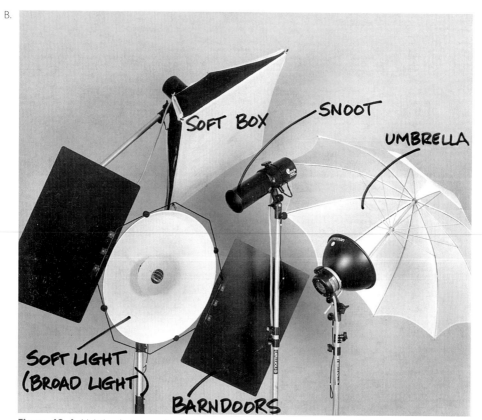

Figure 12-4. Lighting instruments. A) Economy lighting. Tungsten reflector lamps and reflectors with bulbs are commonly available at low cost in hardware and lighting stores. B) Professional lighting. Professional lighting units include strobe (flash) and quartz lamps and are available with a variety of heads and reflectors for more precise control of lighting.

strobes have built-in tungsten modeling lights of a low wattage that are used to aid the photographer in positioning the lights. In this way the intended lighting pattern may be studied and adjusted before the brief flash exposure.

Most studio flash heads feature detachable and interchangeable reflectors. Thus, any head may be used with a variety of reflectors, umbrellas, and other devices to suit the lighting needs of the individual assignment. Like smaller camera-mounted flash units, the light-producing flash tube on a studio strobe head rarely wears out and is capable of thousands of flashes.

Electronic flash is generally replacing incandescent lighting in commercial studios because it produces great quantities of light without much attendant heat. This feature permits the flash head to be enclosed and contained in light-modifying devices such as soft-boxes that might pose a fire hazard with hot lights. Although the initial cost of a professional quality studio strobe system is fairly high, the units consume less power, are less costly to operate, and have a very long lifespan. Figure 12-4 B shows some common studio electronic flash heads and reflectors.

Reflector Types

Both hot lights and studio strobes can be outfitted with a variety of metal reflectors and other accessories designed to modify the quality of the light produced. In general, small reflectors tend to produce a highly directional and specular quality of illumination, while larger reflectors modify the light so that it is more diffused and less directional. The selection of an appropriate reflector is governed by the surface characteristics of the subject and the textural and tonal rendering desired in the final photograph. Some general reflector types and their lighting characteristics are described below.

Floodlights One type of floodlight reflector that may be found on both hot lights and strobe heads is the **pan-reflector light**. This instrument has a large, curved, panlike reflector bowl and generally uses only one light head for its source. Like other floodlights, the pan-reflector light produces a relatively broad, even field of light with some direction. Large pan-reflectors are often used as the key or main light in studio work and may be used

to give the feel of direct sunlight illumination. One advantage of this type of floodlight is that auxiliary equipment can be clipped easily onto the reflector.

Small-diameter pan-reflectors, and/or units having brightly polished inner surfaces will produce more specular light with greater directional traits. Positioned above or to the side of a subject, these small reflectors are often used to accent edges and textures. Using very large-diameter pan-reflectors, or those with satin or painted finishes, results in softer, more diffused lighting. Thus, the size and type of pan-reflector will determine the sharpness and darkness of the shadows and the size of the highlights. Larger, less shiny pan-reflectors will produce open, soft shadows coupled with large, luminous highlights.

Umbrellas A special type of large reflector, called an **umbrella**, often is used to provide extremely even and diffused illumination. Many different materials, including metallic fabrics, are used in their manufacture. In general use, a light head with a small pan-reflector is directed into the hollow of the umbrella, which in turn reflects the light toward the subject. When the light is reflected in this fashion, it is commonly referred to as **bounce light**. Depending on the nature and shape of the material, the light is reflected and diffused in different ways. Normally, the light produced is sufficiently specular to produce clear highlights and shadows, yet it is sufficiently diffuse to give the shadows a soft edge that is especially pleasing for portraits. An umbrella is often used as a key light, as depicted in Figure 12-5.

A plain white fabric umbrella without any silver lining may also be used as a light diffuser. When this is done, the lighting standard is reversed so that the light passes through the umbrella toward the subject. The result approximates the quality of light from a softbox.

Softboxes

Classical painters were known to favor the soft, broad and even illumination produced by north-facing windows. **Softboxes** are the modern studio photographer's equivalent of this kind of lighting. A softbox is usually a large fabric-covered enclosure supported by metal rods. A flash head, placed inside the box, is directed through

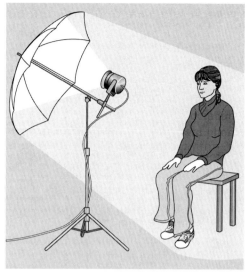

Figure 12-5. Light with umbrella reflector, mounted on lighting standard. This arrangement provides a broad, keylight effect— strong enough to provide highlights and shadows, but diffuse enough to soften the edges.

one or more layers of translucent diffusing material. The sides and back of the box are generally made of metallic-coated cloth to direct and reflect the maximum amount of light through the front opening. Softboxes are usually used only with strobe lights, because their use with hot lights could pose a fire hazard.

Softboxes come in a variety of sizes to light different-size objects. Automobile photographers, for example, use boxes as large as 10 x 12 ft. for their large subjects. Most studios, however, are well served by 3- or 4-ft. square boxes that can be used as both main and fill lights for subjects ranging from portraits to still lifes.

Spotlights

Typically a **spotlight** is used to obtain a narrow, specular beam of light. The spotlight combines a light source, which may be either a flash tube or a hot light, with a small, highly polished reflector and one or more lenses to concentrate the light emanating from the unit. This design produces a small point source of light and focuses the light rays to minimize diffusion.

Spotlights are often used as an addition to a main or key light to add controlled illumination to small areas. This may be done to call visual attention to the area, to provide tonal separation and highlights, or to emphasize the texture and sur-

face of a material. Alternatively, the spotlight itself may be used as the dominant key light to produce a more dramatic, theatrical effect.

Reflector Cards

Any light-colored or white surface, as well as a mirror-bright polished surface, can serve as a **reflector card**. Light reflected by a matte surface, such as paper, cardboard, or cloth, will tend to be diffused, reflecting from the surface in many directions. Light reflected by a mirror or a highly polished, metallic surface will tend to be specular, reflecting from the surface in a single direction. A **matte-white reflector** is often useful for reflecting diffused light into the shadowed areas of the subject. This procedure is sometimes more convenient than placing a fill light in that position, particularly when the key light is opposite. Figure 12-6 shows this arrangement.

Baffles, Screens, Flags, and Snoots

Sometimes a main light source produces unwanted highlights along with the desired highlights. In a portrait, for example, the key light may produce an unwanted highlight on a prominent ear. One method of removing this highlight is to shade the key light from this area with an opaque **baffle**. One kind of baffle is called a **barn-door baffle**. It attaches to the light reflector and has hinged flaps that can be adjusted to shade any part of the light.

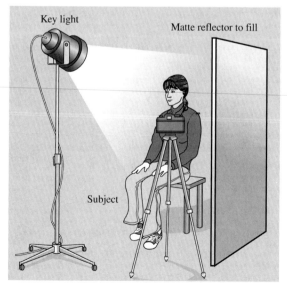

Figure 12-6. Placement of reflector. Keylight provides dominant source for highlights and shadows. Reflector provides fill for shadows.

Another type of baffle is an opaque **head screen** that can be inserted into the light beam and held in place on a separate stand by a clamp. A small screen of this sort, often called a **flag**, can be used for very precise local control of shading. Figure 12-7 shows the use of baffles, screens, and flags.

Because artificial light travels away from its source in all directions, even the light from a spotlight spreads out over short distances. Baffles and flags will keep unwanted light from falling on the subject. Another approach is to use a **snoot** fitted to the front of the light—a long metallic tube that passes light only through its small, circular opening. Thus the light may be further controlled for exact placement on the subject.

Diffusion Screens, Pattern Screens, and Gels

Whereas baffles fully shade or block some portion of the light, diffusion screens, pattern screens, and gel filters alter the quality of the light in some way.

Diffusion screens are introduced into the path of the light to soften and diffuse it. The key light may be too specular, producing sharp edges between the highlights and shadows. To soften these sharp edges, a diffusion screen can be placed in the path of the light. Doing so will change the hard, specular light into a softer, more diffused light. Diffusion screens may be made of ordinary window screen material, light gauze, sheer nylon stocking mate-

rial, or something similar. Usually a diffusion screen is mounted into a frame and clamped to a light standard in the desired position.

A **pattern screen** is used to create a pattern of shadows, usually on a background, often simulating shadows found in nature. For example, inserting a leafy tree branch into the background lighting will produce a leafy pattern of shadows. Similar effects can be obtained with patterns cut from opaque materials, such as cardboard. These cutout patterns may be abstract or representative of natural patterns. Pattern screens of this sort can lend interest to an otherwise uninteresting background.

Gels, or colored filter sheets, are sometimes positioned in front of the light head to produce special effects. A red gel, for example, might be mounted on a background light to color the backdrop in a portrait or product shot. By using a variety of colored gels, a single roll of gray or white background paper can be made to appear any desired color.

Although special photographic gels are sold, almost any sheet of suitably colored acetate can be used. Be sure to mount gels so that they will not touch any hot objects or modeling lights—they may be flammable. When used with hot lights, gel filters must be mounted in a filter frame and positioned some distance away from the lighting unit to avoid discoloration, melting, or combustion.

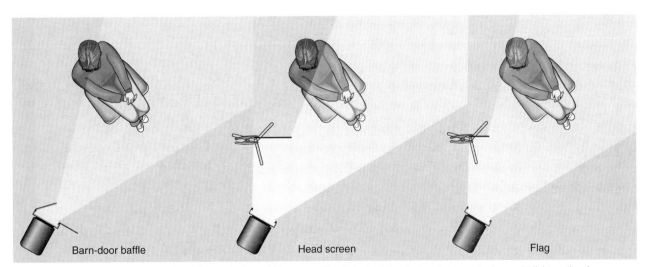

Barn-door baffle   Head screen   Flag

Figure 12-7. Baffles, screens, and flags. These devices aid in controlling light by introducing shadows in the main light path where needed.

Light Standards and Booms

The lighting instruments, reflectors, baffles, flags, screens, and gels all need to be placed carefully and held in place while the setup is being made. A wide range of stands, clamps, extension arms, and mounting hardware is available for this purpose. The term **standard** commonly refers to a weighted or tripod stand, sometimes mounted on casters, designed to stand on the floor and to accept the mounting of lighting and auxiliary equipment. Standards come in many varieties, the most useful having telescoping extensions with manually operated clamps to hold the extensions in place. A **boom** usually refers to a cross member, sometimes counterbalanced, designed to attach to the standard and to hold an item of equipment suspended in the air at a short distance from the standard. Figure 12-8 depicts a light standard and boom with a spotlight affixed.

Having several standards and booms makes possible precise placement of lighting instruments. In the ideal studio, instruments are hung from the

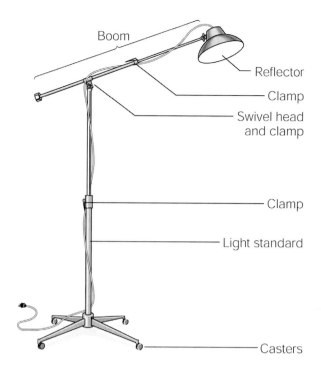

Figure 12-8. Lighting standard and boom.

ceiling on adjustable mounts, eliminating a tangle of wires on the floor and concealing the equipment from the camera. An ideal portable lighting system includes several lightweight instruments, collapsible standards, cords, and connectors, all contained in a carton or case.

Summary

Table 12-1 shows the types of highlights and shadows obtained from various artificial lighting tools.

A Basic Four-Light Setup

Objective 12-D Describe and demonstrate the functions of the key (or main) light, fill light, background light, and accent lights in a basic setup.

Key Concepts key (main) light, vertical placement, high-angle lighting, top lighting, subject-level or eye-level placement, low-level placement, horizontal placement, frontal lighting, 45-degree sidelighting, 90-degree sidelighting, backlighting, rim lighting, Rembrandt lighting, catchlights, fill light, highlight brilliance, background light, accent lights, hair light, backlight or kicker

---

☠ CAUTION ☠

Lighting Hazards

The cords and connectors that provide power to the photo lamps must be of a suitable gauge. Ordinary household lamp cords (#18 gauge) and connectors are usually not adequate for the wattages used by photo lamps and present a hazard if overloaded. Use heavier gauge cord and connectors to power photographic lighting instruments. (For typical U.S. 115 V AC power supply, use #16 gauge for up to 500-W loads or #14 gauge for up to 1500-W loads.)

Be sure not to overload the electric circuits when more than one photo lamp is used on a single circuit. To work out how many lamps can be operated on one circuit, use the formula: volts × amperes = watts. A typical U.S. household electric circuit has a 115-V power supply and a maximum capacity of 15 A. Thus, the total wattage of all loads that can safely be run from one such circuit is: 115 V × 15 A = 1725 W, or approximately three 500-W lamps. Consult an electrician or electrical supply store before setting up a home studio.

Do not place flammable screen, filter, or gel materials too close to, or in contact with, hot light instruments.

Table 12-1. Lighting effects		
Tool	*Type of Highlight*	*Type of Shadow*
Floodlight	Fairly broad and diffused	Indistinct edges; good shadow detail
Umbrella bounce light	Broad; softened specular	Clear; soft edges; good shadow detail
Umbrella diffused light	Medium, softened specular	Soft edges; moderate shadow detail
Softbox	Very broad and diffused	Open shadows full of detail
Spotlight	Small and specular	Sharp edges; little shadow detail
Matte reflector card	Very diffused	Some shadow details; indistinct edge
Polished reflector card	Broad and specular	Sharp edges; little shadow detail
Diffusion screen with spotlight	Narrow; softened specular	Clear, soft edges; some shadow detail

Most lighting setups will benefit from a plan that applies the principle of the single dominant light source. To implement such a plan, imagine that the subject, whether a portrait or an object, is illuminated by some single natural source, such as a window, sunlight, an overhead lamp, a candle, or a fireplace. With this single source in mind, set up the lighting in a way that will simulate lighting from this source. The following basic four-light setup should be useful in developing such a plan.

The Key Light

The **key (main) light** is placed in the position of the assumed single dominant light source. The placement of the key light has a greater effect on the feel and form of the subject than any other light. In placing the key light, the photographer must consider both the vertical and horizontal placement.

Vertical Placement **Vertical placement** involves deciding if the light is to come from above the subject, from the subject's level, or from below the subject. Because most natural sources originate from above, the key light usually is placed above the subject and directed downward. Light emanating from above the subject is called **high-angle lighting** and generally produces a pattern of highlights and shadows that is familiar in nature. Placing the light source directly above the subject produces extreme high-angle lighting, or **top lighting**.

Light emanating from the level of the subject may be referred to as **subject-level** or **eye-level placement**. A key light at this level may simulate window light or lamplight because that is the level at

which we are accustomed to seeing these natural sources.

Light originating from a source below the level of the subject is referred to as **low-level placement**. A key light in this position can be used to simulate a fireplace or campfire because that is the level at which we are accustomed to seeing these sources. Low-level light can also give a mysterious or "other world" feel and is often used for this effect in Hollywood horror movies.

Horizontal Placement **Horizontal placement** involves deciding if the light is to come from in front of the subject, from the side of the subject, or from behind the subject. Light emanating from in front of the subject, approximately on the camera's axis, is referred to as **frontal lighting**. A key light in this position tends to eliminate most modeling and texture shadows and results in a relatively flat, textureless, representation characterized primarily by shape.

Light emanating from the side of the subject is referred to as sidelighting. If **45-degree sidelighting** is used, the key light is placed toward the side of the subject, about 45 degrees off the camera's axis. In this position, the key light produces good modeling and texture shadows and results in natural-appearing surface details and textures. If **90-degree sidelighting** is used, the key light is placed to the extreme side of the subject, 90 degrees off the camera's axis. In this position, the key light illuminates one side of the subject, casts the opposite side in deep shadow, and exaggerates surface textures.

Light emanating from behind the subject is called **backlighting**. If the key light is used in a backlighting position, the front of the subject that is facing the camera is cast in deep shadow, surface textures are not revealed, and the edges around the shape of the subject are brilliantly lighted. This effect is also called **rim lighting**.

Studio photographers select carefully from among these horizontal and vertical placements and various intermediate positions to control which features of the subject are to be emphasized and subordinated. The types of light sources selected and their positions will control how viewers perceive the shape, form, volume, mass, and surface characteristics of the subject. The creative photographer uses light to shape and refine his or her interpretation of the subject.

Typical Key Light Location

For portraits, a favored position for the key light is at approximately 45° to one side of the camera-subject axis and approximately 40° to 60° above the head (see Figure 12-9). When the light is correctly positioned a triangle of light should highlight the cheek on the shadow side of the face. This is often called **"Rembrandt lighting."** The reflections in the eyes produced by the key light, called **catchlights**, should be high in the eyes. For subjects with deep-set eyes, the key light may need to be lowered somewhat to keep the eye sockets from appearing excessively dark.

Recommended Types of Key Lights

For most portrait photography the key light is a flood lamp or broad light source, which produces a diffused light that tends to soften the shadows produced by skin blemishes and wrinkles. A medium-size softbox or a small pan-reflector light bounced from an umbrella is good for this purpose; each produces a soft, directional light. To produce a more dramatic look or to accentuate character lines, many photographers prefer a smaller light source of higher specularity.

In photographing objects, a harder, more specular key light usually helps to accentuate the shape, contour, and texture of the object. A common position for the key light in object photography is above and behind the object. This position, called "key backlighting," provides good definition of volume and form.

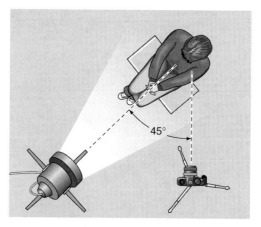

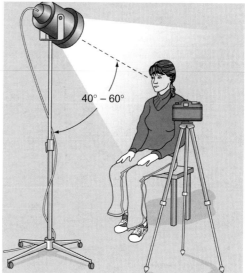

Figure 12-9. Normal placement of key light. A) Top view. B) Frontal view.

The Fill Light

The key light is intended to provide the basic pattern of highlights and shadows that will give the subject its three-dimensional appearance. In nature, however, considerable diffused light is also present to light up the shadows, revealing the detail in the shadow areas. In a basic light setup, therefore, some provision should be made to fill in these shadow areas with secondary, diffused light. That is the purpose of the **fill light**.

The fill light is generally a diffused light source such as a large floodlight, medium umbrella, small softbox, or a matte white reflector. Normally a fill light is placed on the side of the subject opposite the key light and at about the same height as the camera. The intensity and amount of fill illumination can be controlled easily by varying the light-to-subject distance. As the light is moved away from the subject, the amount of fill illumination declines.

The fill light should produce no visible shadow patterns of its own. This is very important to creating the impression of the single dominant light source. The viewer of the final print should be unaware that a light was used in this position. It should appear that the shadow areas are illuminated solely by the diffused lighting normally produced by the dominant source.

In portraiture, the fill light may occasionally produce specular highlights on the cheeks, nose, or forehead of the subject. If these are too intense, this **highlight brilliance** may give the subject an oily or sweaty look. Once the fill light is in place, it can be adjusted slightly from side to side to minimize this effect. Also, the fill light at this position may sometimes produce an additional set of catchlights in the eyes. These secondary catchlights tend to give the subject a directionless gaze and generally are considered undesirable. If they cannot be eliminated in the lighting setup, they can be removed later by spotting them out of the final print or by digital retouching.

The Background Light

Usually the **background light** is a small floodlight placed between the subject and the background. Its purpose is to light the background, not the subject, in a way that will help add tonal separation between the subject and background. This light will give the illusion of depth behind the subject and will separate the subject from the background. Care must be taken to place the lighting instrument in a position where it is not seen by the camera. Pattern screens may be used to add patterns of light and shadow to backgrounds that otherwise might appear uninteresting. Such pattern lighting of the background can be used to simulate a natural setting, such as the pattern sunlight might produce through a paned window or a leafy branch. Gel filters may also be used on the background light to introduce color effects.

Accent Lights

Additional **accent lights** can be placed at various positions to provide highlight accents that will help reveal the three-dimensional quality of the subject. An added highlight on the subject's hair, for example, or at the sides of the face to rim the features, often helps to separate the subject from its background and to add some sparkle to the final print.

One common accent light is called a **hair light**. It is usually a small lighting instrument, such as a snoot or spotlight, mounted on a boom and placed in a top lighting position slightly behind the subject. It may be placed directly overhead or slightly to one side. When it is used off center, it is usually most useful on the side of the head away from the key light. Its beam is directed from behind the subject slightly toward the camera to give the hair a brilliant, halo-like highlight, which not only adds some detail but helps provide additional subject-background separation. Care must be taken, however, that light from the hair light does not fall on the subject's face and produce a secondary set of highlights.

Another common accent light is the **backlight**, or **kicker**, generally a snoot or spotlight placed behind and slightly above the subject's head, usually on the same side of the subject as the key light. If it is directed to the back of the subject's shoulders or to the back of the head, the backlight will rim these features with highlights, not only adding detail but also adding to the subject/background separation.

Care should be taken that accent lights are turned off while light meter readings are being taken; they may falsely inflate the reading, leading to underexposure of the key and fill areas. Care also should be taken that accent lights do not accidentally fall directly on the camera lens; this will create lens flare. Baffles can be used to shield the lens from these lights, or a lens shade can be attached to the camera lens.

Steps in Preparing the Lighting Setup

There is no one best approach to preparing the lighting setup. Most photographers advise that the lighting setup be constructed one light at a time, that each light be set up while all other lights are switched off. Not until all the basic lights are set up are they all switched on at once to view the overall effect. Only at this time are the final adjustments made—instruments are moved slightly to modify their brightness or to alter their angle to the subject, or additional lights are added to fill shadows or to obtain special effects.

Most photographers begin this process with the main or key light, and then add the fill light, background lights, and accents. (See Figure 12-10.) Experience and practice in the placement and adjustment of these components will lead to proficiency in setting up artificial indoor lighting. The step-by-step procedure outlined below is intended to provide a starting point.

Basic Portrait Lighting

Objective 12-E Describe and demonstrate some basic lighting techniques for portrait photography.

Key Concepts broad lighting, short or narrow lighting, butterfly or glamour lighting

To achieve an ideal representation of the subject, the portrait photographer uses several tools—lighting, pose, camera angle, and retouching. One of the more useful and flexible tools is lighting.

Lighting for the portrait follows the same basic principles of lighting discussed previously—a single dominant light source, a dominant set of highlights and shadows, a natural angle of incidence, and the like. But in addition, by placing the

key light properly, the photographer can emphasize the attractive features of the subject and subordinate the less attractive features, such as balding, high forehead, a sharp chin, or deep-set eyes. Features can be highlighted or obscured in shadow; round faces can be narrowed, narrow faces rounded, long noses shortened, broad noses narrowed, and so on.

There are three main types of lighting commonly used for portraits, each based on a different placement of the key light to produce a different effect.

Broad Lighting

Assuming that the subject is facing slightly off camera—that is, slightly to one side or the other of the subject-camera axis—the key light fully illuminates the side of the face turned toward the camera. It also illuminates the cheek on the shadowed side of the face. This type of lighting, termed **broad lighting**, tends to wash out skin textures but helps round out thin or narrow faces. To obtain a broad-lighting setup, place the key light to fully light the side of the face facing the camera. About three-fourths of the face will be in key light, whereas one-fourth will be in fill. Figure 12-11 depicts the basic key and fill positions for broad lighting.

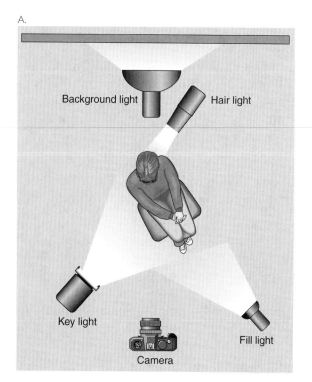

Figure 12-10. Typical four-light setup. A) Top view. B) Front view.

Making a Lighting Setup

1. Decide on the general effect. *Think about the general effect to be produced. Is it soft? Hard? Dark? Bright? Settle on the single dominant source. Does it simulate a natural light source, such as sunlight, window light, or firelight? From what direction will it strike the subject? Plan the placement of the key, fill, background, and accent lights, and the instruments that will be used in each location. Place the lighting instruments approximately in these positions.*

2. Place the key light. *Locate the key light to create the dominant set of highlights and shadows. Place it far enough away that it produces an even light, without hot spots. Place the key light so that the highlights and shadows are modeling the subject in the desired way. Adjust its height and position until the desired highlight pattern is obtained.*

3. Add the fill light. *Use the fill light to flood the set with an even, shadowless, diffused field of illumination. Use the camera's viewing screen to be sure that no conflicting shadows are visible. Move the fill light closer to or farther away from the subject to control the brightness ratio. The brightness ratio can be set visually by changing the light position until the desired feeling is produced, or it can be calculated with a light meter.*

   To calculate the lighting ratio, take a closeup meter reading of the subject with both the key and fill lights on. Note this reading. Now take a similar reading with only the fill light on. Adjust the position of the fill light to obtain a 3-to-1 or 4-to-1 brightness ratio between key-plus-fill and fill alone. (This is a 1 1/2- to 2-stop difference.)

4. Separate the subject from its background. *Do not place the subject too close to its background. Add the background lights. Take care that direct light from these sources does not fall on the subject. Baffles, gels, and diffusion screens are useful for controlling and modifying the background lighting.*

5. Add the accent lights. *When a hair light and/or kickers are added, take care that their light falls only where it is wanted— that is, be careful not to add any secondary highlights or shadows on the subject's face. Flags and snoots are useful for controlling the placement of accent lights.*

6. Make final adjustments. *Examine the subject through the viewfinder with all the lights turned on. Are there unwanted highlights? Shade them off with baffles, flags, or snoots. Are there deep shadow areas that need additional fill? Add reflectors or additional floodlights. Is the subject not fully separated from the background? Add accents and/or background lights. Are the catchlights not properly located? Adjust the key and fill. Pose the subject. Shoot.*

A.
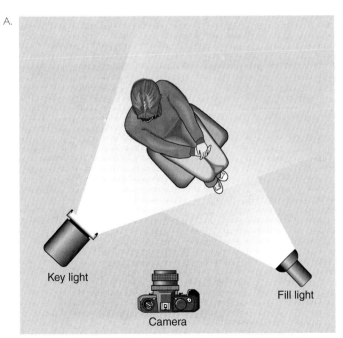

B.

Figure 12-11. Broad lighting. A) Normal key light and fill-light placements for broad lighting. B) Effect of broad lighting.

Short or Narrow Lighting

When the subject is facing slightly off camera, the key light fully illuminates the side of the face turned away from the camera and produces a triangular highlight on the cheek on the shadowed side of the face. This type of lighting, termed **short** or **narrow lighting**, may be used effectively with average oval or round faces. It tends to narrow the face and emphasizes facial contours and textures more than broad lighting. With this setup, about one-fourth of the face is in key light, whereas the three-fourths facing the camera is in fill. Figure 12-12 depicts the basic key and fill positions for short lighting.

Butterfly or Glamour Lighting

In **butterfly** or **glamour lighting**, the key light is placed directly in front of the subject and slightly above the head so that the nose shadow appears directly under the nose and in line with it, forming a shape similar to a butterfly. It may be used successfully with the normal oval face. It is not usually recommended for photographing people with short hair because it tends to highlight the ears, making them undesirably prominent. Figure 12-13 depicts the basic key and fill positions for butterfly lighting.

Enhancing Physical Features

By appropriate arrangements of lighting and poses, certain physical features can be emphasized and others subordinated in portraits. Table 12-2 provides some suggestions for dealing with various physical features of the subject.

Lighting Small Objects

Objective 12-F Describe and demonstrate some common problems and techniques for lighting small objects in product photography.

Key Concepts shape, surface texture, key backlighting, edge accents, texture accents, transillumination, tenting, spraying, dulling

As with other forms of lighting, small-object lighting usually challenges the photographer to create an arrangement of highlight and shadow that will reveal the characteristic shape, contours, and textures of the object. If a natural lighting effect is desired, the same natural lighting standard that was discussed in *Basic Lighting Principles* can be applied. However, natural lighting will not always be desired; the photographer may choose to portray the object in some other lighting environment that better expresses his or her interpretation of the ob-

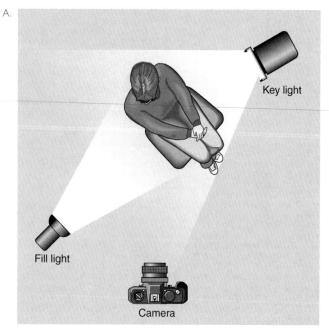

Figure 12-12. Short lighting. A) Normal key light and fill-light placements for short lighting. B) Effect of short lighting.

A.

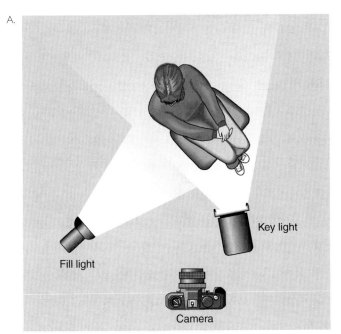

B.

Figure 12-13. Butterfly (glamour) lighting. A) Normal key light and fill-light placements for butterfly lighting. B) Effect of butterfly lighting.

ject. Whatever kind of lighting effect is desired, it is wise to adhere to these basic principles:

■ There should be one dominant source light and one dominant set of highlights and shadows.

■ Shadow detail will usually be illuminated by diffused fill light that is subordinate to the key light.

■ The brightness ratio will usually not exceed 4 to 1.

Table 12-2. Lighting physical features	
Features	*Lighting*
Nose	Avoid profiles if nose uneven. For short noses, shoot from slightly high angle. Raise key lights to lengthen nose shadow. For long noses, vice versa.
Eyes	Lower key lights to reduce shadows in deep-set eye sockets. For large eyes, lower gaze; for small eyes, lift gaze.
Face	For round faces, use short lighting. Increase brightness ratio. Keep sides of face in shadow. For narrow faces, use broad lighting. Lower key light. Reduce lighting ratio. For bony faces, have subject face cameras; use soft diffuse lighting; avoid shadows and highlights.
Prominent Features	Keep lights off prominent features, such as prominent ears, high foreheads, large noses.
Glasses	Use higher key light angle and adjust fill to minimize frame shadows. Rim shadows and hot spots from lenses will need retouching. Consider glassless rims. Tip glasses slightly forward to eliminate reflections.
Wrinkles	Use flat lighting angles and diffuse light to reduce wrinkles; use oblique lighting angles and specular light to emphasize them.
Secondary Catchlights	Arrange lights so that one and only one catchlight appears in each eye in the one o'clock or eleven o'clock position. Remove secondary catchlights by spotting print or etching negative.
Body	View stout persons from the side; thin persons more from the front. Have plump persons lean forward to conceal paunchiness. Use narrow lighting to slim plump persons; use broad lighting to fill out thin ones.

Note: For digital images, spotting, etching, and other retouching techniques can be accomplished in your image-editing program.

- The object will usually be separated visually from its background.
- The major lighting components are the key, fill, background, and accent lights.

Even though the general principles are the same, the approach to lighting objects is often somewhat different. In object photography, the lighting setup is usually determined primarily by the object's **shape** and **surface texture**. Lighting setups for objects with curved surfaces will differ from those for objects with flat surfaces. Transparent objects, shiny metallic objects, and dull, matte-surfaced objects will each require somewhat different lighting treatments to reveal their surface textures.

Often the photographer will want to go beyond the mere recording of an object's physical characteristics to express its psychological meaning or to elicit an emotional response from the viewer. By selecting or arranging the lighting, the photographer can express unique visual ideas. One approach to lighting small objects is described in the following discussion.

The Key Light

In object photography it is generally useful to establish the key light first. Unlike the human face, an object's most important characteristics are often its shape and texture. One effective placement of the key light that reveals shape and texture is above and behind the subject. This **key backlighting** placement illuminates the top of the object with a brilliant highlight and projects the main shadow of the object toward the viewer. The backlight position tends to reveal surface textures, and the main shadow helps establish the shape of the object.

Although it is usually more flattering to a portrait subject if the key light is a diffused light, a hard, specular light is often used for small objects to emphasize their surface details and textures. This will vary, of course, depending on the surface texture of the object. Matte or coarse surfaces are revealed better by a hard, specular key light; however, a shiny surface may be revealed better by a diffused key light.

The Accent Lights

Two types of accents are often useful in lighting small objects: **edge accents** and **texture accents**.

The edge accents help to separate the various subject planes so that the viewer can better perceive the subject's shape. They also separate the subject from its background by providing rim lighting around the outside edges of the object. Edge accents are established primarily by means of additional backlights that tend to produce brilliant edge highlights.

Texture accents are intended to reveal the surface irregularities of the object. Sidelighting is generally used for this purpose, either from above or from below the object, so that the light beam "skids" across the surface of the object and across the grain of the texture to be emphasized. Hard, specular light is most useful for this purpose, because it will tend to create a fine pattern of highlights and shadows that the viewer will perceive as texture. Lighting for texture also requires that the fill lighting be a bit weaker than normal so that the texture shadows are not washed out.

When establishing the accent highlights, take care to create no new major shadow patterns. The key light has established a single dominant shadow of the object. Additional accent lights placed at relatively low angles, shooting upward, will avoid producing new and competing shadows of the object.

The Fill Light

As with the accent lights, it is important that the fill light cast no identifiable shadows of its own. Fill light can be provided by a diffuse flood lamp or by a reflector placed in a frontal position close to the camera-subject axis. The lighting ratio between key and fill areas usually should not exceed 4 to 1. (See *Basic Lighting Principles* on page 398.)

The Background Light

Background light is directed toward the background rather than toward the object itself. One purpose of background light is to provide a light background against which a dark object can be emphasized. Another purpose is to lighten a background that otherwise might appear too dark in the final print. In setting up lighting for the background, take care that no ambient light from this source is cast onto the object—it might wash out the dominant shadows or create a new set of conflicting highlights.

Figure 12-14 demonstrates the effects of one lighting arrangement of key, fill, accent, and background lights for lighting a small object.

Lighting Glass Objects and Shiny Objects

Certain types of objects pose special problems in object photography. Transparent objects, such as glassware, and highly polished, metallic objects require certain special treatments that are worthy of some consideration here.

Glass Objects It is usually a good idea to avoid frontal illumination of glass objects. The reflective surface of the glass produces a profusion of distracting reflections from the light sources. One common method of photographing glass objects is to place them against an illuminated background, such as a white paper background illuminated frontally by a floodlight. Another method is **trans-illumination**, using a background of translucent material illuminated from behind by a floodlight. Figure 12-15 depicts these placements for photographing glass objects.

To add accents to a glass object, the careful addition of limited frontal lights may be helpful. Because the surface of the glass is highly polished, it produces highly specular reflections of any light

A.

B.
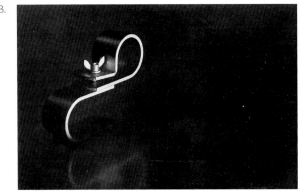

C.
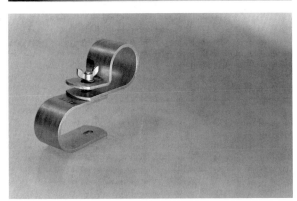

D.

E.

Figure 12-14. Lighting objects. A) Key backlighting. Light placed high and behind object to one side. B) Edge-light accent. Light placed low and to one side. C) Fill lighting. Light placed close to camera at lens height. D) Background lighting. Light directed to background only and masked from object itself. E) Effect of combined key, fill, accent, and background light on object.

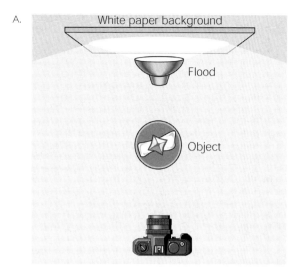

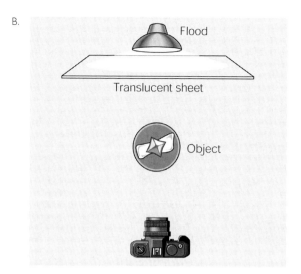

Figure 12-15. Background lighting for glass objects. A) Frontally illuminated background. B) Transilluminated background using translucent screen. C) Bottle with liquid photographed against transilluminated background; no other light source used. Base line is simple black paper cutout.

sources that are visible from the object's position. By placing one or two light sources in front of the object and by using baffles to shape the light sources, very precise highlights can be produced.

Shiny Objects The problem in photographing shiny objects, such as metalware or shiny plastic, is that they are highly reflective and will reflect images of their surroundings. Because most shiny objects have curved surfaces, the patterns of light reflected from them often are confusing and tend to mask the true surface textures of the objects themselves. The trick in photographing shiny objects is to eliminate from the surroundings all other objects that the shiny object might reflect. If

the shiny surface of the object is surrounded with only blank surfaces, it can reflect only plain light without details. Under these conditions, the contours and texture of the shiny object will be revealed without confusion.

To accomplish this, a technique known as **tenting** is commonly used. White paper or other translucent material can be used to erect a tent, which then is transilluminated as evenly as possible with diffused light. Then the shiny object is photographed through a hole in the tent, placed above or to the side of the object. Figure 12-16 depicts tenting arrangements and their effects.

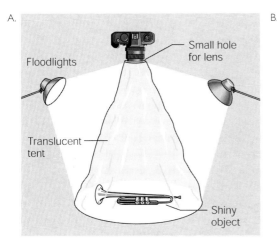

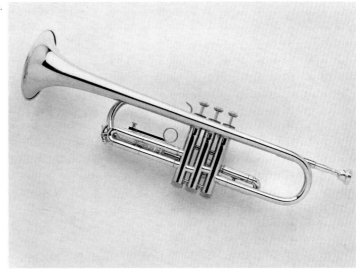

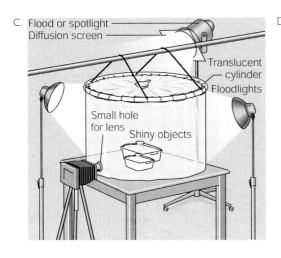

Figure 12-16. Tenting arrangements. A) Photographing objects in tent from above. B) Result of tenting as shown in A. C) Photographing objects in tent from the side. D) Result of tenting as shown in C.

Occasionally a shiny object may appear in an arrangement that also includes other objects that may require stronger, more directional lighting treatments. After the lighting setup has been established, the shiny object may pick up many undesirable, specular highlights from the light sources and reflections of other objects in the scene. Spraying the shiny object with a matting spray is one way to diffuse the reflections from its surface. **Spraying** is often the best solution when both matte and shiny objects are in a scene. However, the spray should not be used indiscriminately on all types of objects—it may damage certain plastics. Both perma-

nent and removable dulling sprays are available. The removable type is generally recommended so that it can be removed from the object once shooting is completed.

Other materials can be used to dull or matte shiny surfaces. **Dulling** can be accomplished also by brushing white cosmetic eyeliner onto the offending surface with a broad, soft brush. This technique is especially useful for dulling small specular highlights from shiny surfaces where a matting spray is too difficult to control.

Questions to Consider

1. What characteristics of light affect the way we see a subject?

2. What characteristics of a subject are revealed by light?

3. What are the differences between specular and diffused light?

4. Describe the principle of the single dominant light source.

5. Explain the functions of main, fill, accent, and background light in photographing any subject.

6. What techniques can be used to obtain good images in dim light without adding artificial light sources?

7. What steps can be taken to control the lighting of a subject when shooting under unmodified, available light?

8. What is meant by the brightness ratio? Explain how to establish a recommended brightness ratio.

9. What is the purpose of each of these artificial lighting tools: floodlights, spotlights, reflectors, baffles and flags, diffusion and pattern screens, gels, light standards, and booms?

10. What is the purpose of each of these light sources in an artificial lighting setup: key light, fill light, background light, accent light?

11. What steps are recommended for preparing a basic four-light artificial lighting setup?

12. Describe the characteristics of each of these types of portrait lighting: broad lighting, short lighting, butterfly lighting.

13. Name some techniques that might be used to subdue these facial features: round face, narrow face, bony face, deep-set eyes, multiple catchlights, wrinkles, prominent ears.

14. Describe how to plan the lighting arrangement for photographing a small object.

15. What are the problems often encountered in photographing transparent and shiny objects, and how may they be solved?

Suggested Field and Laboratory Assignments

1. Shoot a number of interior photographs under available light. Include several examples of each of the following:

   a. lighting exclusively from a window

   b. lighting exclusively from artificial light sources

   c. lighting from both window and artificial light sources

2. Arrange for the use of a studio or set up a temporary one. Shoot a number of portraits, including at least one example of each of the following:

   a. broad lighting

   b. short lighting

   c. butterfly lighting

   d. a portrait using key, fill, background, and accent lights

3. Set up lighting and shoot a number of objects. Include at least one example of each of the following:

   a. round object

   b. rectangular object

   c. glass object

   d. shiny object

   e. matte object

   f. a transparent, a shiny, and a matte object in a single arrangement

Flash Photography

Lisa Billings, "Halloween."

Unit at a Glance

Great photographic subjects are not always accompanied by optimum—or even adequate—lighting conditions. Artificial light is sometimes necessary, and electronic flash is a convenient source. Flash photography allows light to be added for photographs at night or in darkened rooms. Flash also can be used to control the contrast and appearance of pictures taken in sunlight. Flash light is dependable and intense; it can be manipulated to produce the effect of natural lighting, or it can provide stroboscopic, multiple-flash exposures.

This unit covers various types of flash, how electronic flash works, the differences among TTL, dedicated, automatic, and manual flash units, and special features found on flash units. In addition, synchronization, flash accessories, exposure setting with flash, common flash problems, and a variety of special flash lighting techniques are explained.

Principles of Flash Photography

Objective 13-A Describe the equipment used in flash photography and the principles and functions that apply to its use.

Key Concepts flash unit, electronic flash, recycling time, light output, BCPS, manual flash, automatic flash, dedicated flash, hot shoe, PC-socket, synch cord, red-eye mode, slow synch mode, rear curtain flash, exposure value (EV), through-the-lens (TTL), thyristor circuit, angle of illumination, zoom head, swivel head, bare bulb, handle mount, synchronization, X-synch, M-synch, FP-synch, bounce flash, bounce card, extension cord, wireless radio slaves, slave sensor, light stand, reflector, umbrella, snoot, filters, gels, external battery packs

Probably the most practical and widely used artificial light source available to photographers today is the portable **flash unit**. These units are simple to use, safe, and reliable, and attach easily to a camera. They are designed to provide a measured burst of intense light timed to the exact instant that the camera's shutter opens and closes.

Electronic Flash

More than one hundred years ago, English photography pioneer William Henry Fox Talbot discovered that a high-speed electrical spark could be used as a photographic light source. The spark was so brief and so intense that it had the effect of stopping the action of rapidly moving objects.

It was not until the 1930s, however, that this principle was developed into a practical system suitable for photography.

How Electronic Flash Units Work **Electronic flash** operates by passing a pulse of electricity through a gas-filled tube, causing a very brief burst of intense illumination. A modern electronic flash unit consists of (1) a power supply for the electric energy, usually a battery or a household AC circuit; (2) a set of capacitors that store the electric energy to a high potential; (3) a triggering circuit to release the stored electric energy; (4) a glass tube filled with inert gas, usually xenon, to convert the electric energy to light; and (5) a reflector. Because the light-producing gas in the tube is chemically inert, it is not burned or consumed during the flash. Therefore, the unit is reusable and can be fired thousands of times before it must be replaced. The batteries that power these units are designed for rapid recovery and long life and sometimes may be rechargeable, allowing them to be reused, often indefinitely. The light produced by these units is approximately 5500K, the color temperature of sunny, noontime daylight, and is extremely bright. It is also of extremely short duration, making its flashes easier on the subject's eyes.

After each firing, the flash cannot be fired again until its capacitors rebuild their electric charge. The time that it takes a unit to recharge its capacitors is known as its **recycling time**; this varies considerably among units. The most popular units are designed to recycle from a completely discharged state in 2 to 6 seconds. Most units also are equipped with an indicator light to let the photographer know when the flash unit has completed its recycling and is ready to fire again. A useful feature of some units is an adjustment permitting the unit to operate at reduced power, providing an additional control over the amount of light generated at each firing and the recycling time required. The **light output** of electronic flash units is rated in terms of **BCPS** (beam candle-power seconds).

The four major types of electronic flash are manual, automatic, dedicated, and TTL units. With **manual flash** the photographer determines the exposure and sets the camera's aperture by hand. With **automatic flash** the photographer presets the flash unit's film or digital sensor speed and the camera's aperture; the unit then determines the exposure automatically by adjusting the flash output based on light detected by a built-in sensor. **Dedicated flash** integrates automatic flash and the camera into one system. The film speed and other settings are determined automatically, as is proper flash exposure. **TTL**, or through-the-lens, flash units take dedicated systems a step further. They measure the flash light entering the lens and automatically set the camera controls for proper exposure. Working methods for flash are detailed in Objective 13-B, *Determining Flash Exposure Settings.*

Built-In Flash Units Many modern cameras have small, built-in, or pop-up flash units. Most are activated automatically in dim light conditions. Some can be user-activated for special purposes such as fill-in flash. Built-in flash units are very convenient for quick snapshots, but they lack the power needed for flash photography in large rooms or at a distance. Exposure is totally automatic with built-in flash units, and the photographer usually has no control over the camera settings. To overcome these limitations advanced photographers generally select an external flash unit.

Contacts and Cords

Unless an electronic flash is built into the camera, most cameras provide one or more devices for mounting and connecting a flash unit. One device in common use is the **hot shoe**, a built-in mounting bracket that electronically connects a properly designed unit to the shutter. The flash and shutter are directly connected through the hot shoe's electrical contacts, eliminating the need for any kind of connecting cord between the two.

The main drawback of the hot-shoe connector is that it attaches the flash unit to the camera and reduces the photographer's ability to vary lighting positions. To overcome this drawback, some cameras also possess a small **PC-socket** for connecting the camera to a flash unit by means of a flash **synch cord**. With a long cord, the flash unit can be positioned at a distance from the camera. The same effect can be achieved by using a hot-shoe extension that allows a flash extension cord to be attached directly to the camera's hot shoe. Figures 13-2 through 13-5 and 13-10 show these connectors.

Special Features

Some flash units incorporate additional useful features.

Red-eye Mode Sometimes the pupils in a subject's eyes appear red in color photographs taken with flash. This effect, called red-eye, occurs when the flash illuminates the blood vessels in the retina at the back of the eye as the photograph is taken. To minimize this troublesome effect some flash units offer a special **red-eye mode** that prefires the flash one or more times to reduce the subject's pupil size.

Slow Synch Mode A special feature found on many TTL flash systems, **slow synch** allows you to combine a flash photograph with a time exposure. For example, a landscape at night might require an exposure of 3–4 seconds. However, a person included in the foreground might be better exposed with flash. The slow synch mode combines both in one photograph by firing a flash at the beginning of the long exposure.

Rear Curtain Synch Rear curtain synch is similar to slow synch mode except that **rear curtain synch** fires the flash after the time exposure. When photographing a moving subject, rear curtain synch produces a sharply defined flash image in front of a motion-blurred background to depict movement. Slow synch mode would produce the opposite effect.

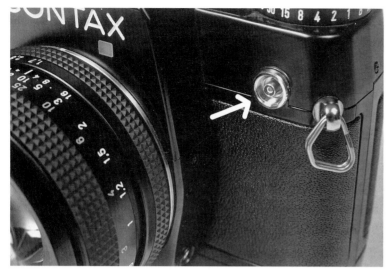

Figure 13-2. A PC-type flash connector.

Figure 13-3. Non-dedicated hot shoe contact.

Figure 13-4. Dedicated hot shoe and flash unit connections. Note that multiple pins allow camera and flash unit to exchange exposure data.

Variable Power Some flash units offer variable power settings. This feature is very useful for fill-in flash work to balance the sunlight exposure. The setting also allows a wide range of lens openings to be selected, providing more control over depth-of-field.

EV Adjustments Some advanced TTL flash units allow the user to adjust the **exposure value** or **EV** setting of the flash light. A setting of EV-1, for example, would give one stop less than normal power. This setting is helpful for fill-in flash work or to use as a means of bracketing flash exposures.

Camera-mounted Sensors Some non-TTL electronic flash units feature removable flash sensors. Mounting the sensor eye on the camera rather than on the flash assures that it always will be pointed at the subject regardless of the flash position. This system makes it possible, for example, to aim and bounce the flash light off a wall behind the photographer while the exposure-determining sensor remains aimed at the subject. Most advanced cameras have built-in flash sensors that measure the flash output **through the lens**. **TTL** sensors of this type give proper flash exposure regardless of where the flash unit is held or aimed.

Thyristor Circuit Early automatic strobe units completely discharged their capacitors even when the flash output was very low, wasting battery power. Modern flashes employ a **thyristor circuit** to preserve the energy in the capacitors following the flash discharge and reuse it during the recharging cycle. The effect of the thyristor circuit design is to conserve energy and to shorten recycling time. At shorter distances, flash durations often will be as brief as 1/50,000 sec., less energy will be spent from the capacitors, and less

Figure 13-5. Shoe-mount electronic flash mounts directly to camera body. Available in dedicated and non-dedicated models. Some have swivel heads for bounce flash work.

time will be required to recycle the capacitors to full charge.

Angle Adjustments Some flash units are designed with the light source and the reflector in fixed positions. This arrangement provides flash coverage within a fixed **angle of illumination**. The angle of illumination is usually designed to correspond to a normal lens's angle of view. With a wide-angle, telephoto, or zoom lens in use, however, the flash unit's normal angle of illumination often will not match the lens's angle of view and will result in uneven illumination. To overcome this discrepancy, some flash units are designed with wide-angle and telephoto adjustments. Many units feature a **zoom head**, which can be set to produce a wide, normal, or narrow angle of illumination to match the lens in use. Other flash units can be outfitted with wide-angle attachments to widen the spread of the light, or telephoto accessories to narrow it.

Swivel Heads Many electronic flash units have a **swivel head** so that the flash unit may be attached to the camera but directed away from the subject. One common way to use the swivel head is to tilt it toward the ceiling or wall so that the flash is bounced off the ceiling toward the subject. This technique is called **bounce flash** and provides a soft key light effect as well as diffused fill light to produce a more natural appearance.

Detachable Reflectors Some flash units have detachable reflectors. If the reflector is detached, light from the unit will travel in all directions. The direct rays from the unit will serve as a key light. The rest of the light from the unit will bounce around among the flat surfaces of the environment and provide a soft, even field of diffused light that serves to fill the shadowed areas. This technique is known as **bare-bulb flash** and is generally available only with advanced electronic flash units.

Handle Mounts Some electronic flash units are designed with an integrated **handle mount** and camera bracket for quick detachment of the unit for off-camera use. The oversize handles of these units often hold additional batteries to increase power and decrease recycling time. (See Figure 13-6.)

Manual Override of Automatic Flash Units Most automatic flash units provide an option for setting flash exposures manually. Setting a unit to manual usually disables the flash sensing eye so that the full flash duration is always produced. Exposure settings are then determined by the photographer with the aid of a calculator dial mounted on the flash unit. Manual operation is often necessary when shooting at long flash-to-subject distances. This is an important feature if the photographer wants to retain full control over exposures under unusual lighting conditions or to obtain special lighting effects.

Synchronization

The method of timing the flash to coincide properly with the shutter is called **synchronization**. To assure correct synchronization, the flash unit and the camera must be set to properly coordinate the timing of the shutter and the flash unit's output. Older cameras, and some professional models, often have a variety of flash synchronization settings or offer a choice of more than one PC terminal for flash connection, such as **X-synch**, **M-**

Figure 13-6. Example of handle-mount flash unit. Handle mounts generally feature greater capacity for more light and/or quicker recycling times than most shoe-mount units. Handle mounts are also available in dedicated versions.

synch, and **FP-synch**. These options differ with respect to the timing of the flash ignition relative to the triggering of the shutter.

M- and FP-synchronization M-synch and FP-synch settings, found on older cameras, are used exclusively with flash bulbs—never with electronic flash. These settings fire the combustible mixture in the flash bulb a few milliseconds *before* the shutter opens so that the light output from the bulb will be at its peak when the picture is made. M and FP settings are rarely found on contemporary cameras, which are generally designed to work solely with electronic flash units.

X-synchronization An electronic flash unit emits a burst of intense light instantly at ignition. **X-synchronization**, therefore, dispenses with the lead time of M- and FP-synch settings and fires the flash a few milliseconds *after* the shutter is released so that the shutter will be fully open when the flash occurs. X-

synchronization should *always* be used with electronic flash units; in fact, electronic flash has become so popular that modern cameras offer only X-synch. If only one flash synchronization is provided on a camera it is intended to be used with electronic flash.

X-synchronization and Focal Plane Shutters A proper setting for electronic flash requires both X-synch and correct shutter speed. Most SLR cameras use *a focal plane shutter*, described in Unit 2, which will not synchronize correctly beyond a given shutter speed. The fastest shutter speed allowable for correct flash synchronization is usually indicated by a colored marking on the shutter speed dial or detailed in the owner's manual. (See Figure 13-7.)

A maximum X-synch shutter speed of 1/60 sec. is common for most SLR cameras, but many advanced focal plane shutters will X-synch at 1/125 sec. or even 1/250 sec. The camera's manual will specify the fastest allowable X-synch shutter speed.

If the shutter is set at a faster shutter speed than is allowable with electronic flash, the focal plane shutter will not be open to the full frame when the flash occurs, and only part of the frame will receive the flash exposure. (See Figure 13-8.)

Figure 13-7. The highest recommended shutter speed for flash synchronization is usually indicated by "X" or other colored markings on the shutter speed dial of focal-plane shutter type cameras.

Figure 13-8. The result of incorrect flash synchronization. Only a portion of the photograph will receive the flash exposure if the shutter speed used is too fast.

Note that using a relatively slow 1/60-sec. shutter does not prohibit stopping action with electronic flash exposure. It is not the shutter speed that stops the action in this case; rather, it is the burst of flash light that usually lasts less than 1/1000 sec. In the relatively dim environments that require flash, the flash duration alone stops the action.

X-synchronization and Between-the-lens Shutters A between-the-lens or leaf shutter, described in Unit 2, permits any shutter speed to be used with X-synchronization. Digital, as well as large- and medium-format, cameras often are equipped with between-the-lens shutters and can synchronize electronic flash pictures even at their fastest shutter speeds—usually 1/500 sec. This is because leaf shutters open fully at all shutter speeds. The availability of the full range of shutter speeds makes it easy to use fill-in flash; however, it has little effect on stopping action, which, as we have seen, is achieved by flash duration rather than by shutter speed.

Flash Accessories

A variety of accessories are available to fit electronic flash units. Some accessories, such as extension cords, slaves, and bounce cards, give the photographer more control over the lighting effect. Other items, such as radio control units and external power packs, offer greater convenience for the working photographer.

Bounce Cards **Bounce flash** is often used instead of direct flash to create a softer, more natu-ral light. For bounce flash, described fully on pages 444–445, the flash is pointed toward the ceiling, where it is diffused and reflected back toward the subject. Not all ceilings make suitable reflectors, however; some may be too high, painted the wrong color, or not sufficiently reflective for small, low-powered flash units. Instead of a ceiling, the photographer may prefer to use a **bounce card**—a reflector, placed over the upward-pointing flash unit—that acts as a substitute ceiling, reflecting and diffusing the light.

Although commercial bounce cards are available, some photographers prefer to make their own from small sheets of stiff white paper or board. Sizes may vary—larger cards capture more light but are harder to carry. Photographers usually select one that will fit conveniently into their gadget bag. To make a bounce card, cut the card into a tapered rectangle that can be attached to the flash head with tape or a rubber band. Then score the card where it meets the top of the flash so that it can be bent to form any angle. (See Figure 13-9.)

Figure 13-9. Various types of commercial bounce cards.

Figure 13-10. A) PC extension cord. B) Dedicated hot-shoe extension cord.

Wireless Radio Slaves **Wireless radio slaves** use radio waves to create the ultimate synch cord. The camera's synch cord is connected to a small transmitter, similar to a garage door opener, and a small radio receiver is attached to the flash unit. The flash unit, as well as additional flash heads, may be placed wherever they are needed—in the ceiling above a basketball gymnasium, for example. The photographer is then free to roam without the bother of cumbersome connecting synch cords. When the camera's shutter is released, the transmitter sends a radio signal to trigger the strobes. (See Figure 13-11.)

Flash Slaves Like the radio transmitter, a **slave sensor** also can trigger a flash to fire without connecting wires. A slave sensor, however, responds to light rather than to radio waves. A slave sensor is simply a photoreceptive cell that connects to flash unit. Light from another flash, perhaps one mounted on a detached camera, triggers the slave to fire the secondary flash. Through this arrangement, two lights can be set up to provide a main frontal light and a side-mounted fill light, which are easily triggered simultaneously without connecting wires. Any number of slaves can be fired from a single main strobe; multiple lights over very large areas are possible.

Extension Cords A flash mounted to the camera is convenient, but the light it produces is not inspiring. Direct flash tends to eliminate distinguishing highlights and shadows and produces a very flat rendering of space and depth. Flash-on-camera also produces a shadow directly behind figures, making them appear like cardboard cutouts. **Extension cords** allow the flash to be removed from the camera and placed elsewhere to improve modeling and texture or to produce other dimensional effects. Most extension cords are simply long PC-synch cords that can be obtained at low cost. For cameras with dedicated or TTL flash, however, special dedicated hot-shoe extension cords are required. (See Figure 13-10.)

Slave sensors are relatively inexpensive and are no larger than a 35mm film canister. Many provide an integrated bracket for mounting the supplemental flash units on tripods or light stands. Some small, inexpensive flash units are even designed with built-in slave cells. These may be battery-powered for use anywhere; others are AC-powered. Some are designed with a screw-in lamp base for use in any convenient lamp fixture to simulate existing room light.

Slaves are an effective way to supplement the relatively weak flash units built into many cam-

Figure 13-11. A) Camera equipped with radio slave transmitter to signal remote flash unit. B) Electronic flash power pack equipped with a radio slave receiver to trigger flash upon receiving signal from radio flash transmitter located at camera position.

eras, allowing flash photography at greater distances. Figure 13-25 shows a typical use of flash slaves.

Light Stands and Reflectors Taking the flash unit off the camera allows the photographer to control the light and shadow effects that give shape and form to subjects. Fine-tuning the lighting effect requires careful light placement. **Light stands** are designed to hold a flash unit in the right place at the right angle. An ideal light stand should be small enough to fit into a gadget bag, yet extendable to great heights; it should weigh little, but be strong enough to support a flash unit and umbrella. Although all of these features may not be found in one light stand, they should guide the photographer in considering which model to purchase.

The quality of illumination from a flash can be varied through the use of **reflectors**. For example, a broader and more flattering portrait light may be obtained by bouncing the flash off an **umbrella-style** reflector. Similarly, a tubular-shaped **snoot** may be used with the flash to spotlight certain features or accent certain objects. A variety of reflectors and panels may be purchased, or they may be fabricated from common household materials such as aluminum foil and sheets of matte board.

Filters and Gels Colored **filter** sheets, sometimes called **gels**, may be placed over a flash unit to produce special effects. A red gel, for example, might be used on a flash to obtain a special effect in a portrait. Coloring the subject red would produce an unreal effect and perhaps add a dramatic quality. Sometimes fill-in flash is filtered in this way for special effects or to enhance separation. When fill-in flash is filtered, the foreground subject receives colored light from the flash, whereas the background retains normal coloration from the sunlight. Thus, color may be used to create a dramatic separation between the subject and the background.

Flash gels in many photographic colors are available for purchase, but any colored, transparent acetate or plastic sheet, such as a transparent report cover, also can be used. When gels are used with non-automatic flash units, exposure must be adjusted to compensate for the reduced light. In general, yellow gels require one stop greater aperture; red, green, or blue filters require two stops. Bracketing exposures is recommended.

One additional gel technique deserves special mention: filtering the flash light to match the color temperature of the available light. Photojournalists and industrial photographers who shoot in warehouses, schools, offices, stores and other areas under fluorescent lighting have developed a special technique for this purpose. They place a green gel (about a CC30G) over the strobe so that the flash light will match the color of the fluorescent light. A complementary magenta filter (CC30M or FLD) is mounted on the camera lens to rectify the color balance, or on digital cameras the white balance is set for fluorescent light. In this way, strobe can be used as fill or kicker illumination, and it will balance with the fluorescent lights. The technique is often adapted to match the color temperature of other light sources by varying the camera and flash filters used.

External Power Packs The batteries in portable flash units often are not large enough to power an extended shoot and still give acceptably short recycle times. For this reason, some professionals choose to connect their flash units to large **external battery packs** that permit extended use. These high-capacity battery packs are connected to the flash unit by an accessory power cord, but the pack itself is typically worn on the photographer's belt or hung from a carrying strap. The packs often contain rechargeable batteries that can provide as many as 2,000 flashes with 1- to 4-sec. recycle times before needing recharge. See Figure 13-12 for an example.

Determining Flash Exposure Settings

Objective 13-B Given shooting conditions, determine appropriate flash exposure settings for manual, automatic, dedicated, and TTL flash photography.

Key Concepts flash-to-subject distance, inverse square law, reflectance, built-in flash, automatic electronic flash, sufficient light indicator, dedicated electronic flash, flash meter, manual flash, guide number

Variables Affecting Exposure with Flash

The intensity of light reflected from the subject and its duration determine exposure. Unless spe-

Figure 13-12. Most flash units can be fitted with an external battery pack. Such devices provide shorter recycling times and more flashes per charge than conventional batteries.

cial flash metering equipment is used, the intensity of the flash cannot be measured, and the amount of light that will be reflected from the subject must be estimated. The variables that will affect the exposure settings are flash output, film speed or digital equivalent, flash-to-subject distance, environmental reflectance, and type of reflector.

Flash Unit Output A major but relatively constant factor that affects exposure is the flash output. Various electronic flash units produce different intensities of light. The output of the flash unit will affect the amount of light reflected from the subject and, consequently, the amount of exposure needed. However, since the flash unit is seldom changed, that factor will remain relatively constant once it is determined.

The light output of the flash, as measured by the manufacturer, usually does not accurately reflect the actual output experienced in the field. Flash output under actual working conditions is often one-half to one stop less than the manufacturer's specifications.

Film Speed Of course, the speed of the film, or digital camera equivalent, will affect exposure. Faster film will require less exposure than slower film, and vice versa, for any given intensity of illumination. As with the flash unit itself, however, the film is not likely to change once the roll is in the camera, and so that factor will remain relatively constant during a shooting session.

Flash-to-subject Distance The main variable factor in determining flash exposure with non-automatic units is the **flash-to-subject distance**, which may change considerably from shot to shot and affect exposure profoundly.

The **inverse square law**, discussed on page 401, states that the amount of light falling on a subject varies inversely as the square of the distance between the light source and the subject. This means that as the flash-to-subject distance is doubled—from eleven to twenty-two feet, for example—the intensity of light falling on the subject from the same flash unit is reduced by a factor of four. A two-stop increase in exposure would be needed to compensate. Moving the flash closer to the subject—from eleven to eight feet, for example—would double the intensity of light falling on the subject, and so require a corresponding one-stop reduction in exposure.

Environmental Reflectance The **reflectance** of objects and surfaces in the surrounding environment also affects the amount of illumination reflected from the scene to the camera. A room with glossy, white walls and ceiling will reflect more of the light from the flash unit onto the subject and back to the camera than will a room with flat, dark-colored walls and ceiling. Shiny, light objects also will reflect more light back to the camera than will dull, dark objects. As the camera is moved from one location to another, the surface textures and coloration of the space might affect exposure profoundly.

Method 1: Automatic Calculation

Three basic methods may be used to determine flash exposure: automatic calculation, flash metering, and manual calculation; we will discuss automatic calculation first. Note that the camera's conventional light meter is *not* used to determine the camera settings for flash photographs.

In general, three types of units provide for automatic calculation of flash exposure: (1) Small built-in or pop-up flash units, (2) automatic electronic flash designed for use with any adjustable camera, and (3) dedicated or TTL electronic flash designed for use with a particular adjustable camera.

Built-in flash units operate without any input from the user. Most pop up or turn themselves on automatically and allow no override controls. They are foolproof to operate, but limited in scope.

Automatic electronic flash units have built-in automatic controls that determine the amount of light that is produced to make the flash exposure. To ready a camera for this type of flash unit, first set the camera's shutter speed to one of the speeds allowable for X-synchronization. Next, set the flash unit's calculator to the ISO speed in use. Finally, reading from the calculator, set the camera's aperture to that recommended for the desired automatic operating range. The flash unit will then control exposure by controlling light output.

A built-in sensor, similar to the photosensitive cell in a light meter, measures the light reflected from the subject. When the flash unit's integrated computer determines that the light is sufficient for proper exposure, it triggers a quenching circuit to terminate the flash. Once they are set, the exposure controls need not be reset as the camera is moved closer to the subject or farther away as long as the shot is made from within the limits of the selected operating range. The quenching circuit adjusts exposure automatically. On more powerful units the user has a choice of several different color-coded ranges that cover situations from close-ups to long distances. (See Figure 13-13.)

Many automatic electronic flash units have a built-in **sufficient light indicator** that signals if the flash exposure was adequate. The flash exposure can be checked before a picture is taken by pressing the unit's open flash or test button and then reading the sufficient light indicator.

Dedicated Flash Units A **dedicated electronic flash** is linked electronically through its hot shoe to the camera for which it is designed. The flash is automatically coupled with the camera, and the system then responds by adjusting exposure for flash pictures. Dedicated flash units vary considerably with the type of camera and the design of the unit. Most automatically choose the proper shutter speed and lens opening for flash; others even adjust the angle of illumination to match the lens in use. (See Figure 13-14.)

Highly automated cameras adjust most of the initial settings automatically when the dedicated flash

Figure 13-13. An automatic flash calculator dial. Various maximum distance ranges can be selected by a color-coded dial. When the camera is set at the corresponding lens opening, the flash will automatically vary its light output for proper exposure.

unit is connected to the hot shoe. Less sophisticated cameras may require the photographer to manually set both the camera and flash unit for automatic operation and for the ISO film or digital sensor, speed in use. Most units usually must be set for the desired operating range as well. Once these initial settings are established, these units will then set the shutter to the speed required for electronic flash and the aperture to the setting that is appropriate for the selected range. As with other automatic units, the flash usually controls its light output to provide proper exposure. Some units, however, may provide a constant light output and adjust the camera aperture instead as the camera is focused on nearer or farther objects.

TTL Dedicated Flash Some dedicated flash units use sensors *inside* the camera to measure the flash intensity *through the lens* (TTL). With computerized control, these units analyze the amount of light that enters the camera and quench the flash when sufficient light has been received. With great accuracy, these units assure proper exposure no matter what lens or filter is used or in what direction the flash is pointed. A TTL dedicated flash also automates otherwise complex fill-in flash operations. When used for fill-in flash, the camera and flash simultaneously set the shutter speed, lens opening, and flash output to provide a balanced correct exposure for the subject and the background. Without the integrated performance of a dedicated flash system, fill-in flash tends to be an intimidating, complicated operation.

If the hot-shoe connector of a dedicated flash unit is examined, additional pins that correspond to contacts on the camera's hot shoe can be seen. These additional connections form the electronic linkage through which the unit manipulates the camera's exposure controls. Although a dedicated electronic flash unit can be used in a manual mode at full output with any adjustable camera, it will operate automatically only when used with its dedicated camera.

Automatic Flash Exposure Problems Automatic flash is not without its drawbacks. Very light or very dark backgrounds can fool the unit into under- or overexposing the subject. To avoid these effects, analyze the scene beforehand to determine whether conditions warrant an adjustment. With automatic flash, the aperture can

Figure 13-14. Dedicated hot shoe contact.

then be adjusted to provide more or less exposure than the calculator indicates. With any form of automatic flash, however, switching over to manual operation and calculating a proper exposure can obtain precise and correct exposure. (See Figure 13-15.)

Method 2: Flash Metering

The second method for determining flash exposure is flash metering. Because a normal light meter cannot usefully measure the brief, intense flash of light from a flash unit, a specially designed **flash meter** must be used instead. Flash meters are designed to integrate both the intensity of the light and its duration so as to record the total light energy that will be available to the picture. The meter is normally held at the subject with its light-receptive dome facing the camera. The flash is then triggered and a measurement is made. Following the flash, the meter displays the correct exposure as a recommended aperture setting. The camera lens is then generally set to this recommended aperture.

Flash meters are available in several designs. Most can serve as conventional light meters in addition to providing their flash function. Some read incident light, some reflected light, and some the light at the film plane. The more advanced flash meters can be used several ways and may also feature spot attachments. (See Figure 13-16.)

Method 3: Manual Calculation

The third means of determining flash exposure is through manual calculation. For manual electronic flash, exposure must be determined by metering or by manual calculation, and the camera must be set by hand. The more advanced automatic and dedicated electronic flash units usually also can be set for manual operation by disabling their automatic features. This is desirable because in some situations the exposures determined automatically will not produce the effect the photographer wants. By selecting manual operation, the photographer gains greater control over the flash exposure and the resulting image.

One way to manually calculate flash exposure is to use a flash exposure calculator. Most **manual electronic flash** units have a built-in calculator dial into which is entered (1) the desired flash output, (2) the ISO film or digital sensor speed, and (3) the flash-to-subject distance. Similar calculators are also published in photographic data books. The calculator indicates an appropriate exposure in an environment of average reflectance. (See Figure 13-17.)

Another method for determining flash exposure involves the use of **guide numbers**. The guide numbers for a flash unit are usually given in the flash unit's manual. Electronic flash output is rated in beam candle-power seconds (BCPS).

A.

B.

C.

D.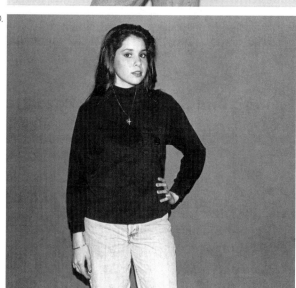

Figure 13-15. Subject failure. A) When presented with a predominantly light colored subject, most automatic flash units tend to underexpose the scene. B) To achieve a correct tonal rendering, open up the camera's lens by 1–2 stops and bracket exposures. C) The opposite exposure problem will occur with predominantly dark colored subjects. Here the automatic flash overexposed the scene. D) To correct this error, close down the lens 1–2 stops and bracket exposures.

Table 13-1 shows a typical guide number table for ISO 125/22° film and digital materials. To determine exposure, divide the guide number by the flash-to-subject distance.

guide number / flash-to-subject distance = f-stop

For example, if your guide number were 56 and the flash-to-subject distance were 10 feet, then a proper f-stop would be 56/10 = 5.6.

Both flash calculator dials and guide numbers are intended as aids. The recommended settings may need to be adjusted to suit specific conditions. If

Table 13-1. Typical guide numbers for electronic flash for ISO 125/22°									
Output of Unit in BCPS	350	500	700	1000	1400	2000	2800	4000	5600	8000
Guide Number	45	55	65	80	95	110	130	160	190	220

A.

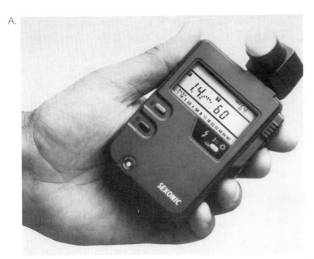

B.

Figure 13-16. Flash metering. A) Flash meter reads out proper f-stop in response to test flash. B) Incident flash meter directed toward camera from subject position and flash test-fired.

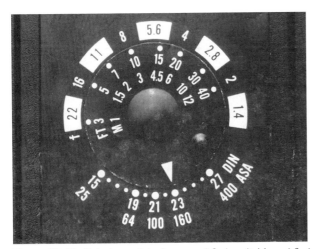

Figure 13-17. Calculator dial of a manual flash unit. Manual flash units require changes to the lens opening whenever the flash to subject changes. For example, with this flash unit set for ISO 160 film, a photograph taken at ten feet would require a lens aperture of f/8. If the photographer backed up to a distance of twenty feet, the aperture would need to be set to f/4.

the final pictures are consistently overexposed, a film speed higher than the film's rated ISO index should be consistently used; if underexposed, a lower film speed should be used. In small rooms with light-colored walls, the aperture should be stopped down one stop; in large, dark rooms, opened up one stop.

Flash Techniques

Objective 13-C Explain and demonstrate several techniques for using flash for lighting a subject, and explain their purposes.

Key Concepts flash-on-camera, red-eye, bounce flash, bounce card, flash-off-camera, reflector card, kicker, open flash, painting with light, stroboscopic, fill-in flash, synchro-sunlight flash, lighting ratio, flash and slash, extension flash

The general principles of photographic lighting discussed in Unit 12 also apply to flash photography. The principle of the single dominant light source applies, as well as the principle of filling in the shadows with some form of diffuse lighting to record shadow details. Accents to rim the edges of the subject, to help reveal its shape and contour, and to separate it from the background are also desirable, as is background lighting.

To achieve these accents with flash may be a bit more difficult only because the effects of lighting placement cannot always be observed in advance. For that reason, practice and experience with floodlights and spotlights provide invaluable knowledge when it comes to anticipating the effects that will result.

Most flash photography is carried out with a single flash unit. Let us first consider some of the techniques for using a single flash unit to provide the key, fill, background, and accent lighting that we consider desirable.

Flash-On-Camera

In most situations a single flash unit mounted on the camera close to the camera-subject axis will be the simplest, most straightforward approach. (See Figure 13-18.)

Figure 13-18. Electronic flash on camera.

This **flash-on-camera** technique is convenient and adequate for many subjects. With flash-on-camera, the flash-to-subject distance is the same as the camera-to-subject distance and can usually be read directly off the camera's focusing scale. This is convenient if a manual flash unit is being used.

Flash-on-camera has several disadvantages, however. As a key-lighting position, it produces a flat, frontal illumination, devoid of the shadows needed for modeling and texture. It tends also to produce bounce-back reflections from shiny walls and objects, and, if the subject is close to the background, it may also produce an unsightly shadow just behind the subject. With color film and digital materials, flash-on-camera sometimes produces an undesirable effect called **red-eye**, in which luminous red spots appear in the center of a subject's eyes.

Bounce Flash

If a flash unit has a swivel head or can be removed from the camera and aimed upward, some of the hazards of flash-on-camera can be avoided by tipping the flash head toward a wall or ceiling and bouncing the light toward the subject. This method is called **bounce flash**, and it provides a soft key-light effect. Some of the light also bounces among other room surfaces before it reaches the subject. This light travels farther and is diffused even more, thus providing fill light from many other directions from a single flash unit mounted on the camera. In very large rooms with high ceilings, in open areas, or in places where the color of the walls or ceiling

may adversely affect the image, a similar effect may be obtained by bouncing the flash off a **bounce card**.

Bounce Flash with Automatic, Dedicated, and TTL Flash Bouncing with an automatic or dedicated flash unit will provide proper exposure as long as the sensor is directed at the subject. If the flash has a swivel head, a detachable eye, or uses TTL metering, the flash is simply directed toward a suitable ceiling or wall, whereas the sensor is directed toward the subject. For units that offer a choice of distance ranges, a range greater than the total distance the bounced light will travel should be selected. Preliminary test flashes are recommended for units equipped with a sufficient light indicator.

If a flash unit is not provided with a swivel head or removable sensor, it must be used in a manual mode rather than automatic mode.

Bounce Exposure with Manual Flash To calculate correct bounce flash exposure with a manual flash unit, figure the flash-to-subject distance as the total distance the key light travels from the flash to the reflecting surface and then to the subject. (See Figures 13-19 and 13-20.) This distance may be used with the guide number or calculator dial in the usual way. The indicated aperture should then be opened one or two stops to com-

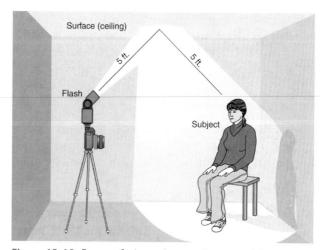

Figure 13-19. Bounce flash produces a pleasant soft lighting but manual exposures can be tricky to calculate. Measure the total distance light travels from flash to the reflecting surface and then back to the subject. Then open up 1–2 stops from the calculated exposure to compensate for light absorbed by the reflecting surface. Most automatic flash units have tilting heads and will automatically calculate correct bounce flash exposure.

Figure 13-20. Bare-bulb flash or bounce flash creates soft highlights and eliminates distracting shadows.

pensate for the additional absorption and diffusion. Further increases should be made for dark or highly textured walls and ceilings, and larger rooms. Bracketing exposures is recommended because the reflectance of ceilings and walls cannot be accurately predicted. Bounce exposure may be determined more accurately with a flash meter.

Wall Bounce Wall bounce is accomplished in exactly the same manner as ceiling bounce, except that the flash is directed at a wall rather than at a ceiling. The principles are the same, and the technique is used for similar purposes. Wall bounce is used to provide soft side lighting; it might be used, for example, to simulate window lighting in a portrait. Again, care should be taken to compensate for nonreflecting or colored walls and ceilings.

Wall bounce with automatic flash can be accomplished only if the flash sensor can be directed at the subject while the flash is directed at the wall. Flash units that lack this feature must be set for manual operation and used accordingly.

Wall bounce with manual flash is accomplished through the same procedures as ceiling bounce flash. The flash is directed toward the wall and the aperture is calculated by guide number or calculator dial, using the total light path distance as the flash-to-subject distance. Again, because walls are not perfect reflectors, the aperture should be opened one or two stops to compensate for lost light. Bracketing exposures is recommended for success.

Flash-Off-Camera

Flash-on-camera, although it is often more convenient, is not usually the most effective flash position. To place the flash unit in a more desirable key-light position, use a flash extension to remove the flash from the camera and use it in an off-camera position.

As we discussed in Unit 12, key lighting from above and to the side of the subject tends to produce the most natural set of highlights and shadows. Using a **flash-off-camera** technique, the flash unit can be held in one hand, high and to one side of the camera, while holding the camera in the other hand. If the camera is placed on a tripod the flash unit can be moved even farther to the side. By using the flash in this position, the modeling of the subject can be improved and textures revealed that add to the three-dimensional effect of the photograph. With a special clamp, the flash unit can be attached to any handy edge, such as a door or chair. Figure 13-21 shows two ways to place the flash unit in a flash-off-camera position.

Flash-off-camera, although it produces a dominant set of highlights and shadows that help to model the subject, does not by itself produce the additional fill light needed to illuminate detail in the shadows. The flash-off-camera technique tends to produce high-contrast prints with deep shadows, but several procedures can be used to enable a single flash unit to produce both key and fill lighting.

Fill Light with Reflectors One way to obtain both key and fill light from an off-camera flash is by using subject reflectors. In this case, the flash unit is held in a good key-light position. Then a **reflector card**, such as a piece of light cardboard, is placed on the fill side of the subject to reflect

A. B.

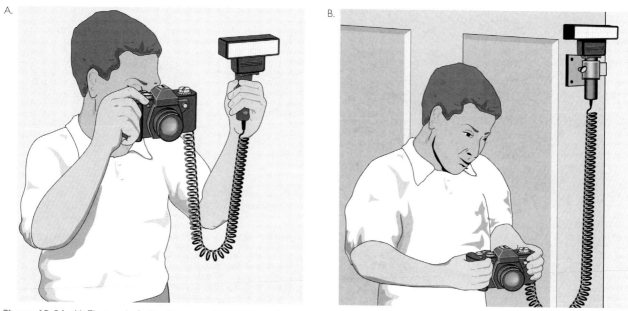

Figure 13-21. A) Electronic flash off-camera. Held high and to one side. B) Flash clamped high on edge of door.

light from the flash into the shadow areas. The same effect can be obtained by placing the subject close to a wall on the fill side. Figure 13-22 depicts the use of the subject reflector.

Bounce Flash Off Camera with Kicker Card
Another way to obtain both key and fill light is to use the bounce flash technique discussed earlier; except with a *small* bounce card attached to the flash. In this way, most of the light is directed toward the ceiling or wall to produce bounce light that serves as the key or main light. A small portion of the light, however, is reflected by the bounce card directly to the subject as a **kicker**. The effect of the kicker is to open up the shadows a bit and to place a visible catchlight in the eyes. If a small bounce card is not handy, three or four fingers may be cupped in front of the flash head for a similar effect.

With flash-off-camera, the bounce flash technique can be used even if the unit does not have a swivel head. Simply point the manual flash unit toward the ceiling or a wall to reflect its light toward the subject. When figuring flash-to-subject distance, be sure to include the entire distance the light travels from the flash unit to reach the subject. If the unit is automatic, be sure the sensor is pointed toward the subject from close to

the camera position. If the flash head and the sensor cannot be directed independently, set the flash unit to manual and calculate the exposure settings.

Flash Diffusion To obtain a soft, diffused key light with flash, use an accessory softbox or throw a clean, white handkerchief over the unit as a hood. Be sure the handkerchief does not block the sensor. Place the unit in a good key-light position off-camera. On automatic units, compensate for the light loss by selecting a longer range setting; on

Figure 13-22. Using subject reflector to fill with electronic flash.

manual units, calculate normal exposure and then increase the obtained aperture one or two stops.

Open Flash Technique One way of making a single flash unit perform as many units is to use the **open flash** method. This technique is useful when ambient light is very dim or absent and the subject is absolutely stationary. At night, or in a darkened room, open the shutter and allow it to stand open. Then carry the off-camera flash unit to several positions in succession, firing it in each location. With this technique, often called "**painting with light**," flash may be fired once from the key-light position, then again from a fill-light position, and a third time from behind to create rim accents. After firing the flash several times, go back and close the shutter.

The open flash technique can be used for night scenes if the distance between the flash unit and the camera is too great for a flash extension cord. Set up the camera and have a helper stand with the flash unit where the flash source is needed. Open the shutter and let it stand open as the helper fires the flash. When the flash has been fired, close the shutter.

Stroboscopic Results A variation of the open flash technique can be used to produce photographs of movement that have a **stroboscopic** or multiple-image effect. Using a black background or a dark, empty space at night, mount the camera on a tripod and open the shutter. Fire the flash repeatedly as quickly as it recycles while the subject slowly moves through an action. Each step of the action will be crisply recorded. If the separate recorded images do not overlap, normal flash exposure should be used; if they overlap significantly, normal flash exposure should be reduced.

Experimenting with Off-camera Flash As with studio spotlights and floodlights, one or more flash units can be used to enhance the subject and to simulate natural lighting sources. Photographers who experiment with off-camera flash in various positions generally are rewarded with more dynamic and dimensional images. High and low lighting angles as well as partial and full sidelighting can alter the modeling and texturing of the subject as well as place shadows to create more interesting and dramatic visual effects. A small flashlight taped onto the strobe head is a helpful tool for visualizing the effects that the flash will produce.

When placing off-camera flash units, consider unorthodox as well as conventional positions. Placing a flash unit outside a window directed toward the interior of a room can simulate sunlight or moonlight; in a fireplace, it can simulate the light from a fire; inside a lampshade, it can simulate an existing light source. Using slave units allows even more control over the placement, quality, and ambience of the light.

Fill-In Flash

Aside from its uses for providing a main source of illumination, the flash unit has another important use strictly as a fill light. As we have seen, pictures taken in bright sunlight tend to have high contrast. The highlights are brilliant, and the shadows are often deep. The range of brightness from highlights to deep shadows often exceeds the latitude of the film or digital sensor; the shadow detail may be lost if the exposure is based on the highlights. Nature does not automatically provide an ideal brightness ratio. In bright sunlight, unless appropriate steps are taken, the brightness ratio may far exceed the latitude of the recording medium.

One way to fill in the shadow areas in a sunlit scene is to use subject reflector cards—matte white or shiny pieces of cardboard—to reflect and diffuse the sunlight into the shadow side of the subject. By properly placing these reflectors, a more favorable brightness ratio between highlights and shadows can be achieved.

Another way to fill in these shadows is to use **fill-in flash**, sometimes called **synchro-sunlight flash**, to provide fill light outdoors in the bright sunlight. The trick is to provide flash illumination just strong enough to fill in the shadows without overpowering the main illumination provided by direct sunlight. This may be done by placing the flash unit at a proper distance from the subject or by reducing the brightness of the flash.

Although these fill-in flash techniques are most commonly used to fill in the shadows when shooting in bright sunlight, they also may be used in other available light situations to provide a more desirable balance between highlights and shadows.

Dedicated or TTL Fill-flash Using fill-in flash with most dedicated systems is automated—an internal computer chooses the ideal flash power, lens opening, and shutter speed to provide a bal-

Calculating Fill-In Flash

1. *Start by setting the shutter to synchronize properly with the flash unit. Then set the aperture properly for the sunlight scene as though flash were not to be used. Suppose that with the shutter set at 1/60 sec. the aperture is set at a meter-recommended f/16.*

2. *Using the calculator dial built into the flash unit, or the guide number system, find the normal distance opposite the f-stop to which the camera is set—in this case, f/16.*

   If the flash is placed at the normal distance, its exposure will exactly balance the brightness of the sunlit highlights—the brightness ratio will be 1 to 1. Although balanced, flat lighting of this kind may sometimes be desirable, the flash exposure should usually be reduced by one or two stops to obtain a greater brightness ratio.

3. *One way to reduce the flash exposure is to reduce the flash output to one-half or one-fourth. With manual flash, a thickness or two of white handkerchief can be placed over the flash head or, if the unit provides for it, the flash unit can be set to one-half or one-fourth power. With automatic units, the range settings can be adjusted to obtain one or two stops less than normal exposure. Check the unit's manual for the recommended method for doing this.*

4. *Another way to reduce the flash exposure with manual flash is to place the unit at a greater-than-normal distance from the subject. For example, if the flash calculator scale indicates that a flash-to-subject distance of 5 feet will exactly balance the sunlit highlights, doubling that distance to 10 feet would reduce the flash intensity to one-fourth the brightness of the sunlit highlights, producing a 4-to-1 brightness ratio. Intermediate distances may be selected to obtain intermediate brightness ratios. (If the camera is also moved to this distance, a proper focal length lens must then be used to obtain the desired framing of the subject.)*

anced fill light. Some dedicated systems even allow the user to select the desired **lighting ratio** between the highlights and shadows. Normally a 2-to-1 ratio between highlights and shadows is desirable for fill-in flash; the direct sun highlights should be twice as bright as the fill-in flash illumination. For a more dramatic effect, the ratio may be increased to accentuate the shadows; for a softer effect, the ratio may be decreased. Ratios from 4 to 1 to 1 1/2 to 1 are commonly used. If your flash system has an exposure value or EV setting use it to change the lighting ratio. EV-2 is equal to a 4-to-1 ratio; EV-1 yields a 2-to-1 ratio.

Fill-flash with Manual and Non-dedicated Flash Without a dedicated system, calculation is required. The objective is to provide fill-in flash to brighten otherwise dark shadows without overpowering the correct sunlight exposure. To do this, normal flash exposure must be reduced by one or two stops. (See Figure 13-23.)

Fill-flash Problems Manual fill-in flash with a focal plane shutter is especially difficult because the range of available X-synch shutter speeds is limited. Often the sun exposure will be too strong for the relatively slow synch speeds available. It may be necessary to use slower speed films and higher-powered flash units to obtain correct fill-in flash exposures under these conditions.

Manual fill-in flash is comparatively easy with between-the-lens shutters because electronic flash can be synched with any shutter speed. On such cameras both shutter speed and aperture can be set for proper sunlight exposure; thus, an equivalent exposure can be selected that will provide the correct aperture for fill-in flash.

Flash and Slash

A variation of fill-in flash combined with a slow shutter speed can produce a combination of blurred motion and sharp images. Dubbed "**flash and slash**" by photojournalists, the technique is often used in indoor available-light situations. The technique is similar to fill-in flash, except that the flash is set to overpower normal exposure by one or more stops, giving proper exposure to the flash light while simultaneously underexposing the ambient light. Slow shutter speeds of 1/8 sec. or longer are usual. When the shutter is released, the instantaneous flash forms a sharp subject image; the slower shutter continues to record a secondary

A.
B.

Figure 13-23. Achieving desired brightness ratio. A) Bright sunlight from side or behind produces excessive brightness ratio, obscuring details in shadow areas. B) Fill-in flash opens up shadow areas and keeps brightness ratio within film's latitude.

ambient light image. Any subject or camera movement during the slow ambient exposure blurs the secondary image. This technique is often effective for depicting motion and for visually separating a subject from its background. (See Figure 13-24 and page 429.)

Multiple-Unit Flash Technique

As we have seen, more than one source of light may be needed to create a desired lighting effect. A single flash used off-camera to improve modeling can create harsh shadows, for example, and although these shadows can be filled by using a reflector, sometimes added control can be obtained

Flash-and-Slash Technique

1. *Choose an ambient lighting situation that will allow shooting at 1/8 sec. or slower—outside at dusk or in a dimly lit room, for example.*

   If you have a TTL flash with a "slow synch" or "rear curtain" feature simply select that mode and you are ready to produce flash-and-slash pictures. With other models follow the remaining steps below.

2. *Set the aperture for a correct flash exposure.*

3. *Use the camera's light meter to determine a shutter speed that will give a one-stop underexposure for the ambient light. For example, adjust the shutter speed until the light meter needle points to the underexposure region. Set the shutter for this speed.*

4. *For more blur, select a slower shutter speed. The slower the shutter speed, the more blur will result from any subject or camera movement.*

Figure 13-24. The flash and slash technique can be used to provide a sense of motion.

Nondedicated Multiple Flash

This example will describe a typical three-light setup for an interior environmental portrait. It will require three small strobe units; two of them should be equipped with slave cells and mounted on light stands or clamps.

1. *Set all flashes to the manual mode. If used in an automatic setting, the sensors in each unit will respond erroneously to the light from all the units.*

2. *Select one stand-mounted flash to serve as the main or key light. Set it to one side of the camera at about a 45% angle to the subject. Raise it until its angle of incidence is also 45%. Use the strobe's calculator dial to figure an exposure based on the flash-to-subject distance. For this example, assume the main flash requires an exposure of f/16.*

3. *Mount a second flash on the camera as the fill light. To obtain a 2-to-1 lighting ratio, the fill light should be half as bright as the main light. (In this example, the output of the fill unit should give correct exposure at f/11.) There are several ways to achieve this:*

   a. *Dial in a lower power setting.*

   b. *Cover the flash head with a neutral density filter or layers of white handkerchief.*

   c. *Change the flash-to-subject distance.*

   d. *Use a bounce flash or bounce-card technique. This might be preferred when providing general room illumination for an environmental portrait.*

4. *Use a third stand-mounted flash and slave as a rim or separation light. Position it almost behind the subject on the side opposite the main light—on a very high or very low stand to prevent its direct light from striking the lens. Use a lens shade. As described above, adjust this unit to give a 2-to-1 brightness ratio—one stop less than the main light—in this example, f/11.*

5. *Check that the camera's shutter speed and synch setting are correct. Then set the aperture to correspond to the main flash unit—in this example, f/16. Test fire to verify that all three units are functioning before making any exposures.*

This setup may be modified to suit any expressive purpose. Various reflectors, bounce cards, snoots, and gels may be used to modify the results. For example, colored gels might be placed over separation lights to create colored rim accents with color photography. A flash meter, if available, can be used to eliminate exposure calculations and to make multiple-flash setups easier to arrange.

by using additional lighting units instead. Similarly, additional lighting units may be useful to illuminate a background, to provide edge accents, or to accomplish any of the other purposes discussed earlier in Unit 12, *Basic Lighting.*

Advanced dedicated cameras now allow two or more battery-powered portable electronic flash units to be used simultaneously. Often the secondary units are called **extension flash** units and are connected to the main unit and camera by multiple dedicated cords. In use, these units are placed to provide the necessary main, fill, accent, and background lighting. One or more units may be used for bounce light to provide soft overall illumination. The dedicated and computerized systems automatically calculate the required exposure.

Multiple flash with non-TTL or nondedicated systems requires more calculation. As above, several conventional battery-powered flash units are used; however, they need not be physically connected either to the camera or to each other. Using a light-sensitive slave cell that is triggered by the flash of the main unit may fire the units instead.

The photo-eye slave cell triggers the slaved flash unit instantaneously when light from the main unit strikes it. The slave units, together with their photo eyes, are generally mounted on light stands or clamped in the positions of fill, background, or accent lights. A portable, multiple-flash lighting system is no more complicated nor costly to assemble and operate than a comparable incandescent lighting system. (See Figure 13-25.)

A.

B.

C.

Figure 13-25. A) Three small flash units were used to create this environmental portrait of an artist in her studio. B) One flash was bounced off a card to provide fill light. Second and third slaved units were mounted on stands and positioned to provide a main light and a rim light. C) An overhead view of the lighting set-up. When the photographer trips the shutter, the camera-mounted flash fires the two slave units. For clarity, the bounce card was removed from the camera's flash for this overhead view.

Using Flash for Action

Objective 13-D Explain and demonstrate how flash can be used to stop fast action.

Key Concepts secondary image

As discussed in Unit 3, stopping fast action requires a very short exposure—usually a very fast shutter that will open and close before the image of the subject can move perceptibly across the image. The requirement for fast shutter speeds normally leads to large aperture settings to maintain proper equivalent exposure. Often, however, even with a large aperture the existing light may be insufficient to obtain the required shutter speed. Additional light and faster exposure may be achieved by using high-speed electronic flash.

Early on, photographers discovered that the bright, brief burst of an electric discharge could provide sufficient light for a short enough interval to stop fast action. Today, the electronic flash unit conveniently produces just such a short burst of intense light—from about 2 milliseconds to as short as 1/50,000 sec. for some automatic units. As long as the shutter is fully open at the moment of the flash, it is the burst of light, not the shutter, which generally determines the duration of exposure. (See Figure 13-26.)

Under bright lighting conditions, take care that the shutter setting is not too slow. Were an electronic flash with a 1/2-sec. shutter speed to be used to shoot a basketball player leaping into the air, the flash would record his image frozen in flight. But the ambient light would also record a blurry **sec-**

Figure 13-26. Stopping fast action with flash.

Famous Photographer

Dr. Harold E. Edgerton, "Drop of Milk," 1931.
© Harold & Esther Edgerton Foundation, 2001, courtesy of Palm Press, Inc.

Drop of Milk

Sir Charles Wheatstone had demonstrated the freezing of extremely fast movement by the abrupt discharge of an electric spark many years before the invention of photography. Even Fox Talbot had experimented with this phenomenon in 1851 to obtain a clear photograph of *The Times* attached to a rapidly spinning wheel exposed by an electric spark discharge of 1/100,000-sec. duration. It was not until Dr. Harold E. Edgerton's development of the stroboscope and related electronic flash equipment in the 1930s, however, that a truly practical method of high-speed, electronic photography became possible.

In his original experiments with the electronic discharge lamp, precursor of the modern electronic flash, Edgerton and his associates at the Massachusetts Institute of Technology demonstrated that previously "unstoppable" action could be stopped by an extremely short burst of intense light. Using bursts of light as short as 1/1,000,000 sec., Edgerton was able to freeze successfully the piercing of an apple by a bullet in flight, the collapse of a bursting balloon, the wings of a flying hummingbird, and the shattering glass of a milk bottle struck with a hammer.

In this photograph of a drop of milk falling onto a plate that was covered with a thin layer of milk, he produced a photograph of unusual beauty showing the crownlike coronet, rimmed with pearllike droplets created by the instantaneous impact. When this photograph was published in 1931 it made an enchanted public aware of the invisible worlds that lay just beyond the realm of natural sight.

During World War II, Edgerton developed this technology into an effective system of night aerial reconnaissance, a system that was used the night before the D-Day Allied invasion of Normandy. Further applying this technology to high-speed, multiple-exposure photography, Edgerton and other scientists explored the movement patterns of such rapidly moving objects and processes as ballet dancers, sports and games, nature studies, explosions, and disturbed air currents—carrying forward the work started by Eadweard Muybridge nearly a half-century earlier. (See Famous Photograph, Unit 4, page 138.)

ondary image while the shutter was opening and closing at 1/2 sec. (See Figure 13-27.) To avoid these secondary images, set the shutter to its highest synch speed. One way to overcome secondary images when using a focal plane shutter is to reduce general illumination on the scene by turning out some of the room lights. Another way is to use slower film or digital film speed settings and higher intensity flash. Alternatively, a controlled secondary image may be deliberately introduced by using the flash-and-slash and/or rear curtain synch technique to obtain an almost cinematic motion effect.

The use of flash to stop action has a fringe benefit, too. Because of the rapid falloff of light intensity over distance, a foreground subject is lighted more intensely than its background. The farther away the background is, the darker it will appear. Thus, when a flash is used as the main light source for an indoor action shot or outdoors at night, the subject/ground contrast in the print will be increased and the subject will be shown against a dark background.

Common Flash Problems

Objective 13-E Name the common problems encountered with flash photography, and give methods for correcting them.

Key Concepts red-eye, secondary images, uneven coverage, near objects brighter than far objects, flash reflection, distracting shadows, empty shadows, partial exposure

With experience, the photographer can develop an ability to predict the effects of flash. Until enough experience is gained, however, the effects are often difficult to predict. Highlights and shadows are not evident in the available light. Improper exposure and unwanted effects may not be discovered until long after the picture opportunity has passed. Some of the flash problems that occur most often are discussed in this section, along with their solutions.

Red-Eye

In color photography, light from the flash may sometimes enter the subject's pupils and be reflected from the retinas, causing luminous red spots to appear in the subject's eyes. This effect, called **red-eye**, is caused by placing the flash unit too close to the camera's lens axis, as when the flash unit is mounted to the top of the camera or when a built-in flash unit is used. Red-eye is especially common in photographs made with compact digital cameras because the flash unit is so very close to the lens.

Figure 13-27. Secondary images with moving subject shot with flash under bright available lighting and slow shutter.

To avoid red-eye, move the flash unit farther from the lens by using the flash-off-camera technique or by mounting the unit on an extender that removes it at least 5 inches from the lens. Another solution is to photograph subjects when they are looking slightly away from the camera. Some modern cameras with built-in flash feature a red-eye mode or preflash system that releases one or more flash bursts an instant before the exposure. This has the effect of contracting the subject's pupils just prior to the flash exposure, thus reducing the effect of red-eye.

Secondary Images

When an electronic flash is used with a slow shutter speed under bright available light, the available light may record a blurry **secondary image** in addition to the image recorded by the electronic flash. Secondary images can occur whenever a slow shutter speed is used with electronic flash, but they tend to occur more often with cameras equipped with focal plane shutters because a slower shutter is usually required. (See Figure 13-27.)

To avoid secondary images, reduce the brightness of the available light if possible. If not, try timing the action shots to record peak action, when the subject is nearly motionless. If a leaf shutter is in use, shoot at a shutter speed fast enough to stop the action even without flash. For focal plane shutters switch to slower film speeds and higher output flash.

Uneven Coverage

If a wide-angle lens is used with a flash unit, the center of the resulting image may be properly exposed, whereas the edges may be underexposed. **Uneven coverage** such as this occurs when the lens's angle of view is greater than the unit's angle of illumination.

Most flash units are designed to match a normal lens's angle of view when used in the normal way. Switching to a shorter focal length lens without making a corresponding adjustment to the flash will produce uneven coverage. To avoid this effect, use the wide-angle adjustment recommended for the flash unit. If the unit lacks such an attachment, place a thickness or two of white handkerchief over the flash unit to diffuse the light over a greater area. Note that this technique reduces the range of automatic units and requires an exposure increase with manual units.

If the lens's angle of view is greater than the flash can handle, bounce flash technique may be used to spread and diffuse the flash or open flash may be used to "paint" the scene with more than one flash. (See Figure 13-28.)

Near Objects Brighter Than Far Objects

Sometimes, with direct flash, nearby objects are overexposed, middle-distance objects are correctly exposed, and more distant objects are underex-

Figure 13-28. Flash units may produce uneven light coverage when used with a wide-angle camera lens. The light fall-off and darkening of the corners can be avoided by placing a sheet of diffusing material or special wide-angle attachment over the flash head.

posed. According to the inverse square law, discussed in Unit 12, *Basic Lighting,* light intensity diminishes over distance. This means that the brightness of objects is determined by their distance from the light source—**near objects are brighter than far objects**.

The inverse square law is a basic law of physics and cannot be changed. Some techniques can be used, however, to avoid foregrounds that are too bright and backgrounds that are too dark. One direct solution is to select a camera angle that places subjects equally distant from the flash. If this is not feasible, another solution is to use bounce flash to diffuse the light to provide more even coverage. A further solution is to place multiple flash units at various subject depths to balance the illumination. (See Figure 13-29.)

Flash Reflection

Sometimes a finished print or slide shows a pronounced bright spot in its center, bright enough to obscure the details within it. This is often caused by shooting perpendicular to a shiny or light surface, so that light from the flash is reflected from the surface directly back into the lens.

Flash reflections of this kind can be avoided by facing blank walls or flat surfaces at an angle, rather than head-on. Mirrors especially should be avoided—if the flash unit can be seen in the mirror, its picture will be taken as it fires. The correction is simple. Change position so that the flash will strike such surfaces at an angle—45 % if possible. Then the flash reflection will be thrown off in another direction and will not bounce back into the taking lens. (See Figure 13-30 A.)

Another source of unsightly flash reflection is eyeglasses worn by subjects. Many a portrait of a bespectacled subject has been ruined by flash reflections from the surface of the glasses. If a subject is wearing glasses, shoot at an angle to the glasses, have the subject turn slightly off-camera, or have the subject tip the glasses slightly downward to direct reflections away from the camera.

Distracting Shadows

When a subject is placed too close to a background and the flash is positioned at an angle, a **distracting shadow** of the subject may appear on the background in the final print.

Shadows of this sort can be predicted easily—flash always casts a shadow. The trick is to anticipate where the shadow will fall. By sighting along a line between the flash and the subject, where

A.

B.

Figure 13-29. Flash fall-off. A) Subjects close to the camera are overexposed by direct flash while objects at a distance receive insufficient light and appear too dark. B) Bounce flash provides a more uniform and natural field of light over a wide range of subject distances.

the shadow will fall can be predicted and steps taken to avoid its appearance in the final print.

Shadows can be positioned harmlessly out of the frame by either moving the subject away from the background or moving the flash unit to another position. Place a subject at least several feet from the background. The subject's shadow will fall out of the camera's view, and the background will be close enough so that it will not be underexposed. Otherwise, try moving the flash unit to a higher or wider angle so that the shadow falls out of the picture's frame. (See Figure 13-30B.)

Empty Shadows

If the highlights of a print are well defined, but the shadow areas are deep black and devoid of detail, it is likely that the brightness ratio exceeded the latitude of the film or digital sensor.

Empty shadows are likely to occur when the flash unit is placed at too extreme an angle to the subject without fill light provided for the shadows. The shadow areas can be filled by using subject reflectors placed opposite the flash unit, by using multiple flash technique to provide illumination to the shadows, or by using bounce flash.

Partial Exposure

Occasionally, only part of an image is properly exposed, whereas the rest is not exposed at all, as if a mask had been placed over part of the picture. **Partial exposure** of this kind occurs when electronic flash is used with a focal plane shutter set at an excessive shutter speed. The flash fires when the shutter is only partially open, causing a portion of the image to remain underexposed. (See Figure 13-8, page 435.)

To avoid this effect, be sure to set the shutter speed correctly to synchronize with the flash. Leaf shutters can be used at all speeds with electronic flash, but focal plane shutters generally are limited to somewhat slower speeds. The maximum shutter speed for electronic flash is generally marked on the camera or stated in the owner's manual.

Flash Maintenance and Safety Recommendations

Objective 13-F List several maintenance and safety recommendations for handling flash equipment.

Key Concepts alkaline batteries, nickel-cadmium or nickel-metal-hydride batteries, zinc-carbon batteries

The following list describes the most sensible procedures to follow when using flash equipment.

1. Keep the electrical contacts on the flash batteries and in the camera and flash unit clean.

A.

B.

Figure 13-30. Flash problems. A) Flash-on-camera shot directly at reflective surfaces produces hot spots and reflections. Slight angle would have directed reflected light away from camera. B) With flash-off-camera a subject too close to a background will produce distracting shadows. Correct by moving subject away from background.

Use a rough cloth or a pencil eraser to clean them periodically.

2. Be sure the photoflash batteries are fresh. **Alkaline batteries** are generally recommended for long life and short recovery time. However, if the manufacturer's recommendations are different, they should be followed.

3. If a flash unit is to be stored for long periods of time, remove the batteries to avoid corrosion and damage.

4. Rechargeable **nickel-cadmium** or **nickel-metal-hydride** batteries are an economical alternative to conventional batteries. They may be used with most flash units, and because they require fewer replacements, their use is ecologically more friendly. Rechargeable batteries give quicker recycle times but fewer flashes per charge than alkaline batteries. Consult the owner's manual for details.

5. Never attempt to recharge conventional alkaline or **zinc-carbon batteries**. Use only special rechargeable batteries and a correctly matched charger.

6. Always turn the unit off and aim it away from yourself while connecting or disconnecting it. Several conditions may cause the unit to fire during connection and disconnection.

7. Never use flash in an explosive atmosphere. Never use flash equipment where there are volatile fumes, such as natural gas or gasoline. Exercise caution when using electronic flash around swimming pools and bathtubs.

8. When multiple flash units are used, position any connecting cords carefully out the way. Tape long connecting cords securely to the floor to prevent anyone from tripping over them during the shoot.

Questions to Consider

1. Describe the ways that flash can be used to stop motion in a frozen moment or to capture the expressive gesture of an action.

2. Find two flash photographs by Annie Leibovitz, two by W. Eugene Smith, and two by Weegee. Describe the flash techniques of these three photographers, and discuss how their use of flash affected the content and visual qualities of their photographs.

3. Examine a current issue of a large metropolitan newspaper. Which photographs were made with flash? How can you tell? What specific flash techniques were used?

4. Describe several ways of using bounce flash with your camera and flash. How do you determine exposure?

Suggested Field and Laboratory Assignments

1. Arrange for the use of an electronic flash unit for your camera. Mount the unit to the camera. Practice setting the unit, shutter, and aperture for subjects at various distances from the flash.

2. Make bounce cards for your flash out of pieces of white cardboard or the equivalent. Make a series of test photographs with a small card, about 5 x 7 in., and with a very large card, about 11 x 14 in. What are the visible differences in the final photographs?

3. Shoot a roll of film or several digital photos using your flash unit. Include at least one example of each of the following. Keep a shooting log describing the technique used, why it was used, what type of flash was used, and exposure data.

    a. Flash-on-camera

    b. Flash-off-camera: flash held in good key-light position

    c. Flash-off-camera: bounce flash

    d. Stop rapid action indoors

    e. Flash-and-slash

    f. Fill-in flash with strong backlight

    g. Fill-in flash with strong sidelight

Subjects and Approaches

Samantha Lawrie, "Study of a shadow becoming an arrow"

Unit at a Glance	Certain subjects have always captured the interest of artists and photographers. When we look at the subjects that continue to fascinate us, we discover that certain themes recur repeatedly, not only in photography, but in painting, graphic arts, sculpture, and other forms of artistic expression. This unit briefly introduces a few of these subjects and discusses how to approach them through photography. We'll examine the principles that can help you make interesting and expressive photographs of scenery, architecture, still life, people, action, human interest, and contemporary events.

Scenery

Objective 14-A Describe some of the principles and techniques of scenic photography.

Key Concepts grand view, intimate view, haze, contrast, actinic light, foreground detail, flat lighting, cross-lighting, backlighting

A visit to a national park, beach, resort, desert, or mountains offers spectacular scenery that virtually begs to be interpreted by a photographer. Photographs of such vast scenic grandeur often fail to measure up to the glorious scenes that inspired them. The endless, breathtaking space has been shrunk into the small borders of a print. A magnifying glass is needed even to see the great distant mountain ranges. The fields of brilliant flowers have merged with the surrounding foliage into a pallid gray mass. It is easy to see why scenic photography poses such a challenge to photographers and provides a lifetime of study for many.

Many factors affect the making of a scenic photograph. As the sun moves across the sky or passes behind a cloud, the lighting continually changes. In spring, summer, winter, or fall, in rain, snow, or sun, each change of season or weather alters the landscape. Add to these factors the myriad of possible viewpoints, moods, land formations, vegetation, and living creatures, and it is apparent that the picture possibilities in even a single landscape are virtually limitless.

As with other types of photography, scenic photography requires first that one learn to see—to study the subject and to visualize the final result. Next, one must learn to execute—to perform the operations necessary to achieve what has been visualized.

As breathtaking as it may seem, the natural landscape is not organized into a two-dimensional frame. Unlike the actual scenery, which has no boundaries and extends off into space in all directions, the scenic photograph is fixed in a single point of view through precisely defined borders at the top, bottom, and sides. Visualizing the landscape within the two-dimensional format of the final print is one of the photographer's major tasks. Because of these limiting edges, successful scenic photography involves deciding carefully what features will appear within them, what features will not appear, and what features will be emphasized.

To make these decisions, it helps to understand what it is about the scene that motivates the photograph. Why is the picture being made in the first place? Is it the way the sunlight filters through the trees that inspires the photograph? Or the awesome height of the cliff face nearby? Or the primitive wariness of the feeding buck? Sound compositional decisions follow naturally when the purpose is clear. Visualize the final result before shooting the picture, and be wary of trying to include too much within the limiting borders of the frame.

Scenic photographs tend to be interesting if a principal feature in the scene is emphasized—one or more animals, a landform, an arrangement of flora. Using the viewfinder as a basic tool allows the photographer to explore the scenic relationships within the top, bottom, and side boundaries of the frame. If the intended center of interest is obscured or dominated by other elements in the frame, the camera can be moved to a different position, or the focal length or depth of field can be changed. By these means, the composition can be altered in the viewfinder until the principal feature of interest is properly related to the rest of the scene.

A vast landscape encompassing miles of space is sometimes termed a **grand view**; a narrow scene measured in yards, an **intimate view**. Whatever the view, the photographer's usual purpose is to convey the character, the mood, and the feeling of the place in a unique visual form rather than to make a simple record. Generally, the photographer hopes to stir the viewer to experience the ideas and feelings that motivated the photograph in the first place. Scenic photographs tend to be more successful if they attempt to reach beyond the mere record to tell the story of a place.

The camera favored by professional landscape photographers has traditionally been the large-format view camera. Bulky and cumbersome though it may be, especially when trudging through the forests or clambering up rocky cliffs, it provides control over the image unmatched by more convenient cameras. Mounted to a tripod, the view camera affords the photographer a studied view of the image on its large, clear ground-glass screen. Its adjustable swings and tilts provide perspective and focus controls for shaping and locating the image to the photographer's vision. And the large-format negative plate provides a medium for representing details in the final image with utmost clarity and precision.

The ubiquitous 35mm camera also serves as a popular tool for landscape photography. The SLR camera is particularly well suited to the physical trials of landscape work. In addition, the SLR camera equipped with a *perspective-control (P-C) lens* provides many of the viewing advantages as well as the perspective and focus controls offered by view cameras. Certainly, the 35mm approach to landscape photography provides an advantage when it comes to spontaneity.

High-resolution digital cameras are increasingly popular tools for landscape photography as they offer immediate review of just-taken shots and the power of image-processing software to modify the image as needed. Colors can be enhanced, modified, or even eliminated from the digital image file to create black-and-white photographs. Additionally many image-processing software programs offer a way to stitch together several shots to make up a single wide-format panorama of a grand vista.

The Grand View

To capture the expanse of a grand view, the photographer will often want to emphasize the elements of distance, such as atmospheric haze, tone and contrast, foreground detail, lighting, and depth of field.

Often a grand view contains natural **haze** because of the distance involved. To eliminate haze in black-and-white photographs so that distant details appear clearer, a haze-penetrating filter, such as a yellow, red, or polarizing filter, may be used. To include natural haze so that aerial perspective is enhanced, a filter may be omitted or a blue filter may be used to exaggerate haze.

Scenic photographs may also benefit from control of **contrast**. Even though white clouds may be set dramatically against a deep blue sky, a black-and-white rendering may rob the final print of these values. Similarly, the stark contrasts between green foliage, blue water and sky, and red-brown earth tones may turn into a dull, pasty gray mass in the final black-and-white print. At high altitudes, at the seashore, or in the snow, the intense ultraviolet light, called **actinic light**, may further drain scenic images of brilliance. Filters often help not only to retain the contrast in a scene but also to improve upon it by emphasizing the features of particular interest. (See Unit 11 *Filters.*)

Foreground detail may also add to the sense of distance. A rock, tree, shrub, or person in the scenic foreground can provide a visual reference by which the viewer of the photograph may judge the scale of distance. Use of both a sharply defined foreground object and a sharp distant scene element can introduce even more depth in the image. This technique of juxtaposition is often called the near-far approach and was often used by the consummate landscape photographer, Ansel Adams.

Lighting is also important to the grand view. The adage "keep the sun at your back" rarely provides the best lighting for grand scenic views. In that position, the sun produces relatively shadowless **flat lighting** that reveals little texture. Similarly, noon sunlight from directly overhead seldom produces the shadow patterns that best reveal landscape features.

Cross-lighting, on the other hand, skimming across the landscape from a relatively low angle, increases image contrast and reveals the contours, textures, and shapes of scenic features. **Backlighting**, striking the scenic features from behind, reveals their shapes and outlines and often pro- duces spectacular rim highlights. Natural cross-lighting and backlighting are most often available when the sun is relatively low on the horizon, during the early morning and late afternoon, times favored by many landscape photographers.

For the grand view, the photographer may want features in the near foreground as well as those in the distant background to appear in sharp focus. To obtain maximum depth of field, it is often use- ful to use extremely small apertures and hyperfo- cal focusing.

Figure 14-2 shows examples of the grand view.

The Intimate View

Great scenic photographs do not need miles of space; many focus on only a few square yards of natural scenery and close-ups of such features as a bough of leaves, a few rocks in a stream, or the gnarled roots of an old tree. Many potentially excit- ing photographs may lie close by as well as in the distance. By paying attention to close-up details, the photographer can learn to convey a sense of the region that produced them.

The intimate view may picture sailboats at a lake- side dock, a rural church, or mailboxes along a country road. Whereas the grand view seeks to pic- ture great scale and distance, the intimate view fo- cuses on particular features closer at hand. Once again, significant foreground detail may provide a useful frame of reference, a feeling of depth, and a means to direct the viewer's attention to the details of particular interest.

As with grand views, intimate views may also benefit from con- trol of contrast. Without controls, contrasts between color elements that show clearly in nature—foli- age, earth tones, sky, water, struc- tures—may fade to insignificance in the gray scale of the final print. However, the important contrasts can be retained, even enhanced in black-and-white images, by the ju- dicious use of filters—red, orange,

Figure 14-2. Grand scenic views. Pictures convey a sense of great distance and magnitude.

or yellow, for example, to lighten earth and wood tones and to darken foliage and sky. These filters also tend to reduce haze that, in an intimate view, may give an unwanted feeling of distance.

Figure 14-3 shows examples of the intimate view.

Scenes with Water

Water may be a part of either a grand or an intimate scenic view, and it sometimes poses problems for the photographer. For example, if a picture of a quiet pond includes a reflection of the shore, the viewer may have to rotate the picture to figure out which side is up. For such scenes, breaking the smooth reflecting surface of the water with a stone or including a strong, unreflected foreground feature often helps the viewer to distinguish up from down and adds interest to the water detail.

Marine scenes, too, may be grand or intimate views, usually dominated by sea and sky. Large foreground waves or rocks may appear as a center of interest; boats, birds, or interesting cloud formations may establish the mood or idea of the scene. Sometimes a marine scene would benefit from the presence of living creatures, creatures that are often camera-shy. When shooting at the shore, try carrying some food along to attract the wildlife (providing such action is legal, of course).

Backlighting and silhouettes can often be used to excellent effect in marine scenes. Light reflecting over the water and toward the camera reflects a myriad of glints, dapples, and sparkles from the surface of the water that enliven the picture and provide a brilliant background against which foreground objects may be silhouetted.

Figure 14-3. Intimate scenic views. Pictures draw attention to close details.

HELPFUL HINT

Shielding the Lens from Sunlight

One caution should be exercised whenever shooting directly toward the sun. Should the sun's rays strike the lens directly, they may produce flares and reflections within the internal structure of the lens. Even the shadowy image of the iris diaphragm may be recorded. To avoid these effects, shield the surface of the lens from direct sunlight with a lens shade. If no lens shade is available, hold a hand, a hat, or any similar object above the lens to shade it from the sun.

To darken the surface of water under blue skies in black-and-white photography, proceed as to darken the blue sky itself. As the surface of the water only reflects the light of the sky, a red, orange, yellow, or polarizing filter will serve to darken the surface of the water. A red filter combined with a polarizing screen will produce spectacular night effects with back- or sidelighted surf.

Contrast Control in Color Landscape Photography

A variety of filters, such as yellow and red, can be used in black-and-white photography to darken skies that would otherwise appear excessively bright in a photograph. Were these same filters to be used in color photography the entire scene would take on a surreal yellow or red hue.

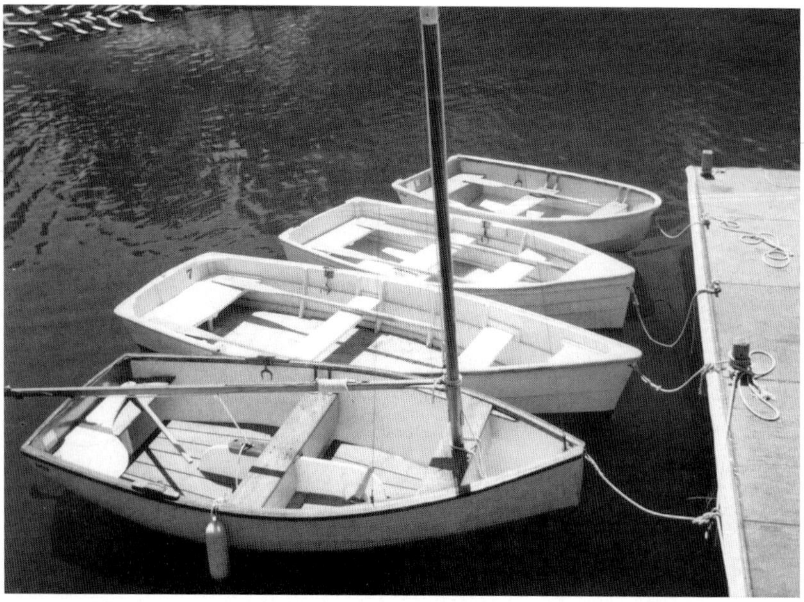

Figure 14-4. Scene with water. Yellow filter used to darken water reflecting expanse of blue sky.

Photographers working in color, whether film or digital, need to employ other tools to darken bright skies. Using a polarizing filter, for example, can dramatically deepen the blue color of both water and sky and increase the apparent contrast with any visible clouds. Alternatively, using a graduated neutral density filter that is gradually tinted darker from bottom to top can be adjusted to darken the sky at the top of the frame without affecting the details nearer to the bottom. These filters are usually rectangular and placed in a special holder in front of the lens.

Digital photographers have another contrast control available—they can make two photographs of the scene, one with correct exposure for the landscape itself and the second with reduced exposure to more dramatically capture the bright sky. The best parts of both images can be combined later using digital imaging software.

Figure 14-4 shows an example of a scene with water.

Architecture

Objective 14-B Describe some of the principles and techniques of architectural photography.

Key Concepts record shot, interpretive shot, keystone effect, perspective-control (P-C) lens

Photographs of buildings or other architectural subjects may be classified as either record or interpretive photographs. A **record shot** is one that attempts to represent all of a structure's essential details from a relatively neutral point of view with a minimum of distortion. An **interpretive shot** attempts to convey an impression of the structure's character and meaning by adopting a unique point of view and emphasizing certain of the structure's features.

Interpretive architectural photography is closely related to outdoor portraiture. The photographer must study the subject and come to know it quite well—its

character, its personality, its moods at different times, in different seasons, and in different weather—and ultimately develop a photographic statement about it. Only then may the photographer select an appropriate point of view, lighting angles, and time of day for picturing the subject. Only then may the photographer decide which features of the structure should be emphasized and which tonal qualities to seek. (See Figures 14-5, 14-6, and 14-7.)

Architectural photography may call for special equipment. For example, the photographer may wish to picture a tall building from across a narrow street or a long bridge from a position near one end of it. Under these conditions a wide-angle lens may be useful to encompass the entire structure from such short range. At other times it may be necessary to capture a feature far up the facade of a building or far out along the span of a bridge. Under these conditions, a telephoto lens may be useful to obtain a close-up image of some distant detail.

Figure 14-6. Interpretive architectural shot. Seeks to capture character of structure by focusing on particular details and to convey photographer's feeling about it.

A.

B.

C.

Figure 14-7. Techniques for interpretive architectural photography. A) Low angle and repetitive forms reveal distinctive character of building. B) Diagonal composition combined with reflections accent dominating structural and surface qualities. C) Bold forms and strong contrast reveal mass of building.

Because architectural subjects are typically large and deep, small apertures are commonly used to assure maximum depth of field. As a consequence, exposure times are typically long and the use of a tripod or other camera support is usually necessary.

Black-and-white photographs of architectural subjects often benefit from the use of contrast filters that increase figure-ground contrast. So that the structure may be separated from its background, for example, it may help to create a dark sky against which the structure will stand out in bold relief.

Ordinarily the pictured structure may gain impact if it does not appear isolated in space. To convey a sense of scale, other objects of known size, such as trees or people, may be included within the frame. So that the viewer may gain a sense of the locale, nearby features, such as other buildings, lakes, or mountains may also be included. These additional features provide the viewer with a frame of reference that contributes to a more complete understanding of the subject.

To photograph an architectural subject, the photographer often must shoot from ground level upward toward the top of the structure. Because its top is more distant than its base, its parallel vertical sides tend to converge in the picture as they recede toward the top. This is called a **keystone effect.** (For more on this topic, see Objective 15-D.) To deal with this and other problems of perspective, the serious architectural photographer often prefers to use a view camera with a full complement of swings and tilts. Ground-glass focusing and composing also are considered essential for this kind of work.

To achieve similar results with an SLR camera, a **perspective-control (P-C) lens** may be used.

This wide-angle lens is designed so that its optical elements may be shifted off-center and the entire lens rotated on its axis. With these adjustments, it is possible to obtain some control over perspective similar to that provided by a view camera, although not to the same degree.

Perspective should be controlled at the time the exposure is made in order to obtain optimal image quality, but that is not always possible with a standard camera and lens. If perspective cannot be controlled at the time the exposure is made, remember that perspective can be corrected partially, and sometimes even completely, during enlargement or digital image processing.

Still Life

Objective 14-C Describe some of the principles and techniques that can be used in photographing still-life subjects.

Key Concepts close-up lens

Still-life photography, because it attempts to convey ideas and feelings from an arrangement of inanimate details and objects, often poses a special challenge for the photographer. The arrangement of the objects and the approach to them should create an image that transcends the objects themselves. If the final image turns out to be little more than a record shot of several lifeless objects, the photograph is likely to convey little meaning. The viewer may be left wondering, I see these objects, but so what? Without an idea as a basis, a still life tends to lack vitality and interest. To succeed, the photograph must invest the image with a life of its own—it must affect the viewer's senses and feelings. It must convey meanings beyond the mere record of the objects themselves. (See Figure 14-8.)

The equipment necessary for still-life photography need not be elaborate. A camera, a camera support, and a few lights are all that are necessary. However, a camera that permits accurate

A.

B.

Figure 14-8. Still life. A) Effective use of perspective, strong graphics, and clean design. B) Strong graphic design achieved by tight cropping to simplify shape. Technique of bleeding objects to edge of frame serves to emphasize composition rather than objects.

viewing and focusing on a ground-glass screen will help to gain greater control over framing and depth of field. SLR and view cameras work well for this purpose. Digital cameras with their LCD preview monitors, also work especially well for close-ups. For extreme close-up work, an accessory **close-up lens** will be useful for focusing at these much closer-than-normal distances. (See Objective 15-E *Close-up and Copy Photography* on page 503.)

Effective pictures can be made with just one light source, preferably a spotlight, and a piece of white cardboard to provide fill if paired with the proper white balance on a digital camera or filtered appropriately for color film. More elaborate setups may be used, of course, to enhance the subject. The basic principles of object photography apply to the lighting of inanimate objects for still-life photographs. (See Objective 12-F *Lighting Small Objects* on page 418.)

Ordinary household tungsten lamps can be used in still-life photography when the subject is small. Especially bright lighting is not needed because the subjects are inanimate and long exposures are possible. Larger subjects, however, may require more than one light source. A camera support, such as a tripod, is a useful aid in composing a still-life image because it helps to hold the camera steady during painstaking framing and focusing, as well as during slow exposures.

People

Objective 14-D Describe and demonstrate some common sense guidelines for photographing people.

Key Concepts characteristic activity

People like to look at pictures of people. Those who study photography for their own pleasure usually find that people—family, friends, and children—are among their most important subjects. Those who study photography for professional reasons soon learn that the ability to capture the feelings and personalities of people in both natural and planned settings is an invaluable asset. Some of the compositional guidelines that were studied earlier apply especially well to photographing people.

1. Avoid distracting backgrounds.

   A photograph of people will benefit from simplicity. The photograph should draw the viewer's attention to the people who are the center of interest. Any kind of background that might confuse or distract the viewer's attention is usually best avoided.

   To simplify shots of people, consider using a neutral background. The sky, with or without clouds, usually provides a flattering neutral background for people. Outdoors, posing the subject in a position for shooting a low-angle shot against the sky is one useful approach.

   The ground, too, may provide a neutral background. By standing on a chair or posing your subject seated on the ground, you may take a high-angle shot. If a high angle shot is not desired, use selective focus to throw the background elements out of focus and so neutralize them.

   The side of a plain building may provide a suitable neutral background for a subject, but such busy patterns as brick or stone are usually best avoided. Indoors, a plain wall or drape may provide an uncluttered background. If background objects must appear in the picture, they may be arranged in such a way that they contribute to the overall composition, rather than distract from it.

   Neutral backgrounds are not necessarily always best, however. If it is relevant, a carefully selected background can help the viewer gain a more complete impression of the subject. Photographing a steel worker against the background of the steel plant, or a farmer against fields of wheat, for example, places such a person in context and gives the viewer a more complete picture. (See Figure 14-9.)

2. Use close-ups.

   The camera should be moved in as close as possible to the subject. A simple guideline is to shoot at a conversational distance. It is desirable to obtain the largest image possible in the viewfinder. A negative or digital image file with a small image element must be enlarged considerably, and this may result in an undesirably grainy print. The larger the image element, the less the needed enlargement and the less its accompanying graininess.

Figure 14-9. Background. A) Background reveals context of subject's activity. B) Background provides strong visual form for composition and sets stage for subject.

This distance may be achieved not only by moving physically closer to the subject, but also by using a long focal length lens. Many photographers prefer this latter approach because it allows them a close-up view without intruding into their subject's personal space.

3. Photograph the subject doing something.

If nothing else, the subject may be engaged in conversation. An animated conversational expression is vastly preferable to a self-conscious smile into the camera. Better yet, the subject may be photographed doing something meaningful—reading a book, arranging some flowers, brushing a horse, examining a stamp collection—something characteristic of that person. Often the most revealing pictures of people, like portraits, depict the central figures engaged in **characteristic activity**, something that interests them and that they do regularly. (See Figure 14-10.)

4. Eliminate distracting objects.

If possible, distracting objects should be removed from the background—the picture on the wall, the lamp, or the monkey in a cage. Light sources, mirrors, or other reflective objects that might form distracting highlights should also be removed. Only those objects that support the central visual idea should be allowed to remain in the background. For example, if the subject is shown painting a picture, brushes, paints, and similar objects may support the central idea. Moving in closer to the subject, either physically or by means of a long lens, is a good way to eliminate extraneous background objects that distract from the subject or that might have to be cropped out of the final print. Selective focus can be used to achieve a similar result.

5. Choose lighting to help portray the subject.

Diffused, flat lighting tends to support such impressions as quiet, inactivity,

473

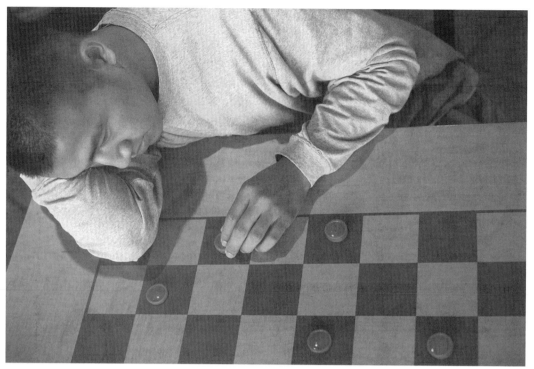

Figure 14-10. Activity. Subject engaged in characteristic activity reveals more of self than one who simply smiles into camera.

passivity, and softness. It also tends to minimize surface textures. Specular, contrasty lighting tends to support such impressions as activity, vitality, aggressiveness, and hardness. When it is used to cross-light the subject, it also tends to reveal surface textures.

The midday sun produces deep, harsh shadows. If subjects face directly into the sun, its glare may cause them to squint unnaturally. The principles of basic lighting discussed in Unit 12 apply to photographing people. (See Figure 14-11.)

Action

Objective 14-E Describe real action, simulated action, and peak action and demonstrate a technique used for photographing each.

Key Concepts real action, peak action, simulated action, blurred movement, time exposures, photo sequence

Action may be classified into three types: real, peak, and simulated. Each requires a different approach to setting the shutter speed.

Real action is what the name implies: movement that occurs as the picture is taken. **Real action** is a halfback's run in a football game, a speeding car, a baseball player in the middle of a swing, a runner during a 100-yard dash. Because the subject is in motion at the moment the shutter snaps, faster shutter speeds are required to stop the action. (See Figure 14-12 B.)

Peak action is the split second when real action slows or even stops. In most action situations, a moment occurs when the action reaches a peak. This moment of **peak action** provides an opportunity for a picture in which action can be stopped with a slower shutter than that required for real action.

Sports are generally thought of as full of real action. Yet most sports have many moments of peak action as well. At the very top of a pole vault, for example, as the vaulter's body reaches the top of its upward flight, movement momentarily slows. The baseball pitcher, for another example, winds up and then unwinds to throw the ball. At that peak moment between winding and unwinding, the action is suspended. Peak action can also be seen in the moment when a diver reaches a high point of ascent before starting the descent, when

A.

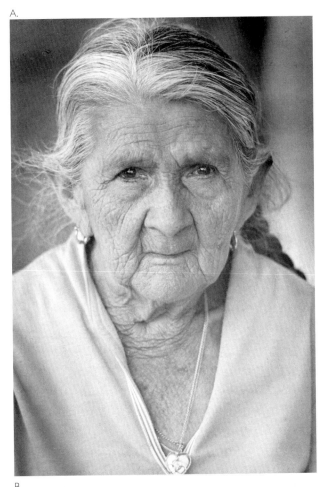

B.

Figure 14-11. Lighting. A) Soft lighting conveys feeling of gentle character. B) Contrasty lighting appropriate to dynamic subject.

the football kicker reaches the top of a punt, when a tennis player reaches the end of a stroke before setting up for the next one.

At the moment of peak action, the action can be stopped with a slower shutter speed and therefore a smaller f/stop, which permits greater depth of field. In low light, the ability to record action with a slower shutter speed may mean the difference between success and failure. (See Figure 14-12 A.)

Simulated action refers more to mental than to physical action. For example, a person talking on a telephone is seen to be in action, yet the action involves little physical movement. The president may appear to be signing new legislation. New officers of an organization appear to be examining a record book. A person is pictured drinking something, writing, or typing. All of these are examples of **simulated action**—the subjects are doing something, but physical movement is hardly present.

As these examples indicate, simulated action, by conveying a sense of activity, reveals more of the subject's personality than does a picture that merely shows the subject grinning benignly into the camera. (See Figure 14-12 C.)

Depicting Action

For a good action picture, it is not always necessary that movement be frozen. Sometimes an effective photo results when the photographer purposely uses a slower shutter speed to obtain the effect of **blurred movement**. The resulting slightly blurred picture may emphasize the impression of movement by tracing the rapid passage of the image through space. At other times, however, when the action is obvious, freezing the action may promote more interest than blurring it. In the case of a high hurdler, for example, a stop action shot might reveal the runner's straining muscles and concentration, whereas a blurred shot would obscure these details. The stop-action shot allows the viewer to study many aspects of an intense moment during continuous action. (See Figure 14-13.)

Whatever the type of action, the sense of movement can be enhanced by appropriate timing and composition. For example, action may be implied if the subject of the picture is off-balance or suspended in midair. Use of compositional lines—especially zigzag and diagonal lines—also en-

A.

B.

C.

Figure 14-12. Types of action. A) Peak action. B) Real action. C) Simulated action.

hances the illusion of movement and action. At night, **time exposures** can be used to capture the action patterns of moving lights or the tracings of exploding fireworks.

Finally, action can be depicted by means of the **photo sequence**. As the viewer's eyes move from picture to picture in a well-designed sequence, a sense of action and movement is conveyed.

Human Interest

Objective 14-F Describe how captivating pictures of people appeal to basic human emotions.

Key Concepts emotion, conflict appeal, sex appeal, achievement appeal, escape appeal

Photographs that appeal to basic human emotions have a special kind of impact. The viewer does not simply observe the image, but reacts emotionally to it. The viewer may laugh, feel sad, or simply empathize with the subject. The range of human **emotion** is extremely wide and complex —far beyond the scope of this discussion. Nevertheless, mention might be made of a few of the emotional appeals that have provided a basis for successful human interest photographs. Some of these subjects are related to conflict, sex, achievement, and escape.

A.

B.

C.

Conflict appeal refers to human interest in witnessing people struggling against others or against the forces of nature or society to achieve their goals. Conflict has been at the center of literature, art, and drama since the beginning of history. In photography, it may be seen in photographs of firefighters battling a blaze, residents sandbagging to fight a flood, ordinary people struggling against disasters. Conflict appeal may also characterize human interest in competitive activities, such as sports, elections, business, and, in a grimmer way, war. Accidents are another context in which we can observe basic human conflict against the forces of nature and society. (See Figure 14-14.)

Sex appeal is so widely recognized as a human interest that it has become a standard phrase in our language. Photographs of attractive men and women, singly, in couples, and in groups, usually appeal to human beings of both sexes. They at-

D.

Figure 14-13. Blurred vs. stop action. A) Intentional blurs enhance feeling of action. B) Implied action. Diagonal composition adds to feeling of dynamic movement. C) Idea of motion expressed by stopping or freezing action at an instant in time. D) Time exposure. Movement expressed by allowing moving subject to create trace across image.

477

Figure 14-14. Conflict appeal. Emotion is evident in competitive sports.

Seeing picture possibilities that appeal to basic human interests such as these is a skill that can be developed. Study photographic subjects and analyze the feelings that a scene generates. Then consider how best to convey those feelings to a viewer. Emotional sensitivity can be developed, and with it the skill to create photographs with strong human interest.

Photojournalism

Objective 14-G Describe some of the principles and techniques of news and documentary photography.

Key Concepts photojournalism, news photography, documentary photography, spot news, long shot, medium shot, close-up, general news, sports news, feature photographs, picture stories, shooting script, lead photograph

Photojournalism is a global concept that refers to the photographic reporting of a wide range of subjects and events of public interest, usually for publication. It includes both **news photography**, which reports events and other subjects of current interest, and **documentary photography**, which photographs subjects that possess some practical or historical significance.

The boundaries are not neat—news photographs often become historically significant and documentary photographs often make the news. What all types of modern photojournalism share is a dedication to objectivity and a commitment to communicate truth. Truthfully reporting an event often leads a photojournalist, as it does other journalists, to seek out a unique point of view that dramatizes the event, that calls attention to its salient details, and that involves viewers both intellectually and emotionally, not only in the event itself, but also in its meaning.

tract the eye and trigger an emotional response. Sex appeal may be observed in action in newspaper and magazine advertisements, in literature, drama, music, and in news stories and articles.

Achievement appeal refers to a human interest in people who have achieved success in some area of human endeavor, such as business, science, athletics, entertainment, culture, or industry. Human beings are interested in others who achieve success, who overcome odds, or who by the workings of chance attain success or celebrity.

Escape appeal refers to a human interest in escaping from everyday reality by fantasizing, daydreaming, or otherwise projecting one's self to another world, real or imagined. A photograph may provide the viewer with an opportunity to escape when it portrays subjects pursuing pleasure and adventure or when it depicts life in faraway places—subjects such as these appeal to the viewer's desire for escape. For a moment the viewer can empathize with the subject and be transported psychologically from the routines of life. (See Figure 14-15.)

Photojournalists are journalists with cameras and, as such, share many of the obligations of other reporters. Although they may not be primarily writers, photojournalists still have an obligation to obtain sufficient information to write a small story or caption to accompany any photograph, explaining the who, what, why, where,

Famous Photographer

W. Eugene Smith

W. Eugene Smith, whose name is nearly synonymous with the modern photo essay, was a moody, seemingly tortured personality, who brought to his work not only technical perfection but an intense, passionate sense of beauty and conscience that shone through his often brutally frank photographs. While still a high school teenager during the depression, he worked as a news photographer for the *Wichita Eagle* and the *Wichita Beacon.* Then and thereafter, a sensitive, compassionate vision and a sense of social purpose permeated his work, whether the subject concerned Pittsburgh steel workers, Welsh coal miners, Haitian fishermen, life in a Spanish village, the work of a country midwife, or life in combat during World War II.

Every photograph he made carried an emotional impact. For Smith, feeling was the essence of a photograph. He once destroyed a batch of his work because he believed it lacked sufficient feeling. "Great depth of field; very little depth of feeling," he explained. His emotional investment in his work is obvious to anyone who views it. "I've never made any picture, good or bad, without paying for it in emotional turmoil," he wrote.

The photo essay, brought to its zenith by Smith and the editors of *Life,* emerged from a simple sequence of pictures into a complex documentary art form with often profound emotional impact. Smith's essays were driven by a strong sense of "story," which dictated image selection, sequence, sizing, placement, and caption text to achieve a final, integrated layout with a singular unity of theme.

His coverage of mercury pollution in the small fishing village of Minimata in 1971 was vintage Smith. The Japanese government had officially charged the Chisso Corporation with having caused widespread environmental pollution and birth defects by carelessly dumping methyl mercury into the bay off the town for years. His brutal, compassionate photographs documenting the horrible physical effects of the poison on the townspeople so angered company officials that they had Smith beaten up and his cameras destroyed. Despite injuries that cost him part of his eyesight, Smith persisted—*Life* and other magazines and newspapers worldwide published his poignant photographs of Japanese people deformed and suffering from mercury poisoning, arousing international indignation and a new awareness of the terrible costs of industrial pollution. Smith went on to publish his own book, *Minimata,* an extended photo essay that exposed the effects of the company's actions on the town.

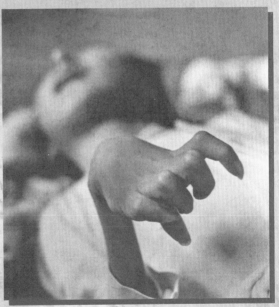

W. Eugene Smith, "Tomoko's Hand," Minimata, Japan, 1972.

After high school Smith received a Photography scholarship to Notre Dame University, but left after a year to become a *Newsweek* photographer. He began a long on-again, off-again relationship with *Life* magazine in 1939, leaving in 1941 to become a war correspondent for Ziff-Davis, and returning again to *Life* in 1944. During World War II, he covered 13 invasions, made 23 combat air missions, and was seriously wounded at Okinawa in 1945. After two years of painful convalescence, he resumed his work for *Life,* remaining until 1955. He was awarded Guggenheim fellowships in 1956, 1957, and 1968. His exhibitions include the University of Oregon; the Rochester Institute of Technology, New York University; the Museum of Modern Art in New York; and the International Museum of Photography in Rochester, New York. Major collections of his work are maintained at the International Museum of Photography, the Museum of Modern Art, and the Art Institute of Chicago.

A.

when, and how of the captured moment and identifying featured people with correctly spelled names. Some photographers make use of a portable tape recorder to keep notes as they move rapidly from one shot to another, thereby avoiding having to stop shooting to write notes.

News Photography

The traditional categories of news photography are news (both spot news and general news), sports, features, and picture stories. The distinctions among these categories, however, are often blurred. Some sports stories may be of news interest and appear in the news sections of the newspaper; some news stories that affect sporting events may appear on the sports pages. Then again, any story may be approached as a feature—capturing an image that has a broad and timeless appeal, unbound by the urgency of a news deadline—or as a picture story—an in-depth exploration of the subject. What is most important in news photography, whether news, sports, features, or picture stories, is reader appeal—learning to rec-

B.

Figure 14-15. Escape appeal. Desire to escape is conveyed in pictures of adventure, sport, and faraway places.

Figure 14-16. Spot news photographers often must place themselves close to the center of action that may threaten their own personal safety. Demonstrations such as this may suddenly turn violent as participants escalate their actions and reactions. © AFP/Corbis.

ognize what interests the news-reading public and telling the story in a visually effective way.

Spot News **Spot news** generally refers to a breaking news event—an unexpected, rapidly changing, newsworthy event of limited duration. As spot news photographers, photojournalists may find themselves covering stories such as crimes, accidents, fires, or natural disasters to a news publication deadline. Spot news photographers must possess an uncommon single-mindedness to get to the scene rapidly, to get into the middle of the action, and to get the story, often under adverse and dangerous conditions. (See Figure 14-16.)

Getting to the scene in a timely way is often the major challenge faced by the spot news photographer. Arriving at the scene of a major fire just as the last glowing embers are being extinguished provides little opportunity to capture a dramatic news shot of the blaze in progress. Most spot news photographers, therefore, equip themselves with a radio scanner to learn about breaking stories early, and good area maps or a global positioning system (GPS) to help them get to the stories fast. (See Figure 14-17).

The photographer should arrive at the scene prepared to start shooting immediately—cameras loaded with film or memory cards, flash units fully charged, and a cool head prepared with a plan. Breaking events are unpredictable and it

rarely pays to wait patiently for a better shot—the shot at that moment may very well be the best that will occur. Saturation shooting—continuous shooting from every conceivable angle—is the general rule for spot news photography. Nevertheless, it pays to have a strategy for approaching fast-moving events.

One way to be sure that the events are fully covered is to look for three basic types of shots—the long shot, the medium shot, and the close-up. The **long shot** establishes the overall scene of the event and the relationships among all the important elements. It is useful for establishing the scale of the event and describing its location. In a fire scene, for example, a long shot might include the fire itself, the firefighters and their equipment, and perhaps even the nearby structures that may be threatened by the fire. If it is a major fire, one photographer might even be dispatched in a helicopter to obtain long aerial shots of the scene that include the surrounding neighborhood.

Figure 14-17. Many photojournalists use hand-held computers equipped with Global Positioning System features to organize their schedules and quickly navigate to news events.

For **medium shots**, the photographer will move in closer to the events so that the important participants and their actions can be seen clearly as well as the background of their activities. In the fire scene, for example, a medium shot might include several firefighters struggling to direct a high-pressure stream of water onto a hot spot of the fire, or using a crane to attempt a rescue from an upper-story window.

For **close-ups**, the photographer moves in even closer to obtain details that provide additional impact. Often so tight that nothing more than a face fills the frame, a close-up of the fire scene might include only the sweaty face of an exhausted firefighter, or a paramedic comforting an injured child.

Of course, varying camera-to-subject distance alone does not guarantee adequate coverage of a spot news event. The photographer must continually look for a point of view that will best dramatize the subject and call attention to the most important details. Furthermore, the photographer cannot stop shooting until the event is concluded, and even then must be alert to subsequent events of possible interest. From beginning to end, the photographer must continually evaluate the news value of all elements of the event and try to capture them in images from various points of view.

General News **General news** refers to newsworthy events and subjects that are planned, expected, or predictable. As general news photogra-

phers, photojournalists may cover such events as meetings, news conferences, stage performances, courtroom proceedings, political and government events, award ceremonies, or funerals. (See Figure 14-18.)

While the major challenge of spot news photographers is getting to the event in time, the challenge for *general* news photographers is to find something interesting and meaningful at the event. Although they have the advantage of knowing when and where an event will take place and can plan well ahead to be there, general news photographers face endless repetitions of cliché events that all look astonishingly alike. After all, what visually distinguishes one meeting from another, one award ceremony from another, one news conference from another, other than the fact that different persons perform the rituals? It is a challenge to the creativity of the general news photographer to seek out and dramatize that which characterizes an event and makes it unique. As with spot news photography, it pays to have a strategy for covering general news events.

The key to shooting interesting general news photographs is to focus attention on the participants—the principals as well as the audiences, observers, and onlookers to the event. Good people pictures make good general news pictures. Seek out medium and close-up shots showing animated, emotional facial expressions, characteristic hand and arm gestures, and actions that reveal relationships, such as the natural embracing, shoving, or com-

Figure 14-18. Free movement for photography is often restricted during congressional hearings, courtroom proceedings, or other formal meetings. The general news photographer often must shoot images such as this from a distance under available light without disturbing the decorum of the event. © AFP/Corbis.

forting actions or the handling of objects that occur naturally between people as the event unfolds. Try to capture the principals in action and avoid the cliché smiles and handshakes, handing off of awards, posed lineups, and document signings that are sure to bore editors and viewers alike.

Because many general news events involve political and government figures, entertainers, or legal proceedings, photographers often face substantial restraints on their movements. It is always a good idea to arrive early to establish an advantageous shooting position; however, photographers often find themselves locked in closely to that position throughout the event. Usually they are not permitted to roam freely about courtrooms or during other government proceedings, and security staff may restrict their movements when government officials or leading entertainers are nearby. Further, most stage events and legal proceedings prohibit the use of flash photography. Therefore, many general news photographers arrive at an event equipped with fast lenses and fast films or digital cameras preset to a high ISO, ready for shooting in available light. Several cameras, each with a different zoom range lens are often used so that long shots, medium shots, and close-ups can be shot from nearly the same position.

Knowing that picture opportunities may be limited during a general news event, general news photographers should remain alert to opportunities both before and after the event. Sometimes the best shots are obtained before the event, during preparations or rehearsals, or after the event when the party is breaking up and the principals move from center stage. At both times the principals tend to be more relaxed and informal, and the photographer has more mobility to gain an advantageous position.

The task of the general news photographer is to recognize the essence of an event and to tell its story in a truthful and interesting way. It is important that the photographs reveal the meaning of the event, and not merely accidental, irrelevant details that contribute nothing toward the viewer's understanding.

Sports News **Sports news** covers a wide range of subjects, including team sports such as football and basketball, individual competitive sports such as tennis and boxing, and personal sports activities such as surfing and skiing. A sports news photographer needs a complete knowledge of the sport, including its fine points, the athletes, the teams, and their equipment to be in the right place at the right time to capture its decisive and dramatic moments. (See Figure 14-19.)

The challenge for the sports photographer is to capture the dramatic shots that best summarize the most significant moments in the action. For the viewer, the sports picture of greatest interest is the knockout punch, the game-winning play, the record-breaking jump, or the turning point in the game. Even though other plays and actions may be wonderful to behold, it is that decisive, significant moment that most captures reader interest. As with other types of news photography, it pays to have a strategy and to be prepared to seize that moment when it happens.

Know the sport. Without an intimate knowledge of the sport, the photographer cannot have the sense of when and where the decisive action will take place and what equipment will be needed to capture it. In many sports, such as in boxing or during the running of a football play, a motor drive may be useful to capture the decisive moment if it

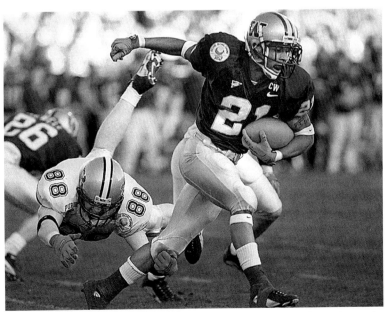

Figure 14-19. Good sports photography requires the photographer to know the sport well enough to anticipate where and when critical action or plays will occur and to be ready to capture these moments on film.

occurs in the midst of very fast and continuous action. Many sports photographers who use a motor drive still prefer to click off their shots one at a time, using the motor drive only to advance the film rapidly between shots. They prefer to use their own instinct to capture the decisive moment rather than hope that the moment will be captured in a mindless, motor-driven sequence of shots.

Know the venue. At local games, photographers are likely to have greater mobility to move around the edges of the action and to position themselves advantageously. At major games of national import, their movements may be more limited and arriving early with long lenses and fast film will provide a better opportunity to obtain a better shooting location. Indoor sports may provide opportunity to move in close to the action with flash while outdoor events may force the photographer farther from the action and require available-light photography. For outdoor events held at night, an early arrival will permit the photographer to obtain light-meter readings at various points on the field.

Know the stats. If any records are about to be broken, the photographer will want to be in position to capture that record-breaking moment.

Know the players and the teams. If photographers understand a team's strategies and the techniques of individual athletes, they will be more likely to anticipate what action will take place, when, and where. In this sense, sports photographers function nearly as the athletes themselves, thrusting and parrying with their cameras in the very heart of the action.

The task of the sports news photographer is to recognize the significant moments during sport action and to capture those moments in a dramatic way. The photographer's task also includes telling the complete story of the event, including spectator reactions, preparations for the event, and follow-up photographs of key players, both winners and losers, and their coaches and staffs.

Features **Feature photographs** differ from news photographs in several different ways. News photographs are timely and interest in them wanes rapidly. A photograph of tonight's winning touchdown pass by the local high school quarterback has great news value in tomorrow's local morning paper. But its news value is close to zero a couple of weeks later. It is no longer news!

A feature photograph, on the other hand, has an enduring quality, unbound by the ephemeral quality of news, maintaining interest value weeks, months, often years later. Sometimes called "evergreens," good feature photographs do not fade with the season, but remain ever fresh.

A feature photograph usually records some commonplace moment in the flow of everyday events, but presents it in a way that arouses immediate empathy in the reader. In a sense, a feature photograph is a moment in the life of Everyperson, dramatizing the trivial adventures that are common to folks like us, and sometimes even to human beings everywhere. A good feature can make you laugh, cry, or just pause for a moment of amazement or recognition. (See Figure 14-20.)

Usually we do not recognize the persons in feature photographs—their identity is not important to our understanding of the picture. In fact, it is our lack of recognition that helps us empathize—the subjects could be anyone, even ourselves, and the meaning would be the same.

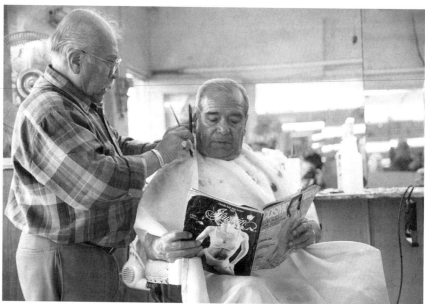

Figure 14-20. Feature photographs possess a timeless quality that transcends the immediacy of news. Not necessarily tied to particular events or personalities, a good feature can be published at any time.

Making good feature photographs is the business of all news photographers. Rarely are news photographers sent out on an assignment to do a feature. Rather, they must be alert to feature opportunities that arise in the normal course of their other news assignments. In the midst of a flood, for example, the photographer might spot a burly rescue worker ministering to a small puppy tucked in his shirt. Years from now it won't matter who that worker was or what disaster it was. Its lasting interest value arises from our recognition that in an extreme situation a tough person reached out to protect a helpless creature.

There is no simple strategy or checklist for making good feature photographs. What is required is an abiding sense of humanity—an ability to empathize with other human beings and to recognize that which makes us human. The photographer must have the capacity to be moved by an event to recognize that others would also be moved. Beyond this recognition that the event has a human-interest appeal, the photographer must have the technical and personal skills to capture the essence of the moment without disturbing it.

Picture Stories A **picture story** is a set of images that work together to tell a story or explore a subject. Sometimes the set of images represents a sequence of events; other times it represents various aspects of a subject, unrelated in time, but connected by the underlying theme or subject. A picture story includes not only photographs, but also the headlines, captions, and accompanying text, all in a carefully coordinated layout of pages.

This form of photojournalism developed during the 1930s when picture magazines were beginning to appear in Europe and America and was brought to perhaps its highest form by *Life* and *Look* magazines in the middle of that decade. The approach to picture stories that these great magazines developed so successfully involved careful research and planning of the story in advance, usually by the editors. Following this approach, the editors would develop an outline of the story, called a **shooting script**, and then assign it to the photographer, who would then set out to photograph a set of related and cohesive images defined by the script.

In the decade that followed, many photographers began to experiment with freer approaches to picture stories, unbound by the preconceived structures of shooting scripts prepared by editors who were often less visually literate than themselves. Led by the work of W. Eugene Smith, these photojournalists would take up a story idea with few preconceptions of what direction it might take. Working without a script, they would immerse themselves in the story, sometimes for extended periods of time, to gain intimate understanding of all its angles and nuances, allowing the story to take shape out of their experiences. Smith's own seminal photo essay on the life of a country doctor, published by *Life* in 1948, grew out of a six-week stay during which he accompanied the doctor night and day, making photographs of the ordinary as well as the extraordinary activities of this dedicated man. His story was a revealing and sensitive portrait that moved readers to a new level of understanding about the work of rural doctors.

Few publications today, however, will fund extended photographic projects of this sort. To photograph long-term projects, photojournalists generally must underwrite them themselves or seek grants from foundations or agencies outside the publishing industry.

As with good features, there are no simple formulas for developing good picture stories. A good story starts with a good idea, and ideas for picture stories arise from the photographer's knowledge and understanding of what interests people and what is interesting about them. Armed with a good idea, however, the photographer may then develop an approach to the story.

Before shooting, it is a good idea to gather as much background information about the subject as possible. This will help the photographer establish rapport with the principals of the story, and also will prepare the photographer to recognize and capture the salient moments when they occur. Try to imagine the headline for the story and the **lead photograph** that best summarizes it. Although these may not actually be used and both may change as the story develops, at any given moment they provide a central point of view to guide shooting and to keep the photographer close to the subject.

Some photographers prefer to develop a shooting outline at this point, one that is flexible and responsive to constantly changing events. Even though the outline may change moment for moment, having an outline will assure that the photographer stays on track and does not overlook shots that are important to the story's continuity.

Famous Photographer

Henri Cartier-Bresson

Henri Cartier-Bresson worked hard to remain unobtrusive, even invisible to the principal actors in the ordinary human dramas from which he squeezed significance with his camera. Perhaps the most influential proponent of candid photography of his generation, Cartier-Bresson dressed plainly and clung to the fringes and shadows of events, better to view the world without disturbing it, and even covered the shiny parts of his equipment with black tape to prevent any sudden reflection from distracting his subjects.

For Cartier-Bresson, timing was the essential ingredient of photography. As events unfold before the eyes of the photographer, he insisted, "there is one moment at which the elements in motion are in balance." It was this "decisive moment," he said, that photography must capture to reveal the essence of an event. For Cartier-Bresson the decisive moment was more than simply freezing movement; it was that single instant in time when all the diverse elements that make up an event align in the photographer's mind in a meaningful pattern that tells all there is to tell about that event.

He always sought to capture an event as a complete composition, often viewing the image upside down in the viewer the better to see its formal organization, and rarely cropping during printing. He once wrote: "To me photography is the simultaneous recognition in a fraction of a second of the significance of an event, as well as the precise organization of forms that give that event its proper expression."

Henri Cartier-Bresson, "Two Prostitutes," Mexico City, 1944. © Henri Cartier-Bresson/Magnum Photos

Seemingly always on the prowl for a "moment of realism," he brought to his search a sharp intelligence, a profound wit, and a sensitive compassion that enabled him to reveal the sad, the grotesque, the bizarre, the embarrassingly comic all without cruelty or bitterness. His work is rich with a sense of humanity and an unerring sensitivity to the customs and foibles of distinct cultures, forcing his viewers to see in ordinary events, wherever they might occur, that which is common to all.

Born in France, Cartier-Bresson first studied painting and literature, but later became entranced by the cinema and the work of Man Ray and Eugene Atget. He started to photograph seriously in 1930, traveling and exhibiting widely. In 1936 he returned to France, worked on Jean Renoir's film, Partie de Campagne, then made his own documentary film about medical aid during the Spanish Civil War. Drafted into the French army in 1939, he served in a photographic unit and was captured in 1940. After three years as a prisoner of war he escaped on his third attempt and joined the Paris underground in 1943. After the war, in 1945, he made a film for the U.S. Office of War Information about French prisoners of war returning home in 1945. His major exhibitions include Madrid, 1934; Mexico City, 1935; Julien Levy Gallery, New York, 1935; Museum of Modern Art, New York, 1946 and 1968; Pavillon de Marsan, at the Louvre, Paris, 1957. Major collections of his work are maintained at the Bibliothèque Nationale in Paris and the Museum of Modern Art in New York. With Robert Capa, David Seymour, William Vandervert, and others, he founded Magnum Photos in 1947.

At best, the outline should serve as a guide rather than a rigid plan; the photographer should remain focused on the story, changing the outline as needed to tell the better story.

Once the photographs have been made they must be edited—a few photographs must be selected to tell the story from the hundreds that were taken —and accompanying text must be written. The photographs and text must then be laid out on the pages in an effective manner. Usually one photograph is selected as a lead photograph that best summarizes and captures the story as a whole, made larger than the others and placed in a dominant position. Then text, captions, and other smaller pictures are arranged to support and explain the lead.

Many photojournalists consider the picture story as the highest form of their profession because it allows them to explore their subjects deeply, digging below the surface to reveal complex issues and subtle nuances of meaning from many points of view. The picture story releases them from the constraints of time—where the single photograph captures a single fleeting moment, the picture story permits photographers to extend their vision through time to document and comment upon complex processes and human activities.

Documentary Photography

Shortly after the invention of photography, Oliver Wendell Holmes, the noted doctor and philosopher, recognized the camera's enormous potential for shaping the world to come and made a remarkable proposal. Wondering what was to become of the millions of photographs that were already gathering on tabletops and in bureau drawers throughout the world, he suggested that these fabulous pictures "will have to be classified and arranged in vast libraries, as books are now." Prophetically, he wrote,

> *We do now distinctly propose the creation of a comprehensive and systematic [photographic] library, where all men can find the special forms they particularly desire to see as artists, or as scholars, or as mechanics, or in any other capacity.*

Clearly Holmes saw the value of photographs as documents—vivid, concrete, and dramatic records for the study of history, science, technology, or any other matter of human interest. From the click of the first camera's shutter, photographers have been recording the sights and events of history—trivial events of family life, the cataclysmic events of war and catastrophe, or the sights of faraway places and people. While some of these photographers were subsidized in their efforts by employers or sponsors, and others were motivated by an expectation of profit, millions made photographs simply because opportunity and interest were there. Most were likely unaware that their photographs might possess some social or historical significance. With a few notable exceptions, these graphic, silent records gathered in private attics and albums for nearly a century before Holmes' "distinct proposal" was formally realized in the founding of the National Archives, which maintains one of the world's great collections of American historical and documentary photographs.

In documentary photography we see a form of photojournalism that is often motivated more by a personal need to record significant sights than to report the news. When John Lloyd Stephens and Frederick Catherwood recorded daguerreotype images of their archeological expedition to the Yucatan in 1841, they were motivated by a scholarly need to record what they did and what they found. Similarly, William Henry Jackson and Timothy O'Sullivan, as official photographers on geological surveys, were motivated to record the sights and features of newly explored territories, not for news reportage, but for the historical record. Others, like John Thomson in London and Eugene Atget in Paris, documented ordinary street life in their respective cities, not for profit and not for news, but to satisfy a need within themselves to show what life was like in their own time. Atget pursued this work for over thirty years, died in poverty, and left a legacy of over ten thousand photographs to future scholars and historians.

Some enormous documentary enterprises cannot be fully explained. For example, all that we know about Mathew Brady's legendary documentation of the American Civil War suggests that Brady himself could never explain why he did it—certainly there was no profit in it and only a small number of his images, copied onto woodcuts, ever appeared in the news media. Yet Brady had a sense of the historical significance of his work and was driven to persist. Similarly, Edward S. Curtis undertook to document the life and culture of the vanishing Indians of North America. Starting in 1896, Curtis endured incredible physical hardships for over thirty years, gathering over forty thousand negatives, mostly large glass plates, before completing his work. Curtis suffered enormous financial hardship for the first decade of his work until he found a patron. Curtis, like Brady, was driven to his work for reasons he found difficult to explain. He felt it needed to be done before the Indian culture vanished altogether.

Many other major documentary projects have been undertaken for reasons other than news value. The work of Jacob Riis, Lewis Hine, and the Farm Security Administration under Roy Stryker are a few notable examples. What distinguishes documentary photography from news is that history provides its primary motivation—a need to record events and sights so that their graphic, visual details can be remembered and perhaps studied by future generations.

Questions to Consider

1. Describe the basic differences in approach that are appropriate for grand and intimate scenic photographs.

2. How can filters be useful in scenic photography?

3. Name several ways to approach a scenic shot.

4. In what situations might backlighting be desirable in scenic photography? In what situations might cross-lighting be desirable?

5. Distinguish between architectural record shots and architectural interpretive shots.

6. How can the converging parallel lines in architectural photography be dealt with?

7. Suggest several ways to provide a frame of reference against which to view an architectural shot.

8. What is the difference between a record shot of objects and a good still-life photograph?

9. Describe the lighting principles that apply to still-life photography.

10. Describe one approach to photographing people. What principles might be applied?

11. Name and explain several types of action.

12. What techniques might be used to enhance movement and action in action photographs?

13. What are human-interest photographs? Give some examples.

14. How do the photographer's feelings about a subject affect his or her approach to photographing it?

15. Describe how you might approach covering a freeway accident with fatalities, a press conference by a political candidate, and a circus performance. What are the major differences in your approach to these subjects?

Suggested Field and Laboratory Assignments

Shoot, process, and print a roll of film or digital images that includes at least the following shots:

a. a grand view scenic photograph

b. an intimate view scenic photograph

c. a record architectural photograph

d. an interpretive architectural photograph

e. a still life

f. people engaged in characteristic activity

g. people in action (real, peak, simulated)

h. an emotional appeal subject

i. a general news subject

j. a spot news subject

k. an action sports subject

l. a feature subject

Special Topics

Will Vocia, "Angel."

Unit at a Glance

The field of photography is constantly evolving as new techniques and technologies emerge. Those who wish to delve a little more deeply into some of the more advanced or specialized areas within the field or who wish a glimpse of some of the more advanced techniques will be interested in the special topics addressed in this unit. The following objectives elaborate upon the fine print, the zone system, processing for permanence, large-format photography, close-up and copy photography, creating a web photo gallery, and law and ethics in photography.

The Fine Print

Objective 15-A Describe the appearance and production of a traditional fine black-and-white photographic print.

Key Concept full-scale print

The Difference in Quality

Many beginning photographers have difficulty making fine prints because they have never seen one. We are usually exposed to great photographs only as relatively poor reproductions in books and magazines. Our expectations of what a good photograph should look like are based on these reproductions.

There is a great difference between looking at a printed reproduction of a photograph and viewing an actual photographic print. An image in a book is made from a halftone plate—a pattern of small dots of black ink absorbed into a sheet of paper. A photographic print on the other hand, consists of sparkling bits of silver suspended over the paper in a gelatin emulsion. A traditional fine photographic print has a sense of internal illumination and a sensuality of tones that no reproduction process can match.

The technical quality of a fine print depends upon the range of tones represented in it and the clarity with which different tones are separated from one another. A **full-scale print** is one in which all tonal values are present and well defined. In a full-scale print, only small areas of specular highlights are reproduced as pure paper white and only small areas of darkest shadow are printed as maximum black. The remaining bright highlights and dark shadows are clearly defined and contain textures, value, and depth. The many middle gray tones are also clearly differentiated with vibrancy and clar-

ity. Altogether, a full-scale print can be defined to contain ten distinct tones from maximum paper white to maximum black. Figure 15-2 shows a full-scale print and identifies the major tone values present in it.

Seeking out and studying original photographic works, in addition to reproductions in books, magazines, and the Internet, can help photographers master the craft of fine printing as well as encourage their expressive growth. Many metropolitan galleries and museums display collections of outstanding original photographic prints. The richness and depth of expression that the original silver prints offer make a lasting impression that can only enhance a photographer's own darkroom work.

Control of Tone and Contrast

Every step in the photographic process contributes to the tonal qualities of the final print. Film selection, image format, lighting, exposure, film processing, paper selection, exposure, print processing, and finishing all work together to determine the print's technical quality.

Achieving good print quality requires that good negative quality be obtained at the outset. Although tone and contrast can be enhanced during printing, the characteristics of the negative limit the range of enhancement that is possible. The factors affecting the negative's tonal rendering, densities and contrast include film selection, image format, lighting, exposure, and film processing.

Film Selection Some films possess more inherent contrast than others. Generally, slower speed films have higher inherent contrast than faster speed films. Slower speed films also tend to have a smaller grain structure.

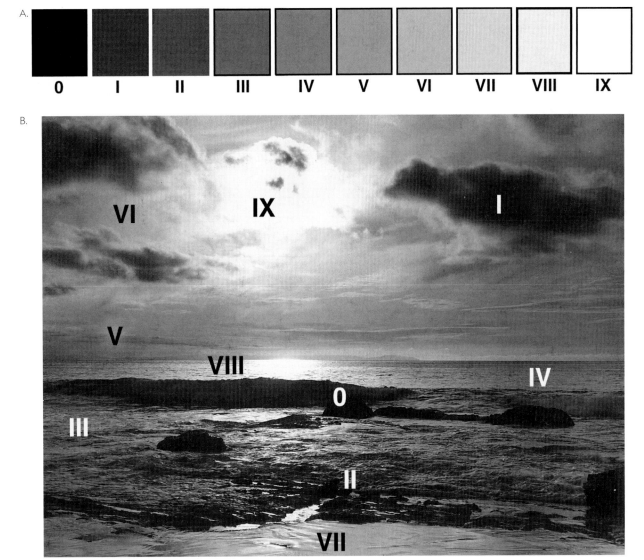

Figure 15-2. Example of a full-scale print. A) Zone system scale. B) Full-scale print showing all tonal values.

Image Format Medium- and large-format negatives have a larger storage capacity for recording information than does the comparatively small 35mm format. Larger negatives permit more details, textures, and tones to be recorded on the film.

Lighting Exposures made in bright sunlight produce higher contrast negatives than exposures made in diffused light. Choose a lighting condition appropriate to the subject and desired effect. Specular lighting may add tonal separation to low-contrast subjects. More diffused lighting may soften the tones of high-contrast subjects.

Exposure Exposure provides density in the thinnest areas of the negative (the shadows). Under-exposure results in the loss of some shadow details in the recorded image. Unrecorded details can never be made to appear in the final print. The combination of exposure and development determine what details appear in the densest areas of the negative (the highlights). Overexposure and/or overdevelopment may result in highlights so dense that they are difficult to print. Bracket your exposures to assure proper exposure.

Film Processing Increasing development time tends to increase negative contrast, while decreasing it tends to reduce negative contrast. Altering development time affects the highlights more than the shadows. Also, some developers tend to increase contrast; others tend to decrease it.

Control of Print Quality

Just as many factors affect negative quality, many factors also affect print quality. Selecting the materials and chemicals used for printing can affect how viewers see and respond to the final print. Within the limits imposed by the negative, final print quality will be affected by paper selection, exposure, the enlarger system, and print processing.

Paper Selection Print contrast is controlled primarily by choice of paper grade (or contrast filter). Some papers have more inherent contrast than others and tend to increase print contrast. Surface texture also affects contrast and the overall tonal range. Glossy surfaces tend to produce a wider range of tones and greater separation than semigloss or matte surfaces. Fiber-based papers generally produce richer tones and a wider tonal range than resin-coated papers.

Exposure Print density is controlled primarily by exposure. Ideally, prints should be exposed so as to reach their optimal density in normal developing time. Overexposure may result in loss of tonal separations and details in the darkest areas. Underexposure may result in the loss of some tonal separations and details in the lightest areas.

Enlarger System The quality, cleanliness, and condition of the enlarger lens affects both sharpness and contrast. A fine enlarging lens capable of producing images that are sharp from corner to corner is essential. The enlarger head should be properly aligned and distribute image-forming light evenly across the picture field. Condenser lighting systems tend to increase contrast and sharpness; diffusion lighting systems tend to decrease contrast and to soften apparent sharpness.

Print Processing Many processing factors can affect print quality. Papers and chemicals should be fresh and pure and used at the proper temperature. Improper use can result in loss of contrast, poor image tone, and stains. Normal development times are most likely to produce optimal contrast and density. Underdevelopment often produces muddy-looking, uneven prints with brownish image tones. Overdevelopment and improper fixing can cause loss of tonal separations in the highlight areas, fog, and chemical stains. Note that some developers increase contrast, while others decrease it.

Characteristics of a Fine Print

When all the factors affecting technical quality in the negative and in the print are under control and working together, optimal technical quality can be expected in the final print. The desirable characteristics of a high quality, full-scale print are:

1. Specular highlights print as white (base white). The presence of any image density in these small highlights reduces image brilliance.

2. Darkest subject tones print as deepest black (maximum density). The lack of deepest black reduces image brilliance and restricts the overall tonal range.

3. Dark objects in the shadows are visible as dark gray tones. Shadow details can be seen.

4. Light objects in the highlights are visible as light gray tones. Highlight details also can be seen.

5. Different tonal values are separate and distinguishable throughout the midtone range. The print has a rich variety of middle grays.

6. Grain is not obtrusive unless used for special effect.

7. Image is clear and sharp except where selective focusing or blurring is used for special effect.

8. Print is totally free of imperfections such as dust specks, stains, scratches, fingerprints, uneven borders, retouching marks, or other, unintended, nonimage blemishes.

Figure 15-2 shows a high quality, full-scale print. However, remember that printed halftone images, such as those appearing in this book, can only approximate a photograph's original tones and contrasts. Nevertheless, the qualities of a good print should become clear. Figure 6-40, page 232, will remind you of the characteristics of poor prints.

The Zone System

Objective 15-B Describe the basic principles of the zone system.

Key Concepts previsualization, zone scale, expansions, contractions

A more comprehensive approach to precise control of tone and contrast is the **zone system**, developed originally by Ansel Adams and Fred Archer. Although normally associated with traditional film photography, the zone system can be applied to digital imaging as well.

The zone system is based on the concept of **previsualization**. This is a process by which the photographer, before exposing the image, visualizes how the final print will appear and plans how to represent the scene's tonal values in the final print. Then, using a light meter, the relative brightness of various parts of the scene are measured and an exposure is determined. With proper development, the various tonal values in the scene will be rendered to their desired levels of density in the negative.

The zone system is based on a printed gray **zone scale**, such as that shown in Figure 15-3. Ten distinct shades, or zones, of gray are represented. The deepest black (maximum print density) of Zone 0 results from no exposure on the negative; the maximum white (minimum print density) of Zone IX results from maximum exposure on the negative. Each successive zone represents double the exposure of the preceding zone —a one f-stop increase. The average shade in a full-scale print is the medium gray of Zone V, which is the same tonality as an 18-percent gray card. Reflected light meters are designed to read Zone V values. For all practical purposes, clear, visible details may be expected only in Zones III through VII.

Table 15-1 explains the zone scale and the exposure adjustments that must be made to a light meter reading to place a subject in a zone other than Zone V.

The density of the low zones (I through IV) is determined mainly by exposure— small changes in exposure greatly affect the amount of detail rendered. The low zones can be placed at any point on the tonal scale by making the exposure adjustments noted to the left of the zone number.

Changes in development have little effect on the low zones.

The density of the high zones (VI through IX) is controlled primarily by the film development. Changing the development will greatly affect the tonal values of the high zones.

Through careful testing of each film/developer combination, photographers can learn to place various subject light values in the zones they desire. By manipulating exposure, they can shift the

A.

B.

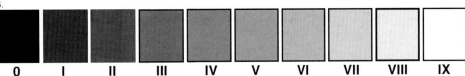

C.

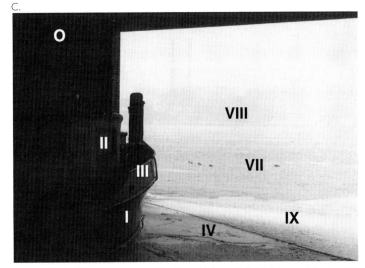

Figure 15-3. Zone system applications. A) In soft flat light or subjects with limited tones the range of densities may be limited to only a few middle tones. B) Zone system scale. C) In stark contrast situations the middle densities may be omitted and only the extremes included.

Table 15-1. The Zone System Scale

Exposure Adjustment	Zone	Description/Normal Subject Values
+4	IX	Pure paper white without tonality or details. The highest zone modern photo materials can handle.
+3	VIII	Very light gray—the least perceptible change of tone from pure white. Zone VIII carries only a suggestion of very light details: sunlight on white walls, white t-shirts, and so on.
+2	VII	Light gray. *The lightest usable detail.* Bright textured detail such as snow or sand, highlights on skin, clouds.
+1	VI	Richly textured light gray. A blue north sky, Caucasian skin, light hair, sand or snow in shadow.
0	V	*Middle gray* value. 18% gray. Green grass, foliage, stone, dark skin, or skin in shadow.
−1	IV	A medium dark value. Important dark shadows, blue jeans, dark hair, shadows under trees. Full detail held.
−2	III	Dark values. *Darkest usable detail.* The darkest area of the print where full detail and texture are rendered. Deep textured shadows.
−3	II	Very dark values. Shadows within shadows. The first slight suggestion of detail and texture.
−4	I	Almost black. The first barely perceptible change from pure black. No detail or texture.
−5	0	Pure black, the blackest tone the paper is capable of creating.

entire tonal range of the image upward or downward in the scale, altering the tonal rendering of various details. Longer than normal development times, or **expansions**, give additional contrast and separation to a flat tonal scene. Alternatively, shorter than normal development times, or **contractions**, can produce a better tonal range from a contrasty tonal scene. Books by Ansel Adams and Minor White, listed in the references, provide extensive explanations of the zone system. See Figure 15-3 for examples of zone system applications.

Processing for Permanence

Objective 15-C Describe the methods and materials used in darkroom print processing for permanence.

Key Concept archival processing

Fiber-based prints that have received normal processing may still contain some residual chemicals that can cause staining and fading over several years. In fact, a poorly processed photograph may begin to deteriorate in only a few months.

Archival processing involves taking special precautions to assure that a print will be as chemically free, stable and long lasting as possible. Any image that may have historical or collectible value should be produced using archival processing procedures. A correctly developed and stored fiber-based photograph may be expected to last several *thousand* years.

Selecting Materials

Producing archival images begins with the selection of the most stable materials. Resin-coated papers may be convenient to use, but their long-term stability is questionable. For maximum stability, high-quality, double-weight, fiber-based enlarging papers are preferred. In addition, many fine art photographers adjust their printing easels to create large, one-inch white borders around the printed image. Such a border acts as a barrier and a "telltale" area to reveal early signs of stains and degradation.

Quality chemistry is also important—use only freshly mixed chemicals and change the baths frequently. The manufacturer's recommendations as to shelf-life and print capacities are usually reduced by 50 percent for archival processing. (See Figure 15-4, showing the steps in archival processing.)

Special Processing and Fixing

Careful processing is important, especially fixing, washing, and drying. Fixing must be thorough enough to remove all residual silver salts; however, prolonged fixing may degrade the fine highlights and hamper washing. For archival processing, many critical workers, including Ansel Adams, prefer two separate fixing baths, both based upon sodium thiosulfate, over a single fixing bath.

In this method, the first fixing bath, which removes most of the harmful byproducts, is used for three minutes. The second bath, which remains fairly free of byproducts, is also used for three minutes. The two baths assure complete fixation. When approximately 8,000 square inches of prints per gallon of fixer has been fixed, the first bath is discarded and is replaced by the second bath. A new batch of fixer is then prepared for the second bath. Many photographers hold their prints in a tank of running water between the first and second fixing bath until a batch of prints accumulates.

Other creative photographers have adopted a single-bath archival fixing method advocated by Ilford. In this method, a single fixing bath, based on ammonium thiosulfate, is used for sixty seconds with continuous agitation. Because the fixing time is so short, the fixer does not penetrate deeply into the paper fibers. Ilford recommends a five-minute first wash after fixing, followed by a ten-minute treatment in a washing aid based on sodium sulfite, and a five-minute final clear water wash. No more than 4,000 square inches of prints should be processed per gallon of fixer with this method.

Toning for Preservation

A very dilute selenium toning solution will protect the print from atmospheric pollution as well as change the image color slightly and intensify the maximum black. To avoid blotchy yellow stains that selenium toner can sometimes produce, wash prints completely before toning or place the print into the toner directly from the fixer without washing at all. Most photographers prefer this latter method. The toner can be combined with a hypo clearing agent to carry out both steps in a single bath by using one part Kodak Rapid Selenium Toner diluted with twenty parts Kodak Hypo-Clearing Agent. The intensity of the tone will vary with the amount of time the print stays in the toning bath. Thoroughly wash all prints after toning and avoid wash temperatures above 68° F (20° C).

Washing

Prints should be washed thoroughly in a washer designed to bring fresh water continuously to the surface of each print. Tray washing is not effective unless the prints are frequently interleaved so that fresh wash water can reach all prints. If a tray must be used, only a few prints should be

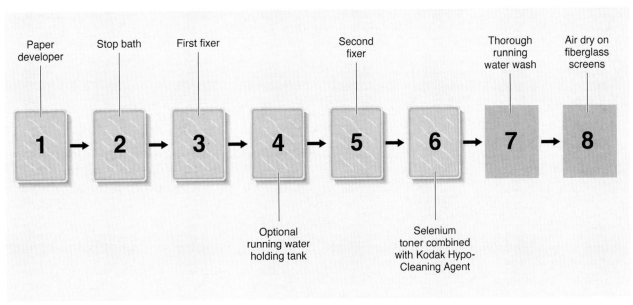

Figure 15-4. The steps in archival processing.

washed at a time; they should be well separated; and the tray should be emptied often to remove accumulated fixer residues. Washer design, water flow, and processing procedures all affect wash time. More than one hour of wash time is often required.

Drying

Air drying prints on a fiberglass screen is a safe way to dry archival prints. You can build a simple dryer easily by stretching fiberglass window screening material over a clean wooden frame. Drying usually requires many hours, depending on ambient temperature and humidity. After drying, stack the prints under a heavy weight to flatten them.

Mounting and Storage

Use only rag or other acid-free mounting board and window mat. Because even archival quality mat board absorbs pollutants from the air and will require replacement, fine prints should not be dry mounted. Instead, use archival photo corners or special tissue hinges to attach the print to the board.

Prints should be stored, interleaved with acid-free tissue, in archival boxes. If prints are displayed, avoid high temperatures, high humidity, and bright lighting conditions.

Large-Format Photography

Objective 15-D Describe a large-format view camera and its basic controls.

Key Concepts camera movements, field camera, monorail camera, standards, covering power, neutral position, rise and fall, lateral shift, swing, tilt, Scheimpflug rule, sheet film holders, corner notches, dark slide, film hangers

Reasons for Using a View Camera

Compared to working with modern electronic, automated, and computerized cameras, using a view camera is like stepping back in time. A view camera is large, heavy, and cumbersome. It must be used on a tripod, loaded with one piece of film at a time, and requires the photographer to hide his head under a dark cloth in order to view an image that is dim, upside down, and backwards. Despite their loss of spontaneity, large-format photographers endure all this because the images a view camera produces cannot be duplicated with standard film and digital cameras.

Most view cameras use 4in x 5in or larger individual sheets of film. These large-format film sheets allow a wealth of details, textures and tonalities to be recorded that cannot be equaled by smaller formats. Moreover, by processing individual film sheets, processing can be tailored to the needs of each subject. In addition, most view cameras permit a range of **camera movements** that give the photographer control over the shape and sharpness of objects in the final image. By altering the position of the camera's front lens board and rear film plane, the photographer can control perspective.

Types of View Cameras

View cameras are the simplest and oldest type of camera. They consist of little more than a lens at one end of a flexible bellows and a ground-glass focusing screen at the other. The two basic designs used for modern view cameras are field and monorail cameras. **Field cameras** are usually lighter, more compact, much easier to carry around, and quicker to set up than their monorail counterparts. On the other hand, **monorail cameras** are much more flexible and offer a greater range of camera movements for image control.

Field cameras Field cameras, sometimes called flat-bed cameras, are usually made from wooden frames that form a U-shaped base. Sometimes the base can telescope in and out to accommodate close focusing or long lenses. Field cameras fold into very small packages for convenience while traveling. The photographer composes and focuses the image directly by viewing it on the camera's ground glass. Compared to monorail cameras, however, field cameras may not be as strong or stable and do not offer the same full range of camera movements.

Light studio work, architectural photographs, and other moderately difficult subjects are best handled with field cameras. They were originally designed for portraits, landscape, and location work and are well suited to these tasks. Besides, the cameras

Famous Photographer

Edward Weston

At the turn of the century two approaches to photography prevailed in America—the east coast approach that was preoccupied with defining the atmosphere of its cities, streets, and interiors, and the west coast approach that was preoccupied with defining the natural landscapes and subjects. Edward Weston, later acclaimed as one of America's great photographic artists, was the quintessential western photographer.

Early in his career Weston utilized all the crafts of processing and printing to produce romantic, impressionistic, soft-focus images that transformed his photographs into works closely akin to painting. By 1911 he had his own studio in Tropico, California, and had achieved an international reputation as a salon photographer. However, the San Francisco Fair of 1915 introduced him to modern art, music, and literature and his work began to break from the salon traditions. By 1922 he had come under the influence of Alfred Stieglitz, Charles Sheeler, and Paul Strand and was clearly striving for an aesthetic based upon objectivity.

In 1923 he moved to Mexico, where he lived and worked for three years with a circle of artists that included Diego Rivera, Orozco, and Siqueiros. By 1925 his photographs demonstrated the pin-sharp, objective, unretouched qualities that characterized new realism in America. Late in 1926 he returned to California, but not to his studio work. With his son, Brett, he took up residence in the mountains near Monterey and with his 8 x 10 inch view camera he began making the photographs of the sea and the shore around Point Lobos and of the dunes at Oceano that many consider to be his finest work. In 1932, with Ansel Adams and Willard Van Dyke, he formed Group f/64, and in 1937 he was the first photographer to be awarded a Guggenheim Fellowship.

He always managed to photograph his subjects with such meticulous precision that he rendered the most mundane subjects into objects of artistic interest. Whether the subject was a blistered and peeling abandoned car, the caked and cracking walls of an adobe house, a farmhouse doorway, a piece of vegetable, or a sweeping vista of orchards or sand dunes, his exacting technique and vision would enable him to surpass documentary realism and to reveal the transcendent beauty of his subject, to communicate his personal feelings, and to affect both the senses and the emotions of his viewers.

Edward Weston. "Artichoke Halved," 1930, photograph by Edward Weston. Collection Center for Creative Photography, The University of Arizona. 1981 Center for Creative Photography, Arizona Board of Regents.

"The camera should be for the recording of life, for rendering the very sustenance and quintessence of the thing itself, whether it be polished steel or palpitating flesh," he wrote. The subject should be "rendered with the utmost exactness: stone is hard, bark is rough, flesh is alive."

His exhibitions include: Mexico City, 1923 and 1924; Museum of Modern Art, New York City, 1946, and Paris, 1950. Major collections of his work are held by Guadalajara State Museum, Los Angeles Public Library, Museum of Modern Art, and the International Museum of Photography in Rochester, New York.

Figure 15-5. An example of a folding wooden field type view camera.

themselves tend to be old, beautiful, polished, wooden artifacts reminiscent of earlier photographic epochs. Edward Weston and Paul Strand are among those who have worked with these old cameras, extracting from them some of the more memorable images that grace photography's history. (See Figure 15-5.)

Monorail Cameras Monorail cameras are mounted by means of front and rear uprights, or **standards**, onto a single metal tube that is attached to the support. (See Figure 15-6.) Although less portable than a field camera, the monorail camera has a larger range of movements. They are the standard choice for studio, product, and architectural photographers who need precise image control.

The monorail camera's design allows it to accept such accessories as an interchangeable bellows and recessed lens boards for wide-angle lenses. Some may even be fitted with reflex viewing attachments and behind-the-lens light meters.

Lenses

The lens, of course, is the true heart of any view camera. Each lens is typically mounted permanently on an interchangeable lens board that may be exchanged with other lens boards with similarly mounted lenses. A normal lens for a view camera with a 4in x 5in film format will have a focal length of approximately 6in (≈150mm). A typical telephoto lens would be 8in (≈210mm); an often-used wide-angle lens would be 3 1/2in (≈90mm). These two lenses would have approximately the same angle of view as 70mm telephoto and 28mm wide-angle lenses on a 35mm camera.

Covering power is another important consideration in lens selection. **Covering power** refers to the size of the circle of illumination produced by a lens—that is, the usable image size. To make full use of the view camera's ability to control perspective, the lens must transmit a usable image that is larger than the film format.

Camera Movements

Conventional cameras are permanently aligned in the **neutral position** so that their lens and film planes are exactly parallel. View cameras can be deliberately unaligned by using **camera movements**. A good view camera should provide for physically repositioning the lens board and ground-glass film plane—the front and back standards. These movements, described below, enable the photographer to precisely control the placement, shape, and sharpness of the image.

Rise and Fall On view cameras, both standards are capable of moving up and down. This movement is called the **rise and fall**. Rise and fall controls the vertical position of the image on the film

Figure 15-6. An example of a monorail type of view camera.

and can be adjusted to include more of the top or bottom of the subject without tilting the camera.

Lateral Shift On many view cameras the standards can be moved sideways in a **lateral shift** and adjusted to include more of the right or left side of the subject. These movements are often used for refining the composition and framing an image without disturbing the tripod.

Swings **Swings** are movements that twist the front or rear boards around a vertical axis. The front swing angles the lens board and is used mainly to control depth of field for horizontally arrayed subjects. The back swing angles the film plane and is used mainly to control the shape and perspective of objects.

Tilts **Tilts** are similar to swings except that they move around a horizontal axis. Thus, the standards may be tilted up and down and also are used to control depth of field and perspective.

Using Camera Movements Effectively Camera movements are made to control the shape of objects, or perspective, and sharpness, or depth of field. As a simplified rule, perspective is generally controlled by adjusting the film plane, and sharpness is usually controlled by adjusting the lens board.

To achieve correct perspective, the film plane must be parallel to the main subject's plane. This can be achieved by using the swings and tilts on the rear standard. The effect of these changes is readily visible on the ground-glass focusing screen.

An optical principle, known as the **Scheimpflug rule**, states that maximum depth of field will be achieved when imaginary lines drawn through the film plane, the plane of the lens board, and the subject plane all meet at some common point in space. In practical terms, the rule is also satisfied when the film plane, lens board, and subject plane are all parallel. This is achieved primarily by means of front swings and tilts and observing the effects of the changes on the ground-glass focusing screen.

For example, if photographing a tall building, tilt the back standard until it is parallel with the building. This will produce a correct perspective by producing an image of the building that is as wide at the top as at the bottom. Then tilt the lens

board until it also is parallel to the subject plane to produce maximum depth of field. Now the Scheimpflug rule is satisfied—all three planes are parallel. Remember, view the effect of the camera movements on the ground-glass focusing screen as you adjust and refine the settings. (See Figure 15-7.)

Using Sheet Film

Most view cameras are designed to use film in sheets rather than rolls. Sheet film must be loaded into carefully cleaned **sheet film holders** that accept one piece of film on each of their two sides. Each sheet of film has a series of **corner notches**, which allow the photographer to determine the type of film and the emulsion position in complete darkness. Once safely in the holders, the film is protected from accidental exposure by a removable **dark slide**. After exposure, the film is given conventional black-and-white processing. Sheet film can be developed in open trays, by using sheet **film hangers**, or in special daylight developing tanks. (See discussion on page 167.)

Common View Camera Accessories

Plenty of sheet film holders, a sturdy tripod, an accurate light meter, a cable release, and a dark cloth are all essential for successful use of a view camera. In addition, some photographers use a Polaroid back on their view camera to check composition with an instant print. Some photographers who like the control of a view camera but who seek the convenience and cost-effectiveness of roll film use roll film adapters on their view cameras. In most cases, a lens hood and a UV filter provide added protection for location work.

Close-up and Copy Photography

Objective 15-E Describe some of the principles and techniques of close-up and copy photography.

Key Concepts close-up photography, image-to-object ratio, photomacrography, photomicrography, microphotography, macrophotography, focal distance, close-up lens, macrolens, ringflash, copying, the copy, copy negative, reproduction, copy stand, copy board, printing frame, line art, continuous-tone image

A.

C.

B.

D.

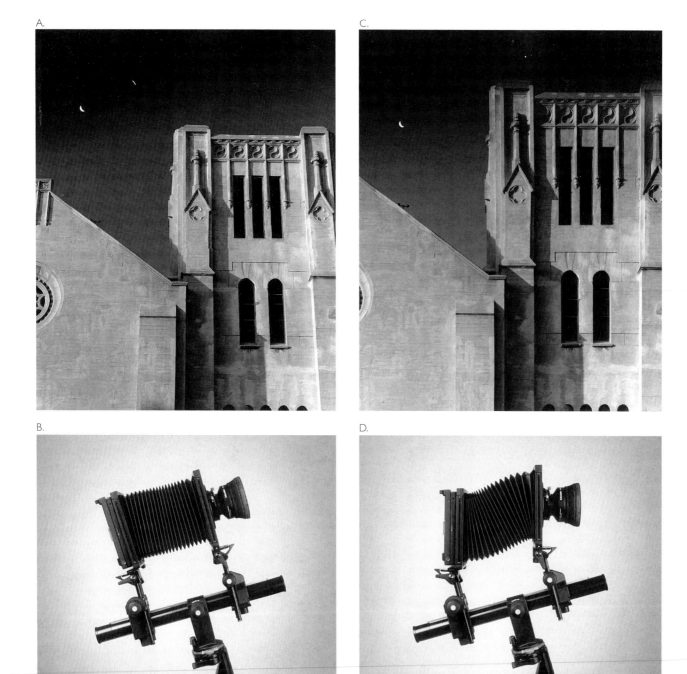

Figure 15-7. A) Convergence results when tall buildings are photographed from a low angle with the camera movements in a neutral position as shown in B. B) The neutral camera movements used for A. C) Correct perspective can be achieved by tilting both the camera's lens board and the film back until they are parallel to the building as shown in D. D) The revised camera movements used for C.

Close-up Photography

Most cameras equipped with a normal lens can take pictures from as close as 1 to 2 feet (0.3 to 0.6 meter). However, this is not usually close enough to get extreme close-ups of small objects such as flowers, small animals, or insects. To obtain really dramatic close-ups of small objects, the camera must be moved much closer to the subject. In order to focus this close to the subject, special lenses or accessories may be needed.

Not all cameras are well suited for close-up work. At close distances, focusing and framing are critical. The slightest misdirection of the camera axis may shift the field of view far off the subject. Depth of field is extremely shallow at close distances, often no more than a small fraction of an inch. Consequently, extremely precise framing and focusing are necessary to assure that essential details are recorded in sharp focus.

The cameras best suited for close-up work are those that permit framing and focusing directly through the camera's picture-taking lens—single-lens reflex, view cameras and digital cameras equipped with small preview monitors. Only these cameras permit one to frame and focus the image precisely as it appears at the focal plane before making the exposure. Close-ups can be made, of course, with viewfinder and twin-lens reflex cameras, but the process requires precise measurement to correct parallax and to obtain correct frame and focus.

Techniques The techniques of photographing objects at close range have been classified in several categories. The term **close-up photography** is used to describe photography between a camera's minimum focusing distance (with a normal lens) and a distance of about two focal lengths from the subject. At the normal minimum focusing distance, the image of an object is recorded at about 1/10 life-size, or at a 1:10 **image-to-object ratio**. When the camera is brought to a distance of two focal lengths from the object, the object is recorded at about life-size, or at a 1:1 image-to-object ratio.

The term **photomacrography** is used to describe the photographing of objects to produce an image larger than life-size. The term **photomicrography** is used to describe the photographing of objects through a microscope to produce an even larger image-to-object ratio. Figure 15-8 distinguishes among the several classes of close-up photography, all of which require the use of special techniques and equipment.

Two other techniques are often confused with these. The term **microphotography** is used to describe techniques for producing extremely small images, such as those used in microelectronic circuits. The term **macrophotography** is used to describe techniques for producing extremely large images, such as photomurals and posters.

Using the View Camera

1. Set up the camera. *Mount the camera on a sturdy tripod, screw in the cable release, and position all camera movements to their middle or neutral position.*

2. Roughly focus and compose. *Set the camera's lens to the largest aperture and open the shutter. Achieve an approximate focus by adjusting the length of the bellows. Use the focusing cloth and a small magnifying glass or jeweler's loupe for a better view. Move the tripod, or use the lateral shift and rise and fall to compose and frame the desired image.*

3. Make any perspective adjustments. *Use the swings and tilts to adjust the position of the rear standard to control the shape of the subject. Generally, the film plane should be aligned so that it is parallel to the subject.*

4. Adjust for sharpness. *Check the focus and, if necessary, adjust the plane of focus with the front swings and tilts according to the Scheimpflug rule. Check final focus carefully.*

5. Make the exposure. *Close the shutter. Take a light meter reading and set the appropriate lens opening and shutter speed. Cock the shutter. Insert a loaded film holder, and remove the front dark slide. Make the exposure by tripping the shutter with the cable release. Replace the dark slide so that the black side faces the lens. By reversing the film holder, another exposure can now be made.*

Equipment In normal operation, the distance between the camera lens and the focal plane, known as the **focal distance**, is about one focal length. To focus on objects closer than the normal minimum, the focal distance must be extended beyond normal. The equipment most commonly used to extend the focal distance are close-up lenses and macrolenses.

Close-up Lenses A **close-up lens** is a simple magnifying lens that screws in front of the normal lens in a manner similar to a filter. Close-up lenses are available in various strengths commonly designated as $+1$, $+2$, $+3$, and so on. The larger the number, the greater the magnification. Close-up lenses may be combined—combining a

Figure 15-8. Close-up photography. A) Reduced, lifesize, and magnified focusing distances. B) Normal focusing distance. A community of bees. C) Close-up photography. A grouping of bees. D) Photomacrography. One individual bee about life size. E) Photomicrography. A bee's face larger than life.

+2 and a +3 lens, for example, has the effect of a +5 close-up lens. Reducing the effective focal length increases the ratio between the focal distance and the focal length.

Close-up lenses require no exposure compensation and they can be used with fixed as well as interchangeable lenses. A disadvantage, however, is that they somewhat degrade image quality.

Macrolenses Designed especially for close-up photography, a **macrolens** is used in place of a camera's normal lens. It is designed for optimal performance in the close-up focusing range but may operate as well as a normal lens in the normal focusing range. Separate, true macrolenses can only be used on cameras with interchangeable lens systems. However many digital and film cameras have zoom lenses that offer a "macro" feature. (See Figure 15-9.)

Figure 15-9. Macro zoom lens. Some zoom lenses feature a macro setting for close-up photography.

Determining Exposure A built-in, through-the-lens (TTL) light-metering system is generally more accurate and convenient than a hand-held light meter for making close-up photographs. Hand-held meters are ill-equipped to distinguish highlight and shadow differences within the close-up's typical narrow field of view. If it is necessary to use an external light meter, determine exposure by using an 18 percent gray card in the object's position (see page 128).

Because close-up focusing distances produce shallow depth of field, select a small aperture to maximize the field of focus.

Lighting Working at close distances requires special lighting techniques. For a balanced light effect, sunlight or a single spotlight may be used as the key light with a reflector of white paper or aluminum foil to bounce fill light into the shadows. For soft, even, shadowless light, the diffused light of an overcast sky can be used as the main light source. If flash is used close to the subject, care must be taken to mute its intensity. Place a layer of white handkerchief over the flash, or use flash-off-camera to improve modeling.

A **ringflash** unit is a circular electronic flash tube that fits around the front element of the lens to provide an even field of shadowless flash

light at close-up distances. These devices are often used to illuminate scientific and medical close-up photographs.

Copy Photography

Copying is a form of close-up photography in which the subjects are two-dimensional, such as drawings, paintings, photographs, or other documents. The products are exact recordings of the originals in every detail of line, tone, and/or color. Because the original subject, termed **the copy**, is two-dimensional, copy photography is not concerned with depth of field; rather, it is concerned with obtaining a sharp, undistorted image over the entire flat surface of the original.

The final print, an exact positive print or transparency of the original, is called a **reproduction**. Sometimes a copy negative is made first. Sometimes a positive transparency is made rather than a copy negative.

As with other close-up photography, SLR, digital, or view cameras afford the most accurate tools for framing and focusing. A camera support, such as a **copy stand** or tripod, helps to achieve stability during exposures. Unlike other forms of photography, however, flat, even, shadowless lighting produces the most faithful reproduction of flat material.

Simple copying setups satisfy most copying needs. Basically, all copy setups consist of (1) a camera;

Figure 15-10. A simple horizontal copying setup.

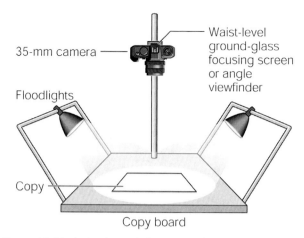

Figure 15-11. A simple vertical copy stand.

(2) a camera support; (3) a **copy board**; (4) a lighting arrangement; and (5) a cable release.

A Simple Horizontal Copying Setup The original may be affixed to a wall, illuminated with a pair of floodlights, and photographed with a camera mounted on a tripod, as shown in Figure 15-10.

The camera axis is aligned with the center of the copy board. The original is kept flat by pinning it to the copy board, by using double-sided tape or magnets, or by placing it in a glass **printing frame**.

A Vertical Copying Setup Vertical copy stands consist of a vertical, tubular post mounted to a copy board. The camera, mounted to a collar assembly that slides up and down the post, can be positioned and locked at any desired height on the post. Flood lamps are mounted to the post or to the copy board. (See Figure 15-11.)

A 35mm SLR camera fitted with a waist-level ground-glass focusing screen or angle viewfinder or a digital camera with a preview monitor is most suitable for a vertical copying setup. This enables the photographer to frame and focus while standing comfortably.

For small- and medium-size copy, a camera with a normal or macro lens must be set up for close-up focusing to obtain an image of satisfactory size. Screw-in close-up lenses are not recommended for copying because of their curvilinear aberrations.

Lighting for Copy Photography For copying, it is essential to illuminate the original uniformly over its whole surface. Uneven lighting will produce a reproduction of uneven density.

Illuminate small originals, 8in x 10in (20cm x 25cm) or smaller, with two flood lamps placed about 30in (75cm) from the center of the copy board and at an angle of 45° to it. For larger originals, use four lamps, one at each corner of the copy board. (See Figure 15-12.)

Most ordinary frosted tungsten (3200 K) lamps or photolamps (3400 K) can be used for black-and-white film. Opalized enlarging lamps and fluorescent tubes also provide a broad, diffused light source. Avoid reflector flood lamps—they often produce an uneven light field.

For color copying, select a film that is balanced for the light source or set a digital camera's white balance to match the lighting. Use a film balanced for tungsten light with tungsten lighting; use a film balanced for daylight with daylight or electronic flash. Avoid fluorescent lighting for copying with color film, as it is difficult to match to a film's color balance.

For best results, all lamps in the copy setup should be of the same type, brightness, and age. Use a lens hood to shield the lens from direct light.

Eliminating Reflections Copy with a shiny surface, such as the varnished surface of an oil painting or a glossy photograph, can create unwanted reflections from the source lamps. Glass covering the copy can sometimes even reflect an image of the copy camera, the photographer, or other objects that then become part of the recorded image.

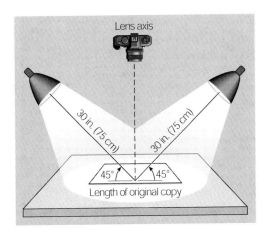

Figure 15-12. A lighting setup for copy photography. Ideal arrangement to provide even field of illumination without reflections.

Try these procedures to eliminate unwanted reflections:

1. Use antiglare photographic glass on top of the copy.
2. Place the source lights at right angles to each other and at 45° to the copy plane.
3. Use polarizing filters over the lamps and over the lens.
4. Use a large aperture to reduce depth of field and throw reflected images out of focus.
5. Shoot through a lens-size hole in a sheet of black cloth inserted between the camera and the copy.

Figure 15-13 shows the use of these techniques.

Retain Important Surface Textures Sometimes it is important to retain or even emphasize the surface texture of the original copy. For example, the surface texture of an oil painting or a tapestry might be important features to include in the reproduction. A faithful reproduction of such an original will retain enough of the surface highlights and reflections to reveal the surface texture. This may require lowering the lights from the suggested 45-degree position.

Determining Exposure for Copying For copying, light meter readings should reveal if there are any variations in the lighting field within the copy frame. A hand-held meter is best suited to this purpose. A TTL meter, on the other hand, can only obtain an average reading of the entire image frame. To obtain an even field of light, reposition the lamps to eliminate any variations of light intensity observed within the copy area.

Adjust exposure as indicated by the light meter to compensate for the overall tonal value of the copy. If the overall tone of the copy is dark, reduce exposure; if the tone is light, increase it. (See *Exposure for Shadows or Highlights*, page 127).

Copying Different Types of Originals The original may consist solely of **line art**, such as a drawing, woodcut, or printed document. In this case, you can obtain maximum contrast between the

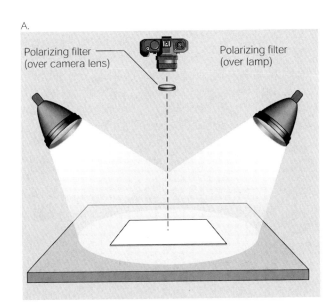

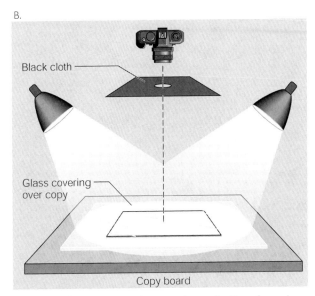

Figure 15-13. Eliminating unwanted reflections. A) By using polarizing filters over light sources and camera lens, reflections from glass or glossy surfaces can be eliminated. B) By shooting through a small hole in a black cloth stretched in front of the camera, reflections of camera and photographer in glass covering of copy frame are eliminated.

lines and the background by using a high-contrast film and developer or by adjustments in the digital darkroom. In black-and-white photography you can also use a filter that transmits the paper color but that absorbs the ink color to increase contrast.

Alternatively, the original may consist of a **continuous-tone image**, such as a black-and-white photograph. In this case you can reproduce the full range of tones present in the original by using a normal-contrast, fine-grain film and soft-working developer that will record a full range of tones between the extremes of black and white.

The original may also consist of a color image, such as a painting, color drawing, or color photograph. In this case, you can record the full range of colors and densities by using a color negative film to make the highest quality prints. You can also use color transparency film, preferably one specially formulated for copying. Instant color print films also can be used to make positive color prints from original copy or from color transparencies.

Appendix G-1 and G-2, on the CD that accompanies this book, describe some of the films commonly used for copying.

Building a Web Photo Gallery

Objective 15-F Create a web photo gallery.

Key Concepts Internet, file server, host server, folder, uploading, web site, home page, browser, World Wide Web, web photo gallery, web authoring program, Hypertext Markup Language (HTML), File Transfer Protocol (FTP), freeware

Many photographers use the Internet to publish their images on the World Wide Web. This provides an inexpensive and rapid medium for sharing photographs of family, friends, and important events with others. For professional photographers, it affords an opportunity to create a portfolio of images to circulate to clients, customers, and prospective purchasers of their photographs and services.

A Brief Overview of How the Internet Works

Anyone with access to a computer can connect to other computers to form a network. All the computers connected in a network can exchange data files, including text, images, multimedia, and program files. Over the years, local networks have connected to other local networks to form an international system of networks called the **Internet**. Much like a telephone system, the Internet makes it possible for any computer on the Internet anywhere in the world to connect to any other computer on the Internet anywhere in the world. Unlike the telephone system, once you are connected to the Internet, connecting to other computers is generally free of additional charges.

A computer that stores many files for use by other computers that are connected to it is called a **file server**. By connecting to a server, any computer can access the files stored on it. Using this system of networks and file servers, it is possible to store your files on a **host server** and make them available to others on demand.

To do this, the host sets up a memory storage area on the host server called a **folder** dedicated just to you. You may then copy files from your computer into this folder. Copying your files from your computer to the host server is called **uploading**. If you organize and format your files properly, you can create a **web site** with an address that others can access from their computers. When someone accesses your web site, the first screen that automatically displays is called the **home page**. In addition to the home page, your web site may consist of many other pages all linked together.

Software programs called **browsers** were developed to make communication over the Internet easier and more graphic. A browser transforms the digital codes contained in the digital files into colorful screen layouts that may include text, images, and multimedia sound and visual effects. Other software tools make it possible to search the entire Internet rapidly for web sites of special interest. Because of the way the computers, networks, and file servers are interconnected on the Internet, the system has come to be known as the **World Wide Web**.

The Internet and the World Wide Web are at the very early stages of their development. Although the Internet itself began in the early 1960s, the World Wide Web and the widespread exchange of graphical and multimedia information began in the early 1990s. Much has yet to be learned about how best to use this immense resource and how it will affect society. For photographers, however, their potential for sharing and exchanging photographic images is at hand.

What Is a Web Photo Gallery?

In general, web sites are created for a myriad of purposes—to provide news and information of all kinds. Web sites are sponsored by individuals, clubs, businesses, and private and government agencies, just to name a few. Private individuals, photographers, galleries, museums, and historical societies often create web sites that feature photographic images. Such a site may be referred to as a **web photo gallery**. Such a gallery may consist of personal family photographs, documentary and news photographs, creative and exhibition photographs, portraits, commercial, or industrial photographs—in short, photographs on any subject or theme that the author wishes. (See Figure 15-14.)

Many software programs, called **web authoring programs**, exist to aid in the creation of web pages. Some are very simple to use; others, more complex. All provide tools for designing the web page layout, and inserting text, images, multimedia files, and links to other pages and other web sites on the World Wide Web. To tie all these various files together, authoring programs usually create master files that use a special programming language called **Hypertext Markup Language (HTML)** that browsers can interpret. Adobe Photoshop, described in Units 8 and 9, provides an authoring tool for creating web photo galleries. (See Step-By-Step Procedure, *Creating a Web Photo Gallery in Photoshop*, p. 512)

To upload files to a host server requires that you set up an account with a Web host server. Host servers generally charge for server space; however, many servers will host your web site free of charge in return for your permission to include advertising on your site. In either case, once an account is established, your files must be uploaded to the server. This is usually done with a software program designed to transfer files using **File Transfer Protocol (FTP)**. Some FTP programs, such as WS_FTPLE and CuteFTP, are available off the Internet free of charge. Using an FTP program, you can upload your files from your computer to your folder on the host server and make your files available to others worldwide. See Appendix M on the CD that accompanies this book for links to FTP programs.

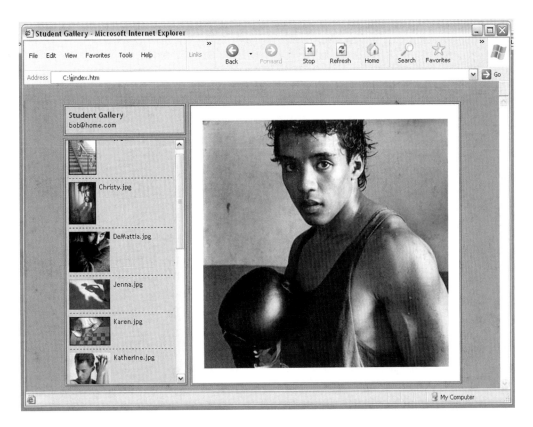

Figure 15-14. The completed web page is assembled automatically in Photoshop.

Creating a Web Photo Gallery in Photoshop

The Web Photo Gallery tool in Adobe Photoshop generates a gallery with easy navigation for viewing images in a browser. To create a Web photo gallery in Photoshop:

1. **Set up the image files**. *Copy all of the digital image files to be included in the gallery into a single folder, called the source folder. Also create a second folder, called the destination folder, which will receive all the files created by Photoshop for your Web photo gallery. (See Figure 15-15.)*

2. **Choose a style and enter your email address.** *Click to FILE —> AUTOMATE —> WEB PHOTO GALLERY. A dialog box displays. (See Figure 15-16.) Under the "Site" section of the dialog box use the STYLES pop-up menu to select how your gallery will be displayed. Note the preview of each style that appears to the right of the dialog box. Enter your email address to have a mail link appear on each page.*

3. **Choose the Source and Destination Locations.** *Specify the locations of both the Source and Destination folders in the "Source Images" section of the dialog box.*

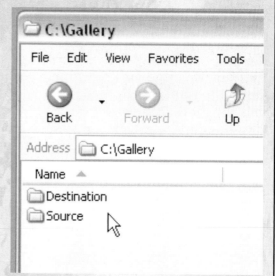

Figure 15-15. Separate sub-folders should be made for source and destination.

4. **Select Options to Customize Your Web Site.** *Toggle the arrow in the "Options" section of the dialog box to "Banner" and enter the title of your gallery. Enter a photographer's name and date if desired.*

5. **Specify Image Size and Color as Desired.** *Next, toggle the arrow in the "Options" section of the dialog box to "Large Images," "Thumbnails," "Custom Colors," and "Security" to make any desired changes to the default sizes and settings.*

6. **View your gallery in a browser.** *When you click OK, Photoshop generates the HTML and JPEG files needed for your Web gallery and saves them in your destination folder. Photoshop generates a master file named index.html that opens automatically whenever someone accesses your folder by addressing your web site address. When the process is complete, Photoshop launches your browser to display your web gallery.*

7. **Share your gallery with others.** *You may use your FTP program to upload the files from the destination folder on your computer to your folder on the host server. Or you may choose to copy all the files in your destination folder onto a removable disk and send it to others. Many prefer to email the files over the Internet. Any of these methods can be used to share your gallery with others.*

Figure 15-16. This dialog box controls the appearance of the page including colors and headings.

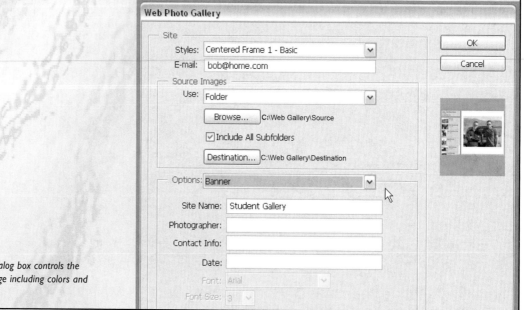

Web Photo Gallery Software Programs In addition to Adobe Photoshop, many other software programs for creating photo galleries for the World Wide Web are available commercially. Some of these are the following:

- ThumbsPlus (Windows & Macintosh)
- Ulead PhotoImpact Album (Windows)
- Jasc Media Center Plus (Windows)

Many other programs are available over the Internet for this purpose free of charge. In general, any programs that are distributed for free use are called **freeware**. Some freeware programs for creating Web photo pages are the following:

- Batch Thumbs (Windows)
- Catalog Wizard (Windows)
- Digi-Cam Web Page Generator (Windows)
- Thumbz Plus (Windows)

Links for installing these programs are provided on the CD that accompanies this book.

Law and Ethics for Photographers

Objective 15-G Describe some of the major principles of law and ethics important to photographers.

Key Concepts privacy, intrusion, trespass, implied consent, publication, tort of privacy, public disclosure of embarrassing private facts, false light, libel, appropriation, model release, Copyright Act of 1976, works for hire, declaration of intent to retain copyright, fair use, implied contract, licensing agreement

Photographers are not entirely free to shoot pictures of anything they wish, anytime, anywhere, in any manner, or to use the pictures however they wish without considering the rights of others. Sometimes the law limits what photographers can and cannot do; sometimes good taste, courtesy, and ethical judgment limit what photographers should and should not do. Except in the area of copyright, however, few laws pertaining to photography are national in scope—most vary from state to state, and practices may vary from community to community.

The following discussion cannot provide definitive answers to specific questions about photography and the law. The answer to any legal question is likely to be "It depends" because legal questions always involve both the law and the facts. Only the courts can determine how the laws pertain to any given set of facts and sometimes small differences of fact may produce completely different judgments.

Moreover, in our legal system, almost anyone can sue almost anyone for almost anything. So avoiding liability does not necessarily guarantee that you will not be sued. Winning is often not the main issue—being sued can be expensive, stressful, and time-consuming even if you prevail. So the risks you take as a photographer should consider your ability and willingness to deal with a lawsuit.

Two areas of law that are of special interest to photographers are those pertaining to privacy and those pertaining to copyright. The laws pertaining to privacy tend to govern photographic activity; the copyright law governs who owns what rights in the photographic works.

Privacy

The law tends to recognize that individuals have certain rights to **privacy** and that the public has certain rights to news and information. Balancing these rights has been the subject of considerable case law.

Invasions of privacy can occur while pictures are being taken or when the photographs are subsequently published. In general, the law defends the rights of photographers to take pictures in public places and, in many cases, in private places open to the public. Similarly, the law tends to protect the privacy rights of property owners and of photographic subjects when they are on private property that is not open to the public.

Even when photography is permitted, such as in a public place, a private place open to the public, or on private property where entry and photography have been permitted, photographers are not necessarily free to use the photographs they take in any way they choose. For example, a photographer may shoot a picture of an acrobat performing in a public parade or, with permission, at a private party, without violating any right of privacy. If the event is newsworthy, the photograph may be published in the news media without violating any right of privacy. However, in neither case could the photographs be sold or used for advertising purposes without violating a right of privacy unless the performer grants permission to use it in that way.

Invasions of privacy may be grouped into four major types, commonly called the four torts of privacy. These include:

1. intrusion upon a person's seclusion, solitude, or private affairs,

2. public disclosure of embarrassing private facts about a person,

3. publicity that places a person in a false light in the public eye, and

4. appropriation of a person's name or likeness for advertising or trade.

Each tort is described briefly with its application to photography.

Intrusion The tort of **intrusion** generally refers to the acts of photography themselves—the presence and actions of the photographer, which may intrude upon the plaintiff's seclusion, solitude, or private affairs.

While closely related to **trespass**, intrusion goes beyond the simple entry upon private property without permission. Even if entry to private property is permitted, any subsequent photographic activity may be regarded as an intrusion upon the expected seclusion of the subjects or into their private affairs. Further, shooting into private property from a public vantage point does not mitigate the intrusion—shooting pictures of people in places where they have a reasonable expectation of privacy is likely to be an invasion of their privacy. Although intrusion is more difficult to prove than trespass, it is usually unethical for a photographer to intrude upon the private lives of people in private places. Since intrusion may occur without trespass, therefore, it is generally a good idea for the photographer to obtain permission not only to enter upon private property but also to photograph subjects who are in private places.

Entering private property, however, that is open to the public is no trespass. Nevertheless, photography on private property that is open to the public, such as most places of business, theaters, and concert halls, may be restricted at the whim of the owner. Generally, unless notices are posted or communicated to the contrary, or the owner verbally refuses permission to photograph on the property, photography may proceed. However, any disruption of the normal flow of business caused by the photographer may be judged an intrusion.

Public places, such as libraries, museums, schools, hospitals, courthouses, and the like, may limit photography to protect the facilities and their users, and to avoid disruption of normal activity. As with private property, unless notice is posted or

---

☠ CAUTION ☠

Protect Your Privacy on the Internet

Before submitting any personal or family information to any Web hosting service or web site that you visit, make sure that they have a privacy policy and that they adhere to it. To be sure that a web site follows their own privacy policy, they should be registered with and display the seal of TRUSTe, a consumer protection organization that maintains records of complaints and litigation against Internet service organizations and web sites.

When you see the TRUSTe seal, you can be assured that the web site will disclose:

- What personal information is being gathered about you

- How the information will be used

- Who the information will be shared with, if anyone

- Choices available to you regarding how collected information will be used

- Safeguards in place to protect your information from loss, misuse, or alteration

- How you can update or correct inaccuracies in your information

Any web site concerned for your privacy and security will spell out to you what they do with the information they gather about you and will endeavor to earn your trust.

otherwise communicated, photography may generally proceed.

Military commanders have generally been judged to have extraordinary rights to search, seize film and cameras, and eject photographers in areas under their control.

Photographers are generally safe to photograph what they see on public streets and thoroughfares without fear of committing an intrusion. Anything that any person might see from the same location with the naked eye may be photographed. This does not mean, however, that the photographer may startle, frighten or intimidate subjects, disrupt their right to go about their normal activities, or that the photographs they take in these places may necessarily be published.

Because celebrities may be considered newsworthy and public persons, they often do not enjoy many of the legal rights of privacy that ordinary persons might enjoy. Although photographers may have an ethical responsibility to be considerate of all their subjects in all places and to respect their privacy in private places, some will often go to extreme lengths to photograph celebrities wherever they may be, sometimes pursuing them relentlessly, harassing them, and interfering with their activities. In some extreme cases the courts have been moved to restrain individual photographers from approaching particular subjects too closely, from unreasonably harassing them or interfering with their activities during photography. Publication of the photographs for purposes other than news would, of course, require the subject's permission.

Gaining access to news events that occur on private property may pose special problems for photographers. Generally, if it is common usage, custom, and practice in a given locality for a news photographer to accompany or follow police or fire officials onto the site of a newsworthy event, the photographer is not likely to be judged guilty of either trespass or intrusion. However, not all police and fire officials may be equally aware of local practices and policies, and individuals may seek to order a news photographer away from the site of a breaking news event or to otherwise restrain photography. Failure to comply may result in the photographer's arrest for disorderly conduct or for obstructing an officer's performance of duty.

In some states, the National Press Photographers Association (NPPA) or regional press photographers associations have established guidelines with state police for news photographers to access news sites. Although not all local police cooperate with these state guidelines, these attempts have gone far to create a more cooperative working relationship between public officials and the news media. Objective 14-G, *Photojournalism,* on page 478, elaborates on some of the special challenges of news photography and photojournalism.

Many potential problems of intrusion may be avoided by using common sense and a few precautions. When photographing people who are aware of the presence of the camera, photographers should verbally identify themselves as photographers and the reasons why they are shooting. It is also good practice to obtain full identification of persons who appear prominently in photographs. Precautions such as these may help to establish **"implied consent"** to being photographed—by not protesting, the subjects implicitly consent to the photographer's actions. However, the concept of implied consent is very subjective and often is difficult to establish in court.

Disclosing Embarrassing Private Facts This tort of privacy and the others that follow generally refer to the publication of photographs rather than to the acts of photography themselves. Although the term "publication" is often thought of as some form of reproduction in print or other media, such a definition is insufficient as it is applied under the laws of privacy. For these purposes, **publication** may include displaying, offering for sale, or even simply showing a photograph to another person.

This **tort of privacy** refers to **public disclosure of embarrassing private facts** that holds persons up to public ridicule, offends public standards of taste, or that publishes private and embarrassing information about them. Although federal case law is uneven in this area, no universal right exists to disclose publicly all private true facts about individuals that the public has no real right to know. Newsworthiness may serve as one defense against legal action under this tort and disclosing information that is a public record, no matter how old, may serve as another. However, circumstances may cloud the issue and notable exceptions remain. For example, reprinting photographs of rehabilitated ex-convicts or reformed prostitutes with their names and descriptions of earlier deeds have been judged invasions of privacy under this tort.

Generally, public persons, such as politicians, relinquish their rights of privacy under this tort. Further, when persons become newsworthy, many of their rights of privacy are lost, including this one. Publication of photographs in news media that disclose embarrassing private facts about newsworthy persons has not generally been held a violation of their rights of privacy—newsworthiness is generally a defense under this tort. But the same photograph may not necessarily be published again, whether in news or other media, after the person has ceased to be newsworthy.

False Light This sort of privacy refers to placing a person in a **"false light"** by incorrectly representing the subject in the public eye. Rather than from the photograph itself, the offense usually results from misrepresentation or misidentification in text accompanying the published photograph, such as in the headline, caption, or story. For example, the photographer might take a picture of a group of students outside the student center with their consent. However, if the photograph were then published to illustrate a story about drug abuse on college campuses, the photograph would place the identifiable students in a false light by implying that they were drug abusers.

Although "false light" rarely results from the photograph itself, it is nonetheless possible. Needless to say, deliberate image alterations by photographic or electronic means that create a false image of the subject and related details are examples. Although such deliberate alterations were a popular form of early news photography, such practices invite lawsuits under this tort today. Nonetheless, distortions and compressions that result accidentally and inadvertently from the use of wide-angle and telephoto lenses can result in image alterations that may cast the subject in a "false light"—for example, by making them appear nearer to persons or objects than they actually were, in conversation with persons to whom they never actually spoke, or in groups of persons they were never in. Careful attention to the headline, caption, and story accompanying the photograph can usually counteract any such inadvertent distortions.

Libel is the printed form of defamation—the wrongful damaging of a person's reputation by communicating a false statement or making a false accusation. As with false light, libel arising from a published photograph usually arises from the accompanying caption or text, even though a photograph alone may be libelous if it conveys a false and defamatory image. Libel actions undertaken under this tort suggest five points that must be proved for the action to succeed:

1. The representation must have been published.
2. The subject must be identified or clearly identifiable.
3. The representation must be false.
4. The representation must be defamatory.
5. Private persons must show that the representation was published through some fault or negligence on the part of the publisher, and not through an honest mistake. Public persons and celebrities must show that the representation was published with actual malice, with knowledge that it was false, or with reckless disregard for the truth.

Appropriation The tort of **appropriation** for advantage of a person's name or likeness has been more a problem for advertisers and commercial photographers than it has for news photographers and photojournalists. The news photographer enjoys many safeguards to the process of reporting the news in the public interest, and public persons and celebrities are often an integral part of the newsworthy landscape. Usually the issue arises with photographs taken of celebrities in public places, which are later used to sell products without their consent. The subjects may not wish to be associated with the product, or they may wish to be paid for their implied endorsement.

Appropriation is considered to possess a proprietary rather than a personal value under the privacy laws; therefore appropriation has monetary value. The image or likeness of a celebrity is what that person trades upon and its trade value may be diminished by uncontrolled exposure. Thus, the appropriation of a celebrity's likeness for gain may be regarded as an appropriation of valuable property.

Famous Photographer

Lewis Wickes Hine

Lewis Wickes Hine first established his reputation as a "conscience with a camera" with his photographic investigations of immigrants at Ellis Island in 1905 while he was still teaching science at the Ethical Culture School in New York. In 1908 he published a strong, illustrated criticism on social conditions that led *Charities and the Commons,* a magazine of social commentary, to hire him away from teaching to make photographic "documents of injustices." His early photographic investigations concerned the plight of the underprivileged brought on by industrialization—the atrocious living conditions of immigrant laborers on the New York State Barge Canal, the growing tenement slums of Chicago and Washington, living and working conditions among Pittsburgh miners and steel workers (later published as *The Pittsburgh Survey*), and the exploitation of children who were forced to perform menial mining and factory labor.

Three years after his first set of child labor photos appeared in *The Pittsburgh Survey,* the National Child Labor Committee appointed him, as a staff photographer, to investigate child labor conditions in the United States. Between 1908 and 1921 he made over 5,000 photographs for the Committee. His brief, but carefully documented sociological records accompanied by his shocking pictures of young children tending dangerous factory machines, working in hazardous coal mines, and hawking newspapers in freezing weather late at night, made the truth vividly clear. He found that over 40,000 children under 16 years of age worked in the cotton industry alone—a massive labor force that not only exploited these children and doomed their futures, but also undercut the wages of an entire adult labor force. Ultimately, an aroused nation demanded and the federal government enacted a protective child-labor law that put an end to such practices.

During World War I, Hine covered the work of the Red Cross and the effects of the war in Europe. Returning home afterwards, he turned to documenting industrial working conditions, emergency relief, rural nursing, and health programs. He wrote, "I wanted to show the things that had to be corrected: I wanted to show the things that had to be appreciated."

Wisconsin born, Hine worked at a succession of labor and factory jobs after high school, learning first hand what he would return to document years later. He took extension courses in art, but decided to pursue a teaching career, for which he enrolled at the University of Chicago in about 1898. In 1901 he took a position teaching science at New York's Ethical Culture School, where he remained for seven years. He studied sociology at Columbia and New York University and was awarded a master's degree in teaching from New

Lewis Wickes Hine, "Little Spinner in a Carolina Cotton Mill," 1909. Courtesy George Eastman House.

York University in 1905. Hine was a self-taught photographer who began photographing seriously at the age of thirty-seven. His exhibitions include: Civic Art Club, New York, 1920; Riverside Museum, New York, 1939; Des Moines Fine Art Association Gallery, Iowa, 1939; Lewis W. Hine traveling exhibition organized by International Museum of Photography, Rochester, New York. Collections of his work are maintained by the International Museum of Photography; Library of Congress; Exchange National Bank of Chicago; Hine Collection, New York Public Library; Tennessee Valley Authority Graphics Division; Prints and Photographs Division, National Archives.

The subject need not be a celebrity, however, for their image to possess proprietary value. Ordinary persons, even professional models, who consent to photography may not wish to have the photographs published for advertising or trade without their permission. Thus, the tort of appropriation gives rise to the need for model releases. A **model release** is simply a written consent to the photography and its subsequent uses. News photographers rarely need model releases to make or publish "hard news" photographs in news publications. For magazine and feature photographs, as distinguished from "hard news" photographs, model releases are generally recommended from featured or identifiable persons in the photographs.

Although not necessary in some states, a valuable consideration for the use of the image, generally a token payment of $1.00 or a copy of the photograph, is usually sufficient to establish a business contract under which the photographer has received consent to shoot and publish the photographs. See Appendix I, on the CD that accompanies this book, for an example of a model release.

Copyright

A copyright can be a valuable asset. The Copyright Act of 1976 affirmed that photographers own the copyrights to their images, except when the images are made as an employee, or when the photographer conveys the copyright to another party in a signed, written agreement.

Copyright is a legal right to control the copying, reproduction, distribution, derivative use, and public display of your photographs and to sue for unauthorized use of your work. This right begins automatically from the moment you record your image in a tangible form, such as on film or in a digital medium and does not require registration with the copyright office or placement of a copyright notice on the image.

To be copyrightable, images must be original. If you make an exact copy a photograph, or a substantially similar copy of another person's copyrighted work, the copy cannot be copyrighted, since it is not original.

Ideas, themes, and concepts are not copyrightable. Only an original expression in a tangible form, such as a photograph, can be copyrighted. You can-not copyright an idea for a photograph; only the actual, original photograph.

The Copyright Act The federal **Copyright Act of 1976** overhauled the copyright system in the United States. The Act created for the first time a separate field of "visual art," including photographs, and extended federal protection to both published and unpublished works. An unpublished, original photograph is automatically protected under the Act from the moment of its creation. To protect it when it is published, the American Society of Media Photographers (ASMP) recommends that all photographs carry a copyright notice, even though the law does not require it. Lack of notice could compromise recovery of damages.

Copyright notice consists of the letter c in a circle (©) followed by the date of first publication and the photographer's name. The word "Copyright" or "Copr." can be substituted for the ©. Either form is recognized, but use of the © symbol can give additional international protection. The words "All Rights Reserved" can also give further international protection. For example, ©1991 (Creator's Name), All Rights Reserved. Sometimes a c in parenthesis [(c)] is used as a substitute for a ©, but this may not be accepted by a court. The law calls for a © or the "Copyright" or "Copr."

Under the Act, the creator of a visual art work retains ownership of the original work for life plus fifty years unless that ownership is sold or given away.

In general, a photographer working as a salaried employee relinquishes copyright to the employer. The Act defines works created by salaried employees as "works for hire," and stipulates that such works are the employer's property unless the employment agreement stipulates otherwise. Works made for hire are protected by copyright for 75 years from the date of publication or 100 years from the date of creation, whichever is shorter.

The Act confers upon the copyright owner four exclusive rights that are of special interest to photographers. These include:

1. the right to reproduce the visual work,
2. the right to prepare derivative works (such as combination prints, croppings, enlargements, manipulated images),

3. the right to distribute the work to the public, and

4. the right to exhibit the work in public.

Under the Act, copyright is automatic upon the creation of the work until the work is published —ownership of the work is vested in the creator of the work or the employer together with the right to register the copyright and to control publication. In the field of copyright, the term publication has been defined in many ways. In this context, publication may be said to occur when the work is offered to another for display, sale, or further distribution, with or without showing the work, when it is printed or distributed, with or without payment, or when it is shown with a reasonable assumption on the part of the viewer that the work may be for sale, such as in a gallery showing. Upon publication, ownership of the work passes into the public domain unless the owner makes a **declaration of intent to retain copyright** by marking the photograph or the transparency mount with a simple copyright declaration where it can be easily seen.

For the photographer to retain copyright of a photograph that appears in a publication, the copyright declaration must appear with the photograph. A credit line is not sufficient. Even though the publication itself may be copyrighted, the copyright protects its contents for the publisher; the photographer needs further protection by having a separate copyright declaration appear with the work, as described above.

It is not necessary to register a copyright immediately. The owner has ninety days after an infringement of copyright to register the work with the Copyright Office and to begin an action against the infringer. To proceed, the copyright declaration must have been attached to the work. If the copyright was registered before the infringement, the owner may seek punitive damages, a sum of money intended to punish the infringer, as well as actual damages, a sum of money intended to compensate the owner for losses suffered as a result of the infringement. If the copyright is registered after the infringement, then the owner may seek only actual damages.

The Copyright Act contains a **"fair use"** provision that allows some uses of copyrighted works without permission and without infringing the copy-

right. Among these are uses that will have a negligible effect upon the work's market potential and uses for nonprofit educational purposes. Thus, copying a copyrighted photograph from a book or exhibit and displaying a transparency of it for classroom discussion would likely fall within the Act's fair use provisions. Making 500 copies for distribution in a course syllabus would not likely be considered fair use because 500 copies might impact upon the work's market potential.

Ownership of Photographs Freelance photographers encounter many situations affecting ownership. Under the general provisions of the Act, freelance photographers shooting on speculation at their own expense generally retain copyright to their own works. If they are contracted to perform photographic work for hire, their works become the property of the employer, unless the photographer and the contractor agree otherwise. The **work-for-hire** rule was established in 1913 when a New York court ruled that an ordinary contract between a photographer and a customer constituted a contract of employment. This decision still holds and is incorporated into the Copyright Act of 1976.

Established freelance photographers often derive a substantial part of their income from the resale of publication rights long after an original photograph was taken. Ownership of the works is, therefore, an important economic consideration that photographers should carefully consider when establishing working agreements with their clients. Unless contracted otherwise, a photograph made to order for a paying client belongs to the client, including the negatives and all rights. Even though the photographer may retain the negatives, they may not be used in any way without the client's permission. Photographs made on speculation at the photographer's own expense belong to the photographer.

Photographers who take photographs on their own that are intended for someone else must exercise care that they do not enter into an **implied contract**. For example, suppose that a photographer verbally agrees to provide photographs of a client's widget, shoots a dozen or so product shots trying to get one that will please the client, and then sends them all to the client to make a selection. Who owns the photographs? Ownership is clouded because no written agreement exists. Perhaps the client believes that the verbal request and agreement constitute a work-for-hire agreement under which the client owns all the photographs. Perhaps the photographer believes that the work was undertaken on a freelance basis, that the photographer owns all the photographs, and that the client is entitled to purchase only those photographs the photographer is willing to sell. Situations such as this need not arise if the terms of engagement are stipulated in a written agreement beforehand.

Freelance photographers should understand that work-for-hire provisions are often included in the fine print of standard commercial contracts. A photographer who wishes to retain the rights to photographs shot for a paying client and to sell them again in the future, must make an agreement with the client stipulating this before shooting begins. A **licensing agreement** is one such type of agreement that, for a fee, gives the client the right to use the photograph under stipulated conditions while leaving the photographer's ownership intact. The licensing agreement can stipulate the fee, restrict use of the photograph to a particular edition of a particular publication, define where the photograph may be distributed, such as only in the United States, specify how the credit line is to read, and state a date for the return of the photographs along with penalties for late or absent returns. An example of a licensing agreement appears in Appendix L on the CD that accompanies this book.

Many periodical publications, understanding licensing agreements, engage freelance photographers under "shoot-and-ship" agreements that commonly grant the assigning publication the first North American publication rights but otherwise leave the photographer's ownership intact. Other clients may be less willing to give up their ownership of works made for hire.

Digital Imaging: Ethical and Social Issues

The new digital technologies have not only changed the working techniques of photographers, they have also given rise to a number of ethical and social issues.

Photojournalism

Photojournalists increasingly must face the sensitive question, to what extent is it ethical for images used for editorial purposes to be altered or manipulated?

In 1903 Edward Steichen recognized that "every photograph is a fake from start to finish, a purely impersonal, unmanipulated photograph being practically impossible." He pointed out that the very acts of regulating exposure and processing for detail and contrast caused the image to be subjectively manipulated.

Although touching up and enhancing photographs to make them more understandable is as old as the medium itself, it is also true that the process has traditionally been tedious and arduous. Digital editing makes photo manipulation much cheaper, easier, and faster and lends itself more readily to ethical abuses.

Even a good intention of making images more understandable can lead to distortion. When photo editing, one must always be aware of how our culture interprets visual symbols. For example, the June 27, 1994 covers of *Newsweek* and *Time* simultaneously offered two different versions of the same police photo of O. J. Simpson. *Newsweek* published the photo without altering it. *Time*, on the other hand, darkened the photo, creating a five o'clock shadow and making a sinister-looking Simpson appear to be lurking in the dark. The image not only made Simpson look guilty, it also prompted the black community to raise the issue of racial insensitivity by suggesting that blacker means guiltier. In an editorial the following week, *TIME*'s managing editor wrote, "The harshness of the mug shot—the merciless bright light, the stubble on Simpson's face, the cold specificity of the picture—had been subtly smoothed and shaped into an icon of tragedy." In other words, the editors changed the photo from a news document to an editorial statement and presented it in a news context. What looked like a real photograph turned out not to be real at all—a violation of the public's trust.

The incident raises many ethical questions. For example:

- Should any news photo, let alone a police photo, be manipulated at all?

- Does the manipulation create an image that is symbolic of complex cultural attitudes?
- Does the manipulation create an image that may be interpreted differently by different ethnic or social groups?

Examples of manipulation abound in the popular press. See, for example, the composite image in Figure 1-43 that conveys the impression that rival Olympic skaters were skating together.

The National Press Photographers Association (NPPA) has adopted an electronic manipulation policy statement that says in part:

As journalists we believe the guiding principle of our profession is accuracy; therefore, we believe it is wrong to alter the content of a photograph in any way that deceives the public.

Most newspaper editors and photojournalists seem to be following the lead of the Associated Press. The AP has traditionally accepted the use of burning, dodging, cropping, and color correction to improve the readability of photographic images used for editorial purposes. The current policy simply extends this principle to electronic image processing. However, they caution that actual retouching should be limited to the removal of scratches and dust spots only. No changes should be made to the content of the image itself if the credibility of the journalism profession is to be maintained.

Similarly, the *Washington Post* policy on photo manipulation states:

Photographs are trusted by our readers to be an accurate recording of an event. Alteration of photographs in any way so as to mislead, confuse or otherwise misrepresent the accuracy of those events is strictly prohibited. Traditional darkroom techniques such as adjustment of contrast and gray scale are permitted.

And the *New York Times* Policy states:

Images in our pages that purport to depict reality must be genuine in every way. No people or objects may be added, rearranged, reversed, distorted or removed from a scene (except for the recognized practice of cropping to omit extraneous outer portions). Adjustments of color or gray scale should be limited to those minimally necessary for clear and accurate reproduction, analogue to the "burning" and "dodging" that formerly took place in darkroom processing of images.

Advertising

Advertising photographers face a similar dilemma. Although the possibility of photo manipulation plays a role in arousing public skepticism in all media, it is exacerbated in the field advertising, a profession already suffering a reputation for questionable ethical behavior. The ready availability of digital enhancement of images only triggers greater doubt.

To what extent is it ethical for images used for advertising purposes to be altered or manipulated? As with other visual media, the image of a print ad is often its most powerful selling message. Today, photo manipulation is so quick and easy and the results so dramatic, that creative advertising need not rely very much on text. In fact, because some of the more effective print advertisements contain very little body copy, increasing pressure is put on photographers and designers to create images that assume the major burden of carrying the ad's message.

For example, the typical fashion magazine either airbrushes or digitally alters photographs of models to advance a certain image of "beauty" to which they seek to inspire their readers. Aside from misrepresenting the true appearance of the models, the practice raises other ethical concerns. For example, does the image of a falsely represented model motivate readers to aspire to unattainable, perhaps even unhealthy standards of glamour? To what extent are these readers undernourishing themselves and plying themselves with layers of cosmetics to achieve some fictitious standard of "beauty" falsely represented in a digitally manipulated image?

Although the advertising profession appears to offer no policy statements to compare with those of the journalism profession, a minimal ethical principle might be to suggest that no alteration of an advertising image should be made that would deceive the public with regard to a product's features, capabilities, or results. This position is supported by the rules and regulations of the Federal Trade Commission governing advertising in general that assert

- Advertising must tell the truth and not mislead consumers
- Claims must be substantiated.

The Federal Trade Commission Act allows the FTC to act in the interest of all consumers to prevent deceptive and unfair acts or practices. The Commission has determined that a representation, omission or practice is deceptive if it is likely to:

- mislead consumers and
- affect consumers' behavior or decisions about the product or service.

In addition, an act or practice is *unfair* if the injury it causes, or is likely to cause, is:

- substantial
- not outweighed by other benefits and
- not reasonably avoidable.

The FTC Act prohibits unfair or deceptive advertising in any medium, including the photographic images embedded in the messages.

Commercial and Creative Photography

Commercial and creative photographers will encounter additional quandaries respecting reproduction rights and copyright. For example, who owns the right to publish an image assembled piece-by-piece by an art director from a file of stock photographs purchased last year? Indeed, who is the artist or creator of such a work? How will copyright violations be handled when small desktop publishing users can easily scan, alter, and reuse previously published photographic material?

These questions and others still need to be resolved, but two guiding principles seem clear:

- If the factual content of a photograph is significantly altered, the alterations should be identified.
- No copyrighted material should be used as a source by a photo-artist without obtaining

prior permission from the copyright holder. Appropriating another's image, or even part of an image, into a new work without permission is wrong and may be a crime.

Photographs in the Courtroom

Despite the fact that photographs can be easily falsified by a number of methods, they are routinely admitted as evidence in court, often with minimal authentication. For example, routine dodging and burning-in can be used to emphasize or eliminate parts of a photograph that may be critical evidence. Although original negatives might provide evidence of the original scene captured by the camera, negatives are rarely used to authenticate photographs unless manipulation is suspected. To make matters worse, today a skilled digital technician using editing software can create a whole new roll of film containing altered images that are virtually undetectable.

Digital Images in the Courtroom Formulating and strictly following standard procedures for the acquisition and handling of digital images can gain their greater acceptance in the courtroom. Key elements of such procedures should include:

- Creating archival, documented reference copies of the original, unenhanced images.
- Archiving original images on an unalterable medium such as a writable CD.
- Maintaining custody of image records and controlling access to images.
- Documenting all processing, editing, and alteration of images.

Sometimes an original photograph is poorly exposed or the details of evidentiary interest are not the primary focus of the photograph. Forensic digital enhancement must be done *solely with the intent to clarify existing information*. However, the ease with which digital images can be altered may make them suspect in the courtroom. Nevertheless, given rigorous procedures and documentation, admission of digitally enhanced photographs is gaining acceptance in the legal community. Some law enforcement agencies are equipping their staff with digital cameras and crime labs are using digital imaging for documentation and for image enhancement. Such enhanced images are increasingly accepted as evidence in the courtroom.

Questions to Consider

1. Describe the characteristics of a fine print and how to produce one.

2. Describe the basic principles of the zone system and the relationship between this system and a full-scale image.

3. What is the purpose of archival processing and how does it differ from normal processing?

4. Describe several situations that might lead a photographer to prefer to use a view camera rather than a 35mm viewfinder or reflex camera? What features of the view camera make it more suitable for these situations?

5. Describe the tools and techniques needed to photograph life-size close-ups of three-dimensional objects.

6. What are the main problems the photographer faces when making a copy of a two-dimensional object, such as an oil painting?

7. Briefly describe the four torts of privacy and the steps a photographer can take to avoid invasions of privacy.

8. Under what conditions do photographers relinquish ownership of their photographic works? How may photographers retain their ownership of works produced for hire?

Suggested Field and Laboratory Assignments

1. Select a subject with a wide range of tonal values. Try to previsualize these tonal values and then photograph it to produce a full-scale print of a subject.

2. Process one print for permanence using techniques of archival processing.

3. Obtain access to a view camera and experiment with the perspective controls.

4. Shoot, process, and print a roll of black-and-white panchromatic film that includes at least one example of each of the following:

   a. close-ups of small objects such as flowers, insects, or coins, to produce a 1:1 or life-size negative image

   b. photomacrographs of similar objects to produce a 2:1 (double life-size) or larger negative image

   c. copy photographs to produce a reproduction of a photograph or other continuous-tone black-and-white original

5. Go on a shoot in a public place and obtain model releases from the subjects of your photographs.

6. Visit the following Website and print out the step-by-step procedure to register your copyright:

   http://www.editorialphoto.com/copyright/index.html

Glossary

1-bit color the lowest number of colors per pixel in which a graphics file can be stored. In 1-bit color, each pixel is either black or white. See Color Depth.

2 1/4-square camera a camera that produces a 2 1/4 x 2 1/4-inch negative format.

24-bit color a display resolution in which each pixel has 24 bits assigned to it, representing 16.7 million colors. 8 bits—or one byte—is assigned to each of the red, green, and blue components of a pixel. See Color Depth.

32-bit color a display resolution setting that is often referred to as true color and offers a color palette of over 16 million colors. See Color Depth.

35mm camera a type of camera designed to use 35mm sprocketed motion picture film, popularly packaged for use in such cameras.

8-bit color/grayscale a display resolution in which each pixel has eight bits assigned to it, providing 256 colors or shades of gray, as in a grayscale image. See Color Depth.

A

AA(A) small battery size(s) used in digital cameras. Available in Alkaline, NiCd and NiMH.

aberration an inherent lens fault that causes the lens to form an unsharp or distorted image.

absorption the assimilation of light by a medium. Absorbed light is neither transmitted nor reflected; it is transformed to another energy form, e.g., heat. See law of transmission and absorption.

accent lights lighting instruments used to produce secondary highlights that reveal the three-dimensional qualities of the subject. See backlight.

acetic acid a colorless, pungent liquid used in photography to halt developing action in film and print processing. It is the primary acid in vinegar.

acid fixer see fix.

actinic light light rays that have powerful effects on photosensitive materials and possess larger-than-normal proportions of ultraviolet and blue wavelengths.

acutance edge sharpness between adjacent tonal areas in a photographic image.

adapter ring a device used to mount filters on the lens barrel of a camera.

ADC Analog-to-digital Converter—(also DAC). Part of digital camera that digitizes CCD electrical charges.

additive color theory theory of mixing light primary colors by adding red, green, and blue to produce white light.

adhesive layer a stratum in photosensitive film or paper that bonds adjacent layers together.

advance see film advance.

AE see Automatic Exposure.

aerial perspective the representation of three dimensions and distance on a two-dimensional surface by means of tonal variations.

AF see Auto-Focus.

agitation the systematic movement of processing chemicals to ensure even immersion of all surfaces in active solutions throughout processing.

air-bells minute bubbles of air or gas that cling to the film surface during processing, preventing processing and causing tiny clear spots or "pin-holes" in the negative.

albumen egg white; used for photographic paper emulsions from about 1850 until replaced by gelatin in the 1880s.

aliasing a stair-stepping effect caused by sampling an image at too low a rate. It makes high texture areas of an image appear as low texture in the sample image.

alkaline battery a type of battery recommended for most flash units. It is not recommended if the unit's electrical contacts are unplated brass or copper. See zinc-carbon battery.

ambient illumination the light existing at the subject location.

ambrotype silver photographic image on glass and backed with a black fabric to produce a weak positive image, popular in the 1860s and 1870s.

analog information a stream of continuously variable data, variations and differences being represented by varying quantities, or amplitudes, e.g. a continuous tone photographic print.

angle of incidence the angle at which incident light strikes an object.

angle of movement the subject's direction of movement in relation to the camera's axis.

angle of view field of view covered by a lens, expressed in degrees.

ANSI American National Standards Institute: formerly ASA. See ASA.

anti-aliasing the process of reducing stair-stepping by smoothing edges where individual pixels are visible.

antihalation backing a dye coating on film designed to prevent halation around intense points of light. See halation.

aperture the opening, usually regulated by a diaphragm, through which light passes into a camera. Aperture size is expressed as an f/number, which signifies the ratio of the focal length of the lens to the effective diameter of the lens. See also maximum aperture.

aperture priority a type of automatic exposure-setting system that requires the photographer to set the aperture manually while the system sets the shutter speed automatically for proper exposure.

APS Advanced Photo System. A film cartridge system that magnetically records all picture data for each frame of film which is then used in photo finishing.

archival processing photographic processing to produce a chemical-free, stable image.

archive long-term storage of data or images.

artifact an undesirable degradation of an electronic image that usually occurs during the electronic capture, manipulation, or output of an image. Any artificial glitch or blemish inadvertently created in or by the digital process.

ASA American Standards Association (now ANSI) system for rating film speed. See film speed rating.

ASA rating see film speed rating.

aspect ratio the ratio of horizontal to vertical dimensions of an image.

at-the-back shutter see focal plane shutter.

at-the-lens shutter see behind-the-lens shutter and between-the-lens shutter.

auto-focus a focusing system that automatically adjusts distance setting by means of emitted sound or infrared light pulses reflected from the subject or by contrast measurements.

automatic diaphragm a device that sets the aperture for proper exposure as the shutter is released.

automatic electronic flash a variable-output flash unit that uses measurements of light reflected from the subject during the flash ignition cycle to govern proper exposure. See thyristor circuit.

automatic exposure an exposure-setting system coupled to a built-in light meter that sets shutter speed, aperture, or both electromechanically.

automatic winder a power-driven device that advances film automatically after each exposure.

Av See Aperture Priority.

available light the light conditions that prevail at the scene you are photographing; existing light.

average gray a point between pure white and pure black representing the typical tone found in nature. The standard tone of average gray is 18 percent gray when 0 percent reflectance = pure black and 100 percent reflectance = pure white. See gray card.

averaging meter a type of exposure meter designed to measure the average brightness reflected from all parts of a scene.

AVI Movie sequence in Windows' Audio Video Interleave format

B

B see bulb.

B setting see bulb.

background light a lighting instrument used especially to illuminate the background.

backlight a light source behind the subject that creates edge highlights or accents. It is also called a kicker.

baffle a device used to shield a portion of the light from striking objects in a scene; a mechanism for introducing a shadow into a field of light.

bandwidth the transmission capacity of a communications channel, usually expressed in bits or bytes per second.

bare bulb flash the use of a flash unit without a reflector, causing both direct and reflected light rays to illuminate the subject.

barn door baffle a baffle with folding leaves that is designed to attach to a lighting instrument and shape the light beam.

base   (1) sheet material that serves as a foundation for coating photographic emulsions. Film bases are transparent and made of acetate or polyester. Print bases are opaque white or tinted, and made usually of paper, but sometimes of glass, metal, or cloth; (2) rigid foundation on which an enlarger is mounted.

base plus fog density   the density of unexposed film that has been developed; film base + fog; fb + f.

base tint   the color of the base material on which a print emulsion is coated. It is also called tint or paper tint.

basic exposure rule   a rule of thumb for determining basic exposure without the aid of a guide or meter: f/16 at 1/ISO for average subjects in sunlight. Variations may be extrapolated for varying conditions.

bayonet mount   a lens-mounting system using flanges by which lens is aligned and seated in the mount and turned slightly to lock it in place.

BCPS   see beam candlepower seconds.

beam candlepower seconds   a measure of the light output of a flash unit; BCPS.

behind-the-lens shutter   shutter located immediately behind the picture-taking lens elements. See leaf shutter.

bellows   a light-tight, accordion-pleated, collapsible unit for adjusting focus, usually made of leather, cloth, or plastic and used between a lens and a camera body or a lens and an enlarger body.

bellows extension   see extension bellows.

bellows unit   see extension bellows.

between-the-lens (BTL) shutter   a shutter located between elements of the picture-taking lens. See leaf shutter.

binary   a numeric system composed of only two symbols, 1 and 0. The binary system is the basis for computer operations that can interpret these symbols as instructions or conditions, such as off/on, zero/one, mark/space, high/low, true/false, yes/no, etc.

bit   one binary digit; a fundamental digital quantity representing either 1 or 0.

bit depth   in digital imaging, the number of bits used to record the brightness of each pixel per color channel. To achieve the illusion of "continuous tone" requires 256 levels of brightness from black (0) to white (255) or 8 bit depth. To represent "full color" RGB, three channels are needed, or 24 bit (3 x 8) depth. To represent CYMK color, four channels are needed, or 32 bit depth.

bitmapped image   an image created from a series of bits and bytes that form pixels. Each pixel can vary in color or gray-scale value. Also known as a raster image, in which the image consists of rows of pixels rather than vector coordinates.

B&W   refers to Black and White imaging. Original form of film photography, still in use today. Some digicams offer a monochrome option.

black body   a theoretical unit of matter, conceived to be unreflecting, that, when heated, is conceived to radiate pure energy; theoretical basis for the Kelvin color temperature scale. See Kelvin.

bleach   a chemical agent capable of dissolving metallic silver and reducing the density of silver images; often potassium ferricyanide is used, or laundry bleach.

bleed   refers to a picture that extends to the extreme edge of a page. A full-page bleed covers an entire page with no borders.

blocked up   negative density of such magnitude as to prevent the passage of light; overexposed and/or overdeveloped negatives may develop such areas, especially in the highlights. Also called burned out.

blue-sensitive   a type of photographic emulsion sensitive to blue and ultraviolet wavelengths and insensitive to red and green.

blur   indistinctness of image caused by movement of camera and/or subject during exposure interval. See also out-of-focus.

blur action   a means of depicting action by intentionally permitting images of moving objects to move across the film surface during exposure to cause blur.

BMP   see Bitmapped image.

boom   an adjustable arm, used with a standard, for mounting lighting equipment.

bounce flash   use of flash unit directed away from the subject so that light is reflected off nearby surfaces toward the subject; usually intended to produce a soft, diffused light. See bounce light.

bounce light any light source directed away from the subject toward some nearby surface, usually matte, so that light is reflected onto the subject indirectly. See bounce flash.

box camera one of the earliest forms of hand-held, roll-film cameras; characterized by fixed-focus lens, simple viewfinder, and limited, if any, adjustments of shutter-speed and aperture.

bracketing the practice of shooting, as a margin for error, several frames of greater and lesser exposure in addition to frames of a "normal" exposure.

brightness the pixel value in an electronic image that represents its lightness value from black to white. Ranges from 0 (black) to 255 (white). See value.

brightness ratio the relative brightness of highlight and shadow areas. A four-to-one brightness ratio indicates that the highlights are four times brighter than the shadows. Also called lighting ratio.

broad lighting a portrait lighting setup characterized by placement of the main light to illuminate the side of the subject's face nearer the camera.

bromide paper a printing paper, typically used for projection printing, in which silver bromide is the principal active ingredient. See halide.

BSI British Standards Institution system for rating film speed. It is used primarily in Great Britain. See film speed rating.

built-in meter an exposure meter integrated into the physical structure of a camera, often electronically coupled to it to form an exposure-setting system.

bulb a shutter setting (B) at which the shutter remains open as long as the shutter release is depressed (the shutter closes as the release returns to a normal position).

burned out see blocked up.

burning-in increasing exposure to a particular area of a photograph during printing. It is a means of increasing print density in selected areas during exposure. It is also called printing in. See also dodging, flashing, vignetting.

busy background a background characterized by peripheral details and contrasts that serve to distract the viewer's attention from the subject and/or to obscure figure-ground relationships in a photographic composition.

butterfly lighting a portrait light setup characterized by placement of the main light in front of and above the subject's head to produce a small shadow directly below the nose.

byte a group of eight binary digits, or bits, treated as a unit.

C

cable release a camera attachment of flexible cable that permits the release of the shutter without touching the camera.

calibration the coordination of one device relative to another, such as a monitor to a printer, or a scanner to a film recorder. The process of adjusting the color of one device to some repeatable standard.

calotype photographic process invented by Fox Talbot about 1840 which was the forerunner of modern negative-positive process; also Talbotype.

camera a light-tight receptacle designed to gather light rays and resolve them as an image. "Camera" is from the Latin word for "room." Modern cameras can record the resolved image permanently by means of light-sensitive film or a digital sensor.

camera angle the orientation of the camera to the subject. See high-angle shot, eye-level shot, and low-angle shot.

camera body the housing into which the lens, shutter, viewer, film-loading feature, and film-advancing feature are fitted.

camera obscura an ancient device for resolving images through a small opening in a darkened room. Used as an artist's aid from the 16th century, it was the forerunner of the modern camera.

camera shake movement of the camera during exposure, causing the photographic image to blur.

camera-to-subject distance see distance.

capture a process by which image bearing light is converted to digital code and stored in a magnetic or optical medium. Capturing an image with a digital camera is analogous to taking a picture with a film camera.

carrier see negative carrier.

carte de visite a popular form of photography in the 1860s and 1870s by which multiple images of individuals and groups were printed on a single small card. The individual images were often used as visiting cards and exchanged as keepsakes.

cartridge a light-tight container, usually disposable, in which lengths of film are dispensed and loaded into cameras designed for their use. It is also called a cassette or magazine.

cassette see cartridge.

cast a slight shift in the apparent color of objects that is produced by variations in the light rays acting upon them.

catchlights highlights in the eyes of the subject produced by reflection of the light sources.

cathode ray tube a visual display device. Often refers to the monitor of a computer terminal.

CC filters see color-compensating filters.

CCD see charge coupled device.

CCD Array Charge-Coupled Device array. A solid-state, semiconductor, light-sensitive device used in scanners and electronic cameras to convert image bearing light into digital signals that are converted into pixel values.

CD Compact Disc. A laser-encoded plastic disc used to store large amounts of data. A variety of CD formats are available for use by computers to store text, images, audio, video, program, and multimedia files. See CD-ROM.

CD Drive a mechanism for reading, playing, and/or recording compact discs.

CD-R a type of CD on which users can record text, images, audio, video, program, and multimedia files once for permanent storage. Not rewritable.

CD-ROM Compact Disc, Read-Only Memory. Generic term used to describe an optical storage technology by which text, images, audio, video, program, and multimedia files are stored. Identical to audio CDs.

CD-RW a type of CD on which users can record text, images, audio, video, program, and multimedia files for permanent or temporary storage. Can be used to erase and rewrite many times.

Celsius (C) a temperature scale in which 0° and 100° respectively represent the freezing and boiling points of water at sea level; also Centigrade (C) scale.

center of interest see central idea.

center-weighted meter a type of exposure meter that bases its measurements mainly on light reflected from the central area of a scene.

centigrade (C) scale see Celsius (C) scale.

central idea the subject of a composition; the key meaning or impression of a composition; the major cognitive or affective representation intended to be communicated by a composition; often associated with a center of interest—a dominant feature or detail within the composition that serves as its main integrating element.

central processing unit (CPU) the main component of a computer system that performs input, output, logical, and arithmetic functions.

CF See Compact Flash

CGA see color graphics adapter.

characteristic curve see H & D curve.

charge coupled device (CCD) a type of light sensitive, electronic matrix that serves as an image receptor in electronic and still video cameras.

charge-injected device (CID) a type of light sensitive, electronic matrix that serves as an image receptor in electronic and still video cameras.

chloride see halide.

chloride paper a printing paper, used primarily for contact printing, whose principal active ingredient is silver chloride.

chloro-bromide paper a printing paper sensitized with a combination of silver bromide and silver chloride.

chroma see hue.

chromagenic film type of film in which the final image is composed of dyes rather than metallic silver.

chromatic aberration an inherent lens fault that causes light rays of different wavelengths to focus in different planes causing loss of resolution in black-and-white images and color-fringing in color images.

CID see charge-injected device.

CIFF Camera Image File Format, a universal method of digicam image storage.

cinch marks parallel exposure marks or scratches in the emulsion caused by physical overwinding or tightening of the film prior to processing.

clearing agent a chemical agent designed to transform fixing compounds into more readily soluble salts to aid in cleansing them from film and prints during washing. Also called hypo neutralizer, hypo eliminator, or hypo clearing bath.

clearing time   the time required after processing to clear a film or print of all residual chemicals.

close-up   a photograph characterized by focus on an object at an apparent distance of no more than a few feet from the camera. It may be achieved by placing the camera within a few feet of the object or optically by the use of appropriate lenses.

close-up lens   a type of magnifying lens designed to be fitted in front of the normal lens to foreshorten focal length and increase focal distance, thereby resulting in close-up focusing distances and image magnification.

close-up photography   photography between a camera's minimum focusing distance and a distance of about two focal lengths from the camera. Generally refers to image magnification of 1/10 lifesize to lifesize.

close-up reading   light-meter measurement taken at a close apparent distance from an object. See close-up.

CMOS   Complimentary Metal Oxide Semiconductor. A type of solid-state, light sensor used in some digital cameras to capture images.

CMS   Color Matching System or Color Management System. A hardware/software configuration designed to ensure color calibration and matching between electronic image displays, such as on video or computer monitors, and any form of hard copy output.

CMY   Cyan, Magenta, Yellow. One of several color encoding systems for reproducing color images, which creates the color spectrum using the three subtractive color primaries.

CMYK   Cyan, Magenta, Yellow, Black. One of several color encoding systems for reproducing color in print, which creates the color spectrum using the three subtractive color primaries plus black. Used in four-color printing to produce a full-color image.

coarse grain   a grain pattern characterized by the grouping of silver grains in the image into relatively large clumps.

coating   a transparent film applied to lens elements and designed to absorb extraneous, non-image-forming light and to increase contrast.

cocking the shutter   loading tension onto the shutter spring mechanism to store the energy needed for its operation.

cold tones   bluish hues associated with the metallic silver image of a print, often emphasized by the use of certain emulsion-developer combinations.

collodion   a viscous solution of guncotton, ether, and alcohol that was used first for bandaging wounds and later as an emulsion medium in wet-plate photography, a process invented by F. Scott Archer in 1851.

color   a visual sensation that permits differential perception of various wavelengths of light generated by the interaction of light and the qualities of the objects perceived.

color balance   the capability of a film to reproduce colors as they are perceived, notwithstanding differences in light sources; a property of color film that specifies under what lighting conditions the film will reproduce colors as perceived.

color composition   the relationships among color details within a photograph; the organization of color elements to support a central idea in a color photograph.

color contrast   the relationship among color values by which colors of complementary hue and varying brightness are composed to achieve emphasis.

color correction   a process of adjusting colors that appear in a digital image or in a print to ensure that the image accurately represents the scene.

color fringes   in color images, color outlines apparent at the edges of color masses caused by chromatic aberration of the lens.

color graphics adapter (CGA)   a relatively low resolution color adapter board used in early IBM PC's and similar computers.

color harmony   the pleasing arrangement of color details in a photograph. See color composition.

color negative   a color image, reversed as to brightness and color, supported on a transparent base for the purpose of making positive prints and transparencies. See negative.

color negative film   a film designed to produce, after processing, a color negative. Compare with color reversal film and color slide film.

color print a positive color image supported on an opaque base of paper or other sheet material; a positive color image designed for unassisted viewing. See print.

color reversal film a film designed to produce, after processing, a positive color transparency; color slide film; film that, after processing, reproduces the colors originally present in the scene. Also called color slide film.

color sensitivity the responsiveness of a photographic emulsion to various wavelengths of light energy.

color slide a positive color image supported on a transparent base, designed primarily for viewing by projection or transillumination; a product of color reversal film; a color transparency.

color slide film see color reversal film.

color temperature a characteristic of visible light, usually measured in Kelvin degrees, measured in terms of the relative dominance of red (lower temperatures) or blue (higher temperatures). See Kelvin.

color transparency a positive color image supported on a transparent base. See color slide, transparency, color reversal film.

color-compensating (CC) filters optically corrected filters, available in various saturations of the six primary and secondary hues, used principally in color photography to modify the overall color balance of the transmitted image.

coma a lens aberration common in high-speed lenses produced by failure of light rays to converge to a common image point

combination printing a printing technique by means of which portions of more than one negative are used to produce a single print.

compact flash Memory cards used for storage of images in digital cameras.

compensating developer a developer that works more vigorously in areas of underexposure than in areas of overexposure.

complementarity see complementary colors.

complementary colors any two hues of light that will, in combination, produce all wavelengths in the visible light spectrum in relative proportions so as to yield white light. The complementaries of the primary colors—red, blue, and green—are the secondary colors—cyan, yellow, and magenta, respectively. Also includes any two hues which, when subtracted from white light, will absorb all wavelengths to yield black.

complements see complementary colors.

composition the arrangement of visual elements in a photograph.

compositional lines see line.

compression a process of encoding data so as to reduce file size for storage. May be classified as "lossy" or "lossless" compression, corresponding to how much original data is lost in the process. Lossless compression provides greater fidelity and less reduction than lossy compression.

compression ratio the relationship between the original size of a data block and its size after compression. A 50:1 ratio indicates that data is compressed to 1/50 its original size. See data compression.

condenser housing the component of an enlarger that holds the condenser lens system in place and provides for its adjustments.

condenser lens a lens used within an enlarger to concentrate light and to direct it through the negative to the lens.

condenser system an adjustable set of condenser lenses designed for use in an enlarger to concentrate light from the source and to distribute it evenly through the negative to the enlarger lens.

conditioning solution also called conditioner. See print conditioning solution.

contact paper a slow-speed printing paper designed for use in contact printing.

contact print a print made by placing the negative in direct contact with photographic paper and exposing the paper to light through the negative.

contact printer a device used to control exposure in making contact prints.

contact proof sheet see contact sheet.

contact proofer see proofer.

contact sheet a set of negatives, contact printed simultaneously on a single sheet of photographic paper.

contamination the introduction, at any stage of processing, of alien or neutralizing agents that produce an unintentional deleterious effect upon the finished product.

continuous spectrum light consisting of all wave-lengths in the visible light spectrum. Compare with discontinuous spectrum.

continuous tone an image in which tonal variations appear gradual and uninterrupted between the extremes of light and dark. Contrast with a halftone image in which tonal variations appear as a matrix of discrete dots of varying sizes.

contrast the differences in density or apparent brightness between adjacent tonal areas of a negative or print image. See gray tone separation, image contrast.

contrast filters (1) filters used with variable-contrast printing papers to control print contrast; (2) filters used in black-and-white photography to increase contrast between gray tone renderings of two colors that might otherwise record at the same density.

contrast grade a contrast characteristic of a printing paper emulsion, identified by a grade number, generally in the range of 0–6. Lower grades signify lower contrast papers; higher grades, higher contrast papers.

contrast index an expression of the relationship between the range of negative densities and the brightness range of the subject. See gamma.

contrast range see contrast.

contrasty see high contrast.

convergence control a technique for manipulating linear perspective by modifying the relationship between parallel lines in a photographic image.

conversion filters filters used primarily with color films to alter the color of available light to conform to the color balance of the film.

converter see teleconverter.

copy to photograph two-dimensional material; the original or material to be copied.

copy board illuminated easel or flat surface to which original is attached for copying.

copy negative negative obtained by photographing two-dimensional material.

copy stand a support that holds camera and copy in position during copying.

correction filters filters used in black-and-white photography to render colors in shades of gray that correspond to their perceived relative brightness.

CPU see central processing unit.

crimp marks crescent-shaped marks in the negative image caused by pinching or crimping the film prior to processing. Usually caused by improperly loading a film reel.

crop to place the boundaries of a photograph, and thus control the locus of edges and borders in relation to the image.

cropper an adjustable frame used as an aid in trimming and framing photographic compositions.

cropping tool in photo-editing software, a tool that simulates the traditional method for trimming and framing photographic compositions.

cross-light lighting from the side of the subject characterized by modeling and textural shadows.

CRT see cathode ray tube.

curtain shutter a type of shutter that effects exposure by opening and closing two or more strips of metal or cloth to create an opening between them that traverses the film surface.

cut film see sheet film.

CW see center-weighted meter.

D

D log E curve see H & D curve.

dark slide see slide.

darkroom a facility designed for the handling, processing, and printing of photosensitive materials and capable of maintaining levels of ambient illumination compatible with these activities.

data in computer terms, raw digital input that is processed, stored, and/or output from a computer.

data compression data processing technique that uses mathematical algorithms to reduce the size of digital files by coding or deleting redundant data. See compression ratio.

daylight in photography, any light source similar in color temperature to standard daylight, 5500–6000 K. At any given time, natural daylight may or may not conform to this standard.

decamired ten mireds. See mired.

dedicated flash   electronic flash unit designed to operate with a specific camera model to automate the setting of many camera functions in response to sensed light intensity.

default setting   in computer programs, a preset parameter or setting that is used during execution of a program unless changed to another value by the user.

definition   the clarity of details in an image. The ability of a lens, photo emulsion, or sensor to produce images of high clarity.

delay   the interval of time between flash ignition and shutter release. See flash synchronization.

dense   characterized by high density. See density.

densitometer   a device used to measure the amount of light transmitted by small negative areas.

density   the mass of metallic silver or dye per unit area in a photographic image, which determines the amount of darkening, light absorption, light reflectance, or light transmission associated with that unit of area.

density range   the range of densities present in a photographic image (DR). See also contrast, tonality.

depth of field   the region within which objects in a resolved image appear in acceptably sharp focus—a zone of sharpness which, for any given lens, varies with the aperture setting and plane of maximum focus; the distance between the nearest and farthest limits of acceptable focus; also zone of sharpness.

depth-of-field scale   a calibrated scale that indicates the depth of field for any given lens at various apertures and distance settings.

desktop publishing   a computer-based process by which text is combined with images in artful two-dimensional layouts to create brochures, newsletters, logos, slide shows, and other forms of published or presented work.

develop   to process exposed photographic materials to transform the recorded image into visible patterns of metallic silver grains. See developer.

developer   a chemical solution that acts upon exposed silver halide crystals, releasing the halogens and leaving a residue of metallic silver.

developing tank   see film processing tank.

diaphragm   a device for controlling the size of the lens aperture by means of a circular iris of overlapping leaves.

diffraction grating   a type of special effect filter used with color film that breaks bright points of light into their spectral components creating a rainbow-like color effect.

diffused light   light scattered in all directions relative to its source, usually as a result of reflection or filtration, and characterized by soft-edged shadows.

diffusing screen   a translucent medium that causes a given degree of diffusion when introduced into the path of light.

diffusion   see diffused light.

diffusion dithering   a method of dithering that distributes pixels randomly than by using a preset pattern. See Dithering.

digital   a description of a system or device that stores and manipulates information in the form of binary numeric data.

digital camera   a device that uses a photosensitive sensor to capture and digitize images that can be manipulated by a computer. A type of filmless camera.

digital image   an image that has been converted into binary code and stored as a file that can then be reconstructed and manipulated by a computer as an array of pixels for display or printing.

digital imaging   a type of electronic photography by which graphic information is digitized, stored, and manipulated in computer-readable form.

digital information   information encoded into discrete, discontinuous, minute data units, called bits, each consisting of a single binary digit, that can be read, stored, and later decoded by a computer program into its original form.

digital zoom   a type of magnification produced by cropping the center part of a captured digital image and expanding it to fill the visual frame. Contrast with optical zoom.

digitize   the process of converting analog information into digital information. The process of converting an image into binary code.

dimmer   a device for controlling the brightness of artificial lighting units by electrical or electronic means.

DIN Deutsche Industrie Normen; a system for designating the speed of light-sensitive materials commonly used in Europe. See film speed rating.

DIN rating see film speed rating.

diopter a measure of the magnifying power of a lens.

disc camera small automatic camera that uses a film cartridge containing a rotating wheel of 15 film frames.

disc film film cartridge containing 15 exposures on a rotating wheel designed for use in a disc camera.

disc or disk media for storing data. "Disc" is often applied to optical storage media (video disc, laser disc, compact disc) while "Disk" is often applied to magnetic storage media (floppy disk, diskette, hard disk). See also Diskette.

discontinuous spectrum light that does not contain all wavelengths in the visible light spectrum; light from which bands of electromagnetic energy of certain wavelengths are absent.

diskette a removable computer storage medium consisting of a thin flexible Mylar disk, coated with a magnetic material on both sides, encased by a hard plastic case, on which data is recorded as magnetic spots.

distance in photography, generally camera-to-subject distance—a critical factor in controlling depth of field and focus in photographic composition.

distance scale the focusing scale of a camera, usually calibrated in feet and meters.

distortion in photography, the alteration of an image, intentional or not, from its true form, usually by the curvature of apparently straight lines or by disproportionate magnification.

dithering a computer method for simulating many colors or shades of gray using only a few. Intermediate colors or tones are achieved by intermixing the nearest bordering colors in a scattering, or dithering, of pixels.

dodging a technique for partially shielding certain portions of a photographic image from exposure during printing in order to reduce print density in those areas. Also called holding back. See also burning-in.

DOF see Depth of Field.

dominant idea see central idea.

dot the smallest spot an imagesetter, or printer, can output. Usually expressed in dots per inch (dpi). Often expressed as pixels per inch (ppi) or halftone cells (lpi or L/S).

double exposure the exposure of a single film frame to more than one image, which has the effect of superimposing images.

double printing see combination printing.

download refers to receiving data files to a local computer from another, or host computer. Contrast with upload.

DPI dots per inch. A measure of scanning or output resolution. Expresses the number of dots a printer can print, or a monitor can display, per inch, both horizontally and vertically. For example, a 600-dpi printer can print $600 \times 600 = 360,000$ dots on one square inch of paper.

DPOF Digital Print Order Format. Memory card format that allows including printing information on your memory card.

DR see density range.

drag and drop a technique for moving an object, such as an image or a block of text, to a different location in a document using a mouse.

drum scanner a high-quality image-capture device that operates by scanning and digitizing an image wrapped around a rapidly spinning drum. Contrast with flatbed scanner.

dry to subject wet film or paper to procedures by which retained moisture will evaporate without visible residue.

dry area a portion of a darkroom, separated from the chemical processing and sink areas, intended solely for the handling of dry materials.

dry mounting a thermoplastic technique for affixing finished prints to a mounting surface by means of a dry, heat-sensitive adhesive. Compare with wet mounting.

dry mounting press a thermal press used for dry mounting.

dry mounting tissue a thin, shellac-impregnated sheeting that becomes adhesive when subjected to heat and pressure in the dry mounting process.

dry plate term used to distinguish the highly popular wet-collodion photographic plates from the newer gelatin-coated plates in the 1880s.

dulling   a technique used to eliminate reflected specular highlights by spraying, powdering, or waxing the reflecting surface.

duplicate   a reproduction that corresponds to its original in every possible respect. A duplicate negative is a photographic reproduction of a negative; a duplicate slide is a photographic reproduction of a positive transparency.

dye   the coloring matter used to color photographic images, usually by means of adhesion to the metallic silver of which the image is formed.

dynamic range   a measure of the range of densities between the brightest and darkest recordable parts of an image or scene. A scene that ranges from bright sunlight to deep shadows is said to have a high dynamic range, while an indoor scene with less contrast has a low dynamic range.

dynamism   an impression of movement, force, and/or energy conveyed by a photographic composition.

E

easel   a device placed at the base of an enlarger and designed to frame the image, hold the enlarging paper in proper position, and create borders during exposure.

edge accents   highlights, produced by light sources behind or to the side of the subject, that define the edges of the subject and are often of intensity equal to or greater than the major highlight area. See rim light.

electromagnetic spectrum   see spectrum.

electronic flash   a photoflash light source produced by electrical discharge through a gas-filled tube and typified by high intensity, short duration, and the approximate color temperature of daylight. Also see strobe.

electronic imaging   a general term used to describe any aspect of the capture, storage, manipulation, and output of pictures by means of electronic devices.

elevator control   a device for raising or lowering the head of an enlarger.

e-mail   electronic mail. Messages sent from one computer to another, usually employing an intermediate server.

emphasis   the relative stress or importance given to a particular detail or feature in a photograph; special prominence, distinctiveness, or vividness given to such a feature.

emulsion   the coating of light-sensitive chemical suspended in a gelatin medium that gives film and photographic paper their photosensitive properties.

enlargement   a photographic reproduction larger than the original from which it was produced. See projection print.

enlarger   a device used to project negative images in varying scale onto photosensitive materials for the purpose of making prints larger or smaller than the original negative.

enlarging   see projection printing.

enlarging lens   a lens designed with a flat field of focus that is especially suitable for enlarging and copying.

enlarging paper   see projection printing paper.

EPS   Encapsulated PostScript. A graphic file format developed by Aldus, Adobe, and Altsys to allow exchange of high-quality vector art, text, and raster images among a variety application programs and computer platforms.

equivalent exposure   a member of a set of differing shutter speed/aperture combinations possessing the same exposure value; given a basic shutter/aperture combination, any alternative shutter/aperture combination that yields the same exposure.

EV   see Exposure Value.

EXIF   refers to exposure and image data stored by a digital camera within an image file.

existing light   see available light.

expiration date   a date assigned to photosensitive materials at the time of manufacture to indicate the limits of their shelf-life when stored under normal conditions, a date beyond which photosensitive materials may not be expected or guaranteed to perform to standard. Actual shelf-life may be extended beyond the expiration date under special conditions of storage.

export   the process of sending data from a local file to another computer, program, file, or device and converting its format as needed to be received.

exposure the product of the intensity of light acting upon a photosensitive material and the time interval during which it does so; the subjection of a photosensitive material to the action of radiant energy.

exposure compensator a mechanism on automatic cameras that permits intentional under- or overexposure.

exposure factor the factor by which exposure must be increased to compensate for greater-than-normal focal distance.

exposure guide a table, usually published for use with a particular photosensitive material indicating proper exposure under various conditions of illumination.

exposure index (EI) see film speed index.

exposure latitude a property of photosensitive material involving the degree of exposure variance possible without significantly degrading image quality.

exposure meter a device used to determine proper exposure by measuring the intensity of light present in the scene in relation to the speed of the film in use.

exposure override a control that allows the photographer to disengage automatic exposure features of a camera for manual exposure setting.

exposure scale an adjustable, graduated, and ordered set of shutter-speed and aperture settings, such as is inscribed on an exposure meter or camera, that indicates equivalent exposures for a given exposure value or photographic situation.

exposure value A number referring to the amount of light needed for a given exposure and used to calculate the shutter speed and aperture at a given ISO speed.

extender see teleconverter.

extension bellows a unit inserted between lens and camera body enabling continuous extension of focal distance for close-up focusing.

extension tubes a set of interlocking hollow tubes designed to be inserted between lens and camera body to increase focal distance for close-up focusing.

eye-level shot a camera-to-subject angle such that the axis of the camera lens is parallel to the ground. Compare high-angle shot and low-angle shot.

F

F see focal length; also see fast peak.

f/- see f/number.

f/number a standardized numerical expression describing the light-admitting characteristics of a lens at a given aperture setting; the ratio of a given aperture diameter to the focal length of a lens. Also f/stop.

f/stop see f/number.

Fahrenheit (F) scale a scale of temperatures in which 32° and 212° respectively represent the freezing and boiling points of water at sea level.

fall-off progressive loss of density in a negative or progressive loss of light intensity over a distance or area.

fast highly sensitive to light; responsive to low levels of light (said of photosensitive paper or film); capable of transmitting relatively large amounts of light per unit of time (said of photographic lenses of relatively large diameter in relation to focal length).

fast peak (F) a type of flashbulb that reaches peak output five milliseconds after ignition; flash synchronization designed for use with such flashbulbs. Rarely used with modern cameras.

fast-speed film see fast.

FB fiber-base

ferrotype a procedure for giving photographic prints a high-gloss finish by drying them while the emulsion is in close contact with a highly polished metal surface; the metal plate used in this procedure.

fiber-base a type of photographic printing paper made with a high quality paper base. Distinguished from resin- coated (RC) papers.

field an analog video image format that uses one-half of the scan lines needed to reproduce a high resolution image. Still video cameras can store 50 images in low resolution field format. See frame.

figure-ground contrast the tonal relationship between foreground and background details.

file a repository of data representing information such as text, audio, video, images, or programs and saved in a storage medium such as a magnetic or optical disk.

file format   a scheme by which data are stored within a file. Some common image file formats include TIFF, JPEG, GIF, BMP, PICT, EPS and others.

fill light   light used to illuminate shadows produced by main light or sunlight; light used to reduce the brightness ratio by increasing illumination in shadow areas.

fill-in flash   the use of flash as secondary, fill light to illuminate shadows produced by main light or sunlight.

film   photosensitive material consisting of a light-sensitive emulsion coating on a transparent base capable of recording a photographic image.

film advance   a mechanism for advancing roll film a prescribed distance within a camera to obtain a succession of evenly spaced exposures; the knob or lever used to advance such film.

film base + fog   see base plus fog density.

film camera   a camera designed to record images and graphics from a computer onto conventional photographic film.

film clip   a spring-loaded device designed to clip onto the end of a strip of film to hold it while it dries.

film holder   a frame designed for handling sheet film. It holds two sheets of film in a light-tight compartment, is inserted into the camera to hold the film in a precise relationship to the lens, and is withdrawn from the camera following exposure.

film pack   a frame designed to hold sheet film. It is loaded with several film sheets that can be used sequentially by manipulating a series of paper tabs without removing the pack from the camera.

film plane   the locus of the film within the camera, usually placed to intersect the focal point of the camera's normal lens.

film processing tank   a light-tight container, used for developing and fixing film, that provides for the entry and egress of fluids through a light trap; also the container used for processing sheet film.

film speed   the relative sensitivity of film to light, as indicated by its film speed index. See speed, film speed rating.

film speed rating   a number indicating the sensitivity to light of a given film. The most common film speed rating systems are ISO, ASA, DIN, BSI, and ANSI.

film speed setting   the mechanism on a photographic device, such as a light meter or camera, by which the film speed index is programmed into the device.

film transport indicator   signalling device that informs the photographer when film is being properly advanced within the camera.

filter   (1) optical. A transparent medium, usually plastic or glass, that absorbs and transmits precisely selected wave-lengths or other components of incident light. (2) Software. A program or sub-program that alters image data in some manner. For example, a software program might filter a blurry picture to make it sharper.

filter drawer   an opening built into an enlarger head designed to accept printing filters.

filter factor   the number by which exposure must be multiplied to compensate for the absorption of light by a filter used during exposure.

filter holder   a device that attached to the front of a lens designed to hold filters in place.

fine grain   a grain pattern characterized by the grouping together of silver grains in the photographic image into relatively small clumps.

fix   to dissolve light-sensitive materials from a photographic emulsion in order to render it chemically stable; the chemical agents employed in the process.

fixed exposure   an exposure-setting system using a single, nonadjustable aperture and shutter-speed combination.

fixed focus   a focusing system without adjustments that is preset to focus within a given distance range.

fixer   the chemicals used to fix film.

fixing bath   see fixer.

flag   a small baffle used to create shadow in a photographic lighting setup.

flare   nonimage-forming light produced by interreflections between lens surfaces; a fogged or dense area produced on the negative as a result of such light on the film in the camera.

flash   in photography, any artificial light source that produces a brief, intense pulse of light, usually synchronized with the opening and closing of a camera's shutter.

flash bar   a type of flash unit consisting of ten individual flashbulbs, each with its own reflector and shield, designed to fire one at a time as successive shots are taken.

flash contacts   the electrical connections that complete the ignition circuit and allow flash equipment to be synchronized to a shutter's action; the metallic connectors by means of which flash units are linked to a camera's circuitry.

flash memory   a nonvolatile memory chip that can retain data without power to the system. Digital cameras with flash memory, for example, can retain image data even when their batteries are exhausted.

flash meter   a type of exposure meter designed to measure the intensity of electronic flash illumination and to output exposure information.

flash peak   the moment in the flash cycle when the flash reaches its maximum intensity; see F, M, FP, X.

flash synchronization   the mechanical coordination of flash ignition and shutter release so that flash peak is timed to occur at a precise moment during the shutter's action; see F-synchronization, M-synchronization, and X-synchronization.

flash unit   generic term referring to any one of many devices used as flash lighting sources.

flashbulb   a consumable lamp containing combustible materials and designed to produce a measured quantity of intense illumination for photographic purposes upon electrical ignition synchronized with a camera's shutter.

flashing   a technique for increasing density in certain portions of a print by means of controlled exposure of the printing paper to raw, white light.

flash-off-camera   a flash technique in which the flash unit is placed or held at a distance from the lens axis.

FlashPix   trade name for a multi-resolution image file format jointly developed by Kodak, HP, Microsoft, and Live Picture. Currently owned by Digital Imaging Group (DIG).

flash-to-subject distance   the distance light travels from the flash unit to the subject; the distance between the unit and the subject if aimed directly; the total distance traveled if bounced off reflecting surfaces.

flat   see low contrast.

flat peak (FP)   a flashbulb burn pattern in which maximum output is reached approximately 20 milliseconds after ignition and is maintained at a relatively constant level for the next 20–25 milliseconds before extinction. Designed for flash bulb use with focal plane shutters. Obsolete in modern cameras.

flatbed scanner   an optical scanner in which the original image is held flat while the sensor passes over or under it to convert images into digital format. Contrast with drum scanner.

floodlight   an artificial light source designed to illuminate a wide area with relatively uniform intensity.

floppy disk   see diskette.

focal distance   the distance between the optical center of a lens and the plane of the focused image it produces.

focal frame   the device used for precise focusing and framing of close-ups with a viewfinder camera.

focal length   the distance between the optical center of a lens and the plane in which the image of an object at infinity is resolved into sharpest focus; the symbol for focal length is F.

focal plane   the plane in which a lens forms a sharp image of an object at infinity. Within a camera, the film is located in the focal plane.

focal plane shutter   a mechanism for controlling exposure that is located slightly forward of and parallel to the camera's focal plane; a camera component designed to initiate, time, and terminate exposure by means of the opening and closing of two overlapping panels.

focal point   the point, characteristic of a given lens, at which the lens resolves parallel light rays to a point of sharp focus.

focus   the adjustment of a lens system to resolve the transmitted light rays in a given plane; to adjust a camera to achieve a clear, sharply defined image of the subject.

focus setting the mechanism by which a lens is adjusted so that a clear, sharply defined image of the subject is formed on the photosensitive material.

focus-free see fixed focus.

focusing magnifier magnifying device designed to assist in focusing the projected image during enlarging.

fog negative or print density produced by nonimage-forming light or chemical action.

fog filter a filter used to diffuse image-forming light to create a soft-edge effect in the image; creates fog-like effects in scenic images.

folding camera a type of camera characterized by a bellows that collapses the lens and shutter assembly into the camera body for ease in carrying and storing.

forced development a technique for developing photographic materials for a longer-than-normal time span, usually to compensate for underexposure.

foreground that portion of a visual composition perceived to be nearest the viewer.

format print or negative dimensions; aspect ratio; the length and width of a photographic product.

FP see flat peak.

FP-synchronization see M-synchronization.

frame (1) to adjust the image within the image boundaries; (2) the boundaries within which the image is presented; (3) an analog video image format that uses twice the number of scan lines needed to reproduce a low resolution image. Still video cameras can store 25 images in high resolution frame format. A complete analog video frame is made up of two fields. See field.

frame grabber a computer expansion board designed to capture and digitize a video image for computer use.

frame numbers numbers printed at the edges of a film during manufacture to aid in identifying specific frames.

framing easel see easel.

freeze action see stop action.

F-synchronization the mechanical synchronization of shutter and flash used with fast peak (F) flashbulbs; a flash synchronization that delays flash ignition five milliseconds after shutter release. No longer in common use.

FTP File Transfer Protocol. A set of standards for transferring files between computers on the Internet.

full frame a negative format using the normal 35mm format (24mm by 36mm).

full stop a full f/stop; a full-stop exposure increase implies a doubling of exposure; a full-stop opening of the lens aperture implies a doubling of the light-transmitting characteristic of the lens.

full-scale print a continuous tone black-and-white photograph characterized by presence of all density values from deepest black to pure (paperbase) white through many clearly differentiated gray tones.

G

gamma (1) A numerical expression of the degree of contrast in a negative relative to the degree of contrast present in the original scene. (2) A measure of contrast applied to an image or an imaging device. Improper gamma adjustment can cause images to appear bleached out, too dark, and to display color imbalances. See also contrast index.

gelatin a chemically neutral medium used as a binder for the photosensitive chemical agents in photographic emulsions.

gelatin square filter a thin, transparent, flexible medium designed to absorb and transmit specified portions of the visible light spectrum. It is usually used in a special holder during the exposure of film or papers.

ghost image see secondary image.

GIF Graphic Interchange Format. A raster oriented graphic file format developed by CompuServe to allow exchange of image files across multiple platforms.

gigabyte (Gb) a measure of computer memory, disk space, or file size consisting of approximately one billion bytes. Actual decimal value is 1,073,741,824 bytes.

glacial acetic acid a concentrated, 99 percent form of acetic acid.

glamour lighting   see butterfly lighting.

glare   a harsh, bright light or reflection of light. See polarized light.

glass filter   a thin, transparent, rigid medium designed to absorb and transmit specific portions of the visible light spectrum used in the exposure of photosensitive materials.

glossing solution   see print conditioning solution.

glossy   characterized by a smooth, glass-like lustre—a surface texture of a photographic print commonly produced by ferrotyping; a print possessing such a finish.

grain   the pattern of the metallic silver particles that form a photographic image. Characteristic grain patterns are produced by the interaction of given combinations of film and developer.

graininess   the degree to which the grain pattern of a photograph is visible or has a tendency to become visible in enlargement; adjective describing coarse grain.

grand view   a photograph that encompasses great distances and relatively large scenic features.

gray card   a neutral test sheet of 18 percent reflectance that can be used as a standard to control tone or color rendering in photographic printing. See average gray.

gray level   the brightness of a pixel. A pixel value that represents its lightness between black and white. Usually a value from 0 to 255, with 0 being black and 255 being white.

gray scale   a term used to describe a range of accurately known shades of gray printed out for use in calibrating those shades on a display or printer. The range of discrete gray tones in an image.

gray tone rendering   the pattern of relative densities recorded on black-and-white film in response to light of various colors or wavelengths.

gray tone separation   the ability of photosensitive material to record at different densities the differences between adjacent tonal areas. See contrast.

ground glass   a plate of frosted glass that functions as a screen for viewing the transilluminated image focused in the focal plane of certain cameras.

guide number   a numerical index reflecting the light output of a flash unit, used for determining exposure when that unit is in use.

guide number table   a table listing guide numbers for given combinations of film speed, flash unit, reflector type, and shutter speed; an aid to determining exposure with any of these combinations.

H

H & D curve   a graph, characteristic of a given photosensitive material, expressing the curvilinear relationship between exposure and density. After the inventors, Hurter and Driffield. Also called characteristic curve and D log E curve.

hair light   spotlight placed to produce highlight accents on the subject's hair.

halation   in photographic images, halo-like blurring around intense points of light caused by reflection of light from the film base back into the emulsion. See antihalation backing.

half-frame   a negative format, using half the normal 35mm format (24mm by 18mm).

half-stop   half an f/stop; an intermediate point between full f/stops, popularly used to increase or decrease exposure approximately 50 percent.

halftone image   a reproduction of a continuous tone image made up of a matrix of tiny dots of various sizes that when viewed in their entirety simulates various shades of gray. Typically used for reproducing photographic images in print media, such as newspapers and magazines.

halide   a light-sensitive compound of silver and one of the halogens, commonly bromine or chlorine, fundamental to most modern photographic emulsions.

hard   see high contrast.

hard copy   computer information output into a tangible form such as a printout on paper.

hardener   a chemical agent introduced in processing to toughen the gelatin medium of a photographic emulsion and thus increase its resistance to abrasion.

haze   a degree of opacity in the air, caused by smoke, dust, or similar particles, which renders distant details less distinct than those nearby; also called aerial or atmospheric haze. Haze is produced in photographic images by the presence of ultraviolet light reflected from such particles.

haze filter   a medium used to reduce aerial haze in a photograph by filtering out ultraviolet light present in the scene.

H-D   see hyperfocal distance.

head screen   a form of baffle.

heliography   early photographic process by which a polished sheet of pewter coated with bitumen of Judea creates an image when exposed to light. Invented by Nièpce in early 1820s.

high contrast   characterized by extreme differences in density between adjacent tonal areas; characterized by extreme highlights and shadows and limited middle tones; also said of lighting situations or photographic materials that tend to produce such tonal differences. Also contrasty, hard.

high-angle shot   a camera-to-subject angle in which the camera is directed downward. Compare eye-level shot and low-angle shot.

high-key   dominated by light or white tones to the exclusion of dark or black tones. Compare with low-key.

highlight area reading   a light meter reading of the brightest areas in a scene.

highlight brilliance   the degree of specularity of highlights, particularly in portraits, as seen from the camera position.

highlights   photographic image densities corresponding to the brightest accents and areas in the original scene; the densest areas of a negative; the least dense areas of a positive print.

histogram   a vertical bar graph displaying the distribution of the tonal values of the pixels in an image. The X-axis represents the tonal value of the pixels (0–255) and the Y-axis represents the number of pixels having that tonal value. Used to identify contrast and dynamic range in photo-editing programs.

holding back   see dodging.

hot shoe contact   a flash synchronization socket providing for simultaneous physical and electrical connection of the flash unit to the camera system.

hot spot   a concentration of light in one area of an otherwise even field of light. Usually an undesirable characteristic.

HTML   hypertext markup language. A standard code that enables multi-media documents on the World Wide Web to be displayed on a wide variety of computer systems.

hue   the property of light determined by the wave-lengths of electromagnetic energy of which it is composed; the color characteristic; chroma.

hyperfocal distance   the distance between the camera lens and the nearest point that will appear in tolerably sharp focus when the camera is set at infinity.

hyperfocal focusing   a technique used to obtain maximum depth of field. When set at the hyperfocal distance, maximum depth of field is achieved; objects will appear in sharp focus from half the hyperfocal distance to infinity. See hyperfocal distance.

hypertext markup language   see HTML.

hypo   see fixer.

hypo clearing bath   see clearing agent.

hypo eliminator   see clearing agent.

hypo neutralizer   see clearing agent.

I

icon   a small picture on a computer screen that represents a computer procedure.

image   an optical counterpart of a scene; in photography and digital imaging, a two-dimensional counterpart of a scene that may be three-dimensional, usually produced by an optical system and formed at the surface of photosensitive material to create a permanent record of the image.

image contrast   see contrast.

image format   see format.

image processing   capturing and manipulating images in order to alter their appearance or to extract information from them.

image resolution   in digital imaging, the number of pixels per unit length of image. For example, pixels per inch, pixels per millimeter, or pixels wide.

image texture   see texture.

image tone   see tone.

image-to-object ratio   the ratio of the size of an object's image as it appears at the focal plane to the object's actual size.

import the process of bringing data into a file from another computer, program, file, or device and converting its format as needed by the receiving file.

in focus an optical situation in which the light rays emanating from a scene are resolved within a focal plane; the optical resolution of light rays into a sharp, clearly defined image.

incandescent light artificial light produced by the glow of a heated substance. It typically refers to electric light illumination.

incident light light rays falling upon or striking a subject.

incident light meter a device designed to measure the intensity of light falling upon or striking a subject. Compare reflected light meter.

index print refers to APS equivalent of a contact sheet; single print displaying the images on a roll of APS film.

indicator stop bath a type of stop bath containing agents that change color, signalling when its effectiveness is exhausted.

infinity (∞) a theoretical distant point at which emanating light rays may be regarded as parallel; in photography, for most practical purposes, any point fifty feet or farther from the camera.

infinity setting the distance setting on an adjustable camera at which all objects 50 feet (15m) or farther from the camera will be recorded in sharp focus.

infrared relating to a band of electromagnetic wavelengths just longer than those perceived as red in the visible light spectrum; describes an invisible band of electromagnetic waves detectable with special equipment and photosensitive materials.

inherent contrast a characteristic of film referring to its capacity to reach a given image contrast in a given development time. Films that reach a given image contrast more quickly have higher inherent contrast.

ink-jet printer a type of printer that forms text and images out of dots created by ink droplets formed by high pressure ink jets.

instant camera a camera that uses instant print film.

instant color print film a film designed to produce a final positive print moments after exposure by means of processing action that is integral to the film and activated by the camera's mechanical operation.

integral tripack the structural design of modern color film by which the color components of light from a scene are separated and the images formed by each color component are recorded on separate emulsions built into a single film.

intensity the brightness of light. Also brightness. See value.

interchangeable lens a lens designed to be mounted on and removed intact from a camera body.

internegative a transparent negative produced from a photographic positive as an intermediate step in reproducing or duplicating the positive.

internet the interconnection of computers and computer servers through phone, cable, and wireless channels that enable computers connected to the Internet to share multi-media information and programs. See World Wide Web.

interpolation resampling. A process whereby software calculates a new value for a pixel based the values of surrounding pixels. An imaging method for increasing the size of a digital image by adding pixels of similar value in the enlarged spaces between existing pixels. For example, to enlarge a 4in x 5in image into an 8in x 10in image having the same resolution, the computer must create the pixels that are not actually there.

intimate view term used to describe a photograph encompassing relatively short distances and small scenic features.

inverse square law a basic principle of physics which, applied to light, states that as light spreads from a source the intensity of its illumination diminishes as the square of the distance from the source.

iris diaphragm see diaphragm, iris.

ISO International Standards Organization. System that rates the speed or light-sensitivity of film or a digital camera's image sensor. See film speed rating.

ISO ratings see film speed ratings.

J

jaggies   the jagged stair-stepping effect often seen in an image whose resolution is so low, or whose magnification is so great, that individual pixels are visible.

JFIF   JPEG File Interchange Format. A minimal graphic file format that enables JPEG images to be exchanged among many different platforms and applications.

JPEG   Joint Photographic Experts Group. A "lossy" compression algorithm that slightly degrades image quality to reduce file size. JPEG is the predominant format used by digital cameras and displayed on the World Wide Web.

K

Kelvin   a unit of measurement, numerically equivalent to degrees Celsius plus 273, used to measure the color temperature of light. After the inventor, W. T. Kelvin.

Kelvin degrees   see Kelvin.

Kelvin temperature   see color temperature, Kelvin.

key backlighting   a lighting setup, characterized by placement of the main light above and behind the subject, often used in small-object photography.

key light   see main light.

keystone effect   an optical effect by which parallel lines appear to converge because of their varying distance from the camera.

kicker   see backlight.

kilobyte   an amount of computer memory, disk space, or document size consisting of approximately one thousand bytes. Actual decimal value is 1024 bytes.

L

lamp   light bulb; an artificial light source, usually consisting of a wire filament within a transparent globe and heated or ignited by electricity.

lamp housing   the component assembly of an enlarger or projector that contains the light source.

large format   see format.

laser printer   a type of printer that forms an image by using a laser to lay down a pattern of charges onto an electrostatically sensitive drum so that it will attract an analogous pattern of carbon based toner. The toner is then transferred and fused by heat and pressure onto paper or transparency material.

latent image   the invisible image recorded on a photographic emulsion following exposure and preceding development; a pattern of chemical changes in a photographic emulsion produced by the action of light, and not normally visible until chemically processed.

latitude   see exposure latitude.

law of transmission and absorption   a principle of the behavior of light that states that a transparent medium, such as a filter, passes light rays of its own apparent color and assimilates light rays of its complementary color.

LCD   liquid crystal display. A device that forms an image by activating a matrix of pixels made up of small crystals. Activated by coded signals from a computer, the crystals appear in various colors and intensities to form a full-color display.

LCD panel   liquid crystal display panel. A device driven by a computer that projects a computer monitor display through an overhead projector.

leader   a length of film or paper preceding usable roll film provided to protect the film and aid in loading the film into a camera.

leaf shutter   a camera component designed to initiate, time, and terminate exposure by means of the opening and closing of an assembly of overlapping, concentric metal leaves.

LED   see light-emitting diode.

lens   a device consisting of one or more elements, usually transparent, designed to direct and focus light; in photography, the device used to focus an image onto a focal plane.

lens barrel   the metal or plastic tube in which the lens elements are mounted.

lens brush   a nonabrasive, soft brush used to clean the surface of a lens.

lens cap   an opaque device used to fit the barrel of a lens to provide protection to the lens surface and to block the passage of light.

lens hood   a detachable device fitted to the lens barrel and designed to shade the lens surface from extraneous, nonimage-forming light so as to maximize contrast and reduce flare. Also see sunshade, lens shade.

lens mount   a mechanism by means of which the lens is attached and held firmly to the camera body.

lens shade   see lens hood.

lens speed   see speed.

lens tissue   a soft, chemically impregnated, nonabrasive paper used for cleaning lenses.

lensboard   a removable panel used as a support for one or more lenses and designed to be mounted onto the body of a camera or enlarger.

lens-cleaning solvent   a liquid used to clean grease and dirt from lens surfaces without affecting the surfaces or their coatings.

light   electromagnetic radiation, including infrared, visible, ultraviolet, and x-rays, that act upon the optical faculties and photographic emulsions.

light balancing filters   see correction filters.

light fog   see fog.

light meter   see exposure meter.

light output   the amount of light produced by a flash unit, usually measured in beam candlepower seconds (BCPS).

light primaries   see primary colors.

light-emitting diode   a small, light-generating device commonly used for indicator and warning lights within camera viewing systems and flash units.

lighting ratio   see brightness ratio.

lighting standard   see standard.

light-tight   capable of preventing the admission of light.

line   an element of visual composition; the arrangement, real or imagined, of outlines, contours, or other connecting elements in an image.

line art   graphic representation made up entirely of lines and marks on a contrasting background, devoid of intermediate tones.

linear perspective   the representation of three dimensions and distance in a two-dimensional plane by means of converging lines and diminishing size.

lines of composition   elements in an image that lead the viewer's attention from detail to detail and often affect the apparent organization of details within the visual structure.

Li-on   Lithium Ion battery. Li-on batteries are lighter and more costly than NiMH or NiCd although they can be charged more rapidly.

liquid crystal display   see LCD.

lithography   a method of printing using ink and a flat plate. Originally, hand-made stone plates were used with ink or crayon; modern lithography uses metal plates prepared by photographic process.

long lens   any lens possessing a focal length longer than is normal for the camera on which it is used. The use of a long lens reduces the angular coverage across the film's diagonal, renders images of distant objects larger than normal, and tends to foreshorten perspective. See telephoto lens.

lossless compression   a method of reducing image file size without loss of information. Reduces the size of files by using internal shorthand that enables all original image data to be completely restored. TIFF is a lossless compression method.

lossy compression   a method of reducing image file size by discarding information that is least perceptible to the human eye, thus producing slight degradation of image quality when restored. JPEG is a lossy compression method.

low contrast   characterized by minimal differences in density between adjacent tonal areas; without contrast; dominated by middle tones to the exclusion of clearly defined highlights and shadows; also said of lighting situations and photographic materials that tend to produce such images. Also flat, soft.

low-angle shot   a camera-to-subject angle in which the camera is directed upward. See eye-level shot and high-angle shot.

low-key   dominated by dark or black tones to the exclusion of white or light tones. Compare high-key.

LPI   lines per inch. The frequency of horizontal and vertical lines in a halftone screen.

LZW   a non-lossy compression scheme (by Lempel, Ziv and Welch). Generally LZW can compress an image down to a ratio of 2:1.

M

M   see medium peak.

macro lens   a type of lens used in place of a camera's normal lens for close-up photography.

macrophotography   techniques used to produce extremely large images such as for photomurals.

macro-zoom lens   a zoom lens with a close-up focusing feature.

magazine   see cartridge.

magnification   an image dimension divided by its corresponding subject dimension; a factor describing the relative sizes of object and image.

main light   the principal light source in a studio setup, which establishes the dominant pattern of highlights and shadows. Also key light, modeling light.

manual exposure   an exposure-setting system requiring the photographer to determine proper exposure and to set both aperture and shutter speed by hand.

manual focus   a focusing system by which the lens is hand-set to an inscribed scale based on the photographer's estimate of camera-to-subject distance.

manual mode   a setting on an automatic camera that enables the photographer to override the automatic functions to select all settings.

marquee   an outline of moving dots that marks off an area selected within a graphic display for further image-editing operations. Typically created when performing such tasks as cropping, cutting, or drawing a mask.

mask   a pattern of defined areas within an image used to limit the effect of image-editing operations. Similar to photographic lith masking in an enlarger.

mass   an element of visual composition; and aggregate of relatively homogeneous tonal densities cohering together such that they appear as one body within a composition.

match indicator   a type of automatic exposure-setting system that requires the photographer to adjust the aperture and/or shutter speed so that an indicator light or needle seen in the viewfinder is properly aligned.

matte   a dull, non-reflective surface texture.

matte white reflector   a reflector with a dull, white surface of relatively high reflectance and diffusing qualities.

maximum aperture   the rated aperture of a lens; its largest useful opening; its aperture when wide open.

maximum depth of field   see depth of field.

medium format   see format.

medium grain   a grain pattern characterized by the grouping together of silver grains in the photographic image into clumps of moderate size.

medium peak (M)   a type of flashbulb that reaches peak output 15–20 milliseconds after ignition. Camera synchronization for common combustible flash bulbs.

medium speed   moderate sensitivity to light of a photographic film or paper; moderate light-transmitting capability of a lens.

medium-speed film   see medium speed.

megabyte (Mb)   an amount of computer memory, disk space, or document size consisting of approximately one million bytes. Actual decimal value is 1,048,576 bytes.

megapixel   one million pixels or more. A unit of measurement used to describe the number of pixels in an image or the capacity of a sensor. The more pixels that exist in an image the higher the resolution and therefore the greater the quality of the image. Actual value is 1,048,576 pixels.

metal oxide sensor (MOS)   a type of image receptor used in place of film in electronic and still video cameras.

metallic silver   see silver.

microphotography   techniques used to produce extremely small images, such as for microelectronics.

microprism   a substructure of a ground-glass focusing screen consisting of a pattern of refracting prisms to enable more accurate focusing.

mired   a unit of measurement, derived from Kelvin, used to measure the color temperature of light; contraction of micro-reciprocal degrees. The mired system simplifies the selection of filters to achieve a desired color balance in color photography.

modeling   revealing by means of lighting the three-dimensional qualities of an object.

modeling light   see main light.

modem a device that converts digital data into electronic signals that can be transmitted over standard phone lines. An abbreviation of Modulator-Demodulator.

modulator-demodulator a device that converts digital computer data into analog signals and vice versa for data exchange over telephone lines.

Moirè pattern a visible pattern that occurs when repetitive patterns are overlaid and viewed simultaneously. Often occurs when two or more halftone screens are misregistered in an image. Interference resulting from overlaying similar patterns. An alias pattern.

monitor a visual output device similar in appearance to a television screen designed to display computer information.

monobath a single solution for rapidly developing and fixing photographic materials.

monochromatic based entirely upon a single or several closely related hues.

monochrome a single hue. See monochromatic.

morphing image metamorphosis. Animated transformation of one digital image to another. A special effect used in motion pictures and video to produce a smooth transformation from one object or shape to another.

MOS see metal oxide sensor.

motor drive a device that automatically advances film under force at a rate of about five frames per second.

mounting adapter a device that enables a given lens to mount to a given camera body.

mouse handheld computer input device which, when rolled across a flat surface, causes corresponding movement of the cursor on the monitor screen. Used to make selections and execute commands.

MOV Apple QuickTime MOVie file.

MP see megapixel.

MPEG Motion JPEG movie file. MPEG 1 was the original format used in CDRoms and Video-CDs. MPEG2 is the standard for DVD movies.

M-synchronization the mechanical synchronization used with medium-peak (M) flashbulbs; provides a 20-millisecond delay between flash ignition and subsequent shutter release. Similar to FP-synchronization designed for use with flat peak (FP) flashbulbs and a focal plane shutter.

multicontrast filter see variable contrast filter.

multicontrast paper see variable-contrast paper.

multigrade paper see variable-contrast paper.

N

narrow lighting see short lighting.

ND filter see neutral density filter.

NEF raw image data file format as used by the Nikon Dl pro digicam.

negative a photographic image in which subject tonalities (and colors) have been reversed from light to dark (and from primaries to complements) and vice versa vis a vis the original scene. Usually the negative is used to make finished positives that possess tonalities (and colors) corresponding to the original scene.

negative carrier a frame-like device used to hold a negative in position in an enlarger during printing.

negative format see format.

neutral background the absence of distracting peripheral details and contrasts in a photographic composition.

neutral density (ND) filter a filter toned to a specific density of gray and used over a camera's lens to reduce the intensity of image-forming light without altering its color balance.

NiCd see nickel cadmium

nickel cadmium a type of rechargeable battery. The original type of rechargeable battery.

nickel metal hydride battery a type of rechargeable battery possessing high energy density, extended recharge properties, and low environmental impact. Recommended for digital cameras.

NiMH see nickel metal hydride battery.

normal contrast a photographic image characterized by the presence of a wide range of tonal densities, including whites, blacks, and a variety of middle gray tones; lighting situations and photographic materials that tend to produce such images.

normal lens any lens possessing a focal length approximately equivalent to the diagonal measurement of the film format of the camera on which it is used. See long lens, short lens.

notching code   pattern of small cutouts in the edges of sheet film which identify the type of film and the emulsion side of the film sheet so it can be identified in the dark.

NTSC   National Television Standards Committee. The broadcast and reception standard for television in the United States, Japan and Canada approved by the committee.

O

object   a visible entity, originally possessing three dimensions; a photographic detail. See subject.

object-at-infinity   an object that is at least 50 feet (15 m) from the camera.

one-shot developer   a developing solution intended to be used once and discarded.

opacity   a medium's ability to block the passage of light; the reciprocal of transmittance.

opaque   resistant to the passage of light.

open bulb   a method of contact print making in which exposure is made with a bare electric light bulb.

open flash   flash technique in which the flash unit is fired manually, often more than once, while the shutter stands open. Sometimes called painting with light.

opening up   increasing the size of the lens aperture to control exposing and focusing.

optical drive   a removable mass storage device for computers that uses a laser beam to access the data.

optical zoom   a type of magnification produced by a camera's lens system by reducing the angle of view so as to fill the visual frame with only the center part of a scene.

optimal exposure   the exposure that yields the maximum contrast with minimum density under given developing conditions.

orthochromatic   a type of emulsion characterized by sensitivity to all wavelengths in the visible light spectrum except red.

outdated film   film unexposed and/or unprocessed after its published expiration date.

outdoor lighting standard   an arrangement of highlights and shadows that reproduces the appearance of natural outdoor light sources, which typically originate from above and to the side of the subject.

out-of-focus   indistinctness of image caused by lack of image resolution and sharpness. Compare blur.

overall reading   a reflected-light meter reading obtained by placing the meter at the camera position and pointing it in the general direction of the scene to be photographed. It records the average light intensity of the entire scene.

overexposure   the action of too much light upon a photographic emulsion.

overexposed negatives, developed normally, are characterized by overall excessive density, loss of detail in highlight areas, overall loss of contrast, and graininess in the final print.

override   to set an automatic camera to disable its automatic functions for manual operation.

P

painting with light   see open flash.

palette   the set of colors that appear in a particular digital image that becomes part of a color look-up table in photo-editing programs. Allows the user to select colors for use in photo editing.

pan   (1) contraction of panchromatic; (2) to swing the camera during exposure to follow a moving subject. Also panning, panoramming.

panchromatic   a type of emulsion characterized by sensitivity to all wavelengths in the visible light spectrum, although only minimally sensitive to green.

panning   see pan.

panoramming   see pan.

paper negative   negative image on a paper base. Characteristic of the calotype process during the 1840s before transparent negative media were available.

paper tint   see base tint, tint.

parallax   the discrepancy between the image seen through a camera's viewfinder and that recorded on the film.

parallel interface   a type of interface that a computer uses to exchange data with other digital devices, such as digital cameras, printers, modems, keyboards, or other computers. Provides for transferring multiple channels of bits concurrently. Contrast with a serial interface that transfers one bit at a time.

pattern screen   a type of baffle that, introduced into a light beam, produces a shadow pattern. Used for background interest.

PC   personal computer.

PC contact   a flash synchronization socket by means of which the camera and flash unit are connected using a short cable.

P-C lens   see perspective control lens.

PCMCIA   Personal Computer Memory Card International Association. An international association that establishes standards and promotes the interoperability of PC Cards in mobile computers, digital cameras, cable TV, set-top boxes, automobiles, and other diverse products.

peak action   a moment when a moving object is relatively motionless due to a change in its direction; e.g. a high jumper at the top of his jump when upward movement has ceased and downward movement has not yet begun. Compare real action, simulated action.

pentaprism   a five-sided prism used to provide correct vertical and horizontal orientation in SLR viewfinders.

perspective   the representation of three dimensional space on a flat surface by means of variations of line, tonality, focus, and image size. See linear perspective, aerial perspective, selective focus.

perspective control (P-C) lens   type of wide-angle lens providing for rotation and shifting of its optical elements to control convergence and depth of field.

photo CD   CD-Recordable media that can be read by CD-ROM drives. The Photo CD provides for storing 100 or more digital images for output to a television or computer monitor, photo-editing program, printer, or for transmission over the Internet. Images can be transferred to a photo CD disc from new or existing films, slides, or other formats.

photo eye   a photoelectric triggering device used to operate slave flash units.

photoflood   an artificial lighting instrument that produces an even, relatively diffused field of light over a broad area.

photographic paper   paper coated with a photosensitive emulsion and used for making photographic prints.

photomacrography   techniques used to produce negative images that are lifesize or larger.

photomicrography   techniques used to photograph objects through a microscope.

photosensitive   subject to chemical change in response to exposure to light.

Photoshop   A widely-used digital image editing software program manufactured by Adobe Systems Inc. that possesses a wide range of tools, including color correction, tonal adjustment, sizing, cropping, retouching, image manipulation, compositing, and many special effects.

pinhole camera   a camera characterized by a tiny hole rather than a lens to resolve admitted light into an image in the film plane.

pinholes   small transparent spots in a negative caused by air-bells where the image failed to develop.

pixel picture element   the single, smallest element in a matrix of elements used to make up an entire digital image.

pixel editing   pixel-by-pixel manipulation of an image.

Plug and Play   PnP. A technology that supports automatic configuration of PC hardware and attached devices. A PnP computer automatically recognizes new attached PnP devices and prompts the user to choose setup options to complete the installation without having to configure the device manually.

PNG   see portable network graphics.

pocket camera   a camera of small size and shape suitable for carrying in a pocket.

point of view   the position from which a scene is viewed; the position from which a photograph is taken; the relationship between the subject and its viewer.

poised action   see peak action.

pola filter   see polarizing filter.

polarized light light composed of electromagnetic waves vibrating predominantly in, or parallel to, a single plane. It is commonly produced by source light reflecting off nonmetallic surfaces, or passing through a polarizing screen.

polarizing filter a filter designed to block or pass polarized light by positioning its axis to oppose or conform to the axis of polarization; a filter designed to block the passage of any light except that which is vibrating in the plane of its axis. Thus, only polarized light is transmitted by such a screen.

portable network graphics (PNG) an extensible file format for lossless portable, well-compressed storage of raster images. A patent-free replacement for GIF similar to JPG, PNG also replaces many common uses of TIFF.

positive a photographic image in black-and-white (or color) in which subject tonalities (and colors) correspond to those in the original scene; the reverse of a negative.

positive print see print.

positive transparency see transparency.

PPI pixels per inch.

press camera historically, a large-format camera, such as a Graflex or Speed Graphic, commonly used by press photographers; currently, any camera used by a press photographer.

previsualization the process of visualizing the final photographic print prior to exposure. In the zone system, a method of analyzing brightness values before exposure to plan a desired range of densities in the final print.

primary colors a set of hues from which all other hues may be derived. The additive light primary colors—red, green, and blue—can, when added together in varying proportions, produce a maximum number of hues, including white (all colors). The subtractive light primary colors—magenta, yellow, and cyan—can, when added together in varying proportions, absorb all hues from white light to pass any specific hue, including black (no color).

print a photographic image, usually understood to be positive, reproduced in final form on an opaque photographic paper, to make a print.

print conditioning solution a photoprocessing agent that functions to soften the gelatin emulsion, thereby reducing curling and generally improving the effect of ferrotyping.

print finishing those procedures subsequent to washing—including drying, ferrotyping, spotting, bleaching, mounting, and similar techniques—intended to produce photographic prints suitable for their intended purposes.

printing the procedures for making prints; making prints.

printing frame a flat, rectangular holder equipped with removable or hinged front glass or back, designed to sandwich copy, negative, and/or printing paper tightly in place for exposure or copying.

printing-in see burning-in.

printing paper see photographic paper.

processing the sequence of steps, usually including developing, stopping, fixing, and washing, necessary to transform a latent photographic image into a permanent image; to subject photographic materials to such a sequence of steps.

programmed automatic exposure a type of automatic exposure-setting system that sets both aperture and shutter speed automatically to obtain proper exposure.

projection the act of causing an image of an original to fall upon a surface by directing and controlling the passage of light onto and/or through the original; the act of reproducing on a surface the image of a transparency, negative or positive, by directing and controlling the passage of light through the transparency.

projection print a print produced by projecting the master image onto the surface of photosensitive material; usually understood to be and often called an enlargement.

projection printing paper relatively fast photosensitive paper used primarily for projection printing. Also see printing paper.

proof sheet see contact sheet.

push process to expose film at a higher-than-normal ISO rating and then to prolong development to compensate for resulting underexposure. See forced development.

Q

quartz light   an extremely intense incandescent lamp designed with a filament bathed in bromine or iodine vapor, having longer life and more constant color temperature than ordinary tungsten-filament lamps.

quench   to terminate flash duration when a predetermined exposure value has been reached. See automatic electronic flash.

QT   see QuickTime.

quicktime   A highly flexible motion video standard format created by Apple that may contain video, audio and even single photographs. Data are stored as MOV files.

R

RAM   Random Access Memory. A component of computer memory used for temporary storage of data and program instructions while a computer is operating.

random access memory (RAM)   see RAM.

range   (1) the distance between the camera and the objects intended to be in focus in a photograph; (2) the spectrum of tones, from lightest to darkest, in a photographic image is referred to as its tone, contrast, or density range.

range of density   the difference between the thickest and thinnest silver deposits on a negative produced by the total range of brightness in the scene.

rangefinder   An electro-mechanical device, usually integrated with a camera's viewfinding system used to focus an image onto the camera's film or sensor plane.

rangefinder camera   a camera with a built-in rangefinder.

range-of-brightness   a method of using a light meter to measure the intensity of light in the important highlight and shadow areas of a scene.

raster image   an image created from a series of bits and bytes that form pixels. Raster images consist of rows of pixels, where each pixel precisely defines its color, size and location within the image. See also bitmapped image.

RAW Image Format   RAW is image data as it comes directly off the CCD without in-camera processing. Typically 8, 10 or 12 bits per pixel.

RC paper   see resin-coated paper.

ready light   an indicator light that activates when an electronic flash unit is fully charged and ready to fire.

real action   movement of the subject at the moment it is photographed. Compare peak action and simulated action.

reciprocity failure   the nonoccurrence of normally expected density changes, resulting from exposures of extremely short or long duration. See reciprocity law.

reciprocity failure (RF) factor   the number by which exposure time must be multiplied to compensate for reciprocity failure.

reciprocity law   a principle of photography stating that a constant density is obtained on a photo-sensitive material if the product of light intensity and exposure duration remains constant. Thus density is postulated to remain constant if, for example, light intensity is halved while exposure duration is doubled, and vice versa. Also see reciprocity failure.

record shot   a photograph that represents a subject objectively and accurately and is devoid of interpretation by the photographer; a theoretical ideal, since any photograph requires the photographer to select, emphasize, and subordinate details in the process of composition.

recycling time   the time interval necessary to recharge an electronic flash unit following discharge.

red eye   the appearance of red pupils in color photographs when flash illumination is reflected off the retina of the subject's eyes back toward the camera. It is avoided by placing the flash unit off the camera axis and/or by directing the subject's gaze off the camera axis.

reducer   a chemical agent capable of dissolving metallic silver, and thereby reducing the density of photographic images. See bleach.

reflectance   the light-reflecting characteristic of an object or surface. Surfaces of high reflectance reflect much of the light incident upon them; subjects of low reflectance absorb much of such light.

reflected-light   light rays that are deflected or bounced from a surface or subject after striking it.

reflected-light meter   a light-measuring device designed to respond to the intensity of light reflected from a surface or subject and to compute proper exposure. Compare incident light meter.

reflection   the partial or complete deflection of light rays from an encountered surface; the production of an image composed of reflected light, as if by a mirror.

reflector   a polished and/or light-colored surface for reflecting light.

reflector floodlight   a lightbulb with a built-in reflector designed to function as a floodlight.

reflector spotlight   a lightbulb with a built-in reflector designed to function as a spotlight.

reflex camera   a camera whose viewfinding mechanism utilizes an inclined mirror to reflect an image onto a ground-glass screen. See single lens reflex and twin lens reflex.

refraction   the deflection of a light ray in passing obliquely from one transparent medium to another in which its velocity is altered.

relative brightness   comparative light reflectance among various elements of a scene to be photographed.

replenisher   a chemical agent added to a developer to restore its strength following use.

reproduction   a print made from a copy negative; an exact positive print or transparency of the original; the end-product of copying.

resampling   see interpolation.

resin-coated (RC) paper   a photosensitive printing paper characterized by a tough, smooth resin coating on the paper base below the emulsion layer.

resize   to alter the resolution or the horizontal or vertical size of an image.

resolution   (1) the number of pixels in a given matrix area. Usually expressed in columns by rows, such as 1,000 by 1,200 pixels; (2) a measurement of the amount of detail in an image file as measured in units per inch such as dpi, ppi, or lpi: dots per inch, pixels per inch, or lines per inch. See also definition.

resolving power   the capability of a lens to form an image in fine detail; the capability of a photographic emulsion to reproduce fine detail in a recorded image.

retaining ring   a device used with an adaptor ring to hold a filter in place in front of a camera's taking lens.

reticulation   a network of wrinkles and cracks in a photographic emulsion, brought about by exposure of the emulsion to extreme temperature changes during processing.

retina   a light-sensitive membrane that lines the interior chamber of the eye upon which the image is formed by the lens.

reversal film   a film designed to produce a positive image after exposure to a positive image; a film that reproduces tonal densities corresponding to those of the image to which it is exposed. Also see color reversal film.

reverse adapter   a device used to invert the position of a normal lens back to front to improve its performance in close-up photography.

rewind button   a mechanism on 35mm cameras used to unlock the takeup spool to permit the film to be wound back into its cartridge.

rewind crank   a mechanism on 35mm cameras used to wind the film from the takeup spool back into its cartridge.

RF   see rangefinder.

RF factor   see reciprocity failure factor.

RGB   Red, Green, Blue. The primary additive colors used to simulate natural color on computer monitors and television sets.

rim light   backlight placed to produce edge accents from the camera's viewpoint. See edge accent.

ringflash   a circular flash unit used at the front of the lens in close-up photography.

roll film   film manufactured in a strip and wound onto a spool, designed for use in a camera that advances the film in measured increments to produce separate negative frames.

ROM   Read Only Memory. One major type of memory that is used in PCs. ROM is "built-in" computer memory containing data that normally can only be read and not written to, as opposed to RAM, which can be both read and written to. Unlike RAM, the data in ROM is not lost when the computer power is turned off.

rule of thirds   an approach to placement of a photographic subject based upon division of the picture space into thirds, both horizontally and vertically.

S

safelight   darkroom illumination of such limited wavelength and brightness that it does not affect the photosensitive materials being handled. Materials of different sensitivities require different safelight.

saturation   concentration of hue. The degree to which a color is undiluted by white light. If a color is 100 percent saturated, it contains no white light. The absence of saturation is no hue at all, or a shade of gray.

scale   the relative sizes of an object in a photographic image and in actuality.

scanner   an optical device that converts analog images, such as photographs, into digital format so they can be stored and manipulated on computers.

SCSI   Small Computer System Interface. A set of evolving ANSI standards that allows personal computers to communicate with peripheral hardware such as disk drives, tape drives, CD-ROM drives, printers, and scanners faster and more flexibly than previous interfaces. Preferred for digital imaging.

second adhesive layer   see adhesive layer.

secondary color   a complement of a primary color; a hue consisting of equal proportions of any two primary colors. In light, the complements of the primary colors red, blue, and green are the secondary colors cyan, yellow, and magenta respectively.

secondary image   the recording of two images, when using flash under bright existing light conditions and a slow shutter speed, one from the flash and a secondary one from the existing light; also ghost image.

selection   (1) the choice of details to appear in a photograph; (2) an area defined for manipulation by an image-editing program.

selective focus   the representation of three dimensions and distance on a two-dimensional surface by means of variations in the sharpness of foreground and background details.

self-timer   a device used to delay release of the shutter a preset interval of time after the shutter release has been pressed. May be built into automatic cameras or used as an accessory with manual cameras.

semigloss finish   a surface texture of a print characterized by a soft, slightly reflective sheen.

sensitivity   the potential of a photographic material or sensor to be affected by the action of light energy. Traditional film with lower ISO requires more light to create the same image than a film with higher ISO. Digital camera sensitivity depends on the sensor (CCD/CMOS device), which is relatively "slow" compared to film, but can be reset on the fly for each shot.

separation   the differentiation of tonal areas within a photographic image; the process of differentiating and recording the primary color components of a photographic image as three distinct black-and-white images.

serial interface   a type of interface that a computer uses to exchange data with other digital devices, such as digital cameras, printers, modems, keyboards, or other computers. A serial interface provides for exchanging one bit of data at a time as a stream of individual bits. Contrast with parallel interface.

series number   an adapter-ring designation that specifies the size of the filters the ring is designed to accept.

server   within a network, a computer that manages network resources and stores files used by users on the network.

shadow area   any mass within a photographic image corresponding to the least illuminated areas in the original scene or subject; the least dense areas of a negative, the densest areas of a print. Also see highlights.

shadow reading   a light-meter reading of the least illuminated areas of a scene, or those that will produce the areas of least density on the film.

shallow depth of field   see depth of field.

sharpening   in a digital context, the enhancing of edge detail. Performed by mathematical formula and applied across an image to enhance the visibility of boundaries between light and dark tones.

sharpness   the apparent clarity and definition of details in a photographic image; a function of such factors as graininess, image resolution, density, and contrast of the negative, which interact to create an impression of sharpness.

sheet film film manufactured and packaged in individual pieces; cut film.

shifts and swings see swings and tilts.

short lens any lens possessing a focal length shorter than is normal for the camera on which it is used. See wide-angle lenses.

short lighting a portrait lighting setup characterized by placement of the main light to illuminate the side of the subject's face farthest from the camera.

short stop see stop bath.

shutter the mechanical component of a camera system by means of which the time interval of exposure is controlled.

shutter priority a type of automatic exposure-setting system that requires the photographer to set the shutter manually while the system sets the aperture automatically for proper exposure.

shutter release a mechanical component of a shutter system by means of which the action of the shutter is activated.

shutter speed (1) the interval of time during which the activated shutter is admitting light into the camera; (2) the calibrated markings on an exposure scale indicating a shutter-speed setting.

silhouette a visual representation of an object's mass and shape, but lacking details within the mass.

silver the metallic element Ag, commonly compounded with halides to form the main active ingredient in most modern photosensitive materials.

silver bromide one of the silver halides.

silver chloride one of the silver halides.

silver density see density.

silver halide see halide.

silver iodide one of the silver halides.

simulated action an impression of activity in the absence of real action. Compare real action and peak action.

single-lens reflex (SLR) a type of camera that has a hinged mirror device through which the viewing and picture-taking functions may be performed by the same lens; SLR.

single use camera An inexpensive alternative if you have no other camera available. Just return the entire camera and collect your prints later.

skylight filter a filter that performs with color film a function similar to that of a haze filter with black-and-white film. It filters ultraviolet light, reduces bluishness, and restores warmth to scenes characterized by excessive ultraviolet light sources.

slave unit a secondary flash unit designed to supplement a primary flash unit through a remote, photo-triggering operation.

slide (1) a positive transparency designed for use in a projector; (2) a component of a film holder that seals the film within against light; a darkslide.

slow minimally sensitive to light; responsive only to relatively high levels of illumination (said of photosensitive paper or film); capable of transmitting relatively small amounts of light per unit of time (said of photographic lenses of relatively small diameter relative to their focal length).

slow-speed film see slow.

SLR see single-lens reflex.

SM see SmartMedia.

small format see format.

SmartMedia A non-volatile flash memory card usually used to store digital camera image files.

smoothing averaging pixel values among neighboring pixels to reduce contrast and simulate an out-of focus effect.

soft see low contrast.

soft focus focus that is slightly diffused, often used to reduce the clarity and definition of details in a photograph.

software coded sequences of instructions, or programs, that tell a computer what operations to perform.

spectrum an ordered series of electromagnetic wave-lengths to which photographic emulsions are sensitive, made up largely of those perceived as light by the human eye.

specular light highly directional, nondiffused light such as that emanating from a relatively small point source or reflected off a highly polished, mirror-like surface.

specularity see specular light.

speed   the relative sensitivity to light of photographic materials; the light-transmitting characteristic of lenses, as expressed by the ratio of their focal length to their maximum aperture diameter; the apparent movement of an object being photographed.

split-image focusing   see split-image rangefinder.

split-image rangefinder   a type of rangefinder in which opposing halves of the image are displaced except when the device is properly focused. Such a rangefinder is commonly built into a camera and integrated with the camera's lens-focusing mechanism.

splitting the frame   a colloquial term for a compositional arrangement in which a strong vertical or horizontal feature splits the picture format into approximately equal halves.

spotlight   a lighting instrument, usually possessing an integrated lens and/or reflector, used to produce a focused, narrow, relatively specular beam of light.

spotmeter   a type of exposure meter, often built into modern cameras, characterized by its capability of measuring light intensity reflected from a very small area within the viewing format.

spotting   a technique for bleaching and/or tinting out undesirable spots on a print, such as those caused by pinholes or dust particles on the negative during printing.

spotting colors   tinting materials, used in spotting, that can be mixed and applied to match print tones.

spraying   a technique for dulling a shiny surface to eliminate specular reflections.

spring tension   the stored energy produced by the compression or expansion of an elastic device.

sprout   a colloquial term for the alignment in a photographic composition of a background detail with a foreground object such that the former appears to be appended to the latter.

square filter   a type of filter, square in shape, requiring a special filter holder to mount it to the camera.

stain   a nonimage-related color or tone on a print, usually produced by chemical oxidation and rarely expected or desired.

standard   a stand, often weighted and castered, for mounting lighting equipment.

standard average gray   eighteen percent gray. See average gray.

star filter   an etched glass filter that produces star-like patterns around specular highlights.

stereo camera   a camera designed to take a pair of photographs simultaneously, as though seen separately by each eye. When mounted side-by-side as a stereograph and viewed through a stereoscope, the photographs are perceived as a three-dimensional image.

stereograph   a pair of photographs mounted side-by-side designed for viewing through a stereoscope.

stereoscope   a device used for viewing stereographs to produce a three-dimensional effect.

still video   a type of video technology that employs video signals to record and display non-moving pictures.

stock solution   any photographic solution used for storage, usually in a concentrated form.

stop   (1) a change in an exposure setting, either aperture or shutter speed, that either doubles or halves exposure; (2) to terminate development by means of a stop bath.

stop action   an approach to photographing real action that seeks to capture an unblurred image of a rapidly moving object by means of extremely short exposure intervals. Also freeze actions.

stop bath   a processing solution of dilute acetic acid, introduced following development to neutralize the action of residual developer promptly prior to fixing.

stop down   to reduce the aperture size of a lens as a control in exposing and focusing.

strobe   a device that produces rapidly flashing bursts of light; derived from "stroboscope," now commonly used to refer to an electronic flash unit. See electronic flash.

strobe peak (X)   a flash burn pattern that reaches maximum output within 1 millisecond after ignition and sustains this level up to 2 milliseconds prior to extinction. See electronic flash, X-synchronization.

studio camera   see view camera.

subbing adhesive layer   adhesive coating used to bind a photographic emulsion to its support. See adhesive layer.

subject   the center of interest or central idea; the person, place, thing, or view photographed. A photograph may include many objects, but usually only one subject. Compare object.

subject speed   see speed.

subordination   the reduction to a subordinate status of a particular detail or feature in a photograph; minimization of the attention-attracting position, size, or clarity given to such a feature. Compare emphasis.

subtractive color theory   theory of mixing light primary colors by subtracting red, green, and blue from white light to produce black by absorbing all wavelengths.

SUC   see single use camera.

sufficient light indicator   a signal light built into automatic cameras and flash units that indicates if the flash illumination has been adequate to obtain proper exposure.

sunshade   see lens hood, lens shade.

superimposed-image focusing   see superimposed-image rangefinder.

superimposed-image rangefinder   a type of rangefinder in which two images of the subject appear to overlap except when the device is properly focused on the subject. Such a rangefinder is commonly built into a camera and integrated with the camera's lens-focusing mechanism.

supplementary lens   a lens used in front of a primary lens to alter its performance. Often used in close-up photography or for special effects.

support   a transparent, firm, chemically stable base upon which is coated the emulsion of a photographic film or plate.

surface texture   see texture.

Sv   see shutter priority.

swings and tilts   the adjustments of the front and rear standards of a studio or view camera. Also shifts and swings.

synchronization   the mechanical-optical method of timing the ignition of a flash unit in coordination with the release of the shutter to obtain optimal exposure. See X-synchronization, M-synchronization, FP-synchronization.

T

T setting   see time.

tacking iron   a hand-held electrical tool used in mounting prints to attach dry-mounting tissue to the mounting surfaces prior to pressing in a dry-mount press.

tagged image file format   A lossless image file format that loses no image information when compressing files.

taking lens   the camera lens that resolves the photographic image on the film; the picture-taking lens (as distinct from other lenses used in viewfinding). Compare viewing lens.

talbotype   see calotype.

tank   see film-processing tank.

teleconverter   a device inserted between lens and camera body to increase the effective focal length of the lens. 2X and 3X teleconverters effectively double and triple the effective focal length respectively. Also extender, converter.

telephoto lens   a type of long lens characterized by its resolution of an image on the film larger than that resolved by a given camera's normal lens.

tenting   a method of lighting through a translucent medium in order to produce an even, diffused field of light devoid of reflected details. It is especially useful for photographing shiny objects.

test exposure   see test print, test strip.

test print   a full-size print exposed in segments for varying exposure intervals in order to determine optimal exposure for printing.

test strip   a narrow strip of printing paper exposed in segments for varying exposure intervals in order to determine optimal exposure.

texture   (1) image texture—an apparent surface characteristic produced by the photographic image; (2) surface texture—a physical surface characteristic of the photographic paper, such as glossy or matte textures; (3) a physical surface characteristic of an object that may be exaggerated or subdued by means of lighting.

texture accents   highlights that reveal the surface irregularities of an object.

texture screen   a device used to produce image texture in a print. See texture.

texturing   emphasizing or revealing surface texture, such as by the use of lighting.

TFT   see thin film transistor.

thermal printer a type of printer that uses heat to transfer image-forming pigment to paper.

thin characterized by low overall print or negative density.

thin emulsion film a type of film characterized by an exceptionally thin photosensitive layer of high resolution and contrast, fine grain, slow to moderate speed, and narrow latitude.

thin film transistor Technology used in LCD screens for displaying images on digicams.

threaded mount a lens-mounting system using screw-threads by which a lens may be aligned with the mount and screwed into place.

through-the-lens A type of viewing and metering system that gathers image-forming light for viewing and/or metering through the camera's picture-taking lens.

thyristor circuit a type of automatic electronic flash that conserves unused energy in its capacitors following each flash to reduce recycling time and extend capacitor life.

TIFF see tagged image file format.

tilt head an adjustable head on an electronic flash unit that can be used to redirect to unit to obtain bounce light.

time (T) a shutter setting (T) at which the shutter remains open following depression of the shutter release until the release is depressed a second time. Rarely seen on modern cameras. Compare bulb.

time and temperature the main variables requiring precise control during chemical processing of photographic materials.

time exposure an exposure interval, usually longer than a few seconds, timed by the photographer while the shutter stands open rather than by the camera's automatic settings.

timer a device used in the darkroom to measure time intervals during processing and printing, often integrated into the design of photographic equipment.

tint a hue of very low saturation. Paper tint or base tint is the color of the paper stock itself.

tintype wet-collodion process on dark-varnished metal plate to produce positive image. Inexpensive process extremely popular in the 1860s and 1870s.

TLR see twin-lens reflex.

tonal range see tonality.

tonality the range in values, in gray or color, present in a photographic image; the range of distinct values that can be discriminated between black and white. See contrast, gray tone separation.

tone white, black, or an intermediate shade of gray; the tint present in the silver image. See tonality, tint.

tone separation the rendering of varying brightness values in a scene as distinctly different shades of gray in a black-and-white print.

toner a chemical agent used to alter the color or tint of the silver image in a black-and-white print. Toners affect only the silver image, not the base tint.

toning see toner.

topcoat an abrasion-resistant material coated onto the surface of a photographic emulsion as a protection.

transillumination illumination produced by lighting through a translucent medium.

translucent capable of transmitting light, but not image; characteristic of a medium that transmits light only at a high level of diffusion.

transmission the passage of light through a medium. See law of transmission and absorption.

transmittance a medium's ability to pass light; the reciprocal of opacity.

transparency a photographic image, positive or negative, recorded on a transparent medium and capable of projection.

transparent capable of transmitting light and image; characteristic of a medium that transmits light at a minimum level of diffusion.

tripod a three-legged, usually foldable, support commonly used for positioning and stabilizing a camera.

T-setting see time (T).

TTL see through-the-lens.

tungsten light conventional artificial light produced by passing an electric current through a tungsten filament in a vacuum or in inert gas. In photography, it usually refers to lamps designed to burn at specific color temperatures (3200 or 3400 K).

tungsten-filament see tungsten light.

tungsten-halogen improved smaller version of tungsten-filament lamp that emits whiter, brighter light.

twin-lens reflex (TLR) a reflex camera characterized by its use of separate but optically similar built-in lens systems to perform the separate functions of viewfinding and picture taking; TLR.

type A a designation identifying color film balanced for tungsten light of 3400 K.

type B a designation identifying color film balanced for tungsten light of 3200 K.

U

ultra-fast film film designed for use under low lighting levels; arbitrarily, film with film-speed rating over ISO 400/27°.

ultraviolet relating to a band of electromagnetic wavelengths just shorter than those perceived as violet in the visible light spectrum; describes an invisible band of electromagnetic waves detectable by most photosensitive silver halide emulsions.

ultraviolet (UV) filter a filter medium that inhibits the passage of ultraviolet light. See skylight filter, haze filter.

umbrella reflector a highly reflectant metallic cloth, stretched over a foldable frame resembling an umbrella, that reflects a soft, directional field of light.

underexposure an amount of exposure inadequate to produce normal density and tonal range on a photosensitive emulsion by means of standard developing procedures.

underwater camera a camera designed for use under water.

underwater housing a container designed to provide a waterproof enclosure for underwater operation of the camera.

uniform resource locator see URL.

unipod a camera support with a single leg.

universal serial bus A high speed data port on digicams, computers, and accessories used for exchanging data.

unsharp masking a process whereby the perceived sharpness of an image is enhanced by increasing the contrast along the edges where different tones meet.

upload refers to transferring data files from a local computer to another, or host computer. Contrast with Download.

URL uniform resource locator. A website address on the World Wide Web. Allows for linking and cross-referencing between websites and documents on the World Wide Web.

USB see universal serial bus.

UV filter see ultraviolet filter.

V

value brightness; the relative presence or absence of black; lightness or darkness. The absence of value is equivalent to zero electromagnetic energy, or no light at all.

variable-contrast filter a type of filter designed for use with variable-contrast printing paper to control, contrast in photographic printing. Also multicontrast and polycontrast filters.

variable-contrast paper a type of printing paper coated with both high contrast and low contrast emulsions, each sensitive to a given band of electromagnetic wavelengths. It is used with variable-contrast filters to control contrast in printing. Also multicontrast, polycontrast, and multigrade paper.

vari-focus lens a variable focal length lens, similar to a zoom lens, that requires re-focusing whenever the focal length is changed; see also zoom lens.

VGA Video Graphics Array. A graphics display standard for PCs that provides a resolution of 640 x 480 pixels in 16 colors and a 4:3 aspect ratio. Introduced in 1990 by IBM and considered today to be the lowest common denominator in graphics display.

video the electronic system by which the visual portion of a television image is generated.

view camera a type of camera characterized by large-format ground-glass viewing of the image in the film plane, and considerable adjustability of the lensboard and film plane to control linear perspective and depth of field.

viewfinder (VF) a mechanism on a camera that indicates to the photographer the details the camera will record and, commonly, the details that will be in focus.

viewing lens   the lens of the viewfinding system, rather than the picture-taking system. The term commonly refers to the lens that forms the viewfinder image in a twin-lens reflex camera. Compare taking lens.

vignetting   (1) a dodging technique for achieving progressive reduction of exposure toward the edges of a picture format, isolating the subject within borders that gradually fade to the value of the base; (2) the progressive reduction of exposure toward the edges of a negative, produced by using a lens or attachment optically inadequate for the camera design.

visible light spectrum   see spectrum.

W

warm tones   brownish hues associated with the metallic silver image of a print, often emphasized by the use of certain emulsion-developer combinations.

wash   to clear active chemicals from photographic materials by rinsing in water.

washed out   a colloquial term describing a print of inadequate density in which a full range of highlight detail has failed to develop, typically as a result of underexposure in printing.

washing aid   see clearing agent.

wavelength   a characteristic of electromagnetic energy which, within the visible light spectrum, activates differential neural sensations that are perceived as color.

weight   the thickness of printing paper stock, e.g., document weight, single weight, double weight.

wet area   a portion of a darkroom, designed especially for handling processing chemicals, solutions, and water so as to minimize the possibility of contaminating chemically sensitive, dry materials such as films and papers.

wet mounting   a technique for affixing finished prints to a surface by means of a liquid or spray adhesive. Compare dry mounting.

wet-plate process   photographic process invented by F. Scott Archer in 1851 and popular more than thirty years by which glass plates were coated with an emulsion of collodion and silver nitrate and loaded into the camera and exposed while still wet.

wetting agent   a water additive that acts to break down surface tension and is used in photography to aid in spot-free drying of film.

white balance   refers to a system of color correction for rendering true colors under differing lighting conditions by determining a "white point" in an image. Most digital cameras set white balance automatically; others allow for manually setting or presetting.

white light   light consisting of virtually all wavelengths in the visible light spectrum; standard daylight; light capable of making normal exposure of photographic emulsions.

wide-angle camera   a camera with a revolving lens and shutter system or a wide-angle optical system, designed for making panoramic photographs.

wide-angle lens   a lens with a shorter focal length and wider angle of coverage than is normal for the camera on which it is used.

winder   see automatic winder.

working solution   any photographic processing solution, usually diluted from its more concentrated stock form. Compare stock solution.

World Wide Web   see WWW.

WWW   World Wide Web. An interconnected network of electronic hypermedia documents available on the Internet. See Internet.

X

XGA   Extended Graphics Array. A high-resolution graphics standard introduced by IBM to replace older video standards by supporting more colors and non-interlaced monitors.

X-synchronization   mechanical synchronization of shutter and flash for use with electronic flash units; X, zero-delay, is designed to make flash contact when the shutter stands fully open.

Z

zero-delay to peak   a flash burn pattern in which peak flash output is reached almost instantaneously upon ignition. Electronic flash units peak with almost zero-delay (actually less than one millisecond) and are used with cameras set for X-synchronization.

zinc-carbon battery   a type of battery recommended for flash units with unplated brass or copper contacts. Compare alkaline battery.

zone focusing   technique for presetting an aperture to obtain a desired depth of field to facilitate shooting subjects at various distances without adjusting the focus.

zone of sharpness   see depth of field.

zone system   a precise method for controlling density and contrast using analysis of brightness values in a scene to plan the exposure and processing necessary to obtain a previsualized result in the final print.

zoom lens   a lens with a continuously adjustable focal length within its design limits.

References

Adams, Ansel, with Robert Baker, *The Camera* (Ansel Adams Photography Series, Book 1). New York: Little Brown and Co., Reprint Edition, 1995.

Adams, Ansel, with Robert Baker (Contributor), *The Negative* (Ansel Adams Photography Series, Book 2). New York: Little Brown and Co., Reprint Edition, 1995.

Adams, Ansel, with Robert Baker, *The Print* (Ansel Adams Photography Series, Book 3). Boston: Bullfinch Press, Reprint Edition, 1995.

Adobe and Photoshop are either registered trademarks of Adobe Systems Incorporated in the United States and/or other countries.

Barrett, Terry, Criticizing Photographs; An Introduction to Understanding Images. *Mountain View: Mayfield Publishing Co., 3rd Edition, 1999.*

Brooks, David, *How to Control and Use Photographic Lighting.* Los Angeles: HPBooks, revised, 1989.

Buell, Hal, *Moments: The Pulitzer Prize Photographs—A Visual Chronicle of Our Time.* New York: Black Dog & Leventhal Publishers, 1999.

Busselle, Michael, *Master Photography—Take and Make Better Pictures.* New York: Rand-McNally, 1978.

Cavallo, Robert M. and Stuart Kahan, *Photography: What's the Law?* New York: Crown Publishers, 1976.

Craven, George M., *Object and Image: An Introduction to Photography.* Englewood Cliffs: Prentice-Hall, 3rd ed., 1990.

Crawford, William, *The Keepers of Light.* New York: Morgan and Morgan, 1979.

Curtis, Edward S., Joseph Epes Brown (Illustrator), *The North American Indians.* New York: Aperture, Inc., 1992.

Davenport, Alma, *The History of Photography: An Overview.* Albuquerque, NM: University of New Mexico Press, 1999.

Davis, Phil, *Photography.* Dubuque: Brown and Benchmark, 7th Edition, 1997.

Davis, Keith F., *An American Century of Photography.* Kansas City, MO., Hallmark Cards, Inc., 1999

Doeffinger, Derek, *The Art of Seeing: A Creative Approach to Photography (Kodak Workshop Series).* New York: Sterling Publications, 4th Ed., 1998.

Doherty, R. J., *Social-Documentary Photography in the USA.* Garden City: AMPHOTO, 1976.

Eastman Kodak Co., *Basic Developing and Printing in Black-and-White.* Rochester: Eastman Kodak Co., Kodak Photo Information Book AJ-2.

Eastman Kodak Co., *Basic Developing and Printing in Color.* Rochester: Eastman Kodak Co., Kodak Photo Information Book AE-13.

Eastman Kodak Co., *Black-and-White Darkroom Techniques.* Rochester: Eastman Kodak Co., Kodak Photo Information Book KW-15. Eastman Kodak, Hubert C. Birnbaum (Ed.), *Existing Light Photography (Kodak Workshop Series).* Rochester, NY: Saunders Photo, 1995.

Eastman Kodak Co., *Close-Up Photography.* Rochester: Eastman Kodak Co., Kodak Publication KW-22.

Eastman Kodak Co., *Color Camera Film—Kodak Consumer Films for Still Cameras.* Rochester: Eastman Kodak Co., Kodak Technical Publication F-507C.

Eastman Kodak Co., *Copying and Duplicating—Photographic and Digital Imaging Techniques.* Rochester: Eastman Kodak Co., Kodak Publication M-1.

Eastman Kodak Co., *Kodak Professional Black-and-White Films, Papers, and Chemicals.* Rochester: Eastman Kodak Company, Kodak Technical Paper F-33.

Eastman Kodak Co., *Using Filters (The Kodak Workshop Series)* New York: Sterling Publications, Revised edition, 1996

Eastman Kodak Co., *The Portrait—Professional Techniques.* Rochester: Eastman Kodak Co., Kodak Publication No. 0-24.

Eastman Kodak Co., *Professional Photographic Illustration Techniques.* Rochester: Eastman Kodak Co., Kodak Professional Data Book 0-16.

Eastman Kodak Co., *Using Filters.* Rochester: Eastman Kodak Co., Kodak Publication KW-13.

Eauclaire, Sally, Jim Dow, and Larry Babis, *American Independents: Eighteen Color Photographers.* New York, Abbeville Press, 1989.

Eggers, Ron, "Expanding a Photographer's Toolbox." In *Photomethods,* October, 1991.

Evening, Martin, *Adobe Photoshop 5.0 for Photographers.* Oxford, England: Focal Press, 1998.

Folts, James A., Ronald P. Lovell, and Fred C. Zwahlen, *Handbook of Photography*. Albany, NY: Delmar Publishers, 5th ed., 2001.

Foss, Kurt, "The Big Squeeze: Compression Makes Time and Photos Fly." In *Photo-Electronic Imaging,* Vol. 34, No. 12, December, 1991.

Foss, Kurt and Jeff Adams, "The Digital Toolbox: Reality and New Realities." In *News Photographer,* October, 1991.

Frizot, Michel (Ed.), *A New History of Photography.* Köln, Germany: Könemann Verlagsgesellschaft mbH, English Language Edition, 1998.

Gassan, Arnold, and A.J. Meek, *Exploring Black and White Photography.* New York: McGraw-Hill Higher Education, 2nd ed., 1992.

Gernsheim, Helmut, *A Concise History of Photography.* Mineola, NY: Dover Publications, 3rd Revised edition, 1986.

Gladstone, Gary, *Corporate & Location Photography (Kodak Pro Workshop Series).* Rochester, NY: Silver Pixel Press, 1998.

Goldberg, Vicki, *The Power of Photography: How Photographs Changed Our Lives.* New York: Abbeville Press, 1993.

Grill, Tom and Mark Scanlon, *Photographic Composition.* Toronto, Canada: Watson-Guptill, 1990.

Grimm, Tom, *The Basic Book of Photography.* New York: Dutton/Plume, 4th ed., 1997.

Hedgecoe, John, *Complete Guide to Photography: A Step-by-Step Course.* New York: Sterling Publishing Co., 1995.

Hedgecoe, John, *The Art of Color Photography.* Woburn, MA: Focal Press, Revised and Updated ed., 1998.

Hirsch, Robert J., *Exploring Color Photography.* New York: McGraw-Hill Higher Education, 3rd ed., 1996.

Hodgson, Pat, *Early War Photographs.* Boston: New York Graphic Society, 1974.

Horenstein, Henry and Russell Hart, *Photography.* Englewood Cliffs: Prentice Hall, 2000.

Horenstein, Henry, *Black & White Photography.* Boston: Little, Brown and Company, 1999.

Horenstein, Henry, with Russell Hart, *Color Photography: A Working Manual.* Boston: Little, Brown and Company, 1995.

Horton, Brian, *The Associated Press Guide to Photojournalism.* New York: McGraw-Hill Professional Publishing, 2nd ed., 2000.

Jacobs, Lou Jr., Megan Lane (Editor), *The Big Picture: The Professional Photographer's Guide to Rights, Rates & Negotiation.* Cincinnati, OH: Writers Digest Books, 2000.

Jones, Bernard Edward (Editor), *Cassell's Cyclopaedia of Photography.* North Stratford, NH: Ayer Company Publishers, 1979. Reprint of *Cassell's Cyclopaedia of Photography.* London: Cassell, 1911.

Jussim, Estelle, *Visual Communication and the Graphic Arts: Photographic Technologies in the Nineteenth Century.* New York: R. R. Bowker Co., 1974.

Jussim, Estelle, The Eternal Moment: Essays on the Photographic Image. New York: Aperture Foundation, 1990

Katzman, Louise, *Photography in California, 1945–1980.* New York: Hudson Hills Press, 1990.

King, Julie Adair, *Digital Photography for Dummies.* Foster City, CA: IDG Books Worldwide, 2000.

Kobre, Kenneth, and Betsy Brill, *Photojournalism: The Professionals' Approach.* Boston: Focal Press, 3rd ed., 1995.

Landt, Artur, *Lenses for 35mm Photography (The Kodak Workshop Series).* New York: Sterling Publications, 1998.

Langford, Michael, *35mm Handbook.* New York: Alfred A Knopf, 3rd ed., 1993.

Langford, Michael (Editor), *Creative Photography.* New York: Readers Digest Association, 1991.

Larish, John, *Fun with Digital Photography.* Rochester, NY: Tiffen, 1996.

Lewis, Greg, *Photojournalism: Content and Technique.* Dubuque: WCB/McGraw-Hill, 1994.

London, Barbara, et al, *Photography.* Englewood Cliffs: Prentice Hall, 7th ed., 2001.

London, Barbara and Jim Stone, *A Short Course in Photography: An Introduction to Black-and-White Photographic Technique.* Englewood Cliffs: Prentice Hall, 4th ed., 2000.

Lucie-Smith, Edward, *The Invented Eye.* New York: Paddington Press, Ltd., 1975.

Lynch, Richard, *Using Adobe Photoshop 6.* Indianapolis, IN: Que, 2001.

Marzio, Peter C., *The Men and Machines of American Journalism.* Washington, D.C.: The Smithsonian Institution, c. 1973.

Mast, Gerald and Bruce A. Kawin, *A Short History of the Movies.* Boston: Allyn and Bacon, 7th ed., 1999.

McClelland, Deke, *Photoshop 6 Bible.* Foster City, CA: IDG Books Worldwide, 2001.

McClelland, Deke, *Photoshop 6 for Dummies.* Foster City, CA: IDG Books Worldwide, 2001.

Miller, Ray, *Building a Home Darkroom (The Kodak Workshop Series).* Rochester, NY: Silver Pixel Press, 4th ed., 1995.

Morse, Mike, "Fitting More Pieces to the Technology Puzzle." In *The Electronic Times,* Vol. III, Number I, September 3, 1991. Published by the National Press Photographer's Association.

Morse, Mike (ed.), *NPPA Special Report: The Electronic Revolution in News Photography.* Durham: National Press Photographer's Association, 1987.

National Archives and Records Service, *The American Image: Photographs from the National Archives, 1860–1960.* New York: Pantheon Books, 1979.

Lester, Paul (ed.), *NPPA Special Report: The Ethics of Photojournalism.* Durham: National Press Photographer's Association, 1990.

Neubart, Jack, *Electronic Flash (Kodak Workshop Series).* Rochester, NY: Silver Pixel Press, 1997.

Newhall, Beaumont, *The History of Photography.* Boston: Little Brown and Co., Revised Edition, 1982.

Petersens Photographic (Ed.), "35mm Film Buying Guide." *Petersens Photographic,* January, 2001.

Petersens Photographic (Ed.), "Advanced Photo System Cameras." *Petersens Photographic,* November, 2000.

Rand, Glenn, *Black & White Photography.* Albany, NY: Delmar Publishers, 2nd ed., 2001.

Raymond, Eric S. (Compiler), *The New Hacker's Dictionary.* MIT Press, 3rd ed., 1996.

Reznicki, Jack, *Studio & Commercial Photography (Kodak Pro Workshop Series).* Rochester, NY: Silver Pixel Press, 1999.

Riis, Jacob A., *How the Other Half Lives: Studies Among the Tenements of New York.* New York: Penguin USA, Reprint edition, 1997. Unabridged republication of the text of the 1901 edition of the original work published by Charles Scribner's Sons of New York in 1890.

Schaub, George, *The Digital Darkroom: Black-And-White Techniques Using Photoshop.* Rochester, NY: Silver Pixel Press, 1999.

Shaw, Susan D., Monona Rossol, *Overexposure: Health Hazards in Photography.* New York: Allworth Press, 1991.

Smith, Joshua P., *The Photography of Invention: American Pictures of the 1980's.* Cambridge: MIT Press, 1989.

Stroebel, Leslie D. (ed.), et al, *Basic Photographic Materials and Processes.* Woburn, MA: Butterworth and Heinemann, 2nd ed., 2000.

Stryker, Roy and Nancy Wood, *In This Proud Land.* Greenwich: New York Graphic Society, 1973.

Swedlund, Charles, *Photography.* Orlando, FL: Harcourt-Brace College & School Division, 3rd ed., 2001.

Taft, Robert, *Photography and the American Scene.* Magnolia, MA: Peter Smith Publications, 1964. Republication of original work published by Macmillan, 1938.

Time-Life Books, *Life Library of Photography.* New York: Time, Inc., 1970–72. A classic series now out of print that includes volumes on Color, Documentary Photography, Light and Film, The Art of Photography, Photographing Nature, Special Problems, Photography as a Tool, The Studio, Caring for Photographs, The Great Themes, Great Photographers, The Camera, and The Print.

White, Minor, *New Zone System Manual: Previsualization, Exposure, Development, Printing.* Hastings-on-Hudson: Morgan and Morgan, 1998.

World Press Photo Foundation (ed.), *World Press Photo 2001.* London: Thames and Hudson, 2001.

Zakia, Richard D. and Leslie Stroebel (Editors), *Focal Encyclopedia of Photography.* Woburn, MA: Focal Press, 1996.

Credits

PHOTOGRAPHY AND

Marvin J. Rosen and David L. DeVries

Kendall/Hunt Publishing Company, 2005

CREDITS

Note: Photographs by the authors and anonymous photographers are not credited.

Cover, ©Patricia Gooden; Unit 1 1-1, Opening photo, Eadweard J. Muybridge, Courtesy Kingston Museum and Heritage Service; 1-2, Rainer Gemma-Frisius, Courtesy Harry Ransom Humanities Research Center, The University of Texas at Austin; 1-3, Joseph Nicéphore Niépce, Courtesy of Harry Ransom Humanities Research Center, The University of Texas at Austin; 1-4, Gaspard-Felix Tournachon-Nadar, Cliché Bibliothéque Nationale de France, Paris; 1-5, Honoré Daumier, Courtesy George Eastman House; pg. 5, Louis J. M. Daguerre, Courtesy Bayerisches Nationalmuseum, Munchen; 1-6, Henry Fox Talbot, Courtesy George Eastman House; 1-7, David Octavius Hill and Robert Adamson, Courtesy George Eastman House; 1-8, Unknown, Courtesy Harry Ransom Humanities Research Center, The University of Texas at Austin; 1-9, Unknown, Courtesy Harry Ransom Humanities Research Center, The University of Texas at Austin; 1-10, Fred Church, Courtesy George Eastman House; 1-11, Roger Fenton, Courtesy George Eastman House; 1-12, Roger Fenton, Courtesy Science Museum, London; 1-13, Unknown, Bettmann/Corbis; 1-14, Adolphe-Eugène Disdéri, Courtesy George Eastman House; 1-15, Culver Pictures; 1-16, Thomas Eakins, Courtesy The Metropolitan Museum of Art; 1-17, Courtesy NASA; 1-18, Oscar G. Rejlander, Courtesy George Eastman House; 1-19, Peter Henry Emerson, Courtesy George Eastman House; 1-20, George Davison, Courtesy George Eastman House; 1-21, Timothy H. O'Sullivan, The Library of Congress; 1-22, Alfred Stieglitz, Courtesy George Eastman House; 1-23, Paul Strand, Courtesy ©Aperture Foundation, Inc., Paul Strand Archive; 1-24, László Moholy-Nagy, Courtesy George Eastman House; 1-25, Edward Weston, Courtesy ©University of Arizona, Collection Center for Creative Photography; 1-26, Julia Margaret Cameron, Courtesy George Eastman House; 1-27, Robert Demachy, Courtesy The Royal Photographic Society, Bath; 1-28, Ansel Adams, Courtesy ©Ansel Adams Publishing Rights Trust/CORBIS; 1-29, Francis Frith, Courtesy George Eastman House; 1-30 Timothy H. O'Sullivan, Courtesy George Eastman House; 1-31, Eugène Atget, Courtesy The Museum of Modern Art, New York; 1-32, Jacob A. Riis, Courtesy The Museum of the City of New York; 1-33, Lewis W. Hine, National Archives, Records of the Children's Bureau; 1-34, Edward S. Curtis, Flury & Company, Seattle; 1-35, Henri Cartier-Bresson, Courtesy ©Henri Cartier-Bresson/Magnum Photos; 1-36 Arthur Rothstein, Farm Security Administration Collection, Library of Congress; 1-37, W. Eugene Smith, Courtesy ©Heirs of W. Eugene Smith/Black Star; 1-38, Yousuf Karsh, Courtesy ©Woodfin Camp & Associates, Inc.; 1-39, Keith Carter, Courtesy of the photographer; 1-40, Jim Dine, Courtesy ©Jim Dine and Pace/McGill Gallery, New York; 1-41, Kenneth Josephson, Courtesy Museum of Art, Rhode Island School of Design; 1-42, Joe Rosenthal, ©Corbis; 1-43, ©1994 by New York Newsday, reprinted by permission; 1-44, Lois Conner, Courtesy ©Lois Conner/Laurence Miller Gallery; 1-45, Peter Campus, Courtesy ©Paula Cooper Gallery, New York. Unit 2 2-1, Opening photo, Michelle Warmotts; 2-3, Jim Marshall; pg. 51, Rusty Hood; 2-5A, Canon, USA; 2-7, E. Leitz, Inc.; 2-8A, Nikon, USA; 2-9A, Mamiya America; 2-12, Michael Tyler; 2-15, Mamiya Corporation; 2-17, Olympus Corporation; 2-18, Nikon, USA; 2-19, Olympus Corporation; 2-20, Courtesy of Steves-Digicams.com; 2-21, Courtesy of Steves-Digicams.com; 2-22, Olympus Corporation; pg. 65, Olympus Corporation; 2-23, Courtesy of Steves-Digicams.com; 2-28, Polaroid Corporation; 2-29A,B, Hasselblad Corporation; 2-31, HP Marketing Corp., Linhof Division; 2-35A, Sean Decker; 2-39, Smith & Son, Inc.; 2-41A, B, Canon U.S.A., Inc.; 2-41C, Minolta Corporation; 2-41D, Julie O'Neil; pg. 87, Stephen T. Horgan, Library of Congress, Washington, D.C. Unit 3 3-1, Opening photo, Lisa Hart; 3-6A, B, C, D, Julie O'Neil; pg. 107 William Henry Jackson, Courtesy The Denver Public Library, Western History Department; 3-14A, B, C, Michael Tyler; 3-14D, Jane Kalinowsky; 3-14D, E, Philipp Eirund; 3-19A, Courtesy Berkey Marketing Companies, Inc.; 3-21, Courtesy Minolta Corporation; 3-23A, B, C, Julie O'Neil, pg. 126A, B, Corbis. Unit 4 4-1, Opening photo, James Bunoan; pg. 138, Eadweard J. Muybridge, Courtesy Kingston Museum and Heritage Service; pg. 148A, David D. Coleman; pg. 149B, Courtesy Beckman-Coulter, Inc.; 4-12, Lexar Media; 4-13, Courtesy of Lexar Media. Unit 5 5-1, Opening photo, Nicole Shibata; 5-3A, B, C, Jim Marshall; 5-4B, Jim Marshall; 5-5, Dimco-Gray Co.; 5-15A, B, Scott Deardorff; pg. 181, Imogen

Index